MYSTICISM

MYSTICISM

A STUDY
IN THE NATURE AND DEVELOPMENT OF
MAN'S SPIRITUAL CONSCIOUSNESS

EVELYN
UNDERHILL

LONDON

METHUEN & CO LTD

ROWMAN AND LITTLEFIELD

TOTOWA: NEW JERSEY

First published 1911
This edition reprinted 1977 by
Methuen & Co Ltd
11 New Fetter Lane
London EC4P 4EE

ISBN 0 416 85850 3

and

Rowman and Littlefield
81 Adams Drive
Totowa New Jersey 07511

ISBN 0 87471 883 X

Printed in Great Britain by
Whitstable Litho Ltd Whitstable Kent

IN HONOREM

OMNIUM ANIMARUM MYSTICARUM

Lume è lassù, che visibile ace
lo Creatore a quella creatura
che solo in lui vedere ha la sua pace.

PAR. XXX. 100

"When love has carried us above all things . . . we receive in
peace the Incomprehensible Light, enfolding us and penetrating us.
What is this Light, if it be not a contemplation of the Infinite,
and an intuition of Eternity? We behold that which we are, and
we are that which we behold; because our being, without losing
anything of its own personality, is united with the Divine Truth."

RUYSBROECK

"Man is the meeting-point of various stages of Reality."

RUDOLPH EUCKEN

PREFACE

THIS book falls naturally into two parts; each of which is really complete in itself, though they are in a sense complementary to one another. Whilst the second and longest part contains a somewhat detailed study of the nature and development of man's spiritual or mystical consciousness, the first is intended rather to provide an introduction to the general subject of mysticism. Exhibiting it by turns from the point of view of metaphysics, psychology, and symbolism, it is an attempt to gather between the covers of one volume information at present scattered amongst many monographs and text-books written in divers tongues, and to give the student in a compact form at least the elementary facts in regard to each of those subjects which are most closely connected with the study of the mystics.

Those mystics, properly speaking, can only be studied in their works: works which are for the most part left unread by those who now talk much about mysticism. Certainly the general reader has this excuse, that the masterpieces of mystical literature, full of strange beauties though they be, offer considerable difficulties to those who come to them unprepared. In the first seven chapters of this book I have tried to remove a few of these difficulties; to provide the necessary preparation; and to exhibit the relation in which mysticism stands to other forms of life. If, then, the readers of this section are enabled by it to come to the encounter of mystical literature with a greater power of sympathetic comprehension than they previously possessed, it will have served the purpose for which it has been composed.

It is probable that almost every such reader, according to

the angle from which he approaches the subject, will here find a good deal which seems to him superfluous. But different types of mind will find this unnecessary elaboration in different places. The psychologist, approaching from the scientific standpoint, eager for morbid phenomena, has little use for disquisitions on symbolism, religious or other. The symbolist, approaching from the artistic standpoint, seldom admires the proceedings of psychology. I believe, however, that none who wish to obtain an idea of mysticism in its wholeness, as a form of life, can afford to neglect any of the aspects on which these pages venture to touch. The metaphysician and the psychologist are unwise if they do not consider the light thrown upon the ideas of the mystics by their attitude towards orthodox theology. The theologian is still more unwise if he refuse to hear the evidence of psychology. For the benefit of those whose interest in mysticism is chiefly literary, and who may care to be provided with a clue to the symbolic and allegorical element in the writings of the contemplatives, a short section on those symbols of which they most often make use has been added. Finally, the persistence amongst us of the false opinion which confuses mysticism with occult philosophy and psychic phenomena, has made it necessary to deal with the vital distinction which exists between it and every form of magic.

Specialists in any of these great departments of knowledge will probably be disgusted by the elementary and superficial manner in which their specific sciences are here treated. But this book does not venture to address itself to specialists. From those who are already fully conversant with the matters touched upon, it asks the indulgence which really kindhearted adults are always ready to extend towards the efforts of youth. Philosophers are earnestly advised to pass over the first two chapters, and theologians to practise the same charity in respect of the section dealing with their science.

The giving of merely historical information is no part of the present plan : except in so far as chronology has a bearing upon the most fascinating of all histories, the history of the spirit of man. Many books upon mysticism have been based on the historical method : amongst them two such very different works as Vaughan's supercilious and unworthy "Hours with the Mystics" and Dr. Inge's scholarly Bampton lectures. It is a method which seems to be open to some objection : since mysticism avowedly deals with the individual not as he stands in relation to the civilization of his time, but as he stands in relation to truths that are timeless. All mystics, said Saint-Martin, speak the same language and come from the same country. As against that fact, the place which they happen to occupy in the kingdom of this world matters little. Nevertheless, those who are unfamiliar with the history of mysticism properly so called, and to whom the names of the great contemplatives convey no accurate suggestion of period or nationality, may be glad to have a short statement of their order in time and distribution in space. Also, some knowledge of the genealogy of mysticism is desirable if we are to distinguish the original contributions of each individual from the mass of speculation and statement which he inherits from the past. Those entirely unacquainted with these matters may find it helpful to glance at the Appendix before proceeding to the body of the work ; since few things are more disagreeable than the constant encounter of persons to whom we have not been introduced.

The second part of the book, for which the first seven chapters are intended to provide a preparation, is avowedly psychological. It is an attempt to set out and justify a definite theory of the nature of man's mystical consciousness : the necessary stages of organic growth through which the typical mystic passes, the state of equilibrium towards which he tends. Each of these stages—and also the characteristically mystical and still largely mysterious experiences of visions and voices, contemplation and ecstasy—though viewed from the standpoint of psychology, is illustrated from the lives of the mystics ; and where possible in their own words. In planning these chapters I have been considerably helped by M. Delacroix's brilliant "Études sur le Mysticisme," though unable to accept his conclusions: and here gladly take the opportunity of acknowledging my debt to him and also to Baron von Hügel's classic "Mystical Element of Religion." This book, which only came into my hands when my own was planned and partly written, has since been a constant source of stimulus and encouragement.

Finally, it is perhaps well to say something as to the exact sense in which the term "Mysticism" is here understood. One of the most abused words in the English language, it has been used in different and often mutually exclusive senses by religion, poetry, and philosophy : has been claimed as an excuse for every kind of occultism, for dilute transcendentalism, vapid symbolism, religious or æsthetic sentimentality, and bad metaphysics. On the other hand, it has been freely employed as a term of contempt by those who have criticized these things. It is much to be hoped that it may be restored sooner or later to its old meaning, as the science or art of the spiritual life.

Meanwhile, those who use the term "Mysticism" are bound in self-defence to explain what they mean by it. Broadly speaking, I understand it to be the expression of the innate tendency of the human spirit towards complete harmony with the transcendental order ; whatever be the theological formula under which that order is understood. This tendency, in great mystics, gradually captures the whole field of consciousness ; it dominates their life and, in the experience called "mystic union," attains its end. Whether that end be called the God of Christianity, the World-soul of Pantheism, the Absolute of Philosophy, the desire to attain it and the movement towards it —so long as this is a genuine life process and not an intellectual speculation—is the proper subject of mysticism. I believe this movement to represent the true line of development of the highest form of human consciousness.

It is a pleasant duty to offer my heartiest thanks to the many kind friends and fellow students, of all shades of opinion, who have given me their help and encouragement. Amongst those to whom my heaviest debt of gratitude is due are Mr. W. Scott Palmer, for much valuable, generous, and painstaking assistance, particularly in respect of the chapter upon Vitalism : and Miss Margaret Robinson, who in addition to many other kind offices, has made all the translations from Meister Eckhart and Mechthild of Magdeburg here given.

Sections of the MS. have been kindly read by the Rev. Dr. Inge, by Miss May Sinclair, and by Miss Eleanor Gregory ; from all of whom I have received much helpful and expert advice. To Mr. Arthur Symons my thanks and those of my readers are specially due ; since it is owing to his generous permission that I am able to make full use of his beautiful translations of the poems of St. John of the Cross. Others who have given me much help in various directions, and to whom most grateful acknowledgments are here offered, are Miss Constance Jones, Miss Ethel Barker, Mr. J. A. Herbert of the British Museum—who first brought to my notice the newly discovered " Mirror of Simple Souls "—the Rev. Dr. Arbuthnot Nairn, Mr. A. E. Waite, and Mr. H. Stuart Moore, F.S.A. The substance of two chapters—those upon " The Characteristics of Mysticism " and " Mysticism and Magic "—has already appeared in the pages of *The Quest* and *The Fortnightly Review*. These sections are here reprinted by kind permission of their respective editors.

E. U.

Feast of St. John of the Cross
1910

CONTENTS

PART I

THE MYSTIC FACT

CHAPTER X

APPENDIX

PART ONE

THE MYSTIC FACT

"What the world, which truly knows *nothing*, calls 'mysticism' is the science of *ultimates*, . . . the science of self-evident Reality, which cannot be 'reasoned about,' because it is the object of pure reason or perception. The Babe sucking its mother's breast, and the Lover returning, after twenty years' separation, to his home and food in the same bosom, are the types and princes of Mystics."

COVENTRY PATMORE,
"The Rod, the Root, and the Flower"

AN INTRODUCTION TO MYSTICISM

CHAPTER I

THE POINT OF DEPARTURE

The mystic type—its persistence--Man's quest of Truth—The Mystics claim to have attained it—The foundations of experience—The Self—its sensations—its concepts—The sense-world—its unreal character—Philosophy—its classic theories of Reality—Naturalism—its failures—Idealism—its limitations—Philosophic Scepticism —the logical end of Intellectualism—Failure of philosophy and science to discover Reality—Emotional and spiritual experience—its validity—Religion—Suffering— Beauty—Their mystical aspects—Mysticism as the science of the Real—Its statements—its practice—It claims direct communion with the Absolute

THE most highly developed branches of the human family have in common one peculiar characteristic. They tend to produce—sporadically it is true, and usually in the teeth of adverse external circumstances—a curious and definite type of personality; a type which refuses to be satisfied with that which other men call experience, and is inclined, in the words of its enemies, to "deny the world in order that it may find reality." We meet these persons in the east and the west; in the ancient, mediaeval, and modern worlds. Their one passion appears to be the prosecution of a certain spiritual and intangible quest: the finding of a "way out" or a "way back" to some desirable state in which alone they can satisfy their craving for absolute truth. This quest, for them, has constituted the whole meaning of life: they have made for it without effort sacrifices which have appeared enormous to other men: and it is an indirect testimony to its objective actuality, that whatever the place or period in which they have arisen, their aims, doctrines and methods have been substantially the same. Their experience, therefore, forms a body of evidence, curiously self-consistent and often mutually explanatory, which must be taken into account before we can add up the sum of the energies and potentialities of the human spirit, or reasonably speculate on its relations to the unknown world which lies outside the boundaries of sense.

All men, at one time or another, have fallen in love with the veiled Isis whom they call Truth. With most, this has been but a passing passion : they have early seen its hopelessness and turned to more practical things. But there are others who remain all their lives the devout lovers of reality : though the manner of their love, the vision which they make unto themselves of the beloved object, varies enormously. Some see Truth as Dante saw Beatrice : a figure adorable yet intangible, found in this world yet revealing the next. To others she seems rather an evil yet an irresistible enchantress : enticing, demanding payment and betraying her lover at the last. Some have seen her in a test tube, and some in a poet's dream : some before the altar, others in the slime. The extreme pragmatists have even sought her in the kitchen ; declaring that she may best be recognized by her utility. Last stage of all, the philosophic sceptic has comforted an unsuccessful courtship by assuring himself that his mistress is not really there.

Under whatsoever symbols they may have objectified their quest, none of these seekers have ever been able to assure the world that they have found, seen face to face, the Reality behind the veil. But if we may trust the reports of the mystics —and they are reports given with a strange accent of certainty and good faith—they have succeeded where all these others have failed, in establishing immediate communication between the spirit of man, entangled as they declare amongst material things, and that " only Reality," that immaterial and final Being, which some philosophers call the Absolute, and most theologians call God. This, they say—and here many who are not mystics agree with them—is the hidden Truth which is the object of man's craving ; the only satisfying goal of his quest. Hence, they should claim from us the same attention that we give to other explorers of countries in which we are not competent to adventure ourselves; for the mystics are the pioneers of the spiritual world, and we have no right to deny validity to their discoveries, merely because we lack the opportunity or the courage necessary to those who would prosecute such explorations for themselves.

It is the object of this book to attempt a description, and also—though this is needless for those who read that description in good faith—a justification of these experiences and the conclusions which have been drawn from them. So remote, however, are these matters from our ordinary habits of thought, that their investigation entails, in all those who would attempt to understand them, a certain definite preparation : a purging of the intellect. As with those who came of old to the Mysteries, purification is here the gate of knowledge. We must come to this encounter with minds cleared of prejudice and convention, must deliberately break with our inveterate habit of taking the " visible world" for granted ; our lazy assumption that somehow science is " real " and metaphysics is not. We must pull down our own card houses—descend, as the mystics say, " into our nothingness "—and examine for ourselves the foundations of all possible human experience, before we are in a position to criticize the buildings of the visionaries, the poets, and the saints. We must not begin to talk of the unreal world of these dreamers until we have discovered—if we can—a real world with which it may be compared.

Such a criticism of reality is of course the business of philosophy. I need hardly say that this book is not written by a philosopher, nor is it addressed to students of that imperial science. Nevertheless, amateurs though we be, we cannot reach our proper starting-point without trespassing to some extent on philosophic ground. That ground covers the whole area of first principles : and it is to first principles that we must go, if we would understand the true significance of the mystic type.

Let us then begin at the beginning : and remind ourselves of a few of the trite and primary facts which all practical persons agree to ignore. That beginning, for human thought, is of course the I, the Ego, the self-conscious subject which is writing this book, or the other self-conscious subject which is reading it ; and which declares, in the teeth of all arguments, I AM.[1]

---

[1] Even this I AM, which has seemed sale ground to most metaphysicians, is of course combated by certain schools of philosophy. " The word *Sum*," said Eckhart

Here is a point as to which we all feel quite sure. No metaphysician has yet shaken the ordinary individual's belief in his own existence. The uncertainties only begin for most of us when we ask what else *is*.

To this I, this conscious self "imprisoned in the body like an oyster in his shell," [1] come, as we know, a constant stream of messages and experiences. Chief amongst these are the stimulation of the tactile nerves whose result we call touch, the vibrations taken up by the optic nerve which we call light, and those taken up by the ear and perceived as sound.

What do these experiences mean? The first answer of the unsophisticated Self of course is, that they indicate the nature of the external world: it is to the "evidence of her senses" that she turns, when she is asked what that world is like. From the messages received through those senses, which pour in on her whether she will or no, batter upon her gateways at every instant and from every side, she constructs that "sense-world" which is the "real and solid world" of normal men. As the impressions come in—or rather those interpretations of the original impressions which her nervous system supplies—she pounces on them, much as players in the spelling-game pounce on the separate letters dealt out to them. She sorts, accepts, rejects, combines: and then triumphantly produces from them a "concept" which *is*, she says, the external world. With an enviable and amazing simplicity she attributes her own sensations to the unknown universe. The stars, she says, *are* bright; the grass *is* green. For her, as for the philosopher Hume, "reality consists in impressions and ideas."

It is immediately apparent, however, that this sense-world, this seemingly real external universe—though it may be useful and valid in other respects—cannot be *the* external world, but only the Self's projected picture of it.[2] It is a work of art, not

long ago, "can be spoken by no creature but by God only: for it becomes the creature to testify of itself *Non Sum*." In a less mystical strain Lotze, and after him Bradley and other modern writers, have devoted much destructive criticism to the concept of the Ego as the starting-point of philosophy: looking upon it as a large, and logically unwarrantable, assumption.

[1] Plato, Phaedrus, § 250.

[2] Thus Eckhart, "Every time that the powers of the soul come into contact with created things, they receive and *create* images and likenesses from the created thing and absorb them. In this way arises the soul's knowledge of created things.

a scientific fact ; and, whilst it may well possess the profound significance proper to great works of art, is dangerous if treated as a subject of analysis. Very slight investigation will be enough to suggest that it is a picture whose relation to reality is at best symbolic and approximate, and which would have no meaning for selves whose senses, or channels of communication, happened to be arranged upon a different plan. The evidence of the senses, then, cannot safely be accepted as evidence of the nature of ultimate reality : useful servants, they are dangerous guides. Nor can their testimony disconcert those seekers whose reports they appear to contradict.

The conscious self sits, so to speak, at the receiving end of a telegraph wire. On any other theory than that of mysticism, it is her one channel of communication with the hypothetical " external world." The receiving instrument registers certain messages. She does not know, and—so long as she remains dependent on that instrument—never can know, the object, the reality at the other end of the wire, by which those messages are sent ; neither can the messages truly disclose the nature of that object. But she is justified on the whole in accepting them as evidence that something exists beyond herself and her receiving instrument. It is obvious that the structural peculiarities of the telegraphic instrument will have exerted a modifying effect upon the message. That which is conveyed as dash and dot, colour and shape, may have been received in a very different form. Therefore this message, though it may in a partial sense be relevant to the supposed reality at the other end, can never be adequate to it. There will be fine vibrations which it fails to take up, others which it confuses together. Hence a portion of the message is always lost ; or, in other language, there are aspects of the world which we can never know.

The sphere of our possible intellectual knowledge is thus strictly conditioned by the limits of our own personality. On

Created things cannot come nearer to the soul than this, and the soul can only approach created things by the voluntary reception of images. And it is through the presence of the image that the soul approaches the created world : for *the image is a Thing, which the soul creates* with her own powers. Does the soul want to know the nature of a stone—a horse—a man ? She forms an image."—Meister Eckhart, Pred. i. (" Mystische Schriften," p. 15).

this basis, not the ends of the earth, but the external termini
of our own sensory nerves, are the termini of our explorations : and to "know oneself" is really to know one's
universe. We are locked up with our receiving instruments :
we cannot get up and walk away in the hope of seeing
whither the lines lead. Eckhart's words are still final for
us : "the soul can only approach created things by the
voluntary reception of images." Did some mischievous
Demiurge choose to tickle our sensory apparatus in a new
way, we should receive by this act a new universe.

The late Professor James once suggested as a useful
exercise for young idealists a consideration of the changes
which would be worked in our ordinary world if the various
branches of our receiving instruments happened to exchange
duties; if, for instance, we heard all colours and saw all
sounds. Such a remark as this throws a sudden light on
the strange and apparently insane statement of the visionary
Saint-Martin, "I heard flowers that sounded, and saw notes
that shone"; and on the reports of certain other mystics
concerning a rare moment of consciousness in which the
senses are fused into a single and ineffable act of perception ; and colour and sound are known as aspects of the
same thing.[1]

Since music is but an interpretation of certain vibrations
undertaken by the ear, and colour an interpretation of other
vibrations performed by the eye, all this is less mad than
it sounds. Were such an alteration of our senses to take
place the world would still be sending us the same messages
—that strange unknown world from which, on this hypothesis,
we are hermetically sealed—but we should have interpreted
them differently. Beauty would still be ours, though speaking
another tongue. The bird's song would then strike our retina
as a pageant of colour: we should see all the magical tones
of the wind, hear as a great fugue the repeated and harmonized
greens of the forest, the cadences of stormy skies. Did we
realize how slight an adjustment of our own organs is needed
to initiate us into such a world, we should perhaps be less

[1] Thus Edward Carpenter says of his own experience of the onset of mystical
consciousness, "The perception seems to be one in which all the senses unite into
one sense" (quoted in Bucke's "Cosmic Consciousness," p. 198).

contemptuous of those mystics who tell us that they apprehended the Absolute as "heavenly music" or "Uncreated
Light": less fanatical in our determination to make the
"real and solid world of common sense" the only standard
of reality. This "world of common sense" is a conceptual
world. It may represent an external universe: it certainly
does represent the activity of the human mind. Within
that mind it is built up: and there most of us are content
"at ease for aye to dwell," like the soul in the Palace of Art.

A direct encounter with absolute truth, then, appears to
be impossible for normal non-mystical consciousness. We
cannot know the reality, or even prove the existence, of the
simplest object: though this is a limitation which few people
realize acutely and most would strenuously deny. But there
persists in the race a type of personality which does realize
this limitation : and cannot be content with the sham realities
that furnish the universe of normal men. It is necessary, as
it seems, to the comfort of persons of this type to form
for themselves some image of the Something or Nothing
which is at the end of their telegraph lines : some "conception
of being," some "theory of knowledge." They are tormented
by the Unknowable, ache for first principles, demand some
background to the shadow show of things. In so far as man
possesses this temperament, he hungers for reality, and must
satisfy that hunger as best he can: staving off starvation,
though he may not be filled.

Now it is doubtful whether any two selves have offered
themselves exactly the same image of the truth outside their
gates : for a living metaphysic, like a living religion, is at
bottom a strictly personal affair—a matter, as Professor James
reminded us, of vision rather than of argument.[1] Nevertheless
such a living metaphysic may—and if sound generally does—
escape the stigma of subjectivism by outwardly attaching itself
to a traditional School; as personal religion may and should
outwardly attach itself to a traditional church. Let us then
consider shortly the results arrived at by these traditional
schools—the great classic theories concerning the nature of
reality. In them we see crystallized the best that the human
intellect, left to itself, has been able to achieve.

[1] "A Pluralistic Universe," p. 10.

1. The most obvious and most generally accepted explanation of the world is of course that of *Naturalism* or Realism : the point of view at once of the plain man and of physical science. Naturalism states simply that we see the real world, though we may not see it very well. What seems to normal healthy people to be there, is approximately there. It congratulates itself on resting in the concrete ; it accepts material things as real. In other words, our corrected and correlated sense impressions, raised to their highest point of efficiency, form for it the only valid material of knowledge : knowledge itself being the classified results of exact observation.

Now such an attitude as this may be a counsel of prudence, in view of our ignorance of all that lies beyond : but it can never satisfy our hunger for reality. It says in effect, " The room in which we find ourselves is fairly comfortable. Draw the curtains, for the night is dark : and let us devote ourselves to describing the furniture." Unfortunately, however, even the furniture refuses to accommodate itself to the naturalistic view of things. Once we begin to examine it attentively, we find that it abounds in hints of wonder and mystery : declares aloud that even chairs and tables are not what they seem.

We have seen that the most elementary criticism, applied to any ordinary object of perception, tends to invalidate the simple and comfortable creed of " common sense " ; that not merely faith, but gross credulity, is needed by the mind which would accept the apparent as the real. I say, for instance, that I " see " a house. I can only mean by this that the part of my receiving instrument which undertakes the duty called vision is affected in a certain way, and arouses in my mind the idea " house." The idea " house " is now treated by me as a real house, and my further observations will be an unfolding, enriching, and defining of this image. But what the external reality *is* which evoked the image that I call " house," I do not know and never can know. It is as mysterious, as far beyond my apprehension, as the constitution of the angelic choirs. Consciousness shrinks in terror from contact with the mighty verb " to be." I may of course call in one sense to " corroborate," as we trustfully say, the evidence of the other ; may approach the house, and touch it. Then the nerves of my hand will be affected by a sensation which I translate as hardness and solidity; the eye by a peculiar and wholly incomprehensible sensation called redness; and from these purely personal changes my mind constructs and externalizes an idea which it calls red bricks. Science herself, however, if she be asked to verify the reality of these perceptions, at once declares that though the material world be real, the ideas of solidity and colour are but hallucination. They belong to the human animal, not to the physical universe: pertain to accident not substance, as scholastic philosophy would say.

"The red brick," says Science, "is a mere convention. In reality that bit, like all other bits of the universe, consists, so far as I know at present, of innumerable atoms whirling and dancing one about the other. It is no more solid than a snowstorm. Were you to eat of Alice-in-Wonderland's mushroom and shrink to the dimensions of the infra-world, each atom might seem to you a planet and the red brick itself a universe. Moreover, these atoms themselves elude me as I try to grasp them. They are only manifestations of something else. Could I track matter to its lair, I might conceivably discover that it has no extension, and become an idealist in spite of myself. As for redness, as you call it, that is a question of the relation between your optic nerve and the light waves which it is unable to absorb. This evening, when the sun slopes, your brick will probably be purple; a very little deviation from normal vision on your part would make it green. Even the sense that the object of perception is outside yourself may be fancy; since you as easily attribute this external quality to images seen in dreams, and to waking hallucinations, as you do to those objects which, as you absurdly say, are "*really there.*"

Further, there is no trustworthy standard by which we can separate the "real" from the "unreal" aspects of phenomena. Such standards as exist are conventional: and correspond to convenience, not to truth. It is no argument to say that most men see the world in much the same way, and that this "way" is the true standard of reality: though for practical purposes we have agreed that sanity consists in sharing the hallucinations of our neighbours. Those who are honest with themselves know that this "sharing" is at best incomplete. By the voluntary adoption of a new conception of the universe, the fitting of a new alphabet to the old Morse code—a proceeding which we call the acquirement of knowledge—we can and do change to a marked extent our way of seeing things : building up new worlds from old sense impressions, and transmuting objects more easily and thoroughly than any magician. " Eyes and ears," said Heracleitus, " are bad witnesses to those who have barbarian souls " : and even those whose souls are civilized tend to see and hear all things through a temperament. In one and the same sky the poet may discover the veritable habitation of angels, whilst the sailor sees only a promise of dirty weather ahead. Hence, artist and surgeon, Christian and rationalist, pessimist and optimist, do actually and truly live in different and mutually exclusive worlds, not only of thought but also of perception. Each, in Professor James's phrase, literally " dichotomizes the Kosmos in a different place." Only the happy circumstance that our ordinary speech is conventional, not realistic, permits us to conceal from one another the unique and lonely world in which each lives. Now and then an artist is born, terribly articulate, foolishly truthful, who insists on " Speaking as he saw." Then other men, lapped warmly in their artificial universe, agree that he is mad : or, at the very best, an " extraordinarily imaginative fellow."

Moreover, even this unique world of the individual is not permanent. Each of us, as we grow and change, works incessantly and involuntarily at the re-making of our sensual universe. We behold at any specific moment not "that which is," but "that which we are"; and personality undergoes many readjustments in the course of its passage from birth through maturity to death. The mind which seeks the Real, then, in this shifting and subjective "natural" world is of necessity thrown back on itself : on images and concepts which owe more to the "seer" than to the "seen." But Reality must be real for all, once they have found it : must exist "in itself" upon a plane of being unconditioned by the perceiving mind. Only thus can it satisfy that mind's most vital instinct, most sacred passion— its " instinct for the Absolute," its passion for truth.

You are not asked, as a result of these antique and elementary propositions, to wipe clean the slate of normal human experience, and cast in your lot with intellectual nihilism. You are only asked to acknowledge that it is but a slate, and that the white scratches upon it which the ordinary man calls facts, and the Scientific Realist calls knowledge, are at best relative and conventionalized symbols of that aspect of the unknowable reality at which they hint. This being so, whilst we must all draw a picture of some kind on our slate and act in relation therewith, we cannot deny the validity—though we may deny the usefulness—of the pictures which others produce, however abnormal and impossible they may seem; since these are sketching an aspect of reality which has not come within our sensual field, and so does not and cannot form part of our world. Yet, as the theologian claims that the doctrine of the Trinity veils and reveals not Three but One, so the varied aspects under which the universe appears to the perceiving consciousness hint at a final reality, or in Kantian language a Transcendental Object, which shall be, not any one, yet all of its manifestations; transcending yet including the innumerable fragmentary worlds of individual conception. We begin, then, to ask what can be the nature of this One; and whence comes the persistent instinct which—receiving no encouragement from sense experience— apprehends and desires this unknown unity, this all-inclusive Absolute, as the only possible satisfaction of its thirst for truth.

2. The second great conception of Being—*Idealism*—has arrived by a process of elimination at a tentative answer to this question. It whisks us far from the material universe, with its interesting array of " things," its machinery, its law, into the pure, if thin, air of a metaphysical world. Whilst the naturalist's world is constructed from an observation of the evidence offered by the senses, the Idealist's world is constructed from an observation of the processes of thought. There are but two things, he says in effect, about which we are sure: the existence of a thinking subject, a conscious Self, and of an object, an Idea, with which that subject deals. We know, that is to say, both Mind and Thought. What we call the universe is really a collection of such thoughts; and these, we agree, have been more or less distorted by the subject, the individual thinker, in the process of assimilation. Obviously, we do not think all that there is to be thought, conceive all that there is to be conceived: neither do we necessarily combine in right order and proportion those ideas which we are capable of grasping.

Reality, says Objective Idealism, is the complete, undistorted Object, the big thought, of which we pick up these fragmentary hints: the world of phenomena which we treat as real being merely its shadow show or " manifestation in space and time."

According to the form of Objective Idealism here chosen from amongst many as typical—for almost every Idealist has his own scheme of metaphysical salvation[1]—we live in a universe which is, in popular language, the Idea, or Dream of its Creator. We, as Tweedledum explained to Alice in the most philosophic of all fairy tales, are "just part of the dream." All life, all phenomena, are the endless modifications and expressions of the one transcendent Object, the mighty and dynamic Thought of one Absolute Thinker in which we are bathed. This Object—or certain aspects of it; and the place of each individual consciousness within the Cosmic Thought, or, as we say, our position in life, must largely determine which these aspects shall be—is interpreted by the senses and conceived by the mind, under limitations which we are accustomed to call matter, space, and time. But we have no reason to suppose that matter, space, and time are necessarily parts of reality; of the ultimate Idea. Probability points rather to their being the pencil and paper with which we sketch it. As our vision, our idea of things, tends to approximate more and more to that of the Eternal Idea, so we get nearer and nearer to reality: for the idealist's reality is simply the Idea, or Thought of God. *This*, he says, is the supreme unity at which all the illusory appearances that make up the widely differing worlds of "common sense," of science, of metaphysics, and of art dimly hint. This is the sense in which it can truly be said that only the supernatural possesses reality; for that world of appearance which we call natural is certainly largely made up of preconception and illusion, of the hints offered by the eternal real world of Idea outside our gates, and the quaint concepts which we at our receiving instruments manufacture from them.

There is this to be said for the argument of Idealism: that in the last resort, the destinies of mankind are invariably guided, not by the concrete "facts" of the sense world, but by concepts

---

[1] There are four main groups of such schemes: (1) Subjective; (2) Objective; (3) Transcendental (Kantian); (4) Absolute (Hegelian). To these must perhaps be added the Immanental Idealism of Professor Eucken.

which are acknowledged by every one to exist only on the mental plane. In the great moments of existence, when he rises to spiritual freedom, these are the things which every man feels to be real. It is by these and for these that he is found willing to live, work, suffer, and die. Love, empire, religion, altruism, fame, all belong to the transcendental world. Hence, they partake more of the nature of reality than any "fact" could do; and man, dimly recognizing this, has ever bowed to them as to immortal centres of energy. Religions as a rule are steeped in idealism: Christianity in particular is a trumpet call to an idealistic conception of life, Buddhism is little less. Over and over again, their Scriptures tell us that only materialists will be damned.

In Idealism we have perhaps the most sublime theory of Being which has ever been constructed by the human intellect: a theory so sublime, in fact, that it can hardly have been produced by the exercise of "pure reason" alone, but must be looked upon as a manifestation of that natural mysticism, that instinct for the Absolute, which is latent in man. But, when we ask the idealist how we are to attain communion with the reality which he describes to us as "certainly there," his system suddenly breaks down; and discloses itself as a diagram of the heavens, not a ladder to the stars. This failure of Idealism to find in practice the reality of which it thinks so much is due, in the opinion of the mystics, to a cause which finds epigrammatic expression in the celebrated phrase by which St. Jerome marked the distinction between religion and philosophy. "Plato located the soul of man in the head; Christ located it in the heart." That is to say, Idealism, though just in its premises, and often daring and honest in their application, is stultified by the exclusive intellectualism of its own methods: by its fatal trust in the squirrel-work of the industrious brain instead of the piercing vision of the desirous heart. It interests man, but does not involve him in its processes: does not catch him up to the new and more real life which it describes. Hence the thing that mattered, the living thing, has somehow escaped it; and its observations bear the same relation to reality as the art of the anatomist does to the mystery of birth.

3. But there is yet another Theory of Being to be considered: that which may be loosely defined as *Philosophic*

Scepticism. This is the attitude of those selves who refuse to accept either the realistic or the idealistic answer to the eternal question : and, confronted in their turn with the riddle of reality, reply that there is no riddle to solve. We of course assume for the ordinary purposes of life that for every sequence a : b : present in our consciousness there exists a mental or material A : B : in the external universe ; and that the first is a strictly relevant, though probably wholly inadequate, expression of the second. The bundle of visual and auditory sensations, for instance, whose sum total I am accustomed to call Mrs. Smith, corresponds with something that exists in the actual as well as in my phenomenal world. Behind my Mrs. Smith, behind the very different Mrs. Smith which the X rays would exhibit, there is, contends the Objective Idealist, a transcendental, or in the Platonic sense an ideal Mrs. Smith, at whose qualities I cannot even guess ; but whose existence is quite independent of my apprehension of it. But though we do and must act on this hypothesis, it remains only a hypothesis ; and it is one which philosophic scepticism will not let pass.

The external world, say the sceptical schools, is—so far as I know it—a concept present in my mind. If my mind ceased to exist, so far as I know the concept which I call the world would cease to exist too. The one thing which for me indubitably *is*, is the self's experience, its whole consciousness. Outside this circle of consciousness I have no authority to indulge in guesses as to what may or may not Be. Hence, for me, the Absolute is a meaningless diagram, a superfluous complication of thought : since the mind, wholly cut off from contact with external reality, has no reason to suppose that such a reality exists except in its own ideas. Every effort made by philosophy to go forth in search of it is merely the metaphysical squirrel running round the conceptual cage. In the completion and perfect unfolding of the set of ideas with which our consciousness is furnished, lies the only reality which we can ever hope to know. Far better to stay here and make ourselves at home : only this, for us, truly is.

This purely subjective conception of Being has found representatives in every school of thought : even including, by a curious paradox, that of mystical philosophy, its one effective antagonist. Thus Delacroix, after an exhaustive and even sympathetic analysis of St. Teresa's progress towards union with the Absolute, ends upon the assumption that the God with whom she was united was the content of her own subconscious mind.[1] Such a mysticism is that of a kitten running after its own tail: a different path indeed from that which the great seekers for reality have pursued. The *reductio ad absurdum* of this doctrine is found in the so-called " philosophy " of New Thought, which begs its disciples to "try quietly to realize that the Infinite is really You."[2] By its utter denial not merely of a knowable, but of a logically conceivable Transcendent, it drives us in the end to the conclusion of extreme pragmatism ; that Truth, for us, is not an immutable reality, but merely that idea which happens to work out as true and useful in any given experience. There is no reality behind appearance, no Isis behind the veil ; therefore all faiths, all figments with which we people that nothingness are equally true, provided they be comfortable and good to live by.

Logically carried out, this conception of Being would permit each man to regard other men as non-existent except within his own consciousness : the only place where a strict scepticism will allow that anything exists. Even the mind which conceives consciousness exists for us only in our own conception of it ; we no more know what we are than we know what we shall be. Man is left a conscious Something in the midst, so far as he knows, of Nothing : with no resources save the exploring of his own consciousness.

Philosophic scepticism is particularly interesting to us in our present inquiry, because it shows us the position in which " pure reason," if left to itself, is bound to end. It is utterly logical ; and though we may feel it to be absurd, we can never prove it to be so. Those persons who are temperamentally inclined to credulity may become naturalists, and persuade themselves to believe in the reality of the sense world. Those with a certain instinct for the Absolute may adopt the more reasonable faith of idealism. But the true intellectualist, who concedes nothing to instinct or emotion, is obliged in the end to adopt some form of sceptical philosophy. The horrors of

---

[1] Delacroix, " Études sur le Mysticisme," p. 62.
[2] E. Towne, " Just how to Wake the Solar Plexus," p. 25.

nihilism, in fact, can only be escaped by the exercise of faith: by a trust in man's innate but strictly irrational instinct for that Real "above all reason, beyond all thought" towards which at its best moments his spirit tends.   If the metaphysician be true to his own postulates, he is compelled at last to acknowledge that we are forced, every one of us, to live, to think, and at last to die, in an unknown and unknowable world : fed arbitrarily and diligently, yet how we know not, by ideas and suggestions whose truth we cannot test but whose pressure we cannot resist. It is not by sight but by faith—faith in a supposed external order which we can never prove to exist, and in the approximate truthfulness and constancy of the vague messages which we receive from it—that ordinary men must live and move. We must put our trust in "laws of nature" which have been devised by the human mind as a convenient epitome of its own observations of phenomena, must, for the purposes of daily life, accept these phenomena at their face value : an act of faith beside which the grossest superstitions of the Neapolitan peasant are hardly noticeable.

The intellectual quest of Reality, then, leads us down one of three blind alleys : (1) To an acceptance of the symbolic world of appearance as the real ; (2) to the elaboration of a theory—also of necessity symbolic—which, beautiful in itself, cannot help us to attain the Absolute which it describes ; (3) to a hopeless but strictly logical scepticism.

In answer to the " Why ? Why ? " of the bewildered and eternal child in us, philosophy, though always ready to postulate the unknown if she can, is bound to reply only, " *Nescio ! Nescio !* " In spite of all her busy map-making, she cannot reach the goal which she points out to us : cannot explain the curious conditions under which we imagine that we know ; cannot even divide with a sure hand the subject and object of thought.   Science, whose business is with phenomena and our knowledge of them, though she too is an idealist at heart, has been accustomed to explain that all our ideas and instincts, the pictured world that we take so seriously, the oddly limited and illusory nature of our experience, appear to minister to one great end : the preservation of life, and consequent fulfilment of that highly mystical hypothesis, the Cosmic Idea.   Each perception, she assures us, serves a useful purpose in this evolu-

tionary scheme : a scheme, by the way, which has been invented
—we know not why—by the human mind, and imposed upon
an obedient universe.

By vision, hearing, smell, and touch, says Science, we find
our way about, are warned of danger, obtain our food. The
male perceives beauty in the female in order that the
species may be propagated. It is true that this primitive
instinct has given birth to higher and purer emotions; but
these too fulfil a social purpose and are not so useless as they
seem. Man must eat to live, therefore many foods give us
agreeable sensations. If he over eats, he dies ; therefore indi-
gestion is an unpleasant pain. Certain facts of which too keen
a perception would act detrimentally to the life-force are, for
most men, impossible of realization : i.e., the uncertainty of life,
the decay of the body, the vanity of all things under the sun.
When we are in good health, we all feel very real, solid, and
permanent ; and this is of all our illusions the most ridiculous,
and also the most obviously useful from the point of view of the
efficiency and preservation of the race.

But when we look a little closer, we see that this brisk
generalization does not cover all the ground—not even that
little tract of ground of which our senses make us free ;
indeed, that it is more remarkable for its omissions than for
its inclusions. Récéjac has well said that "from the moment
in which man is no longer content to devise things useful for
his existence under the exclusive action of the will-to-live, the
principle of (physical) evolution has been violated."[1] Nothing
can be more certain than that man is not so content. He has
been called by utilitarian philosophers a tool-making animal—
the highest praise they knew how to bestow. More surely he is
a vision-making animal ;[2] a creature of perverse and unpractical
ideals, dominated by dreams no less than by appetites—dreams
which can only be justified upon the theory that he moves
towards some other goal than that of physical perfection or
intellectual supremacy, is controlled by some higher and more
vital reality than that of the determinists. One is driven to

[1] " Fondements de la Connaissance Mystique," p. 15.
[2] Or, as St. Thomas Aquinas suggests, a contemplative animal, since " this act
alone in man is proper to him, and is in no way shared by any other being in this
world" (" Summa Contra Gentiles," l. iii. cap. xxxvii., Rickaby's translation).

the conclusion that if the theory of evolution is to include or explain the facts of artistic and spiritual experience—and it cannot be accepted by any serious thinker if these great tracts of consciousness remain outside its range—it must be rebuilt on a mental rather than a physical basis.

Even the most normal, most ordinary human life includes in its range fundamental experiences—violent and unforgettable sensations—forced on us as it were against our will, for which science finds it hard to account. These experiences and sensations, and the hours of exalted emotion which they bring with them—often recognized by us as the greatest, most significant hours of our lives—fulfil no office in relation to her pet "functions of nutrition and reproduction." It is true that they are far-reaching in their effects on character; but they do little or nothing to assist that character in its struggle for physical life. To the unprejudiced eye many of them seem hopelessly out of place in a universe constructed on strictly physico-chemical lines—look almost as though nature, left to herself, tended to contradict her own beautifully logical laws. Their presence, more, the large place which they fill in the human world of appearance, is a puzzling circumstance for deterministic philosophers; who can only escape from the dilemma here presented to them by calling these things illusions, and dignifying their own more manageable illusions with the title of facts.

Amongst the more intractable of these groups of perceptions and experiences are those which we connect with religion, with pain, and with beauty. All three, for those selves which are capable of receiving their messages, possess a mysterious authority far in excess of those feelings, arguments, or appearances which they may happen to contradict. All three, were the universe of the naturalists true, would be absurd; all three have ever been treated with the reverence due to vital matters by the best minds of the race.

A. I need not point out the hopelessly irrational character of all great religions, which rest, one and all, on a primary assumption that can never be intellectually demonstrated, much less proved; the assumption that the supra-sensible is somehow important and real, and can be influenced by the activities of man. This fact has been incessantly dwelt upon by their critics, and has provoked many a misplaced exercise of ingenuity on the part of their intelligent friends. Yet religion —emphasizing and pushing to extremes that general dependence on faith which we saw to be an inevitable condition of our lives—is one of the most universal and ineradicable functions of man, and this although it constantly acts detrimentally to the interests of his merely physical existence, opposes "the exclusive action of the will-to-live," except in so far as that will aspires to eternal life. Strictly utilitarian, almost logical in the savage, religion becomes more and more transcendental with the upward progress of the race. It begins as black magic; it ends as Pure Love. Why did the Cosmic Idea elaborate this religious instinct, if the construction put upon its intentions by the determinists be true?

B. Consider again the whole group of phenomena which are known as "the problem of suffering": the mental anguish and physical pain which appear to be the inevitable result of the steady operation of "natural law" and its voluntary assistants, the cruelty, greed, and injustice of man. Here, it is true, the naturalist seems at first sight to make a little more headway, and is able to point to some amongst the cruder forms of suffering which are clearly useful to the race: punishing us for past follies, spurring to new efforts, warning against future infringements of "law." But he forgets the many others which refuse to be resumed under this simple formula: forgets to explain how it is that the Cosmic Idea involves the long torments of the incurable, the tortures of the innocent, the deep anguish of the bereaved, the existence of so many gratuitously agonizing forms of death. He forgets, too, the strange fact that man's capacity for suffering tends to increase in depth and subtlety with the increase of culture and civilization; ignores the still more mysterious, perhaps most significant circumstance that the highest types have accepted it eagerly and willingly, have found in Pain the grave but kindly teacher of immortal secrets, the conferrer of liberty even the initiator into amazing joys.

Those who "explain" suffering as the result of nature's immense fecundity—a by-product of that overcrowding and stress through which the fittest tend to survive—forget that even were this demonstration valid and complete it would leave the real problem untouched. The question is not, whence come those conditions which provoke in the self the experiences called sorrow, anxiety, pain : but, why do these conditions *hurt* the self? The pain is mental ; a little chloroform, and though the conditions continue unabated the suffering is gone. Why does full consciousness always include the mysterious capacity for misery as well as for happiness—a capacity which seems at first sight to invalidate any conception of the Absolute as Beautiful and Good? Why does evolution, as we ascend the ladder of life, foster instead of diminishing the capacity for useless mental anguish, for long, dull torment, bitter grief? Why, when so much lies outside our limited powers of perception, when so many of our own most vital functions are unperceived by consciousness, does suffering of some sort form an integral part of the experience of man? For utilitarian purposes acute discomfort would be quite enough ; the Cosmic Idea, as the determinists explain it, did not really need an apparatus which felt all the throes of cancer, the horrors of neurasthenia, the pangs of birth. Still less did it need the torments of impotent sympathy for other people's irremediable pain, the dreadful power of feeling the world's woe. We are hopelessly over-sensitized for the part science calls us to play.

Pain, however we may look at it, indicates a profound disharmony between the sense-world and the human self. If it is to be vanquished, either the disharmony must be resolved by a deliberate and careful adjustment of the self to the world of sense, or, that self must turn from the sense-world to some other with which it is in tune.[1] Pessimist and optimist here join hands. But whilst the pessimist, resting in appearance, only sees "nature red in tooth and claw" offering him little hope of escape, the optimist thinks that pain and anguish— which may in their lower forms be life's harsh guides on the path of physical evolution—in their higher and apparently "useless" developments are her leaders and teachers in the upper school of Supra-sensible Reality. He believes that they press the self towards another world, still "natural" for him, though "super-natural" for his antagonist, in which it will be more at home. Watching life, he sees in Pain the complement of Love : and is inclined to call these the wings on which man's

---

[1] All the healing arts, from Æsculapius and Galen to Metchnikoff and Mrs. Eddy, have virtually accepted and worked upon these two principles.

spirit can best take flight towards the Absolute. Hence he can say with À Kempis, " Gloriari in tribulatione non est grave amanti," [1] and needs not to speak of morbid folly when he sees the Christian saints run eagerly and merrily to the Cross.[2]

He calls suffering the " gymnastic of eternity," the " terrible initiative caress of God " ; recognizing in it a quality for which the disagreeable rearrangement of nerve molecules cannot account. Sometimes, in the excess of his optimism, he puts to the test of practice this theory with all its implications. Refusing to be deluded by the pleasures of the sense world, he accepts instead. of avoiding pain, and becomes an ascetic ; a puzzling type for the convinced naturalist, who, falling back upon contempt—that favourite resource of the frustrated reason —can only regard him as diseased.

Pain, then, which plunges like a sword through creation, leaving on the one side cringing and degraded animals ànd on the other side heroes and saints, is one of those facts of universal experience which are peculiarly intractable from the point of view of a merely materialistic philosophy.

C. From this same point of view the existence of music and poetry, the qualities of beauty and of rhythm, the evoked sensations of awe, reverence, and rapture, are almost as difficult to account for. The question *why* an apparent corru- gation of the Earth's surface, called for convenience' sake an Alp, coated with congealed water, and perceived by us as a snowy peak, should produce in certain natures acute sensations of ecstasy and adoration, why the skylark's song should catch us up to heaven, and wonder and mystery speak to us alike in " the little speedwell's darling blue " and in the cadence of the wind, is a problem that seems to be merely absurd, until it is seen to be insoluble. Here Madam How and Lady Why alike are silent. With all our busy seeking, we have not found the sorting house where loveliness is extracted from the flux of things. We know not why " great " poetry should move us to unspeakable emotion, or a stream of notes, arranged in a

---

[1] " De Imitatione Christi," l. ii. cap. vi.

[2] " Such as these, I say, as if enamoured of My honour and famished for the food of souls, run to the table of the Most holy Cross, willing to suffer pain. . . . To these, My most dear sons, trouble is a pleasure, and pleasure and every consolation that the world would offer them are a toil " (St. Catherine of Siena, Dialogo, cap. lxxviii.). Here and throughout I have used Thorold's translation.

peculiar sequence, catch us up to heightened levels of vitality : nor can we guess how a passionate admiration of that which we call "best" in art or letters can possibly contribute to the physical evolution of the race. In spite of many lengthy disquisitions on æsthetics, Beauty's secret is still her own. A shadowy companion, half seen, half guessed at, she keeps step with the upward march of life : and we receive her message and respond to it, not because we understand it but because we *must*.

Here it is that we approach that attitude of the self, that point of view, which is loosely and generally called *mystical*. Here, instead of those broad blind alleys which philosophy showed us, a certain type of mind has always discerned three strait and narrow ways going out towards the Absolute. In religion, in pain, in beauty, and the ecstasy of artistic satisfaction—and not only in these, but in many other apparently useless peculiarities of the empirical world and of the perceiving consciousness—these persons insist that they recognize at any rate the fringe of the real. Down these three paths, as well as by many another secret way, they claim that news comes to the self concerning levels of reality which in their wholeness are inaccessible to the senses : worlds wondrous and immortal, whose existence is not conditioned by the "given" world which those senses report. "Beauty," said Hegel, who, though he was no mystic, had a touch of that mystical intuition which no philosopher can afford to be without, "is merely the Spiritual making itself known sensuously." [1] "In the good, the beautiful, the true," says Rudolph Eucken, "we see Reality revealing its personal character. They are parts of a coherent and substantial spiritual world." [2] Here, some of the veils of that substantial world are stripped off : Reality peeps through, and is recognized dimly, or acutely, by the imprisoned self.

Récéjac only develops this idea when he says,[3] "If the mind penetrates deeply into the facts of æsthetics, it will find more and more, that these facts are based upon an ideal identity between the mind itself and things. At a certain point the harmony becomes so complete, and the finality so close that it

[1] "Philosophy of Religion," vol. ii. p. 8.
[2] "Der Sinn und Wert des Lebens," p. 148.
[3] "Fondements de la Connaissance Mystique," p. 74.

gives us actual emotion. The Beautiful then becomes the sublime; brief apparition, by which the soul is caught up into the true mystic state, and touches the Absolute. It is scarcely possible to persist in this æsthetic perception without feeling lifted up by it above things and above ourselves, in an ontological vision which closely resembles the Absolute of the Mystics."

It was of this underlying reality—this truth of things—that St. Augustine cried in a moment of lucid vision, " Oh, Beauty so old and so new, too late have I loved thee ! " [1] It is in this sense also that " beauty is truth, truth beauty " : and as regards the knowledge of ultimate things which is possible to ordinary men, it may well be that

> " That is all
> Ye know on earth, and all ye need to know."

" Of Beauty," says Plato in an immortal passage, " I repeat again that we saw her there shining in company with the celestial forms ; and coming to earth we find her here too, shining in clearness through the clearest aperture of sense. For sight is the most piercing of our bodily senses : though not by that is wisdom seen ; her loveliness would have been transporting if there had been a visible image of her, and the other ideas, if they had visible counterparts, would be equally lovely. But this is the privilege of Beauty, that being the loveliest she is also the most palpable to sight. Now he who is not newly initiated, or who has been corrupted, does not easily rise out of this world to the sight of true beauty in the other. . . . But he whose initiation is recent, and who has been the spectator of many glories in the other world, is amazed when he sees anyone having a godlike face or form, which is the expression of Divine Beauty ; and at first a shudder runs through him, and again the old awe steals over him. . . ." [2]

---

[1] Aug. Conf., bk. x. cap. xxvii.

[2] Phaedrus, § 250 (Jowett's translation). The reference in the phrase " he whose initiation is recent" is to the rite of admission into the Greek Mysteries. It is believed by some authorities that the neophyte was then cast into an hypnotic sleep by his " initiator," and whilst in this condition a vision of the " glories of the other world " was suggested to him. The main phenomena of " conversion " were thus artificially produced : but the point of attack being the mind rather than the heart, the results, as would appear from the context, were usually transient. See for matter bearing on this point, Rudolf Steiner, " Das Christenthum als mystiche Thatsache."

Most men in the course of their lives have known such Platonic hours of initiation, when the sense of beauty has risen from a pleasant feeling to a passion, and an element of strangeness and terror has been mingled with their joy. In those hours the world has seemed charged with a new vitality; with a splendour which does not belong to it but is poured through it, as light through a coloured window, grace through a sacrament, from that Perfect Beauty which "shines in company with the celestial forms" beyond the pale of appearance. In such moods of heightened consciousness each blade of grass seems fierce with meaning, and becomes a well of wondrous light: a "little emerald set in the City of God." The seeing self is indeed an initiate thrust suddenly into the sanctuary of the mysteries: and feels the "old awe and amazement" with which man encounters the Real. In such experiences as these, a new factor of the eternal calculus appears to be thrust in on us, a factor which no honest seeker for truth can afford to neglect; since, if it be dangerous to say that any two systems of knowledge are mutually exclusive, it is still more dangerous to give uncritical priority to any one system. We are bound, then, to examine this path to reality as closely and seriously as we should investigate the most neatly finished safety-ladder of solid ash which offered a *salita alle stelle*.

Why, after all, take as our standard a material world whose existence is affirmed by nothing more trustworthy than the sense-impressions of "normal men"; those imperfect and easily cheated channels of communication? The mystics, those adventurers of whom we spoke upon the first page of this book, have always declared, implicitly or explicitly, their distrust in these channels of communication. They have never for an instant been deceived by phenomena, nor by the careful logic of the industrious intellect. One after another, with extraordinary unanimity, they have rejected that appeal to the unreal world of appearance which is the standard of all sensible men: affirming that there is another way, another secret, by which the conscious self may reach the actuality which it seeks. More complete in their grasp of experience than the votaries of intellect or of sense, they accept as central for life those spiritual messages which are mediated to the self by religion, by beauty, and by pain. More reasonable than the

rationalists, they find in that very hunger for reality which is
the mother of all metaphysics, an implicit proof that such reality
exists; that there is something else, some final satisfaction,
beyond the ceaseless stream of sensation which besieges consciousness. " In that thou hast sought me, thou hast already
found me," says the voice of Absolute Truth in their ears.
This is the first doctrine of mysticism. Its next is that only
in so far as the self is real can it hope to *know* Reality: like
to like: *Cor ad cor loquitur.* Upon the propositions implicit in
these two laws the whole claim and practice of the mystic life
depends.

" Finite as we are," they say—and here they speak not
for themselves, but for the race—"lost though we seem to be
in the woods or in the wide air's wilderness, in this world of
time and of chance, we have still, like the strayed animals or
like the migrating birds, our homing instinct. . . . We seek.
That is a fact. We seek a city still out of sight. In the contrast with this goal, we live. But if this be so, then already we
possess something of Being even in our finite seeking. For
the readiness to seek is already something of an attainment,
even if a poor one." [1]

Further, in this our finite seeking we are not wholly dependent on that homing instinct. For some, who have climbed
to the hill-tops, that city is not really out of sight   The mystics
see it clearly. They report to us concerning it. Science and
metaphysics may do their best and their worst: but these pathfinders of the spirit never falter in their statements concerning
that independent spiritual world which is the only goal of
" pilgrim man." They say that messages come to him from
that spiritual world, that complete reality which we call
Absolute: that we are not, after all, hermetically sealed from
it. To all selves who will receive it, news comes every hour
of the day of a world of Absolute Life, Absolute Beauty,
Absolute Truth, beyond the bourne of time and place: news
that most of us translate—and inevitably distort in the process
—into the language of religion, of beauty, of love, or of pain.

Of all those forms of life and thought with which humanity
has fed its craving for truth, mysticism alone postulates, and in
the persons of its great initiates proves, not only the existence

[1] Royce, " The World and the Individual," vol. i. p. 181.

of the Absolute, but also this link: this possibility first of
knowing, finally of attaining it. It denies that possible knowledge is to be limited (*a*) to sense impressions, (*b*) to any
process of intellectation, (*c*) to the unfolding of the content of
normal consciousness. Such diagrams of experience, it says,
are hopelessly incomplete. The mystics find the basis of their
method not in logic but in life: in the existence of a discoverable "real," a spark of true being, within the seeking subject
which can, in that ineffable experience which they call the
"act of union," fuse itself with and thus apprehend the reality
of the sought Object. In theological language, their theory of
knowledge is that the spirit of man, itself essentially divine, is
capable of immediate communion with God, the One Reality.[1]

In mysticism that love of truth which we saw as the
beginning of all philosophy leaves the merely intellectual
sphere, and takes on the assured aspect of a personal passion.
Where the philosopher guesses and argues, the mystic lives and
looks; and speaks, consequently, the disconcerting language of
first-hand experience, not the neat dialectic of the schools.
Hence whilst the Absolute of the metaphysicians remains a
diagram—impersonal and unattainable—the Absolute of the
mystics is lovable, attainable, alive.

"Oh, taste and see!" they cry, in accents of astounding
certainty and joy. "Ours is an experimental science. We can
but communicate our system, never its result. We come to
you not as thinkers, but as doers. Leave your deep and absurd
trust in the senses, with their language of dot and dash, which
may possibly report fact but can never communicate personality. If philosophy has taught you anything, she has
surely taught you the length of her tether, and the impossibility
of attaining to the doubtless admirable grazing land which lies
beyond it. One after another, idealists have arisen who, straining
frantically at the rope, have announced to the world their approaching liberty; only to be flung back at last into the little

---

[1] The idea of Divine Union as man's true end is of course of immeasurable
antiquity. Its first definite appearance in the religious consciousness of Europe
seems to coincide with the establishment of the Orphic Mysteries in Greece and
Southern Italy in the sixth century B.C. See Adam, "The Religious Teachers of
Greece," p. 92. It is also found in the Hermetic writings, which vary between the
fifth and second century B.C. Compare Petrie, "Personal Religion in Egypt before
Christianity," p. 102.

circle of sensation.   But here we are, a small family, it is true, yet one that refuses to die out, assuring you that we have slipped the knot and are free of those grazing grounds.   This is evidence which you are bound to bring into account before you can add up the sum total of possible knowledge ; for you will find it impossible to prove that the world as seen by the mystics, 'unimaginable, formless, dark with excess of bright,' is less real than that which is expounded by the youngest and most promising demonstrator of a physico-chemical universe. We will be quite candid with you.   Examine us as much as you like : our machinery, our veracity, our results.   We cannot promise that you shall see what we have seen, for here each man must adventure for himself ; but we defy you to stigmatize our experiences as impossible or invalid.   Is your world of ex- perience so well and logically founded that you dare make of it a standard ?   Philosophy tells you that it is founded on nothing better than the reports of your sensory apparatus and the tradi- tional concepts of the race.   Certainly it is imperfect, probably it is illusion ; in any event, it never touches the foundation of things.   Whereas what the world, which truly knows *nothing*, calls ' mysticism,' is the science of *ultimates* . . . the science of self-evident Reality, which cannot be ' reasoned about,' because it is the object of pure reason or perception." [1]

[1] Coventry Patmore, " The Rod, the Root, and the Flower," " Aurea Dicta," cxxviii.

CHAPTER II

MYSTICISM AND VITALISM

Another philosophic scheme — Vitalism, the " new philosophy " — Driesch,
Bergson, Eucken—The vital principle as the essence of reality—Freedom—Spontaneity — Nietzsche — The inclusive character of vitalistic philosophy : physical,
psychological, spiritual—Vitalism and the mystics—Heracleitus, the father of the
new philosophy—its other connections—its central idea—The World of Becoming
—Reality as dynamic—Life as incessant change—Bergson's theory of the intellect
— of perception — Its relation to mysticism — Reality known by communion —
Intuition—its partial nature — Rudolph Eucken's teaching—a spiritual vitalism—
Reality as an "independent spiritual world"—Man's possible attainment of it—he
is "the meeting-point of various stages of reality"—Rebirth—Denial of the sense
world—Eucken's teaching and mysticism—Mystics the heroic examples of "independent spiritual life"—Vitalism criticized—its central idea only half a truth—The
mystic consciousness of reality two-fold—Being and Becoming—Transcendence and
Immanence—both true—St. Augustine on the Nature of God—Man's instinct for
the Absolute—Mysticism justifies it—reconciles it with a dynamic universe—
Boehme—Revelation by strife—Mystic union—its two forms—its agent, the absolute
element in man—Total mystic experience only expressible in terms of personality—
How is this experience attained?

WE glanced, at the beginning of this inquiry, at the
universes which result from the various forms of
credulity practised by the materialist, the idealist,
and the sceptic. We saw the mystic denying by word and
act the validity of the foundations on which those universes
are built : substituting his living experience for their conceptual
schemes.

But there is another and wholly distinct way of seeing
reality—or, more correctly, one aspect of reality—old as to
its central idea, new as to its applications of that idea. This
scheme of things—this new system, method or attitude—
possesses the merit of accepting and harmonizing many
different forms of experience ; even those supreme experiences
and intuitions peculiar to the mystics. It is the first great

contribution of the twentieth century to the history of man's quest of reality. A true "child of its time," it is everywhere in the air. Many who hardly know its name have been affected by its spirit, and by the vague luminous shadow which is always cast before a coming system of thought. Almost insensibly, it has already penetrated and modified our attitude, not only to philosophy, but to religion, science, art, and practical life. Like the breath of spring, impossible to grasp and difficult to define, it is instinct with fresh life and fertilizes where it goes. It has come upon us from different directions : already possesses representatives on each of the three great planes of thought. Driesch [1] and other biologists have applied it in the sphere of organic life. Bergson,[2] starting from psychology, has taken its intellectual and metaphysical aspects in hand. Rudolph Eucken [3] has developed from, or beside it, a living Philosophy of the Spirit, of man's relations to the Real : the nearest approach, perhaps, which any modern thinker has made to a constructive mysticism.

At the bottom of these three very different philosophies the same principle may be discerned ; the principle, that is to say, of Vitalism, of a free spontaneous and creative life as the very essence of the Real. Not law but aliveness, incalculable and indomitable, is their motto : not human logic, but actual living experience, is their text. The Vitalists, whether the sphere of their explorations be biology, psychology or ethics, see the whole Cosmos, the physical and spiritual worlds, as instinct with initiative and spontaneity : as above all things *free*. For them, nature is "on the dance": one cannot calculate her acts by the nice processes of dialectic. Though she be conditioned, her inherent freedom is greater than the sum of these conditions. Pushing out from within, seeking expression, she buds and breaks forth into spontaneous and original creation.[4]

[1] "The Science and Philosophy of Organism," Gifford Lectures, 1907–8.
[2] "Les Données Immédiates de la Conscience" (1889), "Matière et Mémoire" (1896), "L'Evolution Créatrice" (1907).
[3] "Der Kampf um einen geistigen Lebensinhalt" (1896), "Der Sinn und Wert des Lebens" (1908), &c. See Bibliography.
[4] The researches of Driesch (*op. cit.*) and of de Vries ("The Mutation Theory," 1910) have done much to establish the truth of this contention upon the scientific plane. Note particularly Driesch's account of the spontaneous responsive changes in the embryo sea-urchin, and de Vries' extraordinary description of the escaped stock of Evening Primrose, varying now this way, now that, "as if swayed by a restless internal tide."

The iron laws of the determinists are merely her habits, not her chains: and man, in seeing nature in the terms of "cause and effect," has been the dupe of his own limitations and prejudices.

Bergson, Nietzsche, Eucken, though they differ in their opinion as to life's meaning, are alike in this vision : in the stress which they lay on the supreme importance and value of life—a great Cosmic life transcending and including our own. This is materialism inside out: for here what we call the universe is presented to us as an expression of life, not life as an expression or by-product of the universe. The strange passionate philosophy of Nietzsche, that unbalanced John the Baptist of the modern world, is really built upon an intense belief in this supernal nature and value of Life, Action and Strength : and spoilt by the one-sided individualism which prevented him from holding a just balance between the great and significant life of the Ego and the greater and more significant life of the All.

Obviously, the peculiar merit of the vitalistic philosophy lies in its ability to satisfy so many different thinkers, starting from such diverse points in our common experience. On the phenomenal side it seems able to accept and transfigure the statements of physical science. In its metaphysical aspect it leaves place for those ontological speculations which take their rise in psychology. It is friendly to those who demand an important place for moral and spiritual activity in the universe. Finally—though here we must be content with deduction rather than declaration—it leaves in the hands of the mystics that unique power of attaining to Absolute Reality which they have always claimed : shows them as the true possessors of freedom, the torch-bearers of the race.

Did it acknowledge its ancestors with that reverence which is their due, Vitalism would identify itself with the great name of Heracleitus ; the mystic philosopher, who, in the fifth century B.C., introduced its central idea to the European world.[1] It is—though this statement might annoy some of its interpreters—both a Hellenic and a Christian system of thought : and represents the reappearance of intuitions which have too long been kept in the hiddenness by the leaders of the race. A living

---

[1] The debt to Heracleitus is acknowledged by Professor Schiller. See "Studies in Humanism," pp. 39, 40.

theologian has said, that as in hats so in heresies, the very
latest creation is generally a revival of forgotten fashions of the
past. This law applies with peculiar force to systems of
philosophy, which generally owe more to the judicious resuscita-
tion of that which sleeps, than to the birth of that which
has been newly conceived.

I have said that, so far as its ontology is concerned, this
" new " way of seeing the Real goes back to Heracleitus, whose
" Logos " or Energizing Fire is but another symbol for that free
and living Spirit of Becoming, that indwelling creative power,
which Vitalism acknowledges as the very soul or immanent
reality of things. This eternal and substantial truth the
Vitalists have picked up, retranslated into modern terms and
made available for modern men. In its view of the proper
function of the intellect it has some unexpected affinities with
Aristotle, and after him with St. Thomas Aquinas ; regarding
it as a departmental affair, not—with the Platonists—as the
organ of ultimate knowledge. Its theory of knowledge is close
to that of the mystics : or would be, if those wide-eyed gazers
on reality had interested themselves in any psychological theory
of their own experiences.

A philosophy which can harmonize such diverse elements as
these, is likely to be useful in our present attempt towards
an understanding of mysticism : for it clearly illustrates certain
aspects of perceived reality which other systems ignore. It has
the further recommendation of involving not a mere diagram of
metaphysical possibilities, but a genuine theory of knowledge.
That is to say, its scope includes psychology as well as
philosophy : the consideration, not only of the nature of Reality
but also of the self's power of knowing it ; the machinery of
contact between the mind and the flux of things. Hence there is
about it a wholeness, an inclusive quality very different from the
tidy ring-fenced systems of other schools of thought. It has no
edges, and if it be true to itself should have no negations. It is
a vision, not a map.

Now the primary difference between Vitalism and the
philosophies which we have already considered is this. Its
Word of Power, its central idea, is not Being but Becoming.[1]

[1] See, for the substance of this and the following pages, the works of Henri
Bergson already mentioned. I am here also enormously indebted to the personal

Translated into the language of Platonic theology, not the changeless One, the Absolute, but His energizing Thought—the Son, the Creative Logos—is at once the touchstone of truth, the end of knowledge, the supreme reality which it proposes as accessible to human consciousness.

"All things," said Heracleitus, "are in a state of flux." "Everything happens through strife." "Reality is a condition of unrest." [1] Such is also the opinion of Bergson and his disciples ; who, agreeing in this with the champions of physical science, look upon the Real as dynamic rather than static, as *becoming* rather than *being* perfect, and invite us to see in Time —the precession or flux of things—the very stuff of reality—

> "From the fixed lull of Heaven she saw
>   Time like a pulse shake fierce
> Through all the worlds"—[2]

said Rossetti of the Blessed Damozel. Bergson, seeing from another standpoint, ignores, if he does not deny, the existence of the "fixed lull," the still Eternity, the point of rest ; and finds everywhere the pulse of Time, the vast unending storm of life and love. Reality, says Bergson, is pure creative Life ; a definition which excludes those ideas of perfection and finality involved in the idealist's concept of Pure Being as the Absolute and Un-changing One. This life, as he sees it, is fed from within rather than upheld from without. Its evolves by means of its own inherent and spontaneous creative power. The biologist's Nature "so careful of the type" ; the theologian's Creator external to His universe, and "holding all things in the hollow of His hand" : these are gone, and in their place we have a universe teeming with free individuals, each self-creative, each evolving eternally, yet towards no term.

The first feeling of the philosopher initiated into this system is that of the bewildered traveller who "could not see the wood for trees." The deep instinct of the human mind that there

help of my friend Mr. William Scott Palmer, whose lucid interpretations have done so much towards familiarizing English readers with Bergson's philosophy ; and to Mr. Willdon Carr's paper on "Bergson's Theory of Knowledge," read before the Aristotelian Society, December, 1908.

[1] Heracleitus, Fragments, 46, 84.   [2] First edition, canto x.

must be a unity, an orderly plan in the universe, that the strung-along beads of experience do really form a rosary, though it be one which we cannot repeat, is here deliberately thwarted. Creation, Activity, Movement; this, says Vitalism, rather than any merely apparent law and order, any wholeness, is the essential quality of the Real—*is* the Real : and life is an eternal Becoming, a ceaseless changefulness. Boldly adopting that Hermetic principle of analogy " *Quod inferius sicut quod superius*," [1] which occult and mystical thinkers have always loved, it invites us to see in that uninterrupted change which is the condition of our normal consciousness, a true image, a microcosm of the living universe as a part of which that consciousness has been evolved.

If we accept this theory, we must then impute to life in its fullness—the huge, many levelled, many coloured life, the innumerable worlds which escape the rhythm of our senses; not merely that patch of physical life which those senses perceive—a divinity, a greatness and splendour of destiny far beyond that with which it is credited by those who hold to a physico-chemical theory of the universe. We must perceive in it, as the mystics have done, " the beating of the Heart of God "; and agree with Heracleitus that " there is but one wisdom, to understand the knowledge by which all things are steered through the All." [2]

Union with reality—apprehension of it—will then upon this hypothesis be union with life at its most intense point : in its most dynamic aspect. It will be a deliberate harmony set up with the Logos which that same far-seeing philosopher described as " man's most constant companion." *Ergo*, says the mystic, union with a Personal and Conscious spiritual existence, immanent in the world—one form, one half of the union which I have always sought : since this is clearly life in its highest manifestation. Beauty, Goodness, Splendour, Love, all those words of glamour which exhilarate the soul, are but the man-made names of aspects or qualities picked out by human intuition as characteristic of this intense and eternal Life in which is the life of men.

How, then, may we know this Life, this creative and original soul of things, in which we are bathed ; in which, as in a

river, swept along? Not, says Bergson bluntly, by any intellectual means. The mind which thinks it knows Reality
because it has made a diagram of Reality, is merely the dupe of
its own categories. The intellect is a specialized aspect of the
self, a form of consciousness: but specialized for very different
purposes than those of metaphysical speculation. Life has
evolved it in the interests of life; has made it capable of dealing
with "solids," with concrete things. With these it is at home.
Outside of them it becomes dazed, uncertain of itself; for it is
no longer doing its natural work, which is to *help* life, not to
know it. In the interests of experience, and in order to grasp
perceptions, the intellect breaks up experience, which is in
reality a continuous stream, an incessant process of change and
response with no separate parts, into purely conventional
"moments," "periods," or psychic "states." It picks out
from the flow of reality those bits which are significant for
human life; which "interest" it, catch its attention. From
these it makes up a mechanical world in which it dwells, and
which seems quite real until it is subjected to criticism. It does,
says Bergson, in an apt and already celebrated simile, the work
of a cinematograph: takes snapshots of something which is
always moving, and by means of these successive static representations—none of which are real, because Life, the object
photographed, never was at rest—it recreates a picture of life, of
motion. This picture, this rather jerky representation of divine
harmony, from which innumerable moments are left out, is very
useful for practical purposes: but it is not reality, because it is
not alive.[1]

This "real world," then, is the result of your selective activity,
and the nature of your selection is largely outside your control.
Your cinematograph machine goes at a certain pace, takes its
snapshots at certain intervals. Anything which goes too quickly
for these intervals, it either fails to catch, or merges with preceding and succeeding movements to form a picture with which
it can deal. Thus we treat, for instance, the storm of vibrations which we convert into "sound" and "light." Slacken or

[1] On the complete and undivided nature oɪ our experience in its "Wholeness,"
and the sad work our analytic brains make of it when they come to pull it to pieces,
Bradley has some valuable contributory remarks in his "Oxford Lectures on
Poetry," p. 15.

accelerate its clock-time, change its rhythmic activity, and at once you take a different series of snapshots, and have as a result a different picture of the world. Thanks to the time at which the normal human machine is set, it registers for us what we call, in our simple way, "the natural world." A slight accession of humility or common sense might teach us that a better title would be "*our* natural world."

Now let human consciousness change or transcend its rhythm, and any other aspect of any other world may be ours as a result. Hence the mystics' claim that in their ecstasies they change the conditions of consciousness, and apprehend a deeper reality which is unrelated to human speech, cannot be dismissed as unreasonable. Do not then confuse that intellect, that surface-consciousness which man has trained to be an organ of utility and nothing more, and which therefore can only deal adequately with the "given" world of sense, with that mysterious something in you—inarticulate but inextinguishable —by which you are aware that a greater truth exists. This truth, whose neighbourhood you feel, and for which you long, is Life. You are in it all the while, "like a fish in the sea, like a bird in the air," as St. Mechthild of Hackborn said many centuries ago.[1]

Give yourself, then, to this divine and infinite life, this mysterious Cosmic activity in which you are immersed, of which you are born. Trust it. Let it surge in on you. Cast off, as the mystics are always begging you to do, the fetters of the senses, the "remora of desire"; and making your interests identical with those of the All, rise to freedom, to that spontaneous, creative, artistic life which, inherent in every individual self, is our share of the life of the Universe. You are yourself *vital*—a free centre of energy—did you but know it. You can move to higher levels, to greater reality, truer self-fulfilment, if you will. Though you be, as Plato said, like an oyster in your shell, you can open that shell to the living waters without, draw from the "Immortal Vitality." Thus only—by contact with the real—shall you *know* reality. *Cor ad cor loquitur.*

The Indian mystics declare substantially the same truth when they say that the illusion of finitude is only to be escaped by relapsing into the substantial and universal life, abolishing

[1] "Liber Specialis Gratiae," l. ii. cap. xxvi.

individuality. So too, by a deliberate self-abandonment to that which Plato calls the " saving madness " of ecstasy, did the initiates of Dionysus " draw near to God."   So their Christian cousins assert that " self-surrender " is the only way : that they must die to live, must lose to find : that knowing implies being : that the method and secret which they have always practised consists merely in a meek and loving union—the synthesis of passion and self-sacrifice—with that divine and unseparated life, that larger consciousness in which the soul is grounded, and which they hold to be conterminous with God. In their hours of contemplation, they deliberately empty themselves of the false images of the intellect, neglect the cinematograph of sense. Then only are they capable of transcending the merely intellectual levels of consciousness and perceiving that Reality which " hath no image."

" Pilgrimage to the place of the wise," said Jelalu 'd Din, "is to find escape from the flame of separation."   It is the mystics' secret in a nutshell. "When I stand empty *in* God's will and empty *of* God's will and of all His works and of God Himself," cries Eckhart with his usual violence of language, " *then* am I above all creatures and am neither God nor creature, but I am what I was and evermore shall be." [1] He attains, that is to say, by this escape from a narrow selfhood, not to identity with God—that were only conceivable upon a basis of pantheism—but to an identity with his own substantial life, and through it with the life of a real and living universe; in symbolic language, with " the thought of the Divine Mind" whereby union with that Mind in the essence or ground of the soul becomes possible.

The first great message of this Vitalistic philosophy, this majestic dream of Time and Motion, is then seen to be—Cease to identify your intellect and your self : a primary lesson which none who purpose the study of mysticism may neglect. Become at least aware of, if you cannot " know," the larger, truer self : that free creative self which constitutes your life, as distinguished from the scrap of consciousness which is its servant.

How then, asks the small consciously-seeking personality of the normal man, am I to become aware of this, my

[1] Meister Eckhart, Pred. lxxxvii.

larger self, and of the free, eternal, spiritual life which it lives ?

Here philosophy, emerging from the water-tight compartment in which metaphysics have lived too long retired, calls in psychology ; and tells us that in intuition, in a bold reliance on contact between the totality of the self and the external world—perhaps too in those strange states of lucidity which accompany great emotion and defy analysis—lies the normal man's best chance of attaining, as it were, a dim and sidelong knowledge of this real. Smothered in daily life by the fretful activities of our surface-mind, reality emerges in our great moments ; and, seeing ourselves in its radiance, we know, for good or evil, what we are. "We are not pure intellects . . . around our conceptional and logical thought there remains a vague, nebulous Somewhat, the substance at whose expense the luminous nucleus we call the intellect is formed."[1] In this aura, this diffused sensitiveness, we are asked to find man's medium of communication with the Universal Life.

Such partial, dim and fragmentary perceptions of the Real, however, such "excursions into the Absolute," cannot be looked upon as a satisfaction of man's hunger for Truth. He does not want to peep, but to live. Hence he cannot be satisfied with anything less than a total and permanent adjustment of his being to the greater life of reality. This alone, as Rudolph Eucken has well pointed out, can resolve the disharmonies between the self and the world, and give meaning and value to human life.[2]

The possibility of this adjustment—of union between man's life and that "independent spiritual life" which is the stuff of reality—is the theme alike of mysticism and of Eucken's spiritual vitalism ; or, as he prefers to call it, his Activistic

---

[1] Willdon Carr, *op. cit.*

[2] "It seems as if man could never escape from himself, and yet, when shut in to the monotony of his own sphere, he is overwhelmed with a sense of emptiness. The only remedy here is radically to alter the conception of man himself, to distinguish within him the narrower and the larger life, the life that is straitened and finite and can never transcend itself, and an infinite life through which he enjoys communion with the immensity and the truth of the universe. Can man rise to this spiritual level ? On the possibility of his doing so rests all our hope of supplying any meaning or value to life " (" Der Sinn und Wert des Lebens," p. 81).

Philosophy.[1]   Reality, says Eucken, is an independent spiritual
world, unconditioned by the apparent world of sense.   To know
it and to live in it is man's true destiny.   His point of contact
with it is personality : the inward fount of his being : his heart,
not his head.   Man is real, and in the deepest sense alive, in
virtue of this free personal life-principle within him : but he is
bound and blinded by the ties set up between his surface-
intelligence and the sense-world.   The struggle for reality must
be a struggle on man's part to transcend the sense-world, escape
its bondage.   He must renounce it, and be " re-born " to a
higher level of consciousness ; shifting his centre of interest
from the natural to the spiritual plane.   According to the
thoroughness with which he does this, will be the amount
of real life he enjoys.   The initial break with the " world," the
refusal to spend one's life communing with one's own cinematograph picture, is essential if the freedom of the infinite is to
be attained.   Our life, says Eucken, does not move upon a
single level, but upon two levels at once—the natural and
the spiritual.   The key to the puzzle of man lies in the fact
that he is "the meeting point of various stages of Reality." [2]
All his difficulties and triumphs are grounded in this.   The
whole question for him is, which world shall be central for
him—the real, vital, all-embracing life we call Spirit, or
the lower life of sense ?   Shall " Existence," the superficial
obvious thing, or " Substance," the underlying verity, be his
home ?   Shall he remain the slave of the senses with their
habits and customs, or rise to a plane of consciousness, of
heroic endeavour, in which—participating in the life of spirit—
he knows reality because he is real ?

   The mystics, one and all, have answered this question in
the same sense : and, centuries before the birth of activistic
philosophy, they have proved in their own experience that
its premises are true.   This philosophic diagram, this application of the vitalistic idea to the transcendental world, does
in fact fit the observed facts of mysticism far more closely

   [1] The essentials of Professor Eucken's teaching are present in all his chief works :
but will be found conveniently summarized in " Der Sinn und Wert des Lebens." I
am also greatly indebted to Mr. Boyce Gibson's brilliant exposition " Rudolph
Eucken's Philosophy."
   [2] " Der Sinn und Wert des Lebens," p. 121.

even than it fits the observed facts of man's ordinary mental life.

(1) The primary break with the sense-world. (2) The "new" birth and development of the spiritual consciousness on high levels—in Eucken's eyes an essential factor in the attainment of reality. (3) That ever closer and deeper dependence on and appropriation of the fullness of the Divine Life ; the conscious participation in, and active union with the infinite and eternal. These three imperatives of Eucken's system, as we shall see later, form an exact description of the psychological process through which the mystics pass. If then Eucken be right in pointing to this transcendence as the highest destiny of the race, mysticism becomes the crown of man's ascent towards Reality ; the orderly completion of the universal plan.

The mystics show us this independent spiritual life, this fruition of the Absolute, enjoyed with a fullness to which others cannot attain. They are the heroic examples of the life of spirit ; just as the great artists, the great discoverers, are the heroic examples of the life of beauty and the life of truth. Directly participating, like all artists, in the Divine Life, they are always persons of exuberant vitality : but this vitality expresses itself in unusual forms, hard of understanding for ordinary men. When we see a picture or a poem, hear a musical composition, we accept it as an expression of life, an earnest of the power which brought it forth. But the deep contemplations of the great mystic, his visionary reconstructions of reality, and the fragments of them which he is able to report, do not seem to us—as they are—the equivalents, or more often the superiors of the artistic and scientific achievements of other great men.

Mysticism, then, offers us the history, as old as civilization, of a race of adventurers who have carried to its term the process of a deliberate and active return to the divine fount of things, have surrendered themselves indeed to the life-movement of the universe : hence have lived with an intenser life than other men can ever know. They have transcended the "sense-world" and lived on high levels the spiritual life. Therefore they are types of all that our latent spiritual consciousness, which shows itself in the "hunger for the Absolute," can be made to mean to

us if we develop it ; and have in this respect a unique importance for the race.

It is the mystics, too, who have perfected that method of
intuition, that knowledge by union, the existence of which
philosophy has been driven to acknowledge. But where the
metaphysician obtains at best a sidelong glance at that Being
" unchanging yet elusive," whom he has so often defined but
never discovered, the artist a brief and dazzling vision of the
Beauty which is Truth, they gaze with confidence into the very
eyes of the Beloved.

The mystics, again, declare themselves to know the divinely
real, free, and active " World of Becoming" which Vitalistic
philosophy expounds to us. They are, by their very constitution, acutely conscious of the Divine Immanence and its unresting travail : it is in them and they are in it : or, as they put it
in their blunt theological way, " the spirit of God is within you."
But they are not satisfied with this statement and this knowledge ; and here it is that they part company with the Vitalists.
It is, they think, but half a truth. To know Reality in this
way, to know it in its dynamic aspect, enter into " the great
life of the All" : this is indeed, in the last resort, to know it
supremely from the point of view of man—to liberate from
selfhood the human consciousness—but it is not to know it
from the point of view of God. There are planes of being
beyond this ; countries dark to the intellect, deeps in which
only the very greatest contemplatives have looked. These,
coming forth, have declared with Ruysbroeck that "God according to the Persons is Eternal Work, but according to the
Essence and Its perpetual stillness He is Eternal Rest." [1]

The full spiritual consciousness of the true mystic is
developed not in one, but in two apparently opposite but
really complementary directions :—

" . . . io vidi
Ambo le corte del ciel manifeste." [2]

On the one hand he is intensely aware of, and knows
himself to be at one with that active World of Becoming,
that deep and primal life of the All, from which his own

[1] " De Septem Gradibus Amoris," cap. xiv.   [2] Par. xxx. 95.

life takes its rise. Hence, though he has broken for ever with the bondage of the senses, he perceives in every mani-festation of life a sacramental meaning ; a loveliness, a wonder, a heightened significance, which is hidden from other men. He may, with St. Francis, call the Sun and the Moon, Water and Fire, his brothers and his sisters : or receive, with Blake, the message of the trees. Because of his cultivation of disinterested love, because his outlook is not conditioned by " the exclusive action of the will-to-live," he has attained the power of communion with the living reality of the universe ; and in this respect can truly say that he finds "God in all and all in God." Thus, the skilled spiritual vision of Lady Julian, transcending the limitations of human perception, entering into harmony with a larger world whose rhythms cannot be received by common men, *saw* the all-enfolding Divine Life, the mesh of reality. "For as the body is clad in the cloth," she said, " and the flesh in the skin and the bones in the flesh and the heart in the whole, so are we, soul and body, clad in the Goodness of God and enclosed. Yea, and more homely : for all these may waste and wear away, but the Goodness of God is ever whole." [1] Many mystical poets and pantheistic mystics never pass beyond this degree of lucidity.

On the other hand, the full mystic consciousness also attains to what is, I think, its really characteristic quality. It develops the power of apprehending the Absolute, Pure Being, the utterly Transcendent : or, as its possessor would say, can rise to "passive union with God." This all-round expansion of consciousness, with its dual power of knowing by communion the temporal and eternal, immanent and transcendent aspects of reality—the life of the All, vivid, flowing and changing, and the changeless, conditionless life of the One—is the peculiar mark, the *ultimo sigillo* of the great mystic, and must never be forgotten in studying his life and work.

As the ordinary man is the meeting-place between two stages of reality—the sense-world and the world of spiritual life —so the mystic, standing head and shoulders above ordinary men, is again the meeting-place between two orders. Or, if you like it better, he is able to perceive and react to reality under two modes. On the one hand he knows, and rests in, the

[1] " Revelations of Divine Love," cap. vi.

eternal world of Pure Being, the " Sea Pacific " of the Godhead, indubitably present to him in his ecstasies, attained by him in the union of love. On the other, he knows—and works in— that "stormy sea," the vital World of Becoming which is the expression of Its will. " Illuminated men," says Ruysbroeck, " are caught up, above the reason, into naked vision. There the Divine Unity dwells and calls them. Hence their bare vision, cleansed and free, penetrates the activity of all created things, and pursues it to search it out even to its height." [1]

Though philosophy has striven since thought began—and striven in vain—to resolve the paradox of Being and Becoming, of Eternity and Time, she has failed strangely enough to perceive that a certain type of personality has substituted experience for her guesses at truth, and achieved its solution, not by the dubious processes of thought, but by direct perception. To the great mystic the "problem of the Absolute" presents itself in terms of life, not in terms of dialectic. He solves it in terms of life : by a change or growth of consciousness which—thanks to his peculiar genius—enables him to apprehend that two-fold Vision of Reality which eludes the perceptive powers of other men. It is extraordinary that this fact of experience—a central fact for the understanding of the contemplative type—has hitherto received no attention from writers upon mysticism. As we proceed with our inquiry, its importance, its far-reaching applications in the domains of psychology, of theology, of action, will become more and more evident. It provides the reason why the mystics could never accept the diagram of the Vitalists as a complete statement of the nature of Reality. " Whatever be the limits of your knowledge, we know"—they would say—"that the world has another aspect than this : the aspect which is present to the Mind of God." " Tranquillity according to His essence, activity according to His nature : perfect stillness, perfect fecundity," [2] says Ruysbroeck again, this is the two-fold character of the Absolute. That which to us is action, to Him, they declare, is rest, " His very peace and stillness coming from the brimming fullness of His infinite life." [3] That which to us is Many, to that Transcen-

[1] Ruysbroeck, "Samuel" (Hello, p. 201).
[2] *Ibid.*, " De Vera Contemplatione" (Hello, p. 175).
[3] Von Hügel, "The Mystical Element of Religion," vol. ii. p. 132.

dent Knower is One. Our World of Becoming rests on the bosom of that Pure Being which has ever been the final Object of man's quest : the " river in which we cannot bathe twice " is the stormy flood of life flowing toward that divine sea. " How glorious," says the Voice of the Eternal to St. Catherine of Siena, " is that soul which has indeed been able to pass from the stormy ocean to Me, the Sea Pacific, and in that Sea, which is Myself, to fill the pitcher of her heart." [1]

The evolution of the mystic consciousness, then, brings its possessors to this transcendent point of view : their secret is this unity in diversity, this stillness in strife. Here they are in harmony with Heracleitus rather than with his new interpreters. That most mystical of philosophers discerned a hidden unity beneath the battle, transcending all created opposites ; and, in the true mystical spirit, taught his disciples that " Having hearkened not unto me but unto the Logos, it is wise to confess that all things are *one*." [2] This is the secret at which the idealists' arid concept of Pure Being has tried, so timidly, to hint : and which the Vitalists' more intimate, more actual concept of Becoming has tried, so unnecessarily, to destroy. We shall see the glorious raiment in which the Christian mystics deck it when we come to consider their theological map of the quest.

If it be objected—and this objection has been made by advocates of each school of thought—that the existence of the idealists' and mystics' " Absolute " is utterly inconsistent with the deeply alive, striving spiritual life which the Vitalists identify with reality, I reply that both these concepts at bottom are but symbols of realities which the human mind can never reach : and that the idea of stillness, unity and peace is and has ever been humanity's best translation of its final intuitive perception of God. " ' In the midst of silence a hidden word was spoken to me.' Where is this Silence, and where is the place in which this word is spoken ? It is in the purest that the soul can produce, in her noblest part, in the Ground, even the Being of the Soul." [3] So Eckhart: and here he does but subscribe to a universal tradition. The mystics have always insisted that " Be

---

[1] St. Catherine of Siena, Dialogo, cap. lxxxix.

[2] Heracleitus, *op. cit.*

[3] Meister Eckhart, Pred. i.

still, be still, and *know*" is the condition of man's purest and
most direct apprehensions of reality : that somehow quiet is the
truest and deepest activity : and Christianity when she formulated her philosophy made haste to adopt and express this
paradox.

"*Quid es ergo, Deus meus?*" said St. Augustine, and gave
an answer in which the vision of the mystic, the genius of the
philosopher combined to hint something at least of the flaming
heart of reality, the paradox of the intimacy and majesty of that
all-embracing, all-transcending One. "Summe, optime, poten-
tissime, omnipotentissime, misericordissime, et justissime, secre-
tissime et presentissime, pulcherrime et fortissime ; stabilis et
incomprehensibilis ; immutabilis, mutans omnia : Numquam
novus, nunquam vetus. . . . Semper agens, semper quietus :
colligens et non egens : portans et implens et protegens ; creans
et nutriens et perficiens : quaerens cum nihil desit tibi. . . .
Quid dicimus, Deus meus, vita mea, dulcedo mea sancta? Aut
quid dicit aliquis, cum de te dicit?"[1]

It has been said that "Whatever we may do, our hunger
for the Absolute will never cease." The hunger—that innate
craving for, and intuition of, a final Unity, a changeless good—
will go on, however heartily we may feed on those fashionable
systems which offer us a pluralistic or empirical universe. If,
now, we admit in all living creatures—as Vitalists must do—an
instinct of self-preservation, a free directive force which may be
trusted and which makes for life ; is it just to deny such an
instinct to the human soul? The "entelechy" of the Vitalists,
the "hidden steersman," drives the phenomenal world on and
up. What about that other sure instinct embedded in the race,
breaking out again and again, which drives the spirit on and up ;
spurs it eternally towards an end which it feels to be definite

[1] Aug. Conf., bk. i. cap. iv. "What art Thou, then, my God? . . . Highest,
best, most potent [*i.e.*, dynamic], most omnipotent [*i.e.*, transcendent], most merciful
and most just, most deeply hid and yet most near. Fairest, yet strongest : steadfast,
yet unseizable ; unchangeable yet changing all things ; never new, yet never old. . . .
Ever busy, yet ever at rest ; gathering yet needing not : bearing, filling, guarding ;
creating, nourishing and perfecting ; seeking though Thou hast no wants. . . .
What can I say, my God, my life, my holy joy? or what can any say who speaks of
Thee?" Compare the strikingly similar Sūfi definition of the Nature of God, as
given in Palmer's "Oriental Mysticism," pp. 22, 23. "First and last, End and
Limit of all things, incomparable and unchangeable, always near yet always far," &c.

yet cannot define? Shall we distrust this instinct for the Absolute, as living and ineradicable as any other of our powers, merely because the new philosophy finds it difficult to accommodate and to describe?

"We must," says Plato in the "Timæus," "make a distinction of the two great forms of being, and ask, 'What is that which Is and has no Becoming, and what is that which is always becoming and never Is?'"[1] Without necessarily subscribing to the Platonic answer to this question, I think we may at any rate acknowledge that the question itself is sound and worth asking; that it expresses a perennial demand of human nature: and that the analogy of man's other instincts and cravings assures us that these his fundamental demands always indicate the existence of a supply.[2] The great defect of Vitalism, considered as a system, is that it only professes to answer half of it; the half which Absolute Idealism disdained to answer at all.

We have seen that the mystical experience, the fullest all-round experience in regard to the transcendental world which is attainable by humanity, declares to us that there are two aspects, two planes of discoverable Reality. We have seen also that hints of these two planes—often clear statements concerning them—abound in mystical literature of the personal first-hand type.[3] Pure Being, says Boutroux in the course of his exposition of Boehme,[4] has two characteristic manifestations. It shows itself to us as Power, by means of strife, of the struggle and opposition of its own qualities. But it shows itself to us as Reality, in harmonizing and reconciling within itself these discordant opposites.

Its manifestation as Power, then, is for us in the dynamic World of Becoming, amidst the thud and surge of that life which is compounded of paradox, of good and evil, joy and sorrow, life and death. Here, Boehme declares that the Absolute God is voluntarily self-revealing. But each revelation has as its

<hr/>

[1] Timaeus, § 27.

[2] "A natural craving," said Aquinas, "cannot be in vain"; and the newest philosophy is creeping back to this "mediaeval" point of view. Compare "Summa Contra Gentiles," l. ii. cap. lxxix.

[3] Compare Dante's vision in Par. xxx., where he sees Reality first as the streaming River of Light, the flux of things; and then, when his sight has been purged, as achieved Perfection, the Sempiternal Rose.

[4] E. Boutroux, "Le Philosophe Allemand, Jacob Boehme," p. 18.

condition the appearance of its opposite : light can only be recognized at the price of knowing darkness, life needs death, love needs wrath.   Hence if Pure Being—the Good, Beautiful and True—is to reveal itself, it must do so by evoking and opposing its contrary : as in the Hegelian dialectic no idea is complete without its negative.   Such a revelation by strife, however, is rightly felt by man to be incomplete.   Absolute Reality, the Player whose sublime music is expressed at the cost of this everlasting friction between bow and lyre, is present, it is true, in His music.   But He is best known in that "light behind," that unity where all these opposites are lifted up into harmony, into a higher synthesis : and the melody is perceived, not as a difficult progress of sound, but as a whole.

We have, then, (a) The Absolute Reality which the Greeks, and every one after them, meant by that seemingly chill abstraction which they called Pure Being : that Absolute One, unconditioned and undiscoverable, in Whom all is resumed. Changeless, yet changer of all, this One is the undifferentiated Godhead of Eckhart, the Transcendent Father of ordinary Christian theology.   It is the great contribution of the mystics to humanity's knowledge of the real that they find in this Absolute, in defiance of the metaphysicians, a personal object of love, the goal of their quest, the "Country of the Soul."

(b) But, contradicting the nihilism of Eastern contemplatives, they see also a reality in the dynamic side of things : in the seething pot of appearance.   They are aware of an eternal Becoming, a striving, free, evolving life, not merely as a shadow-show, but as an implicit of their Cosmos : God's manifestation or showing, in which He is immanent, and in which He becomes conscious of Himself.   It is in *this* plane of reality that all individual life is immersed : this is the stream which set out from the Heart of God and "turns again home."

The mystic knows his task to be the attainment of Being, union with the One, the "return to the Father's heart" : for the parable of the Prodigal Son is to him the history of the universe.   This union is to be attained, first by co-operation in that Life which bears him up, in which he is immersed.   He must become conscious of this "great life of the All," merge himself in it, if he would find his way back whence he came. *Vae soli.*   Hence there are really two separate acts of "divine

union," two separate kinds of illumination involved in the
Mystic Way: the dual character of the spiritual consciousness
brings a dual responsibility in its train. First, there is the
union with Life, with the World of Becoming: and parallel with
it the illumination by which the mystic "gazes upon a more
veritable world." Secondly, there is the union with Being, with
the One: and that final, ineffable illumination of pure love
which is called the "knowledge of God." It is by means of the
abnormal development of the third factor, the free, creative
"Spirit," the scrap of Absolute Life which is the ground of his
soul, that the mystic can (*a*) conceive and (*b*) accomplish these
transcendent acts. Only Being can know Being: we "behold
that which we are, and are that which we behold." But there
is a spark in man's soul, say the mystics, which is real—which
in fact *is*—and by its cultivation we may know reality.

Over and over again—as Being and Becoming, as Eternity
and Time, as Transcendence and Immanence, Reality and
Appearance, the One and the Many—these two dominant
ideas, demands, imperious instincts of man's self will reappear ;
the warp and woof of his completed universe. On the one
hand is his ineradicable intuition of a remote, unchanging
Somewhat calling him : on the other there is his longing for and
as clear intuition of an intimate, adorable Somewhat, companion-
ing him. Man's true Real, his only adequate God, must be
great enough to embrace this sublime paradox, to take up these
apparent negations into a higher synthesis. Neither the utter
transcendence of extreme Absolutism, nor the utter immanence
of the Vitalists will do. Both these, taken alone, are declared
by the mystics to be incomplete. They conceive that Absolute
Being who is the goal of their quest as manifesting Himself in
a World of Becoming : agonizing in it, at one with it, yet though
semper agens, also *semper quietus*. The Divine spirit which they
know to be immanent in the heart and in the universe comes
forth from and returns to the Transcendent One ; and this
division of persons in unity of substance completes the "Eternal
Circle, from Goodness, through Goodness, to Goodness."

Absolute Being and Becoming, the All and the One, are
found to be alike inadequate to their definition of this discovered
Real; the "triple star of Goodness, Truth, and Beauty." Speaking always from experience—the most complete experience

that is possible to man—they describe to us an Absolute which overpasses and includes the Absolute of philosophy, far transcends that Cosmic life which it fills and sustains, and is best defined in terms of Transcendent Personality; which because of its richness and of the poverty of human speech, they have sometimes been driven to define only by negations. At once static and dynamic, above life and in it, "all love yet all law," eternal in essence though working in time, this vision resolves the contraries which tease those who study it from without, and swallows up whilst it kindles to life all the partial interpretations of metaphysics and of science.

Here then stands the mystic. By the help of two philosophies, eked out by the resources of symbolic expression, he has contrived to tell us something of his vision and his claim. Confronted by that vision—that sublime reconstruction of eternity—we may surely ask, indeed, are bound to ask, What is the machinery by which this self, akin to the imprisoned and sense-fed self of our daily experience, has contrived to slip its fetters and rise to those levels of spiritual perception on which alone such vision can be possible to man? How has it brought within the field of consciousness those deep intuitions which fringe upon Absolute Life; how developed powers by which it is enabled to arrive at this amazing, this superhuman concept of the nature of Reality? Psychology will do something, perhaps, to help us to an answer to this question; and it is her evidence which we must examine next. But its final solution is the secret of the mystics; and they reply to our questioning, when we ask them, in the direct and uncompromising terms of action, not in the refined and elusive periods of speculative thought.

"Come with us," they say to the bewildered and entangled self, craving for finality and peace, "and we will show you a way out that shall not only be an issue from your prison but also a pathway to your Home. True, you are immersed, fold upon fold, in the World of Becoming; worse, you are besieged on all sides by the persistent illusions of sense. But you too are a child of the Absolute. You bear within you the earnest of your inheritance. At the apex of your spirit there is a little door, so high up that only by hard climbing can you reach it. There the Object of your craving stands and knocks; thence came those persistent messages—faint echoes from the Truth eternally hammering at your gates—which disturbed the comfortable life of sense. Come up then by this pathway, to those higher levels of reality to which, in virtue of the eternal spark in you, you belong. Leave your ignoble ease : your clever prattle : your absurd attempts to solve the apparent contradictions of a Whole too great for your useful little mind to grasp. Trust your deep instincts : use your latent powers. Appropriate that divine, creative life which is the very substance of your being. Remake yourself in its interest, if you would know its beauty and its truth. You can only behold that which you *are*. Only the Real can know Reality."

CHAPTER III

MYSTICISM AND PSYCHOLOGY

Man's craving to know more and love more—His mental machinery—Emotion, Intellect, Will—Their demand of absolute objects—Conation and Cognition—Action and Thought—Importance of emotion—Love and Will—Concentration—Contemplation—The mystic sense—its liberation—Passivity—The Mystic State—Supraliminal and subliminal personality—The " ground of the soul "—The " subconscious mind " —extravagances of this doctrine—The subconscious not the equivalent of the transcendental self—Mystical theory of man's spiritual sense—The New Birth—The Spiritual Self—Synteresis—The Spark of the Soul—the organ of transcendental consciousness—Transcendental Feeling—its expression—The Spark of the Soul sleeps in normal men—The mystic's business is to wake it—Function of contemplation—it alters the field of consciousness—Dual personality—The hidden self of the Mystic— its emergence—Entrancement—Mystical ill-health—Psycho-physical phenomena— Mysticism and hysteria—Mysticism and longevity—The mystics' psychic peculiarities —their wholeness of life—Genius and mysticism compared—Philo on inspiration— The function of passivity—Automatic states—Summary and conclusion

WE come now to consider the mental apparatus which is at the disposal of the self: to ask what it can tell us of the method by which she can escape from the prison of the sense-world, transcend its rhythm, and attain knowledge of—or conscious contact with—Reality. We have seen the normal self close shut within the prison of the senses, and making, by the help of science and of philosophy, a survey of the premises and furniture: testing the thickness of the walls and speculating on the possibility of trustworthy news from without penetrating to her cell. Shut with her in that cell, two forces, the desire to know more and the desire to love more, are ceaselessly at work. Where the first of these cravings predominates, we call the result a philosophical or a scientific temperament; where it is overpowered by the ardour of unsatisfied love, the self's reaction upon things becomes poetic, artistic, and characteristically—though not always explicitly—religious.

We have seen further that a certain number of persons

declare that they have esaped from this prison. Have they
done so, it can only be in order to satisfy these two hungry
desires, for these, and these only, make that a prison which
might otherwise be a comfortable hotel ; and since these desires
are in all of us, active or latent in varying degrees, it is clearly
worth while to discover, if we can, the weak point in the walls,
and that method of attack which is calculated to take advantage
of this one possible way of escape.

Before we attempt to define in psychological language the
way in which the mystic slips the fetters of sense, sets out upon
his journey towards home, it seems desirable to examine the
machinery which is at the disposal of the normal, conscious
self: the creature, or part of a creature, which we recognize
as "ourselves." Psychologists are accustomed to tell us that
the messages from without awaken in that self three main
forms of activity. (1) They arouse in her movements of attraction or repulsion, of desire or distaste, which vary in intensity
from the semi-conscious cravings of the hungry infant to the
passions of the lover, artist, or fanatic. (2) They stimulate in
her a sort of digestive process in which she combines and
cogitates upon the material presented to her ; finally absorbing
a certain number of the resulting concepts and making them
part of herself or of her world. (3) The movements of desire,
or the action of reason, or both in varying combinations, awaken
in her a determination by which percept and concept issue in
action ; bodily, mental, or spiritual.

Hence we say that the main aspects of the self are Emotion,
Intellect, and Will : and that the nature of the individual is
emotional, intellectual, or volitional, according to whether feeling, thought, or will assumes the reins.

Thanks to the watertight-compartment system of popular
psychology, we are apt to personify these qualities ; thinking of
them as sitting, like Clotho, Lachesis, and Atropos, within the
mind, and spinning the flax of experience into the thread of life.
But these three words do not define three separate and mutually
exclusive things ; rather a Trinity in Unity, three aspects,
methods, or moments of the same thing—the self's reaction on
her universe.[1]

[1] There is a tendency on the part of the younger psychologists to rebel against
this traditional diagram. Thus Godfernaux says (*Revue Philosophique*, September,

Now the unsatisfied self in her emotional aspect wants, as we have said, to love more ; her curious intellect wants to know more. Both appetites are aware that they are being kept on a low diet ; that there really is more to love, and more to know, somewhere in the mysterious world without. They know, too, that their own powers of affection and understanding are worthy of some greater and more durable objective than that provided by the illusions of sense. Urged therefore by the cravings of feeling or of thought, consciousness is always trying to run out to the encounter of the Absolute, and always being forced to return. The neat philosophical system, the diagrams of science, the "sunset-touch," are tried in turn. Art and life, the accidents of our humanity, all foster an emotional outlook ; till the moment in which the neglected intellect arises and pronounces such an outlook to have no validity. Metaphysics and science seem to offer to the intellect an open window towards truth ; till the heart looks out and declares this landscape to be a chill desert in which she can find no nourishment. These diverse aspects of things must be either fused or transcended if the whole self is to be satisfied ; for the reality which she seeks has got to meet both claims and pay in full.

When Dionysius the Areopagite divided those angels who stand nearest God into the Seraphs who are aflame with perfect love, and the Cherubs who are filled with perfect knowledge, he only gave expression to the two most intense aspirations of the human soul, and described under an image the unattainable conditions of her bliss.[1]

Now, there is a sense in which it may be said, that the desire of knowledge is a department of the desire of perfeet love : since one aspect of that primal, all inclusive passion is

---

1902), " Feeling, intelligence, will ! When shall we be delivered from this tedious trinity ? When shall we give up, once for all, this classification which corresponds to nothing ? " The classification, however, is retained here as a matter of general convenience. So long as its symbolic character is kept in mind, its advantages probably outweigh its defects.

[1] The wise Cherubs, according to the beautiful imagery of Dionysius, are " all eyes," but the loving Seraphs are " all wings." Whilst the Seraphs, the figure of intensest Love, " *move* perpetually towards things divine," ardour and energy being their characteristics, the characteristic of the Cherubs is receptiveness, their power of absorbing the rays of the Supernal Light. (Dionysius the Areopagite, " De Caelesti Ierarchia," vi. 2, and vii. 1.)

clearly a longing to know, in the deepest, fullest, closest sense, the thing adored. Love's characteristic activity—for Love, all wings, is inherently active, and " cannot be lazy," as the mystics say—is a quest, an outgoing towards an object desired, which only when possessed will be fully known, and only when fully known can be perfectly adored.[1] Intimate communion, no less than worship, is of its essence. Joyous fruition is its proper end. This is true of all Love's quests, whether the Beloved be human or divine—the bride, the Grail, the Mystic Rose, the plenitude of God. But there is no sense in which it can be said that the desire of love is merely a department of the desire of perfect knowledge : for that strictly intellectual ambition includes no adoration, no self-spending, no reciprocity of feeling between Knower and Known. Mere knowledge, taken alone, is a matter of receiving, not of acting : of eyes, not wings : a dead alive business at the best.

There is thus a sharp distinction to be drawn between these two great expressions of life : the energetic love, the passive knowledge. One is related to the eager, outgoing activity, the dynamic impulse to *do* somewhat, physical, mental, or spiritual, which is inherent in all living things and which psychologists call *conation ;* the other to the indwelling consciousness, the passive knowing somewhat, which they call *cognition.*

To go back to our original diagram, " conation " is almost wholly the business of will, but of will stimulated by emotion : for wilful action of every kind, however intellectual it may seem, is always the result of feeling. We act because we want to ; our impulse to "do" is a synthesis of determination and desire. All man's achievements are the result of conation, never of mere thought. " The intellect by itself moves nothing," said Aristotle, and modern psychology has but affirmed this law. Hence his quest of Reality is never undertaken, though it may be greatly assisted, by the intellectual aspect of his consciousness ; for the reasoning powers as such have little initiative. Their province is analytic, not exploratory. They stay at home, dissecting and arranging matter that comes to hand ; and do not adventure

[1] So Récéjac says of the mystics, " They desire to know, only that they may love ; and their desire for union with the principles of things in God, Who is the sum of them all, is founded on a feeling which is neither curiosity nor self-interest " (" Fondements de la Connaissance Mystique," p. 50).

beyond their own region in search of food. Thought does not penetrate far into an object in which the self feels no interest— *i.e.*, towards which she does not experience a "conative" movement of attraction, of desire—for interest is the only method known to us of arousing the will, and securing the fixity of attention necessary to any intellectual process. None think for long about anything for which they do not care ; that is to say, which does not touch some aspect of their emotional life. They may hate it, love it, fear it, want it ; but they must have some feeling about it. Feeling is the tentacle we stretch out to the world of things.

Here the lesson of psychology is the same as that which Dante brought back from his pilgrimage ; the supreme importance and harmonious movement of *il desiro* and *il velle*. *Si come rota ch'egualmente e mossa*,[1] these move together to fulfil the Cosmic Plan. In all human life, in so far as it is not merely a condition of passive "awareness," the law which he found implicit in the universe is the law of the individual mind. Not logic, not "common sense," but *l'amor che move il sole e le altre stelle* is the motive force of the spirit of man : in the inventors, the philosophers, and the artists, no less than in the heroes and in the saints.

The vindication of the importance of feeling in our life, and in particular its primacy over reason in all that has to do with man's contact with the transcendental world, has been one of the chief works of recent psychology. Especially in the sphere of religion it has come to be acknowledged that " God known of the heart" is a better and more valid statement of ultimate experience than " God guessed at by the brain " ; that the active adventure of the spirit is more fruitful and more trustworthy than the dialectic proof. One by one the commonplaces of mysticism are being thus rediscovered by official science, and given their proper place in the psychology of the spiritual life. The steady growth of vitalistic theories of existence, with their tendency to emphasize the purely departmental and utilitarian nature of the intellect, and interpret everything in terms of vitality, assists this process. Thus Leuba has not hesitated to say that " Life, more life, a larger, richer, more satisfying life, is in the last analysis the end of religion,"[2] and we have seen that

---

[1] Par. xxxiii. 143.   [2] The *Monist*, July, 1901, p. 572.

life, as we know it, appears to be far more tightly bound up with will and feeling than with thought.

That which our religious and ethical teachers were wont to call " mere emotion " is now acknowledged to be of the primal stuff of consciousness. Thought is but its servant : a skilled and often arrogant servant, with a constant tendency to usurpation. At bottom, then, we shall find in emotion the power which drives the mental machinery ; a power as strong as steam, though as evanescent unless it be put to work. Without it, the will would be dormant, and the intellect lapse into a calculating machine. As for its transitoriness, incessant change has been defined by Bergson as a necessary condition of consciousness, indeed of life.[1]

Further, " the heart has its reasons which the mind knows not." It is a matter of experience that in our moments of deep emotion, transitory though they be, we plunge deeper into the reality of things than we can hope to do in hours of the most brilliant argument. At the touch of passion doors fly open which logic has battered on in vain : for passion rouses to activity not merely the mind, but the whole vitality of man. It is the lover, the poet, the mourner, the convert, who shares for a moment the mystic's privilege of lifting that Veil of Isis which science handles so helplessly, leaving only her dirty fingermarks behind. The heart, eager and restless, goes out into the unknown, and brings home, literally and actually, " fresh food for thought." Hence those who "feel to think " are likely to possess a richer, more real, if less orderly, experience than those who "think to feel."

This psychological law, easily proved in regard to earthly matters, holds good also upon the supersensual plane. It was expressed once for all by one of the earliest of English mystics when he said of God, " By love He may be gotten and holden, but by thought of understanding never." [2] " The first thing which enlightens our eyes," says Ruysbroeck, is the *vivid emotion* which floods and irradiates consciousness when it receives a message from the spiritual world. This exalted feeling, this desire, not the neat deductions of logic, the apologist's " proofs " of the existence of the Absolute, unseals the eyes to things unseen

[1] H. Bergson, " Les Données Immédiates de la Conscience," cap. ii.
[2] " The Cloud of Unknowing," cap. vi. (B. M. Harl. 674).

before. He continues, "Of this abrupt emotion is born from the side of man the second point: that is to say, a concentration of all the interior and exterior forces in the unity of the spirit and in the bonds of love."[1] Here we see emotion at its proper work, as the spring and stimulant of action ; the movement of desire passing over at once into the act of concentration, the gathering up of all the powers of the self into a state of determined attention, which is the business of the Will.

Now this act of perfect concentration, the passionate focusing of the self upon one point, when it is applied in "the unity of the spirit and the bonds of love" to real and transcendental things, constitutes in the technical language of mysticism the state of meditation or recollection:[2] a condition which is peculiarly characteristic of the mystical consciousness, and is the necessary prelude of pure contemplation, that state in which the mystic enters into communion with Reality.

We have then arrived so far in our description of the mechanism of the mystic. Possessed like other men of powers of feeling, thought, and will, it is essential that his love and his determination, even more than his thought, should be set upon Transcendent Reality. He must feel a strong emotional attraction toward the supersensual Object of his quest: that love which scholastic philosophy defined as the force or power which causes every creature to follow out the trend of its own nature. Of this must be born the will to attain communion with that Absolute Object. This will, this burning and active desire, must crystallize into and express itself by that definite and conscious concentration of the whole self upon the Object, which precedes the contemplative state. We see already how far astray are those who look upon the mystical temperament as passive in type.

Our next concern, then, would seem to be with this condition of contemplation : what it does and whither it leads. What is (a) its psychological explanation and (b) its empirical value ? Now, in dealing with this, and other rare mental conditions, we are of course trying to describe from without that which can only adequately be described from within ; which is as much as to say that only mystics can really write

[1] "L'Ornement des Noces Spirituelles," l. ii. cap. iv. (trans. Maeterlinck).
[2] See below, Pt. II. Cap. VI.

about mysticism. Fortunately, many mystics have so written; and we, from their experiences and from the explorations of psychology upon another plane, are able to make certain elementary deductions. It appears generally from these that the act of contemplation is for the mystic a psychic gateway; a method of going from one state of consciousness to another. In technical language it is the condition under which he shifts his "field of perception" and obtains his characteristic outlook on the universe. That there is such a characteristic outlook, peculiar to no creed or race, is proved by the history of mysticism; which demonstrates plainly enough that there is developed in some men another sort of consciousness, another "sense," beyond those normal qualities of the self which we have discussed. This "sense" has attachments at each point to emotion, to intellect, and to will. It can express itself under each of the aspects which these terms connote. Yet it differs from and transcends the emotional, intellectual, and volitional life of ordinary men. It was recognized by Plato as that consciousness which could apprehend the real world of the Ideas. Its development is the final object of that education which his "Republic" describes. It is called by Plotinus "Another intellect, different from that which reasons and is denominated rational."[1] Its business, he says, is the perception of the supersensual—or, in Neoplatonic language, the *intelligible* world. It is the sense which, in the words of the "Theologia Germanica," has "the power of seeing into eternity,"[2] the "mysterious eye of the soul" by which St. Augustine saw "the light that never changes."[3] It is, says Al Ghazzali, a Persian mystic of the eleventh century, "like an immediate perception, as if one touched its object with one's hand."[4] In the words of his great Christian successor, St. Bernard, "it may be defined as the soul's true unerring intuition, the unhesitating apprehension of truth":[5] which "simple vision of truth," says St. Thomas Aquinas, "ends in a movement of desire."[6]

It is infused with burning love, for it seems to its possessors

[1] Plotinus, Ennead vi. 9.
[2] "Theologia Germanica," cap. vii. (trans. Winkworth).
[3] Aug. Conf., bk. vii. cap. x.
[4] A. Schmölders, "Essai sur les Écoles Philosophique chez les Arabes," p. 68.
[5] "De Consideratione," bk. ii. cap. ii.
[6] "Summa Theologica," ii. ii. q. clxxx. art. 3. eds. 1 and 3.

to be primarily a movement of the heart: with intellectual subtlety, for its ardour is wholly spent upon the most sublime object of thought : with unflinching will, for its adventures are undertaken in the teeth of the natural doubts, prejudices, languors, and self-indulgence of man.   These adventures, looked upon by those who stay at home as a form of the Higher Laziness, are in reality the last and most arduous labours which humanity is called to perform.   They are the only known methods by which we can come into conscious possession of all our powers ; and, rising from the lower to the higher levels of consciousness, become aware of that larger life in which we are immersed, attain communion with the transcendent ·Personality in Whom that life is resumed.

Mary has chosen the better, not the idler part.   In vain does sardonic common sense, confronted with the contemplative type, reiterate the sneer of Mucius, "Encore sont-ils heureux que la pauvre Marthe leur fasse la cuisine."   It remains a paradox of the mystics that the passivity at which they appear to aim is really a state of the most intense activity: more, that where it is wholly absent no great creative action can take place.   In it, the superficial self compels itself to be still, in order that it may liberate another more deep-seated power which is, in the ecstasy of the contemplative genius, raised to the highest pitch of efficiency.

"This restful labouring," said Walter Hilton, "is full far from fleshly idleness and from blind security.   It is full of spiritual working, but it is called rest, for that grace looseth the heavy yoke of fleshly love from the soul and maketh it mighty and free through the gift of spiritual love for to work gladly, softly, and delectably. . . . Therefore it is called an holy *idleness* and a *rest* most busy, and so it is in regard of *stillness* from the great crying of the beastly noise of fleshly desires." [1]

If those who have cultivated this latent power be correct in their statements, the self was mistaken in supposing herself to be entirely shut off from the true external universe.   She has, it seems, certain tentacles which, once she learns to uncurl them, will stretch sensitive fingers far beyond that limiting envelope in which her normal consciousness is contained, and obtain data

[1] Walter Hilton, "The Scale of Perfection," bk. iii. cap. x.

from which she can construct a higher reality than that which can be deduced from the reports of the senses. The fully educated and completely conscious human soul can open, then, as an anemone does, and *know* the ocean in which she is bathed. This act, this condition of consciousness, in which barriers are obliterated, the Absolute flows in on us, and we, rushing out to its embrace, "find and feel the Infinite above all reason and above all knowledge,"[1] is the true "mystical state." The value of contemplation is that it tends to produce this state, and turns the "lower servitude" in which the natural man lives under the sway of his earthly environment to the "higher servitude" of fully conscious dependence on that Reality "in Whom we live and move and have our being."

What then, we ask, is the nature of this special sense—this transcendental consciousness — and how does contemplation liberate it?

Any attempt to answer this question brings upon the scene another aspect of man's psychic life: an aspect which is of paramount importance to the student of the mystic type. We have reviewed the chief aspects under which the normal self reacts upon experience by means of its surface consciousness : a consciousness which has been trained through long ages to deal with those concrete matters which make up the universe of sense. We know, however, that the personality of man is a far deeper and more mysterious thing than the sum of his conscious feeling, thought, and will : that this superficial self—this Ego of which each of us is aware—hardly counts in comparison with those deeps of being which it hides. "There is a root or depth in thee," says Law, "from whence all these faculties come forth as lines from a centre, or as branches from the body of a tree. This depth is called the centre, the fund, or bottom, of the soul. This depth is the unity, the Eternity, I had almost said the infinity of thy soul, for it is so infinite that nothing can satisfy it, or give it any rest, but the infinity of God."[2]

Since normal man, by means of his feeling, thought, and will, is utterly unable to set up relations with spiritual reality, it is clearly in this depth of being—in these unplumbed levels of

---

[1] Ruysbroeck, " De Septem Gradibus Amoris," cap. xiv.
[2] "The Spirit of Prayer" (" Liberal and Mystical Writings of William Law," p. 14).

personality—that we must search, if we would find the organ, the power, by which he is to achieve the mystic quest. That alteration of consciousness which takes place in contemplation can only mean the emergence from this "fund or bottom of the soul" of some faculty which diurnal life keeps hidden "in the deeps."

Modern psychology has summed up man's hiddenness in that doctrine of the subconscious or subliminal personality which looms so large in recent apologetic literature. It has so dwelt upon and defined this vague and shadowy region—which is really less a "region" than a useful name—that it sometimes seems to know more about the subconscious than about the conscious life of man. There it finds, side by side, the sources of his most animal instincts, his least explicable powers, his most spiritual intuitions: the "ape and tiger," and the "soul." Genius and prophecy, table-turning and clairvoyance, hypnotism, hysteria, and "Christian" science—all are explained by the "subconscious mind." In its pious and apologetic moods, it has told us *ad nauseam* that "God speaks to man in the sub-consciousness,"[1] and has succeeded in making the subliminal self into the Mesopotamia of Liberal Christianity. The result is that popular psychology tends more and more to personify and exalt the "subconscious." Forgetting the salutary warning administered by a living writer, when he told us that man has not only a "Shadowy Companion," but a "Muddy Companion" too,[2] it represents the subliminal self as an imprisoned angel, a mystic creature possessed of supernatural powers. Stevenson was far more scientific when he described the subconscious personality of Dr. Jekyll as being Mr. Hyde: for the "subconsciousness" is simply the aggregate of those powers, parts, or qualities of the whole self which at any given moment are not conscious, or that the Ego is not conscious of. Included in the subconscious region of an average healthy man are all those automatic activities by which the life of the body is carried on: all those "uncivilized" instincts and vices, those remains of the ancestral savage which education has forced out of the stream of consciousness; all those aspirations for which the busy life

[1] Cutten, "Psychological Phenomena of Christianity," p. 18. James, "Varieties of Religious Experience," p. 515. Schofield, "The Unconscious Mind," p. 92.
[2] Arthur Machen, "Hieroglyphics," p. 124.

of the world leaves no place. Hence in normal men the best and the worst, the most savage and most spiritual parts of the character, are bottled up "below the threshold." Often the partisans of the "subconscious" forget to mention this.

It follows, then, that whilst we shall find it convenient and indeed necessary to avail ourselves of the symbols and diagrams of psychology in tracking out the mystic way, we must not forget the large and vague significance which attaches to these symbols, or allow ourselves to use the "subconscious" as the equivalent of man's transcendental sense. Here the old mystics, I think, displayed a more scientific spirit, a more delicate power of analysis, than the new psychologists. They, too, were aware that in normal men the spiritual sense lies below the threshold of consciousness. Though they had not at their command the astonishing spatial metaphors of the modern school, and could not describe man's ascent toward God in those picturesque terms of paths and levels, uprushes, margins, and fields, which now come so naturally to investigators of the spiritual life, they leave us in no doubt as to their view of the facts. Further, man's spiritual history primarily meant for them, as it means for us, the emergence of this transcendental sense from its prison; its capture of the field of consciousness, and the opening up of those paths which permit the inflow of a larger spiritual life, the perception of a higher reality. This, in so far as it was an isolated act, was "contemplation." When it was part of the general life process, and permanent, they called it the New Birth, which "maketh alive." The faculty or personality concerned in the "New Birth"—the "spiritual man," capable of the spiritual vision and life, which was dissociated from the "earthly man" adapted only to the natural life—was always distinguished by them very sharply from the total personality, conscious or subconscious. It was something definite; a bit or spot of man which, belonging not to Time but to Eternity, was different in kind from the rest of his human nature, framed in all respects to meet the demands of the merely natural world.

The business of the mystic in the eyes of these old specialists was to remake, transmute, his total personality in the interest of his spiritual self; to bring it out of the hiddenness, and unify himself about it as a centre, thus "putting on divine humanity."

It is interesting to note that the most recent teaching of Rudolph Eucken is in this respect a pure and practical mysticism, though his conclusions have not been reached by the mystic's road. The " redemptive remaking of personality," in conformity with the transcendent or spiritual life of the universe, is for him the central necessity of human life. The life of reality, he says, is spiritual and heroic: an act, not a thought.[1] Further, Eucken, like the mystics, declares that there is a definite transcendental principle in man.[2] He calls it the *Gemüth*, the heart or core of personality; and there, he says, " God and man initially meet." He invites us, as we have seen,[3] to distinguish in man two separate grades of being; "the narrower and the larger life, the life that is straitened and finite, and can never transcend itself, and an infinite life through which he enjoys communion with the immensity and the truth of the universe." [4] At bottom, all the books of the mystics tell us no more and no less; but their practical instructions in the art of self-transcendence, by which man may appropriate that infinite life, far excel those of the philosopher in lucidity and exactness.

The divine nucleus, the point of contact between man's life and the divine life in which it is immersed and sustained, has been given many names in course of the development of mystical doctrine. All clearly mean the same thing, though emphasizing different aspects of its life. Sometimes it is called the Synteresis,[5] the keeper or preserver of his being: sometimes the Spark of the Soul, the *Fünklein* of the German mystics: sometimes its Apex, the point at which it touches the heavens. Then, with a sudden flight to the other end of the symbolic scale, and in order to emphasize its oneness with pure Being, rather than its difference from mere nature, it is called the Ground of the Soul, the foundation or basal stuff whence springs all spiritual life.

---

[1] Boyce Gibson, " Rudolph Eucken's Philosophy," p. 17.
[2] *Ibid.*, p. 104. [3] *Supra*, Cap. II.
[4] Eucken, " Der Sinn und Wert des Lebens," p. 81.
[5] An interesting discussion of the term " Synteresis " will be found in Dr. Inge's " Christian Mysticism," Appendix C, pp. 359, 360.

Clearly all these guesses and suggestions aim at one goal, and are to be understood in a purely symbolic sense ; for, as Malaval observed in answer to his disciples' anxious inquiries on this subject, "since the soul of man is a spiritual thing and thus cannot have divisions or parts, consequently it cannot have height or depth, summit or surface. But because we judge spiritual things by the help of material things, since we know these better and they are more familiar to us, we call the highest of all forms of conception the summit, and the easier way of comprehending things the surface, of the understanding." [1]

Here at any rate, whatever name we may choose to give it, is the organ of man's spiritual consciousness ; the place where he meets the Absolute, the germ of his real life. Here is the seat of that deep "Transcendental Feeling," the "beginning and end of metaphysics" which is, says Professor Stewart, "at once the solemn sense of Timeless Being—of 'That which was and is and ever shall be' overshadowing us—and the conviction that Life is good." "I hold," says the same writer, "that it is in Transcendental Feeling, manifested normally as Faith in the Value of Life, and ecstatically as sense of Timeless Being, and not in Thought proceeding by way of speculative construction, that Consciousness comes nearest to the object of metaphysics, Ultimate Reality." [2]

The existence of such a "sense," such an integral part or function of the complete human being, has been affirmed and dwelt upon not only by the mystics, but by seers and teachers of all times and creeds : by Egypt, Greece, and India, the poets, the fakirs, the philosophers, and the saints. A belief in its actuality is the pivot of the Christian position : the foundation and justification of mysticism, asceticism, the whole machinery of the self-renouncing life. That there is an extreme point at which man's nature touches the Absolute: that his ground, or substance, his true being, is conterminous with the Divine Life which constitutes the underlying reality of

[1] "La Pratique de la Vraye Theologie Mystique," vol. i. p. 204.
[2] J. A. Stewart, "The Myths of Plato," pp. 41, 43. Perhaps I may point out that this Transcendental Feeling—the ultimate material of poetry—has, like the mystic consciousness, a dual perception of Reality : static being and dynamic life. See above, p. 42.

things; this is the basis on which the whole mystic claim of possible union with God must rest. Here, they say, is our link with reality; and in this place alone can be celebrated the "marriage from which the Lord comes."[1]

To use another of their diagrams, it is thanks to the existence within him of this immortal spark from the central fire, that man is implicitly a "child of the infinite." The mystic way must therefore be a life, a discipline, which will so alter the constituents of his mental life as to include this spark within the conscious field, bring it out of the hiddenness, from those deep levels where it sustains and guides his normal existence, and make it the dominant element round which his personality is arranged. The revolution in which this is effected begins with the New Birth, which has been described under other terms by Rudolph Eucken, as the indispensable preliminary of an "independent spiritual life" in man.[2]

Now it is clear that under ordinary conditions, and save for sudden gusts of "Transcendental Feeling" induced by some saving madness such as Religion, Art, or Love, the superficial self knows nothing of the attitude of this silent watcher—this "Dweller in the Innermost"—towards the incoming messages of the external world: nor of the activities which they awake in it. Wholly taken up by the sense-world, and the messages she receives from it, she knows nothing of the relations which exist between this subject and the unattainable Object of all thought. But by a deliberate inattention to the messages of the senses, such as that which is induced by contemplation, the mystic brings the ground of the soul, the seat of "Transcendental Feeling," within the area of consciousness: making it amenable to the activity of the will. The contemplative subject, becoming unaware of his usual and largely fictitious "external world," another and more substantial set of perceptions, which never have their chance under normal conditions, rise to the surface. Sometimes these unite with the normal reasoning faculties. More often, they supersede them. Some such exchange, such "losing to find," appears to be necessary, if man's transcendental powers are to have their full chance.

"The two eyes of the soul of man," says the "Theologia

---

[1] Tauler, Sermon on St. Augustine ("The Inner Way," p. 162).
[2] "Der Sinn und Wert des Lebens," p. 146. See also below, Pt. I. Cap. V.

Germanica" in an apt and vigorous metaphor, "cannot both perform their work at once: but if the soul shall see with the right eye into eternity, then the left eye must close itself and refrain from working, and be as though it were dead. For if the left eye be fulfilling its office toward outward things; that is, holding converse with time and the creatures; then must the right eye be hindered in its working; that is, in its contemplation. Therefore whosoever will have the one must let the other go; for 'no man can serve two masters.'" [1]

There is within us an immense capacity for perception, for the receiving of messages from outside; and a very little consciousness which deals with them. It is as if one telegraph operator were placed in charge of a multitude of lines: all may be in action, but he can only attend to one at a time. In popular language, there is not enough consciousness to go round. Even upon the sensual plane, no one can be aware of more than a few things at once. These fill the centre of our field of consciousness: as the object on which we happen to have focused our vision dominates our field of sight. The other matters within that field retreat to the margin. We know, dimly, that they are there; but we pay them no attention and should hardly miss them if they ceased to exist.

Transcendental matters are, for most of us, always beyond the margin; because most of us have given up our whole consciousness to the occupation of the senses, and permitted them to construct there a universe in which we are contented to remain. Only in certain occult and mystic states: in orison, contemplation, ecstasy and their allied conditions; does the self contrive to turn out the usual tenants, shut the "gateways of the flesh," and let those submerged powers which are capable of picking up messages from another plane of being have their turn. Then it is the sensual world which retreats beyond the margin, and another landscape that rushes in. At last, then, we begin to see something of what contemplation does for its initiates. It is one of the many names applied to that chain of processes which have for their object this alteration of the mental equilibrium: the putting to sleep of that "Normal Self" which usually wakes, and the awakening of that "Transcen-

---

[1] "Theologia Germanica," cap. vii. À Kempis has the same metaphor. Compare "De Imitatione Christi," l. iii. cap. 38.

dental Self" which usually sleeps. To man, "meeting-point of various stages of reality," is given—though he seldom considers it—this unique power of choosing his universe.

The extraordinary phenomenon known as double or disintegrated personality may perhaps give us a hint as to the mechanical nature of the change which contemplation effects. In this psychic malady the total character of the patient is split up; a certain group of qualities are, as it were, abstracted from the surface-consciousness and so closely associated as to form in themselves a complete "character" or "personality"— necessarily poles asunder from the "character" which the self usually shows to the world, since it consists exclusively of those elements which are omitted from it. Thus in the classical case of Miss Beauchamp, the investigator, Dr. Morton Prince, called the three chief "personalities," from their ruling characteristics, "the Saint," "the Woman," and "the Devil."[1]   The totality of character which composed the "real Miss Beauchamp" had split up into these mutually opposing types; each of which was excessive, because withdrawn from the control of the rest. When, voluntarily or involuntarily, the personality which had possession of the field of consciousness was lulled to sleep, one of the others emerged. Hypnotism was one of the means which most easily effected this change.

Now in persons of mystical genius, the qualities which the stress of normal life tends to keep below the threshold of consciousness are of enormous strength. In these natural explorers of Eternity the "transcendental faculty," the "eye of the soul," is not merely present in embryo, but is highly developed; and is combined with great emotional and volitional power. The result of the segregation of such qualities below the threshold of consciousness is to remove from them the friction of those counterbalancing traits in the surface mind with which they might collide. They are "in the hiddenness," as Jacob Boehme would say. There they develop unchecked, until a point is reached at which their strength is such that they break their bounds and emerge into the conscious field : either temporarily dominating the subject as in ecstasy, or permanently transmuting the old self, as in the "unitive life." The attainment of this point is accelerated by such processes as those of contem-

[1] Morton Prince, "The Dissociation of a Personality," p. 16.

plation. These processes—not themselves mystical, but merely the mechanical conditions of mystical experience—are classed by psychologists with the states of dream and reverie, and the conditions loosely called hypnotic. In them the normal surface consciousness is deliberately or involuntarily lulled, and images or faculties from "beyond the threshold" are able to take its place.

Of course these images or faculties may or may not be more valuable than those already present in the surface-consciousness. In the ordinary subject, often enough, they are but the odds and ends for which the superficial mind has found no use. In the mystic, they are of a very different order: and this fact justifies the means which he instinctively employs to secure their emergence. Indian mysticism founds its external system almost wholly on (a) Ascetism, the domination of the senses, and (b) the deliberate practice of self-hypnotization; either by fixing the eyes on a near object, or by the rhythmic repetition of the *mantra* or sacred word. By these complementary forms of discipline, the pull of the phenomenal world is diminished and the mind is placed at the disposal of the subconscious powers. Dancing, music, and other exaggerations of natural rhythm have been pressed into the same service by the Greek initiates of Dionysus, by the Gnostics, by innumerable other mystic cults. That these proceedings do effect a remarkable change in the human consciousness is proved by experience: though how and why they do it is as yet little understood. Such artificial and deliberate production of ecstasy is against the whole instinct of the Christian contemplatives; but here and there amongst them also we find instances in which ecstatic trance or lucidity, the liberation of the "transcendental sense," was inadvertently produced by purely physical means. Thus Jacob Boehme, the "Teutonic theosopher," having one day as he sat in his room "gazed fixedly upon a burnished pewter dish which reflected the sunshine with great brilliance," fell into an inward ecstasy, and it seemed to him as if he could look into the principles and deepest foundations of things.[1] The contemplation of running water had the same effect on St. Ignatius Loyola. Sitting on the bank of a river one day, and facing the stream, which was running deep, "the eyes of his mind were opened, not so as to

[1] Martensen, "Jacob Boehme," p. 7.

see any kind of vision, but so as to understand and comprehend spiritual things . . . and this with such clearness that for him all these things were made new." [1] This method of attaining to mental lucidity by a narrowing and simplification of the conscious field, finds an apt parallel in the practice of Emmanuel Kant, who "found that he could better engage in philosophical thought while *gazing steadily* at a neighbouring church steeple." [2]

It need hardly be said that rationalistic writers, ignoring the parallels offered by the artistic and philosophic temperaments, have seized eagerly upon the evidence afforded by such instances of apparent mono-ideism and self-hypnotization in the lives of the mystics, and by the physical disturbances which accompany the ecstatic trance, and sought by its application to attribute all the abnormal perceptions of contemplative genius to hysteria or other disease. They have not hesitated to call St. Paul an epileptic, St. Teresa the "patron saint of hysterics"; and have found room for most of their spiritual kindred in various departments of the pathological museum. They have been helped in this grateful task by the acknowledged fact that the great contemplatives, though almost always persons of robust intelligence and marked practical or intellectual ability—Plotinus, St. Bernard, the two S.S. Catherine, St. Teresa, St. John of the Cross, and the Sūfi poets Jàmi' and Jelalu 'd Din are cases in point—have often suffered from bad physical health. More, their mystical activities have generally reacted upon their bodies in a definite and special way; producing in several cases a particular kind of illness and of physical disability, accompanied by pains and functional disturbances for which no organic cause could be discovered, unless that cause were the immense strain which exalted spirit puts upon a body which is adapted to a very different form of life.

It is certain that the abnormal and highly sensitized type of mind which we call mystical does frequently, but not always, produce or accompany strange and inexplicable modifications of the physical organism with which it is linked. The supernatural is not here in question, except in so far as we are inclined to give

---

[1] Testament, cap. iii.
[2] Starbuck, "The Psychology of Religion," p. 388.

that name to natural phenomena which we do not understand. Such instances of psycho-physical parallelism as the stigmatizations of the saints—and indeed of other suggestible subjects hardly to be ranked as saints—will occur to anyone.[1] I here offer to the reader another less discussed and more extraordinary example of the modifying influence of the spirit on the supposed "laws" of bodily life.

We know, as a historical fact, unusually well attested by contemporary evidence and quite outside the sphere of hagiographic romance, that both St. Catherine of Siena and her namesake St. Catherine of Genoa—active women as well as ecstatics, the first a philanthropist, reformer, and politician, the second an original theologian and for many years the highly efficient matron of a large hospital—lived, in the first case for years, in the second for constantly repeated periods of many weeks, without other food than the consecrated Host which they received at Holy Communion. They did this, not by way of difficult obedience to a pious vow, but because they could not live in any other way. Whilst fasting, they were well and active, capable of dealing with the innumerable responsibilities which filled their lives. But the attempt to eat even a few mouthfuls—and this attempt was constantly repeated, for, like all true saints, they detested eccentricity [2]—at once made them ill and had to be abandoned as useless.[3]

In spite of the researches of Murisier,[4] Janet,[5] Ribot,[6] and other psychologists, and their persevering attempts to find a pathological explanation which will fit all mystic facts, this and other marked physical peculiarities which accompany the mystical temperament belong as yet to the unsolved problems of humanity. They need to be removed both from the sphere of marvel and from that of disease—into which enthusiastic friends

[1] See, for instances, Cutten, "The Psychological Phenomena of Christianity," cap. viii.

[2] "Singularity," says Gertrude More, "is a vice which Thou extreamly hatest" ("The Spiritual Exercises of the most vertuous and religious Dame Gertrude More," p. 40). All the best and sanest of the mystics are of the same opinion.

[3] See E. Gardner, "St. Catherine of Siena," pp. 12 and 48 ; and F. von Hügel, "The Mystical Element of Religion," vol. i. p. 135.

[4] "Les Maladies des Sentiments Religieux."

[5] "L'État Mentale des Hysteriques," and "Une Extatique" (*Bulletin de l'Institut Psychologique*, 1901).

[6] "La Psychologie des Sentiments," 1896.

and foes force them by turn—to the sphere of pure psychology ; and there studied dispassionately with the attention which we so willingly bestow on the less interesting eccentricities of degeneracy and vice.   Their existence no more discredits the sanity of mysticism or the validity of its results than the unstable nervous condition usually noticed in artists—who share to some extent the mystic's apprehension of the Real— discredits art.   " In such cases as Kant and Beethoven," says Von Hügel justly, " a classifier of humanity according to its psycho-physical phenomena alone would put these great discoverers and creators, without hesitation, amongst hopeless and useless hypochondriacs." [1]

In the case of the mystics the disease of hysteria, with its astounding variety of mental symptoms, its strange power of disintegrating, rearranging and enhancing the elements of consciousness, its tendencies to automatism and ecstasy, has been most often invoked to provide an explanation of the observed phenomena.   This is as if one sought the source of the genius of Taglioni in the symptoms of St. Vitus's dance. Both the art and the disease have to do with bodily movements. So too both mysticism and hysteria have to do with the domination of consciousness by one fixed and intense idea or intuition, which rules the life and is able to produce amazing physical and psychical results.   In the hysteric patient this idea is often trivial or morbid [2] but has become—thanks to the self's unstable mental condition—an obsession.   In the mystic the dominant idea is a great one : so great in fact that when it is received in its completeness by the human consciousness, almost of necessity it ousts all else.   It is nothing less than the idea or perception of the transcendent reality and presence of God.   Hence the mono-ideism of the mystic is rational, whilst that of the hysteric patient is invariably irrational.

On the whole then, whilst psycho-physical relations remain so little understood, it would seem more prudent, and certainly more scientific, to withhold our judgment on the meaning of the psycho-physical phenomena which accompany the mystic life ; instead of basing destructive criticism on facts which are avowedly mysterious and at least capable of more than one

[1] *Op. cit.*, vol. ii. p. 42.
[2] For examples consult Pierre Janet, *op. cit.*

interpretation. To deduce the nature of a compound from the character of its by-products is notoriously unsafe.

Our bodies are animal things, made for animal activities. When a spirit of unusual ardour insists on using its nerve-cells for other activities, they kick against the pricks, and inflict, as the mystics themselves acknowledge, the penalty of "mystical ill-health." "Believe me, children," says Tauler, "one who would know much about these high matters would often have to keep his bed, for his bodily frame could not support it." [1] "I cause thee extreme pain of body," says the voice of Love to Mechthild of Magdeburg. "If I gave myself to thee as often as thou wouldst have me, I should deprive myself of the sweet shelter I have of thee in this world, for a thousand bodies could not protect a loving soul from her desire. Therefore the higher the love the greater the pain." [2]

On the other hand the exalted personality of the mystic—his self-discipline, his heroic acceptance of labour and suffering, and his inflexible will—raises to a higher term that normal power of mind over body which all possess. Also the contemplative state—like the hypnotic state in a healthy person—seems to enhance life by throwing open deeper levels of personality. The self then drinks at a fountain which is fed by the Universal Life : the "life of the Spirit," to use the language of Eucken's philosophy. True ecstasy is notoriously life-enhancing. In it a bracing contact with Reality seems to take place, and as a result the subject is himself more real. Often, says St. Teresa, even the sick come forth from ecstasy healthy and with new strength ; for something great is then given to the soul.[3] Contact has been set up with levels of being which the daily routine of existence leaves untouched. Hence the extraordinary powers of endurance and independence of external conditions which the great ecstatics so often display.

If we see in the mystics, as some have done, the sporadic beginning of a power, a higher consciousness, towards which the race slowly tends ; then it seems likely enough that where it appears nerves and organs should suffer under a stress to which they have not yet become adapted, and that a spirit

[1] Sermon for First Sunday after Easter (Winkworth, p. 302).
[2] " Das Fliessende Licht der Gottheit," pt. ii. cap. xxv.
[3] Vida, cap. xx. § 29. (Here and throughout I use Lewis's translation.)

more highly organized than its bodily home should be able
to impose strange conditions on the flesh. When man first
stood upright, a body long accustomed to go on all fours, legs
which had adjusted themselves to bearing but half his weight,
must have rebelled against this unnatural proceeding; inflicting
upon its author much pain and discomfort if not absolute illness.
It is at least permissible to look upon the strange "psycho-
physical" state common amongst the mystics as just such a
rebellion on the part of a normal nervous and vascular system
against the exigencies of a way of life to which it has not yet
adjusted itself.[1]

In spite of such rebellion, and of the tortures to which it has
subjected them, the mystics, oddly enough, are a long-lived
race : an awkward fact for critics of the physiological school.
To take only a few instances from amongst marked ecstatics,
Mechthild of Magdeburg lived to be eighty-seven, Ruysbroeck to
eighty-eight, Suso to seventy, Julian of Norwich to a hundred,
St. Catherine of Genoa and St. Peter of Alcántara to sixty-
three, Madame Guyon to sixty-nine. It seems as though that
enhanced life which is the reward of mystical surrender enabled
them to triumph over their bodily disabilities : and to live and
do the work demanded of them under conditions which would
have incapacitated ordinary men.

Such triumphs, which take heroic rank in the history of the
human mind, have been accomplished as a rule in the same
way. Like all intuitive persons, all possessors of genius, all
potential artists—with whom in fact they are closely related—
the mystics have, in psychological language, "thresholds of
exceptional mobility." That is to say, a very slight effort, a
very slight departure from normal conditions, will permit their
latent or "subliminal" powers to emerge and occupy the mental
field. A "mobile threshold" may make a man a genius, a
lunatic, or a saint. All depends upon the character of the
emerging powers. In the great mystic, these powers, these
mighty tracts of personality lying below the level of normal

---

[1] Mr. Boyce Gibson has lately drawn a striking parallel between the ferment and
"interior uproar" of adolescence and the profound disturbances which mark man's
entry into a conscious spiritual life. His remarks are even more applicable to the
drastic rearrangement of personality which takes place in the case of the mystic
whose spiritual life is more intense than that of other men. See Boyce Gibson,
"God with Us," 1909, cap. iii.

consciousness, are of unusual richness; and cannot be accounted for in terms of pathology. "If it be true," says Delacroix, "that the great mystics have not wholly escaped those nervous blemishes which mark nearly all exceptional organizations, there is in them a vital and creative power, a constructive logic, an extended scale of realization—in a word a genius—which is, in truth, their essential quality. . . . The great mystics, creators and inventors who have found a new form of life and have justified it . . . join, upon the highest summits of the human spirit, the great simplifiers of the world." [1]

The truth, then, so far as we know it at present, seems to be that those powers which are in contact with the Transcendental Order, and which constitute at the lowest estimate half the self, are dormant in ordinary men, whose time and interest are wholly occupied in responding to the stimuli of the world of sense. With those latent powers sleeps the landscape which they alone can apprehend. In mystics none of the self is always dormant. They have roused the Dweller in the Innermost from its slumbers, and round it have unified their life. Heart, Reason, Will are there in full action, drawing their energy not from the shadow-show of sense, but from the deeps of true Being; where a lamp is lit, and a consciousness awake, of which the sleepy crowd remains oblivious. He who says the mystic is but half a man, states the exact opposite of the truth. Only the mystic can be called a whole man, since in others half the powers of the self always sleep. This wholeness of experience is much insisted on by the mystics. Thus the Divine Voice says to St. Catherine of Siena, "I have also shown thee the Bridge and the three general steps, placed there for the three powers of the soul, and I have told thee how no one can attain to the life of grace unless he has mounted all three steps, that is, gathered together all the three powers of the soul in My Name." [2]

In those abnormal types of personality to which we give the name of genius, we seem to detect a hint of the relations which may exist between these deep levels of being and the crust of consciousness. In the poet, the musician, the great mathematician or inventor, mighty powers lying below the threshold,

[1] Delacroix, "Études sur le Mysticisme," p. iii.   [2] Dialogo, cap. lxxxvi.

hardly controllable by their owner's conscious will, clearly take a major part in the business of perception and conception. In all creative acts, the larger share of the work is done subconsciously : its emergence is in a sense automatic. This is equally true of mystics, artists, philosophers, discoverers, and rulers of men. The great religion, invention, work of art, always owes its inception to some sudden uprush of intuitions or ideas for which the superficial self cannot account; its execution to powers so far beyond the control of that self, that they seem, as their owner sometimes says, to " come from beyond." This is " inspiration," the opening of the sluices, so that those waters of truth in which all life is bathed may rise to the level of consciousness.

The great teacher, poet, artist, inventor, never aims deliberately at his effects. He obtains them he knows not how : perhaps from a contact of which he is unconscious with that creative plane of being which the Sūfis call the Constructive Spirit, and the Kabalists Yesod, and which both postulate as lying next behind the world of sense. " Sometimes," said the great Alexandrian Jew Philo, " when I have come to my work empty, I have suddenly become full ; ideas being in an invisible manner showered upon me, and implanted in me from on high; so that through the influence of divine inspiration, I have become greatly excited, and have known neither the place in which I was, nor those who were present, nor myself, nor what I was saying, nor what I was writing ; for then I have been conscious of a richness of interpretation, an enjoyment of light, a most penetrating insight, a most manifest energy in all that was to be done; having such an effect on my mind as the clearest ocular demonstration would have on the eyes." [1] This is a true creative ecstasy, strictly parallel to the state in which the mystic performs his mighty works.

To let oneself go, be quiet, receptive, is the condition under which such contact with the Cosmic Life may be obtained. " I have noticed that when one paints one should think of nothing: everything then comes better," says the young Raphael to Leonardo da Vinci.[2] The superficial self must here acknowledge its own insufficiency, must become the

[1] Quoted by James (" Varieties of Religious Experience," p. 481) from Clissold's " The Prophetic Spirit in Genius and Madness," p. 67.
[2] Mérejkowsky, " Le Roman de Leonard de Vinci," p. 638.

humble servant of a more profound and vital consciousness. The mystics are of the same opinion. "I tried," says Madame Guyon, speaking of her early failures in contemplation, "to obtain by effort that which I could only obtain by ceasing all effort."[1] "The best and noblest way in which thou mayst come into this Life," says Eckhart, "is by keeping silence and letting God work and speak. Where all the powers are withdrawn from their work and images there is this word spoken . . . the more thou canst draw in all thy powers and forget the creature the nearer art thou to this, and the more receptive."[2]

Thus Boehme says to the neophyte,[3] "When both thy intellect and will are quiet and passive to the expressions of the eternal Word and Spirit, and when thy soul is winged up above that which is temporal, the outward senses and the imagination being locked up by holy abstraction, *then* the eternal Hearing, Seeing, and Speaking will be revealed in thee. Blessed art thou therefore if thou canst stand still from self thinking and self willing, and canst stop the wheel of thy imagination and senses." Then, the conscious mind being passive, the more divine mind below the threshold—organ of our free creative life—can emerge and present its reports. In the words of an older mystic, "The soul, leaving all things and forgetting herself, is immersed in the ocean of Divine Splendour, and illuminated by the Sublime Abyss of the Unfathomable Wisdom."[4]

The "passivity" of contemplation, then, is a necessary preliminary of spiritual energy: an essential clearing of the ground. It withdraws the tide of consciousness from the shores of sense, stops the "wheel of the imagination." "The soul," says Eckhart again, "is created in a place between Time and Eternity : with its highest powers it touches Eternity, with its lower Time."[5] These, the worlds of Being and Becoming, are the two "stages of reality" which meet in the spirit of man. By cutting us off from the temporal plane, the lower kind of reality, Contemplation gives the eternal plane, and the powers which can commu-

---

[1] Vie (ed. Poiret, 1720), t. ii. p. 74.

[2] Meister Eckhart, Pred. i. ("Mystische Schriften," p. 18).

[3] "Three Dialogues of the Supersensual Life," p. 14.

[4] Dionysius the Areopagite, "De Divinis Nominibus," vii. 3.

[5] Pred. xxiii. Eckhart obtained this image from St. Thomas Aquinas, "Summa Contra Gentiles," l. iii. cap. lxi. "The intellectual soul is created on the confines of eternity and time."

nicate with that plane, their chance. In the born mystic these powers are great, and lie very near the normal threshold of consciousness. He has a genius for transcendental—or as he would say, divine—discovery in exactly the same way as his cousins, the born musician and poet, have a genius for musical or poetic discovery. In all three cases, the emergence of these higher powers is mysterious, and not least so to those who experience it. Psychology on the one hand, theology on the other, may offer us diagrams and theories of this proceeding : of the strange oscillations of the developing consciousness, the fitful visitations of a lucidity and creative power over which the self has little or no control ; the raptures and griefs of a vision by turns granted and withdrawn. But the secret of genius still eludes us, as the secret of life eludes the biologist.

The utmost we can say of such persons is, that reality presents itself to them under abnormal conditions and in abnormal terms, and that subject to these conditions and in these terms they are bound to deal with it. Thanks to their peculiar mental make up, one aspect of the universe is for them focused so sharply that in comparison with it all other images are blurred, vague, and unreal. Hence the sacrifice which men of genius—mystics, artists, inventors—make of their whole lives to this one Object, this one vision of truth, is not self-denial, but rather self-fulfilment. They gather themselves up from the unreal, in order to concentrate on the real. The whole personality then absorbs or enters into communion with certain rhythms or harmonies existent in the universe, which the receiving apparatus of other selves cannot take up. " Here is the finger of God, a flash of the Will that can ! " exclaims Abt Vogler, as the sounds grow under his hand. " The numbers *came* ! " says the poet. He knows not how ; certainly not by deliberate intellectation.

So it is with the mystic. Madame Guyon states in her autobiography, that when she was composing her works she would experience a sudden and irresistible inclination to take up her pen ; though feeling wholly incapable of literary composition, and not even knowing the subject on which she would be impelled to write. If she resisted this impulse it was at the cost of the most intense discomfort. She would then begin to write with extraordinary swiftness ; words, elaborate arguments, and appropriate quotations coming to her without reflection, and so quickly that one of her longest books was written in one and a half days.[1]

"In writing I saw that I was writing of things which I had never seen : and during the time of this manifestation, I was given light to perceive that I had in me treasures of knowledge and understanding which I did not know that I possessed."[2]

Similar statements are made of St. Teresa, who declared that in writing her books she was powerless to set down anything but that which her Master put into her mind.[3] So Blake said of "Milton" and "Jerusalem," "I have written the poems from immediate dictation, twelve or sometimes twenty or thirty lines at a time, without premeditation and even against my will. The time it has taken in writing was thus rendered non-existent, and an immense poem exists which seems to be the labour of a long life, all produced without labour or study."[4]

These are, of course, extreme forms of that strange power of automatic composition, in which words and characters arrive and arrange themselves in defiance of their authors' will, of which most poets and novelists possess a trace. Such composition is related to the "automatic writing" of "mediums" and other sensitives; in which the often disorderly and incoherent subliminal mind seizes upon this channel of expression. The subliminal mind of the great mystic, however, is not disorderly. It is richly endowed and keenly observant—a treasure house, not a lumber room—and becomes, in the course of its education, a highly disciplined and skilled instrument of knowledge. When, therefore, its contents emerge, and are presented to the normal consciousness in the form of lucidity, "auditions," visions, automatic writing, or any other translations of the supersensual into the terms of sensual perception, they cannot be discredited because the worthless subconscious field of feebler natures sometimes manifests itself in the same way. Idiots are often voluble : but many orators are sane.

Now, to sum up : what are the chief characteristics which we have found in this sketch-map of the mental life of man ?

(1) We have divided that life, arbitrarily enough, along the

---

[1] Vie, t. ii. pp. 120, 229.   [2] Op. cit., p. 223.
[3] G. Cunninghame Graham, "Santa Teresa," vol. i. p. 202.
[4] "Letters of William Blake," April 25, 1803.

fluctuating line which psychologists call the "threshold of his consciousness" into the surface life and the subconscious deeps.

(2) In the surface life, though we recognized its essential wholeness, we distinguished three outstanding and ever-present aspects : the Trinity in Unity of feeling, thought, and will. Amongst these, we were obliged to give the primacy to feeling, as the power which set the machinery of thought and will to work.

(3) We have seen that the expression of this life takes the two complementary forms of *conation*, or outgoing action, and *cognition*, or indwelling knowledge ; and that the first, which is dynamic in type, is largely dependent on the will stimulated by the emotions ; whilst the second, which is passive in type, is the business of the intellect. They answer to the two main aspects which man discerns in the universal life : Being and Becoming.

(4) Neither conation nor cognition—action nor thought—as performed by this surface mind, concerned as it is with natural existence and dominated by spatial conceptions, is able to set up any relations with the Absolute or Transcendental world. Such action and thought deal wholly with material supplied directly or indirectly by the world of sense. The testimony of the mystics, however, and of all persons possessing an "instinct for the Absolute," points to the existence of a further faculty in man ; an intuitive power which the circumstances of diurnal life tend to keep "below the threshold" of his consciousness, and which thus becomes one of the factors of his "subliminal life." This latent faculty is the primary agent of mysticism, and lives a "substantial" life in touch with the real or transcendental world.

(5) Certain processes, of which contemplation has been taken as a type, so alter the state of consciousness as to permit the emergence of this faculty ; which, according as it enters more or less into the conscious life, makes man more or less a mystic.

The mystic life, therefore, involves the emergence from deep levels of man's transcendental self ; its capture of the field of consciousness ; and the "conversion" or rearrangement of his feeling, thought, and will—his character—about this new centre of life.

We state, then, as the conclusion of this chapter, that the object of the mystic's adventure, seen from within, is the apprehension of, or direct communion with, that transcendental reality which we tried in the last section to define from without.

Here, as in the fulfilment of the highest earthly love, knowledge and communion are the same thing ; we must be " oned with bliss" if we are to be aware of it. The main agent by which we may attain this communion resides in that part of the self which usually lies below the threshold of our consciousness. Thence, in certain natures of abnormal richness and vitality, and under certain favourable conditions, it may be liberated by various devices, such as contemplation. Once it has emerged, however, it takes up, to help it in the work, aspects of the conscious self. The surface must co-operate with the deeps, and at last merge with those deeps to produce that unification of consciousness upon high levels which alone can put a term to man's unrest. The heart that longs for the All, the mind that conceives it, the will that concentrates the whole self upon it, must all be called into play. The self must be surrendered : but it must not be annihilated, as some Quietists have supposed. It only dies that it may live again. Supreme success, says the Lady Julian, in a passage which anticipates the classification of modern psychology, the permanent assurance of the mystic that " we are more verily in heaven than in earth," " cometh of the natural Love of our soul, and of the clear light of our Reason, and of the steadfast Mind." [1]

But what is the order of precedence which these three activities are to assume in the work which is *one ?* All, as we have seen, must do their part ; for the business is nothing less than the movement of man in his wholeness to high levels. But which shall predominate ? On the answer which each gives to this question the ultimate nature of the self, and the nature of that self's experience of reality, will depend. The question for her is really this ; under which aspect of consciousness can she creep most closely to the Thought of God; the real life in which she is bathed? Which, fostered and made dominant, is most likely to put her in harmony with the Absolute ? The Love of

---

[1] Julian of Norwich, " Revelations of Divine Love," cap. lv.

God, which is ever in the hearts and often on the lips of Saints, is the passionate desire for this harmony; the "malady of thought" is its intellectual equivalent. Though we may seem to escape God, we cannot escape this craving; except at the price of utter stagnation. We go back, therefore, to the statement with which this chapter opened: that of the two governing desires which share the prison of the self. We see them now as representing the cravings of the intellect and the emotions for the only end of all quests. The disciplined will— that "conative power"—with all the dormant faculties which it can wake and utilize, can come to the assistance of one of them. Which? The question is a crucial one; for the destiny of the self depends on the partner which the will selects.

CHAPTER IV

THE CHARACTERISTICS OF MYSTICISM

EVER since the world began, man has had two distinct and fundamental attitudes towards the unseen ; and through them has developed two methods of getting in touch with it. For the purpose of our present inquiry, I propose to call these methods the " way of magic " and the " way of mysticism." Having said so much, one must at once add that although in their extreme forms these arts are sharply contrasted with one another, their frontiers are far from being clearly defined : that, starting from the same point, they often confuse the inquirer by using the same language, instruments, and methods. Hence it is that so much which is really magic is loosely and popularly described as mysticism. They represent as a matter of fact the opposite poles of the same thing : the transcendental consciousness of humanity. Between them lie the great religions, which might be described under this metaphor as representing the ordinarily habitable regions of that consciousness. Hence, at one end of the scale, pure mysticism "shades off" into religion—from some points of view seems to grow out of it. No deeply religious man is without a touch of mysticism ; and no mystic can be other than religious, in the psychological if not in the theological sense of the word. At the other end of the scale, as we shall see later on, religion, no less surely, shades off into magic.

The fundamental difference between the two is this : magic wants to get, mysticism wants to give—immortal and antagonistic attitudes, which turn up under one disguise or another in every age of thought. Both magic and mysticism in their full development bring the whole mental machinery, conscious and subconscious, to bear on their undertaking: both claim that they produce in their initiates powers unknown to ordinary men. But the centre round which that machinery is grouped, the reasons of that undertaking, and the ends to which those powers are applied differ enormously. In mysticism the will is united with the emotions in an impassioned desire to transcend the sense-world in order that the self may be joined by love to the one eternal and ultimate Object of love ; whose existence is intuitively perceived by that which we used to call the soul, but now find it easier to refer to as the "Cosmic" or "transcendental" sense. This is the poetic and religious temperament acting upon the plane of reality. In magic, the will unites with the intellect in an impassioned desire for supersensible knowledge. This is the intellectual, aggressive, and scientific temperament trying to extend its field of consciousness, until it includes the supersensual world : obviously the antithesis of mysticism, though often adopting its title and style.

It will be our business later on to consider in more detail the characteristics and significance of magic. Now it is enough to say that we may class broadly as magical all forms of self-seeking transcendentalism. It matters little whether the apparatus which they use be the incantations of the old magicians, the congregational prayer for rain of orthodox Protestants, or the consciously self-hypnotizing devices of "New Thought" : whether the end proposed be the evocation of an angel, the power of transcending circumstance, or the healing of disease. The object of the thing is always the same : the deliberate exaltation of the will, till it transcends its usual limitations and obtains for the self or group of selves something which it or they did not previously possess. It is an individualistic and acquisitive science : in all its forms an activity of the intellect, seeking Reality for its own purposes, or for those of humanity at large.

Mysticism, whose great name is too often given to these supersensual activities, is utterly different from this. It is non-individualistic. It implies, indeed, the abolition of individuality; of that hard·separateness, that "I, Me, Mine" which makes of man a finite isolated thing. It is essentially a movement of the heart, seeking to transcend the limitations of the individual standpoint and to surrender itself to ultimate Reality; for no personal gain, to satisfy no transcendental curiosity, to obtain no other-worldly joys, but purely from an instinct of love. By the word *heart*, of course we here mean not merely "the seat of the affections," "the organ of tender emotion," and the like : but rather the inmost sanctuary of personal being, the synthesis of its love and will, the very source of its energy and life. The mystic is "in love with the Absolute" not in any idle or sentimental manner but in that deep and vital sense which presses forward at all costs and through all dangers towards union with the object beloved. Hence, where the practice of magic—like the practice of science—does not necessarily entail any passionate emotion, though of course it does and must entail interest of some kind, mysticism, like art, cannot exist without it. We must feel, and feel acutely, before we want to act on this hard and heroic scale.

We at once see that these two activities correspond to the two eternal passions of the self, the desire of love and the desire of knowledge : severally representing the hunger of heart and intellect for ultimate truth.

The third attitude towards the supersensual world, that of transcendental philosophy, hardly comes within the scope of the present inquiry; since it is purely academic where both magic and mysticism are practical, and in their methods strictly empirical. Such philosophy is often wrongly called mysticism because it tries to make maps of the countries which the mystic explores. Its performances are useful, as diagrams are useful, so long as they do not ape finality; remembering that the only final thing is personal experience—the personal exploration of the exalted and truth-loving soul.

What then do we really mean by mysticism? A word which is impartially applied to the performances of mediums and the ecstasies of the saints, to "menticulture" and sorcery, dreamy poetry and mediaeval art, to prayer and palmistry, the doctrinal excesses of Gnosticism, and the tepid speculations of the Cambridge Platonists—even, according to William James, to the higher branches of intoxication [1]—soon ceases to have any useful meaning. Its employment merely confuses the inexperienced student, who usually emerges from his struggle with the ever-increasing mass of theosophical and psychical literature possessed by a vague idea that every kind of super-sensual theory and practice is somehow "mystical." Hence it is necessary, if possible, to fix its true characteristics: to restate the fact that Mysticism, in its pure form, is the science of ultimates, the science of union with the Absolute, and nothing else, and that the mystic is the person who attains to this union, not the person who talks about it. Not to *know about*, but to *Be*, is the mark of the real practitioner.

The difficulty lies in determining the point at which super-sensual experience ceases to be merely a practical and interesting extension of sensual experience—an enlarging, so to speak, of the boundaries of existence — and passes over into that boundless life where Subject and Object, desirous and desired, are *one*. No sharp line, but rather an infinite series of gradations separate the two states. Hence we must look carefully at all the pilgrims on the road; discover, if we can, the motive of their travels, the maps which they use, the luggage which they take, the end which they attain.

Now we have said that the end which the mystic sets before him on his pilgrimage is conscious union with a living Absolute. That Divine Dark, that Abyss of the Godhead, of which he sometimes speaks as the goal of his quest, is just this Absolute, the Uncreated Light in which the Universe is bathed, and which —transcending, as it does, all human powers of expression—he can only describe to us as *dark*. But there is—must be—contact "in an intelligible where" between every individual self and this Supreme Self, this All. In the mystic this union is conscious, personal, and complete. More or less according to

---

[1] See "Varieties of Religious Experience," p. 387, "The Drunken Consciousness is a bit of the Mystic Consciousness."

his measure, he has touched the substantial Being of Deity, not merely its manifestation in life. This it is which distinguishes him from the best and most brilliant of other men, and makes his science, in Patmore's words, "the science of self-evident Reality." Gazing with him into that ultimate Abyss, that unsearchable ground whence the World of Becoming comes forth "eternally generated in an eternal Now," we may see only the icy darkness of perpetual negations : but he looks upon the face of Perfect Love.

Just as genius in any of the arts is—humanly speaking—the final term of a power of which each individual possesses the rudiments, so mysticism may be looked upon as the final term, the active expression, of a power latent in the whole race : the power, that is to say, of so perceiving transcendent reality. Few people pass through life without knowing what it is to be at least touched by this mystical feeling. He who falls in love with a woman and perceives—as the lover really does perceive —that the categorical term "girl" veils a wondrous and un-speakable reality : he who, falling in love with nature, sees the light that never was on sea or land—a vaguely pretty phrase to those who have not seen it, but a scientific statement to the rest—he who falls in love with invisible things, or as we say "undergoes conversion": all these have truly known for an instant something of the secret of the world.[1]

> ". . . Ever and anon a trumpet sounds
> From the hid battlements of Eternity,
> Those shaken mists a space unsettle, then
> Round the half-glimpsèd turrets slowly wash again."

At such moments "Transcendental Feeling, welling up from another 'Part of the Soul' whispers to Understanding and Sense that they are leaving out something. What ? Nothing less than the secret plan of the Universe. And what is that secret plan ? The other 'Part of the Soul' indeed comprehends it in silence as it is, but can explain it to the Understanding only in the symbolical language of the interpreter, Imagination—in Vision."[2]

Here, in this spark or "part of the soul" is the fountain

---

[1] Compare above, pp. 24, 26, 57.
[2] J. A. Stewart, "The Myths of Plato," p. 42.

alike of the creative imagination and the mystic life. Now and again something stings it into consciousness, and man is caught up to the spiritual level, catches a glimpse of the "secret plan." Then hints of a marvellous truth, a unity whose note is ineffable peace, shine in created things; awakening in the self a sentiment of love, adoration, and awe. Its life is enhanced, the barrier of personality is broken, man escapes the sense-world, ascends to the apex of his spirit, and enters for a brief period into the more extended life of the All.

This intuition of the Real lying at the root of the visible world and sustaining its life, is present in a modified form in the arts : perhaps it were better to say, *must* be present if these arts are to justify themselves as heightened forms of experience. It is this which gives to them that peculiar vitality, that strange power of communicating a poignant emotion, half torment and half joy, which baffle their more rational interpreters. We know that the picture which is "like a photograph," the building which is at once handsome and commodious, the novel which is a perfect transcript of life, fail to satisfy us. It is difficult to say why this should be so unless it were because these things have neglected their true business ; which was not to reproduce the illusions of ordinary men but to catch and translate for us something of that "secret plan," that reality which the artistic consciousness is able, in a measure, to perceive. "Painting as well as music and poetry exists and exults in immortal thoughts," says Blake.[1] That "life-enhancing power" which has been recognized by modern critics as the supreme quality of good painting,[2] has its origin in this contact of the artistic mind with the archetypal—or, if you like, the transcendental—world : the underlying verity of things.

A living critic, in whom poetic genius has brought about the unusual alliance of intuition with scholarship, testifies to this same truth when he says of the ideals which governed early Chinese painting, " In this theory every work of art is thought of as an incarnation of the genius of rhythm, manifesting the living spirit of things with a clearer beauty and intenser power than the gross impediments of complex matter allow to be transmitted to our senses in the visible world around us. A

[1] "Descriptive Catalogue."
[2] See Rolleston, "Parallel Paths," 1908.

picture is conceived as a *sort of apparition from a more real world of essential life.*" [1]

That "more real world of essential life" is the world in which the "free soul" of the great mystic dwells; hovering like the six-winged seraph before the face of the Absolute. [2]   The artist too may cross its boundaries in his brief moments of creation : but he cannot stay.   He comes back to us, bearing its tidings, with Dante's cry upon his lips—

> ". . . Non eran da ciò le proprie penne
> se non che la mia mente fu percossa
> da un fulgore, in che sua voglia venne." [3]

The mystic may say — is indeed bound to say — with St. Bernard, "My secret to myself."   Try how he will, his stammering and awestruck reports can hardly be understood but by those who are already in the way.   But the artist cannot act thus.   On him has been laid the duty of expressing something of that which he perceives.   He is bound to tell his love. In his worship of Perfect Beauty faith must be balanced by works.   By means of veils and symbols he must interpret his free vision, his glimpse of the burning bush, to other men.   He is the mediator between his brethren and the divine, for art is the link between appearance and reality. [4]

But we do not call every one who has these partial and artistic intuitions of reality a mystic, any more than we call every one a musician who has learnt to play the piano.   The true mystic is the person in whom such powers transcend the merely artistic and visionary stage, and are exalted to the point of genius : in whom the transcendental consciousness can dominate the normal consciousness, and who has definitely surrendered himself to the embrace of Reality.

As artists stand in a peculiar relation to the phenomenal world, receiving rhythms and discovering truths and beauties

---

[1] Laurence Binyon, " Painting in the Far East," p. 9.

[2] " The Mirror of Simple Souls," f. 141 C. (B.M. Add. 37790).

[3] Par. xxxiii. 139. " Not for this were my wings fitted : save only that my mind was smitten by a lightning flash, wherein came to it its desire."

[4] In this connexion Godfernaux (*Revue Philosophique*, February, 1902) has a highly significant remark to the effect that romanticism represents the invasion of secular literature by mystic or religious emotion.   It is, he says, the *secularization of the inner life.*

which are hidden from other men, so this true mystic stands in a peculiar relation to the transcendental world ; there experiencing the onslaught of what must remain for us unimaginable delights. His consciousness is transfigured in a particular way, he lives at different levels of experience from other people : and this of course means that he sees a different world, since the world as we know it is the product of specific scraps or aspects of reality acting upon a normal and untransfigured consciousness. Hence his mysticism is no isolated vision, no arbitrary glimpse of reality, but a complete system of life—a *Syntagma*, to use Eucken's expressive term. As other men are immersed in and react to natural or intellectual life, so the mystic is immersed in and reacts to spiritual life. He moves towards that utter identification with its interests which he calls " Union with God." He has been called a lonely soul. He might more properly be described as a lonely body : for his soul, peculiarly responsive, sends out and receives communications upon every side.

The earthly artist, because perception brings with it the imperative longing for expression, tries to give us in colour, sound or words a hint of his ecstasy, his glimpse of truth. Only those who have tried, know how small a fraction of his vision he can, under the most favourable circumstance, contrive to represent. The mystic too tries very hard to tell an unwilling world the only secret. But in his case, the difficulties are enormously increased. First, there is the huge disparity. between his unspeakable experience and the language which will most nearly approach it. Next, there is the great gulf fixed between his mind and the mind of the world. His audience must be bewitched as well as addressed, caught up to something of his state, before they can be made to understand.

Were he a musician, it is probable that he could give his message to other musicians in the terms of that art, far more accurately than language will ever allow him to do : for we must remember that there is no excuse but that of convenience for the pre-eminence amongst modes of expression which we accord to words. These correspond so well to the physical plane and its adventures, that we forget that they have but the faintest of relations with transcendental things. Even the artist, before he can make use of them, is bound to re-arrange them in accordance with the laws of rhythm : obeying unconsciously the rule by which all arts " tend to approach the condition of music."

So too the mystic. Mysticism, the most romantic thing in the universe, from one point of view the art of arts, their source and also their end, finds naturally enough its closest correspondences in the most purely artistic and most deeply significant of all forms of expression. The mystery of music is seldom realized by those who so easily accept its gifts. Yet of all the arts music alone shares with great mystical literature the power of waking us to response to the life-movement of the universe : brings us—we know not how—news of its exultant passions and its incomparable peace. Beethoven heard the very voice of Reality, and little of it escaped when he translated it for our ears.[1]

The mediaeval mind, more naturally mystical than ours, and therefore more sharply aware of the part which rhythmic harmony plays in the worlds of nature and of grace, gave to music a Cosmic importance, discerning its operation in many phenomena which we now attribute to that dismal figment, Law. "There are three kinds of music," says Hugh of St. Victor, "the music of the worlds, the music of humanity, the music of instruments. Of the music of the worlds, one is of the elements, another of the planets, another of Time. Of that which is of the elements, one is of number, another of weights, another of measure. Of that which is of the planets, one is of place, another of motion, another of nature. Of that which is of Time, one is of the days and the vicissitudes of light and darkness ; another of the months and the waxing and waning of the moon ; another of the years and the changes of spring, summer, autumn and winter. Of the music of humanity, one is of the body, another of the soul, another in the connexion that is between them."[2] Thus the life of the visible and invisible universe consists in a supernal fugue.

[1] Since this passage was written M. Hebert's brilliant monograph " Le Divin " (1907) has come into my hands. I take from his pages two examples of the analogy between mystical and musical emotion. First that of Gay, who had " the soul, the heart, and the head full of music, of another beauty than that which is formulated by sounds." Next, that of Ruysbroeck, who, in a passage that might have been written by Keats, speaks of Contemplation and Love as " two heavenly pipes " which, blown upon by the Holy Spirit, play " ditties of no tone " (*op. cit.*, p. 29).

[2] Hugh of St. Victor, " Didascalicon de Studio Legendi."

One contemplative at least, Richard Rolle of Hampole, " the father of English mysticism," was acutely aware of this music of the soul, discerning in its joyous periods a response to the measured harmonies of the spiritual universe.   In that beautiful description of his inward experience which is one of the jewels of mystical literature, nothing is more remarkable than his constant and deliberate employment of musical imagery.   This alone, it seems, could catch and translate for him the wild rapture of Transcendent Life.   The condition of joyous and awakened love to which the mystic passes when his purification is at an end, is to him, above all else, the state of Song.   He does not "see" Reality : he "hears" it.   For him, as for St. Francis of Assisi, it is a " heavenly melody, intolerably sweet." [1]

"Song I call," he says, " when in a plenteous soul the sweetness of eternal love with burning is taken, and thought into song is turned, and the mind into full sweet sound is changed." [2] He who experiences this joyous exaltation "says not his prayers like other righteous men" but " is taken into marvellous mirth : and, goodly sound being descended into him, as it were with notes his prayers he sings." [3]   So Gertrude More— "O lett me sitt alone, silent to all the world and it to me, that I may learn the song of Love." [4]

Rolle's own experience of mystic joy seems actually to have come to him in this form : the perceptions of his exalted consciousness presenting themselves to his understanding under musical conditions, as other mystics have received them in the form of pictures or words.   I give in his own words the charming account of his passage from the first state of " burning love" to the second state of "songful love"—from *Calor* to *Canor*— when " into song of joy meditation is turned."   " In the night, before supper, as I my psalms sung, as it were the sound of readers or rather singers about me I beheld.   Whilst also, praying to heaven, with all desire I took heed, suddenly, in what

---

[1] " Fioretti."   Delle Istimati. (Arnold's translation.)

[2] Richard Rolle, " The Fire of Love " (Early English Text Society), bk. i. cap. xv.   As the Latin version of the " Incendium Amoris " unfortunately still remains in MS., in this and subsequent quotations from Rolle I have adopted Mesyn's fifteenth - century translation, slightly modernizing the spelling, and sometimes correcting from the Latin his somewhat obscure language.

[3] *Op. cit.*, bk. i. cap. xxiii.   Compare bk. ii. caps. v. and vi.

[4] " Spiritual Exercises," p. 30.

manner I wot not, in me the sound of song I felt ; and likeliest heavenly melody I took, with me dwelling in mind. Forsooth my thought continually to mirth of song was changed : and as it were the same that loving I had thought, and in prayers and psalms had said, in *sound* I showed." [1]

The song, however, is a mystic melody having little in common with its clumsy image, earthly music. Bodily song "lets it"; and "noise of janglers makes it turn again to thought," "for sweet ghostly song accords not with outward song, the which in churches and elsewhere is used. It discords much : for all that is man's voice is formed with bodily ears to be heard ; but among angels tunes it has an acceptable melody, and with marvel it is commended of them that have known it." To others it is incommunicable. "Worldly lovers soothly words or ditties of our song may know, for the words they read : but the tone and sweetness of that song they may not learn." [2]

Such symbolism as this—a living symbolism of experience and action as well as of statement—seems almost essential to mystical expression. The mind must employ some device of the kind if its transcendental perceptions—wholly unrelated as they are to the phenomena with which intellect is able to deal— are ever to be grasped by the surface consciousness. Sometimes the symbol and the perception which it represents become fused in that consciousness ; and the mystic's experience then presents itself to him as "visions" or "voices" which we must look upon as the garment he has himself provided to veil that Reality upon which no man may look and live. The nature of this garment will be largely conditioned by his temperament—as in Rolle's evident bias towards music, St. Catherine of Genoa's leaning towards the abstract conceptions of fire and light—and also by his theological education and environment ; as in the highly dogmatic visions and auditions of St. Gertrude, Suso, St. Catherine of Siena, the Blessed Angela of Foligno ; above all

---

[1] *Op. cit.*, bk. i. cap. xvi.
[2] *Op. cit.*, bk. ii. caps. iii. and xii.   Shelley is of the same opinion :—

"The world can hear not the sweet notes that move
The Sphere whose light is melody to lovers."
("The Triumph of Life.")

of St. Teresa, whose marvellous self-analyses provide the classic account of these attempts of the mind to translate transcendental intuitions into concepts with which it can deal.

The greatest mystics, however—Ruysbroeck, St. John of the Cross, and St. Teresa herself in her later stages—distinguish clearly between the indicible Reality which they perceive and the image under which they describe it. Again and again they tell us with Dionysius and Eckhart, that the Object of their contemplation "hath no image": or with St. John of the Cross that "the soul can never attain to the height of the divine union, so far as it is possible in this life, through the medium of any forms or figures."[1] Therefore the attempt which has sometimes been made to identify mysticism with such forms and figures—with visions, voices, and "supernatural favours"—is clearly wrong.

"The highest and most divine things which it is given us to see and to know," says Dionysius the Areopagite plainly, "are in some way the expression of all That which the sovereign Nature of God includes: an expression which reveals to us That which escapes all thought and which has its seat beyond the heights of heaven."[2]

The mystic, as a rule, cannot wholly do without symbol and image, inadequate to his vision though they must always be: for his experience must be expressed if it is to be communicated, and its actuality is inexpressible except in some side-long way, some hint or parallel which will stimulate the dormant intuition of the reader, and convey, as all poetic language does, something beyond its surface sense. Hence the enormous part which is played in all mystical writings by symbolism and imagery; and also by that rhythmic and exalted language which induces in sensitive persons something of the languid ecstasy of dream. The close connection between rhythm and heightened states of consciousness is as yet little understood. Its further investigation will probably throw much light on ontological as well as psychological problems. Mystical, no less than musical and poetic perception, tends naturally—we know not why—to present itself in rhythmical

[1] "Subida del Monte Carmelo," l. ii. cap. xvi. (Here and throughout I quote from Lewis's translation.)
[2] "De Mystica Theologia," i. 3.

periods : a feature which is also strongly marked in writings obtained in the automatic state. So constant is this law in some cases that Baron von Hügel, in his biography of St. Catherine of Genoa, has adopted the presence or absence of rhythm as a test whereby to distinguish the genuine utterances of the saint from those wrongly attributed to her by successive editors of her legend.[1]

All kinds of symbolic language come naturally to the articulate mystic, who is usually a literary artist as well : so naturally, that he sometimes forgets to explain that his utterance is but symbolic ; a desperate attempt to translate the truth of that world into the beauty of this. It is here that mysticism joins hands with music and poetry : had this fact always been recognized by its critics, they would have been saved from many regrettable and some ludicrous misconceptions. Symbol—the clothing which the spiritual borrows from the material plane—is a form of artistic expression. That is to say, it is not literal but suggestive : though the artist who uses it may sometimes lose sight of this distinction. Hence the persons who imagine that the " Spiritual Marriage " of St. Catherine or St. Teresa veils a perverted sexuality, that the vision of the Sacred Heart involved an incredible anatomical experience, or that the divine inebriation of the Sūfis is the apotheosis of drunkenness, do but advertise their ignorance of the mechanism of the arts : like the lady who thought that Blake *must* be mad because he said that he had touched the sky with his finger.

Further, the study of the mystics, the keeping company however humbly with their minds, brings with it as music or poetry does—but in a far greater degree—a strange exhilaration, as if we were brought near to some mighty source of Being, were at last on the verge of the secret which all seek. The symbols displayed, the actual words employed, when we analyse them, are not enough to account for such effect. It is rather that these messages from the waking transcendental self of another, stir our own deeper selves in their sleep. It were hardly an extravagance to say, that those writings which are the outcome of true and first-hand mystical experience may be known by this power of imparting to the reader the sense of exalted and

[1] Von Hügel, " The Mystical Element in Religion," vol. i. p. 189.

extended life. "All mystics," says Saint-Martin, "speak the same language, for they come from the same country." The deep undying life which nests within us came from that country too : and it recognizes the accents of home, though it cannot always understand what they would say.

Now, returning to our original undertaking, that of defining if we can the characteristics of true mysticism, I think that we have already reached a point at which William James's celebrated "four marks" of the mystic state,[1] Ineffability, Noetic Quality, Transiency, and Passivity, will fail to satisfy us. In their place I propose to set out, illustrate and, I hope, justify four other rules or notes which may be applied as tests to any given case which claims to take rank amongst the mystics.

1. True mysticism is active and practical, not passive and theoretical. It is an organic life-process, a something which the whole self does ; not something as to which its intellect holds an opinion.

2. Its aims are wholly transcendental and spiritual. It is in no way concerned with adding to, exploring, re-arranging, or improving anything in the visible universe. The mystic brushes aside that universe even in its most supernormal manifestations. Though he does not, as his enemies declare, neglect his duty to the many, his heart is always set upon the changeless One.

3. This One is for the mystic, not merely the Reality of all that is, but also a living and personal Object of Love ; never an object of exploration. It draws his whole being homeward, but always under the guidance of the heart.

4. Living union with this One—which is the term of his adventure—is a definite state or form of enhanced life. It is obtained neither from an intellectual realization of its delights, nor from the most acute emotional longings. Though these must be present, they are not enough. It is arrived at by a definite and arduous psychological process—the so-called Mystic Way—entailing the complete remaking of character and the liberation of a new, or rather latent, form of consciousness, which imposes on the self the condition which is sometimes inaccurately called "ecstasy," but is better named the Unitive State.

[1] "Varieties of Religious Experience," p. 380.

Mysticism, then, is not an opinion : it is not a philosophy. It has nothing in common with the pursuit of occult knowledge.   It is not merely the power of contemplating Eternity. It is the name of that organic process which involves the perfect consummation of the Love of God : the achievement here and now of the immortal heritage of man.   Or, if you like it better —for this means exactly the same thing—it is the art of establishing his conscious relation with the Absolute.

The movement of mystic consciousness towards this consummation, is not merely the sudden admission to an overwhelming vision of Truth : it is rather an ordered movement towards ever higher levels of reality, ever closer identification with the Infinite.   "The mystic experience," says Récéjac, "ends with the words, 'I live, yet not I, but God in me.'   This feeling of identification, which is the term of mystical activity, has a very important significance.   In its early stages the mystic consciousness feels the Absolute in opposition to the Self . . . as mystic activity goes on, it tends to abolish this opposition. . . . When it has reached its term the consciousness finds itself possessed by the sense of a Being at one and the same time greater than the Self and identical with it : great enough to be God, intimate enough to be me." [1]

This is the mystic union which is the only possible fulfilment of mystic love : since

> " All that is not One must ever
> Suffer with the wound of Absence,
> And whoever in Love's city
> Enters, finds but room for One
> And but in One-ness, Union." [2]

The history of mysticism is the history of the demonstration of this law upon the plane of reality.

Now, how do these statements square with the practice of the great mystics ; and with the various forms of activity which have been classified at one time or another as mystical ?

(1) *Mysticism is practical, not theoretical.*

This statement taken alone is not of course enough to identify mysticism, since it is equally true of magic, which also

---

[1] " Les Fondements de la Connaissance Mystique," p. 45.

[2] Jámí.   Quoted in " Jelalu 'd Din " (Wisdom of the East Series), p. 25.

H

proposes to itself something to be done rather than something to be believed. It at once comes into collision, however, with the opinions of the group of writers who believe mysticism to be "the reaction of the born Platonist upon religion."

The difference between such devout philosophers and the true mystic, is the difference which the late Father Tyrrell defined as separating theology from revelation.[1] Mysticism, like revelation, is final and personal. It is not merely a beautiful and suggestive diagram of experience, but is of the very stuff of life. In the superb words of Plotinus, it is the soul's solitary adventure : "the flight of the Alone to the Alone."[2] Its vision provides the material, the substance, the actual experience, upon which mystical philosophy cogitates ; as the theologians cogitate upon the individual revelations which form the basis of faith. Hence those whom we are to accept as mystics must have received, and acted upon, intuitions of a Truth which is for them absolute. If we are to acknowledge that they "knew the doctrine" they must have "lived the life," submitted to the interior travail of the Mystic Way, not merely have reasoned about the mystical experiences of others. We could not well dispense with our Christian Platonists and mystical philosophers. They are our stepping stones to higher things; interpret to our dull minds, entangled in the sense-world, the ardent vision of those who speak to us from the dimension of Reality. But they are no more mystics than the milestones on the Dover Road are travellers to Calais. Sometimes their words—the wistful words of those who know but cannot be—produce mystics ; as the sudden sight of a signpost pointing to the sea will rouse the spirit of adventure in a boy. Also there are many instances of true mystics, such as Eckhart, who have philosophized upon their own experiences, greatly to the advantage of the world ; and others —Plotinus is the most characteristic example—of Platonic philosophers who have passed far beyond the limits of their own philosophy, and abandoned the making of diagrams for an experience, however imperfect, of the reality at which these diagrams hint. It were more accurate to reverse the

[1] "Through Scylla and Charybdis," p. 264.
[2] Ennead vi. 9.

epigram above stated, and say, that Platonism is the re-action of the born intellectualist upon mystical truth.

Over and over again the great mystics tell us, not how they speculated, but how they acted. To them, the passage from the life of sense to the life of spirit is a veritable under-taking, which demands effort and constancy. The paradoxical "quiet" of the contemplative is but the outward stillness essential to inward work. Their favourite symbols are those of action : battle, search, and pilgrimage.

> " In an obscure night
> Fevered with love's anxiety
> (O hapless, happy plight !)
> I *went*, none seeing me,
> Forth from my house, where all things quiet be," [1]

said St. John of the Cross, in his poem of the mystic quest.

"It became evident to me," says Al Ghazzali of his own search for mystic truth, "that the Sūfis are men of intuition and not men of words. I recognized that I had learnt all that can be learnt of Sūfiism by study, and that the rest could not be learnt by study or by speech." [2] "Let no one suppose," says the "Theologia Germanica," "that we may attain to this true light and perfect knowledge . . . by hearsay, or by reading and study, nor yet by high skill and great learning." [3] "It is not enough," says Gerlac Petersen, "to know by estimation merely : but we must know by experience." [4]

So Mechthild of Magdeburg says of her revelations, "The writing of this book was seen, heard, and experienced in every limb. . . . I see it with the eyes of my soul, and hear it with the ears of my eternal spirit." [5]

"The invitation of the mystic life is to come and see, the promise of the mystic life is that we shall attain to see." [6] Those who suppose it to be merely a pleasing consciousness

[1] " En una Noche Escura," Stanza I. I quote from Mr. Arthur Symons's beautiful translation, which will be found in vol. ii. of his Collected Poems.
[2] Schmölders, " Les Écoles Philosophiques chez les Arabes," p. 55.
[3] Cap. xix.
[4] " Ignitum cum Deo Soliloquium," cap. xi.
[5] " Das Fliessende Licht der Gottheit," pt. iv. cap. 13.
[6] A. E. Waite, " Studies in Mysticism," p. 53.

of the Divine in the world, a sense of the "otherness" of things, a basking in the beams of the Uncreated Light, are only playing with Reality. True mystical achievement is the most complete and most difficult expression of life which is as yet possible to man. It is at once an act of love, an act of union, and an act of supreme perception; a trinity of experiences which meets and satisfies the three activities of the self. Religion might give us the first and metaphysics the third of these processes. Only Mysticism can offer the middle term of the series; the essential link which binds the three in one. "Secrets," says St. Catherine of Siena, "are revealed to a friend who has become *one thing* with his friend and not to a servant." [1]

(2) *Mysticism is an entirely Spiritual Activity.*

This rule provides us with a further limitation, which of course excludes all the practisers of magic and of magical religion: even in their most exalted and least materialistic forms. As we shall see when we come to consider these persons, their object—not necessarily an illegitimate one—is to improve and elucidate the visible by help of the invisible: to use the supernormal powers of the self for the increase of power, virtue, happiness or knowledge. The mystic never turns back on himself in this way, or tries to combine the advantages of two worlds. At the term of his development he knows God by communion, and this direct intuition of the Absolute kills all lesser cravings. He possesses God, and needs nothing more. Though he will spend himself ceaselessly and tirelessly for other men, become "an agent of the Eternal Goodness," he is destitute of supersensual ambitions, craves no occult knowledge or power. Having his eyes set on eternity, his consciousness steeped in it, he can well afford to tolerate the entanglements of time. "His spirit," says Tauler, "is as it were sunk and lost in the Abyss of the Deity, and loses the consciousness of all creature-distinctions. All things are gathered together in one with the divine sweetness, and the man's being is so penetrated with the divine substance that he loses himself therein, as a drop of water is lost in a cask of strong wine. And thus the man's spirit is so sunk in God in divine union, that he loses all sense of distinction . . . and

[1] Dialogo, cap. lx.

there remains a secret, still union, without cloud or colour." [1]
" I wish not," said St. Catherine of Genoa, " for anything that
comes forth from Thee, but only for Thee, oh sweetest Love ! " [2]
" The Soul," says Plotinus in one of his most profound
passages, "having now arrived at the desired end, and participating of Deity, will know that the Supplier of true life
is then present. She will likewise then require nothing farther ;
for, on the contrary it will be requisite to lay aside other
things, to stop in this alone, amputating everything else with
which she is surrounded." [3]

(3) *The business and method of Mysticism is Love.*

Here is one of the most distinctive notes of true mysticism ;
a note which marks it off from every other kind of transcendental theory and practice, and provides the answer to the
question with which our last chapter closed. It is the eager,
outgoing activity whose driving power is generous love, not the
absorbent, indrawing activity which strives only for new knowledge, that is fruitful in the spiritual as well as in the physical
world.

Having said this, however, we must add—as we did when
speaking of the " heart "—that the word Love as applied to the
mystics is to be understood in its deepest, fullest sense ; as the
ultimate expression of the self's most vital tendencies, not as
the superficial affection or emotion often dignified by this name.
Mystic Love is the offspring of the Celestial Venus ; the deep-
seated desire and tendency of the soul towards its source. [4] It
is a condition of humble access, a life-movement of the self :
more direct in its methods, more valid in its results,—even in the
hands of the least lettered of its adepts—than the most piercing
intellectual vision of the greatest philosophic mind. Over and
over again the mystics insist upon this. " For silence is not
God, nor speaking is not God ; fasting is not God nor eating is
not God ; onliness is not God nor company is not God ; nor
yet any of all the other two such quantities. He is hid between
them, and may not be found by any work of thy soul, but all
only by love of thine heart. He may not be known by reason,
He may not be gotten by thought, nor concluded by under-

[1] Tauler, Sermon for Septuagesima Sunday (Winkworth's translation, p. 253).
[2] Vita e Dottrina, cap. vi.   [3] Ennead vi. 9.
[4] Plotinus, *loc. cit.*

standing ; but he may be loved and chosen with the true lovely will of thine heart. . . . Such a blind shot with the sharp dart of longing love may never fail of the prick, the which is God." [1]

"Come down quickly," says the Incomprehensible Godhead to the soul that has struggled like Zacchæus to the topmost branches of the theological tree, " for I would dwell with you to-day. And this swift descent which God demands is simply an immersion by love and desire in that abyss of the Godhead which the intellect cannot understand. Here, where the intelligence must rest without, love and desire can enter in." [2]

One might compile volumes of extracts from the works of the mystics illustrative of this rule, which is indeed its central principle ; for " Love," says Rolle, " truly suffers not a loving soul to bide in itself, but ravishes it out to the Lover, that the soul is more there where it loves, than where the body is that lives and feels it." " Oh singular joy of love everlasting," he says again, " that ravishes all his to heavens above all worlds, them binding with bands of virtue ! Oh dear charity, in earth that has thee not is nought wrought, whatever it hath ! He truly in thee that is busy, to joy above earthly is soon lifted ! . . . Oh merry love, strong, ravishing, burning, wilful, strong, unslaked, that all my soul brings to thy service, and suffers to think on nothing but thee. . . . Oh clear charity, come into me and take me into thee, and so present me before my Maker. Thou art a savour well tasting, sweetness well smelling, a pleasing odour, a cleansing heat, a comfort endlessly lasting. Thou makest men contemplative, heaven-gate thou openest, mouths of accusers thou dost shut, God thou makest to be seen and multitude of sins thou hidest. We praise thee, we preach thee, by thee the world we quickly overcome, by whom we joy and the heavenly ladder we ascend." [3]

Love to the mystic, then, is (a) the active, conative expression of his will and desire for the Absolute, (b) his innate

---

[1] " An Epistle of Discretion." This beautiful old English tract, probably by the author of the " Cloud of Unknowing," is printed by E. Gardner, " The Cell of Self Knowledge," p. 108.

[2] Ruysbroeck, " L'Ornement des Noces Spirituelles," l. i. cap. xxvi.

[3] " The Mending of Life," cap. xi.

tendency to that Absolute: his spiritual weight. He is only thoroughly natural, thoroughly alive, when he is obeying its voice. For him it is the source of joy: the secret of the universe: the vivifying principle of things. In the words of Récéjac, "Mysticism claims to be able to know the Unknowable without any help from dialectics; and believes that, by the way of love and will, it reaches a point to which thought alone is unable to attain." Again, "It is the heart and never the reason which leads us to the Absolute."[1] Hence in St. Catherine of Siena's exquisite allegory it is the feet of the soul's affection which brings it first to the Bridge, "for the feet carry the body as affection carries the soul."[2]

Page after page of the jewels of mystical literature glow with this intimate and impassioned love of the Absolute; which transcends the dogmatic language in which it is clothed and become applicable to mystics of every race and creed. There is little difference in this between the extremes of Eastern and Western thought: between À Kempis the Christian and Jelalu 'd Din the Moslem saint.

"How great a thing is Love, great above all other goods: for alone it makes all that is heavy light, and bears evenly all that is uneven. . . .

"Love would be aloft, nor will it be kept back by any lower thing. Love would be free, and estranged from all worldly affection, that its inward sight be not hindered: that it may not be entangled by any temporal comfort, nor succumb to any tribulation.

"Nought is sweeter than love, nought stronger, nought higher, nought wider: there is no more joyous, fuller, better thing in heaven or earth. For love is born of God, and cannot rest save in God, above all created things.

"The lover flies, runs, and rejoices: he is free, and cannot be restrained. He gives all for all, and has all in all; for he rests in One Supreme above all, from whom all good flows and proceeds.

"He looks not at the gift, but above all goods turns himself to the giver.

". . . He who loves knows the cry of this voice. For this

[1] "Fondements de la Connaissance Mystique," p. 7.
[2] Dialogo, cap. xxvi.

burning affection of the soul is a loud cry in the ears of God
when it saith 'My God, My Love, Thou art all mine, and I am
all Thine.'" [1]

So much for the Christian.   Now for the Persian mystic.

> "While the thought of the Beloved fills our hearts
> All our work is to do Him service and spend life for Him.
> Wherever He kindles His destructive torch,
> Myriads of lovers' souls are burnt therewith.
> The lovers who dwell within the sanctuary
> Are moths burnt with the torch of the Beloved's face,
> O heart, hasten thither! for God will shine upon you,
> And seem to you a sweet garden instead of a terror.
> He will infuse into your soul a new soul,
> So as to fill you, like a goblet, with wine.
> Take up your abode in His Soul !
> Take up your abode in heaven, oh bright full moon !
> Like the heavenly Scribe, He will open your heart's book,
> That he may reveal mysteries unto you." [2]

Well might Hilton say that "Perfect love maketh God
and the soul to be as if they both together were but one
thing," [3] and Tauler that "the well of life is love, and he who
dwelleth not in love is dead." [4]

"When I love God with my will, I transform myself into
Him," says St. Bernard, "for this is the power or virtue of
love, that it maketh thee to be like unto that which thou
lovest." [5]

These, nevertheless, are objective and didactic utterances ;
though their substance may be—probably is—personal, their
form is not.   But if we want to see what it really means to be
"in love with the Absolute,"—how intensely actual to the
mystic is the Object of his passion, how far removed from the
sphere of pious duty, or of philosophic speculation, how concrete,
positive and dominant such a passion may be—we must study
the literature of autobiography, not that of poetry or exhorta-
tion.   I choose for this purpose, rather than the well-known self-
analyses of St. Augustine, St. Teresa or Suso, which are acces-

[1] "De Imitatione Christi," l. iii. cap. v.
[2] "Jelalu 'd Din" (Wisdom of the East Series), p. 79.
[3] "The Scale of Perfection," p. 339.
[4] Sermon for Thursday in Easter week (Winkworth's translation, p. 294).
[5] Quoted in the "Soliloquies of St. Bonaventura," ex. i.

sible to every one, the more private confessions of that remarkable and neglected mystic Dame Gertrude More, contained in her "Spiritual Exercises."

This nun, great-granddaughter of Sir Thomas More, and favourite pupil of the celebrated Benedictine contemplative, the Ven. Augustine Baker, exhibits the romantic and personal side of mysticism far from perfectly than even St. Teresa, whose works were composed for her daughters' edification. She was an eager student of St. Augustine, "my deere deere Saint," as she calls him more than once. He has evidently influenced her language; but her passion is her own.

Remember that Gertrude More's confessions represent the most secret conversations of her soul with God. They were not meant for publication; but, written for the most part on blank leaves in her breviary, were discovered and published after her death. "She called them," says the title-page with touching simplicity, "*Amor ordinem nescit:* an Ideot's Devotions. Her only spiritual father and directour, Father Baker, styled them *Confessiones Amantis*, A Lover's Confessions. *Amans Deum anima sub Deo despicit universa.* A soul that loveth God despiseth all things that be inferiour unto God."[1]

The spirit of her little book is summed up in two epigrams : epigrams of which her contemporary, Crashaw, might have been proud. "To give all for love, is a most sweet bargain."[2] "O let me love, or not live!"[3]—surely a nobler concept of the devoirs of spiritual chivalry than St. Teresa's more celebrated and uncompromising alternative: *Aut pati aut mori.* Love indeed was her life : and she writes of it with a rapture which recalls at one moment St. Francis de Sales, at another the love songs of the Elizabethan poets.

"Never was there or can there be imagined such a Love, as is between an humble soul and thee. Who can express what passeth between such a soul and thee? Verily neither man nor Angell is able to do it sufficiently. . . . In thy prayse I am only happy, in which, my Joy, I will exullt with all that love thee. For what can be a comfort while I live separated from thee, but only to remember that my God, who is more myne than I am

---

[1] They were printed in 1658, "At Paris by Lewis de la Fosse in the Carme Street at the Signe of the Looking Glasse." I quote from this edition.
[2] P. 138.   [3] P. 181.

my owne, is absolutely and infinitely happy ? . . . Out of this
true love between a soul and thee, there ariseth such a knowledge in the soul that it loatheth all that is an impediment to
her further proceeding in the Love of thee. O Love, Love, even
by naming thee, my soul loseth itself in thee. . . . Nothing can
Satiate a reasonable soul, but only thou : and having of thee,
who art indeed all, nothing could be said to be wanting to her.
. . . *Blessed are the cleane of hart for they shall see God.* O sight
to be wished, desired, and longed for ; because once to have
seen thee is to have learnt all things. Nothing can bring us
to this sight but love.. But what love must it be ? not a sensible
love only, a childish love, a love which seeketh itself more than
the beloved. No, no, but it must be an ardent love, a pure love,
a couradgious love, a love of charity, an humble love, and a
constant love, not worn out with labours, not daunted with any
difficulties. . . . For that soul that hath set her whole love and
desire on thee, can never find any true satisfaction, but only in
thee." [1]

Who will not see that we have here no literary exercise, but
the fruits of an experience of peculiar intensity? It answers
exactly to one of the best modern definitions of mysticism as
" in essence, the concentration of all the forces of the soul upon
a supernatural Object, conceived and loved as a living Person." [2]
" Love and desire," says the same critic, " are the fundamental
necessities ; and where they are absent man, even though he be
a visionary, cannot be called a mystic." [3] Such a definition, of
course, is not complete. It is valuable however because it
emphasizes the fact that all true mysticism is rooted in personality ; and is therefore fundamentally a science of the heart.

" The passion which constrains the stars " also constrains that
starry thing, the soul. Attraction, desire, and union as the
fulfilment of desire, this is the way Life works, in the highest as
in the lowest things. The mystic's outlook, indeed, is the lover's
outlook. It has the same element of wildness, the same quality
of selfless and quixotic devotion, the same combination of
rapture and humility. This parallel is more than a pretty fancy:
for mystic and lover, upon different planes, are alike responding
to the call of the Spirit of Life. The language of human

[1] *Op. cit.*, pp. 9, 16, 25, 35, 138, 175.
[2] Berger, " William Blake," p. 72.   [3] *Ibid.*, p. 74.

passion is tepid and insignificant beside the language in which the mystics try to tell the splendours of their love. They force upon the unprejudiced reader the conviction that they are dealing with an ardour far more burning for an Object far more real.

"This monk can give lessons to lovers!" exclaimed Arthur Symons in astonishment of St. John of the Cross.[1] It would be strange if he could not; since their finite passions are but the feeble images of his infinite one, their beloved the imperfect symbol of his First and only Fair. "I saw Him and sought Him : I had Him and I wanted Him," says Julian of Norwich, in a phrase which seems to sum up all the ecstasy and longing of man's soul. Only this mystic passion can lead us from our prison. Its brother, the desire of knowledge, may enlarge and improve the premises to an extent as yet undreamed of : but it can never unlock the doors.

(4) *Mysticism entails a definite Psychological Experience.*

That is to say, it shows itself not merely as an attitude of mind and heart, but as a form of organic life. It is not a theory of the intellect or a hunger, however passionate, of the heart : but a definite and peculiar development of the whole self, conscious and unconscious, under the spur of such a hunger: a remaking of the whole character on high levels in the interests of the transcendental life. The mystics are emphatic in their statement that spiritual desires are useless unless they involve the movement of the whole self towards the Real.

Thus in the visions of Mechthild of Magdeburg, "The soul spake thus to her Desire, ' Fare forth and see where my Love is. Say to him that I desire to love.' So Desire sped forth, for she is quick of her nature, and came to the Empyrean and cried, ' Great Lord, open and let me in!' Then said the Householder of that place : ' What means this fiery eagerness?' Desire replied, ' Lord, I would have thee know that my lady can no longer bear to live. If Thou wouldst flow forth to her, then might she swim : but the fish cannot long exist that is left stranded on the shore.' ' Go back,' said the Lord, ' I will not let thee in unless thou bring to me that hungry soul, for it is in this alone that I take delight.' "[2]

We have said[3] that the full mystic consciousness is extended

---

[1] *Contemporary Review*, April, 1899.
[2] " Das Fliessende Licht der Gottheit," pt. iii. cap. I.   [3] *Supra*, p. 42.

108 AN INTRODUCTION TO MYSTICISM

in two distinct directions. So too there are two distinct sides to
the full mystical experience. (A) The vision or consciousness
of Absolute Perfection. (B) The inward transmutation to
which that Vision compels the mystic, in order that he may be
to some extent worthy of that which he has beheld : may take
his place within the order of Reality. He has seen the Perfect ;
he wants to be perfect too. The " third term," the necessary
bridge between the Absolute and the Self, can only, he feels, be
moral and spiritual transcendence—in a word, *Sanctity*—for "the
only means of attaining the Absolute lies in adapting ourselves
to It." [1] The moral virtues are for him, then, the obligatory
"ornaments of the Spiritual Marriage" as Ruysbroeck called
them : though far more than their presence is needed to bring
that marriage about. Unless this impulse for moral perfection
be born in him, this travail of the inner life begun, he is no
mystic : though he may well be a visionary, a prophet, a
" mystical " poet.

Moreover, this process of transmutation, this rebuilding of
the self on higher levels, will involve the establishment within
the field of consciousness, the making " central for life," of those
subconscious spiritual perceptions which are the primary
material of mystical experience. The end and object of this
" inward alchemy " will be the raising of the whole self to the
condition in which conscious and permanent union with the
Absolute takes place ; and man, ascending to the summit of his
manhood, enters into that greater life for which he was made.

In its journey towards this union, the subject passes through
certain well-marked phases, which constitute what is known as
the " Mystic Way." This statement rules out from the true
mystic kingdom all merely sentimental and affective piety and
visionary poetry, no less than mystical philosophy. It brings
us back to our first proposition—the concrete and practical
nature of the mystical act.

More than the apprehension of God, then, more than the
passion for the Absolute, is needed to make a mystic. These
must be combined with an appropriate psychological make-up,
with a nature capable of extraordinary concentration, an exalted
moral emotion, a nervous organization of the artistic type. All
these are necessary to the successful development of the mystic

[1] Récéjac, *op. cit.* p. 35.

life process.   In the experience of the mystics who have left us the records of their own lives, the successive stages of this life process are always traceable.   In the second part of this book, they will be found worked out at some length.   Rolle, Suso, Madame Guyon, St. Teresa, and many others have left us valuable self-analyses for comparison : and from them we see how arduous, how definite, and how far removed from mere emotional or intellectual activity, is that educational discipline by which " the eye which looks upon Eternity " is able to come to its own.   " One of the marks of the true mystic," says Leuba, " is the tenacious and heroic energy with which he pursues a definite moral ideal." [1]   " He is," says Pacheu, " the pilgrim of an inward Odyssey." [2]   Though we may be amazed and delighted by his adventures and discoveries on the way, to him the voyage and the end are all.   " The road on which we enter is a royal road which leads to heaven," says St. Teresa.   " Is it strange that the conquest of such a treasure should cost us rather dear ? " [3]

It is one of the many indirect testimonies to the objective reality of mysticism that the stages of this road, the psychology of the spiritual ascent, as described to us by different schools of contemplatives, always present practically the same sequence of states.   The " school for saints " has never found it necessary to bring its curriculum up to date.   The psychologist finds little difficulty, for instance, in reconciling the " Degrees of Orison " described by St. Teresa [4]—Recollection, Quiet, Union, Ecstasy, Rapt, the " Pain of God," and the Spiritual Marriage of the soul —with the four forms of contemplation enumerated by Hugh of St. Victor, or the Sūfi's " Seven Stages " of the soul's ascent to God, which begin in adoration and end in spiritual marriage. [5] Though each wayfarer may choose different landmarks, it is clear from their comparison that the road is one.

(5) As a corollary to these four rules, it is perhaps well to reiterate the statement already made, that *True Mysticism is never self-seeking.*   It is not, as many think, the pursuit of

[1] *Revue Philosophique*, July, 1902.
[2] " Psychologie des Mystiques Chrétiens," p. 14.
[3] " Camino de Perfeccion," cap. xxiii.
[4] In " El Castillo Interior."
[5] See Palmer, " Oriental Mysticism," pt. v. ch. v.

supernatural joys ; the satisfaction of a high ambition. The mystic does not enter on his quest because he desires the happiness of the Beatific Vision, the ecstasy of union with the Absolute, or any other personal reward.

In "that strange, extravagant, and heroic character which calls itself a Christian mystic,"[1] that noblest of all passions, the passion for perfection for Love's sake, far outweighs the desire for transcendental satisfaction. "O Love," said St. Catherine of Genoa, "I do not wish to follow thee for sake of these delights, but solely from the motive of true love."[2] Those who do otherwise are only, in the plain words of St. John of the Cross, "spiritual gluttons":[3] or, in the milder metaphor here adopted, magicians of the more high-minded sort. The true mystic claims no promises and makes no demands. He goes because he must, as Galahad went towards the Grail : knowing that for those who can live it, this alone is life. He never rests in that search for God which he holds to be the fulfilment of his highest duty ; yet he seeks without any certainty of success. He holds with St. Bernard that "He alone is God who can never be sought in vain : not even when He cannot be found."[4] With Mechthild of Magdeburg, he hears the Absolute saying in his soul, "O soul, before the world was I longed for thee : and I still long for thee, and thou for Me. Therefore, when our two desires unite, Love shall be fulfilled."[5]

Like his type, the "devout lover" of romance, then, the mystic serves without hope of reward. By one of the many paradoxes of the spiritual life, he obtains satisfaction because he does not seek it ; completes his personality because he gives it up. "Attainment," says Dionysius the Areopagite in words which are writ large on the annals of Christian ecstasy, "comes only by means of this sincere, spontaneous, and entire surrender of yourself and all things.[6] Only with the annihilation of self-hood comes the fulfilment of love. Were the mystic asked the cause of his often extraordinary behaviour, his austere and steadfast quest, it is unlikely that his reply would contain any

[1] Leuba, *op. cit.*
[2] Vita, p. 8.
[3] "Subida del Monte Carmelo," l. ii. cap. vii.
[4] "De Consideratione," l. v. cap. xi.
[5] "Das Fliessende Licht der Gottheit," pt. vii. cap. 16.
[6] "De Mystica Theologia," i. 1.

reference to sublime illumination or unspeakable delights. It is more probable that he would answer in some such words as those of Jacob Boehme, " I am not come to this meaning, or to this work and knowledge through my own reason or through my own will and purpose; neither have I sought this knowledge nor so much as to know anything concerning it. I sought only for the heart of God, therein to hide myself." [1]

It has been well said that such a search is "not the quest of joy," but "the satisfaction of a craving impelled by the spur of necessity." [2] This craving is the craving of the soul, unable to rest in those symbols of the sensual world which only feed the little tract of normal consciousness, to attain that fulness of life for which she was made : to "lose herself in That which can be neither seen nor touched; giving herself entirely to this sovereign Object without belonging either to herself or to others ; united to the Unknown by the most noble part of herself and because of her renouncement of knowledge ; finally drawing from this absolute ignorance a knowledge which the understanding knows not how to attain." [3] Mysticism, then, is seen as the " one way out " for the awakened spirit of man. It is the healing of that human incompleteness which is the origin of our divine unrest : the inevitable reaction of the fully conscious, fully living soul upon "Eternal Truth, True Love, and Loved Eternity." [4] " I am sure," says Eckhart, " that if a soul knew the very least of all that Being means, it would never turn away from it." [5] The mystics have never turned away : to do so would have seemed to them a self-destructive act. Here, in this world of illusion, they say, we have no continuing city. This statement, to you a proposition, is to us the central fact of life. " Therefore, it is necessary to hasten our departure from hence, and to be indignant that we are bound in one part of our nature, in order that with the whole of our selves, we may fold ourselves about Divinity, and have no part void of contact with Him." [6]

To sum up. Mysticism is seen to be a highly specialized form of that search for reality, for heightened and completed

[1] " Aurora," English translation, 1764, p. 237.
[2] A. E. Waite, " Strange Houses of Sleep," p. 211.
[3] Dionysius the Areopagite, " De Mystica Theologia," i. 3.
[4] Aug. Conf., bk. vii. cap. 10.
[5] " Mystische Schriften," p. 137.   [6] Plotinus, Ennead vi. 9.

life, which we have found to be a constant characteristic of human consciousness. It is largely prosecuted by that "spiritual spark," that transcendental faculty which, though the life of our life, remains below the threshold in ordinary men. Emerging from its hiddenness in the mystic, it gradually becomes the dominant factor in his life; subduing to its service, and enhancing by its saving contact with reality, those vital powers of love and will which we attribute to the heart; rather than those of mere reason and perception, which we attribute to the head. Under the spur of this love and will, the whole personality rises in the acts of contemplation and ecstasy to a level of consciousness at which it becomes aware of a new field of perception. By this awareness, by this "loving sight," it is stimulated to a new life in accordance with the Reality which it has beheld. So strange and exalted is this life, that it never fails to provoke either the anger or the admiration of other men. "If the great Christian mystics," says Leuba, "could by some miracle be all brought together in the same place, each in his habitual environment, there to live according to his manner, the world would soon perceive that they constitute one of the most amazing and profound variations of which the human race has yet been witness." [1]

A discussion of mysticism as a whole will therefore include two branches. First the life process of the mystic: the remaking of his personality; the method by which his peculiar consciousness of the Absolute is attained, and faculties which have been evolved to meet the requirements of the phenomenal, are enabled to do work on the transcendental, plane. This is the "Mystic Way" in which the self passes through the states or stages of development which were codified by the Neoplatonists, and after them by the mediaeval mystics, as Purgation, Illumination, and Ecstasy. Secondly, the content of the mystical field of perception; the revelation under which the contemplative becomes aware of the Absolute. This will include a consideration of the so-called doctrines of mysticism: the attempts of the articulate mystic to sketch for us the world into which he has looked, in language which is only adequate to the world in which the rest of us dwell. Here the difficult question of symbolism, and of symbolic theology comes in: a point upon

[1] *Op. cit.*

which many promising expositions of the mystics have been wrecked. It will be our business to strip off as far as may be the symbolic wrapping, and attempt a synthesis of these doctrines ; to resolve the apparent contradictions of objective and subjective revelations, of the ways of negation and affirmation, emanation and immanence, surrender and deification, the Divine Dark and the Inward Light ; and finally to exhibit, if we can, the essential unity of that experience in which the human soul enters consciously into the Presence of God.

CHAPTER V

MYSTICISM AND THEOLOGY

Mystic diagrams—Theology as used by the Mystics—Their conception of God—
Emanation and Immanence—Emanation discussed—Dante—the Kabalists—Aquinas
—Its psychological aspect—Immanence discussed—the basis of introversion—The
"ground" of soul and universe—Emanation and Immanence compared—both
accepted by the Mystics—Objections to this answered—Emanation and the Mystic
Way—Its reconciliation with Immanence—Both describe experience—are expressions
of temperament—Mystical theology must include both—Theology is the Mystic's
map—Sometimes but not always adequate—Christianity the best of such maps—
It combines the metaphysical and personal aspects of the Divine — reconciles
Emanation and Immanence—provides a congenial atmosphere for the Mystic—
explains his adventures—All Western mystics implicitly Christian—Blake—The
dogma of the Trinity—Division of Persons essential to the description of God—The
indwelling and transcendent aspects of the Divine—St. Teresa—her vision of the
Trinity—Father, Word, Holy Spirit—Threefold division of Reality—Neoplatonic
trinities—Lady Julian on the Trinity—Its psychological justification—Goodness,
Truth, and Beauty—Trinitarian doctrine and the Mystics—Light, Life, Love—The
Incarnation—its mystic aspect—The Repairer—The Drama of Faith—The Eternal
Birth of the Son—The New Birth in Man—Regeneration—Conclusion

IN the last chapter we tried to establish a distinction between
the mystic who tastes supreme experience and the mystical
philosopher who cogitates upon the data so obtained. We
have now, however, to take account of the fact that the true
mystic is also very often a mystical philosopher; though there
are plenty of mystical philosophers who are not and could
never be mystics.

Because it is characteristic of the human self to reflect upon
its experience, to use its percepts as material for the construction
of a concept, most mystics have made or accepted a theory of
their own adventures. Thus we have a mystical philosophy or
theology—the comment of the intellect on the proceedings of
spiritual intuition—running side by side with true or empirical
mysticism : classifying its data, criticizing it, explaining it, and

translating its vision of the supersensible into symbols which are amenable to dialectic.

Such a philosophy is most usually founded upon the formal creed which the individual mystic accepts. It is characteristic of him that in so far as his transcendental activities are healthy he is generally an acceptor and not a rejector of such creeds. The view which regards the mystic as a spiritual anarchist receives little support from history;[1] which shows us, over and over again, the great mystics as faithful sons of the great religions. Almost any religious system which fosters unearthly love is potentially a nursery for mystics: and Christianity, Islam, Brahmanism, and Buddhism each receives its most sublime interpretation at their hands.

Thus St. Teresa interprets her ecstatic apprehension of the Godhead in strictly Catholic terms. Thus Boehme believed to the last that his explorations of eternity were consistent with the teaching of the Lutheran Church. Thus the Sūfis were good Mohammedans, Philo and the Kabalists were orthodox Jews. Thus Plotinus even adapted—though with what difficulty! —the relics of paganism to his doctrine of the Real.

Attempts, however, to limit mystical truth—the direct apprehension of the Divine Substance—to the formulæ of any one religion, are as futile as the attempt to identify a precious metal with the die which converts it into current coin. The dies which the mystics have used are many. Their peculiarities and excrescences are always interesting and sometimes highly significant. Some give a far sharper, more coherent, impression than others. But the gold from which this diverse coinage is struck is always the same precious metal: always the same Beatific Vision of a Goodness, Truth, and Beauty which is *one*. Hence its substance must always be distinguished from the accidents under which we perceive it: for this substance has a cosmic, and not a denominational, importance.

If, however, we are to understand the language of the mystics, it is evident that we must know a little of accident as well as of substance: that is to say, of the principal philosophies or religions which they have used in describing their adventures to the world. This being so, before we venture to

[1] Dr. Rufus Jones ("Studies in Mystical Religion") is at present the most eminent upholder of this opinion.

apply ourselves to the exploration of theology proper, it will be well to consider the two extreme forms under which both mystics and theologians have been accustomed to conceive Reality : that is to say, the so-called " emanation-theory " and " immanence-theory " of the transcendental world.

Emanation and Immanence are formidable words ; which, though perpetually tossed to and fro by amateurs of religious philosophy, have probably, as they stand, little actuality for practical modern men.   They are, however, root-ideas for the maker of mystical diagrams : and his best systems are but attempts towards their reconciliation.   Since the aim of every mystic is union with God, it is obvious that the vital question in his philosophy must be the place which this God, the Absolute of his quest, occupies in the scheme.   Briefly, He has been conceived—or, it were better to say, presented—by the great mystics under two apparently contradictory modes.

(1) The opinion which is represented in its most extreme form by the above-mentioned *Theory of Emanations*, declares His utter transcendence.   This view appears early in the history of Greek philosophy.   It is developed by Dionysius, by the Kabalists, by Dante : and is implied in the language of Rulman Merswin and many other Christian ecstatics.

The solar system is an almost perfect symbol of this concept of the universe ; which finds at once its most rigid and most beautiful expression in Dante's " Paradiso." [1]   The Absolute Godhead is conceived as removed by a vast distance from the material world of sense ; the last or lowest of that system of dependent worlds or states which, generated by or emanating from the Unity or Central Sun, become less in spirituality and splendour, greater in multiplicity, the further they recede from their source.   That Source—Ain Soph, the Great Countenance of the Absolute—can never, say the Kabalists, be discerned by man.   It is the Unplumbed Abyss of later mysticism : the Cloud of Unknowing wraps it from our sight.   Only by its " emanations " or manifested attributes can we attain knowledge of it.

---

[1] " La gloria di colui che tutto move
        per l'universo penetra, e resplende
    in una parte più e meno altrove " (Par. i. 1-3).

The theological ground-plan of the Cantica is epitomized in this introductory verse.

By the outflow of these same manifested attributes and
powers the created universe exists, depending in the last resort
on the *latens deitas :* Who is therefore conceived as external to
the world which He illuminates and vivifies.

St. Thomas Aquinas virtually accepts the doctrine of
Emanations when he writes : [1] "As all the perfections of
Creatures descend in order from God, who is the height of
perfection, man should begin from the lower creatures and
ascend by degrees, and so advance to the knowledge of God. . . .
And because in that roof and crown of all things, God, we find
the most perfect unity ; and everything is stronger and more
excellent the more thoroughly it is one ; it follows that diversity
and variety increase in things, the further they are removed
from Him who is the first principle of all." Suso, whose mystical
system, like that of most Dominicans, is entirely consistent with
Thomist philosophy, is really glossing Aquinas when he writes :
" The supreme and superessential Spirit has ennobled man by
illuminating him with a ray from the Eternal Godhead. . . .
Hence from out the great ring which represents the Eternal
Godhead there flow forth . . . little rings, which may be taken
to signify the high nobility of natural creatures." [2]

Obviously if this theory of the Absolute be accepted the
path of the soul's ascent to union with the divine must be
literally a transcendence : a journey " upward and outward,"
through a long series of intermediate states or worlds till, having
traversed the " Thirty-two paths of the Tree of Life," she at last
arrives, in Kabalistic language, at the Crown : unconditioned
and ineffable Being, the Abyss or Divine Dark of the Dionysian
school, the Neoplatonic One. Such a series of worlds is
symbolized by the Ten Heavens of Dante, the hierarchies of
Dionysius, the Tree of Life or Sephiroth of the Kabalah : and
receives its countersign in the inward experience, in the long
journey of the self through Purgation and Illumination to
Union. " We ascend," says St. Augustine, " thy ways that be
in our heart, and sing a song of degrees ; we glow inwardly
with thy fire, with thy good fire, and we go, because we go
upwards to the peace of Jerusalem." [3]

This theory postulates, under normal and non-mystical con-

[1] " Summa Contra Gentiles," l. iv. cap. i. (Rickaby's translation).
[2] Leben, cap. lvi.   [3] Aug. Conf., bk. xiii. cap. xi.

ditions, the complete separation of the human and the divine ; the temporal and the eternal worlds.   Hence the language of pilgrimage, of exile, of a world which has fallen from perfection into illusion and must make a long and painful return, comes naturally to the mystic who apprehends reality under these terms.   To him the mystical adventure is essentially a "going forth" from his normal self and from his normal universe. Like the Psalmist "in his heart he hath disposed to ascend by steps in this vale of tears" from the less to the more divine. He, and with him the Cosmos—for we must never forget that to mystical philosophy the soul of the individual subject is the microcosm of the soul of the world—has got to retrace the long road to the Perfection from which it originally came forth ; as the fish in Rulman Merswin's Vision of Nine Rocks must struggle upwards from pool to pool until they reach their Origin.

Such a way of conceiving Reality accords with the type of mind which William James has denominated the "sick soul." [1] It is the mood of the contrite, of the penitent, of the utter humility which, appalled by the sharp contrast between itself and the Perfect which it contemplates, can only cry " out of the depths."   It comes naturally to the kind of temperament which leans to pessimism, which sees a "great gulf fixed" between itself and its desire, and is above all things sensitive to the elements of evil and imperfection in its own character and in the normal experience of man.   Permitting these elements to dominate its field of consciousness, wholly ignoring the divine aspect of the World of Becoming, such a temperament con- structs from its perceptions and prejudices the concept of a material world and a normal self which is very far from God.

(2) *Immanence*.   At the opposite pole from this way of sketching Reality is the extreme theory of Immanence, so fashionable amongst liberal theologians at the present time. To the holders of this theory, who belong of necessity to Pro- fessor James's "healthy minded" or optimistic class, the quest of the Absolute is no long journey, but a realization of something which is implicit in the self and in the universe : an opening of the eyes of the soul upon the Reality in which it is bathed. For them earth is literally "crammed with heaven."   "Thou

[1] "Varieties of Religious Experience," Lecture vi.

wert I, but dark was my heart, I knew not the secret transcendent," says Téwekkul Bég, a Moslem mystic of the seventeenth century.[1]   This is always the cry of the temperament
which leans to a theology of immanence, once its eyes are
opened on the light.   "God," says Plotinus, "is not external to
anyone, but is present with all things, though they are ignorant
that He is so."[2]   In other and older words, "The spirit of God
is within you."   The Absolute Whom all seek does not hold
Himself aloof from an imperfect material universe, but dwells
within the flux of things: stands as it were at the very threshold of consciousness and knocks, awaiting the self's slow discovery of her treasures.   "He is not far from any one of us, for
in Him we live and move and have our being," is the pure
doctrine of Immanence: a doctrine whose teachers are drawn
from amongst the souls which react more easily to the touch of
the Divine than to the sense of alienation and of sin, and are
naturally inclined to love rather than to awe.   The truth that
"God and man initially meet where man is most inward "[3]—*i.e.*,
in the spark or ground of the soul—is the cardinal fact in their
experience of the transcendental world.

   Unless safeguarded by limiting dogmas, the theory of
Immanence, taken alone, is notoriously apt to degenerate into
pantheism ; and into those extravagant perversions of the
doctrine of "deification" in which the mystic holds his transfigured self to be identical with the Indwelling God.   It is the
philosophical basis of that practice of introversion, the turning
inwards of the soul's faculties in contemplation, which has been
the "method" of the great practical mystics of all creeds.   That
God, since He is in all—in a sense, *is* all—may most easily be
found within ourselves, is the doctrine of these adventurers ;[4]
who, denying or ignoring the existence of those intervening
"worlds" or "planes" between the material world and the
Absolute, which are postulated by the theory of Emanations,
claim with Ruysbroeck that "by a simple introspection in

----

[1] Quoted by W. L. Lilly, "Many Mansions," p. 140.

[2] Ennead vi. 9.

[3] Boyce Gibson, "Rudolph Eucken's Philosophy," p. 104.

[4] Thus Aquinas says, "Since God is the universal cause of all Being, in whatever
region Being can be found, there must be the Divine Presence " ("Summa Contra
Gentiles," l. iii. cap. lxviii.).   And we have seen that the whole claim of the mystics
ultimately depends on man's possession of pure being in " the spark of the soul."

fruitive love" they "meet God without intermediary." [1] They hear the Father of Lights "saying eternally, without intermediary or interruption, in the most secret part of the spirit, the one unique, and abysmal Word." [2]

This divine essence, or substance, which the introversive mystic finds dwelling, as Ruysbroeck says, at the apex of man's spirit, is the "spark of the soul" of Eckhart, the "ground" of Tauler, the Inward Light of the Quakers, the "Divine Principle" of some modern transcendentalists: the fount and source of all true life. At this point words and definitions fail mystic and theologian alike. A tangle of metaphors takes their place. He is face to face with the "wonder of wonders"—that most real of all experiences, the fusion of human and divine, in a nameless *something* which is "great enough to be God, small enough to be me." Hence at one moment the spark of the soul is presented to us as the divine to which the self attains : at another, as that transcendental aspect of the self which is in contact with God. On either hypothesis it is that in which the mystic encounters Absolute Being: and constitutes his guarantee of God's immediate presence in the human heart ; and, if in the human heart, then in that universe of which man's soul resumes in miniature the essential characteristics.

According to the doctrine of Immanence, creation, the universe, could we see it as it is, would be perceived as the self-development, the self-unfolding of this indwelling Deity. The world is not projected from the Absolute, but rather enshrines It. "I understood," says St. Teresa, "how our Lord was in all things, and how He was in the soul : and the illustration of a sponge filled with water was suggested to me." [3] The world-process then, is the slow coming to fruition of that Divine Spark which is latent alike in the Cosmos and in man. "If," says Boehme, "thou conceivest a small minute circle, as small as a grain of mustard seed, yet the Heart of God is wholly and perfectly therein : and if thou art born in God, then there is in thy-

---

[1] " L'Ornement des Noces Spirituelles," l. ii. cap. lxxi.

[2] *Op. cit.*, l. iii. cap. i.

[3] Relaccion, ix. 10. But this image of a sponge, which also suggested itself to St. Augustine, proved an occasion of stumbling to his more metaphysical mind : tending to confuse his idea of the nature of God with the category of space. *Vide* Aug. Conf., bk. vii. cap. v.

self (in the circle of thy life) the whole Heart of God undivided."[1] The idea of Immanence has seldom been more beautifully expressed.

It is worth noticing that both the theological theories of reality which have been acceptable to the mystics implicitly declare, as modern science does, that the universe is not static but dynamic : a World of Becoming. According to the doctrine of Immanence this universe is free, self-creative. The Divine nests within it : no part is more removed from the Godhead than any other part. " God," says Eckhart, " is nearer to me than I am to myself; He is just as near to wood and stone, but they do not know it."[2]

These two apparently contradictory explanations of the Invisible have both been held, and that in their extreme form, by the mystics : who have found in both adequate and indeed necessary diagrams by which to demonstrate their experience of Reality.[3] Some of the least lettered and most inspired amongst them—for instance, St. Catherine of Siena, Lady Julian of Norwich—and some of the most learned, as Dionysius the Areopagite and Meister Eckhart, have actually used in their rhapsodies language appropriate to both the theories of Emanation and of Immanence. It would seem, then, that both these theories must veil the truth ; and that it is the business of a sound mystical philosophy to reconcile them. It is too often forgotten by quarrelsome partisans of a concrete turn of mind that at best all these transcendental theories are only symbols, methods, diagrams ; feebly attempting the representation of an experience which is always the same, and whose dominant characteristic is its ineffability. Hence they insist with tiresome monotony that Dionysius must be wrong if Tauler be right : that it is absurd to call yourself the Friend of God if unknowableness be that God's first attribute : that Plato's Perfect Beauty and Catherine of Siena's Accepter of Sacrifices cannot be the same : that the " courteous and dear-worthy Lord " who said to Lady Julian, " My darling, I am glad that thou art come to Me, in all thy wo I have ever been with thee,"[4] rules out the formless and

<hr>

[1] " The Threefold Life of Man," cap. vi. § 71.
[2] Eckhart, Pred. lxix. So too we read in the Oxyrhyncus Papyri, " Raise the stone and there thou shalt find Me. Cleave the wood and there am I."
[3] Compare above, cap. ii.   [4] " Revelations of Divine Love," cap. xl.

impersonal One of Plotinus, the "triple circle" of Suso and
Dante.   Finally, that if God be truly immanent in the material
world, it is either sin or folly to refuse that world in order that
we may find Him ; and if introversion be right, a plan of the
universe which postulates intervening planes between Absolute
Being and the phenomenal world must be wrong.

Now as regards the mystics, of whom we hold both these
doctrines, these ways of seeing truth—for what else is a doctrine
but that?—it is well to remind ourselves that their teaching
about the relation of the Absolute to the finite, of God to the
phenomenal world, must be founded in the first instance on
what they know by experience of the relation between that
Absolute and the individual self. This experience is the valid
part of mysticism, the thing which gives to it its unique importance amongst systems of thought, the only source of its
knowledge.   Everything else is really guessing aided by
analogy.   When therefore the mystic, applying to the
universe what he knows to be true in respect of his own
soul, describes Divine Perfection as very far removed from
the material world, yet linked with it by a graduated series
of "emanations"—states or qualities which have each of them
something of the godlike though they be not God—he is trying
to describe the necessary life-process which he has himself
passed through in the course of his purgation and spiritual
ascent from the state of the " natural man " to that other state
of harmony with the spiritual universe, sometimes called
" deification," in which he is able to contemplate, and unite
with, the divine.   We have in the " Divina Commedia " a classic
example of such a two-fold vision of the inner and the outer
worlds : for Dante's journey up and out to the Empyrean
Heaven is really an inward alchemy, an ordering and transmuting of his nature, a purging of his spiritual sight till—
transcending all derived beatitude—it can look for an instant
on the Being of God.

The mystic assumes—because he always assumes an orderly
basis for things—that there is a relation, an analogy, between this
microcosm of man's self and the macrocosm of the world-self.
Hence his experience, the geography of the individual quest,
appears to him good evidence of the geography of the Invisible.
Since he must transcend his natural life in order to attain con-

sciousness of God, he conceives of God as essentially transcendent
to the natural world.   His description of that geography, however
—of his path in a land where there is no time and space, no inner
and no outer, up or down—will be conditioned by his temperament, by his powers of observation, by the metaphor which
comes most readily to his hand, above all by his theological
education.   The so-called journey itself is a psychological
experience: the purging and preparation of the self, its
movement to higher levels of consciousness, its unification
with that more divine but normally subconscious self which
is in touch with the spiritual universe, and its gradual or
abrupt entrance into union with the Real.   Sometimes it
seems to the self that this performance is a retreat inwards
to that "ground of the soul" where, as St. Teresa says,
"His Majesty awaits us": sometimes a going forth from the
Conditioned to the Unconditioned, the "supernatural flight"
of Plotinus and Dionysius the Areopagite.   Both are but images
under which the self conceives the process of attaining conscious union with that God who is "at once immanent and
transcendent in relation to the soul which shares His Life."[1]

He has got to find God.   The quest is long; the end
amazing.   Sometimes his temperament causes him to lay
most stress on the length of the search; sometimes the abrupt
rapture which brings it to a close makes him forget that
preliminary pilgrimage in which the soul is "not outward
bound, but rather on a journey to its centre."   The Habitations
of the Interior Castle through which St. Teresa conducts the
ardent disciple to that hidden chamber which is the sanctuary
of the indwelling God: the hierarchies of Dionysius, ascending
from the selfless service of the angels, past the seraphs' burning
love to the God enthroned above time and space: the mystical
paths of the Kabalistic Tree of Life, which lead from the
material world of Malkuth through the universes of action and
thought, by Mercy, Justice and Beauty to the Supernal
Crown;[2] all these are different ways of seeing this same
pilgrimage.

As every one is born a disciple of either Plato or
Aristotle, so every human soul leans to one of these two

[1] Boyce Gibson, "God with Us," p. 24.
[2] See A. E. Waite, "The Doctrine and Literature of the Kabalah," pp. 36–53.

ways of apprehending reality. The artist, the poet, every one who looks with awe and rapture on created things, acknowledges in this act the Immanent God. The ascetic, and that intellectual ascetic the metaphysician, turning from the created, denying the senses in order to find afar off the Uncreated, Unconditioned Source, is really—though often he knows it not—obeying that psychological law which produced the doctrine of Emanations.

A good map then, a good mystical philosophy, will leave room for both these ways of interpreting experience. It will mark the routes by which many different temperaments claim to have found their way to the same end. It will acknowledge both the aspects under which the *patria splendida* Truth has appeared to its lovers: the aspects which have called forth the theories of emanation and immanence and are enshrined in the Greek and Latin names of God. *Deus*, whose root means day, shining, the Transcendent Light; and *Theos*, whose true meaning is supreme desire or prayer—the Inward Love—do not contradict, but complete each other. They form, when taken together, an almost perfect definition of that Absolute which is the object of the mystic's desire: the Divine Love which, being born in the soul, spurs on that soul to union with the transcendent and Absolute Light which is at once the source, the goal, the life of created things.

The true mystic—the person with a genius for God—hardly needs a map himself. He steers a compass course across the " vast and stormy sea of the divine." It is characteristic of his intellectual humility, however, that he is always willing to use the map of the community in which he finds himself, when it comes to showing other people the route which he has pursued. Sometimes these maps have been adequate. More, they have elucidated the obscure wanderings of the explorer; helped him; given him landmarks; worked out right. Time after time he puts his finger on some spot—some great hill of vision, some city of the soul—and says with conviction, "*Here* have I been." At other times the maps have embarrassed him, have refused to fit in with his description. Then he has tried, as Boehme did and after him Blake, to make new ones. Such maps are often wild in drawing, because good draughtsmanship does not necessarily go with a talent for exploration. Departing from the usual convention, they are hard—sometimes impossible—to understand. As a result, the orthodox have been forced to regard their makers as madmen or heretics: when they were really only practical men struggling to disclose great matters by imperfect means.

Now, without prejudice to individual beliefs and without offering an opinion as to the exclusive truth of any one religious system or revelation—for here we are concerned neither with controversy nor with apologetics—we are bound to allow as a historical fact that mysticism, so far, has found its best map in Christianity. Christian philosophy, especially that Neo-platonic theology which, taking up and harmonizing all that was best in the spiritual intuitions of Greece, India and Egypt, was developed by the great doctors of the early and mediaeval Church, supports and elucidates the revelations of the individual mystic as no other system of thought has been able to do.

We owe to the great fathers of the first five centuries—to Clement of Alexandria and Irenæus, Gregory of Nyssa and Augustine; above all to Dionysius the Areopagite, the great Christian contemporary of Proclus—the preservation of that mighty system of scaffolding which enabled the Catholic mystics to build up the towers and bulwarks of the City of God. The peculiar virtue of this Christian philosophy, that which marks its superiority to the more coldly self-consistent systems of Greece, is the fact that it re-states the truths of metaphysics in terms of personality: thus offering a third term, a "living mediator" between the Unknowable God, the unconditioned Absolute, and the conditioned self. This was the priceless gift which the Wise Men received in return for their gold, frankincense, and myrrh. This solves the puzzle which all explorers of the supersensible have sooner or later to face: *come si convenne l'imago al cerchio*,[1] the reconciliation of Infinite and intimate, both known and felt, but neither understood. Such a third term, such a stepping-stone, was essential if mysticism were ever to attain that active union, that fullness of life which is its object, and develop from a blind and egoistic rapture into fruitful and self-forgetting love.

Where non-Christian mystics, as a rule, have made a forced choice between the two great dogmatic expressions of their

[1] Par. xxxiii. 137.

experience, (a) the long pilgrimage towards a transcendent and unconditioned Absolute, (b) the discovery of that Absolute in the "ground" or divine principle of the self; it has been possible to Christianity, by means of her central doctrine of the Trinity, to find room for both of them and to exhibit them as that which they are in fact—the complementary parts of a whole. Even Dionysius, the godfather of the emanation doctrine, combines with his scheme of descending hierarchies the dogma of an indwelling God: and no writer is more constantly quoted by Meister Eckhart, who is generally considered to have preached Immanence in its most extreme and pantheistic form.

Further, the Christian atmosphere is the one in which the individual mystic has most often been able to develop his genius in a sane and fruitful way; and an overwhelming majority of the great European contemplatives have been Christians of a strong, impassioned and personal type. This alone would justify us in regarding it as representing, at any rate in the West, the formal side of the true tradition: the "path of least resistance" through which that tradition flows. In many cases the very heretics of Christianity have owed their greatness almost wholly to their mystical qualities. The Gnostics, the Fraticelli, the Brethren of the Free Spirit, the Quietists, the Quakers, are instances of this. In others, it was to an excessive reliance on reason when dealing with the suprarational, and a corresponding absence of trust in mystical intuition that heresy was due. Arius and Pelagius are heretics of this type.

The greatest mystics, however, have not been heretics but Catholic saints. In Christianity the "natural mysticism" which, like "natural religion," is latent in humanity, and at a certain point of development breaks out in every race, came to itself; and attributing for the first time true and distinct personality to its Object, brought into focus the confused and unconditioned God which Neoplatonism had constructed from the abstract concepts of philosophy blended with the intuitions of Indian ecstatics, and made the basis of its meditations on the Real. It is a truism that the real claim of Christian philosophy on our respect does not lie in its exclusiveness but in its Catholicity: in the fact that it finds truth in a hundred different systems, accepts and elucidates Greek, Jewish and Indian thought, fuses them in a coherent theology, and says to speculative thinkers of every time and place, "Whom therefore ye ignorantly worship, Him declare I unto you."

The voice of Truth, which spoke once for all on Calvary and there declared the ground plan of the universe, was heard more or less perfectly by all the great seers, the intuitive leaders of men, the possessors of genius for the Real. There are few of the Christian names of God which were not known to the teachers of antiquity. To the Egyptians He was the Saviour, to the Platonists the Good, Beautiful and True, to the Stoics the Father and Companion. The very words of the Fourth Gospel are anticipated by Cleanthes. Heracleitus knew the Energizing Fire of which St. Bonaventura and Mechthild of Magdeburg speak. Countless mystics, from St. Augustine to St. John of the Cross, echo again and again the language of Plotinus. It is true that the differentia which mark off Christianity from all other religions are strange and poignant: but these very differentia make of it the most perfect of settings for the mystic life. Its note of close intimacy, of direct and personal contact with a spiritual reality given here and now— its astonishing combination of splendour and simplicity, of the sacramental and transcendent—all these things minister to the needs of the mystical type.

Hence the Christian system, or some colourable imitation of it, has been found essential by almost all the great mystics of the West. They adopt its nomenclature, explain their adventures by the help of its creed, identify their Absolute with the Christian God. Amongst European mystics the most usually quoted exception to this rule is Blake; yet it is curious to notice that the more inspired his utterance, the more passionately and dogmatically Christian even this hater of the Churches becomes:—

> "We behold
> Where Death eternal is put off eternally. O Lamb
> Assume the dark satanic body in the Virgin's womb!
> O Lamb divine! it cannot thee annoy! O pitying One,
> Thy pity is from the foundation of the world, and thy Redemption
> Begins already in Eternity." [1]

This is the doctrine of the Incarnation in a nutshell: here

[1] "Vala," viii. 237.

St. Thomas himself would find little to correct. Of the two following extracts from " Jerusalem," the first is but a poet's gloss on the Catholic's cry, " *O felix culpa!* " the second is an almost perfect epitome of Christian theology and ethics :—

> " If I were pure, never could I taste the sweets
> Of the forgiveness of sins. If I were holy, I never could behold the tears
> Of Love . . . O Mercy! O divine Humanity!
> O Forgiveness, O Pity and Compassion! If I were pure I should never
> Have known Thee."

> " Wouldst thou love one who never died
> For thee, or ever die for one who had not died for thee?
> And if God dieth not for man, and giveth not Himself
> Eternally for Man, Man could not exist, for Man is Love
> As God is Love. Every kindness to another is a little death
> In the Divine Image, nor can Man exist but by brotherhood." [1]

What needs to be emphasized is this : that whether the dogmas of Christianity be or be not accepted on the scientific and historical plane, they are necessary to an adequate description of mystical experience—at least, of the fully developed dynamic mysticism of the West. We must therefore be prepared in reading the works of the contemplatives for much strictly denominational language ; and shall be wise if we preface the encounter by some consideration of this language, and of its real meaning for those who use and believe it.

No one needs, I suppose, to be told that the two chief features of Christian schematic theology are the dogmas of the Trinity and the Incarnation. They correlate and explain each other : forming together, for the Christian, the " final key " to the riddle of the world. The history of practical Christianity is the history of the attempt to exhibit their meaning in space and time. The history of mystical philosophy is the history—still incomplete—of the demonstration of their meaning in eternity.

Some form of Trinitarian dogma is found to be essential, as a method of describing observed facts, the moment that mysticism begins either (*a*) to analyse its own psychological conditions, or (*b*) to philosophize upon its intuitions of the Absolute. It must, that is to say, divide the aspects under

[1] " Jerusalem," lxi. 44 and xcv. 23.

which it knows the Godhead, if it is to deal with them in a fruitful or comprehensible way. The Unconditioned One, which is, for Neoplatonist and Catholic alike, the final object of the mystic quest, cannot of itself satisfy the deepest instincts of humanity: for man is aware that diversity in unity is a necessary condition if perfection of character is to be expressed. Though the idea of unity alone may serve to define the End—and though the mystics return to it again and again as a relief from that "heresy of multiplicity" by which they are oppressed—it cannot by itself be adequate to the description of the All.

The first question, then, must be—How many of such aspects are necessary to the complete presentment of the mystic's position? How many faces of Reality does he see? At the very least, as we have already seen, he must be aware of two aspects: (*a*) that Holy Spirit within, the immanent spark of the soul, life of his life, of which the contemplative becomes increasingly conscious as his education proceeds ; (*b*) that Transcendent Spirit without, the "Absolute," towards union with which the indwelling and increasingly dominant spirit of love pushes the developing soul. It is the function of ecstasy to fuse these two aspects of God—to bring back, in mystical language, the Lover to the Beloved—but it is no less the function of mystical philosophy to separate them. Over and over again the mystics and their critics acknowledge, explicitly or implicitly, the necessity of this act.

Thus even the rigid monotheism of Israel and Islam cannot, in the hands of the Kabalists and the Sūfis, get away from an essential dualism in the mystical experience. According to the Zohar, says Mr. A. E. Waite, its best modern student, "God is considered as immanent in all that has been created or emanated, and yet is transcendent to all." [1] So too the Sūfis. God, they say, is to be contemplated (*a*) outwardly in the imperfect beauties of the earth ; (*b*) inwardly, by meditation. Further, since He is One, and in all things, "to conceive one's self as separate from God is an error: yet *only when one sees oneself as separate from God, can one reach out to God.*" [2]

Thus Delacroix, speaking purely as a psychologist, and

---

[1] A. E. Waite, "The Doctrine and Literature of the Kabalah," p. 35.

[2] Palmer, "Oriental Mysticism," pt. i. cap. i.

denying to the mystical revelation—which he attributes exclusively to the normal content of the subliminal mind—any transcendental value, writes with entire approval of St. Teresa, that she "set up externally to herself the definite God of the Bible, at the same time as she set up within her soul the confused God of the Pseudo-Areopagite: the One of Neoplatonism. The first is her guarantee of the orthodoxy of the second, and prevents her from losing herself in an indistinction which is non-Christian. The confused God within is highly dangerous. . . . St. Teresa knew how to avoid this peril, and, served by her rich subconscious life, by the exaltation of her mental images, by her faculty of self-division on the one hand, on the other by her *rare powers of unification*, she realized simultaneously a double state in which the two Gods [*i.e.*, the two ways of apprehending God, transcendence and immanence] were guarantees of each other, mutually consolidating and enriching one another: such is the intellectual vision of the Trinity in the Seventh Habitation." [1]

It is probable that St. Teresa, confronted by this astonishing analysis, would have objected that her Trinity, unlike that of her eulogist, consisted of three and not two Persons. His language concerning confused interior and orthodox exterior Gods would certainly have appeared to her delicate and honest mind both clumsy and untrue : nor could she have allowed that the Unconditioned One of the Neoplatonists was an adequate description of the strictly personal Divine Majesty Whom she found enthroned in the inmost sanctuary of the Castle of the Soul.

What St. Teresa really did was to actualize in her own experience, apprehend in the "ground of her soul" by means of her extraordinarily developed transcendental perceptions, the three distinct and personal Aspects of the Godhead which are acknowledged by the Christian religion.

First, the Father, pure transcendent Being, creative Source and Origin of all that Is: the Unconditioned and Unknowable One of the Neoplatonist: Who is to be conceived, *pace* M. Delacroix, as utterly transcendent to the subject rather than "set up within the soul."

[1] Delacroix, "Études sur le Mysticisme," p. 75. The reference in the last sentence is to St. Teresa's "Castillo Interior."

Secondly, in the Person of Christ, Teresa isolated and distinguished the Logos or Creative Word, the expression, outbirth, or manifestation of the Father's thought. Here is the point at which the Divine Substance first becomes apprehensible by the spirit of man ; here that mediating principle "raised up between heaven and earth" which is at once the Mirror of Pure Being and the Light of a finite world. The Second Person of the Christian Trinity is for the believer not only the brightness or manifestation of Deity, but also the personal, inexhaustible, and responsive Fount of all life and Object of all love : Who, because of His taking up (in the Incarnation) of humanity into the Godhead, is of necessity the one and only Bridge between the finite and infinite, between the individual and the Absolute Life, and hence in mystic language the "true Bridegroom" of every human soul.

Thirdly, she recognized within herself the germ of that Absolute Life, the indwelling Spirit which is the source of man's transcendental consciousness and his link with the Being of God. That is to say, the Holy Spirit of Divine Love, the Real Desirous seeking for the Real Desired, without Whose presence any knowledge of or communion with God on man's part would be inconceivable.

In the supreme Vision of the Trinity which is vouchsafed to St. Teresa in the Seventh Habitation of the soul, these three aspects became fused in One. In the deepest recesses of her spirit, in that unplumbed abyss where selfhood ceases to have meaning, and the individual soul is merged in the life of the All, distinction vanished and she " saw God in a point." Such an experience, such an intuition of simple and undifferentiated Godhead—the Unity—beyond those three centres of Divine Consciousness which we call the Trinity of Persons, is highly characteristic of mysticism. The German mystics—temperamentally miles asunder from Teresa—described it as the attainment of the " still wilderness " or " lonely desert of Deity ": the limitless Divine Abyss, impersonal, indescribable, for ever hid in the Cloud of Unknowing, and yet the true Country of the Soul.[1]

[1] See Tauler, Sermon on St. John Baptist, and Third Instruction (" The Inner Way," pp. 97 and 321) ; Suso, " Buchlein von der Wahrheit," cap. v. ; Ruysbroeck, " L'Ornement des Noces Spirituelles," l. iii. caps. ii. and vi.

These propositions, which appear when thus laid down to be hopelessly academic, violently divorced from life, were not for St. Teresa or any other Christian mystic propositions at all; but attempts towards the description of first-hand experience. "How this vision comes to pass," she says, "I know not; but it does come to pass, and the three Persons of the Holy Trinity then show themselves to the soul with a radiance as of fire, which, like a shining cloud, first invades the mind and admirably illuminates it. Then she sees those three distinct Persons, and she knows with a sovereign truth that these three are One in substance, One in Power, One in wisdom, One God: so that those things which we know in this world by faith, the soul, in this light, understands by a sort of vision which is neither the vision of the body nor that of the soul; for it is not a sensible vision. There those three Persons communicate Themselves to the soul, and speak to her and . . . it seems to her that these three divine Persons have never left her: she sees clearly, in the manner which I have described, that they are within her soul, in its most inward part, as it were within a deep abyss. This person, a stranger to learning, knows not how to tell what is this deep abyss, but it is there that she feels within herself this divine companionship." [1]

Mystical writers remind us over and over again, that life as perceived by the human mind shows an inveterate tendency to arrange itself in triads: that if they proclaim the number Three in the heavens, they can also point to it as dominating everywhere upon the earth. Here Christianity did but give form to the deepest instinct of the human mind: an instinct which made Pythagoras call Three the number of God because beginning, middle, and end were contained therein. Thus to Hindu thought the Absolute Godhead was unknowable, but He disclosed three faces to man—Brahma the Creator, Shiva the Destroyer, Krishna the Repairer—and these three were One. So too the Neoplatonists, touched by the spirit of the East, distinguished three worlds; the Sensible or Phenomenal, the Rational or Intellectual, the Intelligible or Spiritual; and three aspects of God—the Unconditioned Absolute, the Logos or Artificer, and the divine Essence or Spirit which is both absolute and created. We have here, as

---

[1] St. Teresa, "El Castillo Interior," Moradas Sétimas, cap. i.

it were, the first sketch of the Christian Trinity; the dry bones awaiting the breath of more abundant life. Corresponding with this diagram of God's nature, they see also three grades of beauty; the Corporeal, the Spiritual, and the Divine.

Man, that "thing of threes," of body, soul and spirit, follows in his path towards unity the Threefold Way: for "our soul," says Lady Julian, "is made-trinity like to the unmade blissful Trinity, known and loved from without beginning, and in the making oned to the Maker."[1] So too we have seen that the psychic self is most easily understood by a division into Emotion, Intellect, and Will. Even the separation of things into Subject and Object implies a third term, the relation between them, without which no thought can be complete. Therefore the very principle of analogy imposes upon man a Trinitarian definition of Reality as the one with which his mind is best able to cope.[2] It is easy for the hurried rationalist to demonstrate the absurdity of this circumstance, but he will find it a very different matter when it comes to disproving it.

"I could wish," says St. Augustine, "that men would consider these three things that are in themselves . . . To Be, To Know, and to Will. For I am, and I know, and I will; I am knowing and willing, and I know myself to be and to will; and I will to be and to know. In these three therefore let him who can, see how inseparable a life there is—even one life, one mind, one essence: finally, how inseparable is the distinction, and yet a distinction. Surely a man hath it before him: let him look into himself and see and tell me. But when he discovers and can see anything of these, let him not think that he has discovered that which is above these Unchangeable: which Is unchangeably and Knows unchangeably and Wills unchangeably."[3]

In one of the best recorded instances of pure mystical vision, Julian of Norwich saw the Trinity of the Divine Nature shining in the phenomenal as well as in the spiritual world.

[1] Julian of Norwich, " Revelations of Divine Love," cap. lv. So St. Thomas says ("Summa Contra Gentiles," l. iv. cap. xxvi), "A likeness of the Divine Trinity is observable in the human mind."

[2] "The three Persons of the Trinity," said John Scotus Erigena, "are less modes of the Divine Substance than modes under which our mind conceives the Divine Substance"—a stimulating statement of dubious orthodoxy.

[3] Aug. Conf., bk. xiii. cap. xi.

"He showed me," she says, "a little thing, the quantity of an hazel nut, in the palm of my hand; and it was as round as a ball. I looked thereupon with the eye of my understanding, and thought, *What may this be?* And it was answered generally thus : *It is all that is made.* . . . In this Little Thing I saw three properties. The first is that God made it, the second is that God loveth it, the third, that God keepeth it. But what is to me verily the Maker, the Keeper, and the Lover, I cannot tell." [1]

Julian the anchoress, a simple and deeply human Englishwoman of middle age dwelling alone in her churchyard cell, with only a tiny window by which to see and hear the outer world, might well be called the poet of the Trinity : that austere and subtle dogma of which the mystics of the fourteenth century write with a passion which will be little understood by those who look upon it as "orthodoxy reduced to mathematics."

That most lovable and poetic of visionaries, who seems in her Revelations of Love to dream before a Crucifix set up in flowery fields, treats this highly metaphysical doctrine with a homely intimacy and a vigorous originality which carry with them at any rate a conviction of her own direct and personal apprehension of the truth which she struggles to describe. "I beheld," she says of a vision which is closely parallel to that of St. Teresa in the "Seventh Habitation of the Soul," and far more lucidly if less splendidly expressed, "the working of all the blessed Trinity : in which beholding, I saw and understood these three properties : the property of the Fatherhood, the property of the Motherhood, and the property of the Lordhood, in one God. In our Father Almighty we have our keeping and our bliss as anent our natural Substance,[2] which is to us by our making, without beginning. And in the Second Person in wit and wisdom we have our keeping as anent our Sense-soul : our restoring and our saving ; for He is our Mother, Brother, and Saviour. And in our good Lord, the Holy Ghost, we have our rewarding and our meed-giving for our living and our travail, and endless overpassing of all that we desire, in His marvellous courtesy, of His high plenteous grace. For all our life is in

[1] *Op. cit.*, cap. v.
[2] *Substance* is here, of course, to be understood in the scholastic sense, as the reality which underlies merely phenomenal existence.

three: in the first we have our Being, in the second we have
our Increasing, and in the third we have our Fulfilling ; the first
is Nature, the second is Mercy, and the third is Grace.[1] . . .
The high Might of the Trinity is our Father, and the deep
Wisdom of the Trinity is our Mother, and the great Love of
the Trinity is our Lord : and all this we have in Nature and
in our Substantial Making."[2]

Again, in a passage of exquisite tenderness, which comes
after the fire and dark of Teresa like cooling waters to the soul :
" As verily as God is our Father, so verily God is our Mother ;
and that shewed He in all [her revelations] and especially in
these sweet words where He saith : *I it am.* That is to say,
*I it am, the Might and the Goodness of the Fatherhood ; I it am,
the Wisdom of the Motherhood ; I it am, the Light and the Grace
that is all blessed Love ; I it am, the Trinity, I it am, the Unity :
I am the sovereign Goodness of all manner of things. I am that
maketh thee to love : I am that maketh thee to long : I it am, the
endless fulfilling of all true desires."* [3]

So Christopher Hervey—

> " The whole world round is not enough to fill
> The heart's three corners, but it craveth still.
> Only the Trinity that made it can
> Suffice the vast triangled heart of Man." [4]

It is a fact that any attempt towards a definition of God
which does not account for and acknowledge these three aspects
is found in experience to be incomplete. They provide objec-
tives for the heart, the intellect, and the will : for they offer to
the Self material for its highest love, its deepest thought, its
act of supreme volition. Under the familiar Platonic terms of
Goodness, Truth, and Beauty, they represent the divine source
and end of Ethics, Science, and Art, the three supreme activities

[1] *I.e.*, the Second Person of the Christian Trinity is the redemptive " fount of
mercy," the medium by which Grace, the free gift of transcendental life, reaches and
vivifies human nature : " permeates it," in Eucken's words, " with the Infinite and
Eternal " (" Der Sinn und Wert des Lebens," p. 181).

[2] " Revelations of Divine Love," cap. lviii.

[3] *Op. cit.*, cap. lix.

[4] " The School of the Heart," Epigram x. This book, which is a free translation of the " Scola Cordis " of Benedict Haeften (1635), is often, but wrongly, attributed
to Francis Quarles.

of man. Thus the ideals of artist, student, and philanthropist, who all seek under different modes the same reality, are gathered up in the mystic's One; as the pilgrimage of the three kings ended in the finding of one Star.

"What is God?" says St. Bernard. "Length, breadth, height, and depth. 'What,' you say, 'you do after all profess to believe in the fourfold Godhead which was an abomination to you?' Not in the least. . . . God is designated One to suit our comprehension, not to describe His character. *His character is capable of division, He Himself is not.* The words are different, the paths are many, but one thing is signified; the paths lead to one Person." [1]

All possible ways of conceiving this One Person are found in the end to range themselves under three heads. He is "above all and through all and in you all," [2] said St. Paul, anticipating the Councils in a flash of mystic intuition, and giving to the infant Church the shortest and most perfect definition of its Triune God. Being, which is above all, manifests itself as Becoming; as the dynamic, omnipresent Word of Life. The Divine Love immanent in the heart and in the world comes forth from, and returns to, the Absolute One. Thus is completed "the Eternal Circle from Goodness, through Goodness, to Goodness." [3] It is true that to these fundamental aspects of the perceived Godhead—that Being, Becoming, and Desire whereto the worlds keep time—the mystics have given many and various names; for they have something of the freedom of true intimates in treating of the Reality which they love. In particular, those symbols of the Absolute which are drawn from the great and formless forces of the universe, rather than from the orthodox but necessarily anthropomorphic imagery of human relationship, have always appealed to them. Their intense apprehension of Spirit seems to find freer and more adequate expression in such terms, than in those in which the notion of space is involved or which are capable of suggesting a concrete picture to the mind. Though they know as well as the philosophers that "there must always be something symbolic in our way of expressing the spiritual life," since "that unfathomable infinite whose spiritual character is first recognized in our human experience, can never reveal itself fully and freely under the limitation of our earthly

[1] "De Consideratione," bk. v. cap. viii.　[2] Ephesians iv. 6.　[3] Compare p. 49.

existence"[1]; yet they ever seek, like the artists they are, some
new and vital image which is not yet part of the debased
currency of popular religion, and conserves its original power of
stinging the imagination to more vivid life.

Thus "the Kingdom of Heaven," says Law, "stands in this
threefold life, where three are one, because it is a manifestation
of the Deity, which is Three and One; the Father has His distinct manifestation in the Fire, which is always generating the
Light; the Son has His distinct manifestation in the Light,
which is always generated from the Fire; the Holy Ghost has
His manifestation in the Spirit, that always proceeds from both,
and is always united with them. It is this eternal unbeginning
Trinity in Unity of Fire, Light, and Spirit, that constitutes
Eternal Nature, the Kingdom of Heaven, the heavenly Jerusalem, the Divine Life, the Beatific Visibility, the majestic
Glory and Presence of God. Through this Kingdom of Heaven,
or Eternal Nature, is the invisible God, the incomprehensible
Trinity, eternally breaking forth and manifesting itself in a
boundless height and depth of blissful wonders, opening and
displaying itself to all its creatures as in an infinite variation
and endless multiplicity of its powers, beauties, joys, and
glories."[2]

Perhaps an easier, better, more beautiful example of these
abstract symbols of the Trinity than Law's Fire, Light, and
Spirit is that of Light, Life, and Love: a threefold picture of
the Real which is constantly dwelt upon and elaborated by the
Christian mystics. Transcendent Light, intangible but un-
escapeable, ever emanating Its splendour through the Universe:
indwelling, unresting, and energizing Life: desirous and directive Love—these are cardinal aspects of Reality to which they
return again and again in their efforts to find words which will
express the inexpressible truth.

(*a*) LIGHT, ineffable and uncreated, the perfect symbol of
pure undifferentiated Being: above the intellect, as St. Augustine reminds us, but known to him who loves.[3] This Uncreated

[1] Eucken, "Der Sinn und Wert des Lebens," p. 131.

[2] "An Appeal to All who Doubt" ("Liberal and Mystical Writings of William
Law," p. 54). Law's symbols are here borrowed from the system of his master,
Jacob Boehme. (See the "De Signatura Rerum" of Boehme, cap. xiv.)

[3] Aug. Conf., bk. vii. cap. x.

Light is the "deep yet dazzling darkness" of the Dionysian school, "dark from its surpassing brightness . . . as the shining of the sun on his course is as darkness to weak eyes."[1] It is Dante's *somma luce*, wherein he saw multiplicity in unity, the ingathered leaves of all the universe[2]: the Eternal Father, or Fount of Things. "For well we know," says Ruysbroeck, "that the bosom of the Father is our ground and origin, wherein our life and being is begun."[3]

(*b*) LIFE, the Son, hidden Steersman of the Universe, the Logos, Fire, or Cosmic soul of things. This out-birth or Concept of the Father's Mind, which He possesses within Himself, as Battista Vernazza was told in her ecstasy,[4] is that Word of Creation which, since It is alive and infinite, no formula can contain: the Word eternally "spoken" or generated by the Transcendent Light. "This is why," says Ruysbroeck again, "all that lives in the hidden unity of the Father lives also in the Son."[5] This life, then, is the flawless expression or character of the Father, *Sapientia Patris*. It is at once the personal and adorable Object of the mystic's adventure—his closest comrade and his beckoning star—and the inmost principle, the sustaining power, of a dynamic universe; for that which intellect defines as the Logos or Cosmic Spirit, contemplative love *knows* as Wonderful, Counsellor, and Prince of Peace.

Since Christ, for the Christian philosopher, *is* Divine Life Itself—the drama of Christianity but expressing this fact and its implications "in a point"—it follows that His active spirit is to be discerned, not symbolically, but in the most veritable sense, in the ecstatic and abounding life of the world. In the rapturous vitality of the birds, in their splendid glancing flight: in the swelling of buds and the sacrificial beauty of the flowers: in the great and solemn rhythms of the sea—there is somewhat of Bethlehem in all these things, somewhat too of Calvary in their self-giving pains. It was this re-discovery of Nature's Christliness which Blake desired so passionately when he sang—

---

[1] Tauler, 3rd Instruction ("The Inner Way," p. 324).
[2] Par. xxxiii. 67, 85.
[3] "L'Ornement des Noces Spirituelles," l. iii. cap. v.
[4] Von Hügel, "The Mystical Element of Religion," vol. i. p. 357.
[5] Ruysbroeck, *op. cit.*, *loc. cit.*

" I will not cease from mental fight,
   Nor shall my sword sleep in my hand,
Till we have built Jerusalem
   In England's green and pleasant land."

Here then it is, on this remote and airy pinnacle of faith, at the utmost boundaries of human speech, that mystical theology suddenly shows herself—not as the puzzle-headed constructor of impossible creeds but as accepting and transmuting to a more radiant life those two profound but apparently contradictory metaphysical definitions of Reality which we have already discussed.[1] Eternal Becoming, God Immanent and dynamic, striving with and in His world : the unresting " flux of things " of Heracleitus, the crying aloud of that Word " which is through all things everlastingly "—the evolutionary world-process beloved of modern philosophers—is here placed once for all in true relation with pure transcendent and unmoved Being ; the Absolute One of Xenophanes and the Platonists. This Absolute is discerned by mystic intuition as the " End of Unity " in whom all diversities must cease ;[2] the Ocean to which that ceaseless and painful Becoming, that unresting river of life, in which we are immersed, tends to return : the Son going to the Father.

(c) LOVE, the principle of attraction, which seems to partake at once of the transcendental and the created worlds. If we consider the Father as Supreme Subject—" origin," as Aquinas says, " of the entire procession of Deity "[3]—and the Son or generated Logos as the Object of His thought, in whom, says Ruysbroeck, " He contemplates Himself and all things in an eternal Now " ;[4] then this personal Spirit of Love, *il desiro e il velle*, represents the relation between the two, and constitutes the very character of the whole. " They breathe forth a spirit," says Ruysbroeck, of the First and Second Persons " which is their will and love." [5] Proceeding, according to Christian doctrine, from Light and Life, the Father and Son— implicit, that is, in both the Absolute Source and dynamic flux of things—this divine and unresting spirit of desire is found

[1] *Supra*, Cap. II.   [2] Tauler, *op. cit., loc. cit.*
[3] " Summa Contra Gentiles," l. iv. cap. xxvi.
[4] " L'Ornement des Noces Spirituelles," l. iii. cap. v.
[5] *Ob. cit.*, l. ii. cap. xxxvii.

enshrined in our very selfhood; and is the agent by which
that selfhood is merged in the Absolute Self. "My love is my
weight," said St. Augustine.[1] It is the spiritual equivalent of
that gravitation which draws all things to their place. Thus
Bernard Holland says in his Introduction to Boehme's "Dialogues," "In a deep sense, the desire of the Spark of Life in the
Soul to return to its Original Source is part of the longing desire
of the universal Life for its own heart or centre. Of this longing,
the universal attraction, striving against resistance, towards a
universal centre, proved to govern the phenomenal or physical
world, is but the outer sheath and visible working." Again,
"Desire is everything in Nature ; does everything. Heaven is
Nature filled with divine Life attracted by Desire."[2]

"The best masters say," says Eckhart, "that the love
wherewith we love is the Holy Spirit.[3] Some deny it. But
this is always true: all those motives by which we are moved
to love, in these is nothing else than the Holy Spirit."[4]

"God wills," says Ruysbroeck, gathering these scattered
symbols to unity again, "that we should come forth from ourselves in this Eternal Light ; that we should pursue in a supernatural manner that image which is our true Life, and that we
should possess it with Him actively and fruitively in eternal
blessedness . . . this going forth of the contemplative is also
in Love : for by fruitive love he overpasses his created essence
and finds and tastes the riches and delights of God, which He
causes to flow without ceasing in the most secret chamber of
the soul, at that place where it is most like unto the sublimity
of God."[5]

Here only, in the innermost sanctuary of being, the soul's
"last habitation," as St. Teresa said, is the truth which these
symbols express truly known : for "as to how the Trinity is

[1] Aug. Conf., bk. xiii. cap. ix.
[2] Introduction to "Three Dialogues of the Supersensual Life," p. xxx.
[3] Probably St. Thomas Aquinas, the usual source of Eckhart's more orthodox
utterances. Compare "Summa Contra Gentiles," l. iv. cap. xxiii : "Since the
Holy Ghost proceeds as the love wherewith God loves Himself, and since God loves
with the same love Himself and other beings for the sake of His own goodness, it is
clear that the love wherewith God loves us belongs to the Holy Ghost. In like
manner also the love wherewith we love God."
[4] Pred. xii.
[5] "L'Ornement des Noces Spirituelles," l. iii. cap. v.

one and the Trinity in the unity of the nature is one, whilst nevertheless the Trinity comes forth from the unity, this cannot be expressed in words," says Suso, " owing to the simplicity of that deep abyss. Hither it is, into this intelligible *where* that the spirit, spiritualizing itself, soars up ; now flying in the measureless heights, now swimming in the soundless deeps, of the sublime marvels of the Godhead ! " [1]

Mystical philosophy, then, has availed itself gladly of the doctrine of the Trinity in expressing its vision of the nature of that Absolute which is found, by those who attain the deep Abyss of the Godhead, to be essentially One. But it is by the complementary Christian dogma of the Incarnation that it has best been able to describe and explain the nature of the inward and personal mystic experience. " Man in the course of his attainment," says a living authority on mysticism, "is at first three—body, soul, and spirit—that is, when he sets out on the Great Quest ; he is two at a certain stage—when the soul has conceived Christ, for the spirit has then descended and the body is for the time being outside the Divine Alliance ; but he is in fine one—that is to say, when the whole man has died in Christ—which is the term of his evolution." [2]

The Incarnation, which is for popular Christianity synonymous with the historical birth and earthly life of Christ, is for the mystic not only this but also a perpetual Cosmic and personal process. It is an everlasting bringing forth, in the universe and also in the individual ascending soul, of the divine and perfect Life, the pure character of God, of which the one historical life dramatized the essential constituents. Hence the soul, like the physical embryo, resumes in its upward progress the spiritual life-history of the race. "The one secret, the greatest of all," says Patmore, is "the doctrine of the Incarnation, regarded not as an historical event which occurred two thousand years ago, but as an event which is renewed in the body of every one who is in the way to the fulfilment of his original destiny." [3]

We have seen that for mystical theology the Second Person

[1] Suso, Leben, cap. lvi.
[2] A. E. Waite, "The Hidden Church of the Holy Grail," p. 539.
[3] "The Rod, the Root, and the Flower," "Homo," xix.

of the Trinity is the Wisdom of the Father, the Word of Life.
The fullness of this Word could therefore only be communicated
to the human consciousness by a Life.   In the Incarnation this
Logos, this divine character of Reality, penetrated the illusions
of the sensual world—in other words, the illusions of all the
selves whose ideas compose that world—and " saved " it by this
infusion of truth.· A divine, suffering, self-sacrificing Personality was then shown as the sacred heart of a living, striving
universe : and for once the Absolute was exhibited in the
terms of finite existence.   Some such event as this breaking
through of the divine and archetypal life into the temporal world
is perceived by the mystical philosopher to be a necessity if man
was ever to see in terms of life· that greatness of life to which
he belongs : learn to transcend the world of sense, and rebuild
his life upon the levels of reality.   Thus it is that the Catholic
priest in the Christmas Mass gives thanks, not for the setting
in hand of any commercial process of redemption, but for a
revelation of reality, " Quia per incarnati Verbi mysterium,
nova mentis nostrae oculis lux tuae claritatis infulsit : ut dum
visibiliter Deum cognoscimus, per hunc in invisibilium amorem
rapiamur."   The very essence of mystical Christianity seems
to be summed up in these lovely words.[1]

    " The Son of God, the Eternal Word in the Father, who is
the glance, or brightness, and the power of the light eternity,"
says Boehme, " must become man and be born in you, if you
will know God : otherwise you are in the dark stable and go
about groping." [2]   " The Word," says Ruysbroeck finely, " is no
other than See.   And this is the coming forth and the birth of
the Son of the Eternal Light, in Whom all blessedness is seen
and known." [3]

    Once at any rate, they say in effect, the measure of that
which it was possible for the Spirit of Life to do and for living
creatures to be, was filled to the brim.   By this event, all
were assured that the ladder of Creation was made whole ; in

---

    [1] " Because by the mystery of the Incarnate Word the new light of Thy brightness
hath shone upon the eyes of our mind : that we, knowing God seen of the eyes, by
Him may be snatched up into the love of that which eye hath not seen " (Missale
Romanum.   Praefatio Solemnis de Nativitate).
    [2] " The Threefold Life of Man," cap. iii. § 31.
    [3] Ruysbroeck, op. cit., l. iii. cap. i.

this hypostatic union, the breach between appearance and reality, between God and man, was healed. The Bridge so made—to use St. Catherine of Siena's allegory again—is eternal, since it was "laid before the foundation of the world" in the "Eternal Now." Thus the voice of the Father says to her in that vision, "I also wish thee to look at the Bridge of My only-begotten Son, and see the greatness thereof, for it reaches from Heaven to earth ; that is, that the earth of your humanity is joined to the greatness of the Deity thereby. I say, then, that this Bridge reaches from Heaven to earth, and constitutes the union which I have made with man. . . . So the height of the Divinity, humbled to the earth, and joined with your humanity, made the Bridge and reformed the road. Why was this done? In order that man might come to his true happiness with the angels. And observe that it is not enough, in order that you should have life, that My Son should have made you this Bridge, unless you walk thereon." [1] "Our high Father God Almighty, which is Being," says Lady Julian, "He knew and loved us from afore any time. Of which knowing, in His marvellous deep charity, and the foreseeing counsel of all the blessed Trinity, He willed that the Second Person should become our Mother." [2]

It is of course this quickening communication of grace to nature, of God to man—this claim to an influx of ultimate reality, possible of assimilation by all—which constitutes the strength of the Christian religion. Instead of the stony diet of the philosophers, it offers to the self hungry for the Absolute that *Panis Angelorum*, the vivifying principle of the world. That is to say, it gives positive and experimental knowledge of and union with a supreme Personality—absorption into His mystical body—instead of the artificial conviction produced by concentration on an idea. It knits up the universe ; shows the phenomenal pierced in all directions by the real, and made one with it. It provides a solid basis for mysticism : a basis which is at once metaphysical and psychological : and shows that state towards which the world's deepest minds have always instinctively aspired, as a part of the Cosmic return through Christ to God.

[1] Dialogo, cap. xxii.
[2] "Revelations of Divine Love," cap. lix.

" Quivi è la sapienza e la possanza
    ch' aprì le strade intra il cielo e la terra
    onde fu già sì lunga disianza." [1]

This is what the Christian mystics mean to express when they declare over and over again that the return to the Divine Substance, the Absolute, which is the end of the soul's ascent, can only be made through the humanity of Christ. The Son, the Word, is the character of the Father : that in which the Ineffable Godhead knows Himself, as we only know ourselves in our own characters. He is thus a double link : the means of God's self-consciousness, the means of man's consciousness of God. How then, asks mystic theology, could such a link complete its attachments without some such process as that which the Incarnation dramatized in time and space? The Principle of Life is also the Principle of Restitution ; by which the imperfect and broken life of sense is mended and transformed into the perfect life of spirit. Hence the title of Repairer applied by Boehme and Saint-Martin to the Second Person of the Trinity.

In the last resort, the doctrine of the Incarnation is the only safeguard of the mystics against the pantheism to which they always tend. The Unconditioned Absolute, so soon as it alone becomes the object of their contemplation, is apt to be conceived merely as Divine Essence ; the idea of Personality evaporates and loving communion is at an end. This is probably the reason why so many of the greatest contemplatives—Suso and St. Teresa are cases in point—have found that deliberate meditation upon the humanity of Christ, difficult and uncongenial as is this concrete devotion to the mystical temperament, was a necessity if they were to retain a healthy and well-balanced inner life.

Further, these mystics see in the historic life of Christ an epitome—or if you will, an exhibition—of the essentials of all spiritual life. There they see dramatized not only the Cosmic process of the Divine Wisdom, but also the inward experience of every soul on her way to union with that Absolute " to which the whole Creation moves." This is why

---

[1] Par. xxxiii. 37. "Here is the Wisdom and the Power which opened the ways betwixt heaven and earth, for which there erst had been so long a yearning."

the expressions which they use to describe the evolution of
the mystical consciousness from the birth of the divine in the
spark of the soul to its final unification with the Absolute
Life are so constantly chosen from the Drama of Faith. In
this drama they see described under veils the supreme and
necessary adventures of the spirit. Its obscure and humble
birth, its education in poverty, its temptation, mortification, and
solitude, its "illuminated life" of service and contemplation, the
desolation of that "dark night of the soul" in which it seems
abandoned by the Divine : the painful death of the self, its
resurrection to the glorified existence of the Unitive Way, its
final reabsorption in its Source—all these, they say, were lived
once in a supreme degree in the flesh. Moreover, the degree
of closeness with which the individual experience adheres
to this Pattern is always taken by them as a standard
of the healthiness, ardour, and success of its transcendental
activities.

> "Apparve in questa forma
> Per dare a noi la norma."

sang Jacopone da Todi. "And he who vainly thinketh otherwise," says the "Theologia Germanica" with uncompromising
vigour, " is deceived. And he who saith otherwise, lieth." [1]
  Those to whom such a parallel seems artificial to the last
degree should remember that according to the doctrine of
mysticism that drama of the self-limitation and self-sacrifice
of the Absolute Life, which was once played out in the phenomenal world—forced, as it were, upon the consciousness of
dim-eyed men—is eternally going forward upon the plane of
reality. To them the Cross of Calvary is implicit in the Rose
of the World. The law of this Infinite Life, which was in
the Incarnation expressing Its own nature to a supreme degree,
must then also be the law of the finite life ; in so far as that life
aspires to transcend individual limitations, rise to freedom,
and attain union with Infinity. It is this governing idea which
justifies the apparently fanciful allegorizations of Christian
history which swarm in the works of the mystics.
  To exhibit these allegorizations in any detail would be
tedious. All that is necessary is that the principle underlying

[1] "Theologia Germanica," cap. xviii.

them should be understood, when anyone can make without difficulty the specific attributions. I give, then, but one example: that which is referred by mystical writers to the Nativity, and concerns the eternal Birth or Generation of the Son or Divine Word.

This Birth is in its first, or Cosmic sense, the welling forth of the Spirit of Life from the Divine Abyss of the unconditioned Godhead. "From our proper Source, that is to say, from the Father and all that which lives in Him, there shines," says Ruysbroeck, "an eternal Ray, the which is the Birth of the Son." [1] It is of this perpetual generation of the Word that Meister Eckhart speaks, when he says in his Christmas sermon, "We are celebrating the feast of the Eternal Birth which God the Father has borne and *never ceases to bear* in all Eternity : whilst this birth also comes to pass in Time and in human nature. Saint Augustine says this Birth is ever taking place." At this point, with that strong practical instinct which is characteristic of the mystics, Eckhart turns abruptly from speculation to immediate experience, and continues, " But if it takes not place in me, what avails it? Everything lies in this, that it should take place in me." [2]

Here in a few words the two-fold character of this Mystic Birth is exhibited. The interest is suddenly deflected from its Cosmic to its personal aspect ; and the individual is reminded that in him, no less than in the Archetypal Universe, real life must be born if real life is to be lived. "When the soul brings forth the Son," he says in another place, "it is happier than Mary." [3]

Since the soul, according to mystic principles, can only perceive Reality in proportion as she is real, know God by becoming God-like, it is clear that this birth is the initial

[1] "L'Ornement des Noces Spirituelles," l. iii. cap. v. The extreme antiquity of this idea is illustrated by the Catholic practice, dating from Patristic times, of celebrating three Masses on Christmas Day. Of these the first, at midnight, commemorates the Eternal Generation of the Son ; the second, at dawn, His incarnation upon earth ; the third His birth in the heart of man. See Kellner, " Heortology" (English translation, London, 1908), p. 156.

[2] Eckhart, Pred. i., " Mystische Schriften," p. 13.   Compare Tauler, Sermon on the Nativity of Our Lady ("The Inner Way," p. 167).

[3] This idea of re-birth is probably of Oriental origin. It can be traced back to Egypt, being found in the Hermetic writings of the third century B.C. See Petrie, " Personal Religion in Egypt before Christianity," p. 167.

necessity. The true and definitely directed mystical life does and must open with that most actual and stupendous, though indescribable phenomenon, the coming forth into consciousness of man's deeper, spiritual self, which ascetical and mystical writers of all ages have agreed to call Regeneration or Re-birth.

We have already considered [1] the New Birth in its purely psychological aspect, as the emergence of the transcendental sense. Here its more profound and mystical side is exhibited, its divine character revealed. By a process which may indifferently be described as the birth of something new or the coming forth of something which has slept—since both these phrases are but metaphors for another and more secret thing—the eye is opened on Eternity ; the self, abruptly made aware of Reality, comes forth from the cave of illusion like a child from the womb and begins to live upon the supersensual plane. Then she feels in her inmost part a new presence, a new consciousness— it were hardly an exaggeration to say a new Person—weak, demanding nurture, clearly destined to pass through many phases of development before its maturity is reached ; yet of so strange a nature, that in comparison with its environment she may well regard it as Divine.

"This change, this upsetting, is called re-birth. *To be born* simply means to enter into a world in which the senses dominate, in which wisdom and love languish in the bonds of individuality. To be *re-born* means to return to a world where the spirit of wisdom and love governs and animal-man obeys." [2] So Eckartshausen. It means, says Jane Lead, "the bringing forth of a new-created Godlike similitude in the soul." [3] This "God-like similitude," or New Man, is described by Saint-Martin as "born in the midst of humiliations, his whole history being that of God suffering within us." [4] He is brought forth, says Eckartshausen again, in the stable previously inhabited by the ox of passion and the ass of prejudice. [5] His mother, says Boehme, is the Virgin Sophia, the Divine Wisdom, or Mirror of the Being of God. With the emergence of this new and sublime factor into the conscious field—this spiritual birth

[1] *Supra*, p. 63.   [2] "The Cloud upon the Sanctuary," p. 77.
[3] "The Enochian Walks with God," p. 3.
[4] A. E. Waite, "Louis Claude de Saint-Martin," p. 263.
[5] *Op. cit.*, p. 81.

—the mystic life begins : as the Christian epoch began with the emergence of Divine Spirit in the flesh. Paradise, says Boehme, is still in the world, but man is not in Paradise unless he be born again. In that case, he stands therein in the New Birth.[1] He has been lifted, as Eucken would say, to the "spiritual level," and there finds Paradise, the Independent Spiritual Life "not alien but his own."[2]

Here then are one or two characteristics of the map which we shall find the Christian mystics most inclined to use. There are, of course, other great landmarks upon it: and these we shall meet as we follow in detail the voyages of the questing soul. One warning, however, must be given to amateur geographers before we go on. Like all other maps, this one at its best can but represent by harsh outline and conventional colour the living earth which those travellers have trod. It is a deliberately schematic representation of Reality, a flat and sometimes arid symbol of great landscapes, rushing rivers, awful peaks: dangerous unless these its limitations be always kept in mind. The boy who defined Canada as "very pink" was not much further off the track than those who would limit the Adorable Trinity to the definitions of the "Athanasian" Creed; however useful that chart may be, and is, within the boundaries imposed by its form.

Further, all such maps, and we who treat of them, can but set down in cold blood and with a dreadful pretence of precision, matters which the true explorers of Eternity were only able to apprehend in the ardours of such a passion, in the transports of such a union as we, poor finite slaves of our frittered emotions, could hardly look upon and live. "If you would truly know how these things come to pass," says St. Bonaventura, in a passage which all students of theology should ever keep in mind, "ask it of grace, not of doctrine; of desire, not of intellect; of the ardours of prayer, not of the teachings of the schools; of the Bridegroom, not of the Master; of God, not of man; of the darkness, not of the day; not of illumination, but of that Fire which enflames all and wraps us in God with great sweetness and most ardent love. The which Fire most truly is God, and the road thereto is through Jerusalem."[3]

[1] "De Signatura Rerum," viii. 47.   [2] "Der Sinn und Wert des Lebens," p. 90.
[3] "De Itinerario Mente in Deo," cap. vii.

CHAPTER VI

MYSTICISM AND SYMBOLISM

IN our study of theology we saw the Christian mystic adopting, as chart and pilot book of his voyages and adventures, the scheme of faith, and diagram of the spiritual world, which is adopted by ordinary Christian men. We saw that he found in it a depth and richness of content which the conventional believer in that theology, the " good churchman," seldom suspects: and that which is here true of the Christian mystic, is true, as regards their respective theologies, of the Pagan, the Mahommedan and the Buddhist as well.

But, since the spiritual adventures of the mystic are not those of ordinary men, it will follow that this map, though always true for him, is not complete. He can press forward to countries which unmystical piety must mark as unexplored. Pushing out from harbour to " the vast and stormy sea of the divine," he can take soundings, and mark dangers the existence of which such piety never needs to prove.

Hence it is not strange that certain maps, artistic representations or symbolic schemes, should have come into being which describe or suggest the special experiences of the mystical consciousness, and the doctrines to which these experiences have given birth. Many of these maps have an uncouth, even an impious appearance in the eyes of those unacquainted with the facts which they attempt to translate : as the charts of the deep-sea sailor seem ugly and unintelligible things to those who have never been out of sight of land.   Others—and these the most pleasing, most easily understood—have already been made familiar, perhaps tiresomely familiar, to us by the poets ; who, intuitively recognizing their suggestive qualities, their links with truth, have borrowed and adapted them to their own business of translating Reality into terms of rhythm and speech. Ultimately, however, they owe their origin to the mystics, or to that mystical sense which is innate in all true poets : and in the last resort it is the mystic's kingdom, and the mystic's experience, which they affect to describe.

Now these special mystical diagrams, these symbolic and artistic descriptions of man's inward history—his secret adventures with God—are almost endless in their variety : since in each we have a picture of the country of the soul seen through a different temperament.   To describe all would be to analyse the whole field of mystical literature, and indeed much other literature as well ; to epitomize in fact all that has been dreamed and written concerning the so-called " inner life "—a dreary and a lengthy task.   But the majority of them, I think, tend to express a comparatively small number of essential doctrines or fundamental ways of seeing things ; and as regards their imagery, these fall into three great classes ; representative of the three principal ways in which man's spiritual consciousness reacts to the touch of Reality, the three primary if paradoxical facts of which that consciousness must be aware.   Hence a consideration of mystic symbols drawn from each of these groups may give us a key with which to unlock some at least of the verbal riddles of the individual adventurer.

Thanks to the spatial imagery inseparable from human thinking and human expression, no direct description of spiritual experience is or can be possible to man.   It must always be symbolic, allusive, oblique : always suggest, but never tell, the truth : and in this respect there is not much to choose between the fluid and artistic language of vision and the arid technicalities of philosophy.   In another respect, however, there is a great deal to choose between them : and here the visionary, not the philosopher, receives the palm.

The greater the suggestive quality of the symbol used, the
more answering emotion it evokes in those to whom it is
addressed, the more truth it will convey. A good symbolism,
therefore, will be more than mere diagram or mere allegory : it
will use to the utmost the resources of beauty and of passion,
will bring with it hints of mystery and wonder, bewitch with
dreamy periods the mind to which it is addressed.   Its
appeal will not be to the clever brain, but to the desirous heart
of man.

The three great classes of symbols which I propose to
consider, play upon three deep cravings of the self, three great
expressions of man's restlessness, which only mystic truth can
fully satisfy. The first is the craving which make him a pilgrim
and wanderer. It is the longing to go out from his normal
world in search of a lost home, a "better country"; an
Eldorado, a Sarras, a Heavenly Syon. The next is that
craving of heart for heart, of the soul for its perfect mate,
which makes him a lover. The third is the craving for inward
purity and perfection, which makes him an ascetic, and in the
last resort a saint.

These three cravings, I think, answer to three ways in which
mystics of different temperaments attack the problem of the
Absolute : three different formulæ under which their transcendence of the sense-world can be described. In describing this
transcendence, and the special adventures involved in it, they
are describing a change from the state of ordinary men, in
touch with the sense-world, responding to its rhythms, to the
state of spiritual consciousness in which, as they say, they are
"in union" with Divine Reality, with God. Whatever be the
theological creed of the mystic, he never varies in declaring
this close, definite, and actual intimacy to be the end of his
quest. "Mark me like the tulip with Thine own streaks," says
the Sūfi.[1] "I would fain be to the Eternal Goodness what his
own hand is to a man," says the German contemplative.[2] "My
me is God, nor do I know my selfhood save in Him," says the
Italian saint.[3]

But, since this Absolute God is for him substance, ground or

[1] Jámi, " Joseph and Zulaikha. The Poet's Prayer."
[2] "Theologia Germanica," cap. x.
[3] St. Catherine of Genoa, Vita e Dottrina, cap. xiv.

underlying Reality of all that *is:* present yet absent, near yet far: He is as much the substance or foundation of the human soul as of the Universe. The seeker for the Real may therefore objectify his quest in two apparently contradictory, yet really mutually explanatory ways. First he may see it as an out-going journey from the world of illusion to the real or transcendental world: a leaving of the visible for the invisible. Secondly, it may appear to him as an inward alteration, re-making or regeneration, by which his personality or character is so changed as to be able to enter into communion with that Fontal Being which he loves and desires; is united with and dominated by the indwelling God who is the fount of its spiritual life. In the first case, the objective idea " God " is the pivot of his symbolism: the Blazing Star, or Magnet of the Universe which he has seen far off: and seeing, has worshipped and desired. In the second case, this is replaced by the subjective idea " Sanctity," with its accompanying consciousness of a disharmony to be abolished. The Mystic Way will then be described, not as a journey, but as an alteration of personality, the transmuting of " earthly " into " heavenly " man. Plainly these two aspects are obverse and reverse of one whole. They represent that mighty pair of opposites, Infinite and Finite, God and Self, which it is the business of mysticism to carry up into a higher synthesis.

Whether the process be considered as outward search or inward change, its object and its end are the same. Man enters into the order of Reality: his desire is met by the Divine Desire, his "separated will" or life becomes one with the great Life of the All.

From what has been said in the last chapter, it will be clear that the two opposing types of symbolism which we have discussed—the outward search and inward change—will be adopted by the two groups of selves whose experience of " union with the Divine " leans (1) to the Transcendent or ex-ternal, (2) to the Immanent or internal way of apprehending Reality: and that a third or intermediate group of images will be necessary to express the experience of those to whom mystic feeling—the satisfaction of love—is the supreme factor in the mystic life. According, then, to whether man's instinct prompts him to describe the Absolute Reality which he knows as a Place, a Person, or a State—all three of course but partial and human symbols of the one Indescribable Truth—so will he tend to adopt a symbolism of one or other of these three types.

A. Those who conceive the Perfect as a beatific vision exterior to them and very far off, who find in the doctrine of Emanations something which answers to their inward experience, will feel the process of their entrance into reality to be a quest, an arduous journey from the material to the spiritual world. They move away from, rather than transmute to another form, the life of sense. The ecstasies of such mystics will answer to the root-meaning of that much perverted word, as a "standing out" from themselves; a flight to happier countries far away. For them, the soul is outward bound towards its home.

B. Those for whom mysticism is above all things an intimate and personal relation, the satisfaction of a deep desire—who can say with Gertrude More, " never was there or can there be imagined such a love, as is between an humble soul and Thee"—will fall back upon imagery drawn largely from the language of earthly passion. Since the Christian religion insists upon the personal aspect of the Godhead, and provides in Christ an object of such intimacy, devotion and desire, an enormous number of Christian mystics necessarily use symbols of this kind.

C. Those who are conscious rather of the Divine as a Transcendent Life immanent in the world and the self, and of a strange spiritual seed within them by whose development man, moving to higher levels of character and consciousness, attains his end, will see the mystic life as involving inward change rather than outgoing search. Regeneration is their watchword, and they will choose symbols of growth or transmutation: saying with St. Catherine of Genoa, " my Being is God, not by simple participation, but by a true transformation of my Being."[1]

These three groups of mystics, then, stand for three kinds of temperament ; and we may fairly take as their characteristic forms of symbolic expression the Mystic Quest, the Marriage of the Soul and the "Great Work" of the Spiritual Alchemists.

[1] Vita e Dottrina, p. 36.

I

The pilgrimage idea, the outgoing quest, appears in mystical literature under two rather different aspects. One is the search for the " Hidden Treasure which desires to be found." Such is the "quest of the Grail " when regarded in its mystic aspect as an allegory of the adventures of the soul. The other is the long, hard journey towards a known and definite goal or state. Such is Dante's "Divine Comedy "; which is, in one of its aspects, a faithful and detailed description of the Mystic Way. The goal of such a quest—the Empyrean of Dante, the Beatific Vision or fulfilment of love—is often called Jerusalem by the Christian Mystics; naturally enough, since that city was for the mediaeval mind the supreme end of pilgrimage. By Jerusalem they mean not only the celestial country, Heaven : but also the spiritual life, which is " itself a heaven." [1]   " Just as a true pilgrim going towards Jerusalem," says Hilton, " leaveth behind him house and land, wife and children, and maketh himself poor and bare from all things that he hath, that he may go lightly without letting. Right so, if thou wilt be a spiritual pilgrim, thou shalt strip thyself naked of all that thou hast . . . then shalt thou resolve in thy heart fully and wholly that thou wilt be at Jerusalem, and at no other place but there." " Jerusalem," he says in this same chapter, " is as much as to say a sight of peace ; and betokeneth contemplation in perfect love of God." [2]

Under this image of a pilgrimage—an image as concrete and practical, as remote from the romantic and picturesque, for the mediaeval writers who used it, as a symbolism of hotel and railway train would be to us—the mystics contrived to summarize and suggest much of the life history of the ascending soul ; the developing spiritual consciousness. The necessary freedom and detachment of the traveller, his departure from his normal life and interests, the difficulties, enemies, and hardships encountered on the road ; the length of the journey, the variety of the country, the dark night which overtakes him, the glimpses of destination far away—all these are seen more

---

[1] This image seems first to have been elaborated by St. Augustine, from whom it was borrowed by Hugh of St. Victor, and most of the mediaeval mystics.

[2] " The Scale of Perfection," bk. ii. pt. ii. cap. iii.

and more as we advance in knowledge to constitute a transparent allegory of the incidents of man's progress from the unreal to the real. Bunyan was but the last and least mystical of a long series of minds which grasped this fact.

The Traveller, says the Sūfī 'Azīz bin Mahommed Nafasī, in whose book, "The Remotest Aim," the pilgrimage-symbolism is developed in great detail, is the Perceptive or Intuitive Sense of Man. The goal to which he journeys is Knowledge of God. This mysterious traveller towards the only country of the soul may be known of other men by his detachment, charity, humility, and patience. These primary virtues, however—belonging to ethical rather than to spiritual life—are not enough to bring his quest to a successful termination. They make him, say the Sūfīs, "perfect in knowledge of his goal but deficient in the power of reaching it." Though he has fraternal love for his fellow-pilgrims, detachment from wayside allurements, tireless perseverance on the road, he is still encumbered and weakened by unnecessary luggage. The second stage of his journey, therefore, is initiated like that of Christian by a casting off of his burden : a total self-renouncement, the attainment of a Franciscan poverty of spirit whereby he becomes "Perfectly Free."

Having got rid of all impediments to the spiritual quest, he must now acquire or develop in their stead the characteristic mystical qualities, or Three Aids of the Pilgrim ; which are called in this system Attraction, Devotion, and Elevation. Attraction is consciousness of the mutual desire existing between man's spirit and the Divine Spirit : of the link of love which knits up reality and draws all things to their home in God. This is the universal law on which all mysticism is based. It is St. Augustine's "Thou hast made us for Thyself and our hearts can find no rest outside of Thee." This "natural magnetism," then, once he is aware of it, will draw the pilgrim irresistibly along the road from the Many to the One. His second aid, Devotion, says the "Remotest Aim" in a phrase of great depth and beauty, is "the prosecution of the journey *to* God and *in* God." [1] It embraces, in fact, the whole contemplative life. It

---

[1] So too Ruysbroeck says that "the just man goes *towards* God by inward love in perpetual activity and *in* God in virtue of his fruitive affection in eternal rest" ("L'Ornement des Noces Spirituelles," l. ii. cap. lxxiii.).

is the next degree of spiritual consciousness after the blind
yielding to the attraction of the Real, and the setting in order
of man's relation to his source.

The Traveller's journey *to* God is complete when he
attains knowledge of Him—"Illumination," in the language
of European mystics.   The point at which this is attained is
called the Tavern, or resting-place upon the road, where he
is fed with the Divine Mysteries.   There are also "Wine
Shops" upon the way, where the weary pilgrim is cheered and
refreshed by a draught of the wine of Divine Love.[1]   Only
when the journey *to* God is completed begins the "Journey *in*
God"—that which the Christian mystics call the Unitive Way—
and this, since it is the essence of Eternal Life, can have no end.
Elevation, the pilgrim's third aid, is the exalted or ecstatic form
of consciousness peculiar to the contemplative, and which allows
the traveller to see the spiritual city towards which he goes.[2]

The Sūfi poet 'Attar, in his mystical poem, "The Colloquy
of the Birds," has described the stages of this same spiritual
pilgrimage with greater psychological insight, as the journey
through "Seven Valleys."   The lapwing, having been asked by
other birds what is the length of the road which leads to the
hidden Palace of the King, replies that there are Seven Valleys
through which every traveller must pass : but since none who
attain the End ever come back to describe their adventures, no
one knows the length of the way.

(1) The first valley, says the lapwing, is the Valley of the
Quest.   It is long and toilsome : and there the traveller must
strip himself of all earthly things, becoming poor, bare, and
desolate : and so stay till the Supernal Light casts a ray on his
desolation.   It is, in fact, Dante's Purgatorio, the Christian Way
of Purgation : the period of self-stripping and purification which
no mystic system omits.

(2) When the ray of Supernal Light has touched the pilgrim
he enters the limitless Valley of Love : begins, that is to say, the
mystic life.   It is Dante's "Earthly Paradise," or, in the traditional system of the mystics, the onset of illumination.

[1] I need not remind the reader of the fact that this symbolism, perverted to the
purposes of his sceptical philosophy, runs through the whole of the Rubaiyat of Omar
Khayyám.
[2] See Palmer's "Oriental Mysticism," pt. i. caps. i., ii., iii., and v.

(3) Hence he passes to the Valley of Knowledge or Enlightenment—the contemplative state—where each finds in communion with Truth the place that belongs to him. No Dante student will fail to see here a striking parallel with those planetary heavens where each soul partakes of the Divine, "not supremely in the absolute sense," as St. Bonaventura has it, but "supremely in respect of *himself.*" The mystery of Being is now revealed to the traveller. He sees Nature's secret, and God in all things. It is the height of illumination.

(4) The next stage is the Valley of Sufficiency, of utter absorption in Divine Love—the Stellar Heaven of the Saints—where Duty is seen to be all in all. This leads to—

(5) The Valley of the Unity, where the naked Godhead is the one object of contemplation. This is the stage of ecstasy, or the Beatific Vision: Dante's condition in the last canto of the "Paradiso." It is transient, however, and leads to—

(6) The Valley of Amazement; where the Vision, far transcending the pilgrim's receptive power, appears to be taken from him and he is plunged in darkness and bewilderment. This is the state which Dionysius the Areopagite, and after him many mediaeval mystics, called the Divine Dark, and described as the truest and closest of all our apprehensions of the Godhead. It is the Cloud of Unknowing: "dark from excessive bright." The final stage is—

(7) The Valley of Annihilation of Self: the supreme degree of union or theopathetic state, in which the self is utterly merged "like a fish in the sea" in the ocean of Divine Love.[1]

Through all these metaphors of pilgrimage to a goal—of a road followed, distance overpassed, fatigue endured—there runs the definite idea that the travelling self in undertaking the journey is fulfilling a destiny, a law of the transcendental life; obeying an imperative need. The chosen Knights are destined or *called* to the quest of the Grail. "All men are *called* to their origin," says Rulman Merswin, and the fishes which he sees in his Vision of Nine Rocks are impelled to struggle as it were "against nature" uphill from pool to pool towards their source.[2]

[1] For the material from which I have here epitomized 'Attar's allegory of the Valleys, I am indebted to Mr. W. S. Lilly's excellent account of the Sūfi poets, in "Many Mansions," p. 130.

[2] Jundt, "Rulman Merswin," p. 27.

All mystical thinkers agree in declaring that there is a mutual attraction between the Spark of the Soul, the free divine germ in man, and the Fount from which it came forth. " We long for the Absolute," says Royce, "only in so far as in us the Absolute also longs, and seeks, through our very temporal striving, the peace that is nowhere in Time, but only, and yet Absolutely, in Eternity." [1] So, many centuries before the birth of American philosophy, Hilton put the same truth of experience in lovelier words. " He it is that desireth in thee, and He it is that is desired. He is all and He doth all if thou couldst see Him."[2]

The homeward journey of man's spirit, then, is due to the push of a divine life within answering to the pull of a divine life without.[3] It is the going of like to like, the fulfilment of a Cosmic necessity : and the mystics, in undertaking it, are humanity's pioneers on the only road to rest. Hence that attraction which the Moslem mystic discerned as the traveller's necessary aid, is a fundamental doctrine of all mysticism : and as a consequence, the symbolism of mutual desire is here inextricably mingled with that of pilgrimage. The spiritual pilgrim goes because he is called ; because he wants to go, must go, if he is to find rest and peace. " God *needs* man," says Eckhart. It is Love calling to love : and the journey, though in one sense a hard pilgrimage, up and out, by the terraced mount and the ten heavens to God, in another is the inevitable rush of the roving comet, caught at last, to the Central Sun. " My weight is my love," said St. Augustine.[4] Like gravitation, it inevitably compels, for good or evil, every spirit to its own place. According to another range of symbols, that love flings open a door, in order that the Larger Life may rush in, and it and the soul be " one thing."

---

[1] Royce, "The World and the Individual," vol. ii. p. 386.

[2] "The Scale of Perfection," bk. ii. pt. ii. cap. v.

[3] Compare Récéjac ("Fondements de la Connaissance Mystique," p. 252). " According to mysticism, morality leads the soul to the frontiers of the Absolute and even gives it an impulsion to enter, but this is not enough. This movement of pure Freedom cannot succeed unless there is an equivalent movement within the Absolute itself."

[4] Aug. Conf., bk. xiii. cap. 9. "All those who love," says Ruysbroeck, "feel this attraction ; more or less according to the degree of their love." ("De Calculo sive de Perfectione filiorum Dei." Quoted by Maeterlinck, introduction to " L'Ornement des Noces Spirituelles," p. lvi.)

Here, then, we run through the whole gamut of symbolic expression; through Transcendence, Desire, and Immanence. All are seen to point to one consummation, diversely and allusively expressed: the imperative need of union between man's separated spirit and the Real, his remaking in the interests of transcendent life, his establishment in that Kingdom which is both " near and far."

"In the book of Hidden Things it is written," says Eckhart, "'I stand at the door and knock and wait' . . . thou needst not seek Him here or there: He is no farther off than the door of the heart. There He stands and waits and waits until He finds thee ready to open and let Him in. Thou needst not call Him from a distance; to wait until thou openest is harder for Him than for thee. He needs thee a thousand times more than thou canst need Him. *Thy opening and His entering are but one moment.*" [1] " God," he says in another place, " can as little do without us, as we without Him." [2] Our attainment of the Absolute is not a one-sided ambition, but a mutual necessity. " For our natural Will," says Lady Julian, " is to have God, and the Good will of God is to have us; and we may never cease from longing till we have Him in fullness of joy." [3]

So, in the beautiful poem or ritual called the " Hymn of Jesus," contained in the apocryphal " Acts of John " and dating from primitive Christian times, the Logos, or Eternal Christ, is thus represented as matching with His own transcendent self-giving desire every need of the soul who stands with Him in the mystical circle of initiation.[4]

The Soul says :—
> " 'I would be saved.'"

Christ replies :—
> " 'And I would save.' Amen."

The Dialogue continues :—
> " 'I would be loosed.'
> 'And I would loose.' Amen.

---

[1] Meister Eckhart, Pred. iii.   [2] *Ibid.*, Pred. xiii.

[3] " Revelations of Divine Love," cap. vi.

[4] The Greek and English text will be found in the " Apocrypha Anecdota " of Dr. M. R. James, series 2 (Cambridge, 1897), pp. 1–25. I follow his translation. It will be seen that I have adopted the hypothesis of Mr. G. R. S. Mead as to the dramatic nature of this poem. See his " Echoes from the Gnosis," 1896.

'I would be pierced.'
'And I would pierce.'   Amen.
'I would be born.'
'And I would bear.'   Amen.
'I would eat.'
'And I would be eaten.'   Amen.
'I would hear.'
'And I would be heard.'   Amen."

*   *   *   *   *

"'I am a Lamp to thee who beholdest Me,
I am a Mirror to thee who perceivest Me,
I am a Door to thee, who knockest at Me,
I am a Way to thee a wayfarer.'"

The same fundamental idea of the mutual quest of the Soul and the Absolute is expressed in the terms of another symbolism by the great Mahommedan mystic :—

"No lover ever seeks union with his beloved,
But his beloved is also seeking union with him.
But the lover's love makes his body lean
While the beloved's love makes her fair and lusty.
When in *this* heart the lightning spark of love arises,
Be sure this love is reciprocated in *that* heart.
When the love of God arises in thy heart,
Without doubt God also feels love for thee."[1]

The mystic vision, then, is of a spiritual universe held tight within the bonds of love:[2] and of the free and restless human soul, having within it the spark of divine desire, the "tendency to the Absolute," only finding satisfaction and true life when united with this Life of God.   Then, in Patmore's lovely image, "the babe is at its mother's breast," "the lover has returned to the beloved."[3]

Whatever their outward sense, the mystic symbols one and all express aspects of this "secret of the world," this primal

[1] "Jelalu 'd Din" (Wisdom of the East Series), p. 77.
[2] So Dante—

"Nel suo profondo vidi che s'interna
    legato con amore in un volume
    cio che per l'universo si squaderna."
                                (Par. xxxiii. 85.)

[3] "The Rod, the Root, and the Flower," "Aurea Dicta," ccxxviii.

verity. But whereas such great visionary schemes as those of
'Attar and of Dante show it in its Cosmic form, in many other
symbols—particularly those which we meet in the writings of
the ecstatic saints—the personal subjective note, the consciousness of an individual relation between that one self and the
Supernal Self, overpowers all such general applications. Then
philosophy and formal allegory must step aside : the sacramental
language of exalted emotion, of profoundly felt experience,
takes its place. The phases of mutual love, of wooing and
combat, awe and delight—the fevers of desire, the ecstasy of
surrender—are drawn upon. "All this lovely dalliance of
private conference," in Hilton's words,[1] is made to contribute
something to the description of the great and secret drama of
the soul.

To such symbolic transcripts of intimate experience belongs
one amazing episode of the spiritual life-history which, because
it has been given immortal expression by the greatest mystical
poet of modern times, is familiar to thousands of readers who
know little or nothing of the more normal adventures incidental
to man's attainment of the Absolute. In "The Hound of
Heaven" Francis Thompson described with an almost terrible
power, not the self's quest of adored Reality, but Reality's quest
of the unwilling self. He shows to us the remorseless, tireless
seeking and following of the soul by the Divine Life to which
it will not surrender : the inexorable onward sweep of "this
tremendous Lover," hunting the separated spirit, "strange
piteous futile thing" that flees Him "down the nights and down
the days." This idea of the love-chase, of the spirit rushing in
terror from the overpowering presence of God, but followed,
sought, conquered in the end, is common to all the mediaeval
mystics : it is the obverse of their general doctrine of the
necessary fusion of human and divine life, "escape from the
flame of separation."

"I chased thee, for in this was my pleasure," says the voice
of Love to Mechthild of Magdeburg ; "I captured thee, for this
was my desire ; I bound thee, and I rejoice in thy bonds ; I
have wounded thee, that thou mayst be united to me. If I
gave thee blows, it was that I might be possessed of thee."[2]

---

[1] "The Scale of Perfection," bk. iii. cap. xv.
[2] "Das Fliessende Licht der Gottheit," pt. i. cap. iii.

So in the beautiful Middle English poem of " Quia amore langueo,"—

> " I am true love that fals was nevere,
> Mi sistyr, mannis soule, I loved hir thus ;
> Bicause we wolde in no wise discevere
> I lefte my Kyngdom glorious.
> I purveyde for hir a paleis precious ;
> She fleyth, I folowe, I soughte hir so.
> I suffride this peyne piteous
> Quia amore langueo." [1]

Meister Eckhart has the same idea of the inexorable Following Love, impossible to escape, expressed under less personal images. "Earth," he says, "cannot escape the sky ; let it flee up or down, the sky flows into it, and makes it fruitful whether it will or no. So God does to man. He who will escape Him only runs to His bosom ; for all corners are open to Him." [2]

All mystics have very strongly this sense of a mysterious spiritual life—a Reality—without, seeking man and compelling him to Its will. It is not for him, they think, to say that he will or will not aspire to the transcendental world.[3] Hence sometimes this inversion of man's long quest of God. The self resists the pull of spiritual gravitation, flees from the touch of Eternity ; and the Eternal seeks it, tracks it ruthlessly down. The Following Love, the mystics say, is a fact of experience, not a poetic idea. "Those strong feet that follow, follow after," once set upon the chase, are bound to win. Man, once conscious of Reality, cannot evade it. For a time his separated spirit, his disordered loves, may wilfully frustrate the scheme of things : but he must be conquered in the end. Then the mystic process unfolds itself inexorably : Love triumphs : the " purpose of the worlds " fulfills itself in the individual life.

II

It was natural and inevitable that the imagery of human love and marriage should have seemed to the mystic the best of

---

[1] " Quia amore langueo," an anonymous fifteenth-century poem. Printed from the Lambeth MS. by the E.E.T.S., 1866-67.

[2] Pred. lxxxviii.

[3] So we are told of St. Francis of Assisi, that in his youth he " *tried* to flee God's hand." Thomas of Celano, Legenda Prima, cap. ii.

all images of his own "fulfilment of life"; his soul's surrender, first to the call, finally to the embrace of Perfect Love. It lay ready to his hand: it was understood of all men: and, moreover, it most certainly does offer, upon lower levels, a strangely exact parallel to the sequence of states in which man's spiritual consciousness unfolds itself, and which form the consummation of the mystic life.

It has been said that the constant use of such imagery by Christian mystics of the mediaeval period is traceable to the popularity of the Song of Solomon. I think that the truth lies rather in the opposite statement: namely, that the mystic loved the Song of Solomon because he there saw reflected, as in a mirror, the most secret experiences of his soul. The sense of a desire that was insatiable, of a personal fellowship so real, inward, and intense that it could only be compared with the closest link of human love, of an intercourse that was no mere spiritual self-indulgence, but was rooted in the primal duties and necessities of life—more, those deepest, most intimate secrets of communion, those self-giving ecstasies which all mystics know, but of which we, who are not mystics, may not speak—all these he found symbolized and suggested, their unendurable glories veiled in a merciful mist, in the poetry which man has invented to honour that august passion in which the merely human draws nearest to the divine.

The great saints who adopted and elaborated this symbolism, applying it to their pure and ardent passion for the Absolute, were destitute of the prurient imagination which their modern commentators too often possess. They were essentially pure of heart; and when they "saw God" they were so far from confusing that unearthly vision with the products of morbid sexuality, that the dangerous nature of the imagery which they employed did not occur to them. They knew by experience the unique nature of spiritual love: and no one can know anything about it in any other way.

Thus for St. Bernard, throughout his deeply mystical sermons on the Song of Songs, the Divine Word is the Bridegroom, the human soul is the Bride: but how different is the effect produced by his use of these symbols from that with which he has been charged by hostile critics! In the place of that "sensuous imagery" which is so often and so earnestly deplored by those

who have hardly a nodding acquaintance with the writings of
the saints, we find images which indeed have once been
sensuous; but which are here anointed and ordained to a holy
office, carried up, transmuted, and endowed with a radiant
purity, an intense and spiritual life.

"'*Let Him kiss me with the kisses of His mouth.*' Who is it
speaks these words? It is the Bride. Who is the Bride? It
is the Soul thirsting for God. . . . She who asks this is held by
the bond of love to him from whom she asks it. Of all the
sentiments of nature, this of love is the most excellent, especially when it is rendered back to Him who is the principle and
fountain of it—that is, God. Nor are there found any expressions equally sweet to signify the mutual affection between the
Word of God and the soul, as those of Bridegroom and of Bride;
inasmuch as between individuals who stand in such relation to
each other all things are in common, and they possess nothing
separate or divided. They have one inheritance, one dwelling-
place, one table, and they are in fact one flesh. If, then,
mutual love is especially befitting to a bride and bridegroom, it
is not unfitting that the name of Bride is given to a soul which
loves." [1]

To women mystics of the Catholic Church, familiar with the
antique and poetic metaphor which called every cloistered nun
the Bride of Christ, that crisis in their spiritual history in which
they definitely vowed themselves to the service of Transcendent
Reality seemed, naturally enough, the veritable betrothal of the
soul. Often, in a dynamic vision, they saw as in a picture the
binding vows exchanged between their spirits and their God. [2]
That further progress on the mystic way which brought with
it a sharp and permanent consciousness of union with the
Divine Will, the constant sustaining presence of a Divine
Companion, became, by an extension of the original simile,
Spiritual Marriage. The elements of duty, constancy, irre-
vocableness, and loving obedience involved in the mediaeval
conception of the marriage tie, made it an apt image of a
spiritual state in which humility, intimacy, and love were the
dominant characteristics. There is really no need to seek a
pathological explanation of these simple facts. Moreover, the

[1] St. Bernard, "Cantica Canticorum," Sermon vii.
[2] *Vide infra*, pt. ii. cap. v.

descriptions of spiritual marriage which the great mystics have
left are singularly free from physical imagery.   " All that I can
say of it, and all that I understand of it," says St. Teresa, " is
that the soul, or rather the Spirit of the Soul [the divine spark,
or part], becomes one thing with God.   That He may show how
much He loves us, God, Who is also spirit, has desired to show
to certain souls how far this love can go : and this, that we may
be excited to praise His generosity.   Despite His infinite
Majesty, He condescends to unite Himself so closely to a
feeble creature, that, like those whom the sacrament of marriage
has united in an irrevocable bond, He would never again be
separated from her.   After the spiritual betrothal it is not thus :
more than once the lovers separate.   In the spiritual marriage,
on the contrary, the soul dwells always with God, in that centre
which I have described." [1]

The great Richard of St. Victor, in one of his most splendid
mystical treatises,[2] has given us perhaps the most daring and
detailed application of the symbolism of marriage to the
adventures of the spirit of man.   He divides the " steep
stairway of love," by which the contemplative ascends to union
with the Absolute, into four stages.   These he calls the betrothal,
the marriage, the wedlock, and the fruitfulness of the soul.[3]   In
the betrothal, he says, the soul " thirsts for the Beloved " ; that
is to say, it longs to experience the delights of Reality.   " The
Spirit comes to the Soul, and seems sweeter than honey."   It
is conversion, the awakening to mystical truth ; the kindling of
the passion for the Absolute.   " Then the Soul, with pertinacity
demands more " : and because of her burning desire she attains
to pure contemplation, and so passes to the second degree of
love.   In this she is " led in bridal " by the Beloved.   Ascending " above herself " in contemplation, she " sees the Sun of
Righteousness."   She is now confirmed in the mystic life ; the
irrevocable marriage vows are made between her spirit and her
God.   At this point she can " see the Beloved," but " cannot yet

---

[1] " El Castillo Interior," Moradas Sétimas, cap. ii.

" De Quatuor Gradibus Violentae Charitatis " (Migne, Patrologia Latina, vol.
cxcvi. col. 1207).

[3] " In primo gradu fit desponsatio, in secundo nuptiae, in tertio copula, in quarto
puerperium. . . . De quarto dicitur, Concepimus, et quasi parturivimus et peperimus
spiritum " (Isa. xviii. 26).   (*Op. cit.*, 1216, D.)

come in to Him," says Richard. This degree, as we shall see later, answers more or less to that which other mystics call the Illuminative Way : but any attempt to press these poetic symbols into a cast-iron series, and establish exact parallels, is foredoomed to failure, and will merely succeed in robbing them of their fragrance and suggestive power. In Richard's " third stage," however, that of union, or wedlock, it is clear that the soul enters upon the " Unitive Way." She has passed the stages of ecstatic and significant events, and is initiated into the Life. She is " deified," " passes utterly *into* God, and is glorified in Him " : is transfigured, he says, by immediate contact with the Divine Substance, into an utterly different quality of being. " Thus," says St. John of the Cross, " the soul, when it shall have driven away from itself all that is contrary to the divine will, becomes transformed in God by love." [1]

"The Soul," says Richard again, " is utterly concentrated on the One." She is " caught up to the divine light." The expression of the personal passion, the intimate relation, here rises to its height. But this is not enough. Where most mystical diagrams leave off, Richard of St. Victor's " Steep stairway of Love " goes on : with the result that this is almost the only symbolic system bequeathed to us by the great contemplatives in which all the implications contained in the idea of the spiritual marriage have been worked out to their term. He saw clearly that the union of the soul with its Source could not be a barren ecstasy. That was to mistake a means for an end ; and to frustrate the whole intention of life, which is, on all levels, fruitful and creative. Therefore he says that in the fourth degree, the Bride who has been so greatly honoured, caught up to such unspeakable delight, sinks her own will and " is humiliated below herself." She accepts the pains and duties, in the place of the raptures of love ; and becomes a source, a " parent " of fresh spiritual life. The *Sponsa Dei* develops into the *Mater Divinæ gratiæ*. That imperative need of life, to push on, to create, to spread, is here seen operating in the spiritual sphere. This forms that rare and final stage in the evolution of the great mystics, in which they return to the world which they forsook ; and there live, as it were, as centres of transcendental energy, the creators of spiritual

[1] " Subida del Monte Carmelo," l. ii. cap. v.

families, the partners and fellow-labourers with the Divine Life.[1]

III

We come now to the symbols which have been adopted by those mystics in whom temperamental consciousness of their own imperfection, and of the unutterable perfection of the Absolute Life to which they aspired, has overpowered all other aspects of man's quest of reality. The "seek, and ye shall find" of the pilgrim, the "by Love shall He be gotten and holden" of the bride, can never seem an adequate description of experience to minds of this type. They are intent on the inexorable truth which must be accepted in some form by both these classes : the crucial fact that "we behold that which we are," or, in other words, that "only the Real can know Reality." Hence the state of the inward man, the "unrealness" of him when judged by any transcendental standard, is their centre of interest. His remaking or regeneration appears to them as the primal necessity, if he is ever to obtain rights of citizenship in the "country of the soul."

We have seen that this idea of the New Birth, the remaking or transmutation of the self, clothed in many different symbols, runs through the whole of mysticism and much of theology. It is the mystic's subjective reading of those necessary psychological changes which he observes taking place within himself as his spiritual consciousness grows. His hard work of renunciation, of detachment from the things which that consciousness points out as illusory or impure, his purifications and trials, all form part of it. If that which is whole or perfect is to come, then that which is in part must be done away : "for in what measure we put off the creature, in the same measure are we able to put on the Creator : neither more nor less." [2]

Of all the symbolic systems in which this truth has been enshrined none is so complete, so picturesque, and now so little understood as that of the "Hermetic Philosophers" or Spiritual Alchemists. This fact would itself be sufficient to justify us in examining some of the chief features of their symbolism.

[1] *Vide infra*, pt. ii. caps. i. and x.
[2] "Theologia Germanica," cap. i.

There is a further excuse for this apparently eccentric proceeding, however, in the fact that the language of alchemy was largely—though not always accurately and consistently—used by the great mystic Jacob Boehme, and after him by his English disciple, William Law. Without, then, some knowledge of the terms which they employed, but seldom explained, the writings of this important school can hardly be understood.

I do not propose in this place to enter upon a long and detailed discussion of the alchemic symbols and their application to the mystic life. These symbols are full of an often deliberate obscurity, which makes their exact interpretation a controversial matter at the best. Moreover, the various authors of the Hermetic writings do not always use them in the same sense, and whilst many of these writings are undoubtedly mystical, others clearly deal with the physical quest of gold : nor have we any sure standard by which to divide class from class.

The elements from which the spiritual alchemists built up their amazing allegories of the mystic life are, however, easily grasped : and these elements, together with the significance generally attributed to them, are as much as those who are not specialists can hope to unravel from this very tangled skein. First, there are the metals, of course the obvious materials of physical alchemy. These are usually called by the names of their presiding planets : thus in Hermetic language Luna means silver, Sol gold, &c. Then there is the Vessel, or Athanor, in which the transmutation of base metal to gold took place : an object whose exact nature is veiled in much mystery. The Fire and various solvents and waters, peculiar to the different alchemistic recipes, complete the apparatus necessary to the "Great Work."

The process of this work, sometimes described in chemical, and sometimes in astrological terms, is more often than not veiled in a strange heraldic and zoological symbolism dealing with Lions, Dragons, Eagles, Vultures, Ravens and Doves : which, delightful in its picturesqueness, is unequalled in its power of confusing the anxious and unwary enquirer. It is also the subject of innumerable and deliberate allegories, which were supposed to convey its secrets to the elect, whilst most certainly concealing them from the crowd. Hence it is that the author of " A Short Enquiry concerning the Hermetic Art" speaks for all investigators of this subject when he describes the " Hermetic science " as a " great Labyrinth, in which are abundance of enquirers rambling to this day, many of them undiscerned by one another." Like him, I too "have taken several Turns in it myself, wherein one shall meet with very few ; for 'tis so large, and almost every one taking a different Path, that they seldom meet. But finding it a very melancholy place, I resolved to get out of it, and rather content myself to walk in the little garden before the entrance, where many things, though not all, were orderly to be seen. Choosing rather to stay there, and contemplate on the Metaphor set up, than venture again into the wilderness." [1]

Coming, then, to the " Contemplation of the Metaphor set up,"—by far the most judicious course for modern students of the Hermetic art—we observe first that the prime object of alchemy was held to be the production of the Philosopher's Stone; that perfect and incorrupt substance, or " noble Tincture," never found upon our imperfect earth in its natural state, which could purge all baser metals of their dross, and turn them to pure gold. The quest of the Stone, in fact, was but one aspect of man's everlasting quest of perfection, his hunger for the Absolute ; and hence an appropriate symbol of the mystic life. But this quest was not conducted in some far off transcendental kingdom. It was prosecuted in the Here and Now, amongst the ordinary things of natural life.

Gold, the Crowned King, or Sol, as it is called in the planetary symbolism of the alchemists, was their standard of perfection, the " Perfect Metal." Towards it, as the Christian towards sanctity, their wills were set. It had for them a value not sordid but ideal. Nature, they thought, is always trying to make gold, this incorruptible and perfect thing ; and the other metals are merely the results of the frustration of her original design. Nor is this aiming at perfection and achieving of imperfection limited to the physical world. *Quod superius, sicut quod inferius.* Upon the spiritual plane also they held that the Divine Idea is always aiming at " Spiritual Gold "— divine humanity, the New Man, citizen of the transcendental world—and " natural man " as we ordinarily know him is a lower metal, silver at best, a departure from the " plan " ; who

[1] " A Short Enquiry Concerning the Hermetic Art," p. 29.

yet bears within himself, if we could find it, the spark or seed of absolute perfection : the " tincture " which makes gold.   " The smattering I have of the Philosopher's Stone," says Sir Thomas Browne, "(which is something more than the perfect exaltation of gold) hath taught me a great deal of divinity, and instructed my belief how that immortal spirit and incorruptible substance of my soul may lie obscure, and sleep awhile within this house of flesh." [1]   This " incorruptible substance " is man's goldness, his perfect principle : for " the highest mineral virtue resides in Man," says Albertus Magnus, "and Gold may be found every where." [2]   Hence the prosecution of a spiritual chemistry is a proper part of the true Hermetic science.

The art of the alchemist, whether spiritual or physical, consists in completing the work of perfection, bringing forth and making dominant, as it were, the " latent goldness " which " lies obscure " in metal or man.   The ideal adept of alchemy was therefore an " auxiliary of the Eternal Goodness."   By his search for the " Noble Tincture " which should restore an imperfect world, he became a partner in the business of creation, assisting the Cosmic Plan.

The proper art of the Spiritual Alchemist, with whom alone we are here concerned, was the production of the spiritual and only valid tincture or Philosopher's Stone, the mystic seed of transcendental life which should invade, tinge, and wholly transmute the imperfect self into spiritual gold.   That this was no fancy of seventeenth-century allegorists, but an idea familiar to many of the oldest writers upon alchemy—whose quest was truly a spiritual search into the deepest secrets of the soul—is proved by the words which bring to an end the first part of the antique " Golden Treatise upon the Making of the Stone," sometimes attributed to Hermes Trismegistus.   " This, O Son," says that remarkable tract, " is the Concealed Stone of Many Colours ; which is born and brought forth in one colour ; know this and conceal it . . . it leads from darkness into light,

---

[1] " Religio Medici," pt. i.

[2] "A Suggestive Enquiry into the Hermetic Mystery," p. 143. This rare and extremely important study of spiritual alchemy was the anonymous work of the late Mrs. Atwood, who attempted to suppress it soon after publication under the impression—common amongst mystics of a certain type—that she had revealed matters which might not be spoken of. In the same way Coventry Patmore destroyed his masterpiece, " Sponsa Dei."

from this desert wilderness to a secure habitation, and from poverty and straits to a free and ample fortune." [1]

Man, then, was for the alchemists " the true laboratory of the Hermetic art "; which concealed in an entanglement of vague and contradictory symbols the life-process of his ascension to that perfect state in which he was able to meet God. This state must not be confused with a merely moral purity, but must be understood as involving utter transmutation into a " new form." It naturally followed from this that the indwelling Christ, the " Corner Stone," the Sun of Righteousness, became, for many of the Christian alchemists, identified with the *Lapis Philosophorum* and with Sol : and was regarded both as the image and as the earnest of this "great work." His spirit was the " noble tincture " which " can bring that which is lowest in the death to its highest ornament or glory," [2] transmutes the natural to the supernatural, operates the " New Birth." "This," says Boehme, "is the noble precious Stone (*Lapis Philosophorum*), the Philosopher's Stone, which the Magi (or wise men) find which *tinctureth nature*, and generateth a new son in the old. He who findeth that, esteemeth more highly of it than of this (outward) world. For the Son is many thousand times greater than the Father." Again, " If you take the *spirit* of the tincture, then indeed you go on a way in which *many have found* Sol ; but they have followed on the way to *the heart* of Sol, where the spirit of the heavenly tincture hath laid hold on *them*, and brought them into the liberty, into the Majesty, where they have *Known* the Noble Stone, *Lapis Philosophorum*, the Philosopher's Stone, and have stood amazed at man's blindness, and seen his labouring in vain. Would you fain find the Noble Stone? Behold we will show it you plain enough, if you be a *Magus*, and worthy, else you shall remain blind still : therefore fall to work thus : for it hath no more but *three numbers*. First tell from *one* till you come to the Cross, which is ten (X) . . . . and *there* lieth the *Stone* without any great painstaking, for it is pure and not defiled with any earthly nature."

" In this stone there lieth hidden, whatsoever God and the

---

[1] Quoted in " A Suggestive Enquiry into the Hermetic Mystery," p. 107. The whole of the "Golden Treatise " will be found set out in this work.

[2] Jacob Boehme, " The Threefold Life of Man," cap. iv. § 23.

Eternity, also heaven, the stars and elements contain and are able to do. There never was from eternity anything better or more precious than this, and it is offered by God and bestowed upon man ; every one may have it . . . it is in a simple form, and hath the power of the whole Deity in it." [1]

Boehme, however, is here using alchemic symbols, according to his custom, in a loose and artistic manner ; for the true Hermetic Philosopher's Stone is not something which can be found but something which must be made. The alchemists, whether their search be for a physical or a spiritual " tincture," say always that this tincture is the product of the furnace and Athanor : and further that it is composed of "three numbers" or elements, which they call Sulphur, Salt, and Mercury. These, when found, and forced into the proper combination, form the " Azoth " or " Philosopher's Egg "—the stuff or First Matter of the Great Work. Sulphur, Salt, and Mercury, however, must not be understood in too literal a sense.

"You need not look for our metallic seed among the elements," says Basil the Monk, "it need not be sought so far back. If you can only rectify the Mercury, Sulphur, and Salt (understand *those of the sages*) until the metallic spirit and body are inseparably joined together by means of the metallic soul, you thereby firmly rivet the chain of love and prepare the palace for the Coronation." [2]

Of these three ingredients, the important one is the spiritual principle, the unseizable Mercury ; which is far from being the metal which we ordinarily know by that name. The Mercury which the alchemists sought—often in strange places—is a hidden and powerful substance. They call it " Mercury of the Wise " ; and he who can discover it, they say, is on the way towards success. The reader in search of mystical wisdom already begins to be bewildered ; but if he persevere in this labyrinth of symbolism, he presently discovers—as Basil the Monk indeed hints—that the Sulphur and the Salt, or " metallic soul and body " of the spiritual chemistry, are the body and the " rational " soul or mind of man—Sulphur his earthly nature,

---

[1] Boehme, "The Threefold Life of Man," cap. vi. § 98; cap. x. §§ 3, 4 ; and cap. xiii. § 1.

[2] "The Golden Tripod of the Monk Basilius Valentinus " (The Hermetic Museum, vol. i. p. 319).

seasoned with intellectual salt. The Mercury is Spirit in its
most mystic sense, the Synteresis or holy Dweller in the Innermost, the immanent spark or Divine Principle of his life. Only
the " wise," the mystically awakened, can know this Mercury,
the agent of man's transmutation : and until it has been discovered,
brought out of the hiddenness, nothing can be done. " This
Mercury or Snowy Splendour, is a Celestial Body drawn from
the beams of the Sun and the Moon. It is the only Agent in
the world for this art." [1] It is the divine-human " spark of the
soul," the bridge between Gold and Silver, God and Man.

The Three Principles being enclosed in the vessel, or
Athanor, which is man himself, and subjected to a gentle fire
—the *Incendium Amoris*—the process of the Great Work, the
mystic transmutation of natural into spiritual man, can begin.
This work, like the ingredients which compose it, has "three
numbers " : and the first matter, in the course of its transmutation, assumes three successive colours: the Black, the White,
and the Red. These three colours are strictly analogous to the
three traditional stages of the Mystic Way : Purgation, Illumination, Union.

The alchemists call the first stage, or Blackness, Putrefaction. In it the three principles which compose the "whole
man " of body, soul and spirit, are " sublimated " till they appear
as a black powder full of corruption, and the imperfect body is
"dissolved and purified by subtle Mercury"; as man is purified by
the darkness, misery, and despair which follows the emergence
of his spiritual consciousness. As psychic uproar and disorder
seems part of the process of mental growth, so " *Solve et coagula* "
—break down that you may build up—is the watchword of the
spiritual alchemist. The " black beast," the passional element,
of the lower nature must emerge and be dealt with before anything further can be done. " There is a black beast in our
forest," says the highly allegorical " Book of Lambspring," " his
name is Putrefaction, his blackness is called the Head of the
Raven ; when it is cut off, Whiteness appears." [2] This Whiteness, the state of Luna, or Silver, the " chaste and immaculate
Queen," is the equivalent of the Illuminative Way : the highest
point which the mystic can attain short of union with the

[1] " A Short Enquiry Concerning the Hermetic Art," p. 17.
[2] " The Hermetic Museum," vol. i. p. 272.

Absolute.   This White Stone is pure, and precious ; but in it
the Great Work of man's spiritual evolution has not yet reached
its term.   That term is the attainment of the Red, the colour of
Perfection or alchemic gold ; a process sometimes called the
" Marriage of Luna and Sol "—the fusion of the human and
divine spirit.   Under this image is concealed the final secret of
the mystic life : that ineffable union of finite and infinite—that
loving reception of the inflowing vitality of God—from which
comes forth the *Magnum Opus :* deified or spiritual man.

     " This," says the author of " A Suggestive Enquiry," " is the
union supersentient, the nuptials sublime, *Mentis et Universi.* . . .
Lo ! behold I will open to thee a mystery, cries the Adept, the
bridegroom crowneth the bride of the north [*i.e.,* she who comes
out of the cold and darkness of the lower nature].   In the
darkness of the north, out of the crucifixion of the cerebral life,
when the sensual dominant is occultated in the Divine Fiat, and
subdued, there arises a Light wonderfully about the summit,
which wisely returned and multiplied according to the Divine
Blessing, is made substantial in life." [1]

     I have said, that side by side with the metallic and planetary
language of the alchemists, runs a strange heraldic symbolism
in which they take refuge when they fear—generally without
reason—that they are telling their secrets too plainly to an
unregenerate world.   Many of these heraldic emblems are used
in an utterly irresponsible manner ; and whilst doubtless con-
veying a meaning to the individual alchemist and the disciples
for whom he wrote, are, and must ever be, unintelligible to other
men.   But others are of a more general application ; and appear
so frequently in seventeenth-century literature, whether mystical
or non-mystical, that some discussion of them may well be
of use.

     Perhaps the quaintest and most celebrated of all these
allegories is that which describes the quest of the Philosopher's
Stone as the " hunting of the Green Lion." [2]   The Green Lion,
though few would divine it, is the First Matter of the Great
Work : hence, in spiritual alchemy, natural man in his whole-

     [1] " A Suggestive Enquiry," p. 354.
     [2] See " A Short Enquiry," p. 17, and " A Suggestive Enquiry," pp. 297 *et seq.*
where the rhymed Alchemic tract called "Hunting the Greene Lyon " is printed
in full.

ness—Salt, Sulphur, and Mercury in their crude state. He is called green because, seen from the transcendent standpoint, he is still unripe, his latent powers undeveloped ; and a Lion, because of his strength, fierceness, and virility. Here the common opinion that a pious effeminacy, a diluted and amiable spirituality, is the proper raw material of the mystic life, is emphatically contradicted. It is not by the education of the lamb, but by the hunting and taming of the wild intractable lion, instinct with vitality, full of ardour and courage, exhibiting heroic qualities on the sensual plane, that the Great Work is achieved. The lives of the saints enforce the same law.

> " Our lyon wanting maturitie
> Is called greene for his unripeness trust me :
> And yet full quickly he can run,
> And soon can overtake the Sun." [1]

The Green Lion, then, in his strength and wholeness is the only creature potentially able to attain Perfection. It needs the adoption and purification of all the wealth and resources of man's nature, not merely the encouragement of his transcendental tastes, if he is to overtake it and achieve the Great Work. The Kingdom of Heaven is taken by violence, not by amiable aspiration. "The Green Lion," says one alchemist, " is the priest by whom Sol and Luna are wed." In other words, the raw stuff of indomitable human nature is the means by which man is to attain union with the Absolute.

The duty of the alchemist, then, the transmuting process, is described as the hunting of the Green Lion through the forest of the sensual world. He, like the Hound of Heaven, is on a love chase down the nights and down the days.

When the lion is caught, when Destiny overtakes it, as the preliminary to the necessary taming process, its head must be cut off. This is called by the alchemists "the head of the Raven," the Crow, or the Vulture, " for its blackness." It represents the fierce and corrupt life of the passions : and its removal is that " death of the lower nature " which is the object of all asceticism—i.e. Purgation. The lion, the whole man, Humanity in its strength, is as it were "slain to the world,"

[1] *Op. cit.*

and then resuscitated ; but in a very different shape. By its
passage through this mystic death or the "putrefaction of the
Three Principles" the "colour of unripeness" is taken away.
Its taming completed, it receives wings, wherewith it may fly
up to Sol, the Perfect or Divine ; and is transmuted, say the
alchemists, into the Red Dragon. This is of course to us a
hopelessly grotesque image : but to the Hermetic philosophers,
whose sense of wonder was yet uncorrupt, it was the deeply
mystical emblem of a new, strange, and transcendental life,
powerful alike in earth and in heaven. As the angel to the
man, so was the dragon to the world of beasts : a creature of
splendour and terror, a super-brute, veritably existent if seldom
seen. We may perhaps realize something of the significance of
this symbol for the alchemic writers, if we remember how sacred
a meaning it has for the Chinese : to whom it is the traditional
emblem of free spiritual life, as the tiger represents the life of
the material plane in its intensest form. Since it is from China
that the practice of alchemy is supposed to have reached the
European world, it may yet be found that the Red Dragon is
one of the most antique and significant symbols of the Hermetic Art.

For the Spiritual Chemistry, then, the Red Dragon represents Deified Man ; whose emergence must always seem like
the birth of some monstrous and amazing creature when seen
from the standpoint of the merely natural world. With his
coming forth, the business of the alchemist, in so far as he be a
mystic, is done. Man has transcended his lower nature, has
received wings wherewith to live on higher levels of reality.
The Tincture, the latent goldness, has been found and made
dominant, the *Magnum Opus* achieved. That the true and
inward business of that Work, when stripped of its many
emblematic veils, was indeed the reordering of spiritual rather
than material elements, is an opinion which rests on a more
solid foundation than personal interpretations of old allegories
and alchemic tracts. The Norwich physician—himself deeply
read in the Hermetic science—has declared to us his own
certainty concerning it in few but lovely words. In them is
contained the true mystery of man's eternal and interior quest
of the Stone : its reconciliation with that other, outgoing quest
of "the Hidden Treasure that desires to be found."

"Do but extract from the corpulency of bodies, or resolve things beyond their First Matter, and you discover the habitation of Angels : which, if I call it the ubiquitary and omnipresent Essence of God, I hope I shall not offend Divinity." [1]

[1] Sir Thomas Browne, "Religio Medici," pt. i.

CHAPTER VII

MYSTICISM AND MAGIC

IT seems hardly necessary to examine in detail the mistakes —or, in ecclesiastical language, the heresies—into which men have been led by a feeble, a deformed, or an arrogant mystical sense. The number of such mistakes is countless; their wildness almost inconceivable to those who have not been forced to study them. Too often it has happened that the loud voices and strange declarations of their apostles have drowned the quieter accents of the orthodox.

It would seem as though the moment of puberty were far more critical in the spiritual than it is in the physical life : the ordinary dangers of adolescence being intensified when they appear upon the higher levels of consciousness. Man, becoming aware of a new power and new desires within him, abruptly subjected to the influx of new life, is dazzled and pleased by every brilliant and fantastic guess, every invitation, which is offered to him. In the condition of psychic disorder which is characteristic of his movement to new states, he is unusually at the mercy of the suggestions and impressions which he receives. Hence in every period of mystical activity we find an outbreak of occultism, illuminism, or other perverted spirituality. In the youth of the Christian Church, side by side with the great Neoplatonists, we have the arrogant and disorderly transcendentalism of the Gnostics: their attempted fusion of the ideals of mysticism and magic. During the Middle Ages and the Renaissance there is the spurious mysticism of the Brethren of the Free Spirit, the occult propaganda of Paracelsus, the Rosicrucians, the Christian Kabalists ; and the innumerable pantheistic, Manichean, mystery-making, and Quietist heresies which made war upon Catholic tradition. Usually owing their existence to the undisciplined will and imagination of some individual adventurer, these died with the death of his influence, and only the specialist in strange faiths now cares to trouble their graves.

But it is otherwise with the root idea whence these perverse activities most usually develop. This cannot be so easily dismissed, nor is it in our interest so to treat it ; for, as Reality is best defined by means of negatives, so the right doctrine is often more easily understood after a consideration of the wrong. In the case of mysticism, which deals largely with the unutterable, and where language at once exact and affirmative is particularly hard to find, such a course is almost certain to help us. Leaving therefore the specifically mystical error of Quietism until we come to the detailed discussion of the states of orison, we will consider some of those other super-normal activities of the self which we have already agreed to classify as magic :[1] and learn through them more of the hidden forces which she has at her command, the dangerous liberty which she enjoys in their regard.

The word "magic" is now out of fashion, though its spirit was never more widely diffused than at the present time. Thanks to the gradual debasement of the verbal currency, it suggests to the ordinary reader the art practised by Mr. Maskelyne. The shelf which is devoted to its literature at the London Library contains many useful works on sleight-of-

[1] *Supra,* p. 84.

hand and parlour tricks. It has dragged with it in its fall the
terrific verb "to conjure," which, forgetting that it once compelled the spirits of men and angels, is now content to produce
rabbits from top-hats. This circumstance would have little
more than philological importance, were it not that the true
adepts of modern occultism—annoyed, one supposes, by this
abuse of their ancient title—tend more and more to arrogate to
their tenets and practices the name of "Mystical Science."
Vaughan, in his rather supercilious survey of the mystics, long
ago classed all forms of white magic, alchemy, and occult
philosophy as "theurgic mysticism," [1] and, on the other side of
the shield, the occultists display an increasing eagerness to claim
the mystics as masters in their school.[2] Even the "three-fold
way" of mysticism has been adopted by them, and relabelled
"Probation, Enlightenment, Initiation." [3]

In our search for the characteristics of mysticism we have
already marked the boundary which separates it from magic :
and tried to define the true nature and intention of occult
philosophy.[4] Now, I think, we may usefully ask of magic
in its turn what it can tell us of the transcendental powers
and consciousness of man. We saw that it represented the
instinctive human "desire to know more" applied to supra-
sensible things. For good or ill this desire and the occult
sciences and magic arts which express it, have haunted
humanity from the earliest times. No student of man dare
neglect their investigation, however distasteful to his intelligence their superficial absurdities may be.

The starting-point of all magic and of all magical religion—
the best and purest of occult activities—is, as in mysticism,
man's inextinguishable conviction that there are other planes
of being than those which his senses report to him ; and its
proceedings represent the intellectual and individualistic results
of this conviction—his craving for the hidden knowledge. It
is, in the eyes of those who practise it, a *moyen de parvenir :*
not the performance of illicit tricks, but a serious and philo-

---

[1] R. A. Vaughan, "Hours with the Mystics," vol. i. bk. i. ch. v.

[2] In a list published by Papus from the archives of the Martinists, we find such
diverse name as Averroes, St. Thomas Aquinas, Vincent of Beauvais, and Swedenborg, given as followers of the occult tradition !

[3] See R. Steiner, "The Way of Initiation," p. 111.

[4] *Supra, loc. cit,*

sophic attempt to solve the riddle of the world. Its result, according to one of the best modern writers upon occult philosophy, " comprises an actual, positive, and realizable knowledge concerning the worlds which we denominate invisible, because they transcend the imperfect and rudimentary faculties of a partially developed humanity, and concerning the latent potentialities which constitute, by the fact of their latency—the interior man. In more strictly philosophical language, the Hermetic science is a method of transcending the phenomenal world and attaining to the reality which is behind phenomena." [1]

Though certain parts of this enormous claim seem able to justify themselves in experience, the whole of it cannot be admitted. The last phrase in particular is identical with the promise which we have seen to be characteristic of mysticism. It presents magic as a pathway to reality. We may as well say at once that this promise is not fulfilled ; for the apparent transcending of phenomena does not necessarily entail the attainment of the Absolute. Such an attainment must, as its first condition, meet and satisfy upon the plane of reality each activity of the self: Love, Will, and Thought. Magic at its best only satisfies two of these claimants ; and this by extending rather than escaping the boundaries of the phenomenal world. At its worst, it satisfies none. It stands for that form of transcendentalism which does abnormal things, but does not lead anywhere : and we are likely to fall victims to some kind of magic the moment that the declaration " I want to know " ousts the declaration " I want to be " from the chief place in our consciousness. The true " science of ultimates " must be a science of pure Being, for reasons which the reader is now in a position to discover for himself: but magic is merely a system whereby the self tries to assuage its transcendental curiosity by an extension of the activities of the will beyond their usual limits, obtaining by this means experimental knowledge of planes of existence usually—but inaccurately—regarded as " supernatural."

It will, no doubt, be felt by those who are not occultists that even this modified claim needs justification. Few recognize that the whole business of the true magician is not with vulgar marvels, but with transcendental matters : fewer still that this

[1] A. E. Waite, " The Occult Sciences," p. 1.

business may be prosecuted with honesty and success. The
search after hidden things has become synonymous with foolish
and disreputable deceits : and the small but faithful company
of Thrice-great Hermes is confused with the army of camp-
followers which preys upon its ranks.

Most persons who do not specialize in the eccentric sciences
are of opinion that in these days the occultist can only be said
to exist in either the commercial or the academic sense. The
Bond Street palmist may represent one class; the annotator
of improper *grimoires* the other. In neither department is the
thing supposed to be taken seriously : it is merely the means
of obtaining money or of assuaging a rather morbid curiosity.

Such a view is far from being accurate. In magic, whether
we choose to regard it as a superstition or a science, we have
at any rate the survival of a great and ancient tradition, the
true splendour and meaning of whose title should hardly have
been lost in a Christian country ; for it claims to be the
science of those Magi whose quest of the symbolic Blazing
Star brought them once, at least, to the cradle of the In-
carnate God. Its laws, and the ceremonial rites which express
those laws, have come down to us from immemorial antiquity.
They enshrine a certain definite knowledge, and a large
number of less definite theories, concerning the sensual and
supersensual worlds, and concerning powers which man,
according to occult thinkers, may develop if he will. Orthodox persons should be careful how they condemn the laws of
magic : for they unwittingly conform to many of them whenever
they go to church. All formal religion is saturated with magic.
The art of medicine will never wholly cast it off : many centuries ago it gave birth to that which we now call modern
science. It seems to possess inextinguishable life. This is
not surprising when we perceive how firmly occultism is rooted
in psychology : how perfectly it is adapted to certain perennial
characteristics of the human mind—its curiosity, its arrogance,
its love of mystery.

Magic, in its perfect and uncorrupted form, claims to be a
practical, intellectual, highly individualistic science, working
towards a declared end : that, namely, of enlarging the sphere
on which the will of man can work and obtaining experimental
knowledge of planes of being usually regarded as transcen-

dental. It is the last descendant of a long line of teaching—the whole teaching, in fact, of the mysteries of Egypt and Greece—which aims at initiating man into the secrets of knowledge, and aspires, egoistically, to an understanding of things. "In every man," says a living occultist, "there are latent faculties by means of which he can acquire for himself knowledge of the higher worlds . . . as long as the human race has existed there have always been schools in which those who possessed these higher faculties gave instruction to those who were in search of them. Such are called the occult schools, and the instruction which is imparted therein is called esoteric science or the occult teaching." [1]

These schools, at least as they exist in the present day, formulate the laws which govern occult phenomena in a manner which seems distressingly prosaic to the romantic inquirer; borrowing from physics and psychology theories of vibration, attraction, mental suggestion and subconscious activity which can be reapplied for their own purposes.

According to its modern teachers, magic is in essence simply an extension of the theory and practice of volition beyond the usual limits. The will, says the occultist, is king, not only of the House of Life, but of the universe outside the gates of sense. It is the key to "man limitless"; the true "ring of Gyges," which can control the forces of nature, known and unknown. This aspect of occult philosophy informs much of the cheap American transcendentalism which is so lightly miscalled mystical by its teachers and converts; Menticulture, "New" or "Higher Thought," and the scriptures of the so-called "New Consciousness." The ingenious authors of "Volo," "The Will to be Well," and "Just How to Wake the Solar Plexus," the seers who assure their eager disciples that by "Concentration" they may acquire not only health but also that wealth which is "health of circumstance," are no mystics. They are magicians; and teach, though they know it not, little else but the cardinal doctrines of Hermetic science, omitting only their picturesque ceremonial accompaniments. [2]

[1] Steiner, "The Way of Initiation," p. 66.
[2] See E. Towne, "Joy Philosophy" (1903) and "Just How to Wake the Solar Plexus" (1904); R. D. Stocker, "New Thought Manual" (1906) and "Soul Culture" (1905); Floyd Wilson, "Man Limitless" (1905). But the literature of the sect is enormous.

These cardinal doctrines, in fact, have varied little since their first appearance early in the world's history: though, like the doctrines of theology, they have needed re-statement from time to time. In setting them out for the enlightenment of the modern reader, I shall quote largely from the works of Eliphas Lévi; the pseudonym under which Alphonse Louis Constant, probably one of the greatest and certainly the most readable occult philosopher of the nineteenth century, offered his conclusions to the world.

Eliphas Lévi found in the old magical tradition, rehandled in the terms of contemporary thought, an adequate theory of the universe and rule of practical life. In his writings, therefore, we see the Hermetic science under its most favourable aspect—*Opus hierarchicum et Catholicum*, as he proudly calls it upon the title-page of his great " Histoire de la Magie." It is the one object of his later works to exhibit—indeed to exaggerate—its connection with true mysticism; to show that it is " Le Clef des Grands Mystères" which will open the gate of that Secret Garden on which the desire of the soul is ever set. The spectacle which he presents is that of a man of eager desires and natural intuitions, set, is is true, upon the quest of reality; but pursuing that quest by strange and twisted paths. It remains for us to examine with his help the nature of these paths and the prospects which they offer to other wayfarers.

The tradition of magic, like most other ways of escape which man has offered to his own soul, originated in the East. It was formulated, developed, and preserved by the religion of Egypt. It made an early appearance in that of Greece. It has its legendary grand master in Hermes Trismegistus, who gave to it its official name of Hermetic Science, and stands towards the magicians in much the same position as Moses occupied in the tradition of the Jews. Fragmentary writings attributed to this personage and contained in the so-called Hermetic books are the primitive scriptures of occultism: and the probably spurious Table of Emerald which is said to have been discovered in his tomb, ranks as the magician's Table of Stone. In Gnosticism, in the superb allegories of the Kabalah, in much of the ceremonial of the Christian Church—finally, in secret associations which still exist in England, France, and Germany

—all that is best and truest in the "secret wisdom" of magical tradition has wandered down the centuries. Its baser offshoots, by which it is unfortunately represented to the crowd, are but too well known and need not be particularized.

Like the world which it professes to interpret, magic has a body and a soul: an outward vesture of words and ceremonies and an inner doctrine. The outward vesture, which is all that the uninitiated are permitted to perceive, is hardly attractive to the judicious eye of common sense. It consists of a series of confusing and often ridiculous symbolic veils: of strange words and numbers, grotesque laws and ritual acts, personifications and mystifications, wrapped one about the other as if the bewilderment of impatient investigators were its one design. The outward vestures of our religious, political, and social systems—which would probably appear equally irrational to a wholly ignorant yet critical observer—offer an instructive parallel to this aspect of occult philosophy.

Stripped of these archaic formulæ, symbols, mystery-mongerings, and other adventitious trappings, magic is found to rest upon three fundamental axioms; none of which can be dismissed as ridiculous by those who listen respectfully to the amazing and ever-shifting hypotheses of fashionable psychology and physics.

(1) The first of these axioms affirms the existence of an imponderable "medium" or "universal agent," which is described as beyond the plane of our normal sensual perceptions, yet interpenetrating and binding up the material world. This agent, which is not luminous and has nothing to do with the stars, is known to the occultists by the unfortunate name of "Astral Light": a term, originally borrowed from the Martinists by Eliphas Lévi, to which the religious rummage-sales of current theosophy have since given a familiarity which treads upon the margin of contempt. To live in conscious communication with the "Astral Light" is to live upon the "Astral Plane," or in the Astral World: to have risen, that is to say, to a new level of consciousness. The education of the occultist is wholly directed towards this end.

This doctrine of the Astral Plane, like most of our other diagrams of the transcendent, possesses not only a respectable ancestry, but also many prosperous relations in the world of

philosophic thought.   Traces of it may even be detected under
veils in the more recent speculations of orthodox physics.   It is
really identical with the " Archetypal World " or *Yesod* of the
Kabalah—the " Perfect Land " of old Egyptian religion—in
which exist the true or spirit forms of all created things.
Perhaps it is connected with the "real world" described by
such visionaries as Boehme and Blake.   A persistent tradition
as to the existence of such a plane of being or of consciousness
is found all over the world : in Indian, Greek, Egyptian, Celtic,
and Jewish thought.   "Above this visible nature there exists
another, unseen and eternal, which, when all things created
perish, does not perish," says the Bhagavad Gita.   According to
the Kabalists it is "the seat of life and vitality, and the
nourishment of all the world." [1]   Vitalism might accept it as
one of those aspects of the universe which can be perceived by
a more extended rhythm than that of normal consciousness.
Various aspects of it have been identified with the "Burning
Body of the Holy Ghost" of Christian Gnosticism and with the
Odic force of the old-fashioned spiritualists.

According to the doctrine of magic the Astral Plane
constitutes the "Cosmic Memory," where the images of all
beings and events are preserved, as they are preserved in the
memory of man.

"The high that proved too high, the heroic for earth too hard,
   The passion that left the ground to lose itself in the sky"—

all are living in the Astral World.   There too the concepts of
future creation are present in their completeness in the Eternal
Now, before being brought to birth in the material sphere.   On
this theory prophecy, and also clairvoyance—one of the great
objects of occult education—consists in opening the eyes of the
mind upon this timeless Astral World: and spiritualists, evoking
the phantoms of the dead, merely call them up from the
recesses of universal instead of individual remembrance.   The
reader who feels his brain to be whirling amidst this medley
of solemn statement and unproven fairy tale must remember
that at best the dogmatic part of the occult tradition can only

[1] A. E. Waite, " Doctrine and Literature of the Kabalah," p. 48.

represent the attempt of an extended consciousness to find an
explanation of its own experiences.

Further, in its strictly undenominational form, the Astral
Light is first cousin to the intangible ether beloved of Sir Oliver
Lodge and other transcendental physicists. In it our whole
selves—not merely our sentient selves—are bathed ; and here
again we are reminded of Vitalism, with its unresting River of
Life. Hence in occult language the all-penetrating Astral is a
" universal agent " : the possible vehicle of hypnotism, telepathy,
clairvoyance, and all those supernormal phenomena which
science has taken out of the hands of the occultists and re-
named metapsychic. This hypothesis also accounts for the
confusing fact of an initial similarity of experience in many
of the proceedings of mystic and occultist. Both must pass
through the plane of consciousness which the concept of the
" Astral " represents, because this plane of perception is the one
which lies " next beyond " our normal life. The transcendental
faculties, once they are freed, become aware of this world : only,
in the case of the mystic, to pass through it as quickly as they
can. The occultist, on the contrary, is willing to rest in the
"Astral" and develop his perceptions of this aspect of the world.
It is the medium in which he works.

From the earliest times, occult philosophy has proclaimed its
knowledge of this medium : always describing its existence as a
scientific fact, outside the range of our normal senses, but susceptible of verification by the trained powers of the initiate.
The possessor of such trained powers, not the wizard or the
fortune-teller, is to be regarded as the true magician : and it is
the first object of occult education, or initiation, to actualize this
supersensual plane of experience, to give the student the power
of entering into conscious communion with it, and teach him to
impose upon its forces the directive force of his own will, as
easily as he imposes that will upon the " material " things of
sense.[1]

(2) This brings us to the second axiom of magic, which also
has a curiously modern air : for it postulates simply the limitless power of the disciplined human will. This dogma has been
" taken over " without acknowledgment from occult philosophy

[1] For a more detailed discussion of this subject the reader is referred to Steiner's
exceedingly curious and interesting little book, " The Way of Initiation."

to become the trump card of menticulture, "Christian Science," and "New Thought." The preachers of "Joy Philosophy," and other dilute forms of mental discipline, are the true priests of transcendental magic in the modern world.[1]

The first lesson of the would-be magus is self-mastery. "By means of persevering and gradual athletics," says Eliphas Lévi, "the powers of the body can be developed to an amazing extent. It is the same with the powers of the soul. Would you govern yourself and others? Learn how to will. How may one learn how to will? This is the first secret of magical initiation; and it was to make the foundations of this secret thoroughly understood that the antique keepers of the mysteries surrounded the approach to the sanctuary with so many terrors and illusions. They did not believe in a will until it had given its proofs; and they were right. Strength cannot prove itself except by conquest. Idleness and negligence are the enemies of the will; and this is the reason why all religions have multiplied their practices and made their cults difficult and minute. The more trouble one gives oneself for an idea, the more power one acquires in regard to that idea. . . . Hence the power of religions resides entirely in the inflexible will of those who practise them."[2]

In its essence, then, magical initiation is a traditional form of mental discipline, strengthening and focussing the will. By it, some of those powers of apprehension which lie below the threshold of ordinary consciousness are liberated, and enabled to report their discoveries to the active and sentient mind. This discipline, like that of the religious life, consists partly in physical austerities and in a deliberate divorce from the world, partly in the cultivation of will-power: but largely in a yielding of the mind to the influence of suggestions which have been selected and accumulated in the course of ages because of their power over that imagination which Eliphas Lévi calls "The eye of the soul." There is nothing supernatural about it. Like the more arduous, more disinterested self-training of the mystic, it is character-building with an object, conducted upon an heroic

[1] Compare the following: "Imagine that all the world and the starry hosts are waiting, alert and with shining eyes, to do your bidding. Imagine that you are to touch the button now, and instantly they will spring to do the rest. The instant you say, "*I can and I will*," the entire powers of the universe are to be set in motion" (E. Towne, "Joy Philosophy," p. 52).

[2] "Rituel de la Haute Magie," pp. 35, 36.

scale. In magic the "will to know" is the centre round which
the personality is rearranged. As in mysticism, subconscious
factors are dragged from the hiddenness to form part of that
personality. The uprushes of thought, the abrupt intuitions
which reach us from the subliminal region, are developed,
ordered, and controlled by rhythms and symbols which have
become traditional because the experience of centuries has
proved, though it cannot explain, their efficacy.

"The fundamental principle," says A. E. Waite, speaking of
occult evocations, "was in the exercise of a certain occult force
resident in the magus and strenuously exerted for the establishment of such a correspondence between two planes of nature as
would effect his desired end. This exertion was termed the
evocation, conjuration, or calling of the spirit, but *that which in
reality was raised was the energy of the inner man ;* tremendously
developed and exalted by combined will and aspiration, this
energy germinated by sheer force a new intellectual faculty of
sensible psychological perception. To assist and stimulate this
energy into the most powerful possible operation, artificial
means were almost invariably used. . . . The synthesis of these
methods and processes was called Ceremonial Magic, which in
effect was a tremendous forcing-house of the latent faculties of
man's spiritual nature." [1]

This is the psychological explanation of those apparently
absurd rituals of preparation, doctrines of signs and numbers,
pentacles, charms, angelical names, the "power of the word"
and all the rest, which go to make up ceremonial magic. The
power of such artifices is known amongst the Indian mystics,
who, recognizing in the *Mantra,* or occult and rhythmic formula,
consciously held and repeated, an invaluable help to the attainment of the true ecstatic states, are not ashamed to borrow them
from the magicians. So, too, the modern American schools of
mental healing and New Thought recommend concentration
upon a carefully selected word as the starting-point of efficacious
meditation. This fact of the enormous psychical effect of
certain verbal combinations, when allowed to dominate the field
of consciousness, is the practical reason of that need of a formal
liturgy which is felt by nearly every great religion : for religion,
on its ceremonial side, is always largely magical. It, too, seeks

[1] "The Occult Sciences," p. 14.

by artificial means to stimulate latent energies. The true magic "word" or spell is untranslatable; because its power resides only partially in that outward sense which is apprehended by the reason, but chiefly in the rhythm, which is addressed to the subliminal mind. Did the Catholic Church choose to acknowledge a law long known to the adepts of magic, she has here an explanation of that instinct which has caused her to cling so strenuously to a Latin liturgy, much of whose amazing and truly magic power would evaporate were it translated into the vulgar tongue. Symbols, religious and other, and symbolic acts which appear meaningless when judged by the intellect alone, perform a similar office. They express the deep-seated instinct of the human mind that it must have a focus on which to concentrate its volitional powers, if those powers are to be brought to their highest state of efficiency. The nature of the focus matters little: its office matters much. I give a short extract from the "Rituel de la Haute Magie," which sufficiently exhibits Lévi's opinion on this subject. Many of its phrases might be fresh from the pen of the newest American psychologist.

". . . All these figures, and acts analogous to them, all these dispositions of numbers and of characters [*i.e.* sacred words, charms, pentacles, &c.] are, as we have said, but instruments for the education of the will, of which they fix and determine the habits. They serve also to concentrate in action all the powers of the human soul, and to strengthen the creative power of the imagination. . . . A practice, even though it be superstitious and foolish, may be efficacious because it is a realization of the will. . . . We laugh at the poor woman who denies herself a ha'porth of milk in the morning, that she may take a little candle to burn upon the magic triangle in some chapel. But those who laugh are ignorant, and the poor woman does not pay too dearly for the courage and resignation which she thus obtains. The wise pass proudly by shrugging their shoulders. They attack superstition with a clamour which shakes the world: and what happens? The houses which they build fall down, and their debris are re-sold to the providers and purchasers of little candles; who willingly allow it to be said that their power is at an end, since they know that their reign is eternal." [1]

---

[1] "Rituel de la Haute Magie," p. 71.

Magic symbols, therefore, from penny candles to Solomon's seal, fall, in modern technical language, into two classes. The first contains instruments of self-suggestion, exaltation, and will direction. To this belong all spells, charms, rituals, perfumes : from the magician's vervain wreath to the "Youth! Health! Strength!" which the student of New Thought repeats when she is brushing her hair in the morning. The second class contains *autoscopes* : *i.e.*, material objects which focus and express the subconscious perceptions of the operator. The dowser's divining rod, fortune-teller's cards, and crystal-gazer's ball, are characteristic examples. Both kinds are rendered necessary rather by the disabilities of the human than by the peculiarities of the superhuman plane : and the great adept, like the great saint, may attain heights at which he can entirely dispense with these "outward and visible signs." "Ceremonies being, as we have said, artificial methods of creating certain habits of the will, they cease to be necessary when these habits have become fixed."[1] This is a point at which the history of magic lights up for us certain peculiarities in the history of mysticism.

These facts, now commonplaces of psychology, have been known and used by students of magic for countless generations. Those who decry the philosophy because of the apparent absurdity of its symbols and ceremonies should remember that the embraces, gestures, grimaces, and other ritual acts by which we all concentrate, liberate, or express love, wrath, or enthusiasm, will ill endure the cold revealing light of a strictly rational inquiry.

(3) To the two dogmas of the "Astral Light" or universal agent and the "power of the will" there is to be added a third : the doctrine of Analogy, or implicit correspondence between appearance and reality, the microcosm of man and the macrocosm of the universe, the seen and the unseen worlds. In this, occultism finds the basis of all its transcendental speculations. *Quod superius sicut quod inferius*—the first words of that Emerald Table which was once attributed to Hermes Trismegistus himself—is an axiom which must be agreeable to all Platonists. It plays an enormous part in the theory of mysticism, which has always assumed that the path of the individual soul towards loving union with the Absolute is

[1] "Rituel de la Haute Magie," p. 139.

strictly analogous with the path on which the universe moves to its consummation in God.

The notion of analogy ultimately determines the religious concepts of every race, and resembles the verities of faith in the breadth of its application : for it embraces alike the appearances of the visible world—which thus become the mirrors of the invisible—the symbols of religion, the tiresome arguments of Butler's " Analogy," the sublime allegories of the Kabalah and the spiritual alchemists, and that childish " doctrine of signatures" on which much of mediaeval science was built.

" Analogy," says Lévi,[1] " is the last word of science and the first word of faith . . . the *sole possible mediator* between the visible and the invisible, between the finite and the infinite." Here Magic clearly defines her own limitations ; stepping incautiously from the useful to the universal, and laying down a doctrine which no mystic could accept—which, carried to its logical conclusion, would turn the adventure of the infinite into a guessing game.

" Analogy," he says again—and this time, perhaps, with more propriety—" is the key of all the secrets of nature : . . . this is why religions seem to be written in the heavens and in all nature : this must be so, for the work of God is the book of God, and in that which he writes one should see the expression of his thought and consequently of his Being, since we conceive of him only as Supreme Thought."[2] Here we have a hint of that idealistic element which is implicit in occultism : as even the wildest heresies retain traces of the truths which they pervert.

The argument by analogy is carried by the occultists to lengths which can hardly be set down in this place. Armed with this torch, they explore the darkest, most terrible mysteries of life : and do not hesitate to cast the grotesque shadows of these mysteries upon the unseen world. The principle of correspondence is no doubt a sound one, so long as it works within reasonable limits. It was admitted into the system of the Kabalah, though that astute philosophy was far from giving to it the importance which it assumes in Hermetic science. It has been accepted eagerly by many of the mystics. Boehme and Swedenborg gladly availed themselves of its method in presenting their intuitions to the world. It is implicitly ac-

[1] " Dogme de la Haute Magie," p. 361 *et seq.*   [2] *Ibid.*, p. 363.

knowledged by thinkers of innumerable other schools : its influence permeates the best periods of literature. Sir Thomas Browne spoke for more than himself when he said, in a well-known passage of the " Religio Medici " : " The severe schools shall never laugh me out of the philosophy of Hermes [*i.e.*, Trismegistus] that this visible world is but a picture of the invisible, wherein, as in a portrait, things are not truly but in equivocal shapes, and as they counterfeit some real substance in that invisible framework." Such a sense of analogy, whatever the " severe schools " may say, is the foundation of every perfect work of art. " Intuitive perception of the hidden analogies of things," says Hazlitt in " English Novelists," " or, as it may be called, his *instinct of the imagination*, is perhaps what stamps the character of genius on the productions of art more than any other circumstance."

The central doctrine of magic may now be summed up thus :—

(1) That a supersensible and real "cosmic medium " exists, which interpenetrates, influences, and supports the tangible and apparent world, and is amenable to the categories both of philosophy and of physics.

(2) That there is an established analogy and equilibrium between the real and unseen world, and the illusory manifestations which we call the world of sense.

(3) That this analogy may be discerned, and this equilibrium controlled, by the disciplined will of man, which thus becomes master of itself and of fate.

We must now examine in more detail the third of these propositions—that which ascribes abnormal powers to the educated and disciplined will : for this assumption lies at the root of all magical practices, alike of the oldest and the newest schools. " Magical operations," says Eliphas Lévi, " are the exercise of a power which is natural, but superior to the ordinary powers of nature. They are the result of a science, and of habits, which exalt the human will above its usual limits."[1] This power of the will is daily gaining recognition in the camps of science, as the chief factor in religion and in therapeutics—the healing of the body and the healing of the soul —for our most advanced theories on these subjects are little more

[1] " Rituel de la Haute Magie," p. 32.

than the old wine of magic in new bottles. The accredited psychological theory of religious "experience," for instance, rests upon the hypothesis that by self-suggestion, by a deliberate cultivation of the "will-to-believe," and similar means, it is possible to shift the threshold of consciousness, and to exhibit those supernormal perceptions which are variously attributed to inspiration and to disease. This is exactly what ceremonial magic professes, in milder and more picturesque language, to do for her initiates: and all such deliberate processes of conversion are, on their psychological side, the results of an involuntary obedience to the laws of Hermetic science. The ancient occultists owed much of their power, and also of their evil reputation, to the fact that they were psychologists before their time.

Recipes for the alteration and exaltation of personality and for the enhancement of will-power, the artificial production of photisms, automatisms, and ecstasy, with the opening up of the subliminal field which accompanies these phenomena—concealed from the profane by a mass of confusing allegories and verbiage—form the backbone of all genuine occult rituals. Their authors were perfectly aware that ceremonial magic has no objective importance, but depends solely on its effect upon the operator's mind. In order that this effect might be enhanced, it was given an atmosphere of sanctity and mystery; its rules were strict, its higher rites difficult of attainment. It constituted at once a test of the student's earnestness and a veil which guarded the sanctuary from the profane. The long and difficult preparations, majestic phrases, and strange ceremonies of an evocation had power, not over the spirit of the dead, but over the consciousness of the living, who was thus caught up from the world of sense to a new plane of perception. For him, not for unknown Powers, were these splendours and these arts displayed. The *rationale* of the evocation of an angel consists, not in summoning spirits from afar, but in opening the operator's eyes upon angels who are always there.

"When the spiritual exaltation of the Magus has been accomplished by . . . various ceremonial practices, the spirit is, in magical language, compelled to appear. That is to say, the operator has passed into a condition when it would be as impossible for a spirit to remain invisible to him as for an ordinary mortal to conceal itself from our common sight, without any intervening shelter, in the blaze of a noonday sun."[1] Thus the whole education of the genuine occult student tends to awaken in him a new view and a new attitude. It adjusts the machinery of his cinematograph to the registering of new intervals in the stream of things, which passed it by before ; and thus introduces new elements into that picture by which ordinary men are content to know and judge the—or rather *their*—universe.

" In the end," says Steiner, with the usual exaggeration of the professional occultist, " it all resolves itself into the fact that man, ordinarily, carries body, soul, and spirit about with him, yet is conscious only of the body, not of the soul and spirit ; and that the student attains to a similar consciousness of soul and spirit also."[2]

So much for the principles which govern occult education. Magic therapeutics, or as it is now called, " mental healing," is but the application of these principles upon another plane. It results, first, from a view of humanity which sees a difference only of degree between diseases of body and of soul, and can state seriously and in good faith that " moral maladies are more contagious than physical, and there are some triumphs of infatuation and fashion which are comparable to leprosy or cholera."[3] Secondly, it is worked by that enhancement of will power, that ability to alter and control weaker forms of life, which we have seen to be the reward of the occult discipline. " All the power of the occult healer lies in his conscious will and all his art consists in producing faith in the patient."[4]

This simple truth was in the possession of the magi at a time when Church and State saw no third course between the burning or beatification of its practitioners. Now, under the polite names of mental hygiene, suggestion, and therapeutics, it is steadily advancing to the front rank of medical shibboleths. Yet it is still the same " magic art " which has been employed for centuries, with varying ritual accompaniments, by the adepts

---

[1] A. E. Waite, "The Occult Sciences," p. 32.
[2] "The Way of Initiation," p. 142.
[3] " Dogme de la Haute Magie," p. 129.
[4] " Rituel," p. 312.

of occult science. The methods of Brother Hilarian Tissot, who is described as curing lunacy and crime by "the unconscious use of the magnetism of Paracelsus," who attributed his cases "either to disorder of the will or to the perverse influence of external wills," and would "regard all crimes as acts of madness and treat the wicked as diseased," [1] anticipated the discoveries of Charcot and Janet.

But in spite of the consistent employment by all the great adepts of their "occult" or supernormal power in the healing and the prevention of disease, on its philosophic side magic, like Christianity, combines a practical policy of pity for the maimed, halt, and blind, with a creed of suffering and renunciation. Here it joins hands with mysticism and proclaims its belief in pain as the schoolmaster of every spirit which desires to transcend the life of sense. Eliphas Lévi, whilst advising the initiate whose conscious will has reached its full strength to employ his powers in the alleviation of pain and prolongation of life, laughs at the student who seeks in magic a method of escaping suffering or of satisfying his own selfish desires. None, he says, knows better than the true magician that suffering is of the essence of the world plan. Only those who face it truly live. "Alas for the man who will not suffer! He will be crushed by griefs." [2] Again—perhaps his finest utterance— "To learn to suffer and to learn to die ; this is the gymnastic of Eternity, the noviciate of immortal life." [3]

Here, then, is the pure theory of magic. It is seen at its best in Eliphas Lévi's works ; because he was, in many respects, greater than the system which he preached. Towards the close of his life the defective and limited nature of that system became clear to him, and in his latest writings he makes no secret of this fact. The chief of these defects is the peculiar temper of mind, the cold intellectual arrogance, the intensely individual point of view which occult studies seem to induce by their conscious quest of exclusive power and knowledge, their implicit neglect of love. At bottom, every student of occultism is striving towards a point at which he may be able to "touch the button " and rely on the transcendental world "springing to do the rest." In this hard-earned acquirement of power over the

[1] "Dogme," p. 134.   [2] "Histoire de la Magie," p. 36.   [3] Ibid., p. 147.

Many, he tends to forget the One. In Lévi's words, " Too deep a study of the mysteries of nature may estrange from God the careless investigator, in whom mental fatigue paralyses the ardours of the heart." [1] When he wrote this sentence Lévi stood, as the greater occultists have often done, at the very frontiers of mysticism. The best of the Hermetic philosophers, indeed, are hardly ever without such mystical hankerings, such flashes of illumination ; as if the transcendental powers of man, once roused from sleep, cannot wholly ignore the true end for which they were made.

In Lévi's case, as is well known, the discord between the occult and mystical ideals was resolved by that return to the Catholic Church which has always amazed and sometimes annoyed his commentators. Characteristically, he " read into " Catholicism much that the orthodox would hardly allow ; so that it became for him, as it were, a romantic gloss on the occult tradition. He held that the Christian Church, nursing mother of the mystics, was also the heir of the magi ; and that popular piety and popular magic veiled the same ineffable truths.

He had more justification than at first appears probable for this apparently wild and certainly heretical statement. Religion, as we have seen, can never entirely divorce herself from magic : for her rituals and sacraments, whatever explanations of their efficacy may be offered by their official apologists, have, and must have if they are to be successful in their appeal to the mind, a magical character. All persons who are naturally drawn towards the ceremonial aspect of religion, are really devotees of the higher magic : are acknowledging the strange power of subtle rhythms, symbolic words and movements, over the human will. An " impressive service " conforms exactly to the description which I have already quoted of a magical rite : it is " a tremendous forcing-house of the latent faculties of man's spiritual nature." Sacraments, too, however simple their beginnings, always tend, as they evolve, to assume upon the phenomenal plane a magical aspect. Those who have observed with understanding, for instance, the Roman rite of baptism, with its spells and exorcisms, its truly Hermetic employment of salt, anointing chrism and ceremonial lights, must have seen in

[1] " Histoire de la Magie," p. 514.

it a ceremony far nearer to the operations of white magic than to the simple lustrations practised by St. John the Baptist.

There are obvious objections to the full working out of this subject in a book which is addressed to readers of all shades of belief; but any student who is interested in this branch of religious psychology may easily discover for himself the numerous and well-marked occult elements in the liturgies of the Christian—or indeed of any other—Church. There are invocative arrangements of the Names of God which appear alike in *grimoire* and in Missal; sacred numbers, ritual actions, perfumes, purifications, words of power, hold as important a place in religion as in magic. In certain minor observances, and charm-like prayers, we seem to stand on the very border-land between magician and priest.

It is inevitable that this should be so. The business of the Church is to appeal to the whole man, as she finds him living in the world of sense. She would hardly be adequate to this task did she neglect the powerful weapons which the occult tradition has put into her hand. She knows, implicitly, that only under those ecstatic conditions which it is the very object of magic to induce, can normal man open his door upon the Infinite, and let those subconscious powers which are the media of all our spiritual experiences emerge and peep for a moment upon the transcendental world. She, who takes the simplest and most common gifts of nature and transmutes them into heavenly food, takes also every discovery which the self has made concerning its own potentialities, and turns them to her own high ends. Founding her external system on sacraments and symbols, on rhythmic invocations and ceremonial acts of praise, insisting on the power of the pure and self-denying will and the "magic chain" of congregational worship, she does but join hands with those Magi whose gold, frankincense, and myrrh were the first gifts that she received.

But she pays for this. She shares the limitations of the system which her Catholic nature has compelled her to absorb. It is true, of course, that she purges it of all its baser elements —its arrogance, its curiosity—true also that she is bound to adopt it because it is the highest common measure which she can apply to the spirituality of that world to which she is sent. But she cannot—and her great teachers have always known that she cannot—extract finality from a method which does not really seek after ultimate things. This method may and does teach men goodness, gives them happiness and health. It can even induce in them a certain exaltation in which they become aware, at any rate for a moment, of the existence of a transcendental world—a stupendous accomplishment. But it will never of itself make them citizens of that world : give to them the freedom of Reality.

" The work of the Church in the world," says Patmore, " is not to teach the mysteries of life, so much as to persuade the soul to that arduous degree of purity at which God Himself becomes her teacher. The work of the Church ends when the knowledge of God begins." [1] Thus in spite of persistent efforts to the contrary, there will always be an inner and an outer Church : the inner Church of the mystics who *know*, the outer Church which, operating beneficently it is true, but—roughly speaking—upon the magical plane, only *knows about*. The New Testament is not without its reminders that this was bound to be the case.[2]

---

[1] "The Rod, the Root, and the Flower," " Knowledge and Science," xxii.
[2] See, amongst other passages, Matt. xiii. 11, 1 Cor. ii. 6, and iii. 1.

PART TWO

THE MYSTIC WAY

"As the Pilgrim passes while the Country permanent remains
So Men pass on; but the States remain permanent for ever."

BLAKE, "Jerusalem."

CHAPTER I

INTRODUCTORY

Our object is to describe the normal development of mystic consciousness—Its difficulty—Mystics differ enormously from one another—No one mystic completely typical— A "composite portrait" necessary — Its characteristics — The developing mystic consciousness oscillates between pain and pleasure states—Its growth is a continuous transcendence—Five great stages: 1. Awakening or Conversion ; 2. Self-knowledge or Purgation ; 3. Illumination ; 4. Surrender, or the Dark Night ; 5. Union—Distinction between Union and Ecstasy—Unitive Life the goal of the Mystic Way—Annihilation of Self the end of Oriental Mysticism—Christian Mysticism denies this interpretation of Union—Finds in it the enhancement not the suppression of life—The Divine Dark—The true Unitive Life active—A state of Divine Fecundity—The "great actives"—Their dual character of action and fruition—St. Catherine of Siena—The proper end of the Mystic Way is Deification

WE are now to turn from general principles and study those principles in action : to describe the psychological process, or "Mystic Way," by which that peculiar type of personality which is able to set up direct relations with the Absolute is usually developed. The difficulty of this description will lie in the fact that all mystics differ one from another ; as all the individual objects of our perception, "living" and "not living," do. The creative impulse in the world, so far as we are aware of it, appears upon ultimate analysis to be free and original, not bound and mechanical : to express itself, in defiance of the determinists, with a certain artistic spontaneity. Man, when he picks out some point of likeness as a basis on which to arrange its productions in groups, is not discovering its methods ; but merely making for his own convenience an arbitrary choice of one or two—not necessarily characteristic—qualities, which happen to appear in a certain number of different persons or things. Hence the most scientific classification is a rough-and-ready business at the best.

When we come to apply such a classification to so delicate and elusive a series of psychological states as those which accompany the "contemplative life," all the usual difficulties seem to be enormously increased. No one mystic can be discovered in whom all the observed characteristics of the transcendental consciousness are resumed, and who can on that account be treated as typical. Mental states which are distinct and mutually exclusive in one case, exist simultaneously in another. In some, stages which have been regarded as essential are entirely omitted: in others, their order appears to be reversed. We seem at first to be confronted by a group of selves which arrive at the same end without obeying any general law.

Take, however, a number of such definitely mystical selves and make of them, so to speak, a "composite portrait": as anthropologists do when they wish to discover the character of a race. From this portrait we may expect a type to emerge, in which all the outstanding characteristics contributed by the individual examples are present together, and minor variations are suppressed. Such a portrait will of course be conventional: but it will be useful as a standard, which can be constantly compared with, and corrected by, isolated specimens.

The first thing we notice about this composite portrait is that the typical mystic seems to move towards his goal through a series of strongly marked oscillations between "states of pleasure" and "states of pain." The existence and succession of these states—sometimes broken and confused, sometimes crisply defined—can be traced, to a greater or less degree, in almost every case of which we possess anything like a detailed record. *Gyrans gyrando vadit spiritus.* The soul, as it treads the ascending spiral of its road towards reality, experiences alternately the sunshine and the shade. These experiences are "constants" of the transcendental life. "The Spiritual States of the Soul are all Eternal," said Blake, with the true mystical genius for psychology.[1]

The complete series of these states—and it must not be forgotten that few individuals present them all in perfection, whilst in many instances several are blurred or appear to be completely suppressed—will be, I think, most conveniently

[1] "Jerusalem," pt. iii.

arranged under five heads. This method of grouping means, of course, the abandonment of the time-honoured threefold division of the Mystic Way, and the apparent neglect of St. Teresa's equally celebrated Seven Degrees of Contemplation; but I think that we shall gain more than we lose by adopting it. The groups, however, must be looked upon throughout as diagrammatic, and only as answering loosely and generally to experiences which seldom present themselves in so rigid and unmixed a form. These experiences, largely conditioned as they are by surroundings and by temperament, exhibit all the variety and spontaneity which are characteristic of life in its highest manifestations : and, like biological specimens, they lose something of their essential reality in being prepared for scientific investigation. Taken all together, they constitute one continuous process of transcendence : the movement of consciousness from lower to higher levels of reality, the steady remaking of character in accordance with the "independent spiritual world." But as the study of physical life is made easier for us by an artificial division into infancy, adolescence, maturity, and old age, so a discreet indulgence of the human passion for map-making will materially increase our chances of understanding the nature of the Mystic Way.

Here, then, is the somewhat arbitrary classification under which we shall study the phases of the mystical life.

(1) The awakening of the Self to consciousness of the Absolute. This experience, usually abrupt and well-marked, is accompanied by intense feelings of joy and exaltation.

(2) The Self, aware for the first time of Divine Beauty, realizes by contrast its own finiteness and imperfection, the manifold illusions in which it is immersed, the immense distance which separates it from the One. Its attempts to eliminate by discipline and mortification all that stands in the way of its progress towards union with God constitute *Purgation* : a state of pain and effort.

(3) When by Purgation the Self has become detached from the "things of sense," and acquired the "ornaments of the spiritual marriage," its joyful consciousness of the Absolute returns in an enhanced form. Like the prisoners in Plato's "Cave of Illusion," it has awakened to knowledge of Reality, has struggled up the harsh and difficult path to the mouth

of the cave. Now it looks upon the sun. This is *Illumination*: a state which includes in itself many of the stages of contemplation, "degrees of orison," visions and adventures of the soul described by St. Teresa and other mystical writers. These form, as it were, a way within the Way: a *moyen de parvenir*, a training devised by experts which will strengthen and assist the mounting soul. They stand, so to speak, for education ; whilst the Way proper represents organic growth. Illumination is the "contemplative state" *par excellence.* It forms, with the two preceding states, the "first mystic life." Many mystics never go beyond it ; and, on the other hand, many seers and artists not usually classed amongst them, have tasted, to some extent, the splendours of the illuminated state. It entails a vision of the Absolute : a sense of the Divine Presence : but not true union with it. It is a state of happiness.

(4) In the development of the great and strenuous seekers after God, this is followed — or sometimes intermittently accompanied—by the most terrible of all the experiences of the Mystic Way : the last and most complete purification of the Self, which is called by some contemplatives the "Mystic pain" or "Mystic death," by others the *Dark Night of the Soul.* The consciousness which had, in Illumination, sunned itself in the sense of the Divine Presence, now suffers under an equally intense sense of the Divine Absence : learning to dissociate the personal satisfaction of mystical vision from the reality of mystical life. As in Purgation the senses were cleansed and humbled, and the energies and interests of the Self were concentrated upon transcendental things : so now the purifying process is extended to the very centre of I-hood, the will. The human instinct for personal happiness must be killed. This is the "spiritual crucifixion" so often described by the mystics : the great desolation in which the soul seems abandoned by the Divine. The Self now surrenders itself, its individuality, and its will, completely. It desires nothing, asks nothing, is utterly passive, and is thus prepared for

(5) *Union*: the true goal of the mystic quest. In this state the Absolute Life is not merely perceived and enjoyed by the Self, as in Illumination : but is *one* with it. This is

the end towards which all the previous oscillations of consciousness have tended. It is a state of equilibrium, of purely
spiritual life; characterized by peaceful joy, by enhanced powers,
by intense certitude. To call this state, as some authorities
do, by the name of Ecstasy, is inaccurate and confusing: since
the term Ecstasy has long been used both by psychologists
and ascetic writers to define that short and rapturous trance
—a state with well-marked physical and psychical accompaniments—in which the contemplative, losing all consciousness
of the phenomenal world, is caught up to a brief and immediate
enjoyment of the Divine Vision. Ecstasies of this kind are
often experienced by the mystic in Illumination, or even on
his first conversion. They cannot therefore be regarded as
exclusively characteristic of the Unitive Way. In some,
indeed—St. Teresa is an example—the ecstatic trance seems
to diminish rather than increase in frequency after the state
of union has been attained.

Union must be looked upon as the true end of mystical
education, the permanent condition of life upon transcendent
levels of reality, of which ecstasies give a foretaste to the soul.
Intense forms of it, described by individual mystics, under
symbols such as those of Mystical Marriage, Deification, or
Divine Fecundity, all prove on examination to be aspects of
this same experience "seen through a temperament."

It is right, however, to state here that Oriental Mysticism
insists upon a further stage beyond that of union, which stage
it regards as the real goal of the spiritual life. This is the total
annihilation or reabsorption of the individual soul in the
Infinite. Such an annihilation is said by the Sūfis to constitute the "Eighth Stage of Progress," in which alone they
truly attain to God. Thus stated it appears to differ little
from the Buddhist's Nirvana, and is the logical corollary of
that pantheism to which the Oriental mystic always tends.
It is at least doubtful, however, whether the interpretation
which has been put upon it by European students be correct.
The passage in which Al Ghazzali attempts to describe it is
certainly more applicable to the Unitive Life as understood
by Christian contemplatives, than to the Buddhistic annihilation
of personality. "The end of Sūfi-ism," he says, "is total
absorption in God. This is at least the relative end to that

part of their doctrine which I am free to reveal and describe. But *in reality it is but the beginning* of the Sūfi life, for those intuitions and other things which precede it are, so to speak, but the porch by which they enter. . . . In this state some have imagined themselves to be amalgamated with God, others to be identical with Him, others again to be associated with Him : but *all this is sin.*" [1]

The doctrine of annihilation as the end of the soul's ascent, whatever the truth may be as to the Moslem attitude concerning it, is decisively rejected by all European mystics, though a belief in it is constantly imputed to them by their enemies : for their aim is not the suppression of life, but its intensification, a change in its form. This change, they say in a paradox which is generally misunderstood, consists in the perfecting of personality by the utter surrender of self. It is true that the more Orientally-minded amongst them, such as Dionysius the Areopagite, do use language of a negative kind which seems almost to involve a belief in the annihilation rather than the mergence of the self in God : but this is because they are trying to describe a condition of supersensible vitality from the point of view of the normal consciousness, to which it can only seem a Nothing, a Dark, a Self-loss.   Further, it will be found that this temperamental language is generally an attempt to describe the conditions of transitory perception, not those of permanent existence : the characteristics, that is to say, of the Ecstatic Trance, in which for a short time the whole self is lifted to transcendent levels, and the Absolute is apprehended by a total suspension of the surface consciousness.

Hence the Divine Dark, the Nothing, is not a state of non-being to which the mystic aspires to attain : it is rather an approximate and imperfect name for the Undifferentiated Godhead, seat of that Supernal Light whence he may, in his ecstasies, bring down fire from heaven to light the world.

In the mystics of the West, the highest forms of Divine Union impel the self to some sort of active, rather than of passive life : and this is now recognized by the best authorities as the true distinction between Christian and non-Christian mysticism. "The Christian mystics," says Delacroix, "move

[1] Schmölders, "Les Écoles Philosophiques chez les Arabes," p. 61.

from the Infinite to the Definite; they aspire to infinitize life and to define Infinity; they go from the conscious to the subconscious, and from the subconscious to the conscious. The obstacle in their path is not consciousness in general, but *self-consciousness*, the consciousness of the Ego. The Ego is the limitation, that which opposes itself to the Infinite : the states of consciousness free from self, lost in a vaster consciousness, may become modes of the Infinite, and states of the Divine Consciousness." [1] So Starbuck : "The individual learns to transfer himself from a centre of self-activity into an organ of revelation of universal being, and to live a life of affection for and one-ness with, the larger life outside." [2]

Hence, the ideal of the great contemplatives, the end of their long education, is to become "modes of the Infinite." Filled with an abounding sense of the Divine Life, of ultimate and adorable reality, sustaining and urging them on, they wish to communicate the revelation, the more abundant life, which they have received. Not spiritual marriage, but divine fecundity is to be their final state. In a sense St. Teresa in the Seventh Habitation, Suso when his great renunciation is made, have achieved the quest ; yet there is nothing passive in the condition to which they have come. Not Galahad, but the Grail-bearer is now their type : and in their life, words or works they are impelled to exhibit that "Hidden Treasure which desires to be found."

"You may think, my daughters," says St. Teresa, "that the soul in this state [of union] should be so absorbed that she can occupy herself with nothing. You deceive yourselves. She turns with greater ease and ardour than before to all that which belongs to the service of God, and when these occupations leave her free again, she remains in the enjoyment of that companionship." [3]

No temperament is less slothful than the mystical one ; and the "quiet" to which the mystics must school themselves in the early stages of contemplation is often the hardest of their tasks. The abandonment of bodily and intellectual activity is only undertaken in order that they may, in the words of Plotinus,

---

[1] "Études sur le Mysticisme," p. 235.
[2] "The Psychology of Religion," p. 147.
[3] "El Castillo Interior," Moradas Sétimas, cap. i.

"energize enthusiastically" upon another plane. Work they must: but this work may take many forms—forms which are sometimes so wholly spiritual that they are not perceptible to practical minds. Much of the misunderstanding and consequent contempt of the contemplative life comes from the narrow and superficial definition of "work" which is set up by a muscular and wage-earning community.

All records of mysticism in the West, then, are also the records of supreme human activity. Not only of "wrestlers in the spirit" but also of great organizers, such as St. Teresa and St. John of the Cross; of missionaries preaching life to the spiritually dead, such as St. Francis of Assisi, St. Ignatius Loyola, Eckhart, Suso, Tauler, Fox; of philanthropists, such as St. Catherine of Genoa; poets and prophets, such as Mechthild of Magdeburg, Jacopone da Todi and Blake; finally, of some immensely virile souls whose participation in the Absolute Life has seemed to force on them a national destiny. Of this St. Bernard, St. Catherine of Siena, and the Blessed Joan of Arc are the supreme examples. "The soul enamoured of My Truth," said God's voice to St. Catherine of Siena, "never ceases to serve the whole world in general." [1]

Utterly remade in the interests of Reality, exhibiting that dual condition of fruition and activity which Ruysbroeck described as the crowning stage of human evolution, the "Supreme summit of the Inner Life," [2] all these lived, as it were, with both hands; towards the finite and towards the Infinite, towards God and man. It is true that in nearly every case such "great actives" have first left the world as a necessary condition of obtaining contact with that Absolute Life which reinforced their own: for a mind distracted by the many cannot apprehend the One. Hence the solitude of the wilderness is an essential part of mystical education. But, having obtained that contact, and established themselves upon transcendent levels—being united with their Source not merely in temporary ecstasies, but by an act of complete surrender—they were impelled to abandon their solitude; and resumed, in some way, their contact with the world in order to become the medium whereby that Life flowed out to other men. To go up

[1] Dialogo, cap. vii.
[2] " L'Ornement des Noces Spirituelles," l. ii. cap. lxxiii.

alone into the mountain and come back as an ambassador to the world, has ever been the method of humanity's best friends. This systole-and-diastole motion of retreat as the preliminary to a return remains the true ideal of Christian Mysticism in its highest development. Those in whom it is not found, however great in other respects they may be, must be considered as having stopped short of the final stage.

Thus St. Catherine of Siena spent three years in hermit-like seclusion in the little room which we still see in her house in the Via Benincasa, entirely cut off from the ordinary life of her family. "Within her own house," says her legend, "she found the desert ; and a solitude in the midst of people."[1] There Catherine endured many mortifications, was visited by ecstasies and visions : passed, in fact, through the states of Purgation and Illumination, which existed in her case side by side. This life of solitude was brought to an abrupt end by the experience which is symbolized in the vision of the Mystic Marriage, and the Voice which then said to her, "Now will I wed thy soul, which shall ever be conjoined and united to Me ! " Catherine, who had during her long retreat enjoyed illumination to a high degree, now entered upon the Unitive State, in which the whole of her public life was passed. Its effect was immediately noticeable. She abandoned her solitude, joined in the family life, went out into the city to serve the poor and sick, attracted and taught disciples, converted sinners, and began that career of varied and boundless activity which has made her name one of the greatest in the history of the fourteenth century. Nor does this mean that she ceased to live the sort of life which is characteristic of mystical consciousness : to experience direct contact with the Transcendental World, to gaze into "the Abyss of Love Divine." On the contrary her astonishing practical genius for affairs, her immense power of ruling men, drew its strength from the long series of visions and ecstasies which accompanied and supported her labours in the world. She "descended into the valley of lilies to make herself more fruitful," says her legend.[2] The conscious vehicle of some "power not herself," she spoke and acted with an authority which might have seemed strange enough in an uneducated daughter

[1] E. Gardner, "St. Catherine of Siena," p. 15.
[2] S. Catherinae Senensis Vitae (Acta SS. Aprilis t. iii.), ii. ii. § 4.

of the people, were it not justified by the fact that all who came into contact with her submitted to its influence.

Our business, then, is to trace from its beginning a gradual and complete change in the equilibrium of the self. It is a change whereby that self turns from the unreal world of sense in which it is normally immersed, to first apprehend, then unite itself with Absolute Reality: finally, possessed by and wholly surrendered to this Transcendent Life, becomes a medium whereby the spiritual world is seen in a unique degree operating directly in the world of sense. In other words, we are to see the human mind advance from the mere perception of phenomena, through the intuition—with occasional contact—of the Absolute under its aspect of Divine Transcendence, to the entire realization of, and union with, Absolute Life under the aspect of Divine Immanence.

The completed mystical life, then, is more than intuitional: it is theopathetic. In the old, frank language of the mystics, it is the *deified life*.

CHAPTER II

THE AWAKENING OF THE SELF

The awakening of transcendental consciousness—Psychologically it is a form of conversion—Generally abrupt—Sometimes gradual—George Fox—An ineffable revelation—A vision of the Divine immanent in the world—General characteristics of mystic conversion—Instances—St. Francis of Assisi—The typical mystic—St. Catherine of Genoa—Madame Guyon—Her character—Her early life and conversion —Rulman Merswin—Suso—Ecstatic conversion—Pascal—Brother Lawrence—The perception of Divine Reality in Nature—The "transfigured world"—Instances— Walt Whitman—Richard Jefferies—Richard Rolle—Heavenly Song—Conversion may take two forms : (1) Expansive and Transcendent ; (2) Personal and Immanent— Their characteristics discussed and compared—Personal love the essential factor—The stimulus which sets the process of transcendence to work

FIRST in the sequence of the mystic states, we must consider that decisive event, the awakening of the transcendental consciousness.

This awakening, from the psychological point of view, appears to be an intense form of the much-discussed phenomenon of "conversion." In particular, it is closely akin to those deep and permanent conversions of the adult type which some religious psychologists call "sanctification."[1] It is a disturbance of the equilibrium of the self, which results in the shifting of the field of consciousness from lower to higher levels, with a consequent removal of the centre of interest from the subject to an object now brought into view : the necessary beginning of any process of transcendence. It must not, however, be confused or identified with religious conversion as ordinarily understood : the sudden and emotional acceptance of theological beliefs which the self had previously either rejected or treated as conventions dwelling upon the margin of consciousness and having no meaning for her actual life. The mechanical process

[1] See Starbuck, "The Psychology of Religion," cap. xxix.

may be much the same ; but the material involved, the results attained, belong to a higher order of reality.

"Conversion," says Starbuck, in words which are really far more descriptive of mystical awakening than of the revivalistic phenomena encouraged by American Protestantism, "is primarily an unselfing. The first birth of the individual is into his own little world. He is controlled by the deep-seated instincts of self-preservation and self-enlargement—instincts which are, doubtless, a direct inheritance from his brute ancestry. The universe is organized around his own personality as a centre." Conversion, then, is "the larger world-consciousness now pressing in on the individual consciousness. Often it breaks in suddenly and becomes a great new revelation. This is the first aspect of conversion : the person emerges from a smaller limited world of existence into a larger world of being. His life becomes swallowed up in a larger whole." [1]

All conversion entails the abrupt or gradual emergence of intuitions from below the threshold, the consequent remaking of the field of consciousness, an alteration in the self's attitude to the world. But in the mystic this process is raised to the nth degree of intensity, for in him it means the first emergence of that genius for the Absolute which is to constitute his distinctive character : an emergence enormous in its effect on every department of his life. Those to whom it happens, often enough, are already "religious" : sometimes deeply and earnestly so. Rulman Merswin, St. Catherine of Genoa, Madame Guyon, George Fox—all these had been bred up in piety, and accepted in its entirety the Christian tradition. They were none the less conscious of an utter change in their world when this opening of the soul's eye took place.

Sometimes the emergence of the mystical consciousness is gradual, unmarked by any definite crisis. The self slides gently, almost imperceptibly, from the old universe to the new. The records of mysticism, however, seem to suggest that this is exceptional : that travail is the normal accompaniment of birth. In another type, of which George Fox is a typical example, there is no conversion in the ordinary sense ; but a gradual and increasing lucidity, of which the beginning has hardly been noticed by the self, intermittently accompanies the

[1] *Op. cit.*, cap. xii.

pain, misery of mind, and inward struggles characteristic of the entrance upon the Way of Purgation. Conversion and purification then go hand in hand, finally shading off into the serenity of the Illuminated State. Fox's "Journal" for the year 1647 contains a vivid account of these "showings" or growing transcendental perceptions of a mind not yet at one with itself, and struggling towards clearness of sight. "Though my exercises and troubles," he says, "were very great, yet were they not so continual but I had some intermissions, and was sometimes brought into such a heavenly joy that I thought I had been in Abraham's bosom. . . . Thus in the deepest miseries, and in the greatest sorrows and temptations that many times beset me, the Lord in His mercy did keep me. I found that there were two thirsts in me; the one after the creatures to get help and strength there; and the other after the Lord, the Creator. . . . It was so with me, that there seemed to be two pleadings in me. . . . One day when I had been walking solitarily abroad and was come home, I was wrapped up in the love of God, so that I could not but admire the greatness of his love. While I was in that condition it was opened unto me by the eternal Light and Power, and I saw clearly therein. . . . But O! then did I see my troubles, trials, and temptations more clearly than ever I had done."[1]

The great oscillations of the typical mystic between joy and pain are here replaced by a number of little ones. The "two thirsts" of the superficial and spiritual consciousness assert themselves by turns. Each step towards the vision of the Real brings with it a reaction. The nascent transcendental powers are easily fatigued, and the pendulum of self takes a shorter swing. "I was swept up to Thee by Thy Beauty, and torn away from Thee by my own weight," says St. Augustine, crystallizing the secret of this experience in an unforgettable phrase.[2]

Most often, however, if we may judge from those first-hand accounts which we possess, mystic conversion is a single and abrupt experience, sharply marked off from the long, dim struggles which precede and succeed it. Normally, it takes the form of a sudden and acute realization of a splendour and adorable reality in the world—or sometimes of its obverse, the

---

[1] Journal of George Fox, cap. i.   [2] Aug. Conf., bk. vii. cap. xvii.

divine sorrow at the heart of things—never before perceived. In so far as I am acquainted with the resources of language, there are no words in which this realization can be described. It is of so actual a nature that in comparison the normal world of past perception seems but twilit at the best. Consciousness has suddenly changed its rhythm and a new aspect of the universe rushes in. The teasing mists are swept away, and reveal, if only for an instant, the sharp outline of the Everlasting Hills. "He who knows this will know what I say, and will be convinced that the soul has then another life." [1]

In most cases, the onset of this new consciousness seems to the self so sudden, so clearly imposed from without rather than developed from within, as to have a supernatural character. The typical case, is, of course, that of St. Paul : the sudden light, the voice, the ecstasy, the complete alteration of life. We shall see, however, when we come to study the evidence of those mystics who have left a detailed record of their pre-converted state, that the apparently abrupt conversion is really, as a rule, the sequel and the result of a long period of restlessness, uncertainty, and mental stress. The deeper mind stirs uneasily in its prison, and its emergence is but the last of many efforts to escape. The temperament of the subject, his surroundings, the vague but persistent apprehensions of a super-sensual reality which he could not find yet could not forget ; all these have prepared him for it. [2]

When, however, the subconscious intuitions, long ago quickened, are at last brought to birth and the eyes are opened on new light—and it is significant that an actual sense of blinding radiance is a constant accompaniment of this state of consciousness—the storm and stress, the vague cravings and oscillations of the past life are forgotten. In this abrupt recognition of reality "all things are made new": from this point the life of the mystic begins. Conversion of this sort may be defined as a sudden, intense, and joyous perception of God immanent in the universe ; of the divine beauty and unutterable splendour of that larger life in which the individual is

---

[1] Plotinus, Ennead vi. 9.

[2] Compare St. Augustine's Confessions, with their description of the years of uncertainty and struggle which prepared him for the sudden and final "Tolle, lege !" that initiated him into the long-sought life of Reality.

immersed, and of a new life to be lived by the self in correspondence with this now dominant fact of existence.   The film
of appearance is abruptly dissolved, and the eternal fairy fields
are disclosed.   For an instant the neophyte sees nature with the
eyes of God.   In that glorious moment "all is beauty ; and
knowing this is love, and love is duty."   But all that is meant
by such a statement as this only the mystics know ; and even
they seem unable to tell.

I will here set down for comparison a few instances of such
mystical conversion ; quoting, where this is available, the actual
description left by the subject of his own experience, or in
default of it, the earliest authentic account.   In these cases,
when grouped together, we shall see certain constant characteristics, from which it may be possible to deduce the psychological law to which they owe their peculiar form.

First in point of time, and first perhaps also in importance
amongst those which I have chosen, is the case of St. Francis of
Assisi ; that great poet and contemplative, that impassioned
lover of the Absolute, whom the unfortunate enthusiasm of his
agnostic admirers has presented to the modern world as a
celestial patron of the Socialist movement and the simple life.
The fact that St. Francis wrote little and lived much, that his
actions were of unequalled simplicity and directness, has
blinded us to the fact that he is a typical mystic : the only
one, perhaps, who forced the most trivial and sordid circumstances of sensual life to become perfect expressions of Reality.

Now the opening of St. Francis's eyes, which took place in
A.D. 1206 when he was twenty-four years old, had been preceded
by a long, hard struggle between the life of the world and the
persistent call of the spirit.   His mind, in modern language, had
not unified itself.   He was a high-spirited boy, full of vitality: a
natural artist, with all the fastidiousness which the artistic
temperament involves.   War and pleasure both attracted him,
and upon them, says his legend, he "miserably squandered and
wasted his time."[1]   Nevertheless, he was vaguely dissatisfied.
In the midst of festivities, he would have sudden fits of abstraction : abortive attempts of the growing transcendental consciousness, still imprisoned below the threshold but aware of
and in touch with the Real, to force itself to the surface and

[1] Thomas of Celano, Legenda Prima, cap. i.

seize the reins. "Even in ignorance," says Thomas of Celano again, "he was being led to perfect knowledge." He loved beauty, for he was by nature a poet and a musician, and shrank instinctively from contact with ugliness and disease. But something within ran counter to this temperamental bias, and sometimes conquered it. He would then associate with beggars, tend the leprous, perform impulsive acts of charity and self-humiliation.[1]

When this divided state, described by the legend as "the attempt to flee God's hand," had lasted for some years, it happened one day that he was walking in the country outside the gates of Assisi, and passed the little church of S. Damiano, "the which" (I again quote from Thomas of Celano's "Second Life") "was almost ruinous and forsaken of all men. And, being led by the Spirit, he went in to pray ; and he fell down before the Crucifix in devout supplication, and *having been smitten by unwonted visitations, found himself another man than he who had gone in.*"

Here, then, is the first stage of conversion. The struggle between two discrepant ideals of life has attained its term. A sudden and apparently "irrational" impulse to some decisive act reaches the surface-consciousness from the seething deeps. The impulse is followed ; and the swift emergence of the transcendental sense results. This "unwonted visitation" effects an abrupt and involuntary alteration in the subject's consciousness : whereby he literally "finds himself another man." He is as one who slept and now awakes.

The crystallization of this new, at first fluid apprehension of Reality in the form of vision and audition : the pointing of the moral, the direct application of truth to the awakened self, follows. "And whilst he was thus moved, straightway—a thing unheard of for long ages!—the painted image of Christ Crucified spoke to him from out its pictured lips. And, calling him by his name, "Francis," it said, "go, repair My house, the which as thou seest is falling into decay." And Francis trembled, being utterly amazed, and almost as it were carried away by these words. And he prepared to obey, for he was wholly set on the fulfilling of this commandment. But *forasmuch as he felt that*

---

[1] Thomas of Celano, Legenda Secunda, cap. v. Compare P. Sabatier, "Vie de S. François d'Assise," cap. ii., where the authorities are fully set out.

the change he had undergone was ineffable, it becomes us to be silent concerning it. . . ." From this time he "gave untiring toil to the repair of that Church. For though the words which were said to him concerned that divine Church which Christ bought with His own Blood, he would not hasten to such heights, but little by little from things of the flesh would pass to those of the Spirit." [1]

In a moment of time, Francis's whole universe had suffered complete rearrangement. There are no hesitations, no uncertainties. The change, which he cannot describe, he knows to be central for life. Not for a moment does he think of disobeying the imperative voice which speaks to him from a higher plane of reality and demands the sacrifice of his career.

Compare now with the experience of St. Francis that of another great saint and mystic, who combined, as he did, the active with the contemplative life. Catherine of Genoa, who seems to have possessed from childhood a religious nature, was prepared for the remaking of her consciousness by years of loneliness and depression, the result of an unhappy marriage. She, like St. Francis—but in sorrow rather than in joy—had oscillated between the world, which did not soothe her, and religion, which helped her no more. At last, she had sunk into a state of dull wretchedness, a hatred alike of herself and of life.

Her emancipation was equally abrupt. In the year 1474, she being twenty-six years old, "The day after the feast of St. Benedict (at the instance of her sister that was a nun), Catherine went to make her confession to the confessor of that nunnery ; but she was not disposed to do it. Then said her sister, ' At least go and recommend yourself to him, because he is a most worthy religious' ; and in fact he was a very holy man. And suddenly, as she knelt before him, she received in her heart the wound of the unmeasured Love of God, with so clear a vision of her own misery and her faults, and of the goodness of God, that she almost fell upon the ground. And by these sensations of infinite love, and of the offences that had been done against this most sweet God, she was so greatly drawn by purifying affection away from the poor things of this world that she was almost beside herself, and for this she cried

[1] Thomas of Celano, Legenda Secunda, cap. vi.

inwardly with ardent love, ' No more world ! no more sin !'
And at this point, if she had possessed a thousand worlds, she
would have thrown all of them away. . . . And she returned
home, kindled and deeply wounded with so great a love of God,
the which had been shown her inwardly, with the sight of her
own wretchedness, that she seemed beside herself. And she
shut herself in a chamber, the most secluded she could find,
with burning sighs. And in this moment she was inwardly
taught the whole practice of orison : but her tongue could say
naught but this—' O Love, can it be that thou hast called me
with so great a love, and made me to know in one instant that
which worlds cannot express?'" This intuition of the Absolute
was followed by an interior vision of Christ bearing the Cross,
which further increased her love and self-abasement. "And
she cried again, ' O Love, no more sins ! no more sins !' And
her hatred of herself was more than she could endure." [1]

Of this experience Von Hügel says, " If the tests of reality
in such things are their persistence and large and rich spiritual
applicability and fruitfulness, then something profoundly real
and important took place in the soul of that sad and weary
woman of six-and-twenty, within that convent-chapel, at that
Annunciation-tide." [2] It is very certain that for St. Catherine,
as for St. Francis, an utterly new life did, literally, begin at this
point. The centre of interest was shifted and the field of
consciousness remade. She "knew in an instant that which
words cannot express." Some veil about her heart was torn
away ; so abruptly, that it left a wound behind. For the first
time she saw and knew the Love in which life is bathed ; and
all the energy and passion of a strong nature responded to
its call.

The conversion of Madame Guyon to the mystic life, as
told by herself in the eighth chapter of part i. of her autobiography—"How a holy Religious caused her to find God
within her heart, with Admirable Results," is its characteristic
title—is curiously like a dilute version of this experience of
St. Catherine's. It, too, followed upon a period of great mental
distress ; also the result of an uncongenial marriage. But since
Madame Guyon's rather unbalanced, diffuse, and sentimental

---

[1] " Vita e Dottrina di Santa Caterina da Genova," cap. ii.
[2] Von Hügel, " The Mystical Element of Religion," vol. ii. p. 29.

character lacks the richness and dignity, the repressed ardours and exquisite delicacy of St. Catherine's mind, so, too, her account of her own interior processes is too often marred by a terrible and unctuous interest in the peculiar graces vouchsafed to her.[1]

Madame Guyon's value to the student of mysticism consists largely in this feeble quality of her surface-intelligence, which hence had little or no modifying or contributory effect upon her spiritual life. True to her own great principle of passivity or " quiet," it lets the interior impulses have their way ; and thus we are able in her case to observe their workings with unusual ease, uncomplicated by the presence of a vigorous intellect or a disciplined will. The wind that bloweth where it listeth whistles through her soul : and the response which she makes is that of a weathercock rather than a windmill. She moves to every current ; she often mistakes a draught for the divine breath ; she feels her gyrations to be of enormous importance. But when it comes to the description of her awakening to the deeper life, a genuine intensity of feeling endows even her effusive style with a certain dignity.

Madame Guyon had from her childhood exhibited an almost tiresome taste for pious observances. At twelve years old she studied St. François de Sales and St. Jeanne Françoise de Chantal ; begged her confessor to teach her the art of mental prayer ; and when he omitted to do so, tried to teach herself, but without result.[2] She wished at this time to become a nun in Madame de Chantal's Order of the Visitation, as St. Catherine at the same age wanted to be an Augustinian canoness ; but as the longings of little girls of twelve for the cloister are seldom taken seriously, we are not surprised to find the refusal of her parents' consent chronicled in the chapter which is headed

---

[1] It is clear from the heading of cap. x. (pt. i.) of her Autobiography that Madame Guyon's editors were conscious, if she was not, of at least some of the extraordinary coincidences between her experiences and those of St. Catherine of Genoa. The parallel between their early years in particular is so exact and descends to such minute details that I am inclined to think that the knowledge of this resemblance, and the gratification with which she would naturally regard it, has governed or modified some at any rate amongst her memories of this past. Such modifications, probably involuntary, have resulted in a curious and hitherto unnoticed case of " unconscious spiritual plagiarism."

[2] Vie, pt. i. cap. iv.

" *Diverses croix chez M. son père.*" Growing up into an unusually beautiful young woman, she went into society, and for a short time enjoyed life in an almost worldly way. Her marriage with Jacques Guyon, however—a marriage of which she signed the articles without even being told the bridegroom's name— put an end to her gaiety. "The whole town was pleased by this marriage ; and in all this rejoicing only I was sad . . . hardly was I married, when the remembrance of my old desire to be a nun overcame me." [1]

Her early married life in her mother-in-law's house was excessively unhappy. She was soon driven to look for comfort in the practices of religion. "Made to love much, and finding nothing to love around her, she gave her love to God," says Guerrier tersely.[2] But she was not satisfied : like most of her fellow-contemplatives, she was already vaguely conscious of something that she missed, some vital power unused, and identified this something with the " orison of quiet," the " practice of the presence of God " which mystically minded friends had described to her. She tried to attain to it deliberately, and naturally failed. " I could not give myself by multiplicity that which Thou Thyself givest, and which is only experienced in simplicity." [3]

When these interior struggles had lasted for nearly two years, and Madame Guyon was nineteen, the long desired, almost despaired of, apprehension came—as it did to St. Catherine—suddenly, magically almost ; and under curiously parallel conditions. It was the result of a few words spoken by a Franciscan friar whom a "secret force" acting in her interest had brought into the neighbourhood, and whom she had been advised to consult. He was a recluse, who disliked hearing the confessions of women, and appears to have been far from pleased by her visit ; an annoyance which he afterwards attributed to her fashionable appearance, "which filled him with apprehension." "He hardly came forward, and was a long time without speaking to me. I, however, did not fail to speak to him and to tell him in a few words my difficulties on the subject of orison. He at once replied, ' Madame, you are seeking without that which you have within. Accustom

---

[1] *Op. cit.*, pt. i. cap. vi.   [2] " Madame Guyon," p. 36.
[3] Vie, pt. i. cap. viii.

yourself to seek God in your own heart, and you will find Him.' Having said this, he left me. The next morning he was greatly astonished when I again visited him and told him the effect which these words had had upon my soul: for, indeed, they were as an arrow, which pierced my heart through and through. I felt in this moment a *profound wound*, which was full of delight and of love—a wound so sweet that I desired that it might never heal. These words had put into my heart that which I sought for so many years, or, rather, they caused me to find that which was there. O, my Lord, you were within my heart, and you asked of me only that I should return within, in order that I might feel your presence. O, Infinite Goodness, you were so near, and I, running here and there to seek you, found you not!" She, too, like St. Catherine, learned in this instant the long-sought practice of orison, or contemplation. "From the moment of which I have spoken, my orison was emptied of all form, species, and images ; nothing of my orison passed through the mind ; but it was an orison of joyous possession in the Will, where the taste for God was so great, pure, and simple that it attracted and absorbed the two other powers of the soul in a profound recollection without action or speech." [1]

Take now the case of a less eminent but not less genuine mystic, who has also left behind him a vivid personal description of his entrance upon the Mystic Way. Rulman Merswin was a wealthy, pious, and respected merchant of Strassburg. In the year 1347, when he was about thirty-six years old, he retired from business in order that he might wholly devote himself to religious matters. It was the time of that spiritual revival within the Catholic Church in Germany which, largely influenced by the great Rhenish mystics Suso and Tauler, is identified with the "Friends of God"; and Merswin himself was one of Tauler's disciples. [2]

One evening, in the autumn which followed his retirement, "about the time of Martinmas," he was strolling in his garden alone. Meditating as he walked, a picture of the Crucifix

---

[1] *Op. cit., loc. cit.*

[2] One of the best English accounts of this movement and the great personalities concerned in it will be found in Rufus Jones, "Studies in Mystical Religion," cap. xiii.

suddenly presented itself to his mind.   In such an imaginary vision as this there is nothing, of course, that can be called in the least degree abnormal.   The thoughts of a devout Catholic, much under the influence of Tauler and his school, must often have taken such a direction during his solitary strolls. This time, however, the mental image of the Cross seems to have given the needed stimulus to subconscious forces which had long been gathering way.   Merswin was abruptly filled with a violent hatred of the world and of his own free-will. "Lifting his eyes to heaven he solemnly swore that he would utterly surrender his own will, person, and goods to the service of God." [1]

This act of complete surrender, releasing as it were the earthbound self, was at once followed by the onset of pure mystical perception.   "The reply from on high came quickly. A brilliant light shone about him : he heard in his ears a divine voice of adorable sweetness ; he felt as if he were lifted from the ground and carried several times completely round his garden." [2] Optical disturbance, auditions, and the sense of levitation, are of course well-marked physical accompaniments of these shift-ings of the level of consciousness.   There are few cases in which one or other is not present ; and in some we find all. Coming to himself after this experience, Merswin's heart was filled by a new consciousness of the Divine, and by a transport

[1] A. Jundt, " Rulman Merswin," p. 19.   M. Jundt has condensed his account, which I here translate, from Merswin's autobiographical story of his conversion, published in *Beiträge zu den theologischen Wissenschaften*, v. (Jena, 1854).   Our whole knowledge of Merswin's existence depends on the group of documents which includes this confession, the " Book of Two Men," the " Vision of Nine Rocks," and his other reputed works.   The authenticity of these documents has been much questioned of recent years, and there can be little doubt that they have suffered severely from the editorial energy of his followers.   Some critics go so far as to regard them as pious fictions useless as evidence of the incidents of Merswin life.   With this view, which is upheld by Karl Reider (Der Gottesfreund von Oberland, 1905), I cannot agree.   The best solution of the many difficulties seems to me to be that involved in the brilliant hypothesis of M. Jundt, who believes that we have in Merswin and the mysterious " Friend of God of the Oberland," who pervades his spiritual career, a remarkable case of dissociated personality.   Merswin's peculiar psychic make-up, as described in his autobiography, supports this view : the adoption of which I shall take for granted in future references to his life.   It is incredible to me that the vivid account of his conversion which I quote should be merely " tendency-literature," without basis in fact.   Compare Jundt's monograph, and also Rufus Jones, *op. cit.* pp. 245–253, where the whole problem is discussed.

[2] Jundt, *op. cit., loc. cit.*

of intense love towards God which made him undertake with
great energy the acts of mortification which he believed
necessary to the purification of his soul. From this time
onwards, his mystical consciousness steadily developed. That
it was a consciousness wholly different in kind from the sincere
piety which had previously caused him to retire from business
in order to devote himself to religious truth, is proved by
the name of *Conversion* which he applies to the vision of the
garden ; and by the fact that he dates from this point the
beginning of his real life.

The conversion of Merswin's greater contemporary, Suso,
seems to have been less abrupt. Of its first stage he speaks
vaguely at the beginning of his autobiography, wherein he says
that " he began to be converted when in the eighteenth year
of his age." [1]   He was at this time, as St. Francis had been,
restless, dissatisfied ; vaguely conscious of something essential
to his peace, as yet unfound.   His temperament, at once deeply
human and ardently spiritual, passionately appreciative of
sensuous beauty yet unable to rest in it, had not " unified itself " : nor did it do so completely until after a period of purgation which is probably unequalled for its austerity in the
history of the mysticism of the West.   " He was kept of God in
this, that when he turned to those things that most enticed him
he found neither happiness nor peace therein.   He was restless,
and it seemed to him that something which was as yet unknown could alone give peace to his heart.   And he suffered
greatly of this restlessness. . . .   God at last delivered him by
a complete conversion. His brothers in religion were astonished
by so quick a change : for the event took them unawares.
Some said of it one thing, and some another : but none could
know the reason of his conversion.   It was God Who, *by a
hidden light*, had caused this return to Himself." [2]

This secret conversion was completed by a more violent
uprush of the now awakened and active transcendental powers.
Suso, whom one can imagine as a great and highly nervous
artist if his genius had not taken the channel of sanctity

[1] " Leben und Schriften " (Diepenbrock), cap. i. Suso's autobiography is
written in the third person. He refers to himself throughout under the title of
" Servitor of the Eternal Wisdom."
[2] *Op. cit., loc. cit.*

instead, was subject all his life to visions of peculiar richness
and beauty. Often enough these visions seem to have floated
up, as it were, from the subliminal region without disturbing
the course of his conscious life; and to be little more than
sharply visualized expressions of his ardour towards and intuition of, divine realities. The great ecstatic vision—or rather
apprehension, for there is nothing material about it—with which
the series opens, however, is of a very different kind; and
represents the characteristic experience of Ecstasy in its fullest
form. It is described with a detail and intensity which make it
a particularly valuable document of the mystical life. It is
doubtful whether Suso ever *saw* more than this: the course
of his long education rather consisted in an adjustment of
his nature to the Reality which he then perceived.

"In the first days of his conversion it happened upon
the Feast of St. Agnes, when the Convent had breakfasted
at midday, that the Servitor went into the choir. He was
alone, and he placed himself in the last stall on the prior's side.
And he was in much suffering, for a heavy trouble weighed
upon his heart. And being there alone, and devoid of all
consolations—no one by his side, no one near him—of a sudden
his soul was rapt in his body, or out of his body. Then did
he see and hear that which no tongue can express.

"That which the Servitor saw had no form neither any manner
of being; yet he had of it a joy such as he might have known
in the seeing of the shapes and substances of all joyful things.
His heart was hungry, yet satisfied, his soul was full of content-
ment and joy: his prayers and hopes were all fulfilled. And
the Friar could do naught but contemplate this Shining Brightness; and he altogether forgot himself and all other things.
Was it day or night? He knew not. It was, as it were, a
manifestation of the sweetness of Eternal Life in the sensations of
silence and of rest. Then he said, 'If that which I see and feel
be not the Kingdom of Heaven, I know not what it can be: for
it is very sure that the endurance of all possible pains were but
a poor price to pay for the eternal possession of so great a joy.'"

The physical accompaniments of ecstasy were also present.
"This ecstasy lasted from half an hour to an hour, and whether
his soul were in the body or out of the body he could not tell.
But when he came to his senses it seemed to him that he

returned from another world. And so greatly did his body suffer in this short rapture that it seemed to him that none, even in dying, could suffer so greatly in so short a time. The Servitor came to himself moaning, and he fell down upon the ground like a man who swoons. And he cried inwardly, heaving great sighs from the depth of his soul and saying, 'Oh, my God, where was I and where am I?' And again, 'Oh, my heart's joy, never shall my soul forget this hour!' He walked, but it was but his body that walked, as a machine might do. None knew from his demeanour that which was taking place within. But his soul and his spirit were full of marvels; heavenly lightnings passed and repassed in the deeps of his being, and it seemed to him that he walked on air. And all the powers of his soul were full of these heavenly delights. He was like a vase from which one has taken a precious ointment, but in which the perfume long remains."

Finally, the last phrases of the chapter seem to suggest the true position of this exalted pleasure-state as a first link in the long chain of mystical development. " This foretaste of the happiness of heaven," he says, "the which the Servitor enjoyed for many days, excited in him a most lively desire for God." [1]

Mystical activity, then, like all other activities of the self, opens with that sharp stimulation of the will which can only be obtained through the emotional life.

Suso was a scholar, and an embryo ecclesiastic. During the period which elapsed between his conversion and his description of it he was a disciple of Meister Eckhart, a student of Dionysius and St. Thomas Aquinas. His writings show familiarity with the categories of mystical theology; and naturally enough this circumstance, and also the fact that they were written for purposes of edification, may have dictated to some extent the language in which his conversion-ecstasy is described.

As against this, I will give two first-hand descriptions of mystical conversion in which it is obvious that theological learning plays little or no part. Both written in France within a few years of one another, they represent the impact of Reality on two minds of very different calibre. One is the secret document in which a great genius set down, in words intended only for his own eyes, the record of a two hours' ecstasy. The other

[1] Leben, cap. iii.

is the plain, unvarnished statement of an uneducated man of the peasant class. The first is, of course, the celebrated Memorial, or Amulet, of Pascal; the second is the Relation of Brother Lawrence.

The Memorial of Pascal is a scrap of parchment on which, round a rough drawing of the Flaming Cross, there are written a few strange phrases, abrupt and broken words; the only news which has come to us concerning one of the strangest ecstatic revelations chronicled in the history of the mystic type. After Pascal's death a servant found a copy of this little document, now lost, sewn up in his doublet. He seems always to have worn it upon his person: a perpetual memorial of the supernal experience, the initiation into Reality, which it describes. Beyond what we can deduce from these few lines, we have no direct knowledge of the processes of Pascal's inner life: but we do know that this abrupt illumination came at the end of a long period of spiritual distress, in which indifference to his ordinary interests was counterbalanced by an utter inability to feel the attractive force of that Divine Reality which his great mind discerned as the only adequate object of desire.

The Memorial opens thus :—

> " L'an de grace 1654
> lundi, 23 novembre, jour de Saint Clément, pape
> et martyr, et autres au martyrologe,
> veille de Saint Chrysogone, martyr et autres,
> depuis environ dix heures et demie du soir jusques
> environ minuit et demie,
> Feu. "

" From half-past ten till half-past twelve, Fire!" That is all, so far as description is concerned; but enough, apparently, to remind the initiate of all that passed. The rest tells us only the passion of joy and conviction which this nameless revelation —this long, blazing vision of Reality—brought in its train. It is but a series of amazed exclamations, crude, breathless words, placed there helter-skelter, the artist in him utterly in abeyance; the names of the overpowering emotions which swept him, one after the other, as the Fire of Love disclosed its secrets, evoked an answering flame of humility and rapture in his soul.

" Dieu d'Abraham, Dieu d'Isaac, Dieu de Jacob,
Non des philosophes et des savants.
Certitude. Certitude. Sentiment. Joie. Paix."

" Not the God of philosophers and of scholars!" cries in amazement this great scholar and philosopher abruptly turned from knowledge to love.

" Oubli du·monde et de tout hormis Dieu," he says again, seeing his universe suddenly swept clean of all but this Transcendertt Fact. Then, " Le monde ne t'a point connu, *mais je t'ai connu*. Joie! joie! joie! pleurs de joie!" Compare with the classic style, the sharp and lucid definition of the " Pensées," the irony and glitter of the "Provinciales," these little broken phrases —this child-like stammering speech—in which a supreme master of language has tried to tell his wonder and his delight. I know few things in the history of mysticism at once more convincing, more poignant than this hidden talisman ; upon which the brilliant scholar and stylist, the merciless disputant, has jotted down in hard, crude words, which yet seem charged with passion —the inarticulate language of love—a memorial of the certitude, the peace, the joy, above all, the reiterated, all-surpassing joy, which accompanied his ecstatic apprehension of God.

" Mon Dieu, me quitterez vous?" he says again ; the fire apparently beginning to die down, the ecstasy drawing to an end. " Que je n'en sois pas séparé éternellement!" "Are you going to leave me? Oh, let me not be separated from you for ever!"—the one unendurable thought which would, said Aquinas, rob the Beatific Vision of its glory were we not sure that it can never fade.[1] But the rhapsody is over, the vision of the Fire has gone ; and the rest of the Memorial clearly contains Pascal's meditations upon his experience, rather than a transcript of the experience itself. It ends with the watchword of all mysticism, Surrender—" Renonciation, totale et douce" in Pascal's words : the only way, he thinks, in which he can avoid continued separation from Reality.[2]

Pascal's long vision of Light, Life, and Love was highly ecstatic ; an indescribable, incommunicable experience, which

[1] "Summa Contra Gentiles," l. iii. cap. lxii.
[2] The complete text of the " Memorial" is printed, among other places, in Faugère's edition of the " Pensées, Fragments et Lettres de Blaise Pascal," 2nd ed., Paris, 1897. Tome i. p. 269.

can only be suggested by his broken words of certitude and joy. By his simple contemporary, Brother Lawrence, that Transcendent Reality Who "is not the God of philosophers and scholars," was perceived in a moment of abrupt intuition, peculiarly direct, unecstatic and untheological in type, but absolutely enduring in its results. Lawrence was an uneducated young man of the peasant class, who first served as a soldier, and afterwards as a footman in a great French family, where he annoyed his masters by breaking everything. When he was between fifty and sixty years of age, he entered the Carmelite Order as a lay brother ; and the letters, "spiritual maxims," and conversations belonging to this period of his life were published after his death in 1691. "He told me," says the anonymous reporter of the conversations, supposed to be M. Beaufort, who was about 1660 Grand Vicar to the Cardinal de Noailles, "that God had done him a singular favour in his conversion at the age of eighteen. That in the winter, seeing a tree stripped of its leaves, and considering that within a little time the leaves would be renewed, and after that the flowers and fruit appear, he received a high view of the Providence and Power of God, which has never since been effaced from his soul. That this view had set him perfectly loose from the world and kindled in him such a love for God that he could not tell whether it had increased in above forty years that he had lived since." [1]

Such use of visible nature as the stuff of ontological perceptions, the medium whereby the self reaches out to the Absolute, is not rare in the history of mysticism. The mysterious, primordial vitality of trees and woods, instinct with energy, yet standing, as it were, upon the borderland of dream, appears—we know not why—to be particularly adapted to it. The silent magic of the forest, the strange and steady cycle of its life, possesses in a peculiar degree this power of unleashing the human soul : is curiously friendly to its cravings, ministers to its inarticulate needs. Unsullied by the corroding touch of consciousness, that life can make a contact with the "great life of the All"; and through its mighty rhythms man can receive a message concerning the true and timeless World of "all that is, and was, and evermore shall be." Plant life of all kinds, indeed, from the "flower in the crannied wall" to the "Woods of

---

[1] Brother Lawrence, "The Practice of the Presence of God," p. 9.

Westermain " can easily become, for selves of a certain type, a
" mode of the Infinite." So obvious does this appear when we
study the history of the mystics, that Steiner has seen fit to
draw from it the hardly warrantable inference that " plants
are just those natural phenomena whose qualities in the higher
world are similar to their qualities in the physical world." [1]

Though the conclusion be not convincing, the fact remains.
The flowery garment of the world is for some mystics a medium
of ineffable perception, a source of exalted joy, the veritable
clothing of God. I need hardly add that such a state of things
has always been found incredible by common sense. " The tree
which moves some to tears of joy," says Blake, who possessed
in an eminent degree this form of sacramental perception, " is
in the Eyes of others only a green thing that stands in the
Way." [2]

Such a perception of the Divine in Nature, of the true and
holy meaning of that rich, unresting life in which we are immersed,
is really a more usual feature of Illumination than of Conversion.
All the most marked examples of it must be referred to that
state ; and will be discussed when we come to its consideration.
Sometimes, however, as in the case of Brother Lawrence, the
first awakening of the self to consciousness of Reality does take
this form. The Uncreated Light manifests Itself in and through
created things. This characteristically immanental discovery
of the Absolute occurs chiefly in two classes : in unlettered men
who have lived close to Nature, and to whom her symbols are
more familiar than those of the Churches or the schools, and in
temperaments of the mixed or mystical type, who are nearer to
the poet than to the true contemplative, for whom as a rule the
Absolute " hath no image." " It was like entering into another
world, a new state of existence," says a witness quoted by
Starbuck, speaking of his own conversion. " Natural objects
were glorified. My spiritual vision was so clarified that I saw
beauty in every material object in the universe. The woods
were vocal with heavenly music." " Oh, how I was changed !
Everything became new. My horses and hogs and everybody
became changed ! " exclaims with naïve astonishment another in
the same collection.[3] " When I went in the morning into the

[1] " The Way of Initiation," p. 134.   [2] " Letters of William Blake," p. 62.
[3] " The Psychology of Religion," p. 120.

fields to work," says a third, " the glory of God appeared in all
His visible creation.   I well remember we reaped oats, and how
every straw and head of the oats seemed, as it were, arrayed in
a kind of rainbow glory, or to glow, if I may so express it, in
the glory of God." [1]

Amongst modern men, Walt Whitman possessed in a
supreme degree the permanent sense of this glory, the " light
rare, untellable, lighting the very light." [2]   But evidences of its
existence and the sporadic power of apprehending it are
scattered up and down the literature of the world.   Its discovery constitutes the awakening of the mystical consciousness
in respect of the World of Becoming: a sharp and sudden break
with the old and obvious way of seeing things.   The human
cinematograph has somehow changed its rhythm, and begins
to register new and more real aspects of the external world.
With this, the self's first escape from the limitations of its
conventional universe, it receives an immense assurance of a
great and veritable life surrounding, sustaining, explaining its
own.   Thus Richard Jefferies says, of the same age as that at
which Suso and Brother Lawrence awoke to sudden consciousness of Reality, " I was not more than eighteen when an inner
and esoteric meaning began to come to me from all the visible
universe." [3]   " I now became lost, and absorbed into the being or
existence of the universe . . . and losing thus my separateness
of being, came to seem like a part of the whole." [4]   " I feel on
the margin of a life unknown, very near, almost touching it—on
the verge of powers which, if I could grasp, would give me an
immense breadth of existence." [5]

What was this " life unknown " but the Life known to the
great mystics, which Richard Jefferies apprehended in these
moments of insight, yet somehow contrived to miss ?

Such participation in the deep realities of the World of
Becoming, the boundless existence of a divine whole—which a
modern psychologist has labelled and described as " Cosmic
Consciousness " [6]—whilst it is not the final object of the mystic's

[1] James, " Varieties of Religious Experience," p. 253.
[2] Whitman, " The Prayer of Columbus."
[3] " The Story of My Heart," p. 181.   [4] *Op. cit.*, pp. 8, 9.
[5] *Op. cit.*, p. 45.
[6] Bucke, " Cosmic Consciousness, a Study in the Evolution of the Human Mind."
Philadelphia, 1905.

journey, is a constant feature of it.   It represents one-half of his characteristic consciousness : an entrance into communion with the second of the Triune Powers of God : the Word which "is through all things everlastingly."   Jefferies stood, as so many mystically minded men have done, upon the verge of such a transcendental life.   The "heavenly door," as Rolle calls it, was ajar but not pushed wide.   He peeped through it to the greater world beyond ; but, unable to escape from the bonds of his selfhood, he did not pass through to live upon the independent spiritual plane.

Rolle, Jefferies's fellow countryman, and his predecessor by close upon six hundred years in the ecstatic love and under-standing of natural things, shall be our last example of the mystical awakening.   He, like his spiritual brother St. Francis, and other typical cases, had passed through a preliminary period of struggle and oscillation between worldly life and a vague but growing spirituality : between the superficial and the deeper self. "My youth was fond, my childhood vain, my young age unclean," [1] but "when I should flourish unhappily, and youth of wakeful age was now come, the grace of my Maker was near, the which lust of temporal shape restrained, and unto ghostly supplications turned my desires, and the soul, from low things lifted, to heaven has borne." [2]

The real "life-changing," however, was sharply and charac-teristically marked off from this preparatory state.   Rolle gives to it the name of Heat : as Song, to his musical soul, represents Illumination, and Sweetness Untrowed the Unitive Way.   "Heat soothly I call when the mind truly is kindled in Love Everlast-ing, and the heart on the same manner to burn not hopingly but verily is felt.   The heart truly turned into fire, gives feeling of burning love."   This burning, it appears, is not to be looked upon as merely symbolic.   In it we seem to have an unusual form of psycho-physical parallelism : a bodily expression of the psychic travail and distress accompanying the "New Birth." "More have I marvelled than I show, forsooth," he says in his prologue, "when I first felt my heart wax warm, and truly, *not imaginingly, but as it were with a sensible fire,* burned.   I was forsooth marvelled, as this burning burst up in my soul, and of an unwonted solace ; for in my ignorance of such healing

[1] "Fire of Love," bk. i. cap. xiii.   [2] *Ibid.*, bk. i. cap. xvi.

abundance, oft have I groped my breast, seeing whether this burning were of any bodily cause outwardly.   But when I knew that only it was kindled of ghostly cause inwardly, and this burning was naught of fleshly love or desire, in this I conceived it was the gift of my Maker." [1]   Further on, he gives another and more detailed account.   " From the beginning, forsooth, of my life-changing and of my mind, to the opening of the heavenly door which Thy Face showed, that the heart might behold heavenly things and see by what way its Love it might seek and busily desire, three years are run except three months or four.   The door, forsooth, biding open, a year near-by I passed unto the time in which the heat of Love Everlasting was verily felt in heart.   I sat forsooth in a chapel and whilst with sweetness of prayer and meditation greatly I was delighted, suddenly in me I felt a merry heat and unknown.   But at first I wondered doubting of whom it should be ; but a long time I am assured that not of the Creature but of my Maker it was, for more hot and gladder I found it." [2]

To this we must add a passage which I cannot but think one of the most beautiful expressions of spiritual joy to be found in mystical literature.   It forms, as it were, a poetic gloss upon the experience just described : its sketch of the ideal mystic life, to the cultivation of which he then set himself, revealing in a few lines the charm of Rolle's character, its simplicity and gaiety, its capacity for ardent love.   In it we see reflected the exquisite and Franciscan candour of soul which enabled him to live in his Yorkshire hermitage, as an earlier brother of the birds did upon the Umbrian hills, close to nature and close to God.

" In the beginning truly of my conversion and singular purpose, I thought I would be like the little bird that for love of her lover longs, but in her longing she is gladdened when he comes that she loves.   And joying she sings, and singing she longs, but in sweetness and heat.   It is said the nightingale to song and melody all night is given, that she may please him to whom she is joined.   How muckle more with greatest sweetness to Christ my Jesu should I sing, that is spouse of my soul by all this present life, that is night in regard of clearness to come." [3]

Glancing back at the few cases here brought together, we

---

[1] " Fire of Love," bk. i. caps. xv. and i.   [2] *Ibid.*, bk. i. cap. xvi.
[3] *Ibid.*, bk. ii. cap. xii.

can see in them, I think, certain similarities and diversities which are often of great psychological interest and importance : and which will be found to govern the subsequent development of the mystic life. We see in particular at this point, before puri- fication, or the remaking of character, begins, the reaction of the natural self, its heart and its mind, upon the uprush of new truth which operates " mystical conversion." This reaction is highly significant, and gives us a clue not only to the future development of the mystic, but to the general nature of man's spiritual consciousness.

We have said[1] that this consciousness in its full develop- ment seems to be extended not in one but in two directions. These directions, these two fundamental ways of apprehending Reality, may be called the Eternal and Temporal, transcendent and immanent, Absolute and dynamic aspects of Truth. They comprise the twofold knowledge of a God Who is both Being and Becoming, near and far : pairs of opposites which ecstasy will carry up into a higher synthesis. But the first awakening of the mystic sense, the first breaking in of the supra-sensible upon the soul, will involve the emergence of one only of these two complementary forms of perception. One side always wakes first : the incoming message always choosing the path of least resistance. Hence mystical conversion tends to belong to one of two distinctive types : tends also as regards its expres- sion to follow that temperamental inclination to objectivize Reality as a Place, a Person, and a State which we found to govern the symbolic systems of the mystics.[2]

There is first, then, the apprehension of a splendour without : an expansive, formless, ineffable vision, a snatching up of the self, as it were, from knowledge of this world to some vague yet veritable knowledge of the next. The veil parts, and the Godhead is perceived under Its aspect of Transcendence. Not the personal touch of love transfiguring the soul, but the imper- sonal glory of a transfigured universe is the dominant note of this experience : and the reaction of the self takes the form of awe and rapture rather than of intimate affection. Of such a kind was the conversion of Suso, and in a less degree of Brother Lawrence. Of this kind also were the Light which Rulman Merswin saw, and the mystical perception of the being of

[1] *Supra*, p. 42.   [2] *Ibid.*, p. 153.

the universe reported by Richard Jefferies and countless others.

This experience, if it is to be complete, if it is to involve the definite emergence of the self from "the prison of I-hood," its setting out upon the Mystic Way, requires an act of concentration on the self's part as the complement of its initial act of expansion. It must pass beyond the stage of metaphysical rapture or fluid splendour, and crystallize into a definite concept, a definite and personal relation set up between the self and the Absolute Life. The vitality and efficiency of the conversion from sense to spirit, says Eucken, depends on the vividness of the apprehension of the new reality *and* on its authority for life.[1] To be a spectator of Reality is not enough. The awakened subject is not merely to perceive transcendent life, but to participate therein. In Jefferies's case this crystallization, this heroic effort towards participation did not take place, and he never therefore laid hold of "the glory that has been revealed." In Suso's it did, "exciting in him a most lively desire for God."

In most cases this crystallization, the personal and imperative concept which the mind constructs from the general and ineffable intuition of Reality, assumes a theological character. Often it presents itself to the consciousness in the form of visions or voices : objective, as the Crucifix which spoke to St. Francis, or mental, as the visions of the Cross in Rulman Merswin and St. Catherine of Genoa. Nearly always, this concept, this intimate realization of the divine, has reference to the love and sorrow at the heart of things, the discord between Perfect Love and an imperfect world ; whereas the complementary vision of Transcendence strikes a note of rapturous joy. " The beatings of the Heart of God sounded like so many invitations which thus spake : Come and do penance, come and be reconciled, come and be consoled, come and be blessed ; come, My love, and receive all that the Beloved can give to His beloved. . . . Come, My bride, and enjoy My Godhead."[2]

It is to this personal touch, to the individual appeal of an immediate Presence, not to the great light and the Beatific Vision, that the awakened self makes its most ardent, most heroic response. Not because he was rapt from himself, but

---

[1] See Boyce Gibson, " Rudolph Eucken's Philosophy," p. 85.
[2] St. Mechthild of Hackborn, " Liber Specialis Gratiæ," l. ii. cap. i.

because the figure on the Cross called him by name, saying, "Repair My Church" did St. Francis, with that simplicity, that disregard of worldly values which constituted his strength, accept the message in a literal sense and set himself instantly to the work demanded; bringing stones, and, in defiance alike of comfort and convention, building up with his own hands the crumbling walls.

In many conversions to the mystic life, the revelation of an external splendour, the shining vision of the transcendent spiritual world, is wholly absent. The self awakes to that which is within, rather than to that which is without: to the Immanent not the Transcendent God, to the personal not the cosmic relation. Where those who look out receive the revelation of Divine Beauty, those who look in receive rather the wound of Divine Love: another aspect of the "triple star." I need not point out that Richard Rolle and Madame Guyon are extreme examples of this type: but it is seen in perhaps a more balanced form in St. Catherine of Genoa.

Both Madame Guyon and St. Catherine compare the anguish and abruptness of that inward revelation, its rending apart of the hard tissues of I-hood and its inevitable setting in relief of their own poor finite selves, to a wound. It is "the wound of Un-measured Love," says the legend of St. Catherine: an image in which we seem to hear the very accents of the saint. "A wound full of delight," says the more effusive Frenchwoman, "I wished that it might never heal." Rolle calls this piercing rapture a great heat: the heat which is to light the Fire of Love. "As it were if the finger were put in fire, it should be clad with feeling of burning: so the soul with love (as aforesaid) set afire, truly feels most very heat." [1]

Love, passionate and all-dominant, here takes the place of that joyous awe which we noticed as the characteristic reaction upon reality in conversions of the Transcendent type. In the deep and strong temperaments of the great mystics this love passes quickly—sometimes instantly—from the emotional to the volitional stage. Their response to the voice of the Absolute is not merely an effusion of sentiment, but an act of will: an act often of so deep and comprehensive a kind as to involve the complete change of the outward no less than of the inward life,

[1] "The Fire of Love," bk. i. cap. i.

"Divine love," says Dionysius, "draws those whom it seizes beyond themselves: and this so greatly that they belong no longer to themselves but wholly to the Object loved." [1]

Merswin's oath of self-surrender: St. Catherine of Genoa's passionate and decisive "No more world! no more sins!": St. Francis's naive and instant devotion to church-restoration in its most literal sense: these things are earnests of the reality of the change. They represent—symbolize as well as they can upon the sensual plane—the inevitable response of every living organism to a fresh external stimulus: its adjustment to the new conditions which that stimulus represents. They complete the process of conversion: which is not one-sided, not merely an infusion into the surface-consciousness of new truth, but rather the beginning of a life-process, a breaking down of the old and building up of the new: a never to be ended give-and-take, now set up between the individual and the Absolute. The Spirit of Life has been born: and the first word it learns to say is *Abba*, Father. It aspires to its origin; to Life in its most intense manifestation: hence all its instincts urge it to that activity which it feels to be inseparable from life. It knows itself a member of that mighty family in which the stars are numbered: the family of the sons of God, who, free and creative, sharing the rapture of a living, striving Cosmos, "shout for joy."

So, even in its very beginning, we see how active, how profoundly organic, how deeply and widely alive is the true contemplative life; how truly on the transcendent as on the phenomenal plane, the law of living things is action and reaction, force and energy. The awakening of the self is to a new and more active plane of being, new and more personal relations with Reality; hence to new and more real work which it must do.

[1] Dionysius the Areopagite, "De Divinis Nominibus," iv. 13.

CHAPTER III

THE PURIFICATION OF THE SELF

Purification the necessary corollary of conversion—The Self's adjustment to Reality—Cleansing of the powers of perception—Acquirement of "goodness"—Self-knowledge—Contrition—St. Catherine of Genoa on Purgatory—Love the agent of purification—Purgation accompanies the whole mystic life ; but the Purgative Way is the completion of conversion—Self-simplification—Cleansing and stripping—Detachment—Poverty, Chastity, and Obedience : the fundamental mystic virtues—Spiritual Poverty : the essence of liberty—Jacopone da Todi on Poverty—St. Francis of Assisi—The "Sacrum Commercium"—Eckhart on Detachment—An attitude not an act—Its various forms—St. Teresa—Antoinette Bourignan—St. Douceline—Perverted detachment—Mortification—The positive aspect of Purgation—The remaking of character—Death of the lower nature—Once the new life is established, mortification ends—"The Mirror of Simple Souls"—St. Catherine of Genoa—The psychological aspect of mortification—Active suffering—The heroic side of purification—Tauler—The conquest of fastidiousness—St. Francis of Assisi—Margery Kempe—St. Catherine of Genoa—Madame Guyon—Purgation essential to all mysticism—Its last stages—The Game of Love—The fluctuating transcendental consciousness—Rulman Merswin—The Passage from Purgation to Illumination—The three factors of the Purgative Way—Conclusion

H ERE, then, stands the newly awakened self: aware, for the first time, of reality, responding to that reality by deep movements of love and of awe. She sees herself, however, to be not merely thrust into a new world, but set at the beginning of a new road. Activity is now to be her watchword, pilgrimage the business of her life. " That a quest there is, and an end, is the single secret spoken." Under one symbol or another, that long slow process of transcendence, of character building, whereby she is to attain freedom, become capable of living upon high levels of reality, is present in her consciousness. Those to whom this secret is not imparted are no mystics, in the exact sense in which that word is here used ; however great their temporary illumination may have been.

What must be the first step of the self upon this road to perfect union with the Absolute? Clearly, a getting rid of all those elements of normal experience which are not in harmony with reality : of illusion, evil, imperfection of every kind. By false desires and false thoughts man has built up for himself a false universe : as a mollusc, by the deliberate and persistent absorption of lime and rejection of all else, can build up for itself a hard shell which shuts it from the external world, and only represents in a distorted and unrecognisable form the ocean from which it was obtained. This hard and wholly unnutritious shell, this one-sided secretion of the surface-consciousness, makes as it were a little cave of illusion for each separate soul. A literal and deliberate getting out of the cave must be for every mystic, as it was for Plato's prisoners, the first step in the individual hunt for reality.

In the plain language of old-fashioned theology "man's sin is stamped upon man's universe." We see a sham world because we live a sham life. We do not know ourselves ; hence do not know the true character of our senses ; hence attribute wrong values to their suggestions and declarations concerning our relation to the external world. That world, which we have distorted by identifying it with our own self-regarding arrangement of its elements, has got to reassume for us the character of Reality, of God. In the purified sight of the great mystics it did reassume this character : their shells were opened wide, they knew the tides of the Eternal Sea. This lucid apprehension of the True is what we mean when we speak of the Illumination which results from a faithful acceptance of the trials of the Purgative Way.

The normal self as it exists in the normal world—the " old Adam " of St. Paul—is wholly incapable of supersensual adventure. All its activities are grouped about a centre of consciousness whose correspondences are with the material world. In the moment of its awakening, it is abruptly made aware of this disability. It knows itself finite. It now inspires to the infinite. It is encased in the hard crust of individuality : it aspires to union with a larger self. It is fettered : it longs for freedom. Its every sense is attuned to illusion : it craves for harmony with the Absolute Truth. "God is the only Reality," says Patmore, "and we are real only as far as we are in His

order and He is in us." [1]   Whatever form, then, the mystical
adventure may take, it must be preceded by a change in the
attitude of the subject ; a change which will introduce it into
the order of Reality, and enable it to set up permanent relations
with an Object which is not normally part of its universe.
Therefore, though the end of mysticism is not goodness, it
entails the acquirement of goodness. The virtues are the
"ornaments of the spiritual marriage" because that marriage
is union with the Good no less than with the Beautiful and the
True.

Primarily, then, the self must be purged of all that stands
between it and goodness : putting on the character of reality
instead of the character of illusion or "sin." It longs ardently
to do this from the first moment in which it sees itself in the
all-revealing radiance of the Uncreated Light. "When once
love openeth the inner eye of the soul for to see this truth,"
says Hilton, "with other circumstances that attend it, then
beginneth the soul to be really humble ; for then through the
sight of God it feeleth and seeth itself as it is, and then doth
the soul forsake the beholding and leaning upon itself." [2]

So, with Dante, the first terrace of the Mount of Purgatory
is devoted to the cleansing of pride and the production of
humility. Such a process is the inevitable—one might almost
say mechanical—result of a vision, however fleeting, of Reality ;
an undistorted sight of the earthbound self. All its life it has
been measuring its candlelight by other candles. Now for the
first time it is out in the open air and sees the sun. "This is
the way," said the voice of God to St. Catherine of Siena in
ecstasy. "If thou wilt arrive at a perfect knowledge and enjoyment of Me, the Eternal Truth, thou shouldst never go outside
the knowledge of thyself; and by humbling thyself in the
valley of humility thou wilt know Me and thyself, from which
knowledge thou wilt draw all that is necessary. . . . In self
knowledge, then, thou wilt humble thyself; seeing that, in
thyself, thou dost not even exist." [3]

The first thing that the self observes, when it turns back
upon itself in that moment of lucidity—enters, as St.
Catherine says, into "the cell of self-knowledge,"—is the

[1] "The Rod, the Root, and the Flower," "Magna Moralia," xxii.
[2] "The Scale of Perfection," bk. iii. cap. vii.   [3] Dialogo, cap. iv.

horrible contrast between its clouded contours and the pure sharp radiance of the Real; between its muddled faulty life, its perverse self-centred drifting, and the clear onward sweep of that Becoming in which it is immersed. It is then that the outlook of rapture and awe receives the countersign of humility. The harbinger of that new self which must be born appears under the aspect of a desire: a passionate longing to escape from the suddenly perceived hatefulness of selfhood, and to conform to Reality, the Perfect which it has seen under its aspect of Goodness, of Beauty, or of Love —to be worthy of it, in fact to be *real*. "This showing," says Gerlac Petersen of that experience, "is so vehement and so strong that the whole of the interior man, not only of his heart but of his body, is marvellously moved and shaken, and faints within itself, unable to endure it. And by this means, his interior aspect is made clear without any cloud, and conformable in its own measure to Him whom he seeks." [1]

The lives of the mystics abound in instances of the "vehemence of this showing": of the deep-seated sense of necessity which urges the newly awakened self to a life of discomfort and conflict, often to intense poverty and pain, as the only way of replacing false experience by true. Here the transcendental consciousness, exalted by a clear intuition of its goal, and not merely "counting" but *perceiving* the world to be obviously well lost for such a prize, takes the reins. It forces on the unwilling surface mind a sharp vision of its own disabilities: its ugly and imperfect life.

The love of Ideal Beauty which is closely bound up with the mystic temperament makes instant response. "No more sins!" was the first cry of St. Catherine of Genoa in that crucial hour in which she saw by the light of love the ugly and distorted nature of her past. She entered forthwith upon the Purgative Way, in which for four years she suffered under a profound sense of imperfection, endured fasting, solitude, and mortification, and imposed upon herself the most repulsive duties in her efforts towards that self-conquest which should make her "conformable in her own measure" to the dictates of that Pure Love which was the aspect of reality that she had seen. It is the

[1] "Ignitum cum Deo Soliloquium," cap. xi.

inner conviction that this conformity—this transcendence of the unreal—is possible and indeed normal, which upholds the mystic during the terrible years of Purgation: so that "not only without heaviness, but with a joy unmeasured he casts back all thing that may him let."[1]

To the true lover of the Absolute, Purgation no less than Illumination is a privilege, a dreadful joy. It is an earnest of increasing life. "Let me suffer or die!" said St. Teresa: a strange alternative in the ears of common sense, but a forced option in the spiritual sphere. However harsh its form, however painful the activities to which it spurs him, the mystic recognizes in this break-up of his old universe an essential part of the Great Work : and the act in which he turns to it is an act of love no less than an act of will. "Burning of love into a soul truly taken all vices purgeth : . . . for whilst the true lover with strong and fervent desire into God is borne, all things him displease that from the sight of God withdraw."[2] His eyes once opened, he is eager for that ordering of his disordered loves which alone can establish his correspondences with Transcendental Life. "Teach me, my only joy," cries Suso, "the way in which I may bear upon my body the marks of Thy Love." "Come, my soul, depart from outward things and gather thyself together into a true interior silence, that thou mayst set out with all thy courage and bury and lose thyself in the desert of a deep contrition."[3]

It is in this torment of contrition, this acute consciousness of unworthiness, that we have the first swing-back of the oscillating self from the initial state of mystic pleasure to the complementary state of pain. It is, so to speak, on its transcendental side, the reflex action which follows the first touch of God. Thus, we read that Rulman Merswin, "swept away by the transports of Divine Love," did not surrender himself to the passive enjoyment of this first taste of Absolute Being, but was impelled by it to diligent and instant self-criticism. He was "seized with a hatred of his body, and inflicted on himself such hard mortifications that he fell ill."[4]

---

[1] Richard Rolle, " The Mending of Life," cap. i.
[2] *Ibid.*, " The Fire of Love," bk. i. cap xxiii.
[3] " Buchlein von der ewigen Weisheit," cap. v.
[4] Jundt, " Rulman Merswin," p. 19.

It is useless for lovers of healthy-mindedness to resent this and similar examples of self-examination and penance: to label them morbid or mediaeval. The fact remains that only such bitter knowledge of wrongness of relation, seen by the light of ardent love, can spur the will of man to the hard task of readjustment.

"I saw full surely," says Julian of Norwich, "that it behoveth needs to be that we should be in longing and in penance until the time that we be led so deep into God that we verily and truly know our own soul." [1]

Dante's whole journey up the Mount of Purgation is the dramatic presentation of this one truth. So, too, the celebrated description of Purgatory attributed to St. Catherine of Genoa [2] is obviously founded upon its author's inward experience of this Purgative Way. In it, she applies to the souls of the dead her personal consciousness of the necessity of purification; its place in the organic process of spiritual growth. It is, as she acknowledges at the beginning, the projection of her own psychological adventures upon the background of the spiritual world: its substance being simply the repetition after death of that eager and heroic acceptance of suffering, those drastic acts of purification which she has herself been compelled to undertake under the whip of the same psychic necessity—that of removing the rust of illusion, cleansing the mirror in order that it may receive the divine light. "It is," she says, "as with a covered object, the object cannot respond to the rays of the sun, not because the sun ceases to shine—for it shines without intermission—but because the covering intervenes. Let the covering be destroyed, and again the object will be exposed to the sun, and will answer to the rays which beat against it in proportion as the work of destruction advances. Thus the souls are covered by a rust—that is, by sin—which is gradually consumed away by the fire of purgatory. The more it is consumed, the more they respond to God their true Sun. Their happiness increases as the rust falls off and lays them open to

---

[1] "Revelations of Divine Love," cap. lvi.

[2] I offer no opinion upon this question of authorship. Those interested may consult Von Hügel, "The Mystical Element of Religion," vol. i., Appendix. Whoever may be responsible for its present form, the Treatise is clearly founded upon first-hand mystic experience: which is all that our present purpose requires.

the divine ray . . . the instinctive tendency to seek happiness in God develops itself, and goes on increasing through the fire of love, which draws it to its end with such impetuosity and vehemence that any obstacle seems intolerable ; and the more clear its vision, the more extreme its pain." [1]

" Mostratene la via di gire al monte !" cry the souls of the newly-dead in Dante's vision,[2] pushed by that "instinctive tendency" towards the purifying flames. Such a tendency, such a passionate desire, the aspiring self must have. No cool, well-balanced knowledge of the need of new adjustments will avail to set it on the Purgative Way. This is a heroic act, and demands heroic passions in the soul.

" In order to overcome our desires and to deny ourselves in all things," says St. John of the Cross, who is the classic authority upon this portion of the mystic quest, " our love and inclination for which are wont so to inflame the will that it delights therein, we require another and greater fire of another and nobler love—that of the Bridegroom—so that having all our joy in Him, and deriving from Him all our strength, we may gain such resolution and courage as shall enable us easily to abandon and deny all besides. It was necessary, in order to subdue our sensual desires, not only to have this love for the Bridegroom, but also to be on fire therewith, and that with anxiety . . . if our spiritual nature were not on fire with other and nobler anxieties—anxieties for that which is spiritual—we should never overcome our natural and sensible satisfactions, nor be able to enter on the night of sense, neither should we have the courage to remain in the darkness, in the denial of every desire." [3]

" It is necessary to be on fire with love, and that with anxiety." Only this deep and ardent passion for a perceived Object of Love can persuade the mystic to those unnatural acts of abnegation on which he kills his lesser love of the world of sense, frees himself from the " remora of desire," unifies all his energies about the new and higher centre of his life. His business, I have said, is transcendence : a mounting up, an attainment of a higher order of reality. Once his eyes have been opened on Eternity, his instinct for the Absolute roused

[1] " Trattato di Purgatorio," caps. ii. and iii.　　[2] Purg. ii. 60.
[3] " Subida del Monte Carmelo," l. i. cap. xiv.

from its sleep, he sees union with that Reality as his duty no less than his joy : sees too that this union can only be consummated on a plane where illusion and selfhood have no place.

The inward voice says to him perpetually at the least seasonable moments, "Dimitte omnia transitora, quaere aeterna." [1] Hence the purgation of the senses and of the character which they have helped to build is always placed first in order in the Mystic Way ; though sporadic flashes of illumination and ecstasy may, and often do, precede and accompany it. Since spiritual no less than physical existence is, as we know it, an endless Becoming, it too has no end. In a sense the whole of the mystical experience in this life consists in a series of purifications, whereby the Finite slowly approaches the nature of its Infinite Source : climbing up the cleansing mountain pool by pool, like the industrious fish in Rulman Merswin's vision, until it reaches its Origin. The greatest of the contemplative saints, far from leaving purgation behind them in their progress, were increasingly aware of their own inadequateness, the nearer they approached to the unitive state : for the true lover of the Absolute, like every other lover, is alternately abased and exalted by his unworthiness and his good fortune. There are moments of high rapture when he knows only that the banner over him is Love : but there are others in which he remains bitterly conscious that in spite of his uttermost surrender there is within him an ineradicable residuum of selfhood which "stains the white radiance of eternity."

In this sense, then, purification is a perpetual process. That which mystical writers mean, however, when they speak of the Way of Purgation, is rather the slow and painful completion of Conversion. It is the drastic turning of the self from the unreal to the real life : a setting of her house in order, an orientation of the mind to Truth. Its business is the getting rid, first of self-love ; and secondly of all those foolish interests in which the surface-consciousness is steeped.

"The essence of purgation," says Richard of St. Victor, "is self-simplification." Nothing can happen until this has proceeded a certain distance : till the involved interests and

"De Imitatione Christi," l. iii. cap. i.

tangled motives of the self are simplified, and the false complications of temporal life are recognized and cast away.

" No one," says another authority in this matter, "can be
enlightened unless he be first cleansed or purified and stripped." [1]
Purgation, which is the remaking of character in conformity
with perceived reality, consists in these two essential acts : the
cleansing of that which is to remain, the stripping of that which
is to be done away.   It may best be studied, therefore, in two
parts : and I think that it will be in the reader's interest if we
reverse the order which the " Theologia Germanica " adopts, and
first consider Negative Purification, or Self-stripping, and next
Positive Purification, or character-adjustment.   These, then,
are the branches into which this subject will here be split.
(1) The Negative Aspect, the stripping or purging away of
those superfluous, unreal, and harmful things which dissipate the
precious energies of the self.   This is the business of Poverty,
or *Detachment*.   (2) The Positive aspect : a raising to their
highest term, their purest state, of all that remains—the permanent elements of character.   This is brought about by
Mortification : the gymnastic of the soul : a deliberate recourse
to painful experiences and difficult tasks.

1. DETACHMENT

Apart from the plain necessity of casting out imperfection and sin, what is the type of "good character" which
will best serve the self in its journey towards union with the
Absolute ?

The mystics of all ages and all faiths agree in their answer.
Those three virtues which the instinct of the Catholic Church
fixed upon as the necessities of the cloistered life—the great
Evangelical counsel of voluntary Poverty with its departments :
Chastity, the poverty of the senses, and Obedience, the poverty
of the will—are also, when raised to their highest term and transmuted by the Fire of Love, the essential virtues of the mystical
quest.

By *Poverty* the mystic means an utter self-stripping, the
casting off of immaterial as well as material wealth, a complete
detachment from all finite things.   By *Chastity* he means an

[1] " Theologia Germanica," cap. xiv.

extreme and limpid' purity of soul, virgin to all but God:
by *Obedience*, that abnegation of selfhood, that mortification of the will which results in a complete humility, a
"holy indifference" to the accidents of life.   These three
aspects of perfection are really one: linked together
as irrevocably as the three aspects of the self.   Their
common characteristic is this: they tend to make the subject
regard itself, not as an isolated and interesting individual,
possessing desires and rights, but as a scrap of the Cosmos,
an ordinary bit of the Universal Life, only important as a part
of the All, an expression of the Will Divine.   Detachment and
purity go hand in hand, for purity is but detachment of the
heart; and where these are present they bring with them that
humble spirit of obedience which expresses detachment of will.
We may therefore treat them as three manifestations of one
thing: which thing is Inward Poverty.   "Blessed are the poor
in spirit, for theirs is the Kingdom of Heaven," is the motto of
all pilgrims on this road.

"God is pure Good in Himself," says Eckhart, "therefore will
He dwell nowhere but in a pure soul.   There He can pour
Himself out: into that He can wholly flow.   What is Purity?
It is that a man should have turned himself away from all
creatures and have set his heart so entirely on the Pure Good that
no creature is to him a comfort, that he has no desire for aught
creaturely, save so far as he may apprehend therein the Pure
Good, which is God.   And as little as the bright eye can endure
aught foreign in it, so little can the pure soul bear anything in
it, any stain on it, that comes between it and God.   To it all
creatures are pure to enjoy; for it enjoyeth all creatures in God,
and God in all creatures." [1]

"To it all creatures are pure to enjoy!"   This is hardly the
popular concept of the mystic; which credits him, in the teeth
of such examples as St. Francis, St. Mechthild of Magdeburg,
Rolle, Suso, and countless others, with a hearty dread of natural
things.   Too many mistaken ascetics of the type of the
Curé d'Ars, who would not smell a rose for fear of sin, have
supported in this respect the vulgar belief; for it is generally
forgotten that though most mystics have practised asceticism as
a means to an end, all ascetics are not mystics.   Whatever may

[1] Meister Eckhart, quoted by Wackernagel, " Altdeutsches Lesebuch," p. 891.

be the case with other deniers of the senses, it is true that the pure soul of the mystic, dwelling on high levels of reality, his eyes set on the Transcendental World, is capable of combining with the perfection of detachment that intense and innocent joy in natural things, as veils and vessels of the divine, which results from seeing "all creatures in God and God in all creatures." "Whoso knows and loves the nobleness of My Freedom," said the voice of God to Mechthild of Magdeburg, "cannot bear to love Me alone, he must also love Me in the creatures."[1] Such a power is characteristic of the illumination which results from a faithful endurance of the Purgative Way; for the corollary of "blessed are the pure in heart" is not merely a poetic statement. The annals of mysticism prove it to be a psychological law.

How then is this contradiction to be resolved: that the mystic who has declared the fundamental necessity of "leaving all creatures" yet finds them pure to enjoy? The answer to the riddle lies in the ancient paradox of Poverty: that we only enjoy true liberty in respect of such things as we neither possess nor desire. "That thou mayest have pleasure in everything, seek pleasure in nothing. That thou mayest know everything, seek to know nothing. That thou mayest possess all things, seek to possess nothing. . . . In detachment the spirit finds quiet and repose, for coveting nothing, nothing wearies it by elation; and nothing oppresses it by dejection, because it stands in the centre of its own humility. For as soon as it covets anything it is immediately fatigued thereby."[2]

It is not love but lust—the possessive case, the very food of selfhood—which poisons the relation between the self and the external world and "immediately fatigues" the soul. Divide the world into "mine" and "not mine," and unreal standards are set up, claims and cravings begin to fret the mind. We are the slaves of our own property. We drag with us not a treasure, but a chain. "Behold," says the "Theologia Germanica," "on this sort must we cast all things from us and strip ourselves of them: we must refrain from claiming anything for our own. When we do this, we shall have the best, fullest, clearest, and noblest knowledge that a man can have, and also the

---

[1] "Das Fliessende Licht der Gottheit," pt. vi., cap. 4.
[2] St. John of the Cross, "Subida del Monte Carmelo," bk. i. cap. xiii.

noblest and purest love and desire."[1] " He will not behold the
Light who attempts to ascend to the vision of the Supreme
whilst he is drawn downwards by those things that are an
obstacle to the vision," says Plotinus, " for he does not ascend
alone, but brings with him that which separates him from the
One : in a word, he is not made one."[2] Accept Poverty, however, demolish ownership, the verb " to have " in every mood
and tense, and this downward drag is at an end. At once the
Cosmos belongs to you and you to it. You escape the heresy
of separateness, are " made one," and merged in "the greater
life of the All." Then, a free spirit in a free world, the self
moves upon its true orbit undistracted by the largely self-
imposed responsibilities of ordinary earthly existence.

This was the truth which St. Francis of Assisi grasped,
and applied with the energy of a reformer and the delicate
originality of a poet to every circumstance of the inner and
the outer life. This noble liberty it is which is extolled by
his spiritual descendant, Jacopone da Todi, in one of his most
magnificent odes :—

> " Poverta alto sapere
>   a nulla cosa sojacere
>   en desprezo possedere
>   tutte le cose create. . . .
>
> Dio non alberga en core strecto
>   tant'e grande quantai affecto
>   povertate ha si gran pecto
>   che ci alberga deitate. . . .
>
> Povertate e nulla havere
>   et nulla cosa poi volere
>   et omne cosa possedere
>   en spirito de libertate."[3]

---

[1] " Theologia Germanica," cap. v.
[2] Ennead vi. 9.
[3] " Oh Poverty, high wisdom ! to be subject to nothing, and by despising all to
possess all created things. . . .
God will not lodge in a narrow heart ; and it is as great as thy love. Poverty
has so ample a bosom that Deity Itself may lodge therein. . . .
Poverty is naught to have and nothing to desire : but all things to possess in
the spirit of liberty."—*Jacopone da Todi.* Lauda lix.

"My little sisters the birds," said St. Francis, greatest adept of that high wisdom, "Brother Sun, Sister Water, Mother Earth." [1] Not my servants, but my kindred and fellow-citizens; who may safely be loved so long as they are not desired. So, in almost identical terms, the dying Hindu ascetic :—

"Oh Mother Earth, Father Sky,
   Brother Wind, Friend Light, Sweetheart Water,
Here take my last salutation with folded hands !
For to-day I am melting away into the Supreme
Because my heart became pure,
And all delusion vanished,
Through the power of your good company."

It is the business of Lady Poverty to confer on her lovers this freedom of the Universe, to eradicate delusion, purify the heart, and initiate them into the "great life of the All." Well might St. Francis desire marriage with that enchantress, who gives back ten-fold all that she takes away. "Holy poverty," he said, "is a treasure so high excelling and so divine that we be not worthy to lay it up in our vile vessels ; since this is that celestial virtue whereby all earthly things and fleeting are trodden underfoot, and whereby all hind-rances are lifted from the soul so that freely she may join herself to God Eternal." [2]

Poverty is the matchmaker between God and the spirit of man. Never will the union to which that spirit tends take place without her good offices, her drastic separation of the unreal from the real. She strips off the clothing which man so often mistakes for himself, transvaluates all his values, and shows him things as they are. Thus, in that beautiful chapter of the "Sacrum Commercium," which describes how the friars, climbing "the steeps of the hill," find Lady Poverty at the summit "enthroned only in her nakedness," we are told that she "preventing them with the blessings of sweetness," said, "Why hasten ye so from the vale of tears to the mount of light ? If, peradventure, it is me that ye seek, lo, I am but as you behold, a little poor one, stricken with storms and far

---

[1] "Fioretti," cap. xvi., and "Speculum," cap. cxx.
[2] *Ibid.*, cap. xiii. (Arnold's translation).

from any consolation." Whereto the brothers answer, "*Only admit us to thy peace ; and we shall be saved.*" [1]

The same truth: the saving peace of utter detachment from everything but Divine Reality—a detachment which makes those who have it the citizens of the world, and enabled the friars to say to Lady Poverty as they showed her from the hill of Assisi the whole countryside at her feet, "Hoc est claustrum nostrum, Domina," [2] is taught by Meister Eckhart in a more homely parable.

There was a learned man who, eight years long, desired that God would show him a man who would teach him the truth. And once when he felt a very great longing a voice from God came to him and said, "Go to the church and there shalt thou find a man who shalt show thee the way to blessedness." And he went thence, and found a poor man whose feet were torn and covered with dust and dirt : and all his clothes were hardly worth three farthings. And he greeted him, saying :—

"God give you good day ! "

He answered : "I have never had a bad day."

"God give you good luck."

"I have never had ill luck."

"May you be happy ! but why do you answer me thus ? "

"I have never been unhappy."

"Pray explain this to me, for I cannot understand it."

The poor man answered, "Willingly. You wished me good day. I never had a bad day ; for if I am hungry I praise God ; if it freezes, hails, snows, rains, if the weather is fair or foul, still I praise God ; am I wretched and despised, I praise God, and so I have never had an evil day. You wished that God would send me luck. But I never had ill luck, for I know how to live with God, and I know that what He does is best ; and what God gives me or ordains for me, be it good or ill, I take it cheerfully from God as the best that can be, and so I have never had ill luck. You wished that God would make me happy. I was never unhappy ; for my only desire is to live in God's will, and I have so entirely yielded my will to God's, that what God wills, I will."

---

[1] "Sacrum Commercium Beati Francisci cum Domina Paupertate," caps. iv. and v. (Rawnsley's translation).　　[2] *Op. cit.*, cap. xxii.

"But if God should will to cast you into hell," said the learned man, "what would you do then?"

"Cast me into hell? His goodness forbids! But if He did cast me into hell, I should have two arms to embrace Him. One arm is true humility, that I should lay beneath Him, and be thereby united to His holy humanity. And with the right arm of love, which is united with His holy divinity, I should so embrace Him that He would have to go to hell with me. And I would rather be in hell and have God, than in heaven and not have God."

Then the Master understood that true abandonment with utter humility is the nearest way to God.

The Master asked further: "Whence are you come?"

"From God."

"Where did you find God?"

"When I forsook all creatures."

"Where have you left God?"

"In pure hearts, and in men of good will."

The Master asked: "What sort of man are you?"

"I am a king."

"Where is your kingdom?"

"My soul is my kingdom, for I can so rule my senses inward and outward that all the desires and powers of my soul are in subjection, and this kingdom is greater than a kingdom on earth."[1]

"What brought you to this perfection?"

"My silence, my high thoughts, and my union with God. For I could not rest in anything that was less than God. Now I have found God; and in God have eternal rest and peace."[2]

Poverty, then, consists in a breaking down of man's inveterate habit of trying to rest in, or take seriously, things which are "less than God": i.e., which do not possess the character of reality. Such a habit is the most fertile of all causes of "world-weariness" and disillusion: faults, or rather spiritual diseases, which the mystics never exhibit, but which few who are without all mystic feeling can hope to escape. Hence the

---

[1] So Ruysbroeck, "Freewill is the king of the soul, he inhabits the highest city of that kingdom: that is to say, the desirous forces of the soul" ("L'Ornement des Noces Spirituelles," l. i. cap. xxiv.).

[2] Meister Eckhart. Quoted in Martensen's monograph, p. 107.

sharpened perceptions of the contemplatives have always seen poverty as a counsel of prudence, a higher form of common sense. It is not with St. Francis, or any other great mystic, a first principle, an end in itself. It was rather a logical deduction from the first principle of their science—the paramount importance to the soul of a clear view of reality.

Here East and West are in agreement: "Their science," says Al Ghazzali of the Sūfis, who practised, like the early Franciscans, a complete renunciation of worldly goods, "has for its object the uprooting from the soul of all violent passions, the extirpation from it of vicious desires, and evil qualities; so that the heart may become detached from all that is not God, and give itself for its only occupation meditation upon the Divine Being." [1]

All those who have felt themselves urged towards the attainment of this transcendental vision, have found that possessions interrupt the view, are centres of conflicting interest in the mind. They assume a false air of importance, force themselves upon the attention, and complicate life. Hence, in the interest of self-simplification, they must be cleared away: a removal which involves for the real enthusiast little more sacrifice than the weekly visit of the dustman. "Having entirely surrendered my own free-will," says Al Ghazzali of his personal experience, "my heart no longer felt any distress in renouncing fame, wealth, or the society of my children." [2]

Others have contrived to reconcile self-surrender with a more moderate abandonment of outward things. Possessions take different rank for almost every human soul; and the true rule of poverty consists in giving up those things which enchain the spirit, divide its interests, and deflect it on its road to the Absolute—whether these things be riches, habits, religious observances, friends, interests, distastes, or desires—not in mere outward destitution for its own sake. It is attitude, not act, that really matters; self-denudation would not be necessary were it not for our ineradicable tendency to attribute false value to things the moment they become our own. "What is poverty of spirit but meekness of mind, by which a man knows his own infirmity?" says Rolle, "seeing that to perfect stable-

---

[1] Schmölders, " Essai sur les Écoles Philosophiques chez les Arabes," p. 54.
[2] Ibid., op. cit., p. 58.

ness he may not come but by the grace of God, all thing that him might let from that grace he forsakes, and only in joy of his Maker he sets his desire. And as of one root spring many branches, so of wilful poverty on this wise taken proceed virtues and marvels untrowed. Not as some that change their clothes and not their souls ; riches soothly it seems these forsake, and vices innumerable they cease not to gather. . . . If thou truly all thing for God forsake, *see more what thou despiseth than what thou forsaketh.*" [1]

From such passages as this it follows that the Poverty of the mystics is a mental rather than a material state. Detachment is the inner reality, of which Franciscan poverty is a sacrament to the world. It is the poor in spirit, not the poor in substance, who are to be spiritually blessed. "Let all things be forsaken of me," says Gerlac Petersen, "so that being poor I may be able in great inward spaciousness, and without any hurt, to suffer want of all those things which the mind of man can desire ; out of or excepting God Himself." [2]

"I am not speaking here of the absence of *things*," says St. John of the Cross, "for absence is not detachment if the desire remains—but of that detachment which consists in suppressing desire and avoiding pleasure. It is this that sets the soul free, even though possession may be still retained." [3]

Every person in whom the mystical instinct awakes soon discovers in himself certain tastes or qualities which interrupt the development of that instinct. Often these tastes and qualities are legitimate enough upon their own plane ; but they are a drain upon the energy of the self, preventing her from attaining that intenser life for which she was made and which demands all her interest and energy. They distract her attention, they fill the field of perception : making of the surface-consciousness so active a thing that it can hardly be put to sleep. "Where can he have that pure and naked vision of unchangeable Truth whereby he see into all things," says Petersen again, "who is so busied in other things, not perhaps evil, which operate . . . upon his thoughts and imagination and

[1] Richard Rolle, "The Mending of Life," cap. iii.
[2] "Ignitum cum Deo Soliloquium," cap. i.
[3] "Subida del Monte Carmelo," l. i. cap. iii.

confuse and enchain his mind . . . that his sight of that unique One in Whom all things are is over-clouded ?"[1]

Now the nature of these distracting factors which "confuse and enchain the mind" will vary with almost every individual. It is impossible to predict in any one case what the things will be which the self must give up in order that the transcendental consciousness may grow. "Does it make any difference whether a bird be held by a slender thread or by a rope, while the bird is bound and cannot fly until the cord that holds it is broken? It is true that a slender thread is more easily broken; still notwithstanding, if it is not broken the bird cannot fly. This is the state of a soul with particular attachments: it never can attain to the liberty of the divine union, whatever virtues it may possess. Desires and attachments affect the soul as the remora is said to affect a ship; that is but a little fish, yet when it clings to the vessel it effectually hinders its progress."[2]

"One man's meat is another man's poison," is a statement that is peculiarly true in regard to questions of detachment. Here each adventurer must—and does—judge for himself; extirpating all those interests which nourish selfhood, however innocent or even useful they may seem in the eyes of the world. The only rule is the remorseless abandonment of everything which is in the way. "When any man God perfectly desires to love, all things as well inward as outward that to God's love are contrary and from His love do let, he studies to do away."[3] This may mean the utter self-stripping of St. Francis of Assisi, who cast off his actual clothing in his relentless determination to have nothing of his own:[4] or the scarcely less drastic proceedings of Antoinette Bourignan, who found that a penny was enough to keep her from God.

"Being one night in a most profound Penitence," says the biographer of this extraordinary woman, "she said from the bottom of her Heart, 'O my Lord! what must I do to please Thee? For I have nobody to teach me. Speak to my soul and it will hear Thee.'" At that instant she heard, as if another had spoken within her, "Forsake all

---

[1] Gerlac Petersen, *op. cit.*, cap. xi.
[2] St. John of the Cross, *op. cit.*, l. i. cap. xi.
[3] Richard Rolle, "The Fire of Love," bk. i. cap. xix.
[4] Thomas of Celano, Legenda Prima, cap. vi.

earthly things. Separate thyself from the love of the creatures. Deny thyself." From this time the more she entered into herself the more she was inclined to abandon all. But she had not the courage necessary for the complete renunciation towards which her transcendental consciousness was pressing her. She struggled to adjust herself to the inner and the outer life, but without success. For such a character as hers, compromise was impossible. "She asked always earnestly, When shall I be perfectly thine, O my God? and she thought He still answered her, *When thou shalt no longer possess anything, and shalt die to thyself.* And where shall I do that, Lord? He answered, *In the Desert.*" At last the discord between her deeper and her superficial self became intolerable. Reinforced by the miseries of an unsympathetic home, still more by a threat of approaching marriage, the inexorable inner powers got their way. She submitted; and having disguised herself in a hermit's dress—she was only eighteen and had no one to help or advise her—"she went out of her chamber about Four in the Morning, taking nothing but one Penny to buy Bread for that Day; and it being said to her in the going out, *Where is thy Faith? In a Penny?* she threw it away. . . . Thus she went away wholly delivered from the heavy burthen of the Cares and Good Things of this World."[1]

An admirable example of the mystic's attitude towards the soul-destroying division of interests, the natural but hopeless human struggle to make the best of both worlds, which sucks at its transcendental vitality, occurs in St. Teresa's purgative period. In her case this state of purification, the war between the real and the superficial self, extended over a long term of years. It ran side by side with the state of Illumination, co-existing with a fully developed contemplative life; and was only brought to an end by that "Second Conversion" which at last unified her scattered interests and set her firmly and for ever on the Unitive Way. The almost virile strength of Teresa's character, which afterwards contributed to the greatness of her achievement in the unitive state, opposed itself to the invading transcendental consciousness; disputed every inch of territory, resisted every demand made upon it by the growing spiritual self. Bit by bit it was conquered, the sphere of

[1] "An Apology for Mrs. Antoinette Bourignan," pp. 269-70.

her deeper life enlarged; until the moment came in which she surrendered, once for all, to her true destiny.[1]

During the years of inward stress, of penance and growing knowledge of the Infinite which she spent in the Convent of the Incarnation, and which accompanied this slow remaking of character, Teresa's only self-indulgence—as it seems, a sufficiently innocent one—was talking to the friends who came down from Avila to the convent-parlour, and spoke to her through the *grille*. Her confessors, unaccustomed to the education of mystical genius, saw nothing incompatible between this practice and the pursuit of a high contemplative life. But as her transcendental consciousness, her states of orison grew stronger, Teresa felt more and more the distracting influence of these glimpses of the outer world. They were a drain upon the energy which ought to be wholly given to that new, deep, more real life which she felt stirring within her, and which could only hope to achieve its mighty destiny by complete concentration upon the business in hand. No genius can afford to dissipate his energies: the mystic genius least of all. Teresa knew that so long as she retained these personal satisfactions, her life had more than one focus; she was not whole-hearted in her surrender to the Absolute. But though her inward voices, her deepest instincts, urged her to give them up, for years she felt herself incapable of such a sacrifice. It was round the question of their retention or surrender that the decisive battle of her life was fought.

"The devil," says her great Augustinian eulogist, Fray Luis de Leon, in his vivid account of these long interior struggles, "put before her those persons most sympathetic by nature; and God came, and in the midst of the conversation discovered Himself aggrieved and sorrowful. The devil delighted in the conversation and pastime, but when she turned her back on them and betook herself to prayer, God redoubled the delight and favours, as if to show her how false was the lure which charmed her at the grating, and that His sweetness was the veritable sweetness. . . . So that these two inclinations warred with each other in

---

[1] St. Teresa's mystic states are particularly difficult to classify. From one point of view these struggles might be regarded as the preliminaries of conversion. She was, however, proficient in contemplation when they occurred, and I therefore think that my arrangement is the right one.

the breast of this blessed woman, and the authors who inspired them each did his utmost to inflame her most, and the oratory blotted out what the grating wrote, and at times the grating vanquished and diminished the good fruit produced by prayer, causing agony and grief which disquieted and perplexed her soul : for though she was resolved to belong entirely to God, she knew not how to shake herself free from the world : and at times she persuaded herself that she could enjoy both, which ended mostly, as she says, in complete enjoyment of neither. For the amusements of the locutorio were embittered and turned into wormwood by the memory of the secret and sweet intimacy with God ; and in the same way when she retired to be with God, and commenced to speak with Him, the affections and thoughts which she carried with her from the grating took possession of her." [1]

Compare with these violent oscillations between the super-ficial and mystical consciousness—characteristic of Teresa's strong volitional nature, which only came to rest after psychic convulsions which left no corner of its being unexplored—the symbolic act of renunciation under which Antoinette Bourignan's "interior self" vanquished the surface intelligence and asserted its supremacy. Teresa must give up her passionate interest in human life. Antoinette, never much tempted in that direction, must give up her last penny. What society was to Teresa's generous, energetic nature, prudence was to the temperamentally shrewd and narrow Antoinette : a distraction, a check on the development of the all-demanding transcendental genius, an unconquered relic of the "lower life."

Many a mystic, however, has found the perfection of detach-ment to be consistent with a far less drastic renunciation of external things than that which these women felt to be essential to their peace. The test, as we have seen, does not lie in the nature of the things which are retained, but in the reaction which they stimulate in the self. "Absolute poverty is thine," says Tauler, "when thou canst not remember whether anybody has ever owed thee or been indebted to thee for anything ; just as all things will be forgotten by thee in the last journey of death." [2] Poverty, in this sense, may be consistent with the

---

[1] Quoted by G. Cunninghame Graham, " Santa Teresa," vol. i. p. 139.
[2] Sermon on St. Paul (" The Inner Way," p. 113)

habitual and automatic use of luxuries which the abstracted self never even perceives. Thus we are told that St. Bernard was reproached by his enemies with the inconsistency of preaching evangelical poverty whilst making his journeys from place to place on a magnificently caparisoned mule, which had been lent to him by the Cluniac monks. He expressed great contrition : but said that he had never noticed what it was that he rode upon.[1]

Sometimes, the very activity which one self has rejected as an impediment becomes for another the channel of spiritual perception. I have mentioned the case of the Curé d'Ars, who, among other inhibitions, refused to allow himself to smell a rose. Sharply opposed to this is the case of St. Francis, who preached to the flowers,[2] and ordered a plot to be set aside for their cultivation when the convent garden was made, "in order that all who saw them might remember the Eternal Sweetness."[3] So, too, we are told of his spiritual daughter, St. Douceline, that "out of doors one day with her sisters, she heard a bird's note. 'What a lovely song!' she said : and the song drew her straightway to God. Did they bring her a flower, *its beauty had a like effect.*"[4] Here we are reminded of Plato. "The true order of going is to use the beauties of Earth as steps along which one mounts upwards for the sake of that other Beauty." This, too, is the true order of Holy Poverty : the selfless use, not the selfish abuse of lovely and natural things.

To say that so difficult a counsel of perfection should sometimes have been practised in excess, is but to say that asceticism is a human, not an inhuman art. Such excesses, however, are found most often amongst those saintly types who have not exhibited true mystic intuition. This intuition, entailing as it does communion with intensest Life, gives to its possessors a sweet sanity, a delicate balance, which guards them, as a rule, from such conceptions of chastity as that of the youthful saint who shut himself in a cupboard for fear he should see his mother pass by : from obedience of the type which identifies the voice of the director with the voice of God ; from detach-

[1] Cotter Morison, " Life and Times of St. Bernard," p. 68.
[2] Thomas of Celano, Legenda Prima, cap. xxix.
[3] *Ibid.*, Legenda Secunda, cap. cxxiv.
[4] Anne Macdonell, " St. Douceline," p. 30.

ment such as that exhibited by the Blessed Angela of Foligno, who, though a true mystic, viewed with murderous delight the deaths of relatives who were " impediments." [1] The detachment of the mystic is just a restoration to the liberty in which the soul was made : it is a state of joyous humility in which he cries, " Nought I am, nought I have, nought I lack." To have arrived at this is to have escaped from external illusion : to be initiated into the purer air of that universe which knows but one rule of action—that which was laid down once for all by St. Augustine when he said, in the most memorable and misquoted of epigrams : " Love, and do what you like."

2. MORTIFICATION

By mortification, I have said, is to be understood the positive aspect of purification : the remaking in relation to reality of the permanent elements of character. These elements, so far, have subserved the interests of the old self, worked for it in the world of sense. Now they must be adjusted to the needs of the new self and to the transcendent world in which it moves. Their focal point is the old self, the lower centre of consciousness ; and the object of mortification is to kill that old self, remove that lower centre, in order that the higher centre, the " new man," may live and breathe. As St. Teresa discovered when she tried to reconcile the claims of friendship and contemplation, one or other has got to go : a house divided against itself cannot stand. " Who hinders thee more," says Thomas à Kempis, "than the unmortified affections of thy own heart ? . . . if we were perfectly dead unto ourselves and not entangled within our own breasts, then should we be able to taste Divine things, and to have some experience of heavenly contemplation." [2]

In psychological language, the process of mortification is the process of setting up " new paths of neural discharge." That is

---

[1] " In that time and by God's will there died my mother, who was a great hindrance unto me in following the way of God : my husband died likewise, and in a short time there also died all my children. And because I had commenced to follow the aforesaid Way, and had prayed God that He would rid me of them, I had great consolation of their deaths, albeit I did also feel some grief" (Beatae Angelae de Fulginio, " Visionum et Instructionum Liber," cap. ix., English translation, p. 5).

[2] " De Imitatione Christi," l. i. caps. iii. and xi.

to say, the mystic life has got to express itself in action : and for this new paths must be cut and new habits formed—all, in spite of the new self's enthusiasm, "against the grain." The energy which wells up incessantly in every living being has to abandon the old road of least resistance and discharge itself in a new and more difficult way. The old paths, left to themselves, must fade and at last die. When they are dead, and the new life has triumphed, Mortification is at an end. The mystics always know when this moment comes. An inner voice then warns them to lay their active penances aside.

Since the greater and stronger the mystic, the stronger and more stubborn his character tends to be, this change of life and turning of energy from the old and easy channels to the new is often a stormy matter. It is a period of actual battle between the inharmonious elements of the self, its lower and higher springs of action : of toil, fatigue, bitter suffering, and many disappointments. Nevertheless, in spite of its etymological associations, the object of mortification is not death but life : the production of health and strength, the health and strength of the human consciousness viewed *sub specie aeternitatis*. "In the truest death of all created things, the sweetest and most natural life is hidden."[1]

"This dying," says Tauler again, "has many degrees, and so has this life. A man might die a thousand deaths in one day, and find at once a joyful life corresponding to each of them. This is as it must be : God cannot deny or refuse this to death. The stronger the death the more powerful and thorough is the corresponding life ; the more intimate the death, the more inward is the life. Each life brings strength, and strengthens to a harder death. When a man dies to a scornful word, bearing it in God's name, or to some inclination inward or outward, acting or not acting against his own will, be it in love or grief, in word or act, in going or staying ; or if he denies his desires of taste or sight, or makes no excuse when wrongfully accused ; or anything else whatever it may be to which he has not yet died, it is harder at first to one who is unaccustomed to it and unmortified than to him who is mortified. . . . A great life makes reply to him who dies in earnest even in the least things, a life which strengthens him immediately to die a greater death ; a

---

[1] Tauler, Sermon on St. Paul ("The Inner Way," p. 114).

death so long and strong, that it seems to him hereafter more joyful, good and pleasant to die than to live, for he finds life in death and light shining in darkness." [1]

No more than detachment, then, is mortification an end in itself. It is a means to the production of a definite kind of efficiency, a definite kind of vitality : like its physical parallel, the exercises of the gymnasium. Once this efficiency, this vitality, is produced, this training accomplished, mortification ends : often with startling abruptness. After a martyrdom which lasted sixteen years, says Suso—speaking as usual in the third person—of his own experience, "On a certain Whitsun Day a heavenly messenger appeared to him, and ordered him in God's name to continue it no more. He at once ceased, and threw all the instruments of his sufferings [irons, nails, hair-shirt, &c.] into a river." [2] From this time onward, austerities of this sort had no part in Suso's life.

The unknown French ecstatic who wrote, and the English contemplative who translated, "The Mirror of Simple Souls," [3] have between them described and explained in bold and accurate language the conditions under which the soul is enabled to abandon that "hard service of the virtues" which has absorbed it during the Purgative Way. The statement of the "French Book" is direct and uncompromising : well calculated to startle timid piety. "Virtues, I take leave of you for evermore!" exclaims the Soul. "Now shall my heart be more free and more in peace than it has been. Forsooth, I wot well your service is too travaillous. Some time I laid my heart in you without any dissevering : ye wot well this. I was in all things to you obedient. O then I was your servant : but now I am delivered out of your thraldom."

To this astounding utterance the English translator has added a singularly illuminating gloss. "I am stirred here," he says, "to say more of the matter, as thus : First when a soul gives her to perfection, she labours busily day and night to get virtues by counsel of reason, and strives with vices at every thought, at every word and deed that she perceives comes of them, and busily ensearches vices, them to destroy. Thus the

---

[1] Tauler, Second Sermon for Easter Day. (This is not included in either of the English collections.)

[2] Suso, Leben, cap. xvii.   [3] B.M. Add. 37790.

virtues be mistresses, and every virtue makes her to war with its contrary, the which be vices. Many sharp pains and bitterness of conscience feels the soul in this war. . . . But so long one may bite on the bitter bark of the nut, that at last he shall come to the sweet kernel : right so, shortly to understand, it fares by these souls that be come to peace. They have so long striven with vices and wrought by virtues that they be come to the nut's kernel, that is to say to the love of God, which is sweetness. And when the soul has deeply tasted this love . . . then the soul is wondrous light and gladsome. Then is she mistress and lady over the virtues, for she has them all within herself. . . . And then this soul takes leave of virtues, as of the thraldom and painful travail of them that she had before. And now she is lady and sovereign and they be subjects."

Jacopone de Todi speaks to the same effect :—

> " La guerra e terminata
>   de le virtu battaglia
>   de la mente travaglia
>   cosa nulla contende." [1]

So too in the case of St. Catherine of Genoa, after a penitential period of four years, during which she was haunted by a constant sense of sin, and occupied by incessant mortifications, " all thought of such mortifications was *in an instant* taken from her mind : in such a manner that, had she even wished to continue such mortifications, she would have been unable to do so . . . the sight of her sins was now taken from her mind, so that henceforth she did not catch a glimpse of them : it was as though they had all been cast into the depths of the sea." [2]   In other words, the new and higher centre of consciousness, finally established, asserted itself and annihilated the old. " La guerra e terminata," all the energy of a strong nature flows freely in the new channels, and mortification ceases, mechanically, to be possible to the now unified or " regenerated " self.

Mortification takes its name from the reiterated statement of all ascetic writers that the senses, or body of desire, with the cravings which are excited by different aspects of the pheno-

---

[1] " The war is at an end : in the battle of virtues, in travail of mind, there is no more striving" (Lauda xci.).

[2] Vita e Dottrina, cap. v.

menal world, have got to be mortified or killed ; which is, of course, but the statement of psychological necessities from another point of view. All those self-regarding instincts—so ingrained that they have become automatic—which impel the self to choose the more comfortable part, are seen by the awakened intuition of the embryo mystic as gross infringements of the law of love. " This then must be the travail and labour of a man, to draw his heart and mind from the fleshly love and liking of all earthly creatures, from vain thoughts and from fleshly imaginations and from the love and vicious feeling of himself, so that the soul shall or may find or take no rest in any fleshly thoughts or worldly affections." [1] The rule of Poverty must be applied to all the circumstances of normal consciousness as well as to the tastes and possessions of the self. Under this tonic influence real life will thrive, unreal life will wither and die.

This mortifying process is rendered necessary, not because the legitimate exercise of the senses is opposed to Divine Reality, but because those senses have usurped a place beyond their station ; become the focus of energy, steadily drained the vitality of the self. " The dogs have taken the children's meat." The senses have grown stronger than their masters, monopolized the field of perception, dominated an organism which was made for greater activities, and built up those barriers of individuality which must one and all be done away before the subject can fulfil its destiny and pass over into the boundless life of the One. It is thanks to this wrong distribution of energy, this sedulous feeding of the cuckoo in the nest, that " in order to approach the Absolute, mystics must withdraw from everything, even themselves." [2] " It is therefore supreme ignorance for any one to think that he can ever attain to the high estate of union with God before he casts away from him the desire of natural things," says St. John of the Cross,[3] " and of supernatural also so far as it concerns self-love, because the distance between them and that which takes place in the state of pure transformation in God is the very greatest." Again, " until the desires be lulled to sleep by the mortification of sensuality, and sensuality

---

[1] Walter Hilton, " The Scale of Perfection," bk. i. pt. iii. cap. i.
[2] Récéjac, " Fondements de la Connaissance Mystique," p. 78.
[3] " Subida del Monte Carmelo," l. i. cap. v.

itself be mortified in them, so that it shall be contrary to the spirit no more, the soul cannot go forth in perfect liberty to the fruition of the union with the Beloved." [1]

The death of selfhood in its narrow obvious sense is, then, the primary object of mortification. All the twisted elements of character which minister to the existence of this unreal yet complex creature are to be pruned away. Then as with the trees of the forest, so with the spirit of man, strong new branches will spring into being, grow towards air and light. " I live, yet not I " is to be the confession of the mystic who has endured this " bodily death." The self-that-is-to-be will live upon a plane where her own prejudices and preferences are so uninteresting as to be imperceptible. She must be weaned from these nursery toys: and weaning is a disagreeable process. The mystic, however, undertakes it as a rule without reluctance: pushed by his vivid consciousness of imperfection, his intuition of a more perfect state necessary to the fulfilment of his love. Often his entrance upon the torments of the Purgative Way, his taking up of the spiritual or material instruments of mortification, resembles in ardour and abruptness that " heroic plunge into Purgatory " of the newly dead when it perceives itself in the light of Love Divine, which is described in the Treatise of St. Catherine of Genoa as its nearest equivalent. " As she, plunged in the divine furnace of purifying love, was united to the Object of her love, and satisfied with all he wrought in her, so she understood it to be with the souls in Purgatory." [2]

This " divine furnace of purifying love " demands from the ardent soul, not only a complete self-surrender and voluntary turning from all impurity, a humility of the most far-reaching kind : but also a deliberate active suffering, a self-discipline in dreadful tasks. As gold in the refiner's fire, so " burning of love into a soul truly taken all vices purgeth." Where detachment may be a counsel of prudence, a practical result of seeing the true values of things, the pain of mortification is seized as a splendid opportunity, a love token, timidly offered by the awakened spirit to that all-demanding Lover from Whom St. Catherine of Siena heard the terrible words " I, Fire, the Acceptor of sacrifices, ravishing away from them their

[1] *Op. cit.*, bk. i. cap. xv.
[2] S. Caterina di Genova, " Trattato di Purgatorio," cap. i.

darkness, give the light." [1] " Suffering is the ancient law of
love," says the Eternal Wisdom to Suso, " there is no quest
without pain, there is no lover who is not also a martyr.
Hence it is inevitable that he who would love so high a thing
as Wisdom should sometimes suffer hindrances and griefs." [2]

The mystics have a profound conviction that Creation,
Becoming, Transcendence, is a painful process at the best.
Those amongst them who are Christians point to the Passion
of Christ as a proof that the cosmic journey to perfection, the
path of the Eternal Wisdom, follows of necessity the Way of
the Cross.   That old dreadful law of the inner life, which
sounds so fantastic and yet is so bitterly true—" No progress
without pain "—asserts itself.   It declares that birth pangs
must be endured in the spiritual as well as in the material
world : that adequate training must always hurt the athlete.
Hence it is that the mystics' quest of the Absolute drives them
to an eager and heroic union with the reality of suffering, as
well as with the reality of joy. [3]

This divine necessity of pain, this necessary sharing in the
travail of a World of Becoming, is beautifully described by Tauler
in one of those " internal conversations " between the contemplative soul and its God, which abound in the works of the
mystics and are familiar to all readers of " The Imitation of
Christ."   " A man once thought," says Tauler, " that God drew
some men even by pleasant paths, while others were drawn by
the path of pain.   Our Lord answered him thus, ' What think
ye can be pleasanter or nobler than to be made most like unto
Me ? that is by suffering.   Mark, to whom was ever offered
such a troubled life as to Me ?   And in whom can I better work
in accordance with My true nobility than in those who are most

---

[1] Dialogo, cap. lxxxv.   [2] Leben, cap. iv.

[3] "This truth, of which she was the living example," says Huysmans of St.
Lydwine, " has been and will be true for every period.   Since the death of Lydwine,
there is not a saint who has not confirmed it.   Hear them formulate their desires.
Always to suffer, and to die ! cries St. Teresa ; always to suffer, yet not to die,
corrects St. Magdalena dei Pazzi ; yet more, oh Lord, yet more ! exclaims St. Francis
Xavier, dying in anguish on the coast of China ; I wish to be broken with suffering in
order that I may prove my love to God, declares a seventeenth century Carmelite, the
Ven. Mary of the Trinity.   The desire for suffering is itself an agony, adds a great
servant of God of our own day, Mother Mary Du Bourg; and she confided to her
daughters in religion that ' if they sold pain in the market she would hurry to buy
it there ' " (J. K. Huysmans, " Sainte Lydwine de Schiedam," 3rd edition, p. 225).

like Me? They are the men who suffer. . . . Learn that My
divine nature never worked so nobly in human nature as by
suffering; and because suffering is so efficacious, it is sent out
of great love. I understand the weakness of human nature at
all times, and out of love and righteousness I lay no heavier load
on man than he can bear. The crown must be firmly pressed
down that is to bud and blossom in the Eternal Presence of My
Heavenly Father. He who desires to be wholly immersed in
the fathomless sea of My Godhead must also be deeply immersed in the deep sea of bitter sorrow. I am exalted far
above all things, and work supernatural and wonderful works
in Myself: the deeper and more supernaturally a man crushes
himself beneath all things, the more supernaturally will he be
drawn far above all things.'" [1]

Pain, therefore, the mystics often court: sometimes in the
crudely physical form which Suso describes so vividly and
horribly in the sixteenth chapter of his Life, more frequently
in those refinements of torture which a sensitive spirit can
extract from loneliness, injustice, misunderstanding—above
all, from deliberate contact with the repulsive accidents
of life.

It would seem from a collation of the evidence that the
typical mystical temperament is by nature a highly fastidious
one. Its passionate apprehension of spiritual beauty, its
intuitive perception of divine harmony, is counterbalanced
by an instinctive loathing of ugliness, a shrinking from the
disharmonies of squalor and disease. Often its ideal of re-
finement is far beyond the contemporary standards of decency:
a circumstance which is alone enough to provide ample opportunity of wretchedness. This extreme sensitiveness, which
appears to form part of the normal psycho-physical make-up
of the mystic, as it often does of the equally highly-strung
artistic type, is one of the first things to be seized upon by
the awakened self as a disciplinary instrument. Then humility's axiom, " Naught is too low for love " is forced to bear the
less lovely gloss, " Naught must be too disgusting."

Two reasons at once appear for this. One is the innate
contempt for phenomena, nasty as well as nice—the longing to
be free from all the fetters of sense—which goes with the

---

[1] Tauler, Sermon on St. Paul ("The Inner Way," p. 114).

passion for invisible things. Those to whom the attractions of earth are only illusion, are inconsistent if they attribute a greater reality to the revolting and squalid incidents of life. St. Francis did but carry his own principles to their logical conclusion, when he insisted that the vermin were his brothers as much as the birds. Real detachment means the death of preferences of all kinds: even of those which seem to other men the very proofs of virtue and fine taste.

The second reason is a nobler one. It is bound up with that principle of self-surrender which is the mainspring of the mystic life. To the contemplative mind, which is keenly conscious of unity in multiplicity—of God in the world—all disinterested service is service of the Absolute which he loves: and the harder it is, the more opposed to his self-regarding and æsthetic instincts, the more nearly it approaches his ideal. The point to which he aspires—though he does not always know it—is that in which all disharmony, all appearance of vileness, is resolved in the concrete reality which he calls the Love of God. Then, he feels dimly, everything will be seen under the aspect of a cosmic and charitable beauty ; exhibiting through the woof of corruption the web of eternal life.

It is told of St. Francis of Assisi, in whom the love of lovely things was always paramount, how he forced himself to visit the lepers whose sight and smell disgusted him: how he served them and even kissed them.[1] " Then as he departed, in very truth that which had aforetime been bitter unto him, to wit, the sight and touch of lepers, now changed into sweetness. For, as he confessed, the sight of lepers had been so grievous unto him that he had been minded to avoid not only seeing them, but even going nigh their dwelling. And if at any time he chanced to pass their abodes, or to see them, albeit he were moved by compassion to do them an alms through another person, yet alway would he turn aside his face, stopping his nostrils with his hand. But through the grace of God he became so intimate a friend of the lepers that, even as he recorded in his will, he did sojourn with them and did humbly serve them."

Also, after his great renunciation of all property, he, once a prosperous young man who had been " dainty in his father's

[1] Thomas of Celano, Legenda Prima, cap. vii. ; 3 Soc. cap. iv.

home," accustomed himself to take a bowl and beg scraps of
food from door to door : and here too, as in the case of the
lepers, that which at first seemed revolting became to him
sweet.   "And when he would have eaten that medley of
various meats," says the legend, " at first he shrank back, for
that he had never been used willingly even to see, much less
to eat, such scraps.   At length, conquering himself, he began
to eat ; and it seemed to him that in eating no rich syrup had
he ever tasted aught so delightsome." [1]

The object, then, of this self-discipline is, like the object of
all purgation, freedom : freedom from the fetters of the senses,
the "remora of desire," from the results of environment and
worldly education, from pride and prejudice, preferences and
distaste : from selfhood in every form.   Its effect is a sharp
reaction to the joy of self-conquest.   The very act that had
once caused in the enchained self a movement of loathing
becomes not merely indifferent, but an occasion of happiness.
So Margery Kempe " had great mourning and sorrowing if she
might not kiss a leper when she met them in the way for the
love of our Lord, *which was all contrary to her disposition* in the
years of her youth and prosperity, for then she abhorred them
most." [2]

I will spare the sensitive reader a detailed account of the
loathsome ordeals by which St. Catherine of Genoa and
Madame Guyon strove to cure themselves of squeamishness [3]
and acquire this liberty of spirit.   They, like St. Francis, St.
Elizabeth of Hungary, and countless other seekers for the Real,
sought out and served with humility and love the sick and the
unclean : associated themselves at all costs with life in its
meanest forms : compelled themselves to contact with the most
revolting substances : and tried to suppress the surface-consciousness by the traditional ascetic expedient of deliberately
opposing all—even its most natural and harmless—inclinations.
" In the first four years after she received the sweet wound from
her Lord," says the Life of Catherine of Genoa, she " made great

[1] 3 Soc. cap. vii.

[2] " A Short Treatise of Contemplation taken out of the boke of Margery Kempe
ancresse of Lynne."   London, 1521.   This has been reprinted by Mr. E. Gardner
in "The Cell of Self-Knowledge," 1910, p. 49.

[3] The curious are referred to the original authorities.   For St. Catherine,
chapter viii. of the Vita e Dottrina : for Madame Guyon, Vie, pt. i. ch. x.

penances : so that all her senses were mortified. And first, so soon as she perceived that her nature desired anything, at once she deprived it thereof, and did so that it should receive all those things that it abhorred. She wore harsh hair, ate no meat nor any other thing that she liked ; ate no fruit neither fresh nor dried . . . and she lived greatly submitted to all persons, and always sought to do all those things which were contrary to her own will ; in such a way that she was always inclined to do more promptly the will of others than her own." . . . "And while she worked such and so many mortifications of all her senses it was several times asked of her 'Why do you do this?' And she answered, ' I do not know, but I feel myself drawn inwardly to do this . . . and I think it is God's will.' " [1]

St. Ignatius Loyola, in the world a highly bred Spanish gentleman of refined personal habits, found in those habits an excellent opportunity of mortification. "As he was somewhat nice about the arrangement of his hair, as was the fashion of those days and became him not ill, he allowed it to grow naturally, and neither combed it nor trimmed it nor wore any head covering by day or night. For the same reason he did not pare his finger or toe nails ; for on these points he had been fastidious to an extreme." [2]

Madame Guyon, a delicate girl of the leisured class, accustomed to the ordinary comforts of her station, seemed impelled to the most primitive and crude forms of mortification in her efforts towards the acquirement of " indifference." But, owing no doubt to the peculiar psychic constitution which afterwards showed itself in the forms of automatism and clairvoyance, her intense concentration upon the transcendental life produced a partial anæsthesia. " Although I had a very delicate body, the instruments of penitence tore my flesh without, as it seemed to me, causing pain. I wore girdles of hair and of sharp iron, I often held wormwood in my mouth." " If I walked, I put stones in my shoes. These things, my God, Thou didst first inspire me to do, in order that I might be deprived even of the most innocent satisfactions." [3]

The developing mystical consciousness made ever sharper and sharper war upon Madame Guyon's delicate and fastidious

---

[1] Vita e Dottrina, cap. v.   [2] Testament, cap. ii. (Rix's translation).
[3] Vie, pt. i. cap. x.

surface-personality. The impulses from below the threshold, so utterly at variance with her own instincts, imposed themselves upon her with an authority which seemed to her to possess all the marks of divine commands. " Thou wert continually with me, Oh my God! and Thou wert so severe a taskmaster that Thou wouldst not let me pass over the smallest things. When I thought of doing anything, Thou didst stop me abruptly and madest me to do without thinking all Thy desires, and all that was most repugnant to my senses, until they were become so docile that they had no longer either desire or distaste for anything. . . . I did nothing of myself, but I let myself be led by my King, who ruled me absolutely in all things." [1]

The procuring of this ascendancy of the "interior man," the transcendental consciousness, over the distracted and normal personality which deals with the manifold illusions of daily life, is, as we have seen, the main business of Purgation. It is, then, almost impossible that any mystic—whatever his religion, character or race—should escape its battles : for none at the beginning of their career are in a position to dispense with its good offices. Neoplatonists and Mahommedans, no less than the Christian ascetics, are acquainted with the Purgative Way. They all know the primal secret of the Spiritual Alchemists, that you must tame the Green Lion before you give him wings. Thus in 'Attar's allegory of the Valleys, the valley of self-stripping and renunciation comes first.[2] So too Al Ghazzali, the Persian contemplative of whom I have already spoken, says of the period immediately following his acceptance of the principles of Sūfi-ism and consequent renunciation of property, " I went to Syria, where I remained more than two years, without any other object than that of living in seclusion and solitude, conquering my desires, struggling with my passions, striving to purify my soul, to perfect my character, and to prepare my heart to meditate upon God." At the end of this period of pure purgation circumstances forced him to return to the world, much to his regret, since he " had not yet attained to the perfect ecstatic state, unless it were in one or two isolated moments." [3]

Such sporadic gleams of ecstatic vision, distributed through the later stages of purification, seem to be normal features of

---

[1] *Op. cit., loc. cit.*   [2] *Supra*, p. 156.

[3] Schmölders, " Essai sur les Écoles Philosophiques chez les Arabes," p. 59.

mystical development. Increasing control of the lower centres, of the surface intelligence and its scattered desires, permits the emergence of the transcendental perceptions. We have seen that Fox in his early stages displayed just such an alternation between the light and shade of the mystic way.[1] So too did that least ascetic of visionaries, Jacob Boehme. " Finding within myself a powerful contrarium, namely the desires that belong to the flesh and blood," he says, " I began to fight a hard battle against my corrupted nature, and with the aid of God I made up my mind to overcome the inherited evil will, to break it, and to enter wholly into the Love of God. . . . This, however, was not possible for me to accomplish, but I stood firmly by my earnest resolution, and fought a hard battle with myself. Now while I was wrestling and battling, being aided by God, a wonderful light arose within my soul. It was a light entirely foreign to my unruly nature, but in it I recognized the true nature of God and man, and the relation existing between them, a thing which heretofore I had never understood, and for which I would never have sought." [2]

In these words Boehme bridges the gap between Purgation and Illumination : showing these two states or ways as co-existing and complementary one to another ; forming the light and dark sides of a developing mystic consciousness. As a fact, they do often exist side by side in the individual experience :[3] and any treatment which exhibits them as sharply and completely separated may be convenient for purposes of study, but becomes at best diagrammatic if considered as a representation of the mystic life. The mystical consciousness, as we have seen, belongs—from the psychological point of view —to that mobile or " unstable " type in which the artistic temperament also finds a place. It sways easily between the extremes of pleasure and pain in its gropings after transcendental reality. It often attains for a moment to heights in which it is not able to rest : is often flung from some rapturous vision of the Perfect to the deeps of contrition and despair.

The mystics have a vivid metaphor by which to describe

[1] *Supra*, p. 215.
[2] Hartmann, "Life and Doctrines of Jacob Boehme," p. 50.
[3] Compare the case of St. Teresa already cited, *supra*, p. 257.

that alternation between the onset and the absence of the joyous transcendental consciousness which forms as it were the characteristic intermediate stage between the bitter struggles of pure Purgation, and the peace and splendour of the Illuminative Life. They call it *Ludus Amoris*, the " Game of Love " which God plays with the desirous soul. It is the " game of chess," says St. Teresa, " in which game Humility is the Queen without whom none can checkmate the Divine King." [1] " Here," says Martensen, " God plays a blest game with the soul." [2] The " Game of Love " belongs emphatically to that state of imperfection, of struggle, oscillation and unrest which precedes the first unification of the self. Once this event has taken place, the new level of reality has been attained, it is known no more. Thus St. Catherine of Siena, that inspired psychologist, was told in ecstasy, " With the souls who have arrived at perfection, I play no more the Game of Love, which consists in leaving and returning again to the soul; though thou must understand that it is not, properly speaking, I, the immovable GOD, Who thus elude them, but rather the sentiment that My charity gives them of Me." [3] In other terms, it is the imperfectly developed spiritual perception which becomes tired and fails, throwing the self back into the darkness and aridity whence it has emerged.

So with Madame Guyon, periods of "dryness "—the orthodox name for such spiritual fatigue—recurred at intervals during the whole of the Illuminated Life. So we are told of Rulman Merswin [4] that after the period of harsh physical mortification which succeeded his conversion came a year of "delirious joy alternating with the most bitter physical and moral sufferings." It is, he says, "the Game of Love which the Lord plays with His poor sinful creature." Memories of all his old sins still drove him to exaggerated penances : morbid temptations "made me so ill that I feared I should lose my reason." These psychic storms reacted upon the physical organism. He had a paralytic seizure, lost the use of his lower limbs, and believed himself to be at the point of death. When he was at his

[1] " Camino de Perfeccion," cap. xvii.
[2] Martensen, " Meister Eckhart," p. 75.
[3] Dialogo, cap. lxxviii.
[4] Jundt, " Rulman Merswin," pp. 19 and 20.

worst, however, and all hope seemed at an end, an inward voice told him to rise from his bed. He obeyed and found himself cured. Ecstasies were frequent during the whole of this period. In these moments of exaltation he felt his mind to be irradiated by a new light, so that he knew, intuitively, the direction which his life was bound to take, and recognized the inevitable and salutary nature of his trials. " God showed Himself by turns harsh and gentle: to each access of misery succeeded the rapture of supernatural grace." In this intermittent style, torn by these constant fluctuations, did Merswin, in whom the psychic instability of the artistic and mystic types is present in excess, pass through the purgative and illuminated states. They appear to have coexisted in his consciousness, first one and then the other emerging and taking control. Hence he did not attain the peaceful condition which is characteristic of full illumination and normally closes the " First Mystic Life." He passed direct from these violent alternations of mystical pleasure and mystical pain to the state which he calls "the school of suffering love." This, as we shall see when we come to its consideration, is strictly analogous to that which other mystics have called the " Dark Night of the Soul" and opens the " Second Mystic Life " or Unitive Way.

Such prolonged coexistence of pain and pleasure states in the developing soul, such delay in the attainment of equilibrium, is not infrequent, and must be taken into account in all attempts towards analysis of the mystic type. Though it is convenient for the purposes of study to practise a certain dissection, and treat as separate matters which are, in the living subject, hopelessly intertwined, we should constantly remind ourselves that such a proceeding is artificial. The struggle of the self to disentangle itself from illusion and attain the Absolute is a life-struggle. Hence, it will and must exhibit in every case something of the freedom and originality of life : will, as a process, obey artistic rather than scientific laws. It will sway now to the light and now to the shade of experience : its oscillations will sometimes be great, sometimes small. Mood and environment, inspiration and information, will all play their part.

There are in this struggle three factors.

(1) The unchanging light of Eternal Reality: that Pure Being "which ever shines and nought shall ever dim."

(2) The web of illusion, here thick, there thin, which hems in, confuses, and allures the sentient self.

(3) That self, always changing, moving, struggling—always, in fact, *becoming*—alive in every fibre, related at once to the unreal and to the real.

In the ever-shifting relations between these three factors, the consequent energy engendered, the work done, we may find a cause of the innumerable forms of stress and travail which are called in their objective form the Purgative Way.   One only of the three is constant: the Absolute to which the soul aspires. Though all else may fluctuate, that goal is changeless.   That Beauty so old and so new, "with whom is no variableness, neither shadow of turning," which is the One of Plotinus, the All of Eckhart and St. John of the Cross, the Eternal Wisdom of Suso, the Unplumbed Abyss of Ruysbroeck, the Pure Love of St. Catherine of Genoa—awaits yesterday, to-day, and for ever the opening of Its creature's eyes.

In the moment of conversion those eyes were opened for an instant: obtained, as it were, a dazzling and unforgettable glimpse of the Uncreated Light.   They must learn to stay open: to look steadfastly into the eyes of Love: so that, in the beautiful imagery of the mystics, the "faithful servant" may become the "secret friend."[1]   Then it is, says Boehme, that "the divine glimpse and beam of joy ariseth in the soul, being a new eye, in which the dark, fiery soul conceiveth the Ens and Essence of the divine light."[2]   So hard an art is not to be acquired abruptly.   On the contrary, it is more in accordance with all that we know of the conditions of growth that its perfect development in the individual should be preceded by a partial acquirement; by bewildering moments of lucidity, by splendid glimpses, whose brevity is due to the weakness of the new and still unpractised "eye which looks upon Eternity," the yet undisciplined strength of the "eye which looks upon Time."   Of such a nature is that play of light and dark, of exaltation and contrition, which bridges the gap

[1] See Denis the Carthusian, "De Contemplatione," bk. iii.   The metaphor is an ancient one and occurs in many mediaeval writers.

[2] "The Epistles of Jacob Boehme," p. 19.

between the Purgative and the Illuminative states. Each by turn takes the field and ousts the other; for "these two eyes of the soul of man cannot both perform their work at once."[1]

To use another and more domestic metaphor, that Divine Child which was, in the hour of the mystic conversion, born in the spark of the soul, must learn like other children to walk alone. Each effort to stand brings with it, first a glorious sense of growth and then a fall: each fall is but the occasion of another struggle towards obtaining the difficult balance which comes when infancy is past. There are many eager trials, many hopes, many disappointments. At last, as it seems suddenly, the moment comes : tottering is over, the muscles have learnt their lesson, they adjust themselves automatically, and the new self suddenly perceives itself—it knows not how— as standing upright and secure. That is the moment which marks the real boundary between the purgative and the illuminative states.

The process of this passage of the "new" or spiritual man from his awakening to the illuminated life, has been set out by Jacob Boehme in language which is at once poetic and precise. "When Christ the Corner-Stone [*i.e.*, the divine principle latent in man] stirreth himself in the extinguished Image of Man in his hearty Conversion and Repentance," he says, "then Virgin Sophia appeareth in the stirring of the Spirit of Christ in the extinguished Image, in her Virgin's attire before the Soul; at which the Soul is so amazed and astonished in its Uncleanness that all its Sins immediately awake in it, and it trembleth before her ; for then the judgment passeth upon the Sins of the Soul, so that it even goeth back in its unworthiness, being ashamed in the Presence of its fair Love, and entereth into itself, feeling and acknowledging itself utterly unworthy to receive such a Jewel. This is understood by those who are of our tribe and have tasted of this heavenly Gift, and by none else. But the noble Sophia draweth near in the Essence of the Soul, and kisseth it in friendly Manner, and tinctureth its dark Fire with her Rays of Love, and shineth through it with her bright and powerful Influence. Penetrated with the strong Sense and Feeling of which, the Soul skippeth in its Body for great Joy, and in the strength of this Virgin Love exulteth,

[1] "Theologia Germanica," cap. vii.

and praiseth the great God for his blest Gift of Grace.   I will
set down here a short description how it is when the Bride thus
embraceth the Bridegroom, for the consideration of the Reader,
who perhaps hath not yet been in this wedding chamber.   It
may be he will be desirous to follow us, and to enter into the
Inner Choir, where the Soul joineth hands and danceth with
Sophia, or the Divine Wisdom."[1]

[1] Jacob Boehme, "The Way to Christ," pt. i. p. 23 (vol. iv. of the complete
English translation of Boehme's works).

CHAPTER IV

THE ILLUMINATION OF THE SELF

IN Illumination we come for the first time to the consideration of that state of consciousness which is popularly
supposed to be peculiar to the mystic: a form of mental
life, a kind of perception, which is radically different from that
of "normal" men. His preceding adventures and experiences
cannot be allowed this quality. His awakening to consciousness of the Absolute—though it be often accompanied by
circumstances of splendour and intensity which seem to mark
it off from other psychic upheavals of that kind—does but
reproduce upon higher levels those characteristic processes of
conversion and falling in love which give depth and actuality
to the religious and passional life. The purification to which
he then sets himself—though this does as a rule possess certain
features which are confined to the phenomena of mystical

development—is again closely related to the mortifications of ascetic, but not necessarily mystical, piety. It is the most exalted form with which we are acquainted of that process of selection and self-discipline—that pruning and training of the human plant—which is the essence of all education and a necessary stage in every kind of transcendence. Here, the mystic does but adopt in a more drastic shape the principles which all who would live with an intense life, all seekers after freedom, all true lovers must accept: though he may justly claim with Ophelia that these wear their rue with a difference.

But in the mighty swing back into sunshine which is the reward of that painful descent into the " cell of self-knowledge," he parts company with these other pilgrims. Those who still go with him a little way—certain prophets, poets, artists, dreamers—do so in virtue of that mystical genius, that instinct for transcendental reality, which seers and creators so often possess. These people have a measure—sometimes a large measure—of illumination : they are the initiates of beauty or of wisdom, as the great mystic is the initiate of love. He has now obtained a veritable foothold in that transcendental world into which they too can penetrate now and again : has acquired the art of fellowship—not yet of union—with the "great life of the All," and thence draws strength and joy. Really and actually, as one whose noviciate is finished, he has "entered the Inner Choir, where the Soul joineth hands and danceth with Sophia, the Divine Wisdom": and, keeping time with the great rhythms of the spiritual universe, feels that he has found his place.

This change of consciousness, however abrupt and amazing it may seem to the self which experiences it, seems to the psychologist a normal incident of that organic process of development which was initiated by the first awakening of the transcendental sense. Responding to the intimations received in that awakening, ordering itself in their interest, concentrating its scattered energies on this one thing, the self emerges from long and varied acts of purification to find that it has pushed through to another order of reality. It has risen to acute consciousness of a world that was always there, and wherein its substantial being—that Ground which is of God—has always stood. Such a consciousness is " Transcendental Feeling" *in excelsis*: a deep, intuitional knowledge of the "secret plan."

As a chorus about its choragus, says Plotinus in a passage which strangely anticipates Boehme's metaphor, so do we all perpetually revolve about the Principle of all Things. But because our attention is diverted by looking at things foreign to the choir—all the foolish complexities of the world of appearance, the little diurnal incidents of that existence which we call life—we are not aware of this. Hence, instead of that free and conscious co-operation in the great life of the All which alone can make personal life worth living, we move like slaves or marionettes, and, oblivious of the whole to which our little steps contribute, fail to observe the measure "whereto the worlds keep time." Our minds being distracted from the Corypheus in the midst, the "energetic Word" who sets the rhythm, we do not behold Him. We are absorbed in the illusions of sense; the "eye which looks on Eternity" is idle. "But when we *do* behold Him," says Plotinus, "then we obtain the end of our wishes, and rest. Then also we are no longer discordant, but form a truly divine dance about Him; in the which dance the soul beholds the Fountain of life, the Fountain of intellect, the Principle of Being, the cause of good, the root of soul."[1] Such a beholding, such a lifting of consciousness from a self-centred to a God-centred world, is of the essence of illumination.

It will be observed that in these passages the claim of the mystic is not yet to supreme communion, to that "flight of the Alone to the Alone" which is the Plotinian image for the utmost bliss of the emancipated soul. A vision, and a knowledge, which is the result of conscious harmony with the divine World of Becoming, is the ideal held out: not self-mergence in the Principle of Life, but willing and harmonious

---

[1] Plotinus, Ennead vi. 9. Compare with this image of the rhythmic dance of things about a divine Corypheus in the midst, those strikingly parallel passages in the Apocryphal "Hymn of Jesus" where the Logos or Christ, standing within the circle of disciples, says, "I am the Word who did play and dance all things." "Now answer to My dancing." "Understand by dancing what I do." Again, "Who danceth not, knoweth not what is being done." "I would pipe, dance ye all!" and presently the rubric declares, "All whose Nature is to dance, doth dance!" (See Dr. M. R. James, "Apocrypha Anecdota," series 2; and G. R. S. Mead, "Echoes from the Gnosis: the Dance of Jesus." Compare *supra*, p. 159.)

revolution about Him, that "in dancing we may know what is done." This distinction holds good in almost every first-hand description of illumination which we possess : and it is this which marks it off from mystic union in all its forms. All pleasurable and exalted states of mystic consciousness in which the sense of I-hood persists, in which there is a loving and joyous relation between the Absolute as object and the self as subject, fall under the head of Illumination : which is really an enormous development of the intuitional life at high levels. All veritable and first-hand apprehensions of the Divine obtained by the use of symbols, as in the religious life; all phases of poetic inspiration, "glimpses of truth," are activities of the illuminated mind.

To "see God in nature," to attain a radiant consciousness of the "otherness" of natural things, is the simplest and commonest form of illumination. Most people, under the spell of emotion or of beauty, have known flashes of rudimentary vision of this kind. Where such a consciousness is permanent, as it is in many poets,[1] there results that partial yet often overpowering apprehension of the Infinite Life immanent in all living things which some modern writers have dignified by the name of "nature-mysticism." Where it is raised to its highest denomination, till the veil is obliterated by the light behind, and "faith has vanished into sight," we obtain such a case as that of Blake, in which the mystic swallows up the poet.

"Dear Sir," says that great genius in one of his most characteristic letters, written immediately after an onset of the illuminated vision which he had lost for many years, "excuse my enthusiasm, or rather madness, for I am really drunk with intellectual vision whenever I take a pencil or graver into my hand."[2] Many a great painter, philosopher, or poet, perhaps every inspired musician, has known this indescribable inebriation of Reality in those moments of transcendence in which his masterpieces were conceived. This is the "saving madness" of which Plato speaks in the "Phaedrus"; the ecstasy of the "God-intoxicated man," the lover, the prophet, and the poet "drunk with life." When the Christian mystic, eager for his birthright, says "Sanguis Christi, inebria me !" he is asking for just such a

---

[1] For instance, Keats, Shelley, Wordsworth, Tennyson, Browning, Whitman.
[2] "Letters of William Blake," p. 171.

gift of supernal vitality, a draught of that Wine of Absolute Life which runs in the arteries of the world.   Those to whom that cup is given attain to an intenser degree of vitality, hence to a more acute degree of perception, a more vivid consciousness, than that which is enjoyed by other men.   It is the prize of which purgation is the price, the passing " from death unto life."

Blake conceived that it was his vocation to bring this mystical illumination, this vision of reality, within the purview of ordinary men : to " cleanse the doors of perception" of the race.   They thought him a madman for his pains.

> " . . . I rest not from my great task
> To open the Eternal Worlds, to open the immortal Eyes
> Of Man inwards into the Worlds of Thought: into Eternity
> Ever expanding in the Bosom of God, the Human Imagination.
> O Saviour, pour upon me thy Spirit of meekness and love,
> Annihilate the Selfhood in me : be thou all my life." [1]

The Mysteries of the antique world were, one and all, attempts—often by the wrong road of a merely magical initiation—to "open the immortal eyes of man inwards " : exalt his powers of perception until they could receive the messages of a higher degree of reality.   In spite of much eager theorizing, it is impossible for us to tell how far they succeeded in this task.   In the case of those who had a natural genius for the Infinite, symbols and rituals which were doubtless charged with ecstatic suggestions, and which often dramatized the actual course of the Mystic Way, may well have brought about some change of consciousness : [2] though hardly that complete rearrangement of character which is an essential part of the mystic's entrance on the true Illuminated State.   Hence Plato only claims that " he whose initiation is recent " can see Immortal Beauty under mortal veils.

> " O blessèd he in all wise,
> Who hath drunk the Living Fountain,

---

[1] "Jerusalem," cap. i.
[2] Compare J. E. Harrison, " Prolegomena to the Study of Greek Religion," caps. ix., x., and xi.; a work which puts the most favourable construction possible on the meaning of Orphic initiation.

> Whose life no folly staineth
> And whose soul is near to God:
> Whose sins are lifted pall-wise
> As he worships on the Mountain." [1]

Thus sang the initiates of Dionysus; that mystery-cult in which the Greeks seem to have expressed all that they knew of the possible movement of consciousness through rites of purification to the ecstasies of the Illuminated Life. The mere crude rapture of illumination has seldom been more vividly expressed. With its half-Oriental fervours, its self-regarding glory in personal purification achieved, and the spiritual superiority conferred by adeptship, may be compared the deeper and lovelier experience of the Catholic poet and saint, who represents the spirit of Western mysticism at its best. His sins, too, had been "lifted pall-wise" as a cloud melts in the sunshine of Divine Love: but here the centre of interest is not the little self which has been thus exalted, but the greater Self which deigns thus to exalt.

> "O burn that burns to heal!
> O more than pleasant wound!
> And O soft hand, O touch most delicate,
> That dost new life reveal,
> That dost in grace abound
> And, slaying, dost from death to life translate." [2]

Here the joy is as passionate, the consciousness of an exalted life as intense: but it is dominated by the distinctive Christian concepts of humility, surrender, and intimate love.

We have seen that all real artists, as well as all pure mystics, are sharers to some degree in the Illuminated Life: are sojourners in, if not true citizens of, the land of heart's desire. They have drunk, with Blake, from that cup of intellectual vision which is the chalice of the Spirit of Life: know something of its divine inebriation whenever Beauty inspires them to create. Some have only sipped it. Some, like John of Parma, have drunk deep; accepting in that act the mystic heritage with all its obligations. But to all who have seen Beauty face to face, the Grail has been administered; and

---

[1] The "Bacchae" of Euripides (translated by Gilbert Murray), p. 83.
[2] St. John of the Cross, "Llama de Amor Viva" (translated by Arthur Symons).

through that sacramental communion they are made participants in the mystery of the world.

In one of the most beautiful passages of the "Fioretti" it is told how Brother Jacques of la Massa, "unto whom God opened the door of His secrets," saw in a vision this Chalice of the Spirit of Life delivered by Christ into the hands of St. Francis, that he might give his brothers to drink thereof.

"Then came St. Francis to give the chalice of life to his brothers: and he gave it first to Brother John of Parma: who, taking it, drank it all in haste, devoutly; and straightway he became all shining like the sun. And after him St. Francis gave it to all the other brothers in order: and there were but few among them that took it with due reverence and devotion and drank it all. Those that took it devoutly and drank it all, became straightway shining like the sun ; but those that spilled it all and took it not devoutly, became black, and dark, and misshapen and horrible to see ; but those that drank part and spilled part, became partly shining and partly dark, and more so or less according to the measure of their drinking or spilling thereof. But the aforesaid Brother John was resplendent above all the rest, the which had more completely drunk the chalice of life, *whereby he had the more deeply gazed into the abyss of the infinite light divine.*" [1]

No image, perhaps, could suggest so accurately as this divine picture the conditions of perfect illumination : the drinking deeply, devoutly, and in haste—that is, without prudent and self-regarding hesitation—of the heavenly Wine of Life ; that wine of which Rolle says that it " fulfils the soul with a great gladness through a sweet contemplation." [2] John of Parma, the hero of the Spiritual Franciscans in whose interest this exquisite allegory was composed, stands for all the mystics, who, "having completely drunk," have attained the power of gazing into the abyss of the infinite light divine. In the brothers who drank part and spilled part, so that they became partly shining and partly dark, "according to the measure of their drinking or spilling thereof," we may see an apt image of the artist, musician, prophet, poet, dreamer, more or less illuminated according to the measure of self-abandonment in which he has

---

[1] "Fioretti," cap. xlviii. (Arnold's translation).
[2] " Richard Rolle of Hampole," ed. Horstman, vol. ii. p. 79.

drunk the cup of ecstasy : but always, in comparison with the radiance of the pure contemplative, " partly shining and partly dark." " Hinder me not," says the soul to the senses in Mechthild of Magdeburg's vision, " I would drink for a space of the unmingled wine." [1]   In the artist, the senses have somewhat hindered the perfect inebriation of the soul.

We have seen that a vast tract of experience—all the experience, in fact, which results from contact between a purged and heightened consciousness and the World of Becoming in which it is immersed ; and much, too, of that which results from contact set up between such a consciousness and the Absolute Itself—is included in that stage of growth which the mystics call the Illuminative Way. This is the largest and most densely populated province of the mystic kingdom. Such disparate visionaries as Suso and Blake, Boehme and Madame Guyon, Mechthild of Magdeburg, Fox, Rolle, St. Teresa, and countless others have left us the record of their sojourn therein. Amongst those who cannot justly be reckoned as pure mystics we can detect in the works of Plato and Heracleitus, Wordsworth, Tennyson, and Walt Whitman certain indications that they too were acquainted, beyond most poets and seers, with the phenomena of the illuminated life. In our study of this degree of transcendence, then, we shall be confronted by a large mass of apparently irreconcilable material : the results of the relation set up between every degree of lucidity, every kind of character, and the suprasensible world.

To say that God is Infinite is to say that He may be apprehended and described in an infinity of ways. That Circle whose centre is everywhere and whose circumference is nowhere, may be approached from every angle with a certainty of being found. Mystical history, particularly that which is concerned with the Illuminative Way, is a demonstration of this fact. Here, in the establishment of the " first mystic life," of conscious correspondence with Reality, the self which has oscillated between two forms of consciousness, has alternately opposed and embraced its growing intuitions of the Absolute, comes for a time to rest. To a large extent, the discordant elements of character have been purged away. The " dark night of the senses " has been endured : though the more terrible " night of the spirit " is yet

[1] " Das Fliessende Licht der Gottheit," pt. i. cap. 43.

to come. Temporally at least the mind has "unified itself" upon high levels, and attained, as it believes, a perdurable consciousness of the divine and veritable world. The depth and richness of its own nature will determine how intense that consciousness shall be.

Whatever its scope, however, this new apprehension of reality at first appears to the Illuminated Self as final and complete. As the true lover is always convinced that he has found in his bride the one Rose of the World, so the mystic is sure that his quest is now fulfilled. In the first glow of his initiation into the "Perfect Land" he can conceive no higher rapture than this : no more intimate adventure of the soul. Ignorant as yet of that final act of communion which over-passes the proceedings of the inward eye and ear, he exclaims with entire assurance, "Beati oculi qui exterioribus clausi, interioribus autem sunt intenti," [1] and, absorbed in this new bliss-ful act of vision, forgets that it belongs to those who are still *in via*. More experience is needed if he is to learn how many more celestial secrets await his discovery ; how powerless is the heavenly food here given to satisfy his "hunger for the Abso-lute"; how far removed from the true End of Being is this basking in the sunbeams of the Uncreated Light, this revolving about the Principle of Things. Only the very greatest souls, the Galahads of the quest, learn this lesson and tread the whole of that "King's Highway" which leads man back to his source. "For the many that come to Bethlehem, there be few that will go on to Calvary." The rest stay here, in this Earthly Paradise, these flowery fields ; where the liberated self wanders at will, describing to us as well as it can now this corner, now that, of the Country of the Soul.

It is in these descriptions of the joy of illumination—in the outpourings of love and rapture belonging to this state—that we shall find the most lyrical passages of mystical literature. Here poet, mystic, and musician are on common ground : for it is only by the oblique methods of the artist, only by the use of æsthetic suggestion and musical rhythm, that the wonder of that vision can be expressed. When essential goodness, truth, and beauty—Light, Life, and Love—are apprehended by the heart, whether the heart be that of lover, painter, saint,

[1] "De Imitatione Christi," l. iii. cap. i.

that apprehension can only be adequately communicated in a living, that is to say, an artistic form.

Here, then, genius and sanctity kiss one another, and each, in that sublime encounter, looks for an instant through the other's eyes.   Hence it is natural and inevitable that the mystic should here call into play all the resources of artistic expression : the lovely imagery of Julian and Mechthild of Magdeburg, Suso's poetic visions, St. Augustine's fire and light, the heavenly harmonies of St. Francis and Richard Rolle. Symbols, too, play a vast part, not only in the description, but also in the machinery of illumination : the intuitions of many mystics presenting themselves directly to the surface-mind in a symbolic form.   We must therefore be prepared for a great variety and fluidity of expression in such writers as have tried to communicate to us the secret of this state of consciousness. We must examine, and even classify in so far as this is possible, a wide variety of experience : some which is recognized by friends and foes alike as purely " mystical," some in which the operation of poetic imagination is clearly discernible, some which involves " psychic phenomena " and other abnormal activities of the mind.   There is no use in being frightened away from investigation by the strange, and apparently irreconcilable aspect of these things.   The wounds of Truth are as faithful as the wounds of a friend.

Now there are three main types of experience which appear over and over again in the history of mysticism ; and always in connection with illumination, rather than any other phase of mystical development.   I think that they may fairly be regarded as its main characteristics, though of course the discussion of them cannot cover all the ground.   In few forms of life is the spontaneity of the individual so clearly seen as here : and in few is the ever-deadly process of classification attended with so many risks.

The three characteristics which I propose to consider are these :—

1. A joyous apprehension of the Absolute : that which many ascetic writers call "the practice of the Presence of God."   This, however, is not to be confused with that unique consciousness of union with the divine which is peculiar to a later stage of mystical development.   The self, though purified, still seems to

itself to exist as a separate entity. It is not immersed in its Origin, but contemplates it. This is the "betrothal" rather than the "marriage" of the soul.

2. This clarity of vision may also be enjoyed in regard to the phenomenal world. The actual physical perceptions are strangely heightened, so that the self perceives an added significance and reality in all natural things : is often convinced that it knows at last "the secret of the world." In Blake's words "the doors of perception are cleansed " so that "everything appears to man as it *is*, infinite." [1]

Plainly, these two forms of perception represent that dual intuition of a Transcendent-Immanent Reality, that stretching of consciousness in two directions until it includes in its span both the World of Pure Being and the World of Becoming,[2] which we found to be one of the distinguishing marks of the mystic type.

3. Along with this two-fold extension of consciousness, the energy of the intuitional or transcendental self is enormously increased. The psychic upheavals of the Purgative Way have tended to make it central for life : to eliminate from the character all those elements which checked its activity. Now it seizes upon the ordinary channels of expression ; and frequently shows itself in such forms as (*a*) auditions, (*b*) dialogues between the surface consciousness and another intelligence which purports to be divine, (*c*) visions, and sometimes (*d*) in automatic writings. This automatic activity of those growing but still largely subconscious powers which constitute the "New Man," increases steadily during the whole of the mystic life.

Illumination, then, tends to appear mainly under one or all of these three forms. Often all are present, though, as a rule, one seems to dominate the rest. The character of each case will be conditioned by the self's psychic make-up, its temperamental leaning towards "pure contemplation," "lucid vision," or automatic expression, emanation or immanence, the metaphysical, artistic, or intimate aspects of truth. The possible combinations between these various factors are as innumerable as the possible creations of Life itself.

In Brother Lawrence's "Practice of the Presence of God,"

[1] "The Marriage of Heaven and Hell," xxii.
[2] *Vide supra*, pp. 42–50.

in St. Bernard's converse with the Word, in Richard Rolle's "state of song," when "sweetest heavenly melody he took, with him dwelling in mind," we may see beautiful expressions of the first form of illuminated consciousness. Jacob Boehme is rightly looked upon as a typical example of the second : which is also found in one of its most attractive forms in St. Francis of Assisi. Suso and St. Teresa, perhaps, may stand for the third, since in thém the visionary and auditory phenomena were peculiarly well marked. The preliminary study of each characteristic in order, will help us to disentangle the many threads which go to the psychical make-up of these great and complex mystic types. The rest of this chapter will, then, be given to the analysis of the two main forms of illuminated consciousness : the self's perception of Reality in the eternal and temporal worlds. The important subject of voices and visions demands a division to itself.

I. THE CONSCIOUSNESS OF THE ABSOLUTE, OR "SENSE OF THE PRESENCE OF GOD"

This consciousness, in its various forms, is perhaps the most constant of all the characteristics of Illumination : and it is this which makes it, for the mystic soul, a pleasure-state of the intensest kind. I do not mean by this that the subject passes months or years in a continuous ecstasy of communion with the Divine. Intermittent periods of spiritual fatigue or "aridity"— the last vestiges of purgation—the oncoming gloom of the Dark Night—all these may be, and often are, experienced at intervals during the Illuminated Life ; as flashes of insight, indistinguishable from illumination, constantly break the monotony of the Purgative Way. But a certain knowledge of this Personal Life omnipresent in the universe has been achieved : and can never be forgotten though it be withdrawn. The "spirit stretching towards God" declares that it has touched Him ; and its normal condition henceforth is an acute and joyous consciousness of His Presence with "many privy touchings of sweet spiritual sights and feeling, measured to us as our simpleness may bear it." [1] Where he prefers less definite or more pantheistic language, the mystic's perceptions may take the form of

[1] Julian of Norwich, " Revelations," cap. xliii.

"harmony with the Infinite"—the same divine music trans-posed to a lower key.

This "sense of God" is not a metaphor. Innumerable decla-rations prove it to be a consciousness as sharp as that which other men have, or think they have, of colour, heat, or light. It is a well-known though usually transitory experience in the religious life : like the homing instinct of birds, a fact which can neither be denied nor explained. " How that presence is felt, may better be known by experience than by any writing," says Hilton, " for it is the life and the love, the might and the light, the joy and the rest of a chosen soul. And therefore he that hath once truly felt it cannot forbear it without pain, neither can he choose but desire it, it is so good in itself and so comfortable. . . . He cometh secretly sometimes when thou art least aware of Him, but thou shalt know Him full well ere He go ; for He wonder-fully stirreth and mightily turneth thy heart into the beholding of His goodness, and then doth thy heart melt delectably as wax against the fire into softness of His love."[1]

Modern psychologists have laboured hard to establish the pathological character of this state of consciousness: to find a place for it in the hospitable domain of " psychic hallucinations."[2] The mystics, however, who discriminate so much more delicately than their critics between true and false transcendental experi-ence, never feel any doubt about the validity of this "sense of the presence." Even when their theology contradicts it, they refuse to be disturbed.

Thus St. Teresa writes of her own experience, with her usual simplicity and directness, " In the beginning it happened to me that I was ignorant of one thing—I did not know that God was in all things : and when He seemed to me to be so near, I thought it impossible. Not to believe that He was present was not in my power ; for it seemed to me, as it were, evident that I felt there His very presence. Some unlearned men used to say to me, that He was present only by His grace. *I could not believe that*, because, as I am saying, He seemed to me to be present Himself : so I was distressed. A most learned man, of the Order of the glorious Patriarch St. Dominic,

---

[1] " The Scale of Perfection," bk. iii. cap. xi.
[2] See Delacroix, " Études sur le Mysticisme," Appendix I. " Hallucinations Psychiques, Sentiment de Présence."

delivered me from this doubt; for he told me that He was present, and how He communed with us : this was a great comfort to me."[1]

Again, "An interior peace, and the little strength which either pleasures or displeasures have to remove this presence (during the time it lasts) of the Three Persons, and that without power to doubt of it, continue in such a manner that I clearly seem to experience what St. John says, *That He will dwell in the soul*, and this not only by grace, but that He will also make her perceive this presence.[2] St. Teresa's strong "immanental" bent comes out well in this passage.

Such a sense of the divine presence goes side by side with the daily life and normal mental activities of its possessor ; who is not necessarily an ecstatic or an abstracted visionary, remote from the work of the world. It is true that the transcendental consciousness has now become, once for all, his centre of interest : that its perceptions and admonitions dominate and light up his daily life. The object of education, in the Platonic sense, has been achieved : his soul has "wheeled round from the perishing world" to "the contemplation of the real world and the brightest part thereof."[3]

In many temperaments of the unstable or artistic type, this intuitional consciousness of the Absolute becomes ungovernable : it constantly breaks through, obtaining forcible possession of the mental field and expressing itself in the "psychic" phenomena of ecstasy and rapture. In others, less mobile, it wells up into an impassioned apprehension, a "flame of love" in which the self seems to "meet God in the ground of the soul." This is "pure contemplation" : that state of deep orison in which the subject seems to be "seeing, feeling and thinking all at once." By this spontaneous exercise of all his powers under the dominion of love, the mystic attains that "Vision of the Heart" which, "more interior, perhaps, than the visions of dream or ecstasy,"[4] stretches to the full those very faculties which it seems to be holding in suspense; as a top "sleeps" when it is spinning fast. *Ego dormio et cor meum*

[1] Vida, cap. xviii. § 20.
[2] "Letters of St. Teresa" (1581), Dalton's translation, No. VII.
[3] "Republic," vii. 518.
[4] Récéjac, "Fondements de la Connaissance Mystique," p. 151.

vigilat. This act of contemplation, this glad surrender to an overwhelming consciousness of the Presence of God, leaves no sharp image on the mind : only a knowledge that we have been lifted up, to a veritable gazing upon That which eye hath not seen.

St. Bernard has left us in one of his sermons a simple, ingenuous and obviously personal account of such "privy touchings," such convincing but elusive contacts of the soul with the Absolute. "Now bear with my foolishness for a little," he says, " for I wish to tell you, as I have promised, how such events have taken place in me. It is, indeed, a matter of no importance. But I put myself forward only that I may be of service to you ; and if you derive any benefit I am consoled for my egotism. If not, I shall but have displayed my foolishness. I confess, then, though I say it in my foolishness, that the Word has visited me, and even very often. But, though He has frequently entered into my soul, I have never at any time been sensible of the precise moment of His coming. I have felt that He was present, I remember that He has been with me ; I have sometimes been able even to have a presentiment that He would come : but never to feel His coming nor His departure. For whence He came to enter my soul, or whither He went on quitting it, by what means He has made entrance or departure, I confess that I know not even to this day ; according to that which is said, *Nescis unde veniat aut quo vadit.* Nor is this strange, because it is to Him that the psalmist has said in another place, *Vestigia tua non cognoscentur.*

"It is not by the eyes that He enters, for He is without form or colour that they can discern ; nor by the ears, for His coming is without sound ; nor by the nostrils, for it is not with the air but with the mind that He is blended. . . . By what avenue then has He entered? Or perhaps the fact may be that He has not entered at all, nor indeed come at all from outside : for not one of these things belongs to out-side. Yet it has not come from within me, for it is good, and I know that in me dwelleth no good thing. I have ascended higher than myself, and lo ! I have found the Word above me still. My curiosity has led me to descend below myself also, and yet I have found Him still at a lower depth. If I have looked without myself, I have found that

He is beyond that which is outside of me; and if within, He was at an inner depth still. And thus have I learned the truth of the words I have read, *In ipso enim vivimus et movemur et sumus.*" [1]

Such a lifting up, such a condition of consciousness as that which St. Bernard is here trying to describe, seems to snatch the spirit for a moment into a state which it is hard to distinguish from that of true "union." This is what the contemplatives call passive or infused contemplation, or sometimes the "orison of union": a brief foretaste of the Unitive State, often enjoyed for short periods in the Illuminative Way, which reinforces their conviction that they have now truly attained the Absolute. It is but a foretaste, however, of that attainment: the precocious effort of a soul still in that stage of "Enlightening"—the equivalent of Illumination,—which the "Theologia Germanica" declares to be "belonging to such as are growing." [2]

This rather fine distinction between temporary union and the Unitive Life is perhaps best brought out in a fragment of dialogue between Soul and Self in Hugh of St. Victor's mystical tract, "De Arrha Animae."

The Soul says, "Tell me, what can be this thing of delight that merely by its memory touches and moves me with such sweetness and violence that I am drawn out of myself and carried away, I know not how? I am suddenly renewed: I am changed: I am plunged into an ineffable peace. My mind is full of gladness, all my past wretchedness and pain is forgot. My soul exults: my intellect is illuminated: my heart is afire: my desires have become kindly and gentle: I know not where I am, because my Love has embraced me. Also, because my Love has embraced me I seem to have become possessed of something, and I know not what it is; but I try to keep it, that I may never lose it. My soul strives in gladness that she may not be separated from That which she desires to hold fast for ever: as if she had found in it the goal of all her desires. She exults in a sovereign and ineffable manner, seeking nought, desiring nought, but to rest in this. Is *this*, then, my Beloved? Tell me that I may know Him, and that if He

---

[1] St. Bernard, "Cantica Canticorum," Sermon lxxiv.
[2] "Theologia Germanica," cap. xiv.

come again I may entreat Him to leave me not, but to stay with me for ever."

Man says, " It is indeed thy Beloved who visits thee ; but He comes in an invisible shape, He comes disguised, He comes incomprehensibly. He comes to touch thee, not to be seen of thee : to arouse thee, not to be comprehended of thee. He comes not to give Himself wholly, but to be tasted by thee : not to fulfill thy desire, but to lead upwards thy affection. He gives a foretaste of His delights, brings not the plenitude of a perfect satisfaction : and the earnest of thy betrothal consists chiefly in this, that He who shall afterwards give Himself to be seen and possessed by thee perpetually, now permits Himself to be sometimes tasted, that thou mayest learn how sweet He is. This shall console thee for His absence : and the savour of this gift shall keep thee from all despair." [1]

The real distinction between the Illuminative and the Unitive Life is that in Illumination the individuality of the subject—however profound his spiritual consciousness, however close his communion with the Infinite—remains separate and intact. His heightened apprehension of reality governs rather than obliterates the rest of his life : and may even increase his power of dealing adequately with the accidents of normal existence. Thus Brother Lawrence found that his acute sense of reality, his apprehension of the Presence of God, and the resulting detachment and consciousness of liberty in regard to mundane things, upheld and assisted him in the most unlikely tasks ; as, for instance, when he was sent into Burgundy to buy wine for his convent, " which was a very unwelcome task to him, because he had no turn for business, and because he was lame, and could not go about the boat but by rolling himself over the casks. That, however, he gave himself no uneasiness about, nor about the purchase of the wine. That he said to God, *It was His business he was about :* and that he afterwards found it very well performed. . . . So likewise in his business in the kitchen, to which he had naturally a great aversion." [2]

The mind, concentrated upon a higher object of interest, is undistracted by its own likes and dislikes ; and performs efficiently the work that is given it to do. Where it does not

---

[1] Hugh of St. Victor, "De Arrha Animae" (Migne, Patrologia Latina, vol. clxxvi.).
[2] "The Practice of the Presence of God," Second Conversation.

do so, then the normal make-up of the subject, rather than its mystical proclivities, must be blamed. St. Catherine of Genoa found in this divine companionship the power which made her hospital a success. St. Teresa was an admirable housewife, and declared that she found her God very easily amongst the pots and pans.[1] Appearances notwithstanding, Mary would probably have been a better cook than Martha, had circumstances forced on her this form of activity.

In persons of feeble or diffuse intelligence, however, this deep absorption in the sense of Divine Reality may easily degenerate into mono-ideism. Then the "black side" of Illumination, a selfish preoccupation with transcendental joys, the "spiritual gluttony" condemned by St. John of the Cross, comes out. "I made many mistakes," says Madame Guyon pathetically, "through allowing myself to be too much taken up by my interior joys. . . . I used to sit in a corner and work, but I could hardly do anything, because the strength of this attraction made me let the work fall out of my hands. I spent hours in this way without being able to open my eyes or to know what was happening to me: so simply, so peacefully, so gently that sometimes I said to myself, 'Can heaven itself be more peaceful than I?'"[2]

Here we see Madame Guyon basking like a pious tabby cat in the beams of the Uncreated Light, and already leaning to the extravagances of Quietism with its dangerous "double character of passivity and beatitude." The heroic aspect of the mystic vocation is wholly in abeyance. The "triumphing spiritual life," which her peculiar psychic make-up permitted her to receive, has been treated as a source of personal and placid satisfactions, not as a well-spring whence new vitality might be drawn for great and self-giving activities.

It has been claimed by the early biographers of St. Catherine of Genoa that she passed in the crisis of her conversion directly through the Purgative to the Unitive Life ; and never exhibited the characteristics of the Illuminative Way. This has been effectually disproved by the Baron von Hügel,[3] though he too is inclined in her case to reject the usual sequence of the mystic

---

[1] G. Cunninghame Graham, "Santa Teresa," vol. i. p. 299.
[2] Vie, pt. i. cap. xvii.
[3] "Mystical Element of Religion," vol. i. p. 105.

states. Yet the description of Catherine's condition after her four great penitential years were ended, as given in cap. vi. of the "Vita e Dottrina," is an almost perfect picture of healthy illumination of the inward or "immanent" type ; and may fruitfully be compared with the passage which I have quoted from Madame Guyon's life.

No doubt there were hours in which St. Catherine's experience, as it were, ran ahead ; and she felt herself not merely lit up by the Indwelling Light, but temporally merged in it. These moments are responsible for such passages as the beautiful fragment in cap. v., which does, when taken alone, seem to describe the true unitive state. "Sometimes," she said, " I do not see or feel myself to have either soul, body, heart, will or taste, or any other thing except Pure Love." [1] Her normal condition of consciousness, however, was clearly not yet that which Julian of Norwich calls being "oned with bliss"; but rather an intense and continuous communion with an objective Reality which she still felt to be distinct from herself. "After the aforesaid four years," says the next chapter of the "Vita," "there was given unto her a purified mind, free, and filled with God : insomuch that no other thing could enter into it. Thus, when she heard sermons or Mass, so much was she absorbed in her interior feelings, that she neither heard nor saw that which was said or done without : but within, in the sweet divine light, she saw and heard other things—being wholly absorbed by their interior light: and it was not in her power to act otherwise." Catherine, then, is still a spectator of the Absolute, does not feel herself to be *one* with it. "And it is a marvellous thing that with so great an interior recollection, the Lord never permitted her to go beyond control. But when she was needed, she always came to herself: so that she was able to reply to that which was asked of her : and the Lord so guided her, that none could complain of her. And she had her mind so filled by Love Divine, that conversation became hard to her : and by this continuous taste and sense of God, several times she was so greatly transported, that she was forced to hide herself, that she might not be seen." It is clear, however, that Catherine herself was aware of the transitory and imperfect nature of this intensely joyous state. Her growing transcendental self, unsatisfied with

[1] Vita e Dottrina, *loc. cit.*

the sunshine of the Illuminative Way, the enjoyment of the
riches of God, already aspired to union with the Divine.   With
her, as with all truly heroic souls, it was love for love, not love
for joy.   " She cried to God because He gave her so many consolations, '*Non voglio quello che esce da te, ma sol voglio te, O
dolce Amore!*'" [1]

"*Non voglio quello che esce da te.*"   When the crescent soul
has come to this, the Illuminative Way is nearly at an end.   It
has seen the goal, "that Country which is no mere vision, but
a home," [2] and is set upon the forward march.   So Gertrude
More: " No knowledge which we can here have of thee can
satisfy my soul seeking and longing without ceasing after thee.
. . . Alas, my Lord God, what is al thou canst give to a loving
soul which sigheth and panteth after thee alone, and esteemeth
al things as dung that she may gain thee?   What is al I say,
whilst thou givest not thyself, who art that one thing which is
only necessary and which alone can satisfy our souls?   Was it
any comfort to St. Mary Magdalen, when she sought thee, to
find two angels which presented themselves instead of thee?
verily I cannot think it was any joy unto her.   For that soul
that hath set her whole love and desire on thee can never find
any true satisfaction but only in thee." [3]

What is the nature of this mysterious mystic illumination?
Apart from the message it transmits, what is the form which
it most usually assumes in the consciousness of the self?   The
illuminatives, one and all, seem to assure us that its apparently
symbolic name is a realistic one ; that it appears to them as a
kind of radiance, a flooding of the personality with new light.
A new sun rises above the horizon and transfigures their twilit
world.   Over and over again they return to light-imagery in
this connection.   Frequently, as in the case of their first conversion, they report an actual and overpowering consciousness

---

[1] " I desire not that which comes forth from Thee; but only I desire Thee, O
sweetest Love !" (Vita e Dottrina, cap. vi.).

[2] Aug. Conf., bk. vii. cap. xx.   Compare St. Teresa : " Rapture is a great help to
recognize our true home and to see that we are pilgrims here ; it is a great thing to
see what is going on there, and to know where we have to live ; for if a person has
to go and settle in another country, it is a great help to him in undergoing the fatigues
of his journey that he has discovered it to be a country where he may live in the most
perfect peace " (Vida, cap. xxxviii., § 8).

[3] "Spiritual Exercises," pp: 26 and 174.

of radiant light, ineffable in its splendour, as an accompaniment of their inward adjustment.

> " Sopr' ogne lengua amore
>   bonta senza figura
>   lume fuor di mesura
>   resplende nel mio core," [1]

sang Jacopone da Todi.   " Light rare, untellable ! " said
Whitman.   " The flowing light of the Godhead," said Mechthild of Magdeburg, trying to describe *what* it was that made
the difference between her universe and that of normal men.
" Infused brightness," says St. Teresa, her delicate powers of
discrimination never, perhaps, used to better effect.   " In comparison with it every other light is something artificial.   It is a
light which knows no night ; but rather, as it is always light,
nothing ever disturbs it." [2]

> " De subito parve giorno a giorno
>   essere aggiunto ! "

exclaims Dante, initiated into the atmosphere of heaven ;
" Lume è lassù " is his constant declaration :

> " Ciò ch' io dico è un semplice lume,"

his last word, in the effort to describe the soul's apprehension of
the Being of God.[3]

It really seems as though the mystics' attainment of new
levels of consciousness did bring with it the power of perceiving
a splendour always there, but beyond the narrow range of our
poor sight ; to which it is only a " luminous darkness " at the
best.   " In Eternal Nature, or the kingdom of Heaven," said
Law, " materiality stands in life and light." [4]   The cumulative
testimony on this point is such as would be held to prove, in
any other department of knowledge, that there is indeed an

[1] " Love above all language, goodness unimagined, light without measure,
shines in my heart " (Jacopone da Todi.   Lauda xci.).
[2] St. Teresa, Vida, cap. xxviii. §§ 7, 8.
[3] Par. i. 61, xxx. 100, xxxiii. 90.
[4] " An Appeal to All who Doubt."   I give the whole passage below, p. 316.

actual light, rare, untellable, "lighting the very light" and awaiting the recognition of men.[1]

Consider the accent of realism with which St. Augustine speaks in the most celebrated passage of the "Confessions": where we seem to see a born psychologist desperately struggling by means of negations to describe an intensely positive state. " I entered into the secret closet of my soul, led by Thee; and this I could do because Thou wast my helper. I entered, and beheld with the mysterious eye of my soul the Light that never changes, above the eye of my soul, above my intelligence. It was not the common light which all flesh can see, nor was it greater yet of the same kind, as if the light of day were to grow brighter and brighter and flood all space. It was not like this, but different: altogether different from all such things. Nor was it above my intelligence in the same way as oil is above water, or heaven above earth, but it was higher because it made me, and I was lower because made by it. He who knoweth the truth knoweth that Light: and who knoweth it, knoweth eternity. Love knoweth it." [2]

Here, as in the case of St. Teresa, St. Catherine of Genoa, and Jacopone da Todi, we have a characteristically " immanental " description of the illuminated state. The self, by the process which mystics call "introversion," the deliberate turning inwards of its attention, its conative powers, discerns Reality within the heart: "the rippling tide of love which flows secretly from God into the soul and draws it mightily back into its source." [3]   But the opposite or transcendental tendency—the splendid Cosmic vision of Infinity exterior to the subject—the expansive, outgoing movement towards a Divine Light,

"Che visible face
lo Creatore a quella creatura
che solo in lui vedere ha la sua pace," [4]

---

[1] It is, of course, arguable that the whole of this light-imagery is ultimately derived from the Prologue of the Fourth Gospel: as the imagery of the Spiritual Marriage is supposed to be derived from the Song of Solomon. But it must be remembered that mystics are essentially realists, always seeking for language adequate to their vision of truth: hence the fact that they have adopted this imagery is a guarantee that it represents something which they know and are struggling to describe.

[2] Aug. Conf., bk. vii. cap. x.   [3] Mechthild of Magdeburg, op. cit., pt. vii. 45.

[4] Par. xxx. 100, "Which makes visible the Creator to that creature who only in beholding Him finds its peace."

the strange, formless absorption in the Divine Dark to which the soul is destined to ascend—these modes of perception are equally characteristic of the Illuminative Way. As in conversion, so here, Reality may be apprehended in either transcendent or immanent, positive or negative terms. It is both near and far ; and for some selves that which is far is easiest to find. To a certain type of mind, the veritable practice of the Presence of God is not the intimate and adorable companionship of the Inward Light, but the awestruck contemplation of the Absolute, the " naked Godhead," source and origin of all that Is. It is an ascent to the supernal plane of perception where, " without veils, in themselves and in their changelessness, the mysteries of theology appear in the midst of the luminous darkness of a silence which is full of profound teaching : a marvellous darkness which shines with rays of splendour, and which, invisible and intangible, inundates with its fires the dazzled and sanctified soul." [1]

With such an experience of eternity, such a vision of the Triune all-including Absolute which " binds the Universe with love," Dante ends his " Divine Comedy " : and the mystic joy with which its memory fills him is his guarantee that he has really seen the Inviolate Rose, the Flaming Heart of things.

> " O abbondante grazia, ond' io presunsi
>   ficcar lo viso per la luce eterna,
>   tanto che la veduta vi consunsi !
> Nel suo profondo vidi che s' interna,
>   legato con amore in un volume,
>   ciò che per l'universo si squaderna ;
> Sustanzia ed accidenti, e lor costume,
>   quasi conflati insieme per tal modo,
>   che ciò ch' io dico è un semplice lume.
> La forma universal di questo nodo
>   credo ch' io vidi, perchè più di largo,
>   dicendo questo, mi sento ch' io godo.
>
> .   .   .   .   .
>
> O, quanto è corto il dire, e come fioco
>   al mio concetto ! e questo, a quel ch' io vidi,
>   è tanto, che non basta a dicer poco.

---

[1] Dionysius the Areopagite, " De Mystica Theologia," i. 1.

O luce eterna, che sola in te sidi,
    sola t' intendi, e, da te intelletta
    ed intendente te, ami ed arridi·!" [1]

In Dante, the transcendent and impersonal aspect of illumination is seen in its most exalted form. It seems at first sight almost impossible to find room within the same system for this expansive vision of the Undifferentiated Light and such intimate and personal apprehensions of Deity as Lady Julian's conversations with her "courteous and dearworthy Lord," St. Catherine's companionship with Love Divine. Yet all these are really reports of the same psychological state : describe the attainment of the same grade of reality.

In a wonderful passage, unique in the literature of mysticism, Angela of Foligno has reported the lucid vision in which she perceived this truth : the twofold apprehension of an Absolute at once humble and omnipotent, personal and transcendent—the unimaginable synthesis of " unspeakable power" and " deep humility."

" The eyes of my soul were opened, and I beheld the plenitude of God, whereby I did comprehend the whole world, both here and beyond the sea, and the Abyss and all things else ; and therein did I behold naught save the divine power in a manner assuredly indescribable, so that through excess of marvelling the soul cried with a loud voice, saying ' This whole world is full of God ! ' Wherefore did I now comprehend that the world is but a small thing ; I saw, moreover, that the power of God was above all things, and that the whole world was filled with it.   Then He said unto me : ' I have shown thee something of My Power,' the which I did so well understand,

[1] Par. xxxiii. 82, 121 :—

" O grace abounding ! wherein I presumed to fix my gaze on the eternal light, so long that I consumed my sight thereon !

In its depths I saw ingathered the scattered leaves of the universe, bound into one book by love.

Substance and accidents, and their relations ; as if fused together in such a manner that what I tell of is a simple light.

And I believe that I saw the universal form of this complexity ; because, as I say this, I feel that I rejoice more deeply. . . .

Oh, but how scant the speech and how faint to my concept ! and that to what I saw is such, that it suffices not to call it ' little.'

O Light Eternal, Who only in Thyself abidest, only Thyself dost comprehend, and, of Thyself comprehended and Thyself comprehending, dost love and smile " that it enabled me better to understand all other things. He said also, 'I have made thee to see something of My Power; behold now, and see My humility.' Then was I given so deep an insight into the humility of God towards man and all other things, that when my soul remembered His unspeakable power and comprehended His deep humility, it marvelled greatly and did esteem itself to be nothing at all." [1]

It must never be forgotten that all apparently one-sided descriptions of illumination—more, all experiences of it—are governed by temperament. "That Light whose smile kindles the Universe" is ever the same; but the self through whom it passes, and by whom we must receive its report, has already submitted to the moulding influences of environment and heredity, Church and State. The very language of which that self avails itself in its struggle for expression, links it with half a hundred philosophies and creeds. The response which it makes to Divine Love will be the same in type as the response which its nature would make to earthly love: but raised to the nth degree. We, receiving the revelation, receive with it all those elements which the subject has contributed in spite of itself. Hence the apprehension of Divine Reality may take almost any form, from the metaphysical ecstasies which we find in Dionysius, and to a less degree in St. Augustine, to the simple, almost "common-sense" statements of Brother Lawrence, the lovely intimacies of Julian or Mechthild.

Sometimes—so rich and varied does the nature of the great mystic tend to be—the exalted and impersonal language of the Dionysian theology goes, with no sense of incongruity, side by side with homely parallels drawn from the most sweet and common incidents of daily life. Suso, in whom illumination and purgation existed side by side for sixteen years, alternately obtaining possession of the mental field, and whose oscillations between the harshest mortification and the most ecstatic pleasure-states were exceptionally violent and swift, is a characteristic instance of such an attitude of mind. His illumination was largely of the intimate and immanental type; but it was not without touches of mystical transcendence, which break out with sudden splendour

[1] B. Angelae de Fulginio, "Visionum et Instructionum Liber," cap. xxii. (English translation, p. 172).

side by side with those tender and charming passages in which
the Servitor of the Eternal Wisdom tries to tell his love.

Thus, he describes in one of the earlier chapters of his
life how " whilst he was thinking, according to his custom, of
the most lovable Wisdom, he questioned himself, and inter-
rogated his heart which sought persistently for love, saying,
' O my heart, whence comes this love and grace, whence comes
this gentleness and beauty, this joy and sweetness of the
heart ? Does not all this flow forth from the Godhead as from
its origin ? Come ! let my heart, my senses and my soul
immerse themselves in the deep Abyss whence come these
adorable things. What shall keep me back ? To-day I will
embrace you, even as my burning heart desires to do.' And at
this moment there was within his heart as it were an emanation
of all good ; all that is beautiful, all that is lovable and desirable
was there spiritually present, and this in a manner which
cannot be expressed. Whence came the habit that every time
he heard God's praises sung or said, he recollected himself in the
depths of his heart and soul, and thought on that Beloved
Object, whence comes all love. It is impossible to tell how often,
with eyes filled with tears, and open heart, he has embraced his
sweet Friend, and pressed Him to a heart overflowing with love.
He was like a baby which a mother holds upright on her knees,
supporting it with her hands beneath its arms. The baby, by
the movements of its little head, and all its little body, tries
to get closer and closer to its dear mother, and shows by its
little laughing gestures the gladness in its heart. Thus did the
heart of the Servitor ever seek the sweet neighbourhood of the
Divine Wisdom, and thus he was as it were altogether filled with
delight." [1]

2. THE ILLUMINATED VISION OF THE WORLD

Very clearly connected with the sense of "the Presence
of God," or power of perceiving the Absolute, is the complementary mark of the illuminated consciousness; the vision of "a
new heaven and a new earth," or an added significance and
reality in the phenomenal world. Such words as those of Julian,
" God is all thing that is good as to my sight, and the goodness

---

[1] Suso, Leben, cap. iv.

that all thing hath, it is He,"[1] seem to provide the link
between the two. Here again we have to distinguish carefully between vaguely poetic language—" the light that never
was," " every common bush afire with God"—and descriptions
which relate to a concrete and definite psychological experience.

This experience, at its best, balances and completes the
experience of the Presence of God at its best. That is to say,
its "note" is sacramental, not ascetic. It entails the expansion rather than the concentration of consciousness, the
discovery of the Perfect One ablaze in the Many, not the for-
saking of the Many in order to find the One. Its characteristic
expression is—

> " The World is charged with the grandeur of God ;
> It will flame out, like shining from shook foil,"

not "turn thy thoughts into thy own soul, where He is hid." It
takes, as a rule, the form of an enormously enhanced mental
lucidity—a sharpening of the senses, as it were—whereby an
ineffable radiance, a beauty and a reality never before suspected,
are perceived by a sort of clairvoyance shining in the meanest
things.

"From the moment in which the soul has received the
impression of Deity in infused orison," says Malaval, " she sees
Him everywhere, by one of love's secrets which is only
known of those who have experienced it. The simple vision
of pure love, which is marvellously penetrating, does not stop at
the outer husk of creation : it penetrates to the divinity which
is hidden within."[2]

Thus Browning makes David declare—

> " I but open my eyes,—and perfection, no more and no less,
> In the kind I imagined full-fronts me, and God is seen God
> In the star, in the stone, in the flesh, in the soul and the clod."[3]

Blake's "To see a world in a grain of sand," Tennyson's
" Flower in the crannied wall," Vaughan's " Each bush and

[1] " Revelations," cap. viii.
[2] Malaval, " De l'Oraison Ordinaire " (" La Pratique de la Vraye Théologie
Mystique," vol. i. p. 342).
[3] " Saul," xvii.

oak doth know I AM," and the like, are exact though over-
quoted reports of "things seen" in this state of consciousness,
this "simple vision of pure love": the value of which is summed
up in Eckhart's profound saying, "The meanest thing that one
knows in God,—for instance, if one could understand a flower
as it has its Being in God—this would be a higher thing
than the whole world!"[1]   Many mystical poets of the type of
Wordsworth and Walt Whitman possessed to a considerable
extent this form of illumination.   It is this which Bucke, the
American psychologist, has analysed in great detail under the
name of "Cosmic Consciousness."[2]   It is seen at its fullest
development in such cases as those of Fox, Boehme, and
Blake.

We will first take the experience of Jacob Boehme, both
because in his case we have a first-hand description which is
particularly detailed and complete, and because he is one of
the best recorded all-round examples of mystical illumination ;
exhibiting, along with an acute consciousness of divine companionship, all those phenomena of visual lucidity, automatism,
and enhanced intellectual powers which properly belong to it,
but are seldom developed simultaneously in the same individual.

In Boehme's life, as described in the Introduction to the
English translation of his Collected Works,[3] there were three
distinct onsets of illumination ; all of the pantheistic and
external type.   In the first, which seems to have happened
whilst he was very young, it is said that "he was surrounded by
a divine Light for seven days, and stood in the highest contemplation and Kingdom of Joy."   This, perhaps, we may
reasonably identify with mystical awakening of the kind
experienced by Suso.   About the year 1600 occurred the
second illumination, initiated by a trance-like state of consciousness, the result of gazing at a polished disc.   To this I have
already referred in an earlier chapter.[4]   This brought with it
that peculiar and lucid vision of the inner reality of the
phenomenal world in which, as he himself says, "he looked into

---

[1] Meister Eckhart ("Mystische Schriften," p. 137).
[2] *Vide supra*, Pt. II. Cap. II., the cases of Richard Jefferies, Brother Lawrence,
and others.
[3] The Works of Jacob Boehme, 4 vols., 1764, vol. i. pp. xii., &c.
[4] *Supra*, p. 69.

the deepest foundations of things." "He believed that it was only a fancy, and in order to banish it from his mind he went out upon the green. But here he remarked that he gazed into the very heart of things, the very herbs and grass, and that actual Nature harmonized with what he had inwardly seen."[1] Of this same experience and the clairvoyance which accompanied it, another biographer says, "Going abroad in the fields to a green before Neys Gate, at Görlitz, he there sat down, and, viewing the herbs and grass of the field in his inward light, he saw into their essences, use and properties, which were discovered to him by their lineaments, figures and signatures. . . . In the unfolding of these mysteries before his understanding, he had a great measure of joy, yet returned home and took care of his family and lived in great peace and silence, scarce intimating to any these wonderful things that had befallen him."[2]

So far as we can tell from his own scattered statements, Boehme must have lived from this time onwards in fairly constant and growing consciousness of the transcendental world : though there is evidence that he, like all other mystics, knew seasons of darkness, "many a shrewd Repulse," and times of struggle with that " powerful contrarium " the lower consciousness. In 1610—perhaps as the result of such intermittent struggles—the vivid illumination of ten years before was repeated in an enhanced form : and it was in consequence of this, and in order that there might be some record of the mysteries upon which he had gazed, that he wrote his first and most difficult book, the " Aurora," or " Morning Redness." The passage in which the "inspired shoemaker " has tried hard to tell us what his vision of Reality was like, to communicate something of the grave and enthusiastic travail of his being, the indicible knowledge of things to which he attained, is one of those which arouse in all who have even the rudiments of mystical perception the sorrow and excitement of exiles who suddenly hear the accents of home. It is a "musical" passage : addresses itself to the whole being, not merely to the intellect. In its movement, and in the quality of its emotion, it is like some romance by Brahms. Those who will listen and be receptive

---

[1] Martensen, " Jacob Boehme," p. 7.
[2] " Life of Jacob Boehme," pp. xiii. and xiv. in vol. i. of his Collected Works, English translation.

will find themselves repaid by a strange sense of extended life, an exhilarating consciousness of truth.   Here, if ever, is a man who is straining every nerve to " speak as he saw " : and it is plain that he saw much—as much, perhaps, as Dante, though he lacked the poetic genius which was needed to give his vision an intelligible form.   The very strangeness of the phrasing, the unexpected harmonies and dissonances which worry polite and well-regulated minds, are earnests of the Spirit of Life crying out for expression from within.   Boehme, like Blake, seems "drunk with intellectual vision "—" a God-intoxicated man."

" In this my earnest and Christian Seeking and Desire," he says, " (wherein I suffered many a shrewd Repulse, but at last resolved rather to put myself in Hazard, than give over and leave off) the Gate was opened to me, that in one Quarter of an Hour I saw and knew more than if I had been many years together at an University, at which I exceedingly admired, and thereupon turned my Praise to God for it.   For I saw and knew the Being of all Beings, the Byss and the Abyss, and the Eternal Generation of the *Holy Trinity*, the Descent and Original of the World, and of all creatures through the Divine Wisdom : knew and saw in myself all the three Worlds, namely, *The Divine*, angelical and paradisical ; and the *dark World*, the Original of the Nature to the Fire ; and then, thirdly, the *external* and *visible World*, being a Procreation or external Birth from both the internal and spiritual Worlds.   And I saw and knew the whole working Essence in the Evil and the Good, and the Original and Existence of each of them ; and likewise how the fruitful bearing Womb of Eternity brought forth. . . . Yet however I must begin to labour in these great mysteries, as a Child that goes to School.   I saw it as in a great Deep in the Internal.   For I had a thorough view of the Universe, as in a Chaos, wherein all things are couched and wrapped up, but it was impossible for me to explain the same.   Yet it opened itself to me, from Time to Time, as in a Young Plant ; though the same was with me for the space of twelve years, and as it was as it were breeding and I found a powerful Instigation within me, before I could bring it forth into external Form of Writing : and whatever I could apprehend with the external Principle of my mind, that I wrote down." [1]

[1] *Op. cit.*, p. xv.

Close to this lucid vision of the reality of things—this sudden glimpse of the phenomenal in the light of the intelligible world—is George Fox's experience at the age of twenty-four, as recorded in his Journal.[1] Here, as in Boehme's case, it is clear that a previous and regrettable acquaintance with the "doctrine of signatures" has to some extent determined the language and symbols under which he describes his intuitive vision of actuality as it exists in the Divine Mind.

"Now was I come up in spirit through the flaming sword into the Paradise of God. All things were new: and all the creation gave another smell unto me than before, beyond what words can utter. . . . The creation was opened to me ; and it was showed me how all things had their names given them, according to their nature and virtue. And I was at a stand in my mind whether I should practise physic for the good of mankind, seeing the nature and virtue of the creatures were so opened to me by the Lord. . . . Great things did the Lord lead me unto, and wonderful depths were opened unto me, beyond what can by words be declared ; but as people come into subjection to the Spirit of God, and grow up in the image and power of the Almighty, they may receive the word of wisdom that opens all things, and come to know the *hidden unity in the Eternal Being*."

"To know the hidden unity in the Eternal Being"—know it with an invulnerable certainty, in the all-embracing act of consciousness with which we are aware of the personality of those we truly love—is to live at its fullest the Illuminated Life, enjoying "all creatures in God and God in all creatures."

Lucidity of this sort seems to be an enormously enhanced form of the true poetic consciousness of "otherness" in natural things—the sense of a unity in separateness, a mighty and actual Life beyond that which eye can see, a glorious reality shining through the phenomenal veil—frequent in those temperaments which are at one with life ; often—as in Blake—a permanent accompaniment of the Illuminative State, and a constant though transitory feature in conversions of all kinds. The self becomes conscious, as it were, of that World of Becoming, that great and many-coloured river of life, in which the little individual life is immersed. Alike in howling gale and singing cricket it

[1] Vol. i. cap. ii,

hears the crying aloud of that "Word which is through all things everlastingly." It participates, actively and open-eyed, in the mighty journey of the Son towards the Father's heart: and seeing with purged sight all things and creatures as they are in that transcendent order, detects in them too that striving of Creation to return to its centre which is the secret of the Universe.

A harmóny is thus set up between the mystic and Life in all its forms. Undistracted by appearance, he sees, feels, and knows it in one piercing act of loving comprehension. "And the bodily sight stinted," says Julian, "but the spiritual sight dwelled in mine understanding, and I abode with reverent dread joying in that I saw."[1] The heart outstrips the clumsy senses, and sees—perhaps for an instant, perhaps for long periods of bliss —an undistorted and more veritable world. All things are perceived in the light of charity, and hence under the aspect of beauty : for beauty is simply Reality seen with the eyes of love. As in the case of another and more beatific Vision, *essere in carità è qui necesse.*[2] For such a reverent and joyous sight the meanest accidents of life are radiant. The London streets are paths of loveliness ; the very omnibuses look like coloured archangels, their laps filled full of little trustful souls.

Often when we blame our artists for painting ugly things, they are but striving to show us a beauty to which we are blind. They have gone on ahead of us, and attained that state of "fourfold vision" to which Blake laid claim ; in which the visionary sees the whole visible universe transfigured, because he has "put off the rotten rags of sense and memory," and "put on Imagination uncorrupt."[3] In this state of lucidity symbol and reality, Nature and Imagination, are seen to be *One :* and in it are produced all the more sublime works of art, since these owe their greatness to the impact of Reality upon the artistic mind. "I know," says Blake again, "that this world is a world of imagination and vision. I see everything I paint in this world, but everybody does not see alike. To the eye of a miser a guinea is far more beautiful than the sun, and a bag worn with the use of money has more beautiful proportions than a vine filled with grapes. The tree which

---

[1] "Revelations," cap. viii.   [2] Par. iii. 77.
[3] "Letters of William Blake," p. 111.

moves some to tears of joy is in the eyes of others only a green thing which stands in the way. Some see Nature all ridicule and deformity, and by these I shall not regulate my proportions; and some scarce see Nature at all. But to the eyes of the man of imagination, Nature is Imagination itself. As a man is, so he sees. As the eye is formed, such are its powers. You certainly mistake, when you say that the visions of fancy are not to be found in this world. To me this world is all one continued vision of fancy or imagination, and I feel flattered when I am told so."[1]

If the Mystic Way be considered as a process of transcendence : a movement of the self towards free and conscious participation in the Absolute Life, and a progressive appropriation of that life by means of the contact which exists in the deeps of man's being—the ground or spark of the soul—between the subject and the transcendental world : then this illuminated apprehension of things, this cleansing of the doors of perception, is surely what we might expect to occur as man moves towards higher centres of consciousness. His surface intelligence, purified from the domination of the senses, is invaded more and more by the transcendent personality, the " New Man" who is by nature a denizen of the independent spiritual world, and whose destiny, in mystical language, is a "return to his Origin." Hence an inflow of new vitality, extended powers of vision, an enormous exaltation of his intuitive powers.

In such moments of clear sight and enhanced perception as that which Blake and Boehme describe, the mystic and the artist do really see *sub specie aeternitatis* the Four-fold River of Life—that World of Becoming in which, as Erigena says, " Every visible and invisible creature is a theophany or appearance of God "—as all might see it, if prejudice, selfhood, or other illusion did not distort their sight. From this loving vision there comes very often that beautiful sympathy with, that abnormal power over, all living natural things, which crops up over and over again in the lives of the mystical saints ; to amaze the sluggish minds of common men, barred by "the torrent of Use and Wont"[2] from all communion alike with their natural and supernatural origin.

Yet is not so very amazing that St. Francis of Assisi, feeling

---

[1] *Op. cit.*, p. 62.   [2] Aug. Conf., bk. i. cap. xvi.

and knowing — not merely "believing" — that every living creature was veritably and actually a "theophany or appearance of God," should have been acutely conscious that he shared with these brothers and sisters of his the great and lovely life of the All. Nor, this being so, can we justly regard him as eccentric because he acted in accordance with his convictions, preached to his little sisters the birds,[1] availed himself of the kindly offices of the falcon,[2] enjoyed the friendship of the pheasant,[3] soothed the captured turtledoves, his "simple-minded sisters, innocent and chaste,"[4] or persuaded his Brother Wolf to a better life.[5]

The true mystic, so often taunted with "a denial of the world," does but deny the narrow and artificial world of self: and finds in exchange the secrets of that mighty universe which he shares with Nature and with God. Strange contacts, unknown to those who only lead the life of sense, are set up between his being and the being of all other things. In that remaking of his consciousness which follows upon the "mystical awakening," the deep and primal life which he shares with all creation has been roused from its sleep. Hence the barrier between human and non-human life, which makes man a stranger on earth as well as in heaven, is done away. Life now whispers to his life: all things are his intimates, and respond to his fraternal sympathy.

Thus it seems quite a simple and natural thing to the Little Poor Man of Assisi, whose friend the pheasant preferred his cell to "the haunts more natural to its state," that he should be ambassador from the terrified folk of Gubbio to his formidable Brother the Wolf. The result of the interview, reduced to ordinary language, could be paralleled in the experience of many persons who have possessed this strange and incommunicable power over animal life.

"O wondrous thing! whenas St. Francis had made the sign of the Cross, right so the terrible wolf shut his jaws and stayed his running: and when he was bid, came gently as a lamb and laid him down at the feet of St. Francis. . . . And St. Francis stretching forth his hand to take pledge of his troth, the wolf

[1] "Fioretti," cap. xiv.
[2] Ibid., "Delle Istimate," 2, and Thomas of Celano, Vita Secunda, cap. cxxvii.
[3] Thomas of Celano, op. cit., cap. cxxix.
[4] "Fioretti," cap. xxii.   [5] Ibid., cap. xxi.

lifted up his right paw before him and laid it gently on the
hand of St. Francis, giving thereby such sign of good faith as he
was able. Then quoth St. Francis, 'Brother Wolf, I bid thee
in the name of Jesu Christ come now with me, nothing doubting,
and let us go stablish this peace in God's name.' And the
wolf obedient set forth with him, in fashion as a gentle lamb;
whereat the townsfolk made mighty marvel, beholding. . . .
And thereafter this same wolf lived two years in Agobio; and
went like a tame beast in and out the houses from door to door,
without doing hurt to any, or any doing hurt to him, and was
courteously nourished by the people; and as he passed thus
wise through the country and the houses, never did any dog
bark behind him. At length after a two years space, brother
wolf died of old age : whereat the townsfolk sorely grieved, sith
marking him pass so gently through the city, they minded them
the better of the virtue and the sanctity of St. Francis." [1]

In another mystic, less familiar than St. Francis to English
readers—Rose of Lima, the Peruvian Saint—this deep sympathy
with natural things assumed a particularly lovely form. To
St. Rose the whole world was a holy fairyland, in which it seemed
to her that every living thing turned its face towards Eternity
and joined in her adoration of God. It is said in her biography
that "when at sunrise, she passed through the garden to go
to her retreat, she called upon nature to praise with her the
Author of all things. Then the trees were seen to bow as she
passed by, and clasp their leaves together, making a harmonious
sound. The flowers swayed upon their stalks, and opened their
blossoms that they might scent the air; thus according to their
manner praising God. At the same time the birds began to
sing, and came and perched upon the hands and shoulders of
Rose. The insects greeted her with a joyous murmur and all
which had life and movement joined in the concert of praise she
addressed to the Lord." [2]

Again—and here we seem to catch an echo of the pure

[1] "Fioretti," cap. xxi. (Arnold's translation). Perhaps I may be allowed to
remind the incredulous reader that the recent discovery of a large wolf's skull in
Gubbio, close to the spot in which Brother Wolf is said to have lived in a cave for two
years after his taming by the Saint, has gone far to vindicate the truth of this beautiful
story : and disconcerted those rationalistic scholars who hold that tradition can do
little else but lie.
[2] De Bussierre, " Le Pérou et Ste. Rose de Lime," p. 256.

Franciscan spirit, the gaiety of the Troubadours of God—during her last Lent, "each evening at sunset a little bird with an enchanting voice came and perched upon a tree beside her window, and waited till she gave the sign for him to sing. Rose, as soon as she saw her little feathered chorister, made herself ready to sing the praises of God, and challenged the bird to this musical duel in a song which she had composed for this purpose. 'Begin, dear little bird,' she said, 'begin thy lovely song! Let thy little throat, so full of sweet melodies, pour them forth : that together we may praise the Lord. Thou dost praise thy Creator, I my sweet Saviour : thus we together bless the Deity. Open thy little beak, begin and I will follow thee : and our voices shall blend in a song of holy joy.'

"At once the little bird began to sing, running through his scale to the highest note. Then he ceased, that the saint might sing in her turn . . . thus did they celebrate the greatness of God, turn by turn, for a whole hour : and with such perfect order, that when the bird sang Rose said nothing, and when she sang in her turn the bird was silent, and listened to her with a marvellous attention. At last, towards the sixth hour, the saint dismissed him, saying, 'Go, my little chorister, go, fly far away. But blessed be my God who never leaves me!'"[1]

The mystic whose illumination takes such forms as these, who feels with this intensity and closeness the bond of love which "binds in one book the scattered leaves of all the universe," dwells in a world for ever shut to the desirous eyes of other men. He pierces the veil of imperfection, and beholds Creation with the Creator's eye. The "Pattern is shown him in the Mount." "The whole consciousness," says Récéjac, "is flooded with light to unknown depths, under the gaze of love, from which nothing escapes. In this state, intensity of vision and sureness of judgment are equal : and the things which the seer brings back with him when he returns to common life are not merely partial impressions, or the separate knowledge of 'science' or 'poetry.' They are rather truths which embrace the world, life and conduct : in a word, *the whole consciousness.*"[2]

It is curious to note in the various diagrams of experience which we have inherited from the more clear-sighted philo-

[1] De Bussierre, "Le Pérou et Ste. Rose de Lime," p. 415.
[2] "Fondements de la Connaissance Mystique," p. 113.

sophers and seers, indications that they have enjoyed prolonged
or transitory periods of this higher consciousness; described by
Récéjac as the marriage of imaginative vision with moral transcendence. I think it at least a reasonable supposition that Plato's
theory of Ideas owed its inception to some intuition of this kind ;
for philosophy, though it prate of pure reason, is more often
found to be based upon psychological experience. The Platonic
statements as to the veritable existence of the Idea of a house,
a table, or a bed, and other such painfully concrete and practical
applications of the doctrine of the ideal, which have annoyed
many metaphysicians, become explicable on such a psychological basis. That illuminated vision in which "all things are
made new" can afford to embrace the homeliest as well as the
sublimest things ; and, as a matter of experience, it does do
this, seeing all objects, as Monet saw the hayrick, as " modes of
light." Blake said that his cottage at Felpham was a shadow
of the angels' houses,[1] and I have already referred to the case of
the converted Methodist who saw his horses and hogs on the
ideal plane.[2]

Again, when Plotinus, who is known to have experienced
ecstatic states, speaks with the assurance of an explorer of an
" intelligible world," and asks us, " What other fire could be a
better image of the fire which is there, than the fire which is
here? Or what other earth than this, of the earth which is
there ? "[3] we seem to detect behind the trappings of Neoplatonic philosophy a hint of the same type of first-hand
experience. The unknown minds to whom we owe the Hebrew
Kabalah found room for it too in their diagram of the soul's
ascent towards Reality. The first "Sephira" above Malkuth,
the World of Matter, or lowest plane upon that Tree of Life
which is formed by the ten emanations of the Godhead, is, they
say, " Yesod," the " archetypal universe." In this are contained
the realities, patterns, or Ideas, whose shadows constitute the
world of appearance in which we dwell. The path of the
ascending soul upon the Tree of Life leads him first from
Malkuth to Yesod : i.e., human consciousness in the course of
its transcendence passes from the normal illusions of men to a
more real perception of the world—a perception which is sym-

---

[1] Letters, p. 75.   [2] Vide supra, p. 231.
        [3] Ennead ii. 9.

bolized by the "archetypal plane" or world of Platonic Ideas. "Everything in temporal nature," says William Law, "is descended out of that which is eternal, and stands as a palpable visible outbirth of it, so when we know how to separate the grossness, death, and darkness of time from it, we find what it is in its eternal state. . . . In Eternal Nature, or the Kingdom of Heaven, materiality stands in life and light; it is the light's glorious Body, or that garment wherewith light is clothed, and therefore has all the properties of light in it, and only differs from light as it is its brightness and beauty, as the holder and displayer of all its colours, powers, and virtues."[1]

When Law wrote this, he may have believed that he was interpreting to English readers the unique message of his master, Jacob Boehme. As a matter of fact he was spreading the news which a long line of practical mystics had been crying for centuries into the deaf ears of mankind. He was saying in the eighteenth century what Gregory of Nyssa had said in the fourth and Erigena in the ninth; telling the secret of that "Inviolate Rose" which can never be profaned because it can only be seen with the eyes of love.

This same belief in the perfect world of archetypes lurking behind the symbols of sense and lending them a measure of its reality, is discoverable in Hermetic philosophy, which is of course largely influenced by Kabalism. It receives practical application in the course of the "occult education" to which neophytes are subjected: a mental and moral training calculated to induce lucid vision of this kind. Such vision—a by-product in true mysticism, never sought for though often achieved—is the end at which magic deliberately aims.[2] No magician was ever found capable of St. Catherine's cry, *Non voglio quello che esce da te.*

That serene and illuminated consciousness of the relation of things inward and outward—of the Hidden Treasure and its Casket, the energizing Absolute and its expression in Time and Space—which we have been studying in this chapter, is at its best a state of fine equilibrium ; a sane adjustment of the inner and outer life. By that synthesis of love and will which is the secret of the heart, the whole world is seen and known in God,

---

[1] "An Appeal to All who Doubt" (Liberal and Mystical Writings of William Law, p. 52).   [2] See Steiner, "The Way of Initiation," cap. v.

and God is seen and known in the whole world. It is a state of exalted emotion : being produced by love, of necessity it produces love in its turn. The sharp division between its inlooking and outlooking forms which I have adopted for convenience of description, is seldom present in the minds of its adepts. They, "cleansed, fed, and sanctified," are initiated into a spiritual universe where such clumsy distinctions have little meaning. All is alike part of the "new life" of peaceful charity : and that progressive abolition of selfhood which is of the essence of mystical development, is alone enough to prevent them from drawing a line between the inward personal companionship and outward impersonal apprehension of the Real. True Illumination, like all real and vital experience, consists rather in the breathing of a certain atmosphere, the living at certain levels of consciousness, than in the acquirement of specific information. It is, as it were, a resting-place upon "the steep stairway of love"; where the self turns and sees all about it a transfigured universe, radiant with that same Light Divine which nests in its own heart and leads it on.

"When man's desires are fixed immovably on his Maker and as for deadliness and corruption of the flesh he is letted," says Rolle of the purified soul which has attained the illuminated state, "then it is no marvel that his strength manly using, first as it were heaven being opened, with his understanding he beholds high heavenly citizens, and afterwards sweetest heat, as it were burning fire, he feels. Then with marvellous sweetness he is taught, and so forth in songful noise he is joyed. This, therefore, is perfect charity, which no man knows but he that hath it took. And he that it has taken, it never leaves : sweetly he lives and sickerly he shall die." [1]

Sweetly, it is true, the illuminated mystic may live ; but not, as some think, placidly. Enlightenment is a symptom of growth : and growth is a living process, which knows no rest. The spirit, indeed, is invaded by a heavenly peace ; but it is the peace, not of idleness, but of ordered activity. "A rest most busy," in Hilton's words : a progressive appropriation of the Divine. The urgent push of an indwelling Spirit aspiring to its home in the heart of Reality is felt more and more, as the invasion of the normal consciousness by the transcendental

[1] Rolle, "The Fire of Love," bk. i. cap. xx.

personality—the growth of the New Man—proceeds towards its term.

Therefore the great seekers for reality are not as a rule long deceived by the exalted joys of Illumination. Intensely aware now of the Absolute Whom they adore, they are aware too that though known He is unachieved. Even whilst they enjoy the rapture of the Divine Presence—of life in a divine, ideal world —something, they feel, makes default. *Sol voglio Te, O dolce Amore.* Hence for them that which they now enjoy, and which passes the understanding of other men, is not a static condition ; often it coexists with that travail of the heart which Tauler has called " stormy love." The greater the mystic, the sooner he realizes that the Heavenly Manna which has been administered to him is not yet That with which the angels are full fed. Nothing less will do : and for him the progress of illumination is a progressive consciousness that he is destined not for the sunny shores of the spiritual universe, but for "the vast and stormy sea of the divine."

" Here," says Ruysbroeck of the soul which has been lit by the Uncreated Light, " there begins an eternal hunger, which shall never more be satisfied. It is the inward eagerness and aspiration of the affective powers and created spirit towards an Uncreated Good. And as the spirit desires fruition, and is indeed invited and urged thereto by God, she continually wishes to attain it. Behold ! here begin the eternal aspiration and eternal effort, of an eternal helplessness ! These men are poor indeed : for they are hungry, greedy, insatiable ! Whatsoever they eat and drink they cannot be satisfied, since theirs is the hunger of eternity. . . . Here there are great feasts of food and drink, of which none know but those who are bidden ; but the full satisfaction of fruition is the one dish that lacks them, and this is why their hunger is ever renewed. Nevertheless there flow in this communion rivers of honey full of all delight ; for the spirit tastes of these delights under every mode that can be conceived. But all this is according to the manner of the creatures, and is below God : and this is why there is here an eternal hunger and impatience. If God gave to man all the gifts which all the saints possess, and all that He has to offer, but without giving Himself, the craving spirit would remain hungry and unfulfilled." [1]

[1] " L'Ornement des Noces Spirituelles," l. ii. cap. liii.

CHAPTER V

VOICES AND VISIONS

This is a controversial subject—Rationalism and Orthodoxy—Both extreme in their conclusions—Literal interpretation fatal to vision—Every kind of automatism is found in the mystic life—Cannot be neglected by its investigators—Visions may often be merely subjective—but sometimes embody transcendental perceptions—Some test necessary—Real mystic vision enhances life—Most visionary activity mixed in type—Is always symbolic in character—A form of artistic expression—Automatisms characteristic of all creative genius—Mystic visions and voices are helps to transcendence—related to life—Delacroix—Audition—the simplest form of automatism—Three kinds of auditions—the Intellectual Word—Madame Guyon—Distinct interior words—St. Teresa—False auditions—St. John of the Cross—Character of the true audition—St. Teresa—Exterior words—Musical audition—Suso—Divine dialogues—Vision—its general character—Most mystics distrust it—Hilton—St. John of the Cross—Madame Guyon—Three classes of vision : intellectual, imaginary, and corporeal—Intellectual vision—its character—St. Teresa—Imaginary vision—it exists in all poets—Its two forms—Symbolic visions—Suso—Dante—St. Mechthild of Hackborn—Visions of Divine Personality—St. Teresa's vision of Christ—its transcendental nature—Active imaginary visions—their character—The mystic marriage of St. Catherine—Transverberation of St. Teresa—Automatic writing in the mystics—St. Catherine of Siena—Blake—St. Teresa—Madame Guyon—Jacob Boehme—Conclusion

WE now come to that eternal battle-ground, the detailed discussion of those abnormal psychic phenomena which appear so persistently in the history of the mystics. That is to say, visions, auditions, automatic script, and those dramatic dialogues between the Self and some other factor—the Soul, Love, Reason, or the Voice of God—which seem sometimes to arise from an exalted and uncontrolled imaginative power, sometimes to attain the proportions of auditory hallucination.

Here, moderate persons are like to be hewn in pieces between the two "great powers" who have long disputed this territory and agreeably occupied their leisure by tearing out each other's hair. On the one hand we have the strangely

named rationalists, who feel that they have settled the matter
once for all by calling attention to the undoubted parallels
which exist between the bodily symptoms of acute spiritual
stress and the bodily symptoms of certain forms of disease.
These considerations, reinforced by those comfortable words
" auto-suggestion " and " psychosensorial hallucination "—which
do but reintroduce mystery in another and less attractive form
—enable them to pity rather than blame the peculiarities of the
great contemplatives. Modern French psychology, in particular, revels in this sort of thing : and would, if it had its way,
fill the wards of the Salpêtrière with patients from the Roman
Calendar. The modern interpreter, says Rufus Jones, finds in
the stigmata of St. Francis of Assisi a point of weakness rather
than a point of strength : not " the marks of a saint," but " the
marks of emotional and physical abnormality." [1]   This is a very
moderate statement of the " rational " position, by a writer who
is in actual sympathy with certain aspects of mysticism. Yet
it may well be doubted whether that flame of living love which
could, for one dazzling instant, weld body and soul in one, was
really a point of weakness in a saint : whether Blake was quite
as mad as some of his interpreters, or the powers of St. Paul
and St. Teresa are fully explained on a basis of epilepsy or
hysteria : whether, finally, it is as scientific as it looks, to lump
together all visions and voices—from Wandering Willy to the
Apocalypse of St. John—as examples of unhealthy cerebral
activity.

As against all this, the intransigeant votaries of the supernatural seem determined to play into the hands of their foes.
They pin themselves, for no apparent reason, to the objective
reality and absolute value of visions, voices, and other experiences which would be classed, in any other department of life,
as the harmless results of a vivid imagination : and claim as
examples of miraculous interference with " natural law " psychic
phenomena which may well be the normal if rare methods by
which a certain type of intuitive genius actualizes its perceptions
of the spiritual world. [2]

[1] "Studies in Mystical Religion," p. 165. Those who wish to study the
" rationalist " argument in an extreme form are directed to the works of Prof. Janet,
particularly " L'Automatisme psychologique " and " L'État mentale des hysteriques."
[2] On the difference in this respect between the "normal" and the "average," see
Granger, "The Soul of a Christian," p. 12.

Materialistic piety of this kind, which would have us believe that St. Anthony of Padua really held the Infant Christ in his arms, and that the Holy Ghost truly told the Blessed Angela of Foligno that He loved her better than any other woman in the Vale of Spoleto, and she knew Him more intimately than the Apostles themselves,[1] is the best friend the "rationalists" possess. It turns dreams into miracles and miracles into dreams ; and drags down the symbolic visions of genius to the level of pious hallucination. Even the profound and beautiful significance of St. Margaret Mary Alacoque's vision of the Sacred Heart—a pictured expression of one of the deepest intuitions of the human soul caught up to the contemplation of God's love—has been impaired by the grossly material interpretation which it has been forced to bear. So, too, the beautiful reveries of Suso, the divine visitations experienced by Francis, Catherine, Teresa and countless other saints, have been degraded in the course of their supposed elevation to the sphere called "supernatural"—a process as fatal to their truth and beauty as the stuffing of birds.[2]

All this, too, is done in defiance of the great mystics themselves, who are unanimous in warning their disciples against the danger of attributing too much importance to "visions" and "voices," or accepting them at their face value as messages from God. Nevertheless, such visions and voices are such frequent accompaniments of the mystic life, that they cannot be left on one side. The messengers of the invisible world knock persistently at the doors of the senses : and not only at those which we refer to hearing and to sight. ' In other words, supersensual intuitions—the contact between man's finite being and the Infinite Being in which it is immersed—can express themselves by means of almost any kind of sensory automatism. Strange sweet perfumes and tastes, physical sensations of touch, inward

---

[1] See B. Angelae de Fulginio, "Visionum et Instructionum Liber," cap. l. (English translation, p. 245).

[2] Ribet's large, learned, and detailed work, "La Mystique Divine," is perhaps the best representative of the extreme "supernaturalist" position. As against the "rationalistic" theory of stigmatization already described, one feels that this writer hardly advances his own cause when he insists on attributing equal validity (a) to the Stigmata as marks of the Divine, (b) to the imprint of a toad, bat, spider "ou de tout autre objet exprimant l'abjection" on the bodies of those who have had commerce with the devil (tome iii. p. 482).

fires, are reported over and over again in connection with such spiritual adventures.[1] Those symbols under which the mystic tends to approach the Absolute easily become objectivized, and present themselves to the consciousness as parts of experience, rather than as modes of interpretation. The knowledge which is obtained in such an approach is wholly transcendental. It consists in an undifferentiated act of the whole consciousness, in which under the spur of love life draws near to Life. Thought, feeling, vision, touch—all are hopelessly inadequate to it: yet all, perhaps, may hint at that intense perception of which they are the scattered parts. "And we shall endlessly be all had in God," says Julian of this supreme experience, " Him verily seeing and fully feeling, Him spiritually hearing and Him delectably smelling and sweetly swallowing."[2]

All those so-called "hallucinations of the senses" which appear in the history of mysticism must, then, be considered soberly, frankly, and without prejudice in the course of our inquiry into the psychology of man's quest of the Real. The question for their critics must really be this: do these automatisms, which appear so persistently as a part of the contemplative life, represent merely the dreams and fancies, the old digested percepts of the visionary, objectivized and presented to his surface-mind in a concrete form ; or, are they ever representations—symbolic, if you like—of some fact, force, or personality, some "triumphing spiritual power," external to himself? Is the vision only a pictured thought: or, is it the violent effort of the self to translate something impressed upon its deeper being, some message received from without,[3] which projects this sharp image and places it before the consciousness ?

The answer seems to be that the voice or vision may be either of these two things: and that pathology and religion have both been over-hasty in their eagerness to snatch at these phenomena for their own purposes. Many—perhaps most— voices do but give the answer which the subject has already

[1] *Vide infra*, quotations from Hilton and St. John of the Cross. Also Rolle, " The Fire of Love," Prologue. E. Gardner, " St. Catherine of Siena," p. 15. Von Hügel, " The Mystical Element in Religion," vol. i. pp. 178–181.

[2] " Revelations of Divine Love," cap. xliii. I have restored the bold language of the original, which is somewhat toned down in modern versions.

[3] Here as elsewhere the reader will kindly recollect that all spatial language is merely symbolic when used in connection with spiritual states.

suggested to itself;[1] many—perhaps most—visions are the pic-
turings of dreams and desires.[2] Some are morbid hallucinations: some even symptoms of insanity. All, probably, borrow
their shape, as apart from their content, from suggestions already
present in the mind of the seer.

But there are some, experienced by minds of great power
and richness, which are crucial for those who have them. These
bring wisdom to the simple and ignorant, sudden calm to those
who were tormented by doubts. They flood the personality
with new light: accompany conversion, or the passage from one
spiritual state to another: arrive at moments of indecision,
bringing with them authoritative commands or counsels opposed
to the inclination of the self: confer a convinced knowledge of
some department of the spiritual life before unknown. Such
visions, it is clear, belong to another and higher plane of experience from the radiant appearances of our Lady, the piteous
exhibitions of the sufferings of Christ, which swarm in the lives
of the saints and contain no feature which is not traceable to
the subject's religious enthusiasms or previous knowledge.[3]
These, in the apt phrase of Godfernaux, are but "images floating on the moving deeps of feeling,"[4] not symbolic messages from
another plane of consciousness. Some test, then, must be
applied, some basis of classification discovered, if we are to
distinguish the visions and voices which seem to be symptoms
of real transcendental activity from those which are only due to
imagination raised to the nth power, to intense reverie, or even
to psychic illness. That test, I think, must be the same as
that which we shall find useful for ecstatic states; namely, their
life-enhancing quality.

Those visions and voices which are the *media* by which the
"seeing self" truly approaches the Absolute; which are the

---

[1] For instance, when Margaret Ebner, the celebrated "Friend of God," heard a
voice telling her that Tauler, who was the object of great veneration in the circle to
which she belonged, was the man whom God loved best, and that He dwelt in him
like melodious music (see Rufus Jones, *op. cit.*, p. 257).

[2] "There are persons to be met with," says St. Teresa, "and I have known them
myself, who have so feeble a brain and imagination that they think they see whatever
they are thinking about, and this is a very dangerous condition" ("El Castillo Interior,"
Moradas Cuartas, cap. iii.).

[3] The book of Angela of Foligno, already cited, contains a rich series of examples.

[4] "Sur la psychologie du Mysticisme" (*Revue Philosophique*, February, 1902).

formulæ under which ontological perceptions are expressed ; are found by that self to be sources of helpful energy, charity, and courage.   They infuse something new in the way of strength, knowledge, direction ; and leave it—physically, mentally, or spiritually—better than they found it.   Those which do not owe their inception to the contact of the soul with external reality—in theological language do not " come from God "—do not have this effect.   At best, they are but the results of the self's turning over of her treasures : at worst, they are the dreams—sometimes the diseased dreams—of an active, rich, but imperfectly controlled subliminal consciousness.

Since it is implicit in the make-up of the mystical tempera-ment, that the subliminal consciousness should be active and rich—and since the unstable nervous organization which goes with it renders it liable to illness and exhaustion—it is not surprising to find that the visionary experience even of the greatest mystics is mixed in type.   Once automatism has established itself in a person, it may as easily become the expression of folly as of wisdom.   In the moments when inspira-tion has ebbed, old forgotten superstitions may take its place. When Julian of Norwich in her illness saw the " horrible showing " of the Fiend, red with black freckles, which clutched at her throat with its paws :[1] when St. Teresa was visited by Satan, who left a smell of brimstone behind, or when she saw him sitting on the top of her breviary and dislodged him by the use of holy water,[2] it is surely reasonable to allow that we are in the presence of visions which tend towards the psychopathic type : and which are expressive of little else but an exhaustion and temporary loss of balance on the subject's part, which allowed her intense consciousness of the reality of evil to assume a concrete form.[3]

Because we allow this, however, it does not follow that all the visionary experience of such a subject is morbid : any more than "Œdipus Tyrannus " invalidates " Prometheus Unbound,"

[1] " Revelations of Divine Love," cap. lxvi.   [2] Vida, cap. xxxi. §§ 5 and 10.
[3] Thus too in the case of St. Catherine of Siena, the intense spiritual strain of that three years' retreat which I have already described (supra, Pt. II. Cap. I.) showed itself towards the end of the period by a change in the character of her visions. These, which had previously been wholly concerned with intuitions of the good and beautiful, now took on an evil aspect and greatly distressed her (Vita (Acta SS.), i. xi. 1 ; see E. Gardner, " St. Catherine of Siena," p. 20)

or occasional attacks of dyspepsia invalidate the whole process of nutrition. The perceptive power and creative genius of mystics, as of other great artists, sometimes goes astray. That visions or voices should sometimes be the means by which the soul consciously assimilates the nourishment it needs, is conceivable: it is surely also conceivable that by the same means it may present to the surface-intelligence things which are productive of unhealthy rather than of healthy reactions.

If we would cease, once for all, to regard visions and voices as objective, and be content to see in them forms of symbolic expression, ways in which the subconscious activity of the spiritual self reaches the surface-mind, many of the disharmonies noticeable in visionary experience, which have teased the devout, and delighted the agnostic, would fade away. Visionary experience is—or at least may be—the outward sign of a real experience. It is a picture which the mind constructs, it is true, from raw materials already at its disposal: as the artist constructs his picture with canvas and paint. But, as the artist's paint and canvas picture is the fruit, not merely of contact between brush and canvas, but also of a more vital contact between his creative genius and visible beauty or truth ; so too we may see in vision, where the subject is a mystic, the fruit of a more mysterious contact between the visionary and a transcendental beauty or truth. Such a vision, that is to say, is the " accident " which represents and enshrines a "substance" unseen : the paint and canvas picture which tries to show the surface consciousness that ineffable sight, that ecstatic perception of good or evil—for neither extreme has the monopoly—to which the deeper, more real soul has attained. The transcendental powers take for this purpose such material as they can find amongst the hoarded beliefs and memories of the self.[1] Hence Plotinus sees the Celestial Venus, Suso the

---

[1] An excellent example of such appropriation of material is related with the utmost ingenuousness by Huysmans ("Sainte Lydwine de Schiedam," p. 258) : " Lydwine found again in heaven those forms of adoration, those ceremonial practices of the divine office, which she had known here below during her years of health. The Church Militant had been, in fact, initiated by the inspiration of its apostles, its popes, and its saints into the liturgic joys of Paradise." In this same vision, which occurred on Christmas Eve, when the hour of the Nativity was rung from the belfries of heaven, the Divine Child appeared on His Mother's knee : just as the crèche is exhibited in Catholic churches the moment that Christmas has dawned.

Eternal Wisdom, St. Teresa the Humanity of Christ, Blake the strange personages of his prophetic books: others more obviously symbolic objects. St. Ignatius Loyola, for instance, in a moment of lucidity, " saw the most Holy Trinity as it were under the likeness of a triple plectrum or of three spinet keys " and on another occasion " the Blessed Virgin without distinction of members." [1]

Visions and voices, then, may stand in the same relation to the mystic as pictures, poems, and musical compositions stand to the great painter, poet, musician. They are the artistic expressions and creative results (a) of thought, (b) of intuition, (c) of direct perception. All would be ready to acknowledge how conventional and imperfect of necessity are those transcripts of perceived Goodness, Truth, and Beauty which we owe to artistic genius : how unequal is their relation to reality. But this is not to say that they are valueless or absurd. So too with the mystic, whose proceedings in this respect are closer to those of the artist than is generally acknowledged. In both types there is a constant and involuntary work of translation going on, by which Reality is interpreted in the terms of appearance. In both, a peculiar mental make-up conduces to this result.

In these subjects, the state of reverie tends easily to a visionary character : thought becomes pictorial, auditory or rhythmic as the case may be. Concrete images, balanced harmonies, elusive yet recognizable, surge up mysteriously without the intervention of the will, and place themselves before the mind. Thus the painter really sees his unpainted picture, the novelist hears the conversation of his characters, the poet receives his cadences ready-made, the musician listens to a veritable music which " pipes to the spirit ditties of no tone." In the mystic, the same type of activity constantly appears. Profound meditation takes a pictorial form. Apt symbols which suggest themselves to his imagination become objectivized. The message that he longs for is heard within his mind. Hence, those "interior voices" and "imaginary visions" which are sometimes—as in Suso—indistinguishable from the ordinary accompaniments of intense artistic activity.

Where, however, artistic "automatisms" spend themselves

[1] Testament, cap. iii.

upon the artist's work, mystical "automatisms" in their highest forms have to do with that transformation of personality which is the essence of the mystic life. They are *media* by which the self measures its approximation to the Absolute and is guided on its upward way. Moreover, they are co-ordinated. The voice and the vision go together: corroborate one another, and "work out right" in relation to the life of the self. Thus St. Catherine of Siena's "mystic marriage" was prefaced by a voice, which ever said in answer to her prayers, " I will espouse thee to Myself in faith"; and the vision in which that union was consummated was again initiated by a voice saying, " I will *this day* celebrate solemnly with thee the feast of the betrothal of thy soul, and even as I promised I will espouse thee to Myself in faith."[1] "Such automatisms as these," says Delacroix, "are by no means scattered and incoherent. They are systematic and progressive: they are governed by an interior aim; they have, above all, a teleological character. They indicate the continuous intervention of a being at once wiser and more powerful than the ordinary character and reason; they are the realization, in visual and auditory images, of a secret and permanent personality of a superior type to the conscious personality. They are its voice, the exterior projection of its life. They translate to the conscious personality the suggestions of the subconscious: and they permit the continuous penetration of the conscious personality by these deeper activities. They establish a communication between these two planes of existence, and, by their imperative nature, they tend to make the inferior subordinate to the superior."[2]

AUDITION

The simplest and as a rule the first way in which automatism shows itself, is in "voices" or auditions. The mystic becomes aware of Something which speaks to him either clearly or implicitly, giving him abrupt and unexpected orders and encouragements. The reality of his contact with the Divine Life is thus brought home to him by a device with which the accidents of human intercourse have made him

---

[1] E. Gardner, " St. Catherine of Siena," p. 25.
[2] Delacroix, "Études sur le Mysticisme," p. 114.

familiar. His subliminal mind, soaked as it now is in transcendental perceptions, "at one with the Absolute," irradiated by the Uncreated Light, but still dissociated from the surface intelligence which it is slowly educating, seems to that surface self like another being. Hence its messages are often heard, literally, as Voices: either (1) the "immediate" or inarticulate voice, which the auditive mystic knows so well, but finds it so difficult to define; (2) the distinct interior voice, perfectly articulate, but recognized as speaking only within the mind; (3) by a hallucination which we have all experienced in dream or reverie, the exterior voice, which appears to be speaking externally to the subject and to be heard by the outward ear. This, the traditional classification of auditions, also answers exactly to the three main types of vision—(1) intellectual, (2) imaginary, (3) corporeal.

Of these three kinds of voices the mystics are unanimous in their opinion that the first and least "marvellous" is by far the best: belonging indeed to an entirely different plane of consciousness from the uttered interior or exterior "word." "Distinct interior words," says Madame Guyon, "are very subject to illusion. The Devil is responsible for many of them: and when they come from our good angel (*for God Himself never speaks in this manner*) they do not always mean that which they say, and one seldom finds that what is thus predicted comes to pass. For when God causes words of this kind to be brought to us by His angels, He understands them in His way, and we take them in ours, and this it is which deceives us. The word which God speaks without intermediary is no other than His WORD [Logos] in the soul: a substantial word, silent and inarticulate, a vivifying and energizing word; as has been said, *dixit et facta sunt*. This word is never for a moment dumb nor sterile: this word is heard ceaselessly in the centre of the soul which is disposed thereto, and returns to its Principle as pure as when it came forth therefrom." [1]

"Let Thy good Spirit enter my heart and there be heard without utterance, and without the sound of words speak all truth," says a prayer attributed to St. Ambrose,[2] exactly descri-

---

[1] Vie, pt. i. cap. ix.
[2] Missale Romanum. Praeparatio ad Missam; Die Dominica.

bing the function of these unmediated or "intellectual words." Dynamic messages of this kind, imperative intuitions which elude the containing formulae of speech, are invariably attributed by the self to the direct action of the Divine. They bring with them an unquestionable authority, an infusion of new knowledge or new life. They are, in fact, not messages but actual "invasions" from beyond the threshold : sudden emergences of that hidden Child of the Absolute which mystics call the "spark of the soul" and of which it has been truly said, "*Abyssus abyssum invocat.*"

"Distinct interior words," on the other hand, are not invariably authoritative for those who hear them : though St. Teresa, whose brilliant self-criticisms are our best source of information on mystical auditions, gives to them a higher place in spiritual experience than Madame Guyon's devotion to "naked orison" will permit her to do. She, too, considers that, though they "come from God," they are not due to direct contact with the Divine : but that they may be distinguished from those "words" which result merely from voluntary activity of the imagination as much by the sense of certitude, peace and interior joy which they produce, as by the fact that they force themselves upon the attention in spite of its resistance, and bring with them knowledge which was not previously within the field of consciousness. That is to say, they are really automatic presentations of the result of mystic intuition, not mere rearrangements of the constituents of thought.[1] Hence they bring to the surface-self new material : have an actual value for life.

Those purely self-created locutions, or rearrangements of thought "which the mind self-recollected forms and fashions within itself"—often difficult to distinguish from true automatic audition—are called by Philip of the Trinity, St. John of the Cross and other mystical theologians "successive words." They feel it to be of the highest importance that the contemplative should learn to distinguish such hallucinations from real transcendental perceptions presented in auditive form.

"I am terrified," says St. John of the Cross, with his customary blunt common sense, "by what passes among us in

[1] "El Castillo Interior," Moradas Sextas, cap. iii.

these days. Anyone who has barely begun to meditate, if he becomes conscious of these words during his self-recollection, pronounces them forthwith to be the work of God, and, considering them to be so, says, ' God has spoken to me,' or, ' I have had an answer from God.' But it is not true: such an one has only been speaking to himself. Besides, the affection and desire for these words, which men encourage, cause them to reply to themselves and then to imagine that God has spoken." [1] These are the words of one who was at once the sanest of saints and the most penetrating of psychologists : words which our modern unruly amateurs of the "subconscious" might well take to heart.

True auditions are usually heard when the mind is in a state of deep absorption without conscious thought : that is to say, at the most favourable of all moments for contact with the transcendental world. They translate into articulate language some aspect of that ineffable apprehension of Reality which the contemplative enjoys : crystallize those clairvoyant intuitions, those prophetic hints which surge in on him so soon as he lays himself open to the influence of the supra-sensible. Sometimes, however, mystical intuition takes the form of a sudden and ungovernable uprush of knowledge from the deeps of personality. Then, auditions may break in upon the normal activities of the self with startling abruptness. It is in such cases that their objective and uncontrollable character is most sharply felt. However they may appear, they are, says St. Teresa, "very distinctly formed ; but by the bodily ear they are not heard. They are, however, much more clearly understood than if they were heard by the ear. It is impossible not to understand them, whatever resistance we may offer. . . . The words formed by the understanding effect nothing, but when our Lord speaks, it is *at once word and work.* . . . The human locution [*i.e.,* the work of imagination] is as something we cannot well make out, as if we were half asleep : but the divine locution is a voice so clear, that not a syllable of its utterance is lost. It may occur, too, when the understanding and the soul are so troubled and distracted that they cannot form one sentence correctly : and yet grand sentences, perfectly arranged, such as the soul in its most recollected state never could have formed,

---

[1] " Subida del Monte Carmelo," l. ii. cap. xxix. 4.

are uttered: and at the first word, as I have said, change it utterly." [1]

St. Teresa's whole mystic life was governed by voices: her active career as a foundress was guided by them. They advised her in small things as in great. Often they interfered with her plans, ran counter to her personal judgment, forbade a foundation on which she was set, or commanded one which appeared imprudent or impossible. They concerned themselves with journeys, with the purchase of houses; they warned her of coming events.[2] She seldom resisted them, though it constantly happened that the action on which they insisted seemed the height of folly: and though they constantly involved her in hardships and difficulties, she never had cause to regret this blind reliance upon decrees which she regarded as coming direct from God, and which certainly did emanate from a life greater than her own, in touch with transcendent levels of consciousness.

So far from mere vague intuitions are the "distinct interior words" which the mystic hears within his mind, that Suso is able to state that the hundred meditations on the Passion thus revealed to him were spoken in German and not in Latin.[3] St. Teresa's own auditions were all of this interior kind—some "distinct" and some "substantial" or inarticulate—as her corresponding visions were nearly all of the "intellectual" or "imaginary" sort: that is to say, she was not subject to sensible hallucination. Often, however, the boundary is overpassed, and the locution seems to be heard by the mystic's outward ear, as in the case of those voices which guided the destinies of the Blessed Joan of Arc, or the Figure upon the Cross which spoke to St. Francis of Assisi. We then have the third form— "exterior words"—which the mystics for the most part regard with suspicion and dislike.

Sometimes audition assumes a musical rather than a verbal character: a form of perception which probably corresponds to the temperamental bias of the self, the ordered sweetness of Divine Harmony striking responsive chords in the music-loving

[1] Vida, cap. xxv. §§ 2, 5, 6. See also for a detailed discussion of all forms of auditions St. John of the Cross, *op. cit.*, l. ii. caps. xxviii. to xxxi.
[2] " El Libro de las Fundaciones " is full of instances.
[3] Suso, " Buchlein von der ewigen Weisheit," Prologue.

soul. The lives of St. Francis of Assisi, St. Catherine of Siena, and Richard Rolle provide obvious instances of this [1] : but Suso, in whom automatism assumed its richest and most varied forms, has also given in his autobiography some characteristic examples.

"One day . . . whilst the Servitor was still at rest, he heard within himself a gracious melody by which his heart was greatly moved. And at the moment of the rising of the morning star, a deep sweet voice sang within him these words, *Stella Maria maris, hodie processit ad ortum.* That is to say, Mary Star of the Sea is risen to-day. And this song which he heard was so spiritual and so sweet, that his soul was transported by it and he too began to sing joyously. . . . And one day—it was in carnival time—the Servitor had continued his prayers until the moment when the bugle of the watch announced the dawn. Therefore, he said to himself, Rest for an instant, before you salute the shining Morning Star. And, whilst that his senses were at rest, behold ! angelic spirits began to sing the fair Respond : ' *Illuminare, illuminare, Jerusalem !* ' And this song was echoed with a marvellous sweetness in the deeps of his soul. And when the angels had sung for some time his soul over-flowed with joy : and his feeble body being unable to support such happiness, burning tears escaped from his eyes." [2]

Closely connected on the one hand with the phenomena of automatic words, on the other with those of prophecy and inspiration, is the prevalence in mystical literature of revelations which take the form of dialogue : of intimate colloquies between Divine Reality and the Soul. The Revelations of Julian of Norwich and St. Catherine of Siena, and many of those of the Blessed Angela of Foligno, appear to have been received by them in this way. We seem as we read them to be present at the outpourings of the Divine Mind, snatching at some form of words on Its way through the human consciousness. We feel on the one hand a "one-ness with the Absolute" on the part of the mystic which has made her really, for the time being, the " voice of God": whilst on the other we recognize in her the persistence of the individual, exalted but not yet wholly absorbed

---

[1] " Fioretti," " Delle Istimate " 2. E. Gardner, " St. Catherine of Siena," p. 15. Rolle, " The Fire of Love," bk. i. cap. xvi.

[2] Leben, cap. vi.

in the Divine, whose questions, here and there, break in upon the revelation which is mediated to it by its deeper mind.

Duologues of this sort are reported with every appearance of realism and good faith by Suso, Tauler, Mechthild of Magdeburg, Angela of Foligno, St. Teresa, and countless other mystics. The third book of the "Imitation of Christ" contains some conspicuously beautiful examples, which may or may not be due to literary artifice. The self, wholly obsessed by the intimate sense of divine companionship, receives its messages in the form of "distinct interior words"; as of an alien voice, speaking within the mind with such an accent of validity and spontaneity as to leave no room for doubt as to its character. Often, as in Julian's Revelations, the discourses of the "Divine Voice," its replies to the eager questions of the self, are illustrated by imaginary visions. Since these dialogues are, on the whole, more commonly experienced in the illuminated than the unitive part of the Mystic Way, that self—retaining a clear consciousness of its own separateness, and recognizing the Voice as personal and distinct from its own soul—naturally enters into a communion which has an almost conversational character, replies to questions or asks others in its turn: and in this dramatic style the content of its intuitions is gradually expressed. We have then an extreme form of that dissociation which we all experience in a slight degree when we "argue with ourselves." But in this case one of the speakers is become the instrument of a power other than itself, and communicates to the mind new wisdom and new life.

The peculiar rhythmical language of genuine mystic dialogue of this kind—for often enough, as in Suso's "Book of the Eternal Wisdom," it is deliberately adopted as a literary device —is an indication of its automatic character.[1] Expression, once it is divorced from the critical action of the surface intelligence, always tends to assume a dithyrambic form. Measure and colour, exaltation of language, here take a more important place than the analytic intellect will generally permit. This feature is easily observable in prophecy, and in automatic writing. It forms an interesting link with poetry which—in so far as it is genuine and spontaneous—is largely the result

[1] Compare p. 95.

of subliminal activity. Life, which eludes language, can yet—
we know not why—be communicated by rhythm: and the
mystic fact is above all else the communication of a greater
Life. Hence we must not take it amiss if the voice of the
Absolute, as translated to us by those mystics who are alone
capable of hearing it, often seems to adopt the "grand
manner."

VISION

Let us pass now from the effort of man's deeper mind to
speak truth to his surface-intelligence, to the effort of the same
mysterious power to *show* truth: in psychological language,
from auditory to visual automatism. "Vision," that vaguest of
words, has been used by the friends and enemies of the mystics
to describe or obscure a wide range of experience: from formless intuition, through crude optical hallucination, to the voluntary visualizations common to the artistic mind. In it we must
include that personal and secret vision which is the lover's
glimpse of Perfect Love, and the great pictures seen by clairvoyant prophets acting in their capacity as eyes of the race.
Of these, the two main classes of vision, says Denis the Carthusian, the first kind are to be concealed, the second declared.
The first are more truly mystic, the second are more prophetic
in type. Even so, and ruling out prophetic vision from our
inquiry, a sufficient variety of experience remains in the purely
mystical class. St. Teresa's fluid and formless apprehension of
the Trinity, her concrete visions of Christ, Mechthild of Magdeburg's poetic dreams, Suso's sharply pictured allegories, even
Blake's soul of a flea, all come under this head.

Now since no one can know much of what it is really like
to have a vision but the visionaries themselves, it will be interesting to see what they have to say on this subject: and to
notice the respects in which their self-criticisms agree with the
conclusions of psychology. We forget, whilst arguing industriously on these matters, that it is really as impossible for
those who have never experienced a voice or vision to discuss
it with intelligence, as it is for stay-at-homes to discuss the
passions of the battle-field on the materials supplied by war
correspondents. No second-hand account of a vision can truly
report the experience of the person whose perceptions or

illusions present themselves in this form. "We cannot," says Récéjac, "remind ourselves too often that the mystic act consists in relations between the Absolute and Freedom which are incommunicable. We shall never know, for instance, what was the state of consciousness of some citizen of the antique world when he gave himself without reserve to the inspiring suggestions of the Sacred Fire or some other image which evoked the infinite."[1]   Neither shall we ever know, unless it be our good fortune to attain to it, the secret of that consciousness which is able to apprehend the Transcendent in visionary terms.

The first thing we notice when we come to this inquiry is that the mystics are all but unanimous in their refusal to attribute importance to any kind of visionary experience.[2]   The natural timidity and stern self-criticism with which they approach auditions is here greatly increased : and this, if taken to heart, might well give pause to their more extreme enemies and defenders. "If it be so," says Hilton of automatisms in general, "that thou see any manner of light or brightness with thy bodily eye or in imagination, other than every man seeth ; or if thou hear any pleasant wonderful sounding with thy ear, or in thy mouth any sweet sudden savour, other than what thou knowest to be natural, or any heat in thy breast like fire, or any manner of delight in any part of thy body, or if a spirit appears bodily to thee as it were an angel to comfort thee or teach thee ; or if any such feeling, which thou knowest well that it cometh not of thyself, nor from any bodily creature, beware in that time or soon after, and wisely consider the stirrings of thy heart ; for if by occasion of the pleasure and liking thou takest in the said feeling or vision thou feelest thy heart drawn . . . from the inward desire of virtues and of spiritual knowing and feeling of God, for to set the sight of thy heart and thy affection, thy delight and thy rest, principally in the said feelings or visions, supposing that to be a part of

---

[1] "Les Fondements de la Connaissance Mystique," p. 149.

[2] Here, as on other points, the exception which proves the rule is Blake. But Blake's visions differed in some important respects from those of his fellow-mystics ; they were "corporeal," not "imaginary" in type, and do not so much represent visualized intuitions as actual and constant perceptions of the inhabitants of that "real and eternal world" in which he held that it was man's privilege to dwell.

heavenly joy or angels' bliss . . . then is this feeling very
suspicious to come from the enemy ; and therefore, though it
be never so liking and wonderful, refuse it and assent not
thereto." [1]   Nearly every master of the contemplative life has
spoken to the same effect: none, perhaps, more strongly than that
stern and virile lover of the Invisible, St. John of the Cross,
who was relentless in hunting down even the most "spiritual"
illusions, eager to purge mind as well as morals of all taint
of the unreal.

"Spiritual men," he says, "are occasionally liable to representations and objects, set before them in a supernatural way.
They sometimes see the forms and figures of those of another
life, saints or angels, good and evil, or certain extraordinary
lights and brightness. They hear strange words, sometimes
seeing those who utter them and sometimes not. They have
a sensible perception at times of most sweet odours without
knowing whence they proceed. . . . Still, though all these may
happen to the bodily senses in the way of God, we must never
rely on them nor encourage them ; yea, rather we must fly
from them, without examining whether they be good or evil.
For, inasmuch as they are exterior and in the body, there is
the less certainty of their being from God. It is more natural
that God should communicate Himself through the spirit—
wherein there is greater security and profit for the soul—than
through the senses, wherein there is usually much danger and
delusion, because the bodily sense decides upon, and judges,
spiritual things, thinking them to be what itself feels them to
be, when in reality they are as different as body and soul,
sensuality and reason." [2]

Again, "in the high state of the union of love, God does
not communicate Himself to the soul under the disguise of
imaginary visions, similitudes or figures, neither is there place
for such, but mouth to mouth. . . . The soul, therefore, that will
ascend to this perfect union with God, must be careful not to
lean upon imaginary visions, forms, figures, and particular intelligible objects, for these things can never serve as proportionate
or proximate means towards so great an end ; yea, rather they

---

[1] "The Scale of Perfection," bk. i. cap. xi.
[2] "Subida del Monte Carmelo," l. ii. cap. xi. The whole chapter should be
read in this connection.

are an obstacle in the way, and therefore to be guarded against and rejected."[1]

So, too, Madame Guyon. Ecstasies, raptures, and visions, she says, are far inferior to "pure orison"—that dumb absorption in God which she learned at the time of her conversion. "Visions are experienced in those powers which are inferior to the will: and they should always have their effect in the will, and afterwards they should lose themselves in the experience of that which one has seen, known, and heard in these states: for without this the soul will never arrive at perfect union. Otherwise, that which she will have, and to which she may even give the name of union, will be only a mediated union, that is to say, an influx of the gifts of God into her powers [i.e., illumination]; but this is not God Himself. It is therefore very important to prevent souls from resting in visions and ecstasies, for this may check them almost for their whole lives. More, these graces are greatly subject to illusion. . . . Of these sort of gifts, the least pure, and those most subject to illusion, are visions and ecstasies. Raptures and revelations [exalted and abrupt intuitions] are not quite so much: though these also are not a little so." "The vision," says Madame Guyon again, "is never God Himself and hardly ever Jesus Christ, as those who have had it suppose . . . it seems to me that the apparitions which we believe to be Jesus Christ Himself are like what we see when the sun is reflected in the clouds so brilliantly that those who are not in the secret think that it is the sun which they see, although it is only his reflection. Thus it is that Jesus Christ is imaged in our minds in what is called *Intellectual Visions*, which are the most perfect. . . . Phantoms and pious pictures also imprint themselves on the imagination. There are also corporeal visions, *the least spiritual of all, and the most subject to illusion.*"[2]

Vision, then, is recognized by the true contemplative as at best a very imperfect, oblique, and untrustworthy method of apprehension : it is ungovernable, capricious, liable to deception, and the greater its accompanying hallucination the more suspicious it becomes. One and all, however, distinguish different classes of visionary experience ; and differentiate sharply between the value of the vision which is "felt" rather than seen, and the

---

[1] "Subida del Monte Carmelo," l. ii. cap. xvi.   [2] Vie, pt. i. cap. ix.

true optical hallucination which is perceived, exterior to the subject, by the physical sight.

We may trace in visions, as we have done in voices—for these are, from the psychologist's point of view, strictly parallel phenomena—a progressive externalization on the self's part of those concepts or intuitions which form the bases of all automatic states. Three main groups have been distinguished by the mystics, and illustrated over and over again from their experiences. These are (1) Intellectual, (2) Imaginary, and (3) Corporeal vision: answering to (1) Substantial or inarticulate, (2) Interior and distinct, (3) Exterior words. With the first two we must now concern ourselves. As to corporeal vision, it has few peculiarities of interest to the student of pure mysticism. Like the "exterior word" it is little else than a more or less uncontrolled externalization of inward memories, thoughts, or intuitions—often, as Madame Guyon acutely observed, of some pious picture which has become imprinted on the mind—which may, in some subjects, attain the dimensions of true sensorial hallucination.

(1) *Intellectual Vision.*—The "intellectual vision," like the "substantial word" as described to us by the mystics, is of so elusive, spiritual, and formless a kind that it is very hard to distinguish it from that act of pure contemplation in which it generally takes its rise. These moods and apprehensions of the soul are so closely linked together—the names applied to them are so often little more than the struggles of different individuals to describe by analogy an experience which is *one*—that we risk a loss of accuracy the moment that classification begins. The intellectual vision, so far as we can understand it, seems to be a *something* not sought but put before the mind, and seen or perceived by the whole self by means of a sense which is neither sight nor feeling, but partakes of the character of both. It is intimate but indescribable: definite, yet impossible to define. There is a passage in the "Consolations" of Angela of Foligno which describes very vividly the sequence of illuminated states which leads up to and includes the intuitions which form the substance of this "formless vision" and its complement the "formless word": and this does far more towards making us realize its nature than the most painstaking psychological analysis could ever do.

" It must be known," says Angela, "that God cometh sometimes unto the soul when it hath neither called nor prayed unto
nor summoned Him.   And He doth instil into the soul a fire
not customary, wherein it doth greatly delight and rejoice ; and
it doth believe that this hath been wrought by God Himself, but
this is not certain.   Presently the soul doth perceive that God is
inwardly within itself because—albeit it cannot behold Him
within—it doth nevertheless perceive that His grace is present
with it, wherein it doth greatly delight.   Yet is not even this
certain.   Presently it doth further perceive that God cometh
unto it with most sweet words, wherein it delighteth yet more,
and with much rejoicing doth it feel God within it ; yet do
some doubts still remain, albeit but few. . . . Further, when God
cometh unto the soul, it is sometimes given unto it to behold
Him ; and it beholdeth Him devoid of any bodily shape or
form, and more clearly than doth one man behold another.
For *the eyes of the soul do behold a spiritual and not a bodily
presence*, of the which I am not able to speak because words and
imagination do fail me.   And in very truth the soul doth
rejoice in that sight with an ineffable joy, and regardeth nought
else, because this it is which doth fill it with most inestimable
satisfaction.   This searching and beholding (wherein God is seen
in such a manner that the soul can behold naught else) is so
profound that much doth it grieve me that I cannot make
manifest aught whatsoever of it ; seeing that it is not a thing
the which can be touched or imagined or judged of." [1]

Intellectual vision, then, seems to be closely connected with
that "consciousness of the Presence of God" which we discussed in the last chapter : though the contemplatives themselves declare that it differs from it. [2]   It is distinguished
apparently from that more or less diffused consciousness of
Divine Immanence by the fact that, although unseen of the
eyes, it can be exactly located in space.   The mystic's general
awareness of the divine is here focussed upon one point—a
point to which some theological or symbolic character is at once
attached.   The result is a sense of presence so concrete, defined,

[1] B. Angelae de Fulginio, " Visionum et Instructionum Liber," cap. lii. (English
translation, p. 24).

[2] " It is not like that presence of God which is frequently felt . . . this is a great
grace . . . but it is not vision " (St. Teresa, Vida, cap. xxvii. § 6).

and sharply personal that, as St. Teresa says, it carries more conviction than bodily sight.   This invisible presence is generally
identified by Christian mystics rather with the Humanity of
Christ than with the unconditioned Absolute.   " In the prayer
of union and of quiet," says St. Teresa again, "certain inflowings of the Godhead are present ; but in the *vision* the Sacred
Humanity also, together with them, is pleased to be our companion and to do us good." [1]   " When one is not thinking at all
of any such favour," she says again, "and has not even had the
idea of meriting it, suddenly one feels at one's side Our Lord
Jesus Christ, *without seeing Him* either with the eyes of the
body or those of the soul. This sort of vision is called intellectual.
I do not know why. . . . Intellectual visions do not go quickly, like
imaginary ones, but last several days, sometimes more than a
year. . . . We know that God is present in all our actions : but
such is the infirmity of our nature, that we often lose sight of
this truth.   Here this forgetfulness is impossible, because Our
Lord, Who is close to the soul, keeps her constantly awake :
and as she has an almost continual love for That which she sees,
or rather feels close to her, she receives the more frequently the
favours of which we have spoken." [2]

In such a state—to which the term "vision" is barely applicable—it will be observed that consciousness is at its highest,
and hallucination at its lowest point.   Nothing is seen, even
with the eyes of the mind : as, in the parallel case of the
"substantial word," nothing is said.   It is pure apprehension :
in the one case of Personality, in the other of knowledge.   " The
immediate vision of the naked Godhead," says Suso of this, " is
without doubt the pure truth : a vision is to be esteemed the
more noble the more intellectual it is, the more it is stripped of
all image and approaches the state of pure contemplation." [3]

We owe to St. Teresa our finest first-hand account of this
strange condition of " awareness."   It came upon her abruptly,
after a period of psychic distress, and seemed to her to be an
answer to her unwilling prayers that she might be " led " by
some other way than that of "interior words " ; which were, in
the opinion of her director, " so suspicious."   " I could not force

---

[1] *Op. cit., loc. cit.*
[2] St. Teresa, " El Castillo Interior," Moradas Sextas, cap. viii
[3] Leben, cap. liv.

myself," she says, " to desire the change, nor believe that I was
under the influence of Satan. Though I was doing all I could
to believe the one and to desire the other, it was not in my power
to do so." She resolved this divided state by making an act of
total surrender to the will of God : and it seems to have been as
the result of this release of stress, this willing receptivity, that
the new form of automatism suddenly developed itself, rein-
forcing and justifying the auditions, and bringing peace and
assurance to the distracted surface-self.

"At the end of two years spent in prayer by myself and
others for this end, namely, that our Lord would either lead me
by another way, or show the truth of this—for now the locutions
of our Lord were extremely frequent—this happened to me. I
was in prayer one day—it was the feast of the glorious St. Peter
—when I saw Christ close by me, or, to speak more correctly,
felt Him ; for I saw nothing with the eyes of the body, nothing
with the eyes of the soul. He seemed to me to be close beside
me ; and I saw, too, as I believe, that it was He who was speaking to me. As I was utterly ignorant that such a vision was
possible, I was extremely afraid at first, and did nothing but
weep ; however, when He spoke to me but one word to reassure
me, I recovered myself, and was, as usual, calm and comforted,
without any fear whatever. Jesus Christ seemed to be by my
side continually, and, as the vision was not imaginary, I saw no
form ; but I had a most distinct feeling that He was always on
my right hand, a witness of all I did ; and never at any time, if
I was but slightly recollected, or not too much distracted, could
I be ignorant of His near presence. I went at once to my confessor in great distress, to tell him of it. He asked in what form
I saw our Lord. I told him I saw no form. He then said :
' How did you know that it was Christ?' I replied that I did
not know how I knew it ; but I could not help knowing that
He was close beside me . . . there are no words whereby to
explain—at least, none for us women, who know so little ;
learned men can explain it better.

"For if I say that I see Him neither with the eyes of the body
nor those of the soul—because it was not an imaginary vision—
how is it that I can understand and maintain that He stands
beside me, and be *more certain of it than if I saw Him?* If it
be supposed that it is as if a person were blind, or in the dark,

and therefore unable to see another who is close to him, the comparison is not exact.   There is a certain likelihood about it, however, but not much, because the other senses tell him who is blind of that presence : he hears the other speak or move, or he touches him ; but in these visions there is nothing like this. The darkness is not felt ; only He renders Himself present to the soul by a certain knowledge of Himself which is more clear than the sun.   I do not mean that we now see either a sun or any other brightness, only that there is a light not seen, which illumines the understanding, so that the soul may have the fruition of so great a good.   This vision brings with it great blessings." [1]

(2) In *Imaginary Vision*, as in " interior words," there is again no sensorial hallucination.   The self sees sharply and clearly, it is true : but is perfectly aware that it does so in virtue of its most precious organ—" that inward eye which is the bliss of solitude." [2]   Imaginary Vision is the spontaneous and auto-matic activity of a power which all artists, all imaginative people, possess.   So far as the machinery employed in it is concerned, there is little real difference except in degree between Words-worth's imaginary vision of the " dancing daffodils" and Suso's of the dancing angels, who " though they leapt very high in the dance, did so without any lack of gracefulness." [3]   Both are admirable examples of " passive imaginary vision " : though in the first case the visionary is aware that the picture seen is supplied by memory, whilst in the second it arises spontaneously like a dream from the subliminal region, and contains elements which may be attributed to love, belief, and direct intuition of truth.

Such passive imaginary vision—by which I mean spontaneous mental pictures at which the self looks, but in the action of which it does not participate—takes in the mystics two main forms : (*a*) purely symbolic, (*b*) personal.

---

[1] St. Teresa, Vida, cap. xxvii. §§ 2–5.

[2] " For oft, when on my couch I lie
    In vacant or in pensive mood,
    They flash upon that inward eye
    Which is the bliss of solitude ;
    And then my heart with pleasure fills,
    And dances with the daffodils."

                    Wordsworth, " The Daffodils."

[3] Leben, cap. vii.

(*a*) In the symbolic form there is no mental deception: the self is aware that it is being shown truth "under an image." Rulman Merswin's "Vision of Nine Rocks" is thus described to us as being seen by him in a sharp picture, the allegorical meaning of which was simultaneously presented to his mind. In Suso's life such symbolic visions abound: he seems to have lived always on the verge of such a world of imagination, and to have imbibed truth most easily in this form. Thus: "It happened one morning that the Servitor saw in a vision that he was surrounded by a troop of heavenly spirits. He therefore asked one of the most radiant amongst these Princes of the Sky to show him how God dwelt in his soul. The angel said to him, 'Do but fix your eyes joyously upon yourself, and watch how God plays the game of love within your loving soul.' And he looked quickly, and saw that his body in the region of his heart was pure and transparent like crystal : and he saw the Divine Wisdom peacefully enthroned in the midst of his heart, and she was fair to look upon. And by her side was the soul of the Servitor, full of heavenly desires ; resting lovingly upon the bosom of God, Who had embraced it, and pressed it to His Heart. And it remained altogether absorbed and inebriated with love in the arms of God its well-beloved."[1]

In such a vision as this, we see the mystic's passion for the Absolute, his intuition of Its Presence in his soul, combining with the constituents of poetic imagination and expressing themselves in an allegorical form. It is really a visualized poem, inspired by a direct contact with truth. Of the same kind are many of those great reconstructions of Eternity in which mystics and seers of the transcendent and outgoing type actualized their profound apprehensions of truth. In such cases, as Beatrice told Dante when he saw the great vision of the River of Light, the thing seen is the shadowy presentation of a transcendent Reality which the self is not yet strong enough to see.

> " E vidi lume in forma di riviera
>   fulvide di fulgore, intra due rive
>   dipinte di mirabil primavera.

---

[1] Suso, Leben, cap. vi.

Di tal fiumana uscian faville vive,
        e d' ogni parte si mettean nei fiori,
        quasi rubin che oro circonscrive.
Poi come inebriate dagli odori,
        riprofondavan sè nel miro gurge,
        e, s'una entrava, un' altra n' uscia fuori."

*   *   *   *   *

                "il sol degli occhi miei
Anco soggiunse : Il fiume, e li topazii
        ch' entrano ed escono, e il rider dell' erbe
        son di lor vero ombriferi prefazii.
Non che da sè sien queste cose acerbe :
        ma è difetto dalla parte tua,
        che non hai viste ancor tanto superbe." [1]

In the last two lines of this wonderful passage, the whole philosophy of vision is expressed. It is an accommodation of the supra-sensible to our human disabilities, a symbolic reconstruction of reality. This symbolic reconstruction is seen as a profoundly significant, vivid, and dramatic dream : and since this dream is directly representative of truth, and initiates the visionary into the atmosphere of the Eternal, it may well claim precedence over that prosaic and perpetual vision which we call the "real world." In it—as in the meaningless dreams of our common experience—vision and audition are often combined. Many of the visions of St. Mechthild of Hackborn are of this complex type. Thus—"She saw in the Heart of God, as it were a virgin exceeding fair, holding a ring in her hand on which was a diamond : with which, incessantly, she touched the Heart of God. Moreover, the soul asked why that virgin thus touched the Heart of God. And the virgin answered, 'I am Divine Love and this stone signifieth the sin of Adam. . . . As soon as Adam sinned, I introduced myself and intercepted the whole of his sin, and by thus ceaselessly touching the Heart of God and moving Him to

---

[1] Par. xxx. 61-81 : " And I saw light in the form of a river blazing with radiance, streaming between banks painted with a marvellous spring. Out of that river issued living sparks and settled on the flowers on every side, like rubies set in gold. Then, as it were inebriated by the perfume, they plunged again into the wondrous flood, and as one entered another issued forth. . . . Then added the Sun of my eyes : The river, the topazes that enter and come forth, the smiling flowers, are shadowy fore-tastes of their reality. Not that these things are themselves imperfect ; but on thy side is the defect, in that thy vision cannot rise so high." This vision probably owes something to Mechthild of Magdeburg's concept of Deity as a Flowing Light.

pity, I suffered Him not to rest until the moment when I took the Son of God from His Father's Heart and laid Him in the Virgin Mother's womb.' . . . Another time, she saw how Love, under the likeness of a fair Virgin, went round about the consistory singing *Alone I have made the circuit of heaven, and I have walked on the waves of the sea.* In these words she understood how Love had subjected to herself the Omnipotent Majesty of God, had inebriated His Unsearchable Wisdom, had drawn forth all His most sweet goodness; and, by wholly conquering His divine justice and changing it into gentleness and mercy, had moved the Lord of all Majesty." [1]

Imaginary vision of this kind is probably far more common than is generally supposed : and can exist without any disturbance of that balance of faculties which is usually recognized as "sane." In many meditative persons it appears, involuntarily, at the summit of a train of thought, which it sometimes illustrates and sometimes contradicts. The picture may show itself faintly against a background of mist; or may start into existence sharply focused, well-lighted, and alive. It always brings with it a greater impression of reality than can be obtained by the more normal operations of the mind.

(*b*) The symbolic and artistic character of the visions we have been discussing is obvious. There is, however, another form of imaginary vision which must be touched on with a gentler hand. In this, the imagery seized upon by the subliminal powers, or placed before the mind by that Somewhat Other of which the mystic is always conscious over against himself, is at once so vivid, so closely related to the concrete beliefs and spiritual passions of the self, and so perfectly expresses its apprehensions of God, that it is not always recognized as symbolic in kind. A simple example of this is the vision of Christ at the moment of consecration at Mass, experienced by so many Catholic ecstatics.[2] Another is the

[1] Mechthild o. Hackborn, "Liber Specialis Gratiae," l. ii. caps. xvii. and xxxv.
[2] For instance, the Blessed Angela ot Foligno, who gives in her "Visions and Consolations" a complete series of such experiences ; ranging from an almost sublime apprehension of Divine Beauty (cap. xxxvii. English translation, p. 222) to a concrete vision of two eyes shining in the Host (cap. xliii. English translation, p. 230). "I did of a certainty behold Him with mine eyes in that sacrament," she says, "poor, suffering, bleeding, crucified, and dead upon the Cross" (cap. xxxviii. p. 223).

celebrated vision in which St. Anthony of Padua embraced the Divine Child. St. Teresa is one of the few mystics who have detected the true character of automatisms of this sort: which bring with them, like their purer forms, the intellectual visions of God, a vivid apprehension of Personality, the conviction of a living presence, rather than the knowledge of new facts. "Now and then," she says of her own imaginary visions of Christ, "it seemed to me that what I saw was an image: but most frequently it was not so. I thought it was Christ Himself, judging by the brightness in which He was pleased to show Himself. Sometimes the vision was so indistinct, that I thought it was an image: but still, not like a picture, however well painted, and I have seen a good many pictures. It would be absurd to suppose that the one bears any resemblance whatever to the other, for they differ as a living person differs from his portrait, which, however well drawn, cannot be life-like, for it is plain that it is a dead thing." [1]

"This vision," she says in another place, "passes like a flash of lightning . . . the word image here employed, does not signify a picture placed before the eyes, but a veritable living image, which sometimes speaks to the soul and reveals great secrets to her." [2]

It seems, then, that this swift and dazzling vision of Divine Personality may represent a true contact of the soul with the Absolute Life—a contact immediately referred to the image under which the Self is accustomed to think of its God. In the case of Christian contemplatives this image will obviously be most usually the historical Person of Christ, as He is represented in sacred literature and art.[3]

"Another time I beheld Christ in the consecrated Host as a child. He appeared certainly to be a child of twelve years of age, very lordly, as though He held the sceptre and the dominion" (cap. xlii. p. 229). (B. Angelae de Fulginio, "Visionum et Instructionum Liber.")

[1] Vida, cap. xxviii. § 11.

[2] "El Castillo Interior," Moradas Sextas, cap. ix.

[3] "On one of the feasts of St. Paul, while I was at Mass, there stood before me the most sacred Humanity as painters represent Him after the resurrection" (St. Teresa, Vida, cap. xxviii. § 4). So too the form assumed by many of the visions of Angela of Foligno is obviously due to her familiarity with the frescoed churches of Assisi and the Vale of Spoleto. "When I did bend my knees upon entering in at the door of the church," she says, "I immediately beheld a picture of St. Francis lying in Christ's bosom. Then said Christ unto me, 'Thus closely will I hold thee,

The life-enhancing quality of such an abrupt apprehension, however, the profound sense of reality which it brings, permit of its being classed not amongst vivid dreams, but amongst those genuine mystic states in which " the immanent God, formless, but capable of assuming all forms, expresses Himself in vision as He had expressed Himself in words." ¹ Certainty and joy are always felt by the self which experiences it. It is as it were a love-letter received by the ardent soul; which brings with it the very fragrance of personality, along with the sign-manual of the beloved.

This concrete vision of Christ has the true mystic quality of ineffability, appearing to the self under a form of inexpressible beauty, illuminated with that unearthly light which is so persistently reported as a feature of all transcendent experience. The artist's exalted consciousness of Beauty as a form of Truth is here seen operating on the transcendental plane. Thus when St. Teresa saw only the Hands of God, she was thrown into an ecstasy of adoration by their shining loveliness.² " If I were to spend many years in devising how to picture to myself anything so beautiful," she says of the imaginary vision of Christ, " I should never be able, nor even know how, to do it ; for it is beyond the scope of any possible imagination here below : the whiteness and brilliancy alone are inconceivable. It is not a brightness which dazzles, but a delicate whiteness, an infused brightness, giving excessive delight to the eyes, which are never wearied thereby nor by the visible brightness which enables us to see a beauty so divine. It is a light so different from any light here below, that the very brightness of the sun we see, in comparison with the brightness and light before our eyes, seems to be something so obscure that no one would ever wish to open his eyes again. . . . In short, it is such that no man, however gifted he may be, can ever in the whole course of his life arrive at any imagination of what it is. God puts it before us so instantaneously, that we could not open our eyes in time to see it, if it were necessary for us to open them at all. But whether our eyes be open or shut, it makes no difference whatever :

and so much closer, that bodily eyes can neither perceive nor comprehend it ' "
(B. Angelae de Fulginio, *op. cit.*, cap. xx. English translation, p. 165).
¹ Delacroix, " Études sur le Mysticisme," p. 116.
² Vida, cap. xxviii. § 2.

for when our Lord wills, we must see it, whether we will or not." [1]

There is another and highly important class of visual automatisms: those which I have chosen to call *Active Imaginary Visions*. Whereas vision of the passive kind is the expression of thought, perception, or desire on the part of the deeper self: active vision is the expression of a change in that self, and generally accompanies some psychological crisis. In this vision, which always has a dramatic character, the self seems to itself to act, not merely to look on. Such visions may possess many of the characters of dream: they may be purely symbolic; they may be theologically "realistic." They may entail a journey through Hell, Purgatory, and Heaven, an excursion into fairyland, a wrestling with the Angel in the Way. Whatever their outward form, they are always connected with inward results. They are the automatic expressions of profound subliminal activity: not merely the *media* by which the self's awareness of the Absolute is strengthened and enriched, but the outward and visible signs of its movement towards new levels of consciousness. Hence we are not surprised to find that a dynamic vision of this sort often initiates the Unitive Life. Such are the imaginary visions reported by St. Francis of Assisi and St. Catherine of Siena at the moment of their stigmatization: the transverberation of St. Teresa; the heavenly visitor who announced to Suso his passage from the "lower school" to the "upper school" of the Holy Spirit. [2] But perhaps the most picturesque and best known example of all such dramas of the soul, is that which is known in art as the "Mystic Marriage of St. Catherine of Siena."

We have already seen that Catherine, who was subject from childhood to imaginary visions and interior words, had long been conscious of a voice reiterating the promise of this sacred betrothal; and that on the last day of the Carnival, A.D. 1366, it said to her, " I will this day celebrate solemnly with thee the

---

[1] St. Teresa, *op. cit.*, cap. xxviii. §§ 7, 8. Angela of Foligno says of an equivalent vision of Christ, " His beauty and adornment cannot be described, and so great was my joy at the sight of Him, that I do think that it will never fade, and there was such certainty with it that I do in no way doubt of the truth thereof " (Angelae de Fulginio, *op. cit.*, cap. xlii. English translation, p. 229).

[2] Leben, cap. xxi.

feast of the betrothal of thy soul, and even as I promised I will espouse thee to Myself in faith." "Then," says her legend, "whilst the Lord was yet speaking, there appeared the most glorious Virgin His Mother, the most blessed John, Evangelist, the glorious apostle Paul, and the most holy Dominic, father of her order; and with these the prophet David, who had the psaltery set to music in his hands; and while he played with most sweet melody the Virgin Mother of God took the right hand of Catherine with her most sacred hand, and, holding out her fingers towards the Son, besought Him to deign to espouse her to Himself in faith. To which graciously consenting the Only Begotten of God drew out a ring of gold, which had in its circle four pearls enclosing a most beauteous diamond; and placing this ring upon the ring finger of Catherine's right hand He said, 'Lo, I espouse thee to Myself, thy Creator and Saviour in the faith, which until thou dost celebrate thy eternal nuptials with Me in Heaven thou wilt preserve ever without stain. Henceforth, my daughter, do manfully and without hesitation those things which by the ordering of My providence will be put into thy hands; for being now armed with the fortitude of the faith, thou wilt happily overcome all thy adversaries.' Then the vision disappeared, but that ring ever remained on her finger, not indeed to the sight of others, but only to the sight of the virgin herself; for she often, albeit with bashfulness, confessed to me that she always saw that ring on her finger, nor was there any time when she did not see it." [1]

It is not difficult to discern the materials from which this vision has been composed. As far as its outward circumstances go, it is borrowed intact from the legendary history of St. Catherine of Alexandria, with which her namesake, the "dyer's

[1] E. Gardner, "St. Catherine of Siena," p. 25. Vita, i. xii. 1, 2 (Acta S.S., *loc. cit.*). In the ring which she always saw upon her finger, we seem to have an instance of true corporeal vision; which finds a curiously exact parallel in the life of St. Teresa. "On one occasion when I was holding in my hand the cross of my rosary, He took it from me into His own hand. He returned it, but it was then four large stones incomparably more precious than diamonds. He said to me that for the future that cross would so appear to me always: *and so it did.* I never saw the wood of which it was made, but only the precious stones. They were seen, however, by no one else" (Vida, cap. xxix. § 8). This class of experience, says Augustine Baker, particularly gifts of roses, rings, and jewels, is "much to be suspected," except in "souls of a long-continued sanctity" ("Holy Wisdom," Treatise iii. § iv. cap. iii.).

daughter of Italy," must have been familiar from babyhood.[1]
Caterina Benincasa showed a characteristic artistic suggestibility
and quickness in transforming the stuff of this old story into the
medium of a profound personal experience : as her contemporaries amongst the Sienese painters took subject, method, and
composition from the traditional Byzantine source, yet forced
them to become expressions of their own overpowering
individuality. The important matter for us, however, is not
the way in which the second Catherine adapted a traditional
story to herself, actualized it in her experience : but the fact
that it was for her the sacramental form under which she became
acutely and permanently conscious of union with God. Long
prepared by that growing disposition of her deeper self which
caused her to hear the reiterated promise of her Beloved, the
vision when it came was significant, not for its outward circumstances, but for its permanent effect upon her life. In it she
passed to a fresh level of consciousness ; entering upon that
state of spiritual wedlock, of close and loving identification with
the interests of Christ, which Richard of St. Victor calls the
" Third Stage of Ardent Love."

Of the same active sort is St. Teresa's great and celebrated
vision, or rather experience, of the Transverberation ; in which
imagery and feeling go side by side in their effort towards
expressing the anguish of insatiable love. " I saw," she says,
" an angel close by me, on my left side, in bodily form. This I
am not accustomed to see unless very rarely. Though I have
visions of angels frequently, yet I see them only by an intellectual vision, such as I have spoken of before. It was our
Lord's will that in this vision I should see the angel in this
wise. He was not large, but small of stature, and most beautiful
—his face burning, as if he were one of the highest angels, who
seem to be all of fire : they must be those whom we call
Cherubim. . . . I saw in his hand a long spear of gold, and at
the iron's point there seemed to be a little fire. He appeared to
me to be thrusting it at times into my heart, and to pierce my
very entrails ; when he drew it out, he seemed to draw them out
also and to leave me all on fire with a great love of God. The
pain was so great that it made me moan ; and yet so surpassing
was the sweetness of this excessive pain that I could not wish to

[1] *Vide* " Legenda Aurea," Nov. xxv.

be rid of it. The soul is satisfied now with nothing less than God. The pain is not bodily, but spiritual; though the body has its share in it, even a large one. It is a caressing of love so sweet which now takes place between the soul and God, that I pray God of His goodness to make him experience it who may think that I am lying."[1]

Finally it should be added that dynamic vision may assume a purely intellectual form; as in the case of the Blessed Angela of Foligno. "Being thus exalted in spirit during the time of Lent, therefore," she says, "I was joined to God in a manner other than was customary for me. Methought I was in the midst of the Trinity in a manner higher and greater than was usual, for greater than usual were the blessings I received, and continually were there given unto me gifts full of delight, and rejoicing most great and unspeakable. All this was so far beyond anything which had heretofore happened unto me that *verily a divine change took place in my soul*, which neither saint nor angel could describe or explain. This divine change, or operation, was so profound that no angel or other creature, howsoever wise, could comprehend it; wherefore do I say again that it seemeth unto me to be evil speaking and blasphemy if I do try to tell of it."[2]

AUTOMATIC SCRIPT

The rarest of the automatic activities reported to us in connection with mysticism is that of "automatic writing." This form of subliminal action has already been spoken of in an earlier chapter[3]; where two of the most marked examples—Blake and Madame Guyon—are discussed. As in the case of voice and vision, so this power of automatic composition may and does exist in various degrees of intensity: ranging from that "inspiration," that irresistible impulse to write, of which all artists are aware, to the extreme form in which the hand of the conscious self seems to have become the agent of another personality. It is probably present to some extent in all the literary work of the great mystics, whose creative power, like

[1] Vida, cap. xxix. §§ 16, 17.
[2] "Visionum et Instructionum Liber," cap. xxvii. (English translation, p. 186).
[3] Pp. 78, 79.

that of most poets, is largely dissociated from the control of the will and the surface intelligence.

St. Catherine of Siena, we are told, dictated her great Dialogue to her secretaries whilst in the state of ecstasy: which probably means a condition of consciousness resembling the "trance" of mediums, in which the deeper mind governs the tongue. Had she been more accustomed to the use of the pen —she did not learn writing until after the beginning of her apostolic life—that deeper mind would almost certainly have expressed itself by means of automatic script. As it is, in the rhythm and exaltation of its periods, the Dialogue bears upon it all the marks of true automatic composition of the highest type. The very discursiveness of its style, its loose employment of metaphor, the strangely mingled intimacy and remoteness of its tone, link it with prophetic literature; and are entirely characteristic of subliminal energy of a rich type, dissociated from the criticism and control of the normal consciousness.[1]

So too the writings of Rulman Merswin, if we accept the ingenious and interesting theory of his psychic state elaborated by M. Jundt,[2] were almost wholly of this kind. So Blake stated on his deathbed that the credit for all his works belonged not to himself, but to his "celestial friends"[3]: *i.e.*, to the inspiration of a personality which had access to levels of truth and beauty unknown to his surface mind.

St. Teresa was of much the same opinion in respect of her great mystical works: which were, she said, like the speech of a parrot repeating, though he cannot understand, the things which his master has taught him. There is little doubt that her powers of composition—as we might expect in one so apt at voice and vision—were largely of the uncontrolled, inspired, or "automatic" kind. She wrote most usually after the reception of Holy Communion—that is to say, when her mystic consciousness was in its most active state—and always swiftly, without hesitations or amendments. Ideas and images welled up from her rich and active subliminal region too quickly, indeed, for her eager, hurrying pen: so that she sometimes exclaimed, "Oh, that I could write with many hands, so that

---

[1] On this point I must respectfully differ from Mr. E. Gardner. See his "St. Catherine of Siena," p. 354.

[2] *Supra*, p. 224.   [3] Berger, "William Blake," p. 54.

none were forgotten !"[1] In Teresa's unitive state, a slight suggestion was enough to change the condition of her consciousness, place her under the complete domination of her deeper mind. Often, she said, when composing the "Interior Castle," her work reacted upon herself. She would suddenly be caught up into the very degree of contemplation which she was trying to describe, and continued to write in this absorbed or entranced condition, clearly perceiving that her pen was guided by a power not her own, and expressed ideas unknown to her surface mind, which filled her with astonishment.

In the evidence given during the process for St. Teresa's beatification, Maria de San Francisco of Medina, one of her early nuns, stated that on entering the saint's cell whilst she was writing this same "Interior Castle" she found her so absorbed in contemplation as to be unaware of the external world. "If we made a noise close to her," said another, Maria del Nacimiento, "she neither ceased to write nor complained of being disturbed." Both these nuns and also Ana de la Encarnacion, prioress of Granada, affirmed that she wrote with immense speed, never stopping to erase or to correct : being anxious, as she said, to "write what the Lord had given her, before she forgot it." They and many others declared that when she was thus writing she seemed like another being : and that her face, excessively beautiful in expression, shone with an unearthly splendour which afterwards faded away.[2]

As for Madame Guyon, whose temperament had in it almost as much of the medium as of the mystic, and whose passion for quietism and mental passivity left her almost wholly at the mercy of subconscious impulses, she exhibits by turns the phenomena of clairvoyance, prophecy, telepathy, and automatic writing, in bewildering profusion.

"I was myself surprised," she says, "at the letters which Thou didst cause me to write, and in which I had no part save the actual movement of my hand : and it was at this time that I received that gift of writing according to the interior mind, and not according to my own mind, which I had never known before. Also my manner of writing was altogether changed,

[1] G. Cunninghame Graham, "Santa Teresa," vol. i. p. 202.
[2] Ibid., pp. 203-4.

and every one was astonished because I wrote with such great facility."[1]

Again, "As soon as I began to read Holy Scripture, I was caused to write the passage that I had read ; and at once, the interpretation of it was given to me. In writing the passage I had not the least thought of the interpretation. Yet no sooner was it written, than it was given to me to explain it, writing with inconceivable swiftness. Before writing, I knew not what I was going to write: in writing, I saw that I wrote things which I had never known, and during the time of this manifestation it was revealed to me that I had in me treasures of knowledge and understanding which I did not know that I possessed. . . . Thou didst make me write with so great a detachment that I was obliged to leave off and begin again as Thou didst choose. Thou didst try me in every way : suddenly Thou wouldst cause me to write, then at once to cease, and then to begin again. When I wrote during the day, I would be suddenly interrupted, and often left words half written, and afterwards Thou wouldst give me whatever was pleasing to Thee. Nothing of that which I wrote was in my mind : my mind, in fact, was so wholly at liberty that it seemed a blank. I was so detached from that which I wrote that it seemed foreign to me. . . . All the faults in my writings come from this : that being unaccustomed to the operations of God, I was often unfaithful to them, thinking that I did well to continue writing when I had time, without being moved thereto, because I had been told to finish the work. So that it is easy to distinguish the parts which are fine and sustained, and those which have neither savour nor grace. I have left them as they are ; so that the difference between the Spirit of God and the human or natural spirit may be seen. . . . I continued always to write, and with an inconceivable swiftness, for the hand could hardly keep up with the dictating spirit : and during this long work, I never changed my method, nor did I make use of any book. The scribe could not, however great his diligence, copy in five days that which I wrote in a single night. . . . At the beginning I made many mistakes, not being yet broken to the operation of the spirit of God which caused me to write. For He made me cease writing when I had time to write and could have done

[1] Vie, pt. ii. cap. ii.

it without inconvenience, and when I felt a great need of sleep,
then it was He made me write. . . . I will add to all that I have
been saying on my writings, that a considerable part of the book
on 'Judges' was lost. Being asked to complete it, I rewrote
the lost portions. Long afterwards, when I was moving house,
these were found in a place where no one could have imagined
that they would be; and the old and new versions were
exactly alike—a circumstance which greatly astonished those
persons of learning and merit who undertook its verification."[1]

A far greater and stronger mystic than Madame Guyon,
Jacob Boehme, was also in his literary composition the more
or less helpless tool of some power other than his normal surface-mind. It is clear from his own words concerning it, that
his first book, the "Aurora," produced after the great illumination
which he received in the year 1610, was no deliberate composition, but an example of inspired or automatic script. This
strange work, full of sayings of a deep yet dazzling darkness,
was condemned by the local tribunal; and Boehme was forbidden to write more. For seven years he obeyed. Then "a
new motion from on high" seized him, and under the pressure
of this subliminal impulse—which, characteristically, he feels
as coming from without not from within—he began to write
again.

This second outburst of composition, too, was almost purely
automatic in type. The transcendental consciousness was
in command, and Boehme's surface-intellect could exert
but little control. "Art," he says of it himself, "has not
wrote here, neither was there any time to consider how to
set it punctually down, according to the Understanding of
the Letters, but all was ordered according to the Direction of
the Spirit, which often went in haste, so that in many words
Letters may be wanting, and in some Places a Capital Letter
for a Word; so that the Penman's Hand, by reason he was not
accustomed to it, did often shake. And though I could have
wrote in a more accurate, fair and plain Manner, yet the
Reason was this, that the burning Fire often forced forward

[1] Vie, pt. ii. cap. xxi. Those who wish to compare this vivid subjective account
of automatic writing with modern attested instances may consult Myers, " Human
Personality," and Oliver Lodge, "The Survival of Man."

with Speed, and the Hand and Pen must hasten directly after it; for it comes and goes as a sudden Shower."[1]

No description could give more vividly than this the spontaneous and uncontrollable character of these automatic states ; the welling-up of new knowledge, the rapid formation of sentences : so quick, that the hand of the subject can hardly keep pace with that "burning Fire," the travail of his inner mind. As in vision, so here, the contents of that inner mind, its hoarded memories, will influence the form of the message : and hence, in Boehme's works, the prevalence of that obscure Kabalistic and Alchemical imagery which baffles even his most eager readers, and which is the result of an earlier acquaintance with the works of Paracelsus, Weigel, and Sebastian Franck.[2] Such language, however, no more discredits the "power behind the pen," than the form under which St. Catherine of Siena apprehended the mystic marriage discredits her attainment of the unitive life. In the fruit of such automatic travail, such a "wrestling with the Angel in the way," the mystic offers to our common humanity the chalice of the Spirit of Life. We may recognize the origins of the ornament upon the chalice: but we cannot justly charge him with counterfeiting the Wine.

We have been dealing throughout this section with means rather than with ends: means snatched at by the struggling self which has not yet wholly shaken itself free from "image," in its efforts to seize somehow—actualize, enjoy, and adore—that Absolute which is the sum of its desires. No one will ever approach an understanding of this phase of the mystical consciousness, who brings to it either a contempt for the minds which could thus simply and sometimes childishly objectivize the Divine, or a superstitious reverence for the image, apart from the formless Reality at which it hints. Between these two extremes lies our hope of grasping the true place of automatisms on the Mystic Way : of seeing in them instances of the adaptation of those means by which we obtain consciousness of the phenomenal world, to an apprehension of that other world whose attainment is humanity's sublimest end.

[1] Works of Jacob Boehme (English translation, vol. i. p. xiv.).
[2] See E. Boutroux, "Le Philosophe Allemand, Jacob Boehme."

CHAPTER VI

INTROVERSION. Part I : RECOLLECTION AND QUIET

Introversion is the characteristic mystic art—Its development accompanies organic growth—It is susceptible of education—The value of tradition—The training of will and attention—Contemplation the only real way of perceiving anything—Its method described—An experiment—Introversion—Ecstasy—the two aspects of contemplative consciousness—The ground of the soul—Philosophic contemplation—The Degrees of Orison—their nature—The end of contemplation—Hilton—Naked orison—All "stages" or degrees of orison arbitrary and diagrammatic—But some division essential to description—Three stages—Recollection, Quiet, Contemplation—Orison grows with the growing self—disciplines the mind, will and heart—St. Teresa's degrees of orison—It is a progress in love—a retreat from circumference to centre—Its end is union—Recollection—a difficult process—Boehme—Meditation—its characteristics—it develops into Recollection—A spiritual gymnastic—St. Teresa—Quiet—its characteristics—largely inexpressible—Suspension of thought—Its development from Recollection—It is a state of humility—Its nature described—Two aspects of Quiet : positive and negative—Eckhart—The Epistle of Private Counsel—St. Teresa —Quiet and Quietism—The " danger-zone " of introversion— Ruysbroeck on Quietism —its evils—It is a perversion of truth—Molinos—Von Hügel—The distinguishing mark of true Quiet—Madame Guyon—Quiet is a transitional state

IN our study of the First Mystic Life, its purification and illumination, we have been analysing and considering a process of organic development; an evolution of personality. This may be called—indifferently—either a movement of consciousness towards higher levels, or a remaking of consciousness consequent on the emergence and growth of a factor which is dormant in ordinary man, but destined to be supreme in the full-grown mystic type. We have seen the awakening of this factor—this spark of the soul—with its innate capacity for apprehending the Absolute. We have seen it attack and conquer the old sense-fed and self-centred life of the normal self, and introduce it into a new universe, lit up by the Uncreated Light. These were the events which, taken together,

constituted the " First Mystic Life " ; a complete round upon
the spiral road which leads from man to God.

What we have been looking at, then, is a life-process, the
establishment of a certain harmony between the self and
Reality : and we have discussed this life-process rather as if
it contained no elements which were not referable to natural
and spontaneous growth, to the involuntary adjustments of the
organism to that extended or transcendental universe of which
it gradually becomes aware.

But side by side with this organic growth goes a specific
kind of activity which is characteristic of the mystic : a form
under which his consciousness works best, and his awareness
of the Infinite is enriched and defined.   Already once or twice
we have been in the presence of this activity, have been obliged
to take its influence into account : as, were we studying other
artistic types, we could not leave the medium in which they
work wholly on one side.

Contemplation is the mystic's medium.   It is to him that
which harmony is to the musician, form and colour to the
artist, measure to the poet : the vehicle by which he can best
apprehend the Good and Beautiful, enter into communion with
the Real.   As " voice " or " vision " is the way in which his
transcendental consciousness presents its discoveries to the
surface-mind, so contemplation is the way in which it makes
those discoveries, perceives the supra-sensible.   The growth of
his effective genius, therefore, is connected with his growth in
this art : and that growth is largely conditioned by education.

The painter, however great his natural powers may be, can
hardly dispense with some technical training ; the musician is
wise if he acquaint himself at least with the elements of
counterpoint.   So too the mystic.   It is true that he sometimes seems to spring abruptly to the heights, to be caught
into ecstasy without previous preparation : as a poet may
startle the world by a sudden masterpiece.   But unless they
be backed by discipline, these sudden and isolated flashes of
inspiration will not long avail for the production of great works.
" Ordina quest' amore, o tu che m'ami " is the one imperative
demand made by Goodness, Truth, and Beauty, by every aspect
of Reality, upon the human soul.   Lover and philosopher, saint,
artist, and scientist, must alike obey or fail.

Transcendental genius, then, obeys the laws which govern all other forms of genius, in being susceptible of culture : and, indeed, cannot develop its full powers without an educative process of some kind. This strange art of contemplation, which the mystic tends naturally to practise during the whole of his career—which develops step by step with his vision and his love—demands of the self which undertakes it the same hard dull work, the same slow training of the will, which lies behind all supreme achievement, and is the price of all true liberty. It is the want of such training—such " supersensual drill "—which is responsible for the mass of vague, ineffectual, and sometimes harmful mysticism which has always existed : the dilute cosmic emotion and limp spirituality which hangs, as it were, on the skirts of the true seekers of the Absolute and brings discredit upon their science.

In this, as in all the other and lesser arts which have been developed by the race, education consists largely in a humble willingness to submit to the discipline, and profit by the lessons, of the past. Tradition runs side by side with experience ; the past collaborates with the present. Each new and eager soul rushing out towards the only end of Love passes on its way the landmarks left by others upon the pathway to Reality. If it be wise it observes them : and finds in them rather helps towards attainment than hindrances to that freedom which is of the essence of the mystic act. This act, it is true, is in the last resort a solitary affair, " the flight of the Alone to the Alone." There is nothing of " social Christianity " in that supreme adventure whereby " God and the soul are made one thing." At the same time, here as elsewhere, man cannot safely divorce his own personal history from that of the race. The best and truest experience does not come to the eccentric and individual pilgrim whose intuitions are his only law : but rather to him who submits personal intuition to the guidance afforded by the general history of the mystic type. Those who refuse this guidance do as a fact expose themselves to all the dangers which crowd about the individualist : from heresy at one end of the scale to madness at the other.

Vae Soli! Nowhere more clearly than in the history of mysticism do we observe the essential solidarity of mankind: the penalty paid by those who will not acknowledge it.

Now the education which tradition has ever prescribed for the mystic, consists in the gradual development of an extraordinary faculty of concentration, a power of spiritual attention. It is not enough that he should naturally be " aware of the Absolute," unless he be able to contemplate it : just as the mere possession of eyesight or hearing, however acute, needs to be supplemented by trained powers of perception and reception if we are really to appreciate—see or hear to any purpose—the masterpieces of Music or of Art. More, Nature herself reveals little of her secret to those who only look and listen with the outward ear and eye. The condition of all valid seeing and hearing of the beautiful and true upon every plane of consciousness lies not in the sharpening of the senses, but in a peculiar attitude of the whole personality : in a self-forgetting attentiveness, a profound concentration, a self-merging, a real communion between the seer and the seen : in a word in *Contemplation*.

Contemplation, then, is a power which we may—and often must—apply to the perception, not only of Divine Reality, but of anything. It is the condition under which all things give up to us the secret of their life. All artists are of necessity in some measure contemplative. " Innocence of eye " is little else than this : and only by its means can they see truly those things which they desire to represent. I invite those to whom these statements seem a compound of cheap psychology and cheaper metaphysics to clear their minds of prejudice and submit this matter to an experimental test. If they will be patient and honest—and unless they belong to that minority which is temperamentally incapable of the simplest contemplative act—they will emerge from the experiment possessed of a little new knowledge as to the nature of the relation between the human mind and the outer world.

All that is asked is that we shall look for a little time, in a special and undivided manner, at some simple, concrete, and external thing.

This object of our contemplation may be almost anything we please : a picture, a statue, a tree, a distant hillside, a growing plant, running water, little living things. We need not, with Kant, go to the starry heavens. " A little thing the quantity of an hazel nut " will do for us, as it did for Lady

Julian long ago.[1] Remember, it is a practical experiment on which we are set ; not an opportunity of pretty and pantheistic meditation.

Look, then, at this thing which you have chosen. Wilfully refuse the messages which countless other aspects of the world are sending, and so concentrate your whole attention on this one act of sight that all other objects are excluded from the conscious field. Do not think, but as it were pour out your personality towards it : let your soul be in your eyes. Almost at once, this new method of perception will reveal unsuspected qualities in the external world. First, you will perceive about you a strange and deepening quietness. Next, you will become aware of a heightened significance, an intensified existence in the thing at which you look. As you, with all your consciousness, lean out towards it, an answering current will meet yours. It seems as though the barrier between its life and your own, between subject and object, had melted away. You are merged with it, in an act of true communion : and you *know* the secret of its being deeply and unforgettably, yet in a way which you can never hope to express.

Seen thus, a thistle has celestial qualities : a speckled hen a touch of the sublime. Our greater comrades, the trees, the clouds, the rivers, initiate us into mighty secrets, flame out at us "like shining from shook foil." The "eye which looks upon Eternity" has been given its opportunity. We have been immersed for a moment in the "life of the All" : a deep and peaceful love unites us with the substance of all things : a "Mystic Marriage" has taken place between the mind and some aspect of the external world. *Cor ad cor loquitur*: Life has spoken to life, but not to the surface-intelligence. That surface-intelligence knows only that the message was true and beautiful : no more.

The price of this experience has been a stilling of that surface-mind, a calling in of all our scattered interests : an entire giving of ourselves to this one activity, without self-consciousness, without reflective thought. To reflect is always to distort : our minds are not good mirrors. The contemplative is contented to absorb and be absorbed : and by this humble access he attains to a plane of knowledge which no intellectual process can come near.

[1] "Revelations of Divine Love," cap. v.

Now this simple experiment exercises on a small scale, and in regard to visible Nature, the faculty by which the mystic apprehends Invisible Reality—enters into communion with the Absolute. It is one thing, of course, to see truthfully for an instant the flower in the crannied wall : another, to bear the full blaze of "eternal Truth, true Love and loved Eternity." Yet both according to their measure are functions of the inward eye.

This humble receptiveness, this still and steady gazing, in which emotion, will, and thought are lost and fused, is the secret of the great contemplative on fire with love of that which he has been allowed to see. But whilst the contemplation of Nature entails an outgoing towards somewhat indubitably external to us : the contemplation of spirit, as it seems to those who practise it, more often entails an ingoing or "introversion" of our faculties ; a "journey towards the centre." The Kingdom of God, they say, is within you : seek it, then, in the most secret habitations of the soul.

The mystic, then, has to learn so to concentrate all his faculties, his very self, upon the invisible and intangible, that all visible things are forgot : to bring it so sharply into focus that everything else is blurred. He must call in his scattered faculties by a deliberate exercise of the will, empty his mind of its swarm of images, its riot of thought. In mystical language he must "sink into his nothingness" : into that blank abiding place where busy, clever Reason cannot come. The whole of this process, this gathering up and turning "inwards" of the powers of the self, this gazing into the ground of the soul, is that which is called *Introversion*.

Introversion is an art which can be acquired, as gradually and as certainly, by the born mystic, as the art of piano-playing can be acquired by the born musician. In both cases it is the genius of the artist which makes his use of the instrument effective : but it is also his education in the use of the instrument which enables that genius to express itself in an adequate way. Such mystical education, of course, presumes a something that can be educated : the "New Birth," the awakening of the deeper self, must have taken place before it can begin. It is a psychological process, and obeys psychological laws : there is in it no element of the unexpected or the supernatural.

In its early stages the practice of introversion is voluntary, difficult, and deliberate ; as are the early stages of learning to read or write. But as reading or writing finally becomes automatic, so as the mystic's training in introversion proceeds, habits are formed : and those contemplative powers which he is educating establish themselves amongst his normal faculties. Sometimes they wholly dominate these faculties, escape the control of the will, and appear spontaneously ; seizing upon the conscious field. Such violent and involuntary invasions of the transcendental powers, when they utterly swamp the surface-consciousness and the subject is therefore cut off from his ordinary "external world," constitute the typical experience of *rapture* or *ecstasy*. It is under the expansive formulæ of such abrupt ecstatic perception, " not by gradual steps, but by sudden ecstatic flights soaring aloft to the glorious things on high," [1] that the mystical consciousness of Divine Transcendence is most clearly expressed. Those wide, exalted apprehensions of the Godhead which we owe to the mystics have been obtained, not by industrious meditation, but by "a transcending of all creatures, a perfect going forth from oneself : by standing in an ecstasy of mind." [2] Hence the experiences peculiar to these ecstatic states have a great value for the student of mystical science. It will be our duty to consider them in some detail in a later section of this book.

The normal and deliberate practice of introversion, on the contrary, is tightly bound up with the sense of Divine Immanence. Its emphasis is on the indwelling God Who may be found " by a journey towards the centre " : on the conviction indeed that "angels and archangels are with us, but He is more truly our own who is not only *with us* but *in* us." [3]

Contemplation—taking that term in its widest sense, as embracing the whole mystic art—establishes communion between the soul and the Absolute by way of these two complementary modes of apprehending that which is One : A. The usually uncontrollable, definitely outgoing, ecstatic experience, the attainment of Pure Being, or "flight to God." B. The

<hr/>

[1] St. Bernard, " De Consideratione," bk. v. cap. iii.
[2] " De Imitatione Christi," l. iii. cap. xxxi.
[3] St. Bernard, *op. cit.*, bk. v. cap. v. So Lady Julian, "We are all in Him enclosed and He is enclosed in us " (" Revelations of Divine Love," cap. lvii.).

more controllable ingoing experience, the breaking down of the barrier between the surface-self and those deeper levels of personality where God is met and known " in our nothingness," and a mysterious fusion of divine and human life takes place. The one, says the Christian mystic, is the " going forth to the Father"; the other is the " marriage with the Son." Both are operated by the Indwelling Spirit, the " spark of the soul." Yet it is probable, in spite of the spatial language which the mystics always use concerning them, that these two experiences, in their most sublime forms, are but opposite aspects of one whole : the complementary terms of a higher synthesis beyond our span. In that consummation of love which Ruysbroeck has called " the peace of the summits " they meet : then distinctions between inward and outward, near and far, cease to have any meaning, in " the dim silence where lovers lose themselves." " To mount to God," says a tract attributed to Albert the Great, " is to enter into one's self. For he who inwardly entereth and intimately penetrateth into himself, gets above and beyond himself and truly mounts up to God." [1]

Says Tauler of this ineffable meeting-place, which is to the intellect an emptiness, and to the heart a fulfilment of all desire, " All there is so still and mysterious and so desolate : for there is nothing there but God only, and nothing strange. . . . This Wilderness is the Quiet Desert of the Godhead, into which He leads all who are to receive this inspiration of God, now or in Eternity." [2] From this " quiet desert," this still plane of being, so near to her though she is far from it, the normal self is separated by all the " unquiet desert " of sensual existence. Yet it stretches through and in her, the stuff of Reality, the very Ground of her being, since it is, in Julian's words, " the Substance of all that is " : linking that being at once with the universe and with God. " God is near us, but we are far from Him, God is within, we are without, God is at home, we are in the far country," said Meister Eckhart, struggling to express the nature of this " intelligible where." [3] Clearly, if the self is ever to become aware of it, definite work must be undertaken, definite powers of perception must be trained : and the

[1] " De Adhaerando Deo," cap. vii.
[2] Third Instruction (" The Inner Way," p. 323).
[3] Eckhart, Pred. lxix.

consciousness which has been evolved to meet the exigencies of the World of Becoming must be initiated into that World of Being from which it came forth.

Plato long ago defined the necessity of such a perception, and the nature of that art of contemplation by which the soul can feed upon the Real, when he said in one of his most purely mystical passages, "When the soul returns into itself and reflects, it passes into . . . the region of that which is pure and ever-lasting, immortal and unchangeable : and, feeling itself kindred thereto, it dwells there under its own control, and has rest from its wanderings." [1] The "contemplation" of Plato and of the Platonic Schools generally, however, is a purely intellectual activity : with him the head and not the heart is the meeting-place between man and the Real. "Anciently," says Augustine Baker, "there was a certain kind of false contemplation, which we may call philosophical, practised by some learned heathens of old, and imitated by some in these days, which hath for its last and best end only the perfection of knowledge and a delightful complacency in it. . . . To this rank of philosophical contemplations may be referred those scholastic wits which spend much time in the study and subtle examination of the mysteries of faith, and have not for their end the increasing of divine love in their hearts." [2]

We cannot long read the works of the mystics without coming across descriptions—often first-hand descriptions of great psychological interest—of the processes through which the self must pass, the discipline which it must undertake, in the course of acquiring the art of contemplation. Most of these descriptions differ as to detail ; as to the divisions adopted, the emotions experienced, the number of "degrees" through which the subject passes, from the first painful attempt to gather up its faculties to the supreme point at which it feels itself to be "lost in God." In each there is that quality of uniqueness which is inherent in every expression of life : in each the temperamental bias and analytical powers of the writer have exerted a further modifying influence. All, however, describe a connected experience, the progressive concentration of the entire self under the spur of love upon the contemplation of transcendental reality. As the Mystic Way involves transcen-

---

[1] Phaedo, 79 c.   [2] "Holy Wisdom," Treatise iii. § iv. cap. i.

dence of character, the movement of the whole man to higher levels of vitality, his attainment of freedom; so the ascent of the ladder of contemplation involves such a transcendence or movement to high levels of liberty, of his perceptive powers.

The steps of the ladder, the substance of the progressive exercises undertaken by the developing self, its education in the art of contemplation, are called, in technical terms, the " degrees of orison " ; or sometimes, by an unfortunate confusion of the English language, the "degrees of prayer." "Prayer," as understood of the multitude, with all its implications of conventional piety, formality, detailed petition—a definite something asked for, and a definite duty done, by means of extemporary or traditional allocutions addressed to the anthropomorphic Deity of popular religion—is wholly incapable of suggesting the nature of those supersensual activities which the mystics mean to express in their use of this term.

"Orison" has nothing in common with petition. It is not articulate ; it has no forms. " It is," says the " Mirror of St. Edmund," " naught else but yearning of soul."[1] On the psychological side it is a steady discipline imposed upon the mystic's rich subliminal mind, a slow preparation of the channels in which that deeper consciousness is to flow : a reducing to some sort of order, a making effective for life, of those involuntary states of passivity, rapture, and intuition which are the characteristic ways in which an uncontrolled, uncultivated genius for the Absolute breaks out. To the subject himself, however, it seems rather a free act of love, a strange and splendid intercourse deliberately undertaken between the soul and the divine, or some aspect of the divine : a wordless " conversation in Heaven."[2] In some of its degrees it is a placid, trustful waiting upon messages from without. In others, it is an inarticulate communion, a wordless rapture, a silent gazing upon God. The mystics have exhausted all the resources of all

---

[1] Cap. xvii.

[2] "I discover all truths in the interior of my soul," says Antoinette Bourignan, " especially when I am recollected in my solitude in a forgetfulness of all Things. Then my spirit communicates with Another Spirit, and they entertain one another as two friends who converse about serious matters. And this conversation is so sweet that I have sometimes passed a whole day and a night in it without interruption or standing in need of meat or drink" (MacEwen, "Antoinette Bourignan, Quietist," p. 109).

tongues in their efforts to tell us of the rewards which await those who will undertake this most sublime and difficult of arts.

As we come to know our friends better by having intercourse with them, so by this deliberate intercourse the self enters more and more deeply into the Heart of Reality. Climbing like Dante step by step up the ladder of contemplation, it comes at last to the Empyrean, "ivi è perfetta, matura ed intera ciascuna disianza."[1] "Journeys end in lovers meeting." The true end of orison, like the true end of that mysticism which it cultivates, is the supreme meeting between Lover and Beloved, between God and the soul. Its method is the method of the mystic life, transcendence : a gradual approximation of the contemplative self to reality : the production within it of those conditions in which union can take place. This entails a concentration, a turning inwards, of all those faculties which the normal self has been accustomed to turn outwards, and fritter upon the manifold illusions of daily life. It means, during the hours of introversion, a retreat from and refusal of the Many, in order that the mind may be able to apprehend the One. " Behold," says Boehme, " if thou desirest to see God's Light in thy Soul, and be divinely illuminated and conducted, this is the short way that thou art to take ; not to let the Eye of thy Spirit enter into Matter or fill itself with any Thing whatever, either in Heaven or Earth, but to let it enter by a naked faith into the Light of the Majesty."[2]

"What this opening of the spiritual eye is," says Hilton, "the greatest scholar on earth cannot imagine by his wit, nor show fully by his tongue ; for it cannot be gotten by study, nor by man's industry alone, but principally by grace of the Holy Ghost and with human industry. I am afraid to speak anything of it, for methinketh that I cannot, it passeth my assay, and my lips are unclean. Nevertheless, because it seems to me that love asketh, yea, love biddeth that I should, therefore shall I say a little more of it, as I hope love teacheth. This opening of the spiritual eye is that lightsome darkness and rich nought that I spake of before, and it may be called purity of spirit and spiritual rest, inward stillness and peace of conscience, highness of thought and loneliness of soul, a lively feeling of grace and

---

[1] Par. xxii. 64.   [2] " Dialogues of the Supersensual Life," p. 66.

privity of heart, the watchful sleep of the spouse and tasting of heavenly savour, burning in love and shining in light, the entry of Contemplation and reforming in feeling . . . these be divers in show of words, yet are they all one in meaning and verity." [1]

"Human industry," says Hilton here, must be joined to "grace." If the spiritual eye is to be opened work must be done. So long as the eye which looks upon Time "fills itself with things" and usurps the conscious field, that spiritual eye which "looks upon Eternity" can hardly act at all : and this eye must not only be opened, it must be trained, so that it may endure to gaze steadfastly at the Uncreated Light. This training and purging of the transcendental sight is described under many images ; "diverse in show of words, one in meaning and verity." Its essence is a progressive cleansing of the mirror, a progressive self-emptying of all that is not real, the attainment of that unified state of consciousness which will permit a pure, imageless apprehension of the final Reality which "hath no image" to be received by the self. "Naked orison," "emptiness," "nothingness," "entire surrender," "peaceful love in life naughted," say the mystics again and again. Where apprehension of the divine comes by way of vision or audition, this is but a concession to human weakness ; a sign, they think, that the senses are not quite killed. It is a translation of the true tongue of angels into a dialect that they can understand. A steady abolition of sense imagery, a cutting off of all possible sources of illusion, all possible encouragements of selfhood and pride—the most fertile of all sources of deception—this is the condition of pure sight ; and the "degrees of orison," the "steep stairs of love" which they climb so painfully, are based upon this necessity.

Now the terms used by individual mystics, the divisions which they adopt in describing the self's progress in this art of orison, are bewildering in their variety. Here, more than elsewhere, has the mania for classification obsessed them. We find, too, when we come to compare them one with another, that the language which they employ is not always so exact as it seems : that they do not all use the traditional terms in the same sense. Sometimes by the word "contemplation" they intend to describe the whole process of intro-

[1] Hilton, "The Scale of Perfection," bk. iii. cap. x.

version : sometimes they reserve it for the "orison of union," sometimes identify it with ecstasy. It has been pointed out by Delacroix that even St. Teresa's classification of her own states is far from lucid, and varies in each of her principal works.[1] Thus in the "Life" she appears to treat Recollection and Quiet as synonymous, whilst in "The Way of Perfection" these conditions are sharply differentiated. In "The Interior Castle" she adopts an entirely different system ; the orison of quiet being there called "tasting of God."[2] Finally, Augustine Baker, in treating of the "Prayer of Interior Silence and Quiet," insists that by the term "Quiet" St. Teresa did not mean this at all, but a form of "supernatural contemplation."[3]

Thus we are gradually forced to the conclusion that the so-called "degrees of orison" so neatly tabulated by ascetic writers are largely artificial and symbolic: that the process which they profess to describe is really, like life itself, one and continuous—not a stairway but a slope—and the parts into which they break it up are diagrammatic. Nearly every mystic makes these breaks in a different place, though continuing to use the language of his predecessors. In his efforts towards self-analysis he divides and subdivides, combines and differentiates his individual moods. Hence the confusion of mind which falls upon those who try to harmonize different systems of contemplation : to identify St. Teresa's "Four Degrees"[4] with Hugh of St. Victor's other four,[5] and with Richard of St. Victor's "four steps of ardent love":[6] or to accommodate upon this diagram Hilton's simple and poetic "three steps of contemplation"[7]— Knowing ; Loving ; and Knowing and Loving—where the dreamer rather than the map-maker speaks. Such fine shades, says Augustine Baker in this connexion, are "nicely distinguished" by the author "rather out of a particular experience

[1] "Études sur le Mysticisme," p. 18.

[2] Vida, cap. xiv. ; "Camino de Perfeccion," cap. xxxi. ; "El Castillo Interior," Moradas Cuartas, cap. ii.

[3] "Holy Wisdom," Treatise iii. § ii. cap. vii.

[4] Meditation, Quiet, a nameless "intermediate" degree, and the Orison of Union (Vida, cap. xi.).

[5] Meditation, Soliloquy, Consideration, Rapture (Hugh of St. Victor, "De Contemplatione ").

[6] "De Quatuor Gradibus Violentae Charitatis." Vide supra, p. 165.

[7] "The Scale of Perfection," bk. i. caps. iv. to viii.

of the effects passing in his own soul, which perhaps are not the same in all " than for any more general reason. [1]

Some diagram, however, some set scheme, the writer on introversion must have, if he is to describe with lucidity the development of the contemplative consciousness : and so long as the methodological nature of this diagram is kept in mind, there can be little objection to the use of it. I propose then to examine under three divisions that continuous and orderly stream of experience, that process of incessant change, by which the mystical consciousness is turned from visible to invisible things. We will give to these three divisions names which will be familiar to all readers of ascetic literature : Recollection, Quiet, and Contemplation. Each of these three parts of the introversive experience may be discerned in embryo in that little experiment at which the reader has been invited to assist : the concentration of mind, the silence, the new perception which results. Each has a characteristic beginning which links it with its predecessor, and a characteristic end which shades off into the next state. Thus Recollection begins in Meditation and develops into the " Orison of Inward Silence," which again melts into the true "Quiet." "Quiet" as it becomes deeper passes into Infused Contemplation : and this grows through Contemplation proper to that Orison of Passive Union which is the highest of the non-ecstatic introversive states. Merely to state the fact thus is to remind ourselves how smoothly continuous is this life-process of the soul.

It is the object of orison, as it is the object of all education, to discipline and develop certain growing faculties. In this case, the faculties are those of the " transcendental self," the " new man "—all those powers which we associate with the " spiritual consciousness." The " Sons of God," however, like the sons of men, begin as babies ; and their first lessons must not be too hard. Therefore the educative process conforms to and takes advantage of every step of the natural process of growth : as we, in the education of our children, make the natural order in which their faculties develop the basis of our scheme of culti-vation. Recollection, Quiet, and Contemplation, then, answer to the order in which the mystic's powers unfold. Roughly speaking, we shall find that the form of spiritual attention which

[1] " Holy Wisdom," *loc. cit.*, § ii. cap. i.

is called "Meditative" or "Recollective" goes side by side with the Purification of the Self; that "Quiet" tends to be characteristic of Illumination: that Contemplation—at any rate in its higher forms—is most constantly experienced by those who have attained, or nearly attained, the Unitive Way. At the same time, just as the self in its "first mystic life" before it has passed through the dark night of the will, often seems to run through the whole gamut of spiritual states, and attain that oneness with the Absolute which it seeks—though as a fact it has not yet reached those higher levels of consciousness on which true and permanent union takes place—so too in its orison. At any point in its career it may experience for brief periods that imageless and overpowering sense of identity with the Absolute Life—that loving and exalted absorption in God—which is called "passive union" and anticipates the consciousness which is characteristic of the deified life. Over and over again in its "prayerful process" it recapitulates in little the whole great process of its life. It runs up for an instant to levels where it is not yet strong enough to dwell. Therefore we must not be too strict in our identification of the grades of education with the stages of growth.

This education, rightly understood, is one coherent process: it consists in a steady and voluntary surrender of the awakened consciousness, its feeling, thought, and will, to the play of those transcendental influences, that inflowing vitality, which it conceives of as divine. In the preparative process of Recollection, the unruly mind is brought into harmony. In "Quiet" the eager will is silenced, the "wheel of imagination" is stilled. In Contemplation, the heart at last comes to its own—*Cor ad cor loquitur*. In their simplest, crudest forms, these three acts are the deliberate concentration upon, the meek resting in, the joyous communing with, the ineffable Object of man's quest. They involve a progressive concentration of the mystic's powers, a gradual handing over of the reins from the surface intelligence to that inner and deeper mind whose growth constitutes the mystical life-process in man. In Recollection the surface-mind still holds, so to speak, the leading strings: but in "Quiet" it surrenders them wholly, allowing consciousness to sink into that "blissful silence in which God works and speaks." This act of surrender, this deliberate negation of thought, is an essential preliminary of the contemplative state. "Lovers put out the candles and draw the curtains when they wish to see the god and the goddess; and in the higher communion the night of thought is the light of perception."[1]

The education of the self in the different degrees of orison has been compared by St. Teresa, in a celebrated passage in her Life, to four ways of watering the garden of the soul so that it may bring forth its flowers and fruits.[2] The first and most primitive of these ways is meditation. This, she says, is like drawing water by hand from a deep well: the slowest and most laborious of all means of irrigation. Next to this is the orison of quiet, which is a little better and easier: for here soul seems to receive some help, *i.e.*, with the stilling of the senses the subliminal faculties are brought into play. The well has now been fitted with a windlass—that little Moorish water-wheel possessed by every Castilian farm. Hence we get more water for the energy we expend: more sense of reality in exchange for our abstraction from the unreal. Also "the water is higher, and accordingly the labour is much less than it was when the water had to be drawn out of the depths of the well. I mean that the water is nearer to it, for grace now reveals itself more distinctly to the soul." In the third stage we leave all voluntary activities of the mind: the gardener no longer depends on his own exertions, contact between subject and object is established, there is no more stress and strain. It is as if a little river now ran through our garden and watered it. We have but to direct the stream. In the fourth and highest stage God Himself waters our garden with rain from heaven "drop by drop." The attitude of the self is now that of perfect receptivity, "passive contemplation," loving trust. Individual activity is sunk in the "great life of the All."

Now the measure of the mystic's real progress is and must always be the measure of his love: for his apprehension is an apprehension of the heart. His education, his watering of the garden of the soul, is a cultivation of this one flower—this Rosa Mystica which has its root in God. The degrees of his orison, then, will be accompanied step by step by those other degrees of exalted feeling-states which Richard of St. Victor

[1] Coventry Patmore, "The Rod, the Root, and the Flower," "Aurea Dicta," xiii.
[2] Vida, cap. ii. §§ 10 and 11.

called the Degrees of Ardent Love. Without their presence, all the drill in the world will not bring him to the true contemplative state, though it may easily produce abnormal powers of perception of the kind familiar to students of the occult.

Our theory of mystic education, then, turns out to be very like our theory of mystic life. In both, there is a progressive surrender of selfhood under the steady advance of conquering love; a stilling of the " I, the Me, the Mine," which is linked by all the senses, and by all its own desires, to the busy world of visible things. This progressive surrender appears in the practice of orison as a progressive inward retreat from circumference to centre; to that ground of the soul, that substantial *somewhat* in man, deep buried for most of us beneath the great rubbish-heap of our surface-interests, where human life and divine life meet. To clear away the rubbish-heap so that he may get down to this treasure-house is from one point of view the initial task of the contemplative. This clearing away is the first part of "introversion": that journey inwards to his own centre where, stripped of all his cleverness and merit, reduced to his "nothingness," he can "meet God without intermediary." This ground of the soul, this strange inward sanctuary to which the normal man so seldom penetrates, is, says Eckhart, "immediately receptive of the Divine Being," and "no one can move it but God alone." [1] There the finite self encounters the Infinite; and, by a close and loving communion with and feeding on the attributes of the Divine Substance, is remade in the interests of the Absolute Life. This encounter, the consummation of mystical culture, is what we mean by contemplation in its highest form. Here we are on the verge of that great self-merging act which is of the essence of pure love: which Reality has sought of us, and we have unknowingly desired of It. Here contemplation and union are one. "Thus do we grow," says Ruysbroeck, "and, carried above ourselves, above reason, into the very heart of love, there do we feed according to the spirit; and taking flight for the Godhead by naked love, we go to the encounter of the Bridegroom, to the encounter of His Spirit, which is His love; and this immense love burns and consumes us in the spirit, and draws us into that union where bliss awaits us." [2]

[1] Pred. i.   [2] Ruysbroeck, "De Contemplatione" (Hello, p. 153).

RECOLLECTION

The beginning of the process of introversion, the first mechanical act in which the self turns round towards the inward path, will not merely be the yielding to an instinct, the indulgence of a natural taste for reverie; it will be a voluntary and purposeful undertaking. Like conversion, it entails a break with the obvious, which must, of necessity, involve and affect the whole normal consciousness. It will be evoked by the mystic's love, and directed by his reason; but can only be accomplished by the strenuous exercise of his will. These preparatory labours of the contemplative life—these first steps upon the ladder—are, says St. Teresa, very [hard, and require greater courage than all the rest.[1] All the scattered interests of the self have here to be collected; there must be a deliberate and unnatural act of attention, a deliberate expelling of all discordant images from the consciousness—a hard and ungrateful task. Since, at this point, the transcendental faculties are still young and weak, the senses not wholly mortified, it needs a stern determination, a " wilful choice," if we are to succeed in concentrating our attention upon the whispered messages from within, undistracted by the loud voices which besiege us from without.

" How," says the Disciple to the Master in one of Boehme's " Dialogues," " am I to seek in the Centre this Fountain of Light which may enlighten me throughout and bring my properties into perfect harmony? I am in Nature, as I said before, and which way shall I pass through Nature and the light thereof, so that I may come into the supernatural and supersensual ground whence this true Light, which is the Light of Minds, doth arise; and this without the destruction of my nature, or quenching the Light of it, which is my reason?

" *Master.* Cease but from thine own activity, steadfastly fixing thine Eye upon *one Point.* . . . For this end, gather in all thy thoughts, and by faith press into the Centre, laying hold upon the Word of God, which is infallible and which hath called thee. Be thou obedient to this call, and be silent before the Lord, sitting alone with Him in thy inmost and most hidden

[1] Vida, cap. xi. § 17.

cell, thy mind being centrally united in itself, and attending His Will in the patience of hope. So shall thy Light break forth as the morning, and after the redness thereof is passed, the Sun himself, which thou waitest for, shall arise unto thee, and under his most healing wings thou shalt greatly rejoice : ascending and descending in his bright and health-giving beams. Behold, this is the true Supersensual Ground of Life." [1]

In this short paragraph Boehme has caught and described the psychological state in which all introversion must begin : the primary simplification of consciousness—the steadfast fixing the soul's eye upon *one point ;* the turning inwards of the whole conative powers for a purpose rather believed in than known, " by faith pressing into the centre."

The unfortunate word *Recollection,* which the hasty reader is apt to connect with remembrance, is the traditional term by which mystical writers define just such a voluntary concentration, such a first collecting or gathering in of the attention of the self to its " most hidden cell." That self is as yet unacquainted with the strange, changeless, and indescribable plane of silence which so soon becomes familiar to those who attempt even the lowest activities of the contemplative life ; where the noises of the world are never heard, and the great adventures of the spirit take place. It stands here between two planes of being ; the Eye of Time is still awake. It knows that it wants to enter the inner world, that "interior palace where the King of Kings is guest" [2]: but it must find some device to help it over the threshold—rather, in the language of modern psychology, to shift that threshold and permit its subliminal intuition of the Absolute to emerge.

This device is as a rule the practice of meditation, in which the state of Recollection usually begins : that is to say, the deliberate consideration of and dwelling upon some one aspect of Reality—an aspect most usually chosen from amongst the religious beliefs of the self. Thus Hindu mystics will brood upon a sacred word, whilst Christian contemplatives set before their minds one of the names or attributes of God, a fragment of Scripture, an incident of the life of Christ ; and allow—indeed encourage—this consideration, and the ideas and feelings

---

[1] " Dialogues of the Supersensual Life," p. 56.
[2] St. Teresa, " Camino de Perfeccion," cap. xxx.

which flow from it, to occupy the whole mental field. This powerful suggestion, kept before the consciousness by an act of will, overpowers the stream of small suggestions which the outer world pours incessantly upon the mind. The self, concentrated upon this image or idea, dwelling on it more than thinking about it, as one may gaze upon a picture that one loves, falls gradually and insensibly into the condition of reverie; and, protected by this holy day-dream from the more distracting dream of life, sinks into itself, and becomes in the language of asceticism "recollected" or gathered together. Although it is deliberately ignoring the whole of its usual "external universe," its faculties are wide awake: all have had their part in the wilful production of this state of consciousness: and this it is which marks off meditation and recollection from the higher or "infused" degrees of orison.

Such meditation as this, says Richard of St. Victor, is the activity proper to a mystic who has attained the first degree of ardent love. By it, "God enters into the mind," and "the mind also enters into itself"; and thus receives in its inmost cell the "first visit of the Beloved." It is a kind of half-way house between the perception of Appearance and the perception of Reality. To one in whom this state is established consciousness seems like a blank field, save for the "one point" in its centre, the subject of the meditation. Towards this focus the introversive self seems to press inwards from every side; still faintly conscious of the buzz of the external world outside its ramparts, but refusing to respond to its appeals. Presently the subject of meditation begins to take on a new significance; to glow with life and light. The contemplative suddenly feels that he knows it, in the complete, vital, but indescribable way in which one knows a friend. More, that through it hints are coming to him of mightier, nameless things. It ceases to be a picture, and becomes a window through which, by straining all his faculties, the mystic peers out into the spiritual universe and apprehends to some extent—though how, he knows not—the veritable presence of God.

In these meditative and recollective states, the self still feels very clearly the edge of its own personality: its separateness from the Somewhat Other, the divine reality set over against the soul. It is aware of that reality: the subject of its meditation becomes a symbol through which it receives a distinct message from the transcendental world. But there is yet no conscious fusion with a greater Life; no resting in the divine atmosphere as in the "Quiet"; no involuntary and ecstatic lifting up of the soul to direct apprehension of truth, as in contemplation. Recollection is a perfectly definite psychic condition, which has perfectly logical psychic results. Originally induced by meditation, or the dreamy pondering upon certain aspects of the Real, it develops, by way of the strenuous control exercised by the will over the understanding, a power of cutting the connexion between the self and the external world, and retreating at will to the inner world of the spirit.

"True recollection," says St. Teresa, "has characteristics by which it can be easily recognized. It produces a certain effect which I do not know how to explain, but which is well understood by those who have experienced it. . . . It is true that recollection has several degrees, and that in the beginning these great effects are not felt, because it is not yet profound enough. But support the pains which you first feel in recollecting yourself, despise the rebellion of nature, overcome the resistance of the body, which loves a liberty which is its ruin, learn self-conquest, persevere thus for a time, and you will perceive very clearly the advantages which you gain from it. As soon as you apply yourself to orison, you will at once feel your senses gather themselves together : they seem like bees which return to the hive and there shut themselves up to work at the making of honey : and this will take place without effort or care on your part. God thus rewards the violence which your soul has been doing to itself; and gives to it such a domination over the senses that a sign is enough when it desires to recollect itself, for them to obey and so gather themselves together. At the first call of the will, they come back more and more quickly. At last after many and many exercises of this kind, God disposes them to a state of absolute repose and of perfect contemplation." [1]

Such a description as this makes it clear that "recollection" is a form of spiritual gymnastics; less valuable for itself than for the training which it gives, the powers which it develops. In it, says St. Teresa again, the soul enters with its God into

[1] "Camino de Perfeccion," cap. xxx.

that Paradise which is within itself, and shuts the door behind
it upon all the things of the world. "You should know, my
daughters," she continues, "that this is no supernatural act, but
depends upon our will, and that therefore we can do it with that
ordinary assistance of God which we need for all our acts and
even for our good thoughts. For here we are not concerned
with the silence of the faculties, but with a simple retreat of
these powers into the ground of the soul. There are various
ways of arriving at it, and these ways are described in different
books. There it is said that we must abstract the mind from
exterior things, in order that we may inwardly approach God :
that even in our work we ought to retire within ourselves,
though it be only for a moment : that this remembrance of a
God who companions us within, is a great help to us ; finally,
that we ought little by little to habituate ourselves to gentle and
silent converse with Him, so that He may make us feel His
presence in the soul." [1]

QUIET

More important for us, because more characteristically
mystical, is the next great stage of orison : that curious and
extremely definite mental state which mystics call the Interior
Silence, or "Orison of Quiet." This represents the results for
consciousness of a further degree of that inward retreat which
Recollection began.

Out of the deep, slow brooding and pondering on some
mystery, some incomprehensible link between himself and the
Real, the contemplative—perhaps by way of a series of moods
which his analytic powers may cause him "nicely to distinguish"
—glides, almost insensibly, on to a plane of perception for
which human speech has few equivalents. It is a plane which
is apparently characterized by an immense increase in the
receptivity of the self, and by an almost complete suspension
of the reflective powers. The strange silence which is the
outstanding quality of this state—almost the only note in regard
to it which the surface-intelligence can secure—is not describable.
Here, as Samuel Rutherford said of another of life's secrets,
"*Come and see* will tell you much : *come nearer* will say more."

[1] *Op. cit.*, cap. xxxi.

Here the self has passed beyond the stage at which its perceptions are capable of being dealt with by thought. It cannot
any longer " take notes ": can only surrender itself to the stream
of an inflowing life, and to the direction of a larger will. Busy,
teasing, utilitarian thought would only interfere with this process:
as it interferes with the vital processes of the body if it once
gets them under its control. That thought, then, already
disciplined by Recollection, gathered up, and forced to work in
the interests of the transcendental mind, is now to be entirely
inhibited.

As Recollection becomes deeper, the self slides into a
dreamy consciousness of the Infinite. The door tight shut on
the sensual world, it becomes aware that it is immersed in a
more real world which it cannot define. It rests quietly in this
awareness : quite silent, utterly at peace. In the place of the
struggles for complete concentration which mark the beginning
of Recollection, there is now an entire surrender of the will and
activity, of the very power of choice : and with this surrender to
something bigger, as with the surrender of conversion, comes an
immense relief of strain. This is " Quiet " in its most perfect
form : this sinking, as it were, of the little child of the Infinite
into its Father's arms.

The giving up of I-hood, the process of self-stripping, which
we have seen to be the very essence of the purification of the
self, finds its correspondence in this part of the contemplative
experience. Here, in this complete cessation of man's proud
effort to do somewhat of himself, Humility, who rules the Fourth
Degree of Love, begins to be known in her paradoxical beauty
and power. Consciousness here loses to find, and dies that it
may live. No longer, in Rolle's pungent phrase, is it a
" Raunsaker of the myghte of Godd and of His Majeste." [1]
Thus the act by which it passes into the Quiet is a sacrament
of the whole mystic quest : of the turning from doing to
being, the abolition of separateness in the interests of the
Absolute Life.

The state of " Quiet," we have said, entails an utter suspension
of the surface-consciousness : yet consciousness of the subject's
personality remains. It follows, generally, on a period of
deliberate and loving recollection, of a slow and steady with-

[1] Prose Treatises of Richard Rolle (E.E.T.S. 20), p. 42.

drawal of the attention from the channels of sense. To one who is entering into this state of orison, the external world seems to get further and further away : till at last nothing but the paramount fact of his own existence remains. So startling, very often, is the deprivation of all his accustomed mental furniture, of the noise and flashing of the transmitting instruments of sense, that the negative aspect of his state dominates consciousness ; and he can but describe it as a nothingness, an emptiness, a "naked" orison. He is there, as it were poised, resting, waiting, he does not know for what : only he is conscious that all, even in this utter emptiness, is well. Presently, however, he becomes aware that *Something* fills this emptiness ; something omnipresent, intangible, like sunny air. Ceasing to attend to the messages from without, he begins to notice that which has always been within. His whole being is thrown open to its influence : it permeates his consciousness.

There are, then, two aspects of the Orison of Quiet : the aspect of deprivation, of emptiness which begins it, and the aspect of acquisition, of something found, in which it is complete. In its description, all mystics will be found to lean to one side or the other, to the affirmative or negative element which it contains. The austere mysticism of Eckhart and his followers, their temperamental sympathy with the Neoplatonic language of Dionysius the Areopagite, caused them to describe it—and also very often the higher state of contemplation to which it leads—as above all things an emptiness, a sublime dark, an ecstatic deprivation. They will not profane its deep satisfactions by the inadequate terms proper to earthly peace and joy : and, true to their school, fall back on the paradoxically suggestive powers of negation. To St. Teresa, and mystics of her type, on the other hand, even a little and inadequate image of its rapture seems better than none. To them it is a sweet calm, a gentle silence, in which the lover apprehends the presence of the Beloved : a God-given state, over which the self has little control.

In Eckhart's writings enthusiastic descriptions of the Quiet, of inward silence and passivity, as the fruit of a deliberate recollection, abound. In his view, this psychical state of Quiet is pre-eminently that in which the soul of man begins to be united with its "ground," Pure Being. The emptying of the field of consciousness, its cleansing of all images—even of

those symbols of Reality which are the subjects of meditation—
is the necessary condition under which alone this encounter
can take place.

"The soul," he says, "with all its powers, has divided and
scattered itself in outward things, each according to its functions :
the power of sight in the eye, the power of hearing in the ear,
the power of taste in the tongue, and thus they are the less able
to work inwardly, for every power which is divided is imperfect.
So the soul, if she would work inwardly, must call home all her
powers and collect them from all divided things to one inward
work. . . . If a man will work an inward work, he must pour all
his powers into himself as into a corner of the soul, and must
hide himself from all images and forms, and then he can work.
Then he must come into a forgetting and a not-knowing. He
must be in a stillness and silence, where the Word may be
heard. One cannot draw near to this Word better than by
stillness and silence : then it is heard and understood in utter
ignorance. When one knows nothing it is opened and revealed.
Then we shall become aware of the Divine Ignorance, and our
ignorance will be ennobled and adorned with supernatural knowledge. And when we simply keep ourselves receptive, we are
more perfect than when at work."[1]

The psychic state of Quiet has a further value for the mystic,
as being the intellectual complement and expression of the
moral state of humility and receptivity : the very condition,
says Eckhart, of the New Birth. "It may be asked whether
this Birth is best accomplished in Man when he does his work
and *forms and thinks himself into God*, or when he keeps
himself in Silence, stillness and peace, so that God may speak
and work in him ; . . . the best and noblest way in which thou
mayst come into this work and life is by keeping silence and
letting God work and speak. When all the powers are withdrawn from their work and images, there is this word spoken."[2]

Eckhart's view of the primary importance of " Quiet " as
essentially *the* introverted state is shared by all those mediaeval
mystics who lay stress on the psychological rather than the
objective aspect of the spiritual life. They regard it as the
necessary preliminary of all contemplation ; and describe it as
a normal phase of the inner experience, possible of attainment

[1] Meister Eckhart, Pred. ii.   [2] *Ibid.*, Pred. i.

by all those who have sufficiently disciplined themselves in patience, recollection, and humility.

In a certain old English mystical work which still remains in MS.—one of that group of treatises of the fourteenth century of which " The Cloud of Unknowing " is the best known—there is a curious and detailed instruction on the disposition of mind proper to this orison of silence. It clearly owes much to the teaching of the Areopagite, something perhaps to Eckhart himself, and something surely—if we may judge by its vivid and exact instructions—to personal experience. " When thou comest by thyself," says the master to the disciple for whom this " pystle " was composed, " think not before what thou shalt do after: but forsake as well good thoughts as evil thoughts, and pray not with thy mouth, but lift thee right well. . . . And look that nothing live in thy working mind but a naked intent stretching unto God, not clothed in any special thought of God in thyself, how He is in Himself or in any of His works, but only that He is as He is. Let Him be so, I pray thee, and make Him on none otherwise speech nor search in Him by subtilty of wit: but *believe by thy ground.* This naked intent freely fastened and grounded by very belief, shall be nought else to thy thought and thy feeling but a naked thought and a blind feeling of thine own being. . . . That darkness be thy mirror and thy mind whole. Think no further of thyself than I bid thee do of thy God, so that thou be oned with Him in spirit as in thought, without departing and scattering, for he is thy being and in Him thou art that thou art: not only by cause and by being, but also He is in thee both thy cause and thy being. And therefore think on God as in this work as thou dost on thyself, and on thyself as thou dost on God, that He is as He is and thou art as thou art, and that thy thought be not scattered nor departed but privied in Him that is All." [1]

" Let Him be so, I pray thee ! " It is an admonition against spiritual worry, an entreaty to the individual, already at work twisting experience to meet his own conceptions, to let things be as they are, to receive and be content. Leave off doing, that you may be. Leave off analysis, that you may know. " That meek darkness be thy mirror "—humble receptivity is the watchword of this state. " In this," says Eckhart finely, " the

[1] " An Epistle of Private Counsel " (B.M. Harl. 674).

soul is of equal capacity with God. As God is boundless in giving, so the soul is boundless in receiving. And as God is almighty in His work, so the soul is an abyss of receptivity : and so she is formed anew with God and in God. . . . The disciples of St. Dionysius asked him why Timotheus surpassed them all in perfection. Then said Dionysius, ' Timotheus is receptive of God.' And thus thine ignorance is not a defect but thy highest perfection, and thine inactivity thy highest work. And so in this work thou must bring all thy works to nought and all thy powers into silence, if thou wilt in truth experience this birth within thyself." [1]

It is interesting to contrast these descriptions of the Quiet with St. Teresa's temperamental reaction on the same psychological state. Where the English mystic's teaching is full of an implied appeal to the will, the Spanish saint is all for the involuntary, or, as she would call it, the " supernatural " actions of the soul. " This true orison of quiet," she says, "has in it an element of the supernatural. We cannot, in spite of all our efforts, procure it for ourselves. It is a sort of peace in which the soul establishes herself, or rather in which God establishes the soul, as He did the righteous Simeon. All her powers are at rest. She understands, but otherwise than by the senses, that she is already near her God, and that if she draws a little nearer, she will become by union one with Him. She does not see this with the eyes of the body, nor with the eyes of the soul. . . . It is like the repose of a traveller who, within sight of the goal, stops to take breath, and then continues with new strength upon his way. One feels a great bodily comfort, a great satisfaction of soul : such is the happiness of the soul in seeing herself close to the spring, that even without drinking of the waters she finds herself refreshed. It seems to her that she wants nothing more : the faculties which are at rest would like always to remain still, for the least of their movements is able to trouble or prevent her love. Those who are in this orison wish their bodies to remain motionless, for it seems to them that at the least movement they will lose this sweet peace . . . they are in the palace close to their King, and they see that He begins to give them His kingdom. It seems to them that they are no longer in the world, and they wish neither to hear nor to see it, but only

[1] Eckhart, Pred. ii.

God. . . . There is this difference between the orison of
quiet and that in which the whole soul is united to God;
that in this last the soul has not to absorb the Divine Food,
God deposits it with her, she knows not how. The orison
of quiet, on the other hand, demands, it seems to me, a
slight effort, but it is accompanied by so much sweetness
that one hardly feels it." [1]

"A slight effort," says St. Teresa. "A naked intent
stretching," says the "Pystle of Private Counsel." In these
words lies the difference between the true and healthy mystic
state of "Quiet" and its morbid perversion in "Quietism":
the difference between the tense stillness of the athlete and
the limp passivity of the sluggard, who is really lazy, though
he looks resigned. True "Quiet" is a means, not an end:
is actively embraced, not passively endured. It is an incident
in the self's growth in contemplation; a bridge which leads
from its old and unco-ordinated life of activity to its new,
unified life of deep action—the real "mystic life" of man.
This state is desired by the mystic, not in order that consciousness may remain a blank, but in order that the "Word
which is Alive" may be written thereon. Too often, however,
this primary fact has been ignored, and the Interior Silence
has been put by wayward transcendentalists to other and
less admirable use.

"Quiet" is the danger-zone of introversion. Of all the
forms of mystical activity, perhaps this has been the most
abused, the least understood. Its theory, seized upon,
divorced from its context, and developed to excess, produced
the foolish and dangerous exaggerations of Quietism: and
these, in their turn, caused a wholesale condemnation of the
principle of passivity, and made many superficial persons
regard "naked orison" as an essentially heretical act. [2] The
accusation of Quietism has been hurled at many mystics
whose only fault was a looseness of language which laid
them open to misapprehension. Others, however, have
certainly contrived, by a perversion and isolation of the

---

[1] "Camino de Perfeccion," cap. xxxiii. The whole chapter, which is a marvel
of subtle analysis, should be read in this connexion.

[2] Note, for instance, the cautious language of "Holy Wisdom," Treatise iii. § iii.
cap. vii.

teachings of great contemplatives on this point, to justify the deliberate production of a half-hypnotic state of passivity. With this meaningless state of "absorption in nothing at all" they were content ; claiming that in it they were in touch with the divine life, and therefore exempt from the usual duties and limitations of human existence. "Quietism," usually, and rather unfairly, spoken of in connexion with Madame Guyon, already existed in a far more dangerous and perverted form in the Middle Ages: and was denounced with violence by Ruysbroeck, one of the greatest masters of true introversion whom the Christian world has known.

"It is important, in the spiritual life," he says, "that we should know, denounce, and crush all quietism. These quietists remain in a state of utter passivity, and in order that they may the more tranquilly enjoy their false repose they abstain from every interior and exterior act. Such a repose is treason to God, a crime of *lèse-majesté*. Quietism blinds a man, plunging him into that ignorance which is not superior, but inferior, to all knowledge: such a man remains seated within himself, useless and inert. This repose is simply laziness, and this tranquillity is forgetfulness of God, one's self and one's neighbour. It is the exact opposite of the divine peace, the opposite of the peace of the Abyss; of that marvellous peace which is full of activity, full of affection, full of desire, full of seeking, that burning and insatiable peace which we pursue more and more after we have found it. Between the peace of the heights and the quietism of the depths there is all the difference that exists between God and a mistaken creature. Horrible error! Men seek it themselves, they establish themselves comfortably within themselves, and no longer seek God even by their desires. Yet it is not He whom they possess in their deceitful repose." [1]

There can be no doubt that for selves of a certain psychical constitution, this " deceitful repose" is only too easy of attainment. They can by wilful self-suggestion deliberately produce this emptiness, this inward silence, and luxuriate in its peaceful effects. To do this from self-regarding motives, or to do it to excess—to let "peaceful enjoyment" swamp "active love"—is a mystical vice : and this perversion of the spiritual

---

[1] Hello, p. 17. Hello has here condensed Ruysbroeck's teaching on this point, which fills the last four chapters of bk. ii. of "L'Ornement des Noces Spirituelles."

faculties, like perversion of the natural faculties, brings degeneration in its train. It leads to the absurdities of "holy indifference," and ends in the complete stultification of the mental and moral life. The true mystic never tries deliberately to enter the orison of quiet: with St. Teresa, he regards it as a supernatural gift, beyond his control, though fed by his will and love. That is to say, where it exists in a healthy form, it exists as a natural state, resulting from the normal development of the inner life ; not as a self-induced one, a psychic trick.

The balance to be struck in this stage of introversion can only be expressed, it seems, in paradox. The true condition of quiet, according to the great mystics, is at once active and passive : it is pure surrender, but a surrender which is not limp self-abandonment, but rather the free and constantly renewed self-giving and self-emptying of a burning love. The departmental intellect is silenced, but the totality of character is flung open to the influence of the Real. Personality is not lost : only its hard edge is gone. A "rest most busy," says Hilton. Like the soaring of an eagle, says Augustine Baker, when "the flight is continued for a good space with a great swiftness, but withal with great stillness, quietness and ease, without any waving of the wings at all, or the least force used in any member, being in as much ease and stillness as if she were reposing in her nest." [1]

"According to the unanimous teaching of the most experienced and explicit of the specifically Theistic and Christian mystics," says Von Hügel, "the appearance, the soul's own impression, of a cessation of life and energy of the soul in periods of special union with God, or of great advance in spirituality, is an appearance only. Indeed this, at such times strong, impression of rest springs most certainly from an unusually large amount of actualized energy, an energy which is now penetrating, and finding expression by every pore and fibre of the soul. The whole moral and spiritual creature expands and rests, yes ; but this very rest is produced by Action, "unperceived because so fleet, so near, so all-fulfilling." [2]

The great teachers of Quietism, having arrived at and experienced the psychological state of "quiet" : having known the ineffable peace and certainty, the bliss which follows on its act

[1] "Holy Wisdom," Treatise iii. § iii. cap. vii.
[2] Von Hügel, "The Mystical Element of Religion," vol. ii. p. 132.

of complete surrender, its utter and speechless resting in the Absolute Life, believed themselves to have discovered in this half-way house the goal of the mystic quest. Therefore, whilst much of their teaching remains true, as a real description of a real and valid state experienced by almost all contemplatives in the course of their development, the inference which they drew from it, that in this mere blank abiding in the deeps the soul had reached the end of her course, was untrue and bad for life.

Thus Molinos gives in the Spiritual Guide many unexceptional maxims upon Interior Silence : " By not speaking nor desiring, and not thinking," he says justly enough of the contemplative spirit, " she arrives at the true and perfect mystical silence wherein God speaks with the soul, communicates Himself to it, and in the abyss of its own depth teaches it the most perfect and exalted wisdom. He calls and guides it to this inward solitude and mystical silence, when He says that He will speak to it alone in the most secret and hidden part of the heart." Here Molinos speaks the language of all mystics, yet the total result of his teaching was to suggest to the ordinary mind that there was a peculiar virtue in doing nothing at all, and that all deliberate spiritual activities were bad.[1]

A good deal of the pseudo-mysticism which is industriously preached at the present time is thus crudely quietistic. It speaks much of the necessity of "going into the silence," and even, with a strange temerity, gives preparatory lessons in subconscious meditation : a proceeding which might well provoke the laughter of the saints. The faithful, being gathered together, are taught by simple exercises in recollection the way to attain the " Quiet." By this mental trick the modern transcendentalist naturally attains to a state of vacant placidity, in which he rests : and " remaining in a distracted idleness and misspending the time in expectation of extraordinary visits," believes—with a faith which many of the orthodox might envy —that he is here " united with his Principle." But, though the psychological state which contemplatives call the orison of quiet is a very common condition of mystical attainment, it is not by itself mystical at all. It is a state of preparation : a way of opening the door. That which comes in when the door is opened will

---

[1] He goes so far as to say in one of his " condemned " propositions, " Oportet hominem suas potentias annihilare," and " velle operari active est Deum offendere."

be that which we truly and passionately desire. The will makes plain the way : the heart—the whole man—conditions the guest. The true contemplative, coming to this plane of utter stillness, does not desire " extraordinary favours and visitations," but the privilege of breathing for a little while the atmosphere of Love. He is about that which St. Bernard called " the business of all businesses " : goes, in perfect simplicity, to the encounter of Perfection, not to the development of himself.

So, even at this—seemingly the most " passive "—stage of his progress, his operations are found on analysis to have a dynamic and purposive character : his very repose is the result of stress. He is a pilgrim that still seeks his country. Urged by his innate tendency to transcendence, he is on his way to higher levels, more sublime fulfilments, greater self-giving acts. Though he may have forsaken all superficial activity, deep, urgent action still remains. " The possession of God," says Ruysbroeck, " demands and supposes perpetual activity. He who thinks otherwise deceives himself and others. All our life as it is in God is immersed in blessedness : all our life as it is in ourselves is immersed in activity. And these two lives form *one*, self-contradictory in its attributes ; rich and poor, hungry and fulfilled, active and quiet." [1] The essential difference between this true " active " Quiet and Quietism of all kinds has been admirably expressed by Baron von Hügel. " Quietism, the doctrine of the One Act ; passivity in a literal sense, as the absence or imperfection of the power or use of initiative on the soul's part, in any and every state ; these doctrines were finally condemned, and most rightly and necessarily condemned ; the Prayer of Quiet and the various states and degrees of an ever-increasing predominance of Action over Activity—an action which is all the more the soul's very own, because the more occasioned, directed, and informed by God's action and stimulation—these and the other chief lines of the ancient experience and practice remain as true, correct, and necessary as ever." [2]

The " ever - increasing predominance of Action over Activity "—the deep and vital movement of the whole self, too deeply absorbed for self-consciousness, set over

[1] " De Contemplatione," Hello, p. 147.
[2] " The Mystical Element of Religion," vol. ii. p. 143.

against its fussy surface-energies—here is the true ideal of orison. This must inform all the self's effort towards union with the absolute Life and Love which waits at the door. It is an ideal which includes Quiet as surely as it excludes Quietism.

As for that doctrine of the One Act here mentioned, which was preached by the more extreme quietists; it, like all else in this movement, was the perversion of a great mystical truth. It taught that the turning of the soul towards Reality, the merging of the will in God, which is the very heart of the mystic life, was *One Act*, never to be repeated. This done, the self had nothing more to do but to rest in the Divine Life, be its unresisting instrument. Pure passivity and indifference were its ideal. All activity was forbidden it, all choice was a negation of its surrender, all striving was unnecessary and wrong. It needed only to rest for ever more and "let God work and speak in the silence." This doctrine is so utterly at variance with all that we know of the laws of life and growth, that it hardly seems to stand in need of condemnation. Such a state of indifference—which the quietists strove in vain to identify with that state of Pure Love which "seeketh not its own" in spiritual things—cannot coexist with any of those "degrees of ardent charity" through which man's spirit must pass on its journey to the One: and this alone is enough to prove its non-mystical character.

It is only fair to Madame Guyon to say that she cannot justly be charged with preaching this exaggeration of passivity, whatever inferences a loose and fluid style may have allowed her enemies and more foolish followers to draw from her works. "Some persons," she says, "when they hear of the orison of quiet, falsely imagine that the soul remains stupid, dead, and inactive. But unquestionably it acteth therein, more nobly and more extensively than it had ever done before, for God Himself is the Mover and the soul now acteth by the agency of His Spirit. . . . Instead, then, of promoting idleness, we promote the highest activity, by inculcating a total dependence on the Spirit of God as our moving principle, for in Him we live and move and have our being. This meek dependence on the Spirit of God is indispensably necessary to reinitiate the soul in its primeval unity and simplicity, that it may thereby attain the

end of its creation. . . . Our activity should therefore consist in
endeavouring to acquire and maintain such a state as may be
most susceptible of divine impressions, most flexile to all the
operations of the Eternal Word. Whilst a tablet is unsteady,
the painter is unable to delineate a true copy : so every act of
our own selfish and proper spirit is productive of false and
erroneous lineaments, it interrupts the work and defeats the
design of this Adorable Artist. We must, then, remain
tranquil and move only when He moves us." [1]

In another metaphor, the contemplative's progress must
involve an advance from the active and laborious watering of
the soul's garden which he practised in Meditation, to that state
of transcendence in which the river of life flows through it
unchecked : wells up, as St. Teresa says in another place, from
a hidden spring, and does not enter by an aqueduct from
without. [2]

The true mystics, in whom the Orison of Quiet develops
to this state of receptivity, seldom use in describing it the
language of " holy indifference." Their love and enthusiasm
will not let them do that. It is true, of course, that they are
indifferent to all else save the supreme claims of love : but then,
it is of love that they speak. *Ego dormio et cor meum vigilat.*
"This," says St. Teresa, "is a sleep of the powers of the soul,
which are not wholly lost, nor yet understanding how they are at
work. . . . To me it seems to be nothing else than a death, as
it were, to all the things of this world, and a fruition of God. I
know of no other words whereby to describe it or explain
it ; neither does the soul then know what to do—for it knows
not whether to speak or be silent, whether it should laugh or
weep. It is a glorious folly, a heavenly madness, wherein true
wisdom is acquired ; and to the soul a kind of fruition most full
of delight. . . . The faculties of the soul now retain only the
power of occupying themselves wholly with God ; not one of
them ventures to stir, neither can we move one of them without
making great efforts to distract ourselves—and, indeed, I do not
think we can do it at all at this time." [3]

[1] " Moyen Court," cap. xxi. Madame Guyon's vague and shifting language, however, sometimes lays her open to other and more strictly "quietistic" interpretations.
[2] " El Castillo Interior," Moradas Cuartas, cap. iii.
[3] Vida, cap. xvi. §§ 1 and 4.

Here, then, we see the Orison of Silence melting into true contemplation: its stillness is ruffled by its joy. The Quiet reveals itself as an essentially transitional state, introducing the self into a new sphere of activity.

The second degree of ardent love, says Richard of St. Victor, *binds*, so that the soul which is possessed of it is unable to think of anything else: it is not only "insuperable," but also "inseparable." [1] He compares it to the soul's bridal; the definitive, irrevocable act, by which permanent union is initiated. The feeling-state which is the equivalent of the Quiet is just such a passive and joyous yielding-up of the virgin soul to its Bridegroom; a silent marriage-vow. It is ready for all that may happen to it, all that may be asked of it—to give itself and lose itself, to wait upon the pleasure of its Love. From this inward surrender the self emerges to the new life, the new knowledge which is mediated to it under the innumerable forms of Contemplation.

[1] "De Quatuor Gradibus Violentae Charitatis" (Migne, Patrologia Latina, vol. cxcvi. col. 1215 b).

CHAPTER VII

INTROVERSION. Part II: CONTEMPLATION

WE must now consider under the general name of Contemplation all those more advanced states of introversion in which the mystic attains somewhat: the results and rewards of the discipline of Recollection and Quiet. If this course of spiritual athletics has done its work, he has now brought to the surface, trained and made efficient for life, a form of consciousness—a medium of communication with reality—which remains undeveloped in ordinary men. Thanks to this faculty, he is now able to perform the characteristic mystic act: to obtain a temporary union with "that spiritual fount closed to all reactions from the world of sense, where, without witnesses of any kind, God and our Freedom meet." [1]

In the degrees of Recollection, the self trained itself in spiritual attention: and at the same time lifted itself to a new

[1] Récéjac, "Fondements de la Connaissance Mystique," p. 176.

level of perception where, by means of the symbol which formed the gathering-point of its powers, it received a new inflow of life. In the degrees of Quiet it passed on to a state characterized by a tense stillness, in which it rested in that Reality at which, as yet, it dared not look. Now, in Contemplation, it is to transcend alike the stages of symbol and of silence : and "energize enthusiastically" on those high levels which are dark to the intellect but radiant to the heart. We must expect this contemplative activity to show itself in many different ways and take many different names, since its type will be largely governed by individual temperament. It appears under the forms which ascetic writers call "ordinary" and "extraordinary," "infused" or "passive" Contemplation ; and as that "orison of union" which we have already discussed.[1] Sometimes, too, it shows itself under those abnormal psycho-physical conditions in which the intense concentration of the self upon its overpowering transcendental perceptions results in the narrowing of the field of consciousness to a point at which all knowledge of the external world is lost, all the messages of the senses are utterly ignored. The subject then appears to be in a state of trance, characterized by physical rigidity and more or less complete anæsthesia. These are the conditions of Rapture or Ecstasy : conditions of which the physical resemblances to certain symptoms of hysteria have so greatly reassured the enemies of mysticism.

Rapture and Ecstasy differ from Contemplation proper in being wholly involuntary states. Rapture, says St. Teresa, who frequently experienced it, is absolutely irresistible ; we cannot hinder it. Whereas the orison of union, which is one of the forms in which pure Contemplation appears at its highest point of development, is still controlled to a large extent by the will of the subject, and "may be hindered, although that resistance be painful and violent."[2] There is thus a sharp natural division—a division both physical and psychical—established between the contemplative and the ecstatic states : and we shall do well to avail ourselves of it in our examination of their character.

First, then, as to Contemplation proper : what is it ? It is a supreme manifestation of that indivisible "power of knowing"

[1] *Supra*, p. 294.   [2] St. Teresa, Vida, cap. xx. §§ 1 and 3.

which lies at the root of all our artistic and spiritual satisfactions. In it, man's "made Trinity" of thought, love, and will, becomes a Unity: and feeling and perception are fused, as they are in all our apprehensions of beauty, and best contacts with life. It is an act, not of the Reason, but of the whole personality working under the stimulus of mystic love. Hence, its results feed every aspect of that personality: minister to its instinct for the Good, the Beautiful, and the True. Psychologically it is an induced state, in which the field of consciousness is greatly contracted: the whole of the self, its conative powers, being sharply focused, concentrated upon one thing. We pour ourselves out or, as it sometimes seems to us, *in* towards this overpowering interest: seem to ourselves to reach it and be merged with it. Whatever the thing may be, in this act we *know* it, as we cannot know it by the mere ordinary devices of thought.

The turning of our attention from that crisp and definite world of multiplicity, that cinematograph-show, with which intelligence is accustomed and able to deal, has loosed new powers of perception which we never knew that we possessed. Instead of sharply perceiving the fragment, we feel the solemn presence of the whole. Deeper levels of personality are opened up, and go gladly to the encounter of the universe. That universe, or some Reality hid between it and ourselves, responds to "the true lovely will of our heart." Our ingoing concentration is balanced by a great outgoing sense of expansion, of new worlds made ours, as we receive the inflow of its life.

Delacroix has described with great subtlety the psychological character of pure contemplation.

"When contemplation appears," he says: "(*a*) It produces a general condition of indifference, liberty, and peace, an elevation above the world, a sense of beatitude. The Subject ceases to perceive himself in the multiplicity and division of his general consciousness. He is raised above himself. A deeper and a purer soul substitutes itself for the normal self. (*b*) In this state, in which consciousness of I-hood and consciousness of the world disappear, the mystic is conscious of being in immediate relation with God Himself; of participating in Divinity. Contemplation installs a method of being and of knowing. Moreover, these two things tend at bottom to become one. The mystic has more and more the impression of being that which he knows, and of knowing that which he is." [1] Temporally rising, in fact, to levels of freedom, he knows himself real, and therefore knows Reality.

Now, the object of the mystic's contemplation is always some aspect of the Infinite Life : of "God, the one Reality." Hence, the enhancement of vitality which artists or other unself-conscious observers may receive from their communion with scattered manifestations of Goodness, Truth, and Beauty, is in his case infinitely increased. His uniformly rapturous language is alone enough to prove this. In the contemplative act, his whole personality, directed by love and will, transcends the sense-world, casts off its fetters, and rises to freedom : becoming operative on those high levels where, says Tauler, "reason cannot come." There it apprehends the supra-sensible by immediate contact, and knows itself to be in the presence of the "Supplier of true Life." Such Contemplation—such attainment of the Absolute—is the *whole act* of which the visions of poets, the intuition of philosophers, give us hints.

It is a brief act. The very greatest of the contemplatives have been unable to sustain the brilliance of this awful vision for more than a very little while. "A flash," "an instant," "the space of an Ave Maria," they say.

"My mind," says St. Augustine, in his account of his first purely contemplative glimpse of the One Reality, "withdrew its thoughts from experience, extracting itself from the contradictory throng of sensuous images, that it might find out what that light was wherein it was bathed. . . . And thus, with the flash of one hurried glance, it attained to the vision of *That Which Is*. And then at last I saw Thy invisible things understood by means of the things that are made, but I could not sustain my gaze : my weakness was dashed back, and I was relegated to my ordinary experience, bearing with me only a loving memory, and as it were the fragrance of those desirable meats on the which as yet I was not able to feed." [2]

This fragrance, as St. Augustine calls it, remains for ever with those who have thus been initiated, if only for a moment, into the atmosphere of the Real : and this—the immortal and indescribable memory of their communion with That Which Is—gives to their work the perfume of the "Inviolate

[1] "Études sur le Mysticisme," p. 370.   [2] Aug. Conf., bk. vii. cap. xvii.

Rose," and is the secret of its magic power. But they can never tell us in exact and human language *what* it was that they attained in their ecstatic flights towards the thought of God : their momentary mergence in the Absolute Life.

" That Which Is," says Augustine ; " The One," "the Supplier of true Life," says Plotinus ; "the energetic Word," says St. Bernard ; " Eternal Light," says Dante ; " the Abyss," says Ruysbroeck ; "Pure Love," says St. Catherine of Genoa—poor symbols of Perfection at the best. But, through and by these oblique utterances, they give us the far more valuable assurance that the Object of their discovery is one with the object of our quest.

William James has well observed that "ineffability" and "noetic quality" are the constant characteristics of the contemplative experience.[1] Those who have seen are quite convinced : those who have not seen, can never be told. There is no certitude to equal the mystic's certitude : no impotence more complete than that which falls on those who try to communicate it. " Of these most excellent and divine workings in the soul, whereby God doth manifest Himself," says Angela of Foligno, " Man can in no wise speak or even stammer." [2] Over and over again, however, he has tried to speak : and the greater part of mystical literature is concerned with these attempts. Under a variety of images, by a deliberate exploitation of the musical and suggestive qualities of words—often, too, by the help of desperate paradoxes, those unfailing stimulants of man's intuitive power—he tries to tell others somewhat of that veritable country which "eye hath not seen." His success—partial though it be—can only be accounted for upon the supposition that somewhere within us lurks a faculty which has known this country from its birth ; which dwells in it, partakes of Pure Being, and can under certain conditions be stung to consciousness. Then "transcendental feeling," waking from its sleep, acknowledges that these explorers of the Infinite have really gazed upon the secret plan.

Now Contemplation is not, like meditation, one simple state, governed by one set of psychic conditions. It is a name for a large group of states, partly governed—like all other forms of

---

[1] " Varieties of Religious Experience," p. 380.

[2] B. Angelae de Fulginio, " Visionum et Instructionum Liber," cap. xxvii. (English translation, p. 189).

mystical activity—by the temperament of the subject, and accompanied by feeling-states which vary from the extreme of quietude or "peace in life naughted" to the rapturous and active love in which "thought into song is turned." Some kinds of Contemplation are inextricably entwined with the phenomena of "intellectual vision" and "inward voices." In others we find what seems to be a development of the "Quiet": a state which the subject describes as a blank absorption, a darkness, or "contemplation *in caligine*."[1] Sometimes the contemplative tells us that he passes through this darkness to the light:[2] sometimes it seems to him that he stays for ever in the "beneficent dark."[3] In some cases the soul says that even in the depths of her absorption, she "knows her own bliss": in others she only becomes aware of it when contemplation is over and the surface-intelligence reassumes the reins.

In this welter of personal experiences, it becomes necessary to adopt some basis of classification, some rule by which to distinguish true Contemplation from other introversive states. Such a basis is not easy to find. I think, however, that there are two marks of the real condition: (A) Totality, and (B) Self-Mergence: and these we may safely use in our attempt to determine its character.

(A) Whatever terms he may employ to describe it, and however faint or confused his perceptions may be, the mystic's experience in Contemplation is the experience of the All. It is the Absolute which he has attained: not, as in meditation or vision, some partial symbol or aspect thereof.

(B) This attainment is brought about, this knowledge gained, by way of participation, not by way of observation. The passive receptivity of the Quiet is here developed into an active, outgoing self-donation. A "give and take"—a divine osmosis —is set up between the finite and the infinite life. Not only does the Absolute pour in on the self, but that self rushes out willingly to lose itself in it. That dreadful consciousness of a narrow and limiting I-hood which dogs our search for freedom and full life, is done away. For a moment, at least, the independent spiritual life is achieved. The contemplative is merged

---

[1] Compare Baker, "Holy Wisdom," Treatise iii. § iv. cap. iv.

[2] See Hilton, "The Scale of Perfection," bk. ii. cap. vi.

[3] *Vide infra*, p. 414.

in it " like a bird in the air, like a fish in the sea " : loses to find and dies to live.

"We must," says Dionysius the Areopagite, "contemplate things divine by *our whole selves standing out of our whole selves ;* becoming wholly of God." [1] This is the " passive union " of Contemplation : a temporary condition in which the subject receives a double conviction of ineffable happiness and ultimate reality. He may try to translate this conviction into " something said " or " something seen " : but in the end he will be found to confess that he can tell nothing, save by implication. The essential fact is that he was *there :* as the essential fact for the returning exile is neither landscape nor language, but the homely spirit of place.

" To see and to have seen that Vision," says Plotinus in one of his finest passages, " is reason no longer. It is more than reason, before reason, and after reason, as also is the vision which is seen. And perhaps we should not here speak of *sight :* for that which is seen—if we must needs speak of seer and seen as two and not one—is not discerned by the seer, nor perceived by him as a second thing. . . . Therefore this vision is hard to tell of : for how can a man describe as other than himself that which, when he discerned it, seemed not other, but one with himself indeed ? " [2]

Ruysbroeck, who continued in the mediaeval world the best traditions of Neoplatonic Mysticism, also describes a condition of supreme insight, a vision of Truth, obviously the same as that at which Plotinus hints. " Contemplation," he says, " places us in a purity and a radiance which is far above our understanding . . . and none can attain to it by knowledge, by subtlety, or by any exercise : but he whom God chooses to unite to Himself, and to illuminate by Himself, he and no other can contemplate God. . . . But few men attain to this divine contemplation, because of our incapacity and of the hiddenness of that light wherein alone we can contemplate. And this is why none by his own knowledge, or by subtle examination, will ever really understand these things. For all words and all that one can learn or understand according to the mode of the creatures, are foreign to the truth that I have seen and far below it. But

---

[1] " De Divinis Nominibus," vii. 1.
[2] Ennead vi. 9, 10.

he who is united to God, and illumined by this truth—he can understand Truth by Truth.[1]

This final, satisfying knowledge of reality—this understanding of Truth by Truth—is, at bottom, that which all men desire. The saint's thirst for God, the philosopher's passion for the Absolute, is nothing else than this crying need of the spirit, variously expressed by the intellect and by the heart. The guesses of science, the diagrams of metaphysics, the intuitions of artists ; all are pressing towards this. Yet it is to be found of all in the kingdom of the contemplatives : that " little city set on an hill" which looks so small to those outside its gates.

Man's soul, says Hilton, " perceiveth full well that there is somewhat above itself that it knoweth not, nor hath not yet, but would have it, and burningly yearneth after it ; and that is nought else than the sight of *Jerusalem* outwardly, which is like to a city which the *Prophet Ezechiel* saw in his visions. He saith that he saw a city upon a hill towards the south, that to his sight when it was measured was no more in length and breadth than a reed, that is six cubits and a palm of length. But as soon as he was brought into the city, and looked about him, then he saw that it was wondrous great, for he saw many halls, and chambers both open and secret ; he saw gates and porches without and within, and many more buildings than I now speak of, and it was in length and breadth many hundred cubits, that it seemed a wonder to him that this city was so long and so large within, that seemed so little to his sight when he was without. This city betokeneth the perfect love of God set upon the hill of *Contemplation*, which to the sight of a soul that without the feeling of it travelleth in desire towards it seemeth somewhat, but it seemeth but a little thing, no more than a rood, that is six cubits and a palm in length. By six cubits are understood the perfection of man's work ; and by the palm, a little touch of *Contemplation*. He seeth well that there is such a thing that passeth the deservings of all the workings of man, like as a palm is surpassed by six cubits, but he seeth not within what it is ; yet if he can come within the city of *Contemplation*, then seeth he much more than at first." [2]

As in the case of vision, so here all that we who " with-

[1] Ruysbroeck, " L'Ornement des Noces Spirituelles," l. iii. cap. i.
[2] " The Scale of Perfection," bk. ii. cap. vi.

out the feeling travel in desire" can really know concerning Contemplation—its value for life, the knowledge it confers—must come from those who have " come within the city " : have, in the metaphor of Plotinus, " taken flight towards the Thought of God." What, in effect, can they tell us about the knowledge of reality which they attained in that brief communion with the Absolute?

They tell us chiefly, when we come to collate their evidence, two apparently contradictory things. They speak, almost in the same breath, of an exceeding joy, a Beatific Vision, an intense communion, and a " loving sight " : and of an exceeding emptiness, a barren desert, an unfathomable Abyss, a nescience, a Divine Dark.

Over and over again these two pairs of opposites occur in all first-hand descriptions of pure contemplation : Remoteness and Intimacy, Darkness and Light. Bearing in mind that these four groups of symbols all describe the same process seen " through a temperament," and represent the reaction of that temperament upon Absolute Reality, we may perhaps by their comparison obtain some faint idea of the indescribable Somewhat at which they hint.

Note first that the emotional accompaniments of his perceptions will always and necessarily be the stuff from which the mystic draws suggestive language by which to hint at his experience of supernal things. His descriptions will always lean to the impressionistic rather than to the scientific side. The " deep yet dazzling darkness," the " unfathomable abyss," the Cloud of Unknowing, the " embrace of the Beloved," all represent, not the Transcendent but his relation with the Transcendent : not an object observed but an overwhelming impression felt, by the totality of his being during his communion with a Reality which is One.

It is not fair, however, to regard Contemplation on this account as pre-eminently a " feeling state," and hence attribute to it, as many modern writers do, a merely subjective validity. It is, of course, accompanied, as all humanity's supreme and vital acts are accompanied, by feelings of an exalted kind : and since such emotions are the least abnormal part of it, they are the part which the subject finds easiest to describe. These elusive combinations of Fear, Amazement, Desire, and Joy are

more or less familiar to him. The accidents of sensual life have
developed them. His language contains words which are
capable of suggesting them to other men. But his total
experience transcends mere feeling, just as it transcends mere
intellect. It is a complete act of perception, inexpressible by
these departmental words : and its agent is the *whole man*, the
indivisible personality whose powers and nature are only
partially hinted at in such words as Love, Thought, or Will.

The plane of consciousness, however—the objective somewhat—of which this personality becomes aware in contemplation, is not familiar to it ; neither is it related to its systems of
thought. Man, accustomed to dwell amongst spatial images
adapted to the needs of daily life, has no language that will fit
it at all. So, a person hearing for the first time some masterpiece of classical music, would have no language in which to
describe it objectively ; but could only tell us how it made him
feel. This is one reason why feeling-states seem to preponderate
in all descriptions of the mystic act. Earthly emotions provide
a parallel which enables the subject to tell us by implication
something of that which he felt : but he cannot tell us—for
want of standards of comparison—what it was that induced him
thus to feel. His best efforts to fit words to this elusive somewhat generally result in the evaporation alike of its fragrance
and of its truth. As St. Augustine said of Time, he knows what
it is until he is asked to define it.

How symbolic and temperamental is all verbal description
of mystical activity, may be seen by the aspect which contemplation takes in the music-loving soul of Richard Rolle ; who
always found his closest parallels with Reality, not in the
concepts of intimate union, or of self-loss in the Divine Abyss,
but in the idea of the soul's participation in a supernal harmony
—that sweet minstrelsy of God in which " thought into song is
turned."

" To me," he says, " it seems that contemplation is joyful
song of God's love taken in mind, with sweetness of angels'
loving. This is jubilation, that is the end of perfect prayer and
high devotion in this life. This is that mirth in mind, had
ghostily by the lover everlastingly, with great voice out-
breaking. . . . Contemplative sweetness not without full great
labour is gotten, and with joy untold it is possessed. Forsooth,

it is not man's merit but God's gift; and yet from the beginning to this day never might man be ravished in contemplation of Love Everlasting, but if he before parfitely all the world's vanity had forsaken." [1]

We must, then, be prepared to accept, sift, and use many different descriptions of evoked emotion in the course of our enquiry into the nature of the contemplative's perceptions of the Absolute. We find on analysis that these evoked emotions separate themselves easily into two groups. Further, these two groups answer to the two directions in which the mystic consciousness of Reality is extended, and to the pairs of descriptions of the Godhead which we have found throughout to be characteristic of mystical literature : *i.e.*, the personal and spatial, immanental and transcendental, indwelling Life and Unconditioned Source : (*a*) the strange, dark, unfathomable Abyss of Pure Being always dwelt upon by mystics of the metaphysical type, and (*b*) the divine and loved Companion of the soul whose presence is so sharply felt by those selves which lean to the concept of Divine Personality.

A. The Contemplation of Transcendence.—The first group of feeling-states, allied to those which emphasize the theological idea of Divine Transcendence, is born of the mystic's sense of his own littleness, unworthiness, and incurable ignorance in comparison with the ineffable greatness of the Absolute Godhead which he has perceived, and in which he desires to lose himself : of the total and incommunicable difference *in kind* between the Divine and everything else. Awe and self-abasement and the paradoxical passion for self-loss in the All, here govern his emotional state. All affirmative statements seem to him blasphemous, so far are they from an ineffable truth which is "more than reason, before reason, and after reason." To this group of feelings, which usually go with an instinctive taste for Neoplatonism, an iconoclastic distrust of personal imagery, we owe all negative descriptions of supreme Reality. For this type of self God is the Unconditioned, for whom we have no words, and whom all our poor symbols insult. To see Him is to enter the Darkness, the "Cloud of Unknowing," and "know only that we know nought." Nothing else can satisfy this exaggerated spiritual

[1] Richard Rolle, "The Mending of Life," cap. xii.

humility, which easily degenerates into that subtle form of pride which refuses to acquiesce in its own limitations.

"There is none other God but He that none may know, which may not be known," says this contemplative soul. "No, soothly, no! Without fail, No, says she. He only is my God that none can one word of say, nor all they of Paradise one only point attain nor understand, for all the knowing that they have of Him."[1]

When they tried very hard to be geographically exact, to define and describe their apprehension of and contact with the Unconditioned One, who is the only Country of the Soul, contemplatives of this type became, like their great master the Areopagite, impersonal and remote. They seem to have been caught up to some measureless height, where the air is too rarefied for the lungs of common men. When we ask them the nature of the life on these summits, they are compelled as a rule to adopt the Dionysian concept of Divine Darkness, or the parallel idea of the fathomless Abyss, the Desert of the Godhead, the Eckhartian "still wilderness where no one is at home."

Oddly enough, it is in their language concerning this place or plane of reality, in which union with the Super-essential Godhead takes place—this "lightsome darkness and rich nought"—that they come nearer to distinct affirmation, and consequently offer more surprises to sentimental and popular piety, than in any other department of their work. Unquestionably this language, these amazing tidings of a "still desert," a "vast sea," an "unplumbed abyss" in which the "emptiness," the "nothing," the "Dark" on which the self entered in the Orison of Quiet is infinitely increased, yet positive satisfaction is at last attained, does correspond with a definite psychological experience. It is not merely the convention of a school. These descriptions, incoherent as they are, have a strange note of certainty, a stranger note of passion, an odd realism of their own: which mean, wherever we meet them, that experience not tradition is their source.

Driven of necessity to a negation of all that their surface-minds have ever known—with language, strained to the uttermost, failing them at every turn—these contemplatives are still able to communicate to us a definite somewhat, news as to

[1] "The Mirror of Simple Souls," cap. iii.

a given and actual Reality, an unchanging Absolute; and a beatific union with it, most veritably attained. They agree in their accounts of it, in a way which makes it obvious that all these reporters have sojourned in the same land, and experienced the same spiritual state. Moreover, our own inmost minds bear witness for them. We meet them half-way. We know instinctively and irrefutably that they tell true; and they rouse in us a passionate nostalgia, a bitter sense of exile and of loss.

One and all, these explorers of the Infinite fly to language expressive of great and boundless spaces. In their withdrawal from the busy, fretful sense-world they have sunk down to the "ground" of the soul and of the universe: Being, the Substance of all that Is. Multiplicity is resolved into Unity: a unity with which the perceiving self is merged. Thus the mystic, for the time of this "union with the Divine," does find himself, in Tauler's words, to be "simply in God."

"The great wastes to be found in this divine ground," says that great master, "have neither image nor form nor condition, for they are neither here nor there. They are like unto a fathomless Abyss, bottomless and floating in itself. Even as water ebbs and flows, up and down, now sinking into a hollow, so that it looks as if there were no water there, and then again in a little while rushing forth as if it would engulf everything, so does it come to pass in this Abyss. This, truly, is much more God's Dwelling-place than heaven or man. A man who verily desires to enter will surely find God here, and himself simply in God; for God never separates Himself from this ground. God will be present with him, and he will find and enjoy Eternity here. There is no past nor present here, and no created light can reach unto or shine into this divine Ground; for here only is the dwelling-place of God and His sanctuary.

"Now this Divine Abyss can be fathomed by no creatures; it can be filled by none, and it satisfies none; God only can fill it in His Infinity. For this abyss belongs only to the Divine Abyss, of which it is written: *Abyssus abyssum invocat.* He who is truly conscious of this ground, which shone into the powers of his soul, and lighted and inclined its lowest and highest powers to turn to their pure Source and true Origin, must diligently examine himself, and remain alone, listening to the voice which cries in the wilderness of this ground.   This ground is so desert and bare, that no thought has ever entered there.   None of all the thoughts of man which, with the help of reason, have been devoted to meditation on the Holy Trinity (and some men have occupied themselves much with these thoughts) have ever entered this ground.   For it is so close and yet so far off, and so far beyond all things, that it has neither time nor place.   It is a simple and unchanging condition. A man who really and truly enters, feels as though he had been here throughout eternity, and as though he were one therewith." [1]

Many other mystics have written to the same effect : have described with splendour the ineffable joys and terrors of the Abyss of Being "where man existed in God from all Eternity," the soul's adventures when, " stripped of its very life," it " sails the wild billows of the sea divine."   But their words merely amaze the outsider and give him little information.   The contemplative self who has attained this strange [country can only tell an astonished and incredulous world that here his greatest deprivation is also his greatest joy ; that here the extremes of possession and surrender are the same, that ignorance and knowledge, light and dark, are *One*.   Love has led him into that timeless, spaceless world of Being which is the peaceful ground, not only of the individual striving spirit, but also of the striving universe ; and he can but cry with Philip, "*It is enough.*"

" Here," says Maeterlinck, "we stand suddenly at the confines of human thought, and far beyond the Polar circle of the mind.   It is intensely cold here ; it is intensely dark ; and yet you will find nothing but flames and light.   But to those who come without having trained their souls to these new perceptions, this light and these flames are as dark and as cold as if they were painted.   Here we are concerned with the most exact of sciences : with the exploration of the harshest and most uninhabitable headlands of the divine ' Know thyself ' : and the midnight sun reigns over that rolling sea where the psychology of man mingles with the psychology of God." [2]

On one hand " flames and light "—the flame of living love

---

[1] Tauler, Sermon on St. John the Baptist (" The Inner Way," pp. 97–99).

[2] Maeterlinck, Introduction to Ruysbroeck's " L'Ornement des Noces Spirituelles," p. v.

which fills the universe—on the other the " quiet desert of Godhead," the Divine Dark. Under these two types, one affirmative, one negative, resumed in his most daring paradox, nearly the whole of man's contemplative experience of the Absolute can be and is expressed. We have considered his negative description of Utmost Transcendence : that confession of " divine ignorance " which is a higher form of knowledge. But this is balanced, in a few elect spirits, by a positive contemplation of truth, an ecstatic apprehension of the " secret plan."

Certain rare mystics seem able to describe to us a Beatific Vision experienced here and now : a knowledge by contact of the Flaming Heart of Reality which includes in one great whole the planes of Being and Becoming, the " fixed point of Deity," the Eternal Father, and His manifestation in the " energetic Word." We saw something of this power, which is characteristic of mystical genius of a high order, when we studied the characteristics of Illumination. Its finest literary expression is found in that passage of the " Paradiso " where Dante tells us how he pierced, for an instant, the secret of the Empyrean. Already he had enjoyed a symbolic vision of two-fold Reality, as the moving River of Light and the still white Rose.[1] Now these two aspects vanished, and he saw the One.

> ". . . la mia vista, venendo sincera,
> e più e più entrava per lo raggio
> dell' alta luce, che da sè è vera.
> Da quinci innanzi il mio veder fu maggio
> che il parlar nostro ch' a tal vista cede,
> e cede la memoria a tanto oltraggio.
> Qual è colui che somniando vede,
> chè dopo il sogno la passione impressa
> rimane, e l' altro alla mente non riede ;
> Cotal son io, chè quasi tutta cessa
> mia visione, ed ancor mi distilla
> nel cor lo dolce che nacque da essa.
>
> *   *   *   *
>
> Io credo, per l' acume ch' io soffersi
> del vivo raggio, ch' io sarei smarrito,
> se gli occhi miei da lui fossero aversi.
> E mi ricorda ch' io fui più ardito
> per questo a sostener tanto ch' io giunsi
> l' aspetto mio col Valor infinito.
>
> *   *   *   *

---

[1] Par. xxx. 61–128. Compare p. 343.

Così la mente mia, tutta sospesa,
  mirava fissa, immobile ed attenta,
  e sempre del mirar faceasi accesa.
A quella luce cotal si diventa,
  che volgersi da lei per altro aspetto
  è impossibil che mai si consenta.
Pero che il Ben, ch' è del volere obbietto,
  tutto s'accoglie in lei, e fuor di quella
  è difettevo ciò che li' è perfetto." [1]

Intermediate between the Dantesque apprehension of eternal Reality and the contemplative communion with Divine Personality, is the type of mystic whose perceptions of the supra-sensible are neither wholly personal nor wholly cosmic and transcendental in type. To him, God is pre-eminently the Perfect—Goodness, Truth, and Beauty, Light, Life, and Love—discovered in a moment of lucidity at the very door of the seeking self. Here the symbols under which He is perceived are still the abstractions of philosophy : but in the hands of the mystic these terms cease to be abstract, are stung to life. Such contemplatives preserve the imageless and ineffable character of the Absolute, but are moved by its contemplation to a joyous and personal love.

Thus " upon a certain time," says Angela of Foligno, " when I was at prayer and my spirit was exalted, God spake unto me many gracious words full of love. And when I looked I beheld God who spake with me. But if thou seekest to know that which I beheld, I can tell thee nothing, save that I beheld a fullness and a clearness, and felt them within me so abundantly that I can in no wise describe it, nor give any likeness thereof.

[1] Par. xxxiii. 52–63, 76–81, 97–105. " My vision, becoming purified, entered deeper and deeper into the ray of that Supernal Light which in itself is true. Thenceforth my vision was greater than our language, which fails such a sight ; and memory too fails before such excess. As he who sees in a dream, and after the dream is gone the impression or emotion remains, but the rest returns not to the mind, such am I : for nearly the whole of my vision fades, and yet there still wells within my heart the sweetness born therefrom. . . . I think that by the keenness of the living ray which I endured I had been lost, had I once turned my eyes aside. And I remember that for this I was the bolder so long to sustain my gaze, as to unite it with the Power Infinite. . . . Thus did my mind, wholly in suspense, gaze fixedly, immovable and intent, ever enkindled by its gazing. In the presence of that Light one becomes such, that never could one consent to turn from it to any other sight. Because the Good, which is the object of the will, is therein wholly gathered ; and outside of this, that is defective which therein is perfect."

For what I beheld was not corporal but as though it were in
heaven. Thus I beheld a beauty so great that I can say nought
concerning it, save that I saw the supreme Beauty which con-
taineth within itself all of Good." Again, " I beheld the ineffable fullness of God : but I can relate nothing of it, save that
I have seen the plenitude of Divine Wisdom wherein is all
Goodness." [1]

  B. *The Contemplation of Immanence.*—The second group of
contemplatives is governed by that " Love which casteth out
fear" : by a predominating sense of the nearness, intimacy,
and sweetness, rather than the strangeness and unattainable
transcendence of that same Infinite Life at whose being
the first group could only hint by amazing images which
seem to be borrowed from the poetry of metaphysics.
They are, says Hilton, in a lovely image, "Feelingly fed with
the savour of His invisible blessed Face." [2] All the feelings
which flow from joy, confidence, and affection, rather than those
which are grouped about rapture and awe—though awe is
always present in some measure, as it is always present in all
perfect love—here contribute towards a description of the Truth.

  These contemplatives tell us of their attainment of That
which Is, as the closest and most joyous of all communions ; a
coming of the Bridegroom ; a rapturous immersion in the
Uncreated Light. " Nothing more profitable, nothing merrier
than grace of contemplation ! " cries Rolle, "that lifts us from
this low and offers to God. What is grace of contemplation but
beginning of joy? what is parfiteness of joy but grace confirmed ? " [3]

  In such " bright contemplation " as this, says the " Mirror of
Simple Souls," " the soul is full gladsome and jolly." Utter peace
and wild delight : every pleasure-state known to man's normal
consciousness, is inadequate to the description of her joy.
She has participated for an instant in the Divine Life : knows
all, and knows nought. She has learnt the world's secret, not
by knowing, but by being : the only way of really knowing
anything.

[1] B. Angelae da Fulginio, "Visionum et Instructionum Liber," caps. xxi. and
xxiii. (English translation, pp. 169, 174).
[2] ".The Scale of Perfection," bk. iii. cap. xi.
[3] " The Mending of Life," cap. xii.

Where the dominant emotion is that of intimate affection : and where the training or disposition of the mystic inclines him to emphasize the personal and Incarnational rather than the abstract and Trinitarian side of Christianity, the contemplative of this type will always tend to describe his secret to us as above all things an experience of adorable Friendship.   Reality is for him a Person, not a State.   In the " orison of union " it seems to him that an absolute communion, a merging of his self with this other and strictly personal Self takes place.   " God," he says, then "meets the soul in her Ground ": *i.e.*, in that world of Pure Being to which, by divine right, she belongs. Clearly, the " degree of contemplation," the psychological state, is here the same as that in which the mystic of the impersonal type attained the "Abyss."   But from the point of view of the subject this joyful and personal encounter of Lover and Beloved will be a very different experience from the soul's immersion in that " desert of Deity," as described by Eckhart and his school.   " In this oning," says Hilton, " consisteth the marriage which passeth betwixt God and the soul, that shall never be dissolved or broken." [1]

St. Teresa is the classic example of this intimate and affective type of contemplation : but St. Gertrude, Suso, Julian, Mechthild of Magdeburg, and countless others, provide instances of its operation.   We owe to it all the most beautiful and touching expressions of mystic love.

Julian's " I saw Him and sought Him : and I had Him, I wanted Him " expresses in epigram its combination of rapturous attainment and insatiable desire : its apprehension of a Presence at once friendly and divine.   So too does her description of the Tenth Revelation of Love when " with this sweet enjoying He showed unto mine understanding in part *the blessed Godhead,* stirring then the poor soul to understand, as it may be said, that is, to think on the endless Love that was without beginning, and is, and shall be ever.   And with this our good Lord said full blissfully, *Lo, how that I loved thee,* as if He had said, *My darling, behold and see thy Lord, thy God that is thy Maker, and thine endless joy." [2]

" The eyes of my soul were opened," says Angela of

---

[1] " The Scale of Perfection," bk. i. pt. i. cap. viii.
[2] " Revelations of Divine Love," cap. xxiv.

Foligno, " and I beheld love advancing gently towards me, and I beheld the beginning but not the end. Unto me there seemed only a continuation and eternity thereof, so that I can describe neither likeness nor colour, but immediately that this love reached me, I did behold all these things more clearly with the eyes of the soul then I could do with the eyes of the body. This love came towards me after the manner of a sickle. Not that there was any actual and measurable likeness, but when first it appeared unto me it did not give itself unto me in such abundance as I expected, but part of it was withdrawn. Therefore do I say after the manner of a sickle. Then was I filled with love and inestimable satiety." [1]

It is to Mechthild of Magdeburg, whose contemplation was emphatically of the intimate type, that we owe the most perfect definition of this communion of the mystic with his Friend. "Orison," she says, "draws the great God down into the small heart: it drives the hungry soul out to the full God. It brings together the two lovers, God and the soul, into a joyful room where they speak much of love." [2]

We have already seen that the doctrine of the Trinity makes it possible for Christian mystics, and, still more, for Christian mysticism as a whole, to reconcile this way of apprehending reality with the " negative " and impersonal perception of the ineffable One, the Absolute which " hath no image." Though they seem in their extreme forms to be so sharply opposed as to justify Eckhart's celebrated distinction between the unknowable totality of the Godhead and the knowable personality of God, the " image " and the " circle " are yet aspects of one thing. Instinctive monists as they are, all the mystics feel—and the German school in particular have expressed—Dante's conviction that these two aspects of reality, these two planes of being, however widely they seem to differ, are *One*.[3] Both are ways of describing that Absolute Truth, " present yet absent, near, yet far," that Triune Fact, *di tre colori e d' una continenza*, which is God. Both are necessary if we are to form any idea of that com-

---

[1] B. Angelae de Fulginio, *op. cit.*, cap. xxv. (English translation, p. 178).
[2] " Das Fliessende Licht der Gottheit," pt. v. cap. 13.
[3] Par. xxxiii. 137.

plete Reality: as, when two men go together to some
undiscovered country, one will bring home news of its great
spaces, its beauty of landscape, another of its geological
formation, or the flora and fauna that express its life; and
both must be taken into account before any just estimate
of the real country can be made.

Since it is of the essence of the Christian religion to
combine personal and metaphysical truth, a transcendent
and an immanent God,[1] it is not surprising that we should
find in Christianity a philosophic and theological basis for
this paradox of the contemplative experience.   Most often,
though not always, the Christian mystic identifies the personal
and intimate Lover of the soul, of whose elusive presence
he is so sharply aware, with the person of Christ; the unknowable and transcendent Godhead with that *eterna luce*,
the Undifferentiated One in Whom the Trinity of Persons
is resumed.

Temperamentally, most practical contemplatives lean to
either one or other of these apprehensions of Reality: to a
personal and immanental meeting in the "ground of the
soul," or to the austere joys of the "naughted soul" abased
before an impersonal Transcendence which no language but
that of negation can define.   In some, however, both types
of perception seem to exist together: and they speak alter-
natively of light and darkness, of the rapturous encounter
with Love and of supreme self-loss in the naked Abyss;
the desert of the essence of God.   Ruysbroeck is the perfect
example of this type of contemplative; and his works contain numerous and valuable passages descriptive of that
synthetic experience which resumes the personal and transcendental aspects of the mystic fact.

"When we have become *Voyant*," he says—that is to say,
when we have attained to spiritual lucidity—"we are able to
contemplate in joy the eternal coming of the Bridegroom; and
this is the second point on which I would speak.   What, then,
is this eternal coming of our Bridegroom?   It is a perpetual
new birth and a perpetual new illumination: for the ground
whence the Light shines and which is Itself the Light, is living
and fruitful: and hence the manifestation of the Eternal Light

[1] Compare *supra*, Pt. I. Cap V.

is renewed without interruption in the most secret part of our souls. Behold! all human works and active virtues are here transcended; for God discloses Himself only at the apex of the soul. Here there is nought else but an eternal contemplation of, and dwelling upon the Light, by the Light and in the Light. And the coming of the Bridegroom is so swift, that He comes perpetually, and He dwells within us with His abysmal riches, and He returns to us as it were anew in His Person, with such new radiance, that He seems never to have come to us before. For His coming consists, outside all Time, in an *Eternal Now*, always welcomed with new desires and with new Joys. Behold! the delights and the joys which this Bridegroom brings in His coming are fathomless and limitless, for they are Himself: and this is why the eyes of the soul, by which the lover contemplates the Bridegroom, are opened so widely that they can never close again. . . . Now this active meeting, and this loving embrace, are in their essence fruitive and unconditioned; for the infinite Undifferentiation of the Godhead is so dark and so naked of all image, that it conceals within itself all the divine qualities and works, all the properties of the Persons, in the all-enfolding richness of the Essential Unity, and forms a divine fruition in the Abyss of the Ineffable One. And here there is an over-passing fruition of, and an outflowing immersion in, the nudity of Pure Being; where all the Names of God, and all manifestations, and all divine knowledge, which are reflected in the mirror of divine truth, are absorbed into the Ineffable Simplicity, the Absence of image and of knowledge. For in this limitless Abyss of Simplicity, all things are embraced in the bliss of fruition; but the Abyss itself remains uncomprehended, except by the Essential Unity. The Persons and all that which lives in God, must give place to this. For there is nought else here but an eternal rest, enwrapped as it were in the fruition of the immersion of love: and this is the Being, without image, that all interior souls have chosen above all other thing. This is the dim silence where all lovers lose themselves." [1]

Here Ruysbroeck, beginning with a symbol of the Divine Personality as Bridegroom of the Soul, which would have been congenial to the mind of St. Catherine of Siena, ends upon the summits of Christian metaphysics; with a description of the

[1] Ruysbroeck, " L'Ornement des noces Spirituelles," bk. iii. caps. iii. and vi.

loving immersion of the self in that Unconditioned One who transcends the Persons of theology and beggars human speech. We seem to see him desperately clutching at words and similes which may, he hopes, give some hint of the soul's fruition of Reality : its immeasurable difference in kind from the dreams and diagrams of anthropomorphic religion. His strange statements in respect of this Divine Abyss are on a par with those which I have already quoted from the works of those other contemplatives, who, refusing to be led away by the emotional aspect of their experience, have striven to tell us—as they thought—not merely what they felt but what they beheld. Ruysbroeck's great mystical genius, however, the depth and wholeness of his intuition of Reality, does not allow him to be satisfied with a merely spatial or metaphysical description of the Godhead. The " active meeting " and the " loving embrace " are, he sees, an integral part of the true contemplative act. In " the dim silence where lovers lose themselves," a Person meets a person : and *this* it is, not the philosophic Absolute, which " all interior souls have chosen above all other thing."

We must now look more closely at the method by which the contemplative attains to his unique communion with the Absolute Life : the kind of activity which seems to him to characterize his mergence with Reality. As we might expect, that activity, like its result, is of two kinds : personal and affirmative, impersonal and negative. It is obvious that where Divine Perfection is conceived as the soul's companion, the Bridegroom, the Beloved, the method of approach will be very different from that which ends in the self's immersion in the paradoxical splendour of the Abyss, the " still wilderness where no one is at home." It is all the difference between the preparations for a wedding and for an expedition to the Arctic Seas. Hence we find, at one end of the scale, that extreme form of personal and intimate communion—the going forth of lover to beloved—which the mystics call " the orison of union ": and at the other end, the " dark contemplation," by which alone selves of the transcendent and impersonal type claim that they draw near to the Unconditioned One.

Of the dim and ineffable contemplation of Unnameable Transcendence, the imageless absorption in the Absolute, Dionysius the Areopagite of course provides the classic example. It was he who gave to it the name of Divine Darkness : and all later mystics of this type borrow their language from him. His directions upon the subject are singularly explicit : his descriptions, like those of St. Augustine, glow with an exultant sense of a Reality attained, and which others may attain if they will but follow where he leads.

" As for thee, oh well beloved Timothy," he says, "exercise thyself ceaselessly in mystical contemplation. Leave on one side the senses and the operations of the understanding, all that which is material and intellectual, all things which *are*, and all things which *are not* ; and, with a supernatural flight, go and unite thyself as closely as possible with That which is above all essence and all idea. For it is only by means of this sincere, spontaneous, and entire surrender of thyself and all things, that thou shalt be able to precipitate thyself, free and unfettered, into the mysterious radiance of the Divine Dark." [1] Again, " The Divine Dark is nought else but that inaccessible light wherein the Lord is said to dwell. Although it is invisible because of its dazzling splendours and unsearchable because of the abundance of its supernatural brightness, nevertheless, whosoever deserves to see and know God rests therein ; and, by the very fact that he neither sees nor knows, is truly *in* that which surpasses all truth and all knowledge." [2]

It has become a commonplace with writers on mysticism to say, that all subsequent contemplatives took from Dionysius this idea of " Divine Darkness," and entrance therein as the soul's highest privilege : took it, so to speak, ready-made and on faith, and incorporated it in their tradition. But to argue thus is to forget that mystics are above all things practical people. They do not write for the purpose of handing on a philosophical scheme, but in order to describe something which they have themselves experienced ; something which they feel to be of

[1] Dionysius the Areopagite, "De Mystica Theologia," i. 1.
[2] *Ibid.*, Letter to Dorothy the Deacon. This passage seems to be the source of Vaughan's celebrated verse in " The Night "—

> " There is in God, some say,
> A deep but dazzling darkness, as men here
> Say it is late and dusky because they
>   See not all clear.
> O for that Night ! where I in Him
> Might live invisible and dim."

transcendent importance for humanity.   If, therefore, they persist—and they do persist—in using this simile of "darkness" in describing their adventures in contemplation, it can only be because it fits the facts.   No Hegelian needs to be told that we shall need the addition of its opposite before we can hope to approach the truth : and it is exactly the opposite of this "dim ignorance" which is offered us by mystics of the "joyous" or "intimate" type, who find their supreme satisfaction in the positive experience of "union," the "mystical marriage of the soul."

What, then, do those who use this image of the "dark" really mean by it?   They mean this: that God in His absolute Reality is unknowable—is dark—to man's intellect : which is, as Bergson has reminded us, adapted to very different purposes than those of divine intuition.   When, under the spur of mystic love, the whole personality of man comes into contact with that Reality, it enters a plane of experience to which none of the categories of the intellect apply.   Reason finds itself, in a very actual sense, "in the dark"—immersed in the Cloud of Unknowing.   This dimness and lostness of the mind, then, is a necessary part of the mystic's ascent to the Absolute.   That Absolute will not be "known of the heart" until we acknowledge that It is "unknown of the intellect"; and obey the Dionysian injunction to "leave the operations of the understanding on one side."   The movement of the contemplative must be a movement of the whole man : he is to "precipitate himself, free and unfettered," into the bosom of Reality.   Only when he has thus transcended sight and knowledge, can he be sure that he has also transcended the world with which they are competent to deal, and is *in* that which surpasses all essence and all idea.

God is Light : but, as Dionysius says, a Light inaccessible to us—at least, to most of us.   We know Him best, when we confess that our minds know Him not at all ; when, in Boehme's words, we "stop the wheel of imagination."   This acknowledgment of our intellectual ignorance, this humble surrender—the mental equivalent of the moral surrender which precedes the Unitive Life—is the entrance into the "Cloud of Unknowing" : the first step towards mystical knowledge of the Absolute. "For Truth and Humility are full true sisters," says Hilton, "fastened together in love and charity, and there is no distance of counsel betwixt them two." [1]

" Thou askest me and sayest," says the author of the " Cloud of Unknowing," " How shall I think upon Himself and what is He? To this I cannot make thee other answer but thus: I wot not.

" For thou hast brought me, with thy question, into that same darkness and cloud of unknowing that I would thou wert in thyself. For of all other creatures and their works and of God Himself a man may have fulhead of knowledge, and well of them think; but of God Himself can no man think, and therefore I will leave all that I can think upon, and choose to my love that thing that I cannot think. And why? Because He may well be loved, but not thought on. By love he may be gotten and holden, but by thought never. . . . Go up towards that thick Cloud of Unknowing with a sharp dart of longing love, and go not thence for anything that befall." [2]

So long, therefore, as the object of the mystic's contemplation is amenable to thought, is something which he can " know," he may be quite sure that it is not the Absolute; but only a partial image or symbol of the Absolute.

To find that final Reality, he must enter into the " Cloud of Unknowing "—must pass beyond the plane on which the intellect can work.

"When I say darkness," says this same great mystic, " I mean thereby a lack of knowing. And therefore it is not called a cloud of the air, but a Cloud of Unknowing, that is between thee and thy God." [3]

The business of the contemplative, then, is to enter this cloud: the " good dark," as Hilton calls it. The deliberate inhibition of thought which takes place in the " orison of quiet " is one of the ways in which this entrance is effected : intellectual surrender, or " self-naughting," is another. He who, by dint of detachment and introversion, enters the " nothingness " or " ground of the soul," enters also into the " Dark ": a statement which seems simple enough until we try to realize what it means.

---

[1] " The Scale of Perfection," bk. iii. cap. xiii.
[2] " The Cloud of Unknowing," cap. vi. (B.M. Harl. 674.)
[3] *Ibid.*, cap. iv.

" O where," says the bewildered disciple in one of Boehme's dialogues, " is this naked Ground of the Soul void of all Self? And how shall I come at the hidden centre, where God dwelleth and not man? Tell me plainly, loving Sir, where it is ; and how it is to be found of me, and entered into?

" *Master*. There where the soul hath slain its own Will and willeth no more any Thing as from itself. . . .

" *Disciple*. But how shall I comprehend it ?

" *Master*. If thou goest about to comprehend it, then it will fly away from thee ; but if thou dost surrender thyself wholly up to it, then it will abide with thee, and become the Life of thy Life, and be natural to thee." [1]

The author of the " Cloud of Unknowing" is particularly explicit as to the sense of dimness and confusion which overwhelms the self when it first enters this Dark ; a proceeding which is analogous with that annihilation of thought in the interests of passive receptivity which we have studied in the " Quiet."

" The first time thou dost it," he says of the neophyte's first vague steps in contemplation, " thou findest but a darkness, and as it were a cloud of unknowing—to wit, a dark mist, which seemeth to be between thee and the light that thou aspirest to—and thou knowest naught saving that thou feelest in thy will a certain naked intent unto God, that is, a certain imperfect and bare intent (as it showeth at the first sight) to come to a thing, without convenient means to come to the thing intended. This cloud (howsoever thou work) is evermore between thee and thy God, and letteth to thee, that thou mayest not see Him clearly by light of understanding in thy reason, nor feel Him by sweetness of love in thine affection. And therefore shape thyself to abide in this darkness so long as thou mayest, evermore crying after Him whom thou lovest, for if ever thou shalt feel Him or see Him (in such sort as He may be seen or felt in this life), it behoveth always to be in this cloud and darkness." [2]

From the same century, but from a very different country and temperament, comes another testimony as to the supreme value of this dark contemplation of the Divine : this absorption,

[1] Boehme, " Three Dialogues of the Supersensual Life," p. 71.
[2] " The Cloud of Unknowing," cap. iii. I have inserted the missing phrases from Collins's text.

beyond the span of thought or emotion, in the "substance of all that Is." It is one of the most vivid and detailed accounts of this strange form of consciousness which we possess; and deserves to be compared carefully with the statements of "The Cloud of Unknowing," and of St. John of the Cross. We owe it to that remarkable personality, the Blessed Angela of Foligno, who was converted from a life of worldliness to become not only a Christian and a Franciscan, but also a Platonist. In it we seem to hear the voice of Plotinus speaking from the Vale of Spoleto.

"There was a time," she says, "when my soul was exalted to behold God with so much clearness that never before had I beheld Him so distinctly. But love did I not see here so fully, rather did I lose that which I had before and was left without love. _Afterward did I see Him darkly_, and this darkness was the greatest blessing that could be imagined, and no thought could conceive aught that would equal this. . . . And by that blessing (most certain, and including also that darkness) have I attained unto all my hope, and inasmuch as now I see clearly, I have all that I desired to have or to know. Here likewise do I see all Good; and seeing it, the soul cannot think that it will depart from it, or it from the Good, or that in future it must ever leave the Good. The soul delighteth unspeakably therein, yet it beholdeth naught which can be related by the tongue or imagined in the heart. It seeth nothing, yet seeth all things, because it beholdeth this Good darkly—and the more darkly and secretly the Good is seen, the more certain is it, and excellent above all things. Wherefore is all other good which can be seen or imagined doubtless less than this, because all the rest is darkness. And even when the soul seeth the divine power, wisdom, and will of God (which I have seen most marvellously at other times), it is all less than this most certain Good. Because this is the whole, and those other things are but part of the whole. Another difference is, that albeit those other things are unspeakable yet they do bring great joy which is felt even in the body. But seen thus darkly, the Good bringeth no smile upon the lips, no fervour or devotion or love into the heart, for the body doth not tremble or become moved or distressed as it doth at other times. And the cause

thereof is, that the soul seeth, and not the body, which reposeth
and sleepeth, and the tongue is made dumb and cannot speak.
. . . Unto this most high power of beholding God ineffably
through such great darkness was my spirit uplifted but three
times and no more ; and although I beheld Him countless
times, and always darkly, yet never in such an high manner
and through such great darkness. . . . And to me it seemeth that
I am fixed in the midst of It and that It draweth me unto
Itself more than anything else the which I ever beheld, or
any blessing I ever yet received, so there is nothing which can
be compared unto It." [1]

These words, and indeed the whole idea which lies at the
bottom of "dark contemplation," will perhaps be better understood in the light of Baron von Hügel's deeply significant saying :
" Souls loving God in His Infinite Individuality will necessarily
love Him beyond their intellectual comprehension of Him ;
the element of devoted trust, of free self-donation to One
fully known *only through and in such an act*, will thus remain
to man for ever.",[2]   Hence, the contemplative act, which is
an act of loving and self-forgetting concentration upon the
Divine—the outpouring of man's little and finite personality
towards the Absolute Personality of God—will, in so far as
it transcends thought, mean darkness for the intellect ; but
it may mean radiance for the heart.   Psychologically, it will
mean the necessary depletion of the surface-consciousness, the
stilling of the mechanism of thought, in the interests of another
centre of consciousness.   Since this new centre makes enormous
demands on the self's stock of vitality its establishment
means, during the time that it is active, the withdrawal of
energy from other centres.   Thus the "night of thought"
becomes the strictly logical corollary of the "light of perception."

No one has expressed this double character of the Divine
Dark—its "nothingness" for the dissecting knife of reason,
its supreme fruitfulness for expansive, active love—with so
delicate an insight as St. John of the Cross.   In his work the
Christian touch of personal rapture vivifies the exact and
sometimes arid descriptions of the Neoplatonic mystics.   A

[1] B. Angelae de Fulginio, " Visionum et Instructionum Liber " (English translation, p. 181).
[2] " The Mystical Element of Religion," vol. ii. p. 257.

great poet as well as a great mystic, in his poem on the
"Obscure Night," he brings to bear on this actual and ineffable
experience of the introverted soul all the highest powers of
artistic expression, all the resources of musical rhythm, the
suggestive qualities of metaphor.

> "Upon an obscure night
> Fevered with Love's anxiety
> (O hapless, happy plight!)
> I went, none seeing me,
> Forth from my house, where all things quiet be.
>
> By night, secure from sight
> And by a secret stair, disguisedly,
> (O hapless, happy plight!)
> By night, and privily
> Forth from my house, where all things quiet be.
>
> Blest night of wandering
> In secret, when by none might I be spied,
> Nor I see anything;
> Without a light to guide
> Save that which in my heart burnt in my side.
>
> That light did lead me on,
> More surely than the shining of noontide
> Where well I knew that One
> Did for my coming bide;
> Where He abode might none but He abide.
>
> O night that didst lead thus,
> O night more lovely than the dawn of light;
> O night that broughtest us,
> Lover to lover's sight,
> Lover to loved, in marriage of delight!
>
> Upon my flowery breast
> Wholly for Him and save Himself for none,
> There did I give sweet rest
> To my beloved one:
> The fanning of the cedars breathed thereon."[1]

Observe in these verses the amazing fusion of personal
and metaphysical imagery; each contributing by its suggestive
qualities to a total effect which conveys to us, we hardly
know how, the obscure yet flaming rapture of the mystic,

[1] "En una Noche Escura." This translation, by Mr. Arthur Symons, will be
found in vol. ii. of his Collected Poems.

the affirmation of his burning love and the accompanying negation of his mental darkness and quiet—that "hapless, happy plight." All is here: the secrecy of the contemplative's true life unseen of other men, his deliberate and active abandonment of the comfortable house of the senses, the dim, unknown plane of being into which his ardent spirit must plunge—a "night more lovely than the dawn of light"—the Inward Light, the fire of mystic love, which guides his footsteps "more surely than the shining of noon-tide: the self-giving ecstasy of the consummation "wholly for Him, and save Himself for none," in which lover attains communion with Beloved "in marriage of delight."

In his book, "The Dark Night of the Soul," St. John has commented upon the opening lines of this poem: and the passages in which he does this are amongst the finest and most subtle descriptions of the psychology of contemplation which we possess.

"The soul," he says, ' calls the dim contemplation, by which it goes forth to the union of love, a secret stair; and that because of two properties of it which I am going to explain. First, this dark contemplation is called secret, because it is, as I have said before, the mystical theology which theologians call secret wisdom, and which according to St. Thomas is infused into the soul more especially by love. This happens in a secret hidden way, in which the natural operations of the understanding have no share. . . . Moreover, the soul has no wish to speak of it; and beside, it can discover no way or proper similitude to describe it by, so as to make known a knowledge so high, a *spiritual impression so delicate and infused*. Yea, and if it could have a wish to speak of it, and find terms to describe it, it would always remain secret still. Because this interior wisdom is so simple, general, and spiritual, that it enters not into the understanding under any form or image subject to sense, as is sometimes the case; the imagination, therefore, and the senses—as it has not entered in by them, nor is modified by them—cannot account for it, nor form any conception of it, so as to speak in any degree correctly about it, though the soul be distinctly conscious that it feels and tastes this strange wisdom. The soul is like a man who sees an object for the first time, the like of which he has never seen before; he

handles it and feels it, yet he cannot say what it is, nor tell
its name, do what he can, though it be at the same time an
object cognisable by the senses.   How much less, then, can
that be described, which does not enter in by the senses. . . .
This is not the only reason why it is called secret and why it
is so.   There is another, namely, the mystical wisdom has the
property of hiding the soul within itself. For beside its ordinary
operation, it sometimes so absorbs the soul and plunges it
in this secret abyss that the soul sees itself distinctly as far
away from, and abandoned by, all created things ; it looks upon
itself as one that is placed in a wild and vast solitude whither
no human being can come, as in an immense wilderness without
limits ; a wilderness the more delicious, sweet, and lovely, the
more it is wide, vast, and lonely, where the soul is the more
hidden, the more it is raised up above all created things.

   " This abyss of wisdom now so exalts and elevates the soul—
orderly disposing it for the science of love—that it makes it not
only understand how mean are all created things in relation
to the supreme wisdom and divine knowledge, but also how
low, defective, and, in a certain sense, improper, are all the
words and phrases by which in this life we discuss divine
things ; and how utterly impossible it is by any natural means,
however profoundly and learnedly we may speak, to understand and see them as they are, except in the light of mystical
theology.   And so the soul in the light thereof discerning this
truth, namely, that it cannot reach it, and still less explain it, by
the terms of ordinary speech, justly calls it Secret." [1]

   In this important passage we have a reconciliation of the
four chief images under which contemplation has been
described : the darkness and the light, the wilderness and the
union of love.   That is to say, the self's paradoxical feeling
of an ignorance which is supreme knowledge, and of solitude
which is intimate companionship.   On the last of these anti-
theses, the " wilderness that is more delicious, sweet, and lovely,

   [1] St. John of the Cross, " Noche Escura del Alma," l. ii. cap. xvii. (Lewis's
translation).   It is perhaps advisable to warn the reader that in this work St. John
applies the image of " darkness " to three absolutely different things : i.e., to the
Way of Purgation, which he calls the " night of sense " ; to dim contemplation, or
the Dionysian " Divine Dark " ; and to the true " dark night of the soul," which he
calls the " night of the spirit."   The result has been a good deal of confusion,
in modern writers on mysticism, upon the subject of the " Dark Night."

the more it is wide, vast, and lonely," I cannot resist quoting as a gloss upon the dignified language of the Spanish mystic the quaint and simple words of Richard Rolle.

"In the wilderness . . . speaks the loved to the heart of the lover ; as it were a bashful lover, that his sweetheart before men entreats not, nor friendly-wise but commonly and as a stranger he kisses. A devout soul safely from worldly business in mind and body departed . . . anon comes heavenly joy, and it marvellously making merry melody, to it springs whose token it takes, that now forward worldly sound gladly it suffers not. This is ghostly music, that is unknown to all that with worldly business lawful or unlawful are occupied. No man there is that this has known, but he that has studied to God only to take heed." [1]

Doubtless the "dark transcendence" reported and dwelt upon by all mystics of the Dionysian type, is nearest the truth of all our apprehensions of God :[2] though it can be true only in the paradoxical sense that it uses the suggestive qualities of negation—the Dark whose very existence involves that of Light—to hint at the infinite Affirmation of All that Is. But the nearer this language is to the Absolute, the further it is from ourselves. Unless care be taken in the use of it, the absence of falsehood may easily involve for us the absence of everything else. Man is not yet pure spirit, has not attained the Eternal. He is *in via*, and will never arrive if impatient amateurs of Reality insist on cutting the ground from under his feet. Like Dante, he needs a ladder to the stars, a ladder which goes the whole way from the human to the divine. Therefore the philosophic exactitude of these descriptions of the dark must be balanced, as they are in St. John of the Cross, by the personal, human, and symbolic affirmations of Love, if we would avoid a distorted notion of the Reality which the contemplative attains in his supreme " flights towards God." Consciousness has got to be helped across the gap which separates it from its Home.

The "wilderness," the dread Abyss, must be made homely by the voice of "the lover that His sweetheart before men entreats not." Approximate as we know such an image of our

[1] " The Fire of Love," bk. ii. cap. vii.
[2] Compare Baker, " Holy Wisdom," Treatise iii. § iv. cap. iv.

communion with the Absolute to be, it represents a real aspect
of the contemplative experience which eludes the rule and
compass of metaphysical thought.   Blake, with true mystic
insight, summed up the situation as between the two extreme
forms of contemplation when he wrote :—[1]

> "God appears, and God is Light
> To those poor souls who dwell in night:
> But doth a human form display
> To those who dwell in realms of day."

In the "orison of union" and the "Spiritual Marriage,"
those contemplatives whose temperament inclines them to
"dwell in realms of day" receive just such a revelation of the
"human form"—a revelation which the Christian dogma of
the Incarnation brings to a point.   They apprehend the personal and passionate aspect of the Infinite Life ; and the love, at
once intimate and expansive, all-demanding and all-renouncing,
which plays like lightning between it and the desirous soul.
"Thou saidst to me, my only Love, that Thou didst will to
make me Thyself; and that Thou wast all mine, with all that
Thou hadst and with all Paradise, and that I was all Thine.
That I should leave all, or rather the nothing ; and that (then)
Thou wouldst give me the all.   And that Thou hadst given
me this name—at which words I heard within me 'dedi te in
lucem gentium'—not without good reason.   And it seemed
then, as though I had an inclination for nothing except the
purest Union, without any means, in accordance with that
detailed sight which Thou hadst given me.   So then I said
to Thee : These other things, give them to whom Thou wilt ;
give me but this most pure Union with Thee, free from every
means."[2]

"Our work is the love of God," cries Ruysbroeck.   "Our
satisfaction lies in submission to the Divine Embrace."   This
utter and abrupt submission to the Divine Embrace is the
essence of that form of contemplation which is called the
Orison of Union.   "Surrender" is its secret: a personal surrender, not only of finite to Infinite, but of bride to Bride-

---

[1] "Auguries of Innocence."
[2] Colloquies of Battista Vernazza: quoted by Von Hügel, "The Mystical
Element of Religion," vol. i. p. 350.

groom, heart to Heart. This surrender, in contemplatives of
an appropriate temperament, is of so complete and ecstatic a
type that it involves a more or less complete suspension of
normal consciousness, an entrancement ; and often crosses
the boundary which separates contemplation from true ecstasy,
producing in its subject physical as well as psychical effects. In
this state, says St. Teresa, " There is no sense of anything : only
fruition, without understanding what that may be the fruition
of which is granted. It is understood that the fruition is of
a certain good, containing in itself all good together at once ;
but this good is not comprehended. The senses are all occupied in this fruition in such a way, that not one of them is at
liberty so as to be able to attend to anything else, whether
outward or inward. . . . But this state of complete absorption,
together with the utter rest of the imagination—for I believe
that the imagination is then wholly at rest—lasts only for a
short time ; though the faculties do not so completely recover
themselves as not to be for some hours afterwards as if in
disorder. . . . He who has had experience of this will understand it in some measure, for it cannot be more clearly
described, because what then takes place is so obscure. All
I am able to say is, that the soul is represented as being close
to God ; and that there abides a conviction thereof so certain
and strong that it cannot possibly help believing so. All the
faculties fail now, and are suspended in such a way that, as
I said before, their operations cannot be traced. . . . The will
must be fully occupied in loving, but it understands not how
it loves ; the understanding, if it understands, does not understand how it understands. It does not understand, as it seems
to me, because, as I said just now, this is a matter which
cannot be understood."[1]   Clearly, the psychological situation
here is the same as that in which mystics of the impersonal
type feel themselves to be involved in the Cloud of Unknowing,
or Divine Dark.

" Do not imagine," says Teresa in another place, " that this
orison, like that which went before [*i.e.*, the quiet] is a sort of
drowsiness : I say drowsiness, because in the orison of divine
savours or of quiet it seemed that the soul was neither
thoroughly asleep, nor thoroughly awake, but that it dozed.

[1] Vida, cap. xviii. §§ 2, 17, 19.

Here, on the contrary, the soul is asleep; entirely asleep as regards herself and earthly things. During the short time that union lasts she is, as it were, deprived of all feeling, and though she wishes it, she can think of nothing. Thus she needs no effort in order to suspend the action of her intellect or even the action of love . . . she is, as it were, absolutely dead to things of the world, the better to live in God."

It may be asked, in what way does such contemplation as this differ from unconsciousness. The difference, according to St. Teresa, consists in the definite *somewhat* which takes place during this inhibition of the surface-consciousness: a "somewhat" of which that surface-consciousness becomes aware when it awakes. Work has been done during this period of apparent passivity. The deeper self has escaped, has risen to freedom, and brings back tidings of the place to which it has been. We must remember that Teresa is here speaking from experience, and that her temperamental peculiarities will modify the form which this experience takes. "The soul," she says, "neither sees, hears, nor understands whilst she is united to God; but this time is usually very short, and seems to be even shorter than it is. God establishes Himself in the interior of this soul in such a way that, when she comes to herself, *it is impossible for her to doubt that she has been in God and God in her;* and this truth has left in her so deep an impression that, though she passed several years without being again raised to this state, she could neither forget the favour she received nor doubt its reality. . . . But you will say, how can the soul see and comprehend that she is in God and God in her, if during this union she is not able either to see or understand? I reply, that then she does not see it, but that afterwards she sees it clearly: not by a vision, but by a certitude which rests with her, and which God alone can give." [1]

[1] "El Castillo Interior," Moradas Quintas, cap. i.

CHAPTER VIII

ECSTASY AND RAPTURE

Ecstasy is the last term of Contemplation—Mystics regard it as a very favourable state—Its physical aspect—The trance—an abnormal bodily state—Healthy and unhealthy trances—their characteristics—St. Catherine of Genoa—Psychological aspect of ecstasy—Complete mono-ideism—A temporary unification of consciousness—Often helped by symbols—St. Catherine of Siena—Description of healthy ecstasy—It entails a new perception of Reality—Mystical aspect of Ecstasy—a state of "Pure Apprehension"—the completion of the Orison of Union—Sometimes hard to distinguish from it—The real distinction is in entrancement—St. Teresa on union and ecstasy—Results of ecstasy confirm those of contemplation—no sharp line possible between the two—Many cases cannot be classified—Rolle on two forms of Rapture—The mystic in ecstasy claims that he attains the Absolute—The nature of his consciousness—a concentration of his whole being on one act—A perception of Eternity—Suso—the Neoplatonists—Plotinus—Self-mergence—Jacopone da Todi—Ecstatic vision—Rapture—its distinction from Ecstasy—it indicates psycho-physical disharmony—St. Teresa on Rapture—Levitation—Rapture always entails bodily immobility—generally mental disorder—Its final result good for life—Ecstatic states contribute to the organic development of the self

SINCE the primal object of all contemplation is the production of that state of intimate communion in which the mystics declare that the self is "in God and God is in her," it might be supposed that the orison of union represented the end of mystical activity, in so far as it is concerned with the attainment of a transitory but exalted consciousness of "oneness with the Absolute." Nearly all the great contemplatives, however, describe as a distinct, and regard as a more advanced phase of the spiritual consciousness, the group of definitely ecstatic states in which the concentration of interest on the Transcendent is so complete, the gathering up and pouring out of life on this one point so intense, that the subject is entranced, and becomes, for the time of the ecstasy, wholly unconscious of the external world. In pure contemplation he refused to attend to that external world : it was there, a blurred image, at the fringe of his conscious field, but he deliberately left it on one side. In ecstasy he *cannot* attend to it. None of its messages reach him: not even those most insistent of all messages which are translated into the terms of bodily pain.

Mystics of all ages have agreed in regarding such ecstasy as an exceptionally favourable state; the one in which man's spirit is caught up to its most immediate vision of the divine. The word has become a synonym for joyous exaltation, for the inebriation of the Infinite. The induced ecstasies of the Dionysian mysteries, the metaphysical raptures of the Neoplatonists, the voluntary or involuntary trance of Indian mystics and Christian saints—all these, however widely they may differ in transcendental value, agree in claiming such value, in declaring that this change in the quality of their consciousness brought with it an expansive and unforgettable apprehension of the Real.

Clearly, this apprehension will vary with the place of the subject in the spiritual scale. The ecstasy is simply the psycho-physical agent by which it is obtained. "It is hardly a paradox to say," says Myers, "that the evidence for ecstasy is stronger than the evidence for any other religious belief. Of all the subjective experiences of religion, ecstasy is that which has been most urgently, perhaps to the psychologist most convincingly asserted; and it is not confined to any one religion. . . . From the medicine man of the lowest savages up to St. John, St. Peter, and St. Paul, with Buddha and Mahomet on the way, we find records which, though morally and intellectually much differing, are in psychological essence the same." [1]

There are three distinct aspects under which the ecstatic state may be studied: (*a*) the physical, (*b*) the psychological, (*c*) the mystical. Many of the deplorable misunderstandings and still more deplorable mutual recriminations which surround its discussion come from the refusal of experts in one of these three branches to consider the results arrived at by the other two.

A. Physically considered, Ecstasy is a trance; more or less deep, more or less prolonged. The subject may slide into it

[1] " Human Personality and its Survival of Bodily Death," vol. ii. p. 260.

gradually from a period of absorption in, or contemplation of, some idea which has filled the field of consciousness : or, it may come on suddenly, the appearance of the idea—or even some word or symbol suggesting the idea—abruptly throwing the subject into an entranced condition. This is the state which mystical writers call Rapture. The distinction, however, is a conventional one: and the works of the mystics describe many intermediate forms.

During the trance, breathing and circulation are depressed. The body is more or less cold and rigid, remaining in the exact position which it occupied at the oncoming of the ecstasy, however difficult and unnatural this pose may be. Sometimes entrancement is so deep that there is complete anæsthesia, as in the case which I quote from the life of St. Catherine of Siena.[1] Credible witnesses report that Bernadette, the visionary of Lourdes, held the flaming end of a candle in her hand for fifteen minutes during one of her ecstasies. She felt no pain, neither did the flesh show any marks of burning. Similar instances of ecstatic anæsthesia abound in the lives of the saints.

The trance includes, according to the testimony of the ecstatics, two distinct phases—(a) the short period of lucidity and (b) a longer period of complete unconsciousness, which may pass into a death-like catalepsy, lasting for hours ; or, as once with St. Teresa, for days. " The difference between union and trance," says Teresa, " is this : that the latter lasts longer and is more visible outwardly, because the breathing gradually diminishes, so that it becomes impossible to speak or to open the eyes. And though this very thing occurs when the soul is in union, there is more violence in a trance ; for the natural warmth vanishes, I know not how, when the rapture is deep, and in all these kinds of orison there is more or less of this. When it is deep, as I was saying, the hands become cold and sometimes stiff and straight as pieces of wood ; as to the body, if the rapture comes on when it is standing or kneeling, it remains so ; and the soul is so full of the joy of that which Our Lord is setting before it, that it seems to forget to animate the body and abandons it. If the rapture lasts, the nerves are made to feel it."[2]

Such ecstasy as this, so far as its merely physical symptoms go, is not of course the peculiar privilege of the mystics. It is an abnormal bodily state, caused by a psychic state : and this causal psychic state may be healthy or unhealthy, the result of genius or disease. It is common in the strange and little understood type of personality called "sensitive" or mediumistic: it is a well-known symptom of certain mental and nervous illnesses. A feeble mind concentrated on one idea—like a hypnotic subject gazing at one spot—easily becomes entranced ; however trivial the idea which gained possession of his consciousness. Taken alone then, and apart from its content, ecstasy carries no guarantee of spiritual value. It merely indicates the presence of certain abnormal psycho-physical conditions : an alteration of the normal equilibrium, a shifting of the threshold of consciousness, which leaves the body, and the whole usual "external world" outside instead of inside the conscious field, and even affects those physical functions—such as breathing—which are almost entirely automatic. Thus ecstasy, physically considered, may occur in any person in whom (1) the threshold of consciousness is exceptionally mobile and (2) there is a tendency to dwell upon one governing idea or intuition. Its worth depends entirely on the objective worth of that idea or intuition.

In the hysterical patient, thanks to an unhealthy condition of the centres of consciousness, any trivial or irrational idea, any one of the odds and ends stored up in the subliminal region, may thus become fixed, dominate the mind, and produce entrancement. Such ecstasy is an illness : the emphasis is on the pathological state which makes it possible. In the mystic, the idea which fills his life is so great a one—the idea of God—that, in proportion as it is vivid, real, and intimate, it inevitably tends to monopolize the field of consciousness. His ecstasy is an expression of this fact : and here the emphasis is on the overpowering strength of spirit, not on the feeble and unhealthy state of body or mind.[1] This true ecstasy, says

[1] St. Thomas proves ecstasies to be inevitable on just this psychological ground. "The higher our mind is raised to the contemplation of spiritual things," he says, "the more it is abstracted from sensible things. But the final term to which contemplation can possibly arrive is the divine substance. Therefore the mind that sees the divine substance must be totally divorced from the bodily senses, either by death or *by some rapture*" ("Summa Contra Gentiles," l. iii. cap. xlvii., Rickaby's translation).

Godfernaux, is not a malady, but "the extreme form of a state which must be classed amongst the ordinary accidents of conscious life." [1]

The mystics themselves are fully aware of the importance of this distinction. Ecstasies, no less than visions and voices, must, they declare, be subjected to unsparing criticism before they are recognized as divine : whereas some are undoubtedly "of God," others are no less clearly "of the devil."

"The great doctors of the mystic life," says Malaval, "teach that there are two sorts of rapture which must be carefully distinguished. The first are produced in persons but little advanced in the Way, and still full of selfhood ; either by the force of a heated imagination which vividly apprehends a sensible object, or by the artifice of the Devil. These are the raptures which St. Teresa calls, in various parts of her works, Raptures of Feminine Weakness. The other sort of Rapture is, on the contrary, the effect of pure intellectual vision in those who have a great and generous love for God. To generous souls who have utterly renounced themselves, God never fails in these raptures to communicate high things." [2]

All the mystics agree with Malaval in finding the test of a true ecstasy, not in its outward sign, but in its inward grace, its after-value : and here psychological science would be well advised to follow their example. The ecstatic states, which are supreme instances of the close connexion between body and soul, have bodily as well as mental results : and those results are as different and as characteristic as those observed in healthy and in morbid organic processes. If the concentration has been upon the highest centre of consciousness, the organ of spiritual perception—if a door has really been opened by which the self has escaped for an instant to the vision of That Which Is—the ecstasy will be good for life. The entrancement of disease, on the contrary, is always bad for life. Its concentration being upon the lower instead of the higher levels of mentality, it depresses rather than enhances the vitality, the fervour, or the intelligence of its subject : and leaves behind it an enfeebled will, and often moral and

[1] " Sur la Psychologie du Mysticisme " (*Revue Philosophique*, February, 1902).
[2] Malaval, " La Pratique de la Vraye Théologie Mystique," vol. i. p. 89.

intellectual chaos : [1] "Ecstasies that do not produce considerable profit either to the persons themselves or others, deserve
to be suspected," says Augustine Baker, "and when any marks
of their approaching are perceived the persons ought to divert
their minds some other way." [2] It is all the difference between a healthy appetite for nourishing food and a morbid
craving for garbage. The same organs of digestion are used in
satisfying both : yet he would be a hardy physiologist who
undertook to discredit all nutrition by a reference to its
degenerate forms.

Sometimes both kinds of ecstasy, the healthy and the
psychopathic, are seen in the same person. Thus in the
cases of St. Catherine of Genoa and St. Catherine of Siena it
would seem that as their health became feebler and the nervous
instability always found in persons of genius increased, their
ecstasies became more frequent ; but these were not healthy
ecstasies, such as those which they experienced in the earlier
stages of their careers, and which brought with them an access
of vitality. They were the results of the increasing weakness
of the body, not of the overpowering strength of the spirit :
and there is evidence that Catherine of Genoa, that acute
self-critic, was conscious of this fact. "Those who attended on
her did not know how to distinguish one state from the other.
And hence on coming to, she would sometimes say, "Why did
you let me remain in this quietude, from which I have almost
died ? " [3]

Her earlier ecstasies were very different from this. They
had in a high degree the positive character of exaltation and
life-enhancement consequent upon extreme concentration upon
the Absolute; as well as the merely negative character of
annihilation of the surface-consciousness. She came from
them with renewed health and strength, as from a resting in
heavenly places and a feeding on heavenly food : and side by
side with this ecstatic life fulfilled the innumerable duties of
her active profession as hospital matron and spiritual mother of
a large group of disciples. "Many times," says her legend,

---

[1] Pierre Janet (" The Major Symptoms of Hysteria," p. 316) says that a lowering
of the mental level is an invariable symptom or " stigma " of hysteria.

[2] " Holy Wisdom," Treatise iii. § iv. cap. iii.

[3] Von Hügel, " The Mystical Element of Religion," vol. i. p. 206.

"she would hide herself in some secret place and there stay: and being sought she was found upon the ground, her face hidden in her hands, altogether beyond herself, in such a state of joy as is beyond thought or speech : and being called —yea, even in a loud voice—she heard not. And at other times she would go up and down: . . . as if beyond herself, drawn by the impulse of love, she did this. And certain other times she remained for the space of six hours as if dead : but hearing herself called, suddenly she got up, and answering she would at once go about all that needed to be done, even the humblest things.[1]   And in thus leaving the All, she went without any grief, because she fled all selfhood [*la proprietà*] as if it were the devil. And when she came forth from her hiding-place, her face was rosy as it might be a cherub's ; and it seemed as if she might have said, 'Who shall separate me from the love of God ? ' " [2]   "Very often," says St. Teresa, describing the results of such rapturous communion with Pure Love as that from which St. Catherine came joyous and rosy-faced, "he who was before sickly and full of pain comes forth healthy and even with new strength : for it is something great that is given to the soul in rapture." [3]

B. Psychologically considered, all ecstasy is a form—the most perfect form—of the state which is technically called "complete mono-ideism." That withdrawal of consciousness from circumference to centre, that deliberate attention to *one thing*, which we discussed in Recollection, is here pushed— voluntarily or involuntarily—to its logical conclusion. It is (1) always paid for by psycho-physical disturbances ; (2) rewarded in healthy cases by an enormous lucidity, a supreme intuition in regard to the one thing on which the self's interest has been set.

Such ecstasy, then, is an extremely exalted form of contemplation, and might be expected to develop naturally from that state. "A simple difference of degree," says Maury, "separates ecstasy from the action of forcibly fixing an idea

---

[1] This power of detecting and hearing the call of duty though she was deaf to everything else is evidently related to the peculiarity noticed by Ribot ; who says that an ecstatic hears no sounds, save, in some cases, the voice of one specific person, which is always able to penetrate the trance. ("Les Maladies de la Volonté," p. 125.)

[2] Vita e Dottrina, cap. v.   [3] Vida, cap. xx. § 29.

in the mind.   Contemplation implies exercise of will and the power of interrupting the extreme tension of the mind.   In ecstasy, which is contemplation carried to its highest pitch, the will, although in the strictest sense able to provoke the state, is nevertheless unable to suspend it." [1]

In "complete mono-ideism" then, the attention to one thing, and the inattention to all else, is so entire, that the subject is entranced.   Consciousness has been withdrawn from those centres which receive and respond to the messages of the external world : he neither sees, feels, nor hears.   The *Ego dormio et cor meam vigilat* of the contemplative ceases to be a metaphor, and becomes a realistic description.   It must be remembered that the whole trend of mystical education has been towards the production of this fixity of attention.   Recollection and Quiet lead up to it.   Contemplation cannot take place without it.   All the mystics assure us that a unification of consciousness, in which all outward things are forgot, is the necessary prelude of union with the Divine : for consciousness of the Many and consciousness of the One are mutually exclusive states.

Ecstasy, for the psychologist, is just such a unification in its most extreme form.   The absorption of the self on the one idea, the one desire, is so profound—and in the case of the great mystics so impassioned—that everything else is blotted out.   The tide of life is withdrawn, not only from those higher centres which are the seats of perception and of thought, but also from those lower centres which govern the physical life. The whole vitality of the subject is so concentrated on the transcendental world—or, in the case of morbid ecstatics, on the idea which dominates their minds—that body and brain alike are depleted of their energy in the interests of this supreme act.

Since mystics have, as a rule, the extreme susceptibility to suggestions and impressions which is characteristic of all artistic and creative types, it is not surprising to find that their ecstasies are often evoked, abruptly, by the exhibition of, or concentration upon, some loved and special symbol of the divine.   Such symbols form the rallying-points about which are gathered a whole group of ideas and intuitions. Their presence—sometimes the sudden thought of them—will

[1] A. Maury, " Le Sommeil et les Rêves," p. 235.

be enough, in psychological language, to provoke a discharge of
energy along some particular path : that is to say, to stir to
life all those ideas and intuitions which belong to the self's
consciousness of the Absolute, to concentrate vitality on them,
to shift the field of consciousness and initiate the self into
that world of perception of which they are, as it were, the
material keys. Hence the profound significance of symbols
for some mystics : their paradoxical clinging to outward
forms whilst declaring that the spiritual and intangible alone
is real.

For the Christian mystics, the sacraments and mysteries of
faith have always provided such a *point d'appui*; and these
symbols often play a large part in the production of their
ecstasies. In the case of St. Catherine of Siena, and also
very often in that of her namesake of Genoa, the reception of
Holy Communion was the prelude to ecstasy. Julian of Norwich [1] and St. Francis of Assisi [2] became entranced whilst
gazing on the crucifix. We are told of Denis the Carthusian
that towards the end of his life, hearing the *Veni Creator* or
certain verses of the psalms, he was at once rapt in God and
lifted up from the earth.[3]

Of St. Catherine of Siena, her biographer says that "she
used to communicate with such fervour that immediately afterwards she would pass into the state of ecstasy, in which for
hours she would be totally unconscious. On one occasion,
finding her in this condition, they (the Dominican friars)
forcibly threw her out of the church at midday, and left her
in the heat of the sun watched over by some of her companions
till she came to her senses." Another, "catching sight of her
in the church when she was in ecstasy, came down and pricked
her in many places with a needle. Catherine was not aroused
in the least from her trance, but afterwards, when she came
back to her senses, she felt the pain in her body and perceived
that she had thus been wounded." [4]

It is interesting to compare with this objective description,
the subjective account of ecstatic union which Catherine gives

[1] " Revelations of Divine Love," cap. iii.
[2] *Vide supra*, p. 218.
[3] D. A. Mougel, "Denys le Chartreux," p. 32.
[4] E. Gardner, "St. Catherine of Siena," p. 50.

in her Divine Dialogue. Here, for once, we have the deeper
self of the mystic giving in a dramatic form its own account
of its inward experiences : hence we here see the inward side
of that outward state of entrancement which was all that
onlookers were able to perceive. As usual in the Dialogue,
the intuitive perceptions of the deeper self are attributed by
Catherine to the Divine Voice speaking in her soul.

" Oftentimes, through the perfect union which the soul has
made with Me, she is raised from the earth almost as if the
heavy body became light. But this does not mean that the
heaviness of the body is taken away, but that the union of
the soul with Me is more perfect than the union of the body
with the soul ; wherefore the strength of the spirit, united with
Me, raises the weight of the body from the earth, leaving it as
if immoveable and all pulled to pieces in the affection of the
soul. Thou rememberest to have heard it said of some
creatures, that were it not for My Goodness, in seeking
strength for them, they would not be able to live ; and I
would tell thee that, in the fact that the souls of some do
not leave their bodies, is to be seen a greater miracle than in
the fact that some have arisen from the dead, so great is the
union which they have with Me. I, therefore, sometimes for a
space withdraw from the union, making the soul return to the
vessel of her body . . . from which she was separated by the
affection of love. From the body she did not depart, because
that cannot be except in death ; the bodily powers alone departed, becoming united to Me through affection of love. The
memory is full of nothing but Me, the intellect, elevated, gazes
upon the object of My Truth ; the affection, which follows the
intellect, loves and becomes united with that which the intellect
sees. These powers, being united and gathered together and
immersed and inflamed in Me, the body loses its feeling, so that
the seeing eye sees not, and the hearing ear hears not, and the
tongue does not speak ; except as the abundance of the heart
will sometimes permit it for the alleviation of the heart and the
praise and glory of My Name. The hand does not touch and
the feet walk not, because the members are bound with the
sentiment of Love." [1]

A healthy ecstasy so deep as this seems to be the exclusive

[1] Dialogo, cap. lxxix.

prerogative of the mystics : perhaps because so great a passion, so profound a concentration, can be produced by nothing smaller than their flaming love of God. But as the machinery of contemplation is employed more or less consciously by all types of creative genius : by inventors and philosophers, by poets, prophets, and musicians, by all the followers of the "Triple Star," no less than by the mystic saints : so too, this apotheosis of contemplation, the ecstatic state, does appear in a less violent form, acting healthily and normally, wherever we have the artistic and creative personality in a complete state of development. It accompanies the prophetic intuitions of the seer, the lucidity of the great metaphysician, the artist's supreme perception of beauty or truth. As the saint is "caught up to God," so these are "caught up" to their vision : their partial apprehensions of the Absolute Life. Those joyous, expansive outgoing sensations, characteristic of the ecstatic consciousness, are theirs also. Their great creations are translations to us, not of something they have thought, but of something they have known, in a moment of ecstatic union with the "great life of the All."

We begin, then, to think that the "pure mono-ideism," which the psychologist identifies with ecstasy, though doubtless a part, is far from being the whole content of this state. True, the ecstatic is absorbed in his one idea, his one love : he is in it and with it : it fills his universe. But this unified state of consciousness does not merely pore upon something already possessed. When it only does this, it is diseased. Its true business is pure perception. It is outgoing, expansive : its goal is something beyond itself. The rearrangement of the psychic self which occurs in ecstasy is not merely concerned with the normal elements of consciousness. It is a temporary unification of consciousness around that centre of transcendental perception which mystics call the "spark of the soul." Those deeper layers of personality which normal life keeps below the threshold are active in it : and these are fused with the surface personality by the governing passion, the transcendent love which lies at the basis of all sane ecstatic states.

The result is not merely a mind concentrated on one idea, nor a heart fixed on one desire, nor even a mind and a heart united in the interests of a beloved thought : but a whole being welded into one, all its faculties, neglecting their normal universe, grouped about a new centre, serving a new life, and piercing like a single flame the barriers of the sensual world. Ecstasy is the psycho-physical state which generally accompanies and expresses this brief synthetic act.

C. Therefore, whilst on its physical side ecstasy is an entrancement, on its mental side a complete unification of consciousness: on its mystical side it is an exalted act of perception. It represents the greatest possible extension of the spiritual consciousness in the direction of Pure Being : the "blind intent stretching" here receives its reward in a profound experience of Eternal Life. In this experience the departmental activities of thought and feeling, the consciousness of I-hood, of space and time—all that belongs to the World of Becoming and our own place therein—are suspended. The vitality which we are accustomed to split amongst these various things, is gathered up to form a state of "pure apprehension" : a vivid intuition of —or if you like conjunction with—the Transcendent. For the time of his ecstasy the mystic is, for all practical purposes, as truly living in the supersensual world as the normal human animal is living in the sensual world. He is experiencing the highest and most joyous of those temporary and unstable states in which his consciousness escapes the limitations of the senses, rises to freedom, and is united for an instant with the "great life of the All."

Ecstasy, then, from the contemplatives' point of view, is the development and completion of the orison of union : and he is not always at pains to distinguish the two degrees, a fact which adds greatly to the difficulties of students.[1] In both states—though he may, for want of better language, describe his experience in terms of sight—the Transcendent is perceived by contact, not by vision : as, enfolded in darkness with one whom we love, we obtain a knowledge far more complete than that conferred by the sharpest sight, the most perfect mental analysis. In Ecstasy, the apprehension is perhaps more definitely "beatific" than in the orison of union. Such memory of his feeling-states as the ecstatic brings back with him is more often concerned with an exultant certainty—a conviction that

[1] In the case of Dante, for instance, we do not know whether his absorption in the Eternal Light did or did not entail the condition of trance.

he has known for once the Reality which hath no image, and solved the paradox of life—than with meek self-loss in that Cloud of Unknowing where the contemplative in union is content to meet his Beloved. The true note of ecstasy, how-ever, its only valid distinction from infused contemplation, lies in *entrancement*; in " being ravished out of fleshly feeling," as St. Paul caught up to the Third Heaven,[1] not in "the lifting of mind unto God." This, of course, is an outward distinction only, and a rough one at that, since entrancement has many degrees : but it will be found the only practical basis of classification.

Probably none but those who have experienced these states know the actual difference between them. Even St. Teresa's psychological insight fails her here, and she is obliged to fall back on the difference between voluntary and involuntary absorption in the divine : a difference, not in spiritual values, but merely in the psycho-physical constitutions of those who have perceived these values. " I wish I could explain with the help of God," she says, " wherein union differs from rapture, or from transport, or from flight of the spirit, as they call it, or from trance, which are all one. I mean that all these are only different names for that *one and the same thing, which is also called ecstasy.* It is more excellent than union, the fruits of it are much greater, and its other operations more manifold, for union is uniform in the beginning, the middle, and the end, and is so also interiorly; but as raptures have ends of a much higher kind, they produce effects both within and without [*i.e.,* both physical and psychical]. . . . A rapture is absolutely irre-sistible ; whilst union, inasmuch as we are then on our own ground, may be hindered, though that resistance be painful and violent." [2]

From the point of view of mystical psychology, our interest in ecstasy will centre in two points. (1) What has the mystic to tell us of the Object of his ecstatic perception ? (2) What is the nature of the peculiar consciousness which he enjoys in his trance ? That is to say, what news does he bring us as to the Being of God and the powers of man ?

It may be said generally that on both these points he bears out, amplifies, and expresses under formulæ of greater splendour,

---

[1] 2 Cor. xii. 1–6.   [2] Vida, cap. xx. §§ 1 and 3.

with an accent of greater conviction, the general testimony of the contemplatives. In fact, we must never forget that an ecstatic is really nothing else than a contemplative of a special kind, with a special psycho-physical make-up. Moreover, we have seen that it is not always easy to determine the exact point at which entrancement takes place, and deep contemplation assumes the ecstatic form. The classification, like all classifications of mental states, is an arbitrary one. Whilst the extreme cases present no difficulty, there are others less complete, which form a graduated series between the deeps of the " Quiet " and the heights of " Rapture." We shall never know, for instance, whether the ecstasies of Plotinus and of Pascal involved true bodily entrancement, or only a deep absorption of the " unitive " kind. So, too, the language of many Christian mystics when speaking of their " raptures " is so vague and metaphorical that it leaves us in great doubt as to whether they mean by Rapture the abrupt suspension of normal consciousness, or merely a sudden and agreeable elevation of soul.

" Ravishing," says Rolle, " as it is showed, in two ways is to be understood. One manner, forsooth, in which a man is ravished out of fleshly feeling; so that for the time of his ravishing plainly he feels not in flesh, nor what is done of his flesh, and yet he is not dead but quick, for yet the soul to the body gives life. And on this manner saints sometime are ravished to their profit and other men's learning; as Paul ravished to the third heaven. And on this manner sinners also in vision sometime are ravished, that they may see joys of saints and pains of damned for their correction.[1] And many other as we read of. Another manner of ravishing there is, that is lifting of mind into God by contemplation. And this manner of ravishing is in all that are perfect lovers of God, and in none but in them that love God. And as well this is called a ravishing as the other ; for with a violence it is done, and as it were against nature." [2]

It is, however, very confusing to the anxious inquirer when

[1] Compare Dante, Letter to Can Grande, sect. 28, where he adduces this fact of " the ravishing of sinners for their correction," in support of his claim that the " Divine Comedy " is the fruit of experience, and that he had indeed " navigated the great Sea of Being " of which he writes.
[2] Richard Rolle, " The Fire of Love," bk. ii. cap. vii.

—as too often—" lifting of mind by contemplation " is " as well called a ravishing as the other," and ecstasy is used as a synonym for gladness of heart.   Here, so far as is possible, these words will be confined to their strict meaning and not applied generally to the description of all the outgoing and expansive states of the transcendental consciousness.

What does the mystic claim that he attains in this abnormal condition—this irresistible trance?   The price that he pays is a heavy one, involving much psycho-physical wear and tear.

He declares that his rapture or ecstasy includes a moment— often a very short, and always an indescribable moment—in which he enjoys a supreme knowledge of or participation in Divine Reality.   He tells us under various metaphors that he then attains Pure Being, his Source, his Origin, his Beloved: " is engulphed in the very thing for which he longs, which is God." [1] " Oh, wonder of wonders," cries Eckhart, " when I think of the union the soul has with God !   He makes the enraptured soul to flee out of herself, for she is no more satisfied with anything that can be named.   The spring of Divine Love flows out of the soul and draws her out of herself into the unnamed Being, into her first source, which is God alone." [2]

This momentary attainment of the Source, the Origin, is the theme of all descriptions of mystic ecstasy.   In Rulman Merswin's " Book of the Nine Rocks," that brief and overwhelming rapture is the end of the pilgrim's long trials and ascents. " The vision of the Infinite lasted only for a moment : when he came to himself he felt inundated with life and joy.   He asked, " Where have I been ? " and he was answered, " In the upper school of the Holy Spirit.   There you were surrounded by the dazzling pages of the Book of Divine Wisdom.[3]   Your soul plunged therein with delight, and the Divine Master of the school has filled her with an exuberant love by which even your physical nature has been transfigured." [4]

Another Friend of God, Ellina von Crevelsheim, who was of so abnormal a psychic constitution that her absorption in the

---

[1] Dante, *loc. cit.*

[2] Eckhart, " On the Steps of the Soul " (Pfeiffer, p. 153).

[3] Compare Par. xxxiii. 85 (*vide supra*, p. 160).

[4] Jundt, " Rulman Merswin," p. 27.   Note that this was a "good ecstasy," involving healthful effects for life.

Divine Love caused her to remain dumb for seven years, was "touched by the Hand of God" at the end of that period, and fell into a five-days' ecstasy, in which "pure truth" was revealed to her, and she was lifted up to an immediate experience of the Absolute. There she "saw the interior of the Father's heart," and was "bound with chains of love, enveloped in light, and filled with peace and joy." [1]

In this transcendent act of union the mystic sometimes says that he is "conscious of nothing." But it is clear that this expression is figurative, for otherwise he would not have known that there had been an act of union : were his individuality abolished, it could not have been aware of its attainment of God. What he appears to mean is that consciousness so changes its form as to be no longer recognizable : or describable in human speech. In the paradoxical language of Richard of St. Victor, "In a wondrous fashion remembering we do not remember, seeing we do not see, understanding we not understand, penetrating we do not penetrate." [2] In this wholly indescribable but most actual state, the whole self, exalted and at white heat, is unified and poured out in one vivid act of impassioned perception, which leaves no room for reflection or self-observation. That aloof "somewhat" in us which watches all our actions, splits our consciousness, has been submerged. The mystic is attending exclusively to Eternity, not to his own perception of Eternity. That he can only consider when the ecstasy itself is at an end.

> "All things I then forgot,
>   My cheek on Him Who for my coming came,
>   *All ceased, and I was not,*
>   Leaving my cares and shame
> Among the lilies, and forgetting them." [3]

This is that state of perfect unity of consciousness, of utter concentration on an experience of love, which excludes all conceptual and analytic acts. Hence, when the mystic says that his faculties were suspended, that he "knew all and knew

[1] Jundt, "Les Amis de Dieu," p. 39. Given also by Rufus Jones, "Studies in Mystical Religion," p. 271.
[2] "Benjamin Major."
[3] St. John of the Cross, "En una Noche Escura."

nought," he really means that he was so concentrated on the Absolute that he ceased to consider his separate existence : so merged in it that he could not perceive it as an object of thought, as the bird cannot see the air which supports it, nor the fish the ocean in which it swims. He really "knows all" but "thinks" nought : "perceives all," but "conceives nought."

The ecstatic consciousness is not self-conscious : it is intuitive, not discursive. Under the sway of a great passion, possessed by a great Idea, it has become "a single state of enormous intensity."[1] In this state, it transcends all our ordinary machinery of knowledge, and plunges deep into the Heart of Reality. A fusion which is the anticipation of the unitive life takes place : and the ecstatic returns from this brief foretaste of freedom saying, in the words of a living mystical philosopher, "I know, as having known, the meaning of Existence ; the sane centre of the universe—at once the wonder and the assurance of the soul."[2] "This utter transformation of the soul in God," says St. Teresa, describing the same experience in the official language of theology, "continues only for an instant : yet while it continues no faculty of the soul is aware of it, or knows what is passing there. Nor can it be understood while we are living on the earth ; at least God will not have us understand it, because we must be incapable of understanding it. *I know it by experience.*"[3]

The utterances of those who know by experience are here of more worth than all the statements of psychology, which are concerned of necessity with the "outward signs" of this "inward and spiritual grace." To these we must go if we would obtain some hint of that which ecstasy may mean to the ecstatic.

"When the soul, forgetting itself, dwells in that radiant darkness," says Suso, "it loses all its faculties and all its qualities, as St. Bernard has said. And this, more or less completely, according to whether the soul—whether in the body or out of the body—is more or less united to God. This forgetfulness of self is, in a measure, a transformation in God ; who then

[1] Ribot, "Psychologie de l'Attention," cap. iii.
[2] B. P. Blood. See William James, "A Pluralistic Mystic," in the *Hibbert Journal*, July, 1910.
[3] Vida, cap. xx. § 24.

becomes, in a certain manner, all things for the soul, as Scripture saith. In this rapture the soul disappears, but not yet entirely. It acquires, it is true, certain qualities of divinity, but does not naturally become divine. . . . To speak in the common language, the soul is rapt, by the divine power of resplendent Being, above its natural faculties, into the nakedness of the Nothing."[1]

Here, of course, Suso is trying to describe his rapturous attainment of God in the negative terms of Dionysian theology. It is likely enough that much of the language of that theology originated, not in the abstract philosophizings, but in the actual ecstatic experience, of the Neoplatonists, who—Christian and Pagan alike—believed in, and sometimes deliberately induced, this condition as the supreme method of attaining the One. The whole Christian doctrine of ecstasy, on its metaphysical side, really descends from that great practical transcendentalist Plotinus: who is said to have attained this state three times, and has left in his Sixth Ennead a description of it obviously based upon his own experiences. " Then," he says, " the soul neither sees, nor distinguishes by seeing, nor imagines that there are two things ; but becomes as it were another thing, and not itself. Nor does that which pertains to itself contribute anything there. But becoming wholly absorbed in Deity, she is *One*, conjoining as it were centre with centre. For here concurring they are One ; but when they are separate, they are two. . . . Therefore in this conjunction with Deity there were not two things, but the perceiver was one with the thing perceived, as not being *Vision* but *Union*; whoever becomes one by mingling with Deity, and afterwards recollects this union, will have within himself an image of it. . . . For then there was not anything excited with him who had ascended thither ; neither anger, nor desire of anything else, nor reason, nor a certain intellectual perception, nor, in short, was he himself moved, if it be needful also to assert this ; but, being as it were in an ecstasy, or *energizing enthusiastically*, he became established in quiet and solitary union."[2] Ecstasy, says Plotinus in another part of the same treatise, is " an expansion or accession, a desire of contact, rest, and a striving after conjunction." All the phases of the contemplative experience seem to be summed up in this phrase.

---

[1] Leben, cap. lv.   [2] Ennead vi. 9.

It has been said by some critics that the ecstasy of Plotinus was wholly different in kind from the ecstasy of the Christian saints: that it was a philosophic rhapsody, something like Plato's "saving madness," which is also regarded on wholly insufficient evidence as being an affair of the head and entirely unconnected with the heart. At first sight the arid metaphysical language in which Plotinus tries to tell his love, offers some ground for this view. But whatever philosophic towers of Babel he may build on it, the ecstasy itself is a practical matter; and has its root, not in reason, but in a deep-seated passion for the Absolute which is far nearer to the mystic's love of God than to any intellectual curiosity, however sublime. The few passages in which it is mentioned tell us what his mystical genius drove him to do: and not what his philosophical mind encouraged him to think or say. At once when we come to these passages we notice a rise of temperature, an alteration of values. Plotinus the ecstatic is sure, whatever Plotinus the metaphysician may think, that the union with God is a union of hearts: that "by love He may be gotten and holden, but by thought never." He, no less than the mediaeval contemplatives, is convinced—to quote his own words—that the Vision is only for the desirous ; for him who has that "loving passion" which "causes the lover to rest in the object of his love."[1] The simile of marriage, of conjunction as the soul's highest bliss, which we are sometimes told that we owe in part to the unfortunate popularity of the Song of Solomon, in part to the sexual aberrations of celibate saints, is found in the work of this hard-headed Pagan philosopher: who was as celebrated for his practical kindness and robust common sense as for his transcendent intuitions of the One.

The greatest of the Pagan ecstatics, then, when speaking from experience, anticipates the Christian contemplatives. His words, too, when compared with theirs, show how delicate are the shades which distinguish ecstasy such as this from the highest forms of orison ; how clumsy are those psychologists who find in "passivity and annihilation of the will" its governing state. "Energizing enthusiastically"—not in itself, or by means of its poor scattered faculties, but in the Divine Life, to which it is conjoined for an instant of time "centre to centre," "per-

[1] *Op. cit., loc. cit.*

ceiver and perceived made one "—this is as near as the subtle intellect of Alexandria can come to the reality of that experience in which the impassioned mono-ideism of great spiritual genius conquers the rebellious senses and becomes, if only for a moment, operative on the highest levels accessible to the human soul. Self-mergence, then—that state of transcendence in which, the barriers of selfhood abolished, we "receive the communication of Life and of Beatitude, in which all things are consummated and all things are renewed "[1]—is the secret of ecstasy, as it was the secret of contemplation. On their spiritual side the two states cannot, save for convenience of description, be divided. Where contemplation becomes expansive, out-going, self-giving, and receives a definite fruition of the Absolute in return, its content is already ecstatic. Whether its outward form shall be so depends on the body of the mystic, not on his soul.

> " Se l' acto della mente
>   è tutto consopito,
>   en Dio stando rapito,
>   ch' en sé non se retrova.

> *   *   *

> En mezo de sto mare
>   essendo sì abyssato,
>   gia non ce trova lato
>   onde ne possa uscire.

> De sé non può pensare
>   né dir como è formato
>   però che, trasformato,
>   altro si ha vestire.

> Tutto lo suo sentire
>   en ben sì va notando,
>   belleza contemplando
>   la qual non ha colore."[2]

Thus sang Jacopone da Todi of the ecstatic soul : and here the

[1] Ruysbroeck, " De Contemplatione " (Hello, p. 144).
[2] "The activity of the mind is lulled to rest : wrapped in God, it can no longer find itself. . . . Being so deeply engulphed in that ocean now it can find no place to issue therefrom. Of itself it cannot think, nor can it say what it is like : because, transformed, it hath another vesture. All its perceptions have gone forth to gaze upon the Good, and contemplate that Beauty which has no likeness " (Lauda xci.).

descriptive powers of one who was both a poet and a mystic bring life and light to the dry theories of psychology.

He continues—and here, in perhaps the finest of all poetic descriptions of ecstasy, he seems to echo at one point Plotinus, at another Richard of St. Victor : to at once veil and reveal, by means of his perfect command of the resources of rhythm, the utmost secrets of the mystic life :—

> " Aperte son le porte
> facta ha conjunctione
> et è in possessione
> de tutto quel de Dio.
>
> Sente que non sentio,
> que non cognove vede,
> possede que non crede,
> gusta senza sapore.
>
> Però ch' à sé perduto
> tutto senza misura,
> possede quel altura
> de summa smesuranza.
>
> Perché non ha tenuto
> en sé altra mistura,
> quel ben senza figura
> receve en abondanza." [1]

This ineffable " awareness," *en dio stando rapito*, this union with the Imageless Good, is not the only—though it is the purest—form taken by ecstatic apprehension. Many of the visions and voices described in a previous chapter were experienced in the entranced or ecstatic state, generally when the first violence of the rapture was passed. St. Francis and St. Catherine of Siena both received the stigmata in ecstasy : almost all the entrancements of Suso, and many of those of St. Teresa and Angela of Foligno, entailed symbolic vision, rather than pure perception of the Absolute. More and more, then, we are forced to the opinion that ecstasy, in so far as it is not a

---

[1] " The doors are flung wide : conjoined to God, it possesses all that is in Him. It feels that which it felt not : sees that which it knew not, possesses that which it believed not, tastes, though it savours not.   Because it is wholly lost to itself, it possesses that height of Unmeasured Perfection.   Because it has not retained in itself the mixture of any other thing, it has received in abundance that Imageless Good " (*op. cit.*).

synonym for joyous and expansive contemplation, is really the name of the outward condition rather than of any one kind of inward experience.

RAPTURE

In all the cases which we have been considering—and they are characteristic of a large group—the onset of ecstasy has been seen as a gradual, though always involuntary, process. Generally it has been the culminating point of a period of contemplation. The self, absorbed in the orison of quiet or of union, or some analogous concentration on its transcendental interests, has passed over the limit of these states, and slid into a still ecstatic trance, with its outward characteristics of rigid limbs, cold, and depressed respiration.

The ecstasy however, instead of developing naturally from a state of intense absorption in the Divine Vision, may seize him abruptly and irresistibly when he in his normal state of consciousness. This is strictly that which ascetic writers mean by Rapture. We have seen that the essence of the mystic life consists in the remaking of personality: its entrance into a conscious relation with the Absolute. This process is accompanied in the mystic by the development of an art expressive of his peculiar genius: the art of contemplation. His practice of this art, like the practice of poetry, music, or any other form of creation, may follow normal lines, at first amenable to the control of his will, and always dependent on his own deliberate attention to the supreme Object of his quest; that is to say, on his orison. His mystic states, however they may end, will owe their beginning to a voluntary act upon his part: a turning from the visible to the invisible world. Sometimes, however, his genius for the transcendent becomes too strong for the other elements of character, and manifests itself in psychic disturbances—abrupt and ungovernable invasions from the subliminal region—which make its exercise parallel to the "fine frenzy" of the prophet, the composer, or the poet. Such is *Rapture*: a violent and uncontrollable expression of genius for the Absolute, which temporarily disorganizes and may permanently injure the nervous system of the self. Often, but not necessarily, Rapture—like its poetic equivalent—yields results of great splendour and value for life. But it is an accident, not an implicit of mystical experience : an indication of disharmony between the subject's psycho-physical make-up and his transcendental powers.

Rapture, then, may accompany the whole development of selves of an appropriate type. We have seen that it is a common incident in mystical conversion. The violent uprush of subliminal intuitions by which such conversion is marked disorganizes the normal consciousness, overpowers the will and the senses, and entails a more or less complete entrancement. This was certainly the case with Suso and Rulman Merswin, and probably with Pascal : whose "Certitude, Peace, Joy" sums up the exalted intuition of Perfection and Reality— the conviction of a final and unforgettable knowledge—which is characteristic of all ecstatic perception.

In her Spiritual Relations, St. Teresa speaks in some detail of the different phases or forms of expression of these violent ecstatic states : trance, which in her system means that which we have called ecstasy, and transport, or "flight of the spirit," which is the equivalent of rapture. "The difference between trance and transport," she says, "is this. In a trance the soul gradually dies to outward things, losing the senses and living unto God. But a transport comes on by one sole act of His Majesty, wrought in the innermost part of the soul with such swiftness that it is as if the higher part thereof were carried away, and the soul were leaving the body." [1]

Rapture, says St. Teresa in another place, "comes in general as a shock, quick and sharp, before you can collect your thoughts, or help yourself in any way ; and you see and feel it as a cloud, or a strong eagle rising upwards and carrying you away on its wings. I repeat it : you feel and see yourself carried away, you know not whither." [2] This carrying-away sensation may even assume the concrete form which is known as levitation : when the upward and outward sensations so dominate the conscious field that the subject is convinced that she is raised bodily from the ground. "It seemed to me, when I tried to make some resistance, as if a great force beneath my feet lifted me up. I know of nothing with which to compare it ; but it was much more violent than the other spiritual visitations, and I was therefore as one ground to pieces. . . . And further, I confess that it threw me into a great fear, very great indeed at

---

[1] Relaccion viii. 8 and 10.   [2] Vida, cap. xx. § 3.

first; for when I saw my body thus lifted up from the earth, how could I help it? Though the spirit draws it upwards after itself, and that with great sweetness if unresisted, the senses are not lost ; *at least I was so much myself as to be able to see that I was being lifted up.*" [1]

So Rulman Merswin in the rapture which accompanied his conversion, was carried round the garden with his feet off the ground : [2] and St. Catherine of Siena, in a passage which I have already quoted, speaks of the strength of the spirit, which raises the body from the earth.[3]

The subjective nature of this feeling of levitation is practically acknowledged by St. Teresa when she says, "When the rapture was over, my body seemed frequently to be buoyant, as if all weight had departed from it ; so much so, that now and then I scarcely knew that my feet touched the ground. But during the rapture the body is very often as it were dead, perfectly powerless. It continues in the position it was in when the rapture came upon it—if sitting, sitting." [4] Obviously here the outward conditions of physical immobility coexisted with the subjective sensation of being " lifted up."

The self's consciousness when in the condition of rapture may vary from the complete possession of her faculties claimed by St. Teresa to a complete entrancement. However abrupt and ungovernable the on-coming of the transport is, it does not follow that the mystic instantly loses his surface-consciousness of what is taking place. "There remains the power of seeing and hearing ; but it is as if the things heard and seen were at a great distance far away." [5] They have retreated, that is to say, to the fringe of the conscious field, but may still remain just within it. Though the senses may not be entirely entranced, however, it seems that the power of movement is always lost : and that, as in ecstasy, breathing and circulation are much diminished.

"When the Divine Bridegroom desires to enrapture the soul, He orders all the doors of its habitations, even those of the castle and its outworks, to be closed. In fact, hardly has one entered the rapture, when one ceases to breathe ;

---

[1] St. Teresa, *op. cit., loc. cit.,* §§ 7 and 9.
[2] *Supra*, p. 224.
[3] Dialogo, cap. lxxix.
[4] Vida, cap. xx, § 23.
[5] *Ibid.*

and if sometimes one retains for a few moments the use of one's other senses, one cannot, nevertheless, speak a single word. At other times, all the senses are instantly suspended ; the hands and the whole body become so intensely cold that the soul seems to be separated therefrom. Sometimes it is difficult to know whether one still breathes. Rapture lasts but a short time, at least at this high degree : the extreme suspension is relaxed, and the body seems to regain life, that it may die anew in the same manner, and make the soul more living than before." [1]

This spiritual storm, then, in St. Teresa's opinion, enhances the vitality of those who experience it : makes them " more living than before." It initiates them into " heavenly secrets," and if it does not do this it is no " true rapture," but a " physical weakness such as women are prone to owing to their delicacy of constitution." Its sharpness and violence, however, leaves considerable mental disorder behind it : " for the rest of the day, and sometimes for several days, the will seems overcome, the understanding is beside itself : the soul seems incapable of applying itself to anything else but the Love of God ; and she applies herself to this with the more ardour that she feels nothing but disgust for created things." [2]

But when equilibrium is re-established, the true effects of this violent and beatific intuition of the Absolute begin to invade the normal life. The self which has thus been caught up to the highest levels of Reality, is stung to new activity by the strength of its impressions. It now desires an eternal union with that which it has beheld ; with which for a brief moment it has been merged. The peculiar talent of the mystic ; that wild genius, that deep-seated power of perceiving Reality which his contemplations have ordered and developed, and his ecstasies express, here reacts upon his life-process, his slow journey from the Many to the One. His nostalgia has been increased by a glimpse of the homeland. His intuitive apprehension of the Absolute, which assumes in ecstasy its most positive form, spurs him on towards that total and permanent union with the Divine which is his goal. " Such great graces,"

[1] St. Teresa, " El Castillo Interior," Moradas Sextas, cap. iv.
[2] *Op. cit., loc. cit.*

says St. Teresa, "leave the soul avid of total possession of that Divine Bridegroom who has conferred them." [1]

Hence the ecstatic states do not merely lift the self to an abnormal degree of knowledge : they enrich her life, contribute to the remaking of her consciousness, develop and uphold the "strong and stormy love which drives her home." They give her the clearest vision she can have of that transcendent standard to which she must conform : entail her sharpest consciousness of the inflow of that Life on which her little striving life depends. Little wonder, then, that—though the violence of their onset may often try his body to the full—the mystic comes forth from a "good ecstasy" as Pascal from the experience of the Fire, humbled yet exultant, marvellously strengthened ; and ready, not for any passive enjoyments, but rather for the struggles and hardships of the Way, the deliberate pain and sacrifice of love.

In the third Degree of Ardent Love, says Richard of St. Victor, love paralyses action. Union (*copula*) is the symbol of this state : ecstasy is its expression. The desirous soul, he says finely, no longer thirsts *for* God but *into* God. The pull of its desire draws it into the Infinite Sea. The mind is borne away into the abyss of Divine Light, and, wholly forgetful of exterior things, knows not even itself, but passes utterly into its God. In this state, all earthly desire is absorbed in the heavenly glory. "Whilst the mind is separated from itself, and whilst it is borne away into the secret place of the divine mystery and is surrounded on all sides by the fire of divine love, it is inwardly penetrated and inflamed by this fire, and utterly puts off itself and puts on a divine love : and being conformed to that Beauty which it has beheld, it passes utterly into that other glory." [2]

Thus does the state of ecstasy contribute to the business of deification ; of the remaking of the soul's substance in conformity with the Goodness, Truth, and Beauty which is God. "Being conformed to that beauty which it has beheld, it passes utterly into that other glory "; into the flaming heart of Reality, the deep but dazzling darkness of its home.

---

[1] St. Teresa, *op. cit.*, cap. vi.
[2] "De Quatuor Gradibus Violentae Charitatis" (paraphrase).

CHAPTER IX

THE DARK NIGHT OF THE SOUL

We return to a study of the mystical life-process—The swing-back from illumination—The Dark Night—(1) Its psychological character—A period of psychic fatigue—Reaction from the strain of mystical lucidity—The sorting-house of the spiritual life—Its on-set is gradual—Madame Guyon—A state of mental chaos—The transition to new levels of consciousness—Mystical adolescence—Psycho-spiritual parallelism—Augustine Baker—(2) Its mystical character—Takes many forms—Emotional, Intellectual, Volitional—A completion of Purgation—The final purification of self-hood—The passage from Luna to Sol—Always painful—Its principal forms—(a) The loss of the presence of God—St. John of the Cross—Madame Guyon—Extinction of the transcendental consciousness—(b) The acute sense of imperfection—St. John of the Cross—(c) Loss of mystic feeling—Spiritual ennui—Ruysbroeck—(d) Intellectual impotence—Loss of will-power—St. Teresa—(e) The pain of God, or dark ecstasy—St. Teresa—All these are aspects of one state—The purification of the whole Personality—An episode in character building—Essential to the attainment of Reality—William Law—Surrender—St. Catherine of Siena—Adaptation to environment—St. John of the Cross—A process beyond the self's control—Self-naughting—Spiritual Poverty—Tauler—The Dark an incident of the movement to union—Its gradual disappearance—Madame Guyon—An "example from life"—Suso—Reasons for this choice—His entrance on the night—The Vision of the Upper School—The Vision of Knighthood—His education in manliness—The ideal of spiritual chivalry—The final trial—Its human characteristics—Suso and the Baby—The last crisis—The act of surrender—The passing of the Dark Night

WE have wandered during the last few chapters from our study of the mystical life-process in man, the organic growth of his transcendental consciousness, in order to examine the by-products of that process, its characteristic forms of self-expression : the development of its normal art of contemplation or introversion, and the visions and voices, ecstasies and raptures which are frequent—though not essential—accompaniments of its activity, of the ever-increasing predominance of its genius for the Real.

But the mystic, like other persons of genius, is man first and artist afterwards. We shall make a grave though common

mistake if we forget this and allow ourselves to be deflected
from our study of his growth in personality by the wonder and
interest of his art. Being, not Doing, is the first aim of the
mystic ; and hence should be the first interest of the student of
mysticism. We have considered for convenience' sake all the
chief forms of mystical activity at the half-way house of the
transcendental life : but these activities are not, of course,
peculiar to any one stage of that life. Ecstasy, for instance,
is as common a feature of mystical conversion as of the last
crisis, or " mystic marriage " of the soul :[1] whilst visions and
voices—in selves of a visionary or auditory type—accompany
and illustrate every phase of the inward development. They
lighten and explain the trials of Purgation as often as they
express the joys of Illumination, and frequently mark the crisis
of transition from one mystic state to the next.

One exception, however, must be made to this rule. The
most intense period of that great swing-back into darkness
which usually divides the "first mystic life," or Illuminative
Way, from the "second mystic life," or Unitive Way, is
generally a period of utter blankness and stagnation, so far
as mystical activity is concerned. The "Dark Night of the
Soul," once fully established, is seldom lit by visions or made
homely by voices. It is of the essence of its miseries that the
once-possessed power of orison or contemplation is now wholly
lost. The self is tossed back from its hard won point of
vantage. Impotence, blankness, solitude, are the epithets by
which those immersed in this dark fire of purification describe
their pains. It is this extraordinary episode in the life-history
of the mystic type to which we have now come.

We have already noticed [2] the chief psychological characteristics of all normal mystical development. We have seen
that the essence of this development consists in the effort to
establish a new equilibrium, to get, as it were, a firm foothold
upon transcendent levels of reality ; and that in its path
towards this consummation the self experiences a series of
oscillations between " states of pleasure " and " states of pain."
Put in another way it is an orderly movement of the whole
consciousness towards higher centres, in which each intense and

progressive affirmation fatigues the immature transcendental powers, and is paid for by a negation ; either a swing-back of the whole consciousness, a stagnation of intellect, a reaction of the emotions, or an inhibition of the will.

Thus the exalted consciousness of Divine Perfection which the self acquired in its "mystical awakening" was balanced by a depressed and bitter consciousness of its own inherent imperfection, and the clash of these two perceptions spurred it to that laborious effort of accommodation which constitutes the "Purgative Way." The renewed and ecstatic awareness of the Absolute which resulted, and which was the governing characteristic of Illumination, brings with it of necessity its own proper negation : the awareness, that is to say, of the self's continued separation from and incompatibility with that Absolute which it has perceived.   During the time in which the illuminated consciousness is fully established, the self, as a rule, is perfectly content : believing that in this sublime vision of Eternity, this intense and loving consciousness of God, it has reached the goal of its quest.   Sooner or later, however, psychic fatigue sets in ; the state of illumination begins to break up, the complementary negative consciousness appears, and shows itself as an overwhelming sense of darkness and deprivation. This sense is so deep and strong that it breaks all communication set up between the self and the Transcendent ; swamps its intuitions of Reality ; and plunges that self into the state of negation and unutterable misery which is called the Dark Night.

Now we may look at the Dark Night, as at most other incidents of the Mystic Way, from two points of view : (1) We may see it, with the psychologist, as a moment in the history of mental development, governed by the more or less mechanical laws which so conveniently explain to him the psychic life of man : or (2) with the mystic himself, we may see it in its spiritual aspect as contributing to the remaking of character, the growth of the "New Man" ; his "transmutation in God."

(1) Psychologically considered, the Dark Night is an example of the operation of the law of reaction from stress. It is a period of fatigue and lassitude following a period of sustained mystical activity.   "It is one of the best established laws of the nervous system," says Starbuck, "that it has

periods of exhaustion if exercised continuously in one direction, and can only recuperate by having a period of rest." [1]
However spiritual he may be, the mystic—so long as he is
in the body—cannot help using the machinery of his nervous
and cerebral system in the course of his adventures. His
development, on its psychic side, consists in the taking over of
this nervous machinery, the capture of its centres of consciousness, in the interests of his growing transcendental life. In so
far, then, as this is so, that transcendental life will be partly
conditioned by psychic necessities, will be amenable to the
laws of reaction and of fatigue. Each great step forward
will entail a period of lassitude and exhaustion in that mental machinery which he has pressed into service and probably
overworked. When the higher centres have become exhausted
under the great strain of a developed illuminated life, with
its accompanying periods of intense lucidity, of deep contemplation, perhaps of visionary and auditory phenomena, the
swing-back into the negative state occurs almost of necessity.

This is the psychological explanation of those strange
and painful episodes in the lives of great saints, and also of
lesser initiates of the spiritual sphere: when, perhaps after a
long, life passed in close contact with the transcendental
order, of full and growing consciousness of the "presence of
God," the whole inner experience is suddenly swept away,
and only a blind reliance on past convictions saves them
from unbelief.[2] The great contemplatives, those destined to
attain the full stature of the mystic, emerge from this period
of destitution, however long and drastic it may be, as from a
new purification. It is for them the gateway to a higher
state. But persons of lesser genius cannot pass this way. If
they enter the Night at all, it is to succumb to its dangers
and pains. This "great negation" is the sorting-house of
the spiritual life. Here we part from the "nature mystics,"
the mystic poets, and all who shared in and were contented
with the illuminated vision of reality. Those who go on are
the great and strong spirits, who do not seek to *know*, but
are driven to *be*.

[1] "Psychology of Religion," p. 24.
[2] An example of this occurred in the later life of Ste. Jeanne Françoise de Chantal.
See "The Nuns of Port Royal," by M. E. Lowndes (1909), p. 284.

We are to expect, then, as a part of the conditions under which human consciousness appears to work, that for every affirmation of the mystic life there will be a negation waiting for the unstable self. This rule is of universal application. The mystic's progress in orison, for instance, is marked by just such an alternation of light and shade: of "dark contemplation" and sharp intuitions of Reality. So too in selves of extreme nervous instability, each separate joyous ecstasy entails a painful or negative ecstasy. The states of darkness and illumination coexist over a long period, alternating sharply and rapidly. Many seers and artists pay in this way, by agonizing periods of impotence and depression, for each violent outburst of creative energy.

The periods of rapid oscillation between a joyous and a painful consciousness occur most often at the beginning of a new period of the mystic way: between Purgation and Illumination, and again between Illumination and the Dark Night: for these mental states are, as a rule, gradually not abruptly established. Mystics call such oscillations the "Game of Love" in which God plays, as it were, "hide and seek" with the questing soul. I have already quoted a characteristic instance from the life of Rulman Merswin,[1] who passed the whole intervening period between his conversion and entrance on the Dark Night or "school of suffering love" in such a state of disequilibrium. Thus too Madame Guyon, who has described at great length and with much elaboration of detail all her symptoms and sufferings during the oncoming and duration of the Night—or, as she calls its intensest period, the Mystic Death—traces its beginning in short recurrent states of privation, or dullness of feeling, such as ascetic writers call "aridity": in which the self loses all interest in and affection for those divine realities which had previously filled its life. This privation followed upon, or was the reaction from, an "illuminated" period of extreme joy and security, in which, as she says, "the presence of God never left her for an instant"; so that it seemed to her that she already enjoyed the Beatific Vision. "But how dear I paid for this time of happiness! For this possession, which seemed to me entire and perfect; and the more perfect the more it was secret, and foreign to the

[1] *Vide supra*, p. 274.

senses, steadfast and exempt from change; was but the preparation for a total deprivation, lasting many years, without any support or hope of its return." [1] Between this state of happiness and the " total deprivation " or true " dark night " comes the intermediate condition of alternating light and darkness. As Madame Guyon never attempted to control any of her states, but made a point of conforming to her own description of the "resigned soul" as "God's weathercock," we have in her an unequalled opportunity of studying the natural sequence of development.

"I endured," she says, "long periods of privation, towards the end almost continual: but still I had from time to time inflowings of Thy Divinity so deep and intimate, so vivid and so penetrating, that it was easy for me to judge that Thou wast but hidden from me and not lost. For although during the times of privation it seemed to me that I had utterly lost Thee, a certain deep support remained, though the soul knew it not: and she only became aware of that support by her subsequent total deprivation thereof. Every time that Thou didst return with more goodness and strength, Thou didst return also with greater splendour; so that in a few hours Thou didst rebuild all the ruins of my unfaithfulness and didst make good to me with profusion all my loss.   But it was not thus in those times of which I am going to speak." [2]

Here we have, from the psychological point of view, a singularly perfect example of the violent oscillations of consciousness on the threshold of a new state. The old equilibrium, the old grouping round a centre characterized by pleasure-affirmation has been lost; the new grouping round a centre characterized by pain-negation is not yet established. Madame Guyon is standing, or rather swinging, between two worlds, the helpless prey of her own shifting and uncontrollable psychic and spiritual states. But slowly the pendulum approaches its limit: the states of privation, as she says, "become almost continual," the reactions to illumination become less and less. At last they cease entirely, the new state is established, and the Dark Night has really set in.

The theory here advanced that the "Dark Night" is, on its

---

[1] Vie, pt. i. cap. xx.   [2] Op. cit., cap. xxi.

psychic side, partly a condition of fatigue, partly a state of transition, is borne out by the mental and moral disorder which seems, in many subjects, to be its dominant character. When they are in it everything seems to "go wrong" with them. They are tormented by evil thoughts and abrupt temptations, lose grasp not only of their spiritual but also of their worldly affairs. Their health often suffers, they become "odd" and their friends forsake them ; their intellectual life is at a low ebb. In their own words "trials of every kind," "exterior and interior crosses," abound.

Now "trials," taken *en bloc*, mean a disharmony between the self and the world with which it has to deal. Nothing is a trial when we are able to cope with it efficiently. Things try us when we are not adequate to them : when they are abnormally hard or we abnormally weak. This aspect of the matter becomes prominent when we look further into the history of Madame Guyon's experiences. Thanks to the unctuous and detailed manner in which she has analyzed her spiritual griefs, this part of her autobiography is a psychological document of unique importance for the study of the "Dark Night."

As her consciousness of God was gradually extinguished, a sort of mental and moral chaos seems to have invaded Madame Guyon, and to have accompanied the more spiritual destitution and miseries of her state. "So soon as I perceived the happiness of any state, or its beauty, or the necessity of a virtue, it seemed to me that I fell incessantly into the contrary vice : as if this perception, which though very rapid was always accompanied by love, were only given to me that I might experience its opposite, in a manner which was all the more terrible because of the horror which I still felt for it. It was then, O my God, that the evil which I hated, that I did : and the good which I loved, that I did not.[1] I was given an intense perception of the purity of God ; and so far as my feelings went, I became more and more impure : for in reality this state is very purifying, but I was then very far from understanding this. . . . My imagination was in a state of appalling confusion, and gave me no rest. I could not speak of Thee, oh my God, for I became utterly stupid ; nor could I even grasp what was

---

[1] Apparently Romans vii. 15, paraphrase ; Madame Guyon's quotations of Scripture seldom agree with the Vulgate.

said when I heard Thee spoken of. Instead of that heavenly peace in which my soul had been as it were confirmed and established, there was nothing but the sorrow of hell. . . . I found myself hard towards God, insensible to His mercies; I could not perceive any good thing that I had done in my whole life. The good appeared to me evil; and—that which is terrible—it seemed to me that this state must last for ever. For I did not believe it to be a state, but a true falling away. For if I had been able to believe that it was a state, or that it was necessary or agreeable to God, I should not have suffered from it at all."[1]

In the midst of all this wretchedness she felt, she says, that this world as well as the next was now leagued against her. "External crosses" of every kind, loss of health and friendship, domestic vexations, increased and kept pace with her interior griefs. Self-control and power of attention were diminished. She seemed stupefied and impotent, unable to follow or understand even the services of the Church, incapable of all orison and all good works; perpetually attracted by those worldly things which she had renounced, yet quickly wearied by them. The neat edifice of her first mystic life was in ruins, the state of consciousness which accompanied it was disintegrated, but nothing arose to take its place.

"It is an amazing thing," says Madame Guyon naïvely, "for a soul that believed herself to be advanced in the way of perfection, when she sees herself thus go to pieces all at once."[2]

So, too, Suso, when he had entered the "upper school" of the spiritual life, was tormented not only by temptations and desolations, but by outward trials and disabilities of every kind: calumnies, misunderstanding, difficulties, pains. "It seemed at this time as if God had given permission both to men and demons to torment the Servitor," he says.[3] This sense of a generally inimical atmosphere, and of the dimness and helplessness of the Ego oppressed by circumstance, is like the vague distress and nervous sensibility of adolescence, and comes in part from the same cause: the intervening period of chaos between the break-up of an old state of equilibrium and the establishment of the new. The self in its necessary movement

[1] *Op. cit.*, cap. xxiii.   [2] "Les Torrents," pt. i. cap. vii. § 2.
[3] Leben, cap. xxii.

towards higher levels of reality, loses and leaves behind certain elements of its world, long loved but now outgrown: as children must make the hard transition from nursery to school. Destruction and construction here go together: the exhaustion and ruin of the illuminated consciousness is the signal for the onward movement of the self towards other centres: the feeling of deprivation and inadequacy which comes from the loss of that consciousness, is an indirect stimulus to new growth. The self is being pushed into a new world where it does not feel at home; has not yet reached the point at which it enters into conscious possession of its second, or adult life.

" Thou hast been a child at the breast, a spoiled child," said the Eternal Wisdom to Suso. " Now I will withdraw all this." In the resulting darkness and confusion, when the old and known supports are thus withdrawn, the self can do little but surrender itself to the inevitable process of things: to the operation of that unresting Spirit of Life which is pressing it on towards a new and higher state, in which it shall not only see Reality but *be* real.

Psychologically, then, the " Dark Night of the Soul " is due to the double fact of the exhaustion of an old state, and the growth towards a new state of consciousness. It is a " growing pain " in the great organic process of the self's attainment of the Absolute. The great mystics, creative geniuses in the realm of character, have known instinctively how to turn these psychic disturbances to spiritual profit. Parallel with the mental oscillations, upheavals and readjustments, through which an unstable psycho-physical type moves to new centres of consciousness, run the spiritual oscillations of a striving and ascending spiritual type. *Gyrans gyrando vadit spiritus.* The machinery of consciousness, over-stretched, breaks up, and seems to toss the self back to an old and lower level, where it loses its apprehensions of the transcendental world; as the child, when first it is forced to stand alone, feels weaker than it did in its mother's arms.

" For first He not only withdraws all comfortable observable infusions of light and grace, but also deprives her of a power to exercise any perceptible operations of her superior spirit and of all comfortable reflections upon His love, plunging her into the depth of her inferior powers," says Augustine Baker, the skilled director of souls, here anticipating the modern psychologist. "Here consequently," he continues, "her former calmness of passions is quite lost, neither can she introvert herself; sinful motions and suggestions do violently assault her, and she finds as great difficulty (if not greater) to surmount them as at the beginning of a spiritual course. . . . If she would elevate her spirit, she sees nothing but clouds and darkness. She seeks God, and cannot find the least marks or footsteps of His Presence ; something there is that hinders her from executing the sinful suggestions within her, but what that is she knows not, for to her thinking she has no spirit at all, and, indeed, she is now in a region of all other most distant from spirit and spiritual operations—I mean, such as are perceptible." [1]

Such an interval of chaos and misery may last for months, or even for years, before the consciousness again unifies itself and a new centre is formed. Moreover, the negative side of this new centre, this new consciousness of the Absolute, often discloses itself first. The self realizes, that is to say, the inadequacy of its old state, long before it grasps the possibility of a new and higher state. This realization will take two forms : (*a*) Objective : the distance or absence of the Absolute which the self seeks ; (*b*) Subjective : the self's weakness and imperfection. Both apprehensions constitute a direct incentive to action. They present, as it were, a Divine Negation which the self must probe, combat, resolve.

The Dark Night, therefore, largely the product of natural causes, is the producer in its turn of mystical energy; and hence of supernatural effects.

(2) So much for psychology. We now turn from a consideration of purely psychic processes to study the mystical or transcendental aspects of the Dark Night : to see what it has meant for those mystics who have endured it, and for those spiritual specialists who have studied it in the interests of other men.

As in other departments of mystical activity, so here, we must beware of any generalization which tempts us to look upon the "Dark Night" as a uniform experience, a neatly-defined state which appears under the same conditions, and attended by the same symptoms, in all the selves who have passed

[1] "Holy Wisdom," Treatise iii. § iv. cap. v.

through its pains. It is a name for the painful and negative
state which normally intervenes between the Illuminative and
the Unitive Life—no more. Different types of contemplatives
have interpreted it to themselves and to us in very different
ways; each type of illumination being in fact balanced by its
own appropriate type of "dark."

In some temperaments it is the emotional aspect—the
anguish of the lover who has suddenly lost the Beloved—which
predominates: in others, the intellectual darkness and confusion
overwhelms everything else. Some have felt it, with Madame
Guyon and St. John of the Cross, as a "passive purification," a
state of limp misery, in which the self does nothing, but lets
Life have its way with her. Others, with Suso and the virile
mysticism of the German school, have put a more manly interpretation on its pains; finding in it a period of strenuous
activity running counter to all the inclinations of the natural
man. Those elements of character which were unaffected by
the first purification of the self—left as it were in a corner when
the consciousness moved to the level of the illuminated life—
are here roused from their sleep, purged of illusion, and forced
to join the growing stream; the "torrent" in Madame Guyon's
imagery, which sets towards the Infinite Sea.

The Dark Night, then, is really a deeply human process, in
which the self which thought itself so spiritual, so firmly established upon the supersensual plane, is forced to turn back, to
leave the Light, and pick up those qualities which it had left
behind. Only thus, by the transmutation of the *whole man*, not
by a careful and departmental cultivation of that which we like
to call his "spiritual" side, can Divine Humanity be formed:
and the formation of Divine Humanity—the remaking of man
"according to the pattern showed him in the mount"—is the
mystic's only certain ladder to the Real. "My humanity," said
the Eternal Wisdom to Suso, "is the road which all must tread
who would come to that which thou seekest." [1] This "hard
saying" might almost be used as a test by which to distinguish
the true and valid mystical activity of man from its many and
specious imitations. The self in its first purgation has cleansed
the mirror of perception; hence, in its illuminated life, has seen
Reality. In so doing it has transcended the normal perceptive

[1] " Buchlein von der ewigen Weisheit," cap. ii.

powers of "natural" man, immersed in the illusions of sense. Now, it has got to *be* reality: a very different thing. For this, a new and more drastic purgation is needed—not of the organs of perception, but of the very shrine of self: that "heart" which is the seat of personality, the source of its love and will. In the stress and anguish of the Night, when it turns back from the vision of the Infinite, to feel the limitations of the finite again, the self loses the power to Do; and learns to surrender its will to the operation of a larger Life, that it may Be. As the alchemist, when he has found Luna, or Silver, is not content, but tosses it back into the crucible in order that he may complete the "great work" and transmute it into Philosophic Gold: so that Indwelling Spirit which is the Artist of man's destinies, labouring at his transmutation from unreal to real, tosses back the illuminated self into the melting-pot that it may become the raw material of Divine Humanity, the "noble stone."

We must remember, in the midst of this cold-blooded analysis, that the mystic life is a life of love: that the Object of the mystic's final quest and of his constant intuition is an object of wild adoration and supreme desire. "With Thee a prison would be a rose garden, oh Thou ravisher of hearts: with Thee Hell would be Paradise, oh Thou cheerer of souls," said Jelalu 'd 'Din.[1] Hence for the mystic who has once known the Beatific Vision, there can be no greater grief than the withdrawal of this Object from his field of consciousness; the loss of this companionship, the extinction of this Light. Therefore, whatever form the "Dark Night" assumes, it must entail bitter suffering: far worse than that endured in the Purgative Way. Then the self was forcibly detached from the imperfect. Now the Perfect is withdrawn, leaving behind an overwhelming yet impotent conviction of something supremely wrong, some final Treasure lost. We will now look at a few of the characteristic forms under which this conviction is translated to the surface-consciousness.

A. To those temperaments in which consciousness of the Absolute took the form of a sense of divine companionship, and for whom the objective idea "God" had become the central fact of life, it seems as though that God, having shown Himself, has

[1] From the "Mesnevi." Quoted in the Appendix to "The Flowers or Rose Garden of Sādi."

now deliberately withdrawn His Presence, never perhaps to manifest Himself again. "He acts," says Eckhart, "as if there were a wall erected between Him and us."[1] The "eye which looked upon Eternity" has closed, the old dear sense of intimacy and mutual love has given place to a terrible blank.

"The greatest affliction of the sorrowful soul in this state," says St. John of the Cross, "is the thought that God has abandoned it, *of which it has no doubt;* that He has cast it away into darkness as an abominable thing . . . the shadow of death and the pains and torments of hell are most acutely felt, that is, the sense of being without God, being chastised and abandoned in His wrath and heavy displeasure. All this and even more the soul feels now, for a fearful apprehension has come upon it that thus it will be with it for ever. It has also the same sense of abandonment with respect to all creatures and that it is an object of contempt to all, especially to its friends."[2]

So, too, Madame Guyon felt this loss of her intuitive apprehension of God as one of the most terrible characteristics of the "night." "After Thou hadst wounded me so deeply as I have described, Thou didst begin, oh my God, to withdraw Thyself from me : and the pain of Thy absence was the more bitter to me, because Thy presence had been so sweet to me, Thy love so strong in me. . . . That which persuaded me, oh my God, that I had lost Thy love, was that instead of finding new strength in that strong and penetrating love, I had become more feeble and more impotent . . . for I knew not then what it is to lose one's own strength that we may enter into the strength of God. I have only learned this by a terrible and long experience. . . . Thy way, oh my God, before Thou didst make me enter into the state of death, was the way of the dying life : sometimes to hide Thyself and leave me to myself in a hundred weaknesses, sometimes to show Thyself with more sweetness and love. The nearer the soul drew to the state of death, the more her desolations were long and weary, her weaknesses increased, and also her joys became shorter, but purer and more intimate, until the time in which she fell into total privation."[3]

---

[1] Meister Eckhart, pred. lvii. So too St. Gertrude in one of her symbolic visions saw a thick hedge erected between herself and Christ.

[2] "Noche Escura del Alma" (Lewis's translation), l. ii. cap. vi.

[3] Vie, pt. i. cap. xxiii.

When this total privation, this "mystic death," as Madame
Guyon calls it—describing its episodes with much imagery of a
macabre and even revolting type—is fully established it involves
not only the personal "Absence of God," but the apparent
withdrawal or loss of that impersonal support, that transcendent Ground or spark of the soul, on which the self has long
felt its whole real life to be based. Hence, its last medium of
contact with the spiritual world is broken ; and as regards all
that matters, it does indeed seem to be "dead." "That *Somewhat* which supports us in our ground is that which it costs us
most to lose, and which the soul struggles with most violence to
retain : because, the more delicate it is, the more divine and
necessary it appears. . . . For what else does a soul desire in
her labours, but to have this witness in her ground that she is a
child of God ? And the goal of all spirituality is this experience.
Nevertheless, she must lose this with the rest . . . and this is
what works the true 'death of the soul,' for whatever miseries
she might have, if this Somewhat in which the soul's life consists
were not lost, she would be able to support herself and never
die. . . . It is then the loss of this imperceptible thing, and the
experience of this destitution, which causes the 'death.'" [1]
Contact, that is to say, between consciousness and the "spark
of the soul" is here broken off : and the transcendental faculties
retreating to their old place "below the threshold," are "dead"
so far as the surface-mind is concerned.

B. In those selves for whom the subjective idea "Sanctity"
—the need of conformity between the individual character and
the Transcendent—has been central, the pain of the Night is
less a deprivation than a new and dreadful kind of lucidity.
The vision of the Good brings to the self an abrupt sense of
her own hopeless and helpless imperfection : a black "conviction of sin," far more bitter than that endured in the Way of
Purgation, which swamps everything else. "That which makes
her pain so terrible is that she is, as it were, overwhelmed by
the purity of God, and this purity makes her see the least atoms
of her imperfections as if they were enormous sins, because of
the infinite distance there is between the purity of God and the
creature." [2]

---

[1] "Les Torrents," pt. i. cap. vii.
[2] Madame Guyon, *op. cit.*, pt. i. cap. vii.

"This," says St. John of the Cross again, "is one of the chief sufferings of this purgation. The soul is conscious of a profound emptiness, and destitution of the three kinds of goods, natural, temporal, and spiritual, which are ordained for its comfort; it sees itself in the midst of the opposite evils, miserable imperfections and aridities, emptiness of the understanding and abandonment of the spirit in darkness."[1]

C. Often combined with the sense of sin and the "absence of God" is another negation, not the least amazing and distressing part of the sufferings of the self suddenly plunged into the Night. This is a complete emotional lassitude: the disappearance of all the old ardours, now replaced by a callousness, a boredom, which the self detests but cannot overcome. It is the dismal condition of spiritual *ennui* which ascetic writers know so well under the name of "aridity," and which psychologists look upon as the result of emotional fatigue. To a person in this state, says Madame Guyon, "everything becomes insipid. She finds no taste in anything. On the contrary every act disgusts her."[2] It seems incredible that the eager love of a Divine Companion, so long the focus of her whole being, should have vanished: that not only the transcendent vision should be withdrawn, but her very desire for and interest in that vision should grow cold. Yet the mystics are unanimous in declaring that this is a necessary stage in the growth of the spiritual consciousness.

"When the sun begins to decline in the heavens," says Ruysbroeck, "it enters the sign Virgo; which is so called because this period of the year is sterile as a virgin." This is the autumn season in the cycle of the soul, when the summer heat grows less. "It completes the yearly travail of the Sun." "In the same manner, when Christ, that glorious sun, has risen to His zenith in the heart of man, as I have taught in the Third Mode, and afterwards begins to decline, to hide the radiance of His divine sunbeams, and to forsake man; then the heat and impatience of love grow less. Now that occultation of Christ, and the withdrawal of His light and heat, are the first work and the new coming of this Mode. Now Christ says inwardly to man, *Come forth in the manner*

---

[1] "Noche Escura del Alma," *loc. cit.*
[2] "Les Torrents," pt. i. cap. vii.

which I now show you : and man comes forth and finds himsèlf to be poor, miserable, and abandoned. Here all the storm, the fury, the impatience of his love, grow cool : glowing summer turns to autumn, all its riches are transformed into a great poverty. And man begins to complain because of his wretchedness : for where now are the ardours of love, the intimacy, the gratitude, all the pleasures of grace, the interior consolation, the secret joy, the sensible sweetness ? How have all these things failed him ? And the burning violence of his love, and all the gifts which he received ? How has all this died in him ? And he like some learned clerk who has lost all his learning and his works . . and of this misery there is born the fear of being lost, and as it were a sort of half-doubt: and this is the lowest point to which one can fall without despair." [1]

D. This stagnation of the emotions has its counterpart in the stagnation of the will and intelligence, which has been experienced by some contemplatives as a part of their negative state. As regards the will, there is a sort of moral dereliction: the self cannot control its inclinations and thoughts. In the general psychic turmoil, all the evil part of man's inheritance, all the lower impulses and unworthy ideas which have long been sternly, almost automatically imprisoned below the threshold, force their way into the field of consciousness. " I had thoughts of all the sins," says Madame Guyon, " though without committing them ; and these thoughts seemed to my mind to be realities because I felt that my heart was occupied by created things." [2]

Where visual and auditory automatism is established, these irruptions from the subliminal region often take the form of evil visions, or of voices making coarse or sinful suggestions to the self. Thus St. Catherine of Siena, in the interval between her period of joyous illumination and her " spiritual marriage," was tormented by visions of fiends, who filled her cell and " with obscene words and gestures invited her to lust." She fled from her cell to the church to escape them, but they pursued her there : and she obtained no relief from this obsession until she ceased to oppose it. She cried, " I have

[1] Ruysbroeck, " L'Ornement des Noces Spirituelles," l. ii. cap. xxviii.
[2] Vie, pt. i. cap. xxiii.

chosen suffering for my consolation, and will gladly bear these and all other torments in the name of the Saviour, for as long as it shall please His Majesty." With this act of surrender, the evil vision fled : Catherine swung back to a state of affirmation, and was comforted by a vision of the Cross.[1]

An analogous psychological state was experienced by St. Teresa ; though she fails to recognize it as an episode in her normal development, and attributes it, with other spiritual adventures for which she can find no other explanation, to the action of the Devil. " The soul," she says, "laid in fetters, loses all control over itself, and all power of thinking of anything but the absurdities he puts before it, which, being more or less unsubstantial, inconsistent, and disconnected, serve only to stifle the soul, so that it has no power over itself; and accordingly—so it seems to me—the devils make a football of it, and the soul is unable to escape out of their hands. It is impossible to describe the sufferings of the soul in this state. It goes about in quest of relief, and God suffers it to find none. The light of reason, in the freedom of its will, remains, but it is not clear; it seems to me as if its eyes were covered with a veil. . . . Temptations seem to press it down, and make it dull, so that its knowledge of God becomes to it as that of something which it hears of far away." This dullness and dimness extends to ordinary mental activity, which shares in the lassitude and disorder of the inner life. " If it seeks relief from the fire by spiritual reading, it cannot find any, just as if it could not read at all. On one occasion it occurred to me to read the life of a saint, that I might forget myself and be refreshed with the recital of what he had suffered. Four or five times, I read as many lines ; and though they were written in Spanish, I understood them less at the end than I did when I began : so I gave it up. It so happened to me on more occasions than one."[2] If we are reminded of anything here, it is of the phenomenon of " dark contemplation." That dimness of mind which we there studied, is here extended to the most normal activities of the surface intelligence. The Cloud of Unknowing, rolling up, seems to envelop the whole self. Contemplation, the " way within the way," has epitomized

---

[1] E. Gardner, "St. Catherine of Siena," p. 20.

[2] Vida, cap. xxx. §§ 13 and 14.

the greater process of the mystic life. In both, the path to Light lies through a meek surrender to the confusion and ignorance of the "Dark." The stress and exasperation felt in this dark, this state of vague helplessness, by selves of an active and self-reliant type, is exhibited by Teresa in one of her half-humorous self-revealing flashes. "The Devil," she says of it, "then sends so offensive a spirit of bad temper that I think I could eat people up!" [1]

All these types of "darkness," with their accompanying and overwhelming sensations of impotence and distress, are common in the lives of the mystics. We have seen them exhibited at length in Madame Guyon's writings. Amongst innumerable examples, Suso and Rulman Merswin also experienced them : Tauler constantly refers to them : Angela of Foligno speaks of a "privation worse than hell." It is clear that even Mechthild of Magdeburg, that sunshiny saint, knew the sufferings of the loss and absence of God. "Lord," she says in one place, "since Thou hast taken from me all that I had of Thee, yet of Thy grace leave me the gift which every dog has by nature : that of being true to Thee in my distress, when I am deprived of all consolation. This I desire more fervently than Thy heavenly Kingdom!" [2] In such a saying as this, the whole "value for life" of the Dark Night is abruptly revealed to us : as an education in selfless constancy, a "school of suffering love."

E. There is, however, another way in which the self's sense of a continued imperfection in its relation with the Absolute—of work yet remaining to be done—expresses itself. In persons of a very highly strung and mobile type, who tend to rapid oscillations between pain and pleasure states, rather than to the long, slow movements of an ascending consciousness, attainment of the Unitive Life is sometimes preceded by the abrupt invasion of a wild and unendurable desire to "see God" : to apprehend the Transcendent in Its fulness : which can only, they think, be satisfied by death. As they begin to outgrow their illuminated consciousness, these selves begin also to comprehend how partial and symbolic that consciousness—even at its best—has been : and their move-

---

[1] *Op. cit., loc. cit.*

[2] "Das Fliessende Licht der Gottheit," pt. ii. cap. 25.

ment to union with God is foreshadowed by a passionate and uncontrollable longing for ultimate Reality. This passion is so intense, that it causes acute anguish in those who feel it. It brings with it all the helpless and desolate feelings of the Dark Night; and sometimes rises to the heights of a negative rapture, an ecstasy of deprivation. St. Teresa is perhaps the best instance of this rather rare method of apprehending the self's essential separation from its home, which is also the subject of a celebrated chapter in the "Traité de l'Amour de Dieu" of St. Francis de Sales.[1] Thanks to her exceptionally mobile temperament, her tendency to rush up and down the scale of feeling, Teresa's states of joyous rapture were often paid for by such a "great desolation"—a dark ecstasy or "pain of God:" "As long as this pain lasts," she says, "it is impossible to the soul to think of anything that has to do with her own being: from the first instant all her faculties are suspended as far as this world is concerned, and they only preserve their activity in order to increase her martyrdom. Here I do not wish to be accused of exaggeration. I am sure, on the contrary, that what I say is less than the truth; for lack of words in which it may be expressed. This, I repeat, is an entrancement of the senses and the faculties as regards all which does not contribute to make the soul feel this pain. For the understanding perceives very clearly why the soul is in affliction, far from her God: and our Lord increases her grief in showing her in a vivid light His sovereign loveliness. The pain thus grows to such a degree of intensity that in spite of oneself one cries aloud. This is what happened to the person of whom I have spoken [St. Teresa herself] when she was in this state. In spite of her patience, in spite of her familiarity with suffering, she could not suppress those cries: because, as I have said, this is not a pain which is felt in the body, but in the depths of the soul. This person then learned how much more intense are the pains of the soul than those of the body."[2]

Moreover, the intense and painful concentration upon the Divine Absence which takes place in this "dark rapture"

---

[1] L. vi. cap. xiii.
[2] "El Castillo Interior," Moradas Sextas, cap. xi.

induces all the psycho-physical marks of ecstasy. " Although this ecstasy lasts but a short time, the bones of the body seem to be disjointed by it. The pulse is as feeble as if one were at the point of death, but whilst the natural heat of the body is lacking and almost extinguished, the soul on the contrary feels itself so burned up by the fire of its love, that with a few more degrees it would escape, as it desires, and throw itself into the arms of God. . . . You will tell me, perhaps, that there is imperfection in this desire to see God : and this humbled soul ought to conform herself to His will Who keeps her still in this exile. Before, I answer, she could do this ; and this consideration helped her to endure her life. But now, impossible ! She is no longer mistress of her reason, and can think of nothing but the causes of her affliction. Far from her Sovereign Good, how could she desire to live ? She feels in an extraordinary solitude : neither the creatures here below, nor even the inhabitants of heaven, are companionable to her, if He whom she loves be not in the midst of them. There is no alleviation to be found in this world : all, on the contrary, torments her. She is like a person suspended in the air, who can neither plant her foot upon the earth, nor raise herself to heaven. She burns with a consuming thirst, and cannot drink at the well which she desires. There is nothing in this world which can soothe the violence of that thirst : and besides, the soul would not consent to quench it with any other water than that of which our Lord spoke to the Samaritan woman, and this water is denied her." [1]

Now all these forms of the Dark Night—the " Absence of God," the sense of sin, the dark ecstasy, the loss of the self's old passion, peace and joy, and its apparent relapse to lower spiritual and mental levels—are considered by the mystics themselves to constitute aspects or parts of one and the same process : the final purification of the will or stronghold of personality, that it may be merged without any reserve " in God where it was first." The function of this process upon the Mystic Way is to cure the soul of the innate tendency to seek and rest in spiritual joys ; to confuse Reality with the joy given by the contemplation of Reality. It

---

[1] St. Teresa, *op. cit.*, *loc. cit.* Compare the Vida, cap. xx. §§ 11 to 14.

is the completion of that ordering of disordered loves, that transvaluation of values, which the Way of Purgation began. The ascending self must leave these childish satisfactions; make its love absolutely disinterested, strong, and courageous, abolish all taint of spiritual gluttony. A total abandonment of the personal standard, of that trivial and egotistic quest of personal success which thwarts the great movement of the Flowing Light, is the supreme condition of man's participation in Reality. This is true not only of the complete participation which is possible to the great mystic, but of those unselfish labours in which the initiates of science or of art become to the Eternal Goodness "what his own hand is to a man." " Think not," says Tauler, " that God will be always caressing His children, or shine upon their head, or kindle their hearts as He does at the first. He does so only to lure us to Himself, as the falconer lures the falcon with its gay hood. . . . We must stir up and rouse ourselves and be content to leave off learning, and no more enjoy feeling and fire, and must now serve the Lord with strenuous industry and at our own cost." [1]

This manly view of the Dark Night as a growth in responsibility—an episode of character-building—in which, as the " Mirror of Simple Souls " has it, " the soul leaves that pride and play wherein it was full gladsome and jolly," is characteristic of the German mystics. We find it again in Suso, to whom the angel of his tribulation gave no sentimental consolations ; but only the stern command, " *Viriliter agite* "— " Be a man ! " " Then first," says Tauler again, " do we attain to the fullness of God's love as His children, when it is no longer happiness or misery, prosperity or adversity, that draws us to Him or keeps us back from Him. What we should then experience none can utter ; but it would be something far better than when we were burning with the first flame of love, and had great emotion, but less true submission." [2]

In Illumination, the soul, basking in the uncreated Light, identified the Divine Nature with the divine light and sweetness which it then enjoyed. Its consciousness of the

[1] Sermon for the 4th Sunday in Lent (Winkworth's translation, p. 280).
[2] *Op. cit., loc. cit.*

transcendent has been felt chiefly as an increase of personal
vision and personal joy. Thus, in that apparently selfless
state, the "I, the Me, the Mine," though spiritualized, still
remained intact. The mortification of the senses was more
than repaid by the rich and happy life which this mortification conferred upon the soul. But before real and permanent
union with the Absolute can take place : before the whole
self can learn to live on those high levels where—its being
utterly surrendered to the Infinite Will—it can be wholly
transmuted in God, merged in the great life of the All; this
separated life, this dependence on personal joys, must be done
away. The spark of the soul, the fast-growing germ of
divine humanity, must so invade every corner of character
that the self can only say with St. Catherine of Genoa, "My
me is God : nor do I know my selfhood except in God."[1]

The various torments and desolations of the Dark Night
,constitute this last and drastic purgation of the spirit; the
doing away of separateness, the annihilation of selfhood, even
though all that self now claims for its own be the Love
of God. Such a claim—which is really a claim to entire
felicity, since the soul which possesses it needs nothing more
—is felt by these great spirits to sully the radiance of their
self-giving love. "All that I would here say of these inward
delights and enjoyments," says William Law, "is only this ;
they are not holiness, they are not piety, they are not perfection ; but they are God's gracious allurements and calls
to seek after holiness and spiritual perfection . . . and ought
rather to convince us that we are as yet but *babes*, than
that we are really *men* of God. . . . This alone is the true
Kingdom of God opened in the soul when, stripped of all
selfishness, it has only one love and one will in it ; when it
has no motion or desire but what branches from the Love
of God, and resigns itself wholly to the Will of God. . . .
To sum up all in a word : Nothing hath separated us
from God but our own will, or rather our own will is our
separation from God. All the disorder and corruption and
malady of our nature lies in a certain fixedness of our own
will, imagination, and desire, wherein we live to ourselves,
are our own centre and circumference, act wholly from our-

[1] Vita e Dottrina, cap. xiv.

selves, according to our own will, imagination, and desires. There is not the smallest degree of evil in us but what arises from this selfishness, because we are thus all in all to ourselves. . . . To be humble, mortified, devout, patient in a certain degree, and to be persecuted for our virtues, is no hurt to this selfishness ; nay, *spiritual-self* must have all these virtues to subsist upon, and his life consists in seeing, knowing, and feeling the bulk, strength, and reality of them. But still, in all this show and glitter of virtue, there is an unpurified bottom on which they stand, there is a selfishness which can no more enter into the Kingdom of Heaven than the grossness of flesh and blood can enter into it. What we are to feel and undergo in these last purifications, when the deepest root of all selfishness, as well spiritual as natural, is to be plucked up and torn from us, or how we shall be able to stand in that trial, are both of them equally impossible to be known by us beforehand." [1]

The self, then, has got to learn to cease to be its "own centre and circumference" : to make that final surrender which is the price of final peace. In the Dark Night the starved and tortured spirit learns through an anguish which is, as Madame Guyon says, "itself an orison" to accept lovelessness for the sake of Love, Nothingness for the sake of the All ; dies without any sure promise of life, loses when it hardly hopes to find. It sees with amazement the most sure foundations of its transcendental life crumble beneath it, dwells in a darkness which seems to hold no promise of a dawn. This is what the German mystics call the "upper school of true resignation" or of "suffering love" ; the last test of heroic detachment, of manliness, of spiritual courage. Though such an experience is "passive" in the sense that the self can neither enter nor leave it at will, it is a direct invitation to active endurance, a condition of stress in which work is done. Thus, when St. Catherine of Siena was tormented by hideous visions of sin, she was being led by her deeper self to the heroic acceptance of this subtle form of torture, almost unendurable to her chaste and delicate mind. When these trials had brought her to the point at which she ceased to resist them, but exclaimed, " I have chosen suffering

[1] "Christian Regeneration" (The Liberal and Mystical Writings of William Law, pp. 158–60).

for my consolation," their business was done. They ceased.
More significant still, when she asked, " Where wast Thou, Lord
when I was tormented by this foulness?" the Divine Voice
answered, " I was in thy heart." [1]

" In order to raise the soul from imperfection," said the Voice
of God to St. Catherine in her Dialogue, " I withdraw Myself
from her sentiment, depriving her of former consolations . . .
which I do in order to humiliate her, and cause her to seek Me
in truth, and to prove her in the light of faith, so that she come
to prudence.   Then, if she love Me without thought of self, and
with lively faith and with hatred of her own sensuality, she
rejoices in the time of trouble, deeming herself unworthy of
peace and quietness of mind.   Now comes the second of the
three things of which I told thee, that is to say : how the soul
arrives at perfection, and what she does when she is perfect.
That is what she does.   Though she perceives that I have
withdrawn Myself, she does not, on that account, look back ;
but perseveres with humility in her exercises, remaining barred
in the house of self-knowledge, and, continuing to dwell therein,
awaits with lively faith the coming of the Holy Spirit, that is of
Me, who am the Fire of Love. . . . This is what the soul does
in order to rise from imperfection and arrive at perfection, and
it is to this end, namely, that she may arrive at perfection, that I
withdraw from her, not by grace, but by sentiment.   Once more
do I leave her so that she may see and know her defects, so that
feeling herself deprived of consolation and afflicted by pain, she
may recognize her own weakness, and learn how incapable she
is of stability or perseverance, thus cutting down to the very
root of spiritual self-love: for this should be the end and
purpose of all her self-knowledge, to rise above herself, mounting the throne of conscience, and not permitting the sentiment
of imperfect love to turn again in its death-struggle, but, with
correction and reproof, digging up the root of self-love with the
knife of self-hatred and the love of virtue." [2]

" Digging up the root of self-love with the knife of self-
hatred "—here we see the mystical reason of that bitter self-
contempt and sense of helplessness which overwhelms the soul
in the Dark Night.   Such a sense of helplessness is really, the
mystics say, a mark of progress : of deeper initiation into that

[1] *Vide supra*, p. 469.   [2] Dialogo, cap. lxiii.

sphere of reality to which it is not yet acclimatized, and which brings with it a growing consciousness of the appalling disparity between that Reality, that Perfection, and the imperfect soul.

The self is in the dark because it is blinded by a Light greater than it can bear. " The more clear the light, the more does it blind the eyes of the owl, and the stronger the sun's rays the more it blinds the visual organs; overcoming them, by reason of their weakness, and depriving them of the power of seeing. So the divine light of contemplation, when it beats on the soul not yet perfectly enlightened, causes spiritual darkness, not only because it surpasses its strength, but because it blinds it and deprives it of its natural perceptions. . . . As eyes weakened and clouded by humours suffer pain when the clear light beats upon them, so the soul, by reason of its impurity, suffers exceedingly when the divine light really shines upon it. And when the rays of this pure light shine upon the soul, in order to expel its impurities, the soul perceives itself to be so unclean and miserable that it seems as if God had set Himself against it, and itself were set against God. . . . Wonderful and piteous sight! so great are the weakness and impurity of the soul that the hand of God, so soft and so gentle, is felt to be so heavy and oppressive, though neither pressing nor resting on it, but merely touching it, and that, too, most mercifully ; for He touches the soul, not to chastise it, but to load it with His graces." [3]

The Dark Night then, whichever way we look at it, is a state of disharmony ; of imperfect adaptation to environment. The self, unaccustomed to that direct contact of the Absolute which is destined to become the Source of its vitality and its joy, feels the "soft and gentle touch" of the Following Love as unbearable in its weight. The "self-naughting" or "purification of the will," which here takes place, is the struggle to resolve that disharmony, to purge away the somewhat which still sets itself up in the soul as separate from the Divine : and makes the clear light of reality a torment instead of a joy. So deeply has the soul now entered into the great stream of spiritual life, so dominant has her transcendental faculty become, that this process is accomplished in her whether she will or no: and in this sense it is, as ascetic writers sometimes call it, a "passive purgation." So long as the subject still feels himself to be *somewhat* he

[3] St. John of the Cross, " Noche Escura del Alma," l. ii. cap. v.

has not yet annihilated selfhood and come to that ground where his being can be united with the Being of God.

Only when he learns to cease thinking of himself at all, in however depreciatory a sense ; when he abolishes even such selfhood as lies in a desire for the sensible presence of God, will that harmony be attained. This is the " naughting of the soul," the utter surrender to the great movement of the Absolute Life, which is insisted upon at such length by all writers upon mysticism. Here, as in purgation, the condition of access to higher levels of vitality is a death : a deprivation, a detachment, a clearing of the ground. Poverty leaps to the Cross : and finds there an utter desolation, without promise of spiritual reward. The satisfactions of the spirit must now go the same way as the satisfactions of the senses. Even the power of voluntary sacrifice and self-discipline is taken away. A dreadful *ennui*, a dull helplessness, takes its place. The mystic motto, *I am nothing, I have nothing, I desire nothing*, must now express not only the detachment of the senses, but the whole being's surrender to the All.

The moral condition towards which the interior travail is directed is that of an utter humility. " Everything depends," says Tauler, on " a fathomless sinking in a fathomless nothingness." He continues, " If a man were to say, ' Lord, who art Thou, that I must follow Thee through such deep, gloomy, miserable paths ? ' the Lord would reply, ' I am God and Man, and far more God.' If a man could answer then, really and consciously from the bottom of his heart, ' Then I am nothing and less than nothing ' ; all would be accomplished, for the Godhead has really no place to work in, but ground where all has been annihilated.[1] As the schoolmen say, when a new form is to come into existence, the old must of necessity be destroyed. . . . And so I say : ' If a man is to be thus clothed upon with this Being, all the forms must of necessity be done away that were ever received by him in all his powers—of perception, knowledge, will, work, of subjection, sensibility and self-seeking.' When St. Paul saw nothing, he saw God. So also when Elias wrapped his face in his mantle, God came. All strong rocks are broken here, all on which the spirit can rest must be done away. Then, when all forms have ceased to

---

[1] *I.e.*, the pure essence of the soul, purged of selfhood and illusion.

exist, in the twinkling of an eye the man is transformed. Therefore thou must make an entrance. Thereupon speaks the Heavenly Father to him: "Thou shalt call Me Father, and shalt never cease to enter in; entering ever further in, ever nearer, so as to sink the deeper in an unknown and unnamed abyss; and, above all ways, images and forms, and above all powers, to lose thyself, deny thyself, and even unform thyself." In this lost condition nothing is to be seen but a ground which rests upon itself, everywhere one Being, one Life. It is thus, man may say, that he becomes unknowing, unloving, and senseless." [1]

It is clear that so drastic a process of unselfing is not likely to take place without stress. It is the negative aspect of "deification": in which the self, deprived of "perception, knowledge, will, work, self-seeking"—the I, the Me, the Mine—loses itself, denies itself, unforms itself, drawing "ever nearer" to the One, till "nothing is to be seen but a ground which rests upon itself"—the Ground of the soul, which is God.

"Everywhere one Being, one Life"—this is the goal of mystical activity; the final state of equilibrium towards which the self is moving, or rather struggling, in the dimness and anguish of the Dark Night. "The soul," says Madame Guyon in a passage of unusual beauty, "after many a redoubled death, expires at last in the arms of Love; but she is unable to perceive these arms. . . . Then, reduced to Nought, there is found in her ashes a seed of immortality, which is preserved in these ashes and will germinate in its season. But she knows not this; and does not expect ever to see herself living again." Moreover, "the soul which is reduced to the Nothing, ought to dwell therein; without wishing, since she is now but dust, to issue from this state, nor, as before, desiring to live again. She must remain as something which no longer exists: and this, in order that the Torrent may drown itself and lose itself in the Sea, never to find itself in its selfhood again: that it may become one and the same thing with the Sea." [2]

So Hilton says of the "naughted soul," "the less that it thinketh that it loveth or seeth God, the nearer it nigheth

[1] Sermon on St. Matthew ("The Inner Way," pp. 204, 205).
[2] "Les Torrents," pt. i. cap. viii.

for to perceive the gift of this blessed love; for then is love master, and worketh in the soul, and maketh it forget itself, and for to see and look on only how love worketh: and then is the soul more suffering than doing, and that is pure love." [1]

The "mystic death" or Dark Night is therefore an aspect or incident of the self's self-loss in the Abyss of the Divine Life; of that mergence and union of the soul with the Absolute which is the whole object of the mystical evolution of man. It is the last painful break with the life of illusion, the tearing away of the self from that World of Becoming in which all its natural affections and desires are rooted, to which its intellect and senses correspond; and the thrusting of it into that World of Being where at first, weak and blinded, it can but find a wilderness, a "dark." No transmutation without fire, say the alchemists: No cross, no crown, says the Christian. All the great experts of the spiritual life agree—whatever be their creeds, their symbols, their explanation—in describing this stress, tribulation, and loneliness, as an essential part of the way from the Many to the One.

The Dark Night, then, brings the self to the threshold of that completed life which is to be lived in intimate union with Reality. It is the Entombment which precedes the Resurrection, say the Christian mystics; ever ready to describe their life-process in the language of their faith. Here as elsewhere—but nowhere else in so drastic a sense—the self must "lose to find and die to live."

The Dark Night, as we have seen, tends to establish itself gradually; the powers and intuitions of the self being withdrawn one after another, the intervals of lucidity becoming rarer, until the "mystic death" or state of total deprivation is reached. So, too, when the night begins to break down before the advance of the new or Unitive Life, the process is generally slow, though it may be marked—as for instance in Rulman Merswin's case—by visions and ecstasies.[2] One after another, the miseries and disharmonies of the Dark Night give way: affirmation takes the place of nega-

[1] "The Scale of Perfection," bk. iii. cap. v.
[2] Jundt, "Rulman Merswin," p. 22.

tion: the Cloud of Unknowing is pierced by rays of light. "When the old state of deprivation has reached its term," says Madame Guyon, "this dead self feels little by little, yet without feeling, that its ashes revive and take a new life: but this happens so gradually that it seems to her that it is but a fancy, or a sleep in which one has had a happy dream. . . . And in this consists the last degree; which is the beginning of the Divine and truly Interior Life which contains an infinite number of degrees, and wherein one may always go forward without end, even as this Torrent can always go forward in the Sea, and take therefrom the more qualities the longer it sojourns there." [1]

The act of utter surrender then, which is produced by the Dark Night, has given the self its footing in Eternity: the abandonment of the old centres of consciousness has permitted movement towards the new. In each such forward movement, the Transcendental Self, that spark of the soul which is united to the Absolute Life, has invaded more and more the seat of personality; advanced in that unresting process which involves the remaking of the self in conformity with the Eternal World. In the misery and apparent stagnation of the Dark Night, in that dimness of the spiritual consciousness, that dullness of its will and love, work has been done; and the last great stage of the inward transmutation accomplished. The self which comes forth from the night is no separated self, conscious of the illumination of the Uncreated Light, but the New Man, the transmuted humanity, whose life is *one* with the Absolute Life of God. "The instant the two houses of the soul [the sensual and the spiritual] are tranquil and confirmed," says St. John of the Cross, "with the whole household of its powers and desires sunk in sleep and silence, as to all things of heaven and earth, the Divine Wisdom immediately in a new bond of loving possession unites itself to the soul, and that is fulfilled which is written, 'While quiet silence contained all things and the night was in the midway of her course, Thy omnipotent Word sallied out of heaven from the royal seats' (Wisdom xviii. 14). The same truth is set before us in the Canticle, where the Bride, after passing by those who took her veil away and

[1] "Les Torrents," pt. i. cap. viii.

wounded her, saith, 'When I had a little passed by them I found Him whom my soul loveth' (Cant. iii. 4)."[1]

.   .   .   .   .

So far, we have considered the Dark Night of the Soul from a somewhat academic point of view. We have tried to dissect and describe it: have seen it through the medium of literature rather than of life. Such a proceeding has obvious disadvantages when dealing with any organic process: and in its application to the spiritual life of man, these disadvantages are increased. Moreover, our chief example, "from the life," Madame Guyon, valuable as her passion for self analysis makes her to the student of mystic states, cannot be looked upon as a wholly satisfactory witness. Her morbid sentimentalism, her absurd "spiritual self-importance" has to be taken into account and constantly remembered in estimating the value of her psychological descriptions. If we want to get a true objective idea of the Dark Night, we must see it in its wholeness as a part of the general life-process; not as a departmental experience. We must study the reactions of a self which is passing through this stage of development upon its normal environment, the content of its diurnal existence; not only on its intuition of the Divine.

As a pendant to this chapter, then, we will look at this "state of pain" as it expressed itself in the life of a mystic whose ardent, impressionable, and poetic nature reacted to every aspect of the contemplative experience, every mood and fluctuation of the soul. I choose this particular case— the case of Suso—(1) because it contains many interesting and unconventional elements; showing us the Dark Night not as a series of specific events, but as a stage of development largely conditioned by individual temperament: (2) because, being described to us at first hand, in the pages of his singularly ingenuous Autobiography, it is comparatively free from the reverent and corrupting emendations of the hagiographer.

Suso's "Life," from the 22nd chapter onwards, is one of the most valuable documents which we possess for the study of this period of the Mystic Way. We see in it—more clearly

---

[1] "Noche Escura del Alma," l. ii. cap. xxiv.

perhaps than its author can have done—the remaking of his consciousness, his temperamental reactions to the ceaseless and inexorable travail of his deeper self: so different in type from those of Madame Guyon and St. Teresa.   There is a note of virile activity about these trials and purifications, an insistence upon the heroic aspect of the spiritual life, which most of us find far more sympathetic than Madame Guyon's elaborate discourses on resignation and holy passivity, or even St. Teresa's "dark ecstasies" of insatiable desire.

The chapter in which Suso's entrance into this "Second Mystic Life" of deprivation is described is called "How the Servitor was led into the School of True Resignation." Characteristically, this inward experience expressed itself in a series of dramatic visions; visions of that "dynamic" kind which we have noticed as a common accompaniment of the crisis in which the mystic self moves to a new level of consciousness.[1]   It followed the long period of constant mortification and intermittent illumination which lasted, as he tells us, from his eighteenth to his fortieth year: and constituted the first cycle of his spiritual life.   At the end of that time, "God showed him that all this severity and these penances were but a good beginning, that by these he had triumphed over the unruly sensual man: but that now he must exert himself in another manner if he desired to advance in the Way."[2]

In two of these visions—these vivid interior dramas—we seem to see Suso's developed mystical consciousness running ahead of its experience, reading the hidden book of its own future, probing its own spiritual necessities; and presenting the results to the backward and unwilling surface-mind. This growing mystic consciousness is already aware of fetters which the normal Suso does not feel.   Its eyes open upon the soul's true country, it sees the path which it must tread to perfect freedom; the difference between the quality of that freedom and the spirituality which Suso thinks that he has attained.   The first of these visions is that of the Upper School; the second is that in which he is called to put upon him the armour of a knight.

"One night after matins, the Servitor being seated in his

---

[1] *Vide supra*, p. 348.   [2] Leben, cap. xx.

chair, and plunged in deep thought, he was rapt from his senses. And it seemed to him that he saw in a vision a magnificent young man descend from Heaven before him, and say, "Thou hast been long enough in the Lower School, and hast there sufficiently applied thyself. Come, then, with me ; and I will introduce thee into the highest school that exists in this world.[1] There, thou shalt apply thyself to the study of that science which will procure thee the veritable peace of God ; and which will bring thy holy beginning to a happy end." Then the Servitor rose, full of joy ; and it seemed to him that the young man took him by the hand and led him into a spiritual country, wherein there was a fair house inhabited by spiritual men : for here lived those who applied themselves to the study of this science. As soon as he entered it, these received him kindly, and amiably saluted him. And at once they went to the supreme Master, and told him that a man was come, who desired to be his disciple and to learn his science. And he said, "Let him come before me, that I may see whether he please me." And when the supreme Master saw the Servitor, he smiled on him very kindly, and said, "Know that this guest is able to become a good disciple of our high science, if he will bear with patience the hard probation : for it is necessary that he be tried inwardly."

"The Servitor did not then understand these enigmatic words. He turned toward the young man who had brought him and asked, "Well, my dear comrade, what then is this Upper School and this science of which you have spoken to me ?" The young man replied thus : "In this Upper School they teach the science of Perfect Self-abandonment ; that is to say, that a man is here taught to renounce himself so utterly that, in all those circumstances in which God is manifested, either by Himself or in His creatures, the man applies himself only to remaining calm and unmoved, renouncing so far as is possible all human frailty." And

---

[1] These expressions, the Upper and Lower School of the Holy Spirit, as applied to the first and second mystic life, were common to the whole group of "Friends of God," and appear frequently in their works. *Vide supra*, p. 441, Rulman Merswin's "Vision of Nine Rocks," where the man who has "gazed upon his Origin" is said to have been in the Upper School of the Holy Spirit ; *i.e.*, to have been united to God.

shortly after this discourse, the Servitor came to himself . . . and, talking to himself, he said, " Examine thyself inwardly, and thou wilt see that thou hast still much self-will: thou wilt observe, that with all thy mortifications which thou hast inflicted on thyself, thou canst not yet endure external vexations. Thou art like a hare hiding in a bush, who is frightened by the whispering of the leaves. Thou also art frightened every day by the griefs that come to thee: thou dost turn pale at the sight of those who speak against thee: when thou dost fear to succumb, thou takest flight; when thou oughtest to present thyself with simplicity, thou dost hide thyself. When they praise thee, thou art happy: when they blame thee, thou art sad. Truly it is very needful for thee that thou shouldst go to an Upper School." [1]

Some weeks later, when he had been rejoicing in the new bodily comfort which resulted from his relinquishment of all outward mortifications, Suso received a still more pointed lesson on his need of moral courage. He was sitting on his bed and meditating on the words of Job " Militia est." " The life of man upon the earth is like unto that of a knight " : [2] " and during this meditation, he was once more rapt from his senses, and it seemed to him that he saw coming towards him a fair youth of manly bearing, who held in his hands the spurs and the other apparel which knights are accustomed to wear. And he drew near to the Servitor, and clothed him in a coat of mail, and said to him, " Oh, knight! hitherto thou hast been but a squire, but now it is God's will that thou be raised to knighthood." And the Servitor gazed at his spurs, and said with much amazement in his heart, " Alas, my God! what has befallen me? what have I become? must I indeed be a knight? I had far rather remain in peace." Then he said to the young man, " Since it is God's will that I should be a knight I had rather have won my spurs in battle; for this would have been more glorious." The young man turned away and began to laugh: and said to him, " Have no fear! thou shalt have battles enough. He who would play a valiant part in the spiritual chivalry of God must endure more numerous and more dreadful combats than any which were encountered by the proud heroes of ancient

---

[1] Leben, cap. xxi.   [2] Job vii. 1 (Vulgate).

days, of whom the world tells and sings the knightly deeds. It is not that God desires to free thee from thy burdens; He would only change them, and make them far heavier than they have ever been." Then the Servitor said, " Oh, Lord, show me my pains in advance, in order that I may know them." The Lord replied, " No, it is better that thou know nothing, lest thou shouldst hesitate. But amongst the innumerable pains which thou wilt have to support, I will tell thee three. The first is this. Hitherto it is thou who hast scourged thyself, with thine own hands : thou didst cease when it seemed good to thee, and thou hadst compassion on thyself. Now, I would take thee from thyself, and cast thee without defence into the hands of strangers who shall scourge thee. Thou shalt see the ruin of thy reputation. Thou shalt be an object of contempt to blinded men ; and thou shalt suffer more from this than from the wounds made by the points of thy cross.[1] When thou didst give thyself up to thy penances thou wert exalted and admired. Now thou shalt be abased and annihilated. The second pain is this : Although thou didst inflict on thyself many cruel tortures, still by God's grace there remained to thee a tender and loving disposition. It shall befall thee, that there where thou hadst thought to find a special and a faithful love, thou shalt find nought but unfaithfulness, great sufferings, and great griefs. Thy trials shall be so many that those men who have any love for thee shall suffer with thee by compassion. The third pain is this : hitherto thou hast been but a child at the breast, a spoiled child. Thou hast been immersed in the divine sweetness like a fish in the sea. Now I will withdraw all this. It is my will that thou shouldst be deprived of it, and that thou suffer from this privation ; that thou shouldst be abandoned of God and of man, that thou shouldst be publicly persecuted by the friends of thine enemies. I will tell it thee in a word : all thou shalt undertake, that might bring thee joy and consolation, shall come to nothing, and all that might make thee suffer and be vexatious to thee shall succeed." [2]

[1] During the years of purgation Suso had constantly worn a sharp cross, the points of which pierced his flesh.

[2] Leben, cap. xxii.

Observe here, under a highly poetic and visionary method of presentation, the characteristic pains of the Dark Night as described by Madame Guyon, St. John of the Cross, and almost every expert who has written upon this state of consciousness. Desolation and loneliness, abandonment by God and by man, a tendency of everything to "go wrong," a profusion of unsought trials and griefs—all are here. Suso, naturally highly strung and unbalanced, sensitive and poetic, suffered acutely in this mental chaos and multiplication of woes. He was tormented by a deep and heavy depression, so that "it seemed as though a mountain weighed on his heart": by doubts against faith: by temptations to despair.[1] These miseries lasted for about ten years. They were diversified and intensified by external trials, such as illnesses and false accusations; and relieved, as the years of purgation had been, by occasional visions and revelations.

Suso's natural tendency was to an enclosed life: to secret asceticisms, dreams, outbursts of fervent devotion, long hours of rapt communion with the Eternal Wisdom whom he loved. Half artist, half recluse, utterly unpractical, he had all the dreamer's dread of the world of men. His deeper mystical self now ran counter to all these preferences. Like the angel which said to him in the hour of his utmost prostration and misery, " *Viriliter agite !* "[2] it pressed him inexorably towards the more manly part; pushing him to action, sending him out from his peaceful if uncomfortable cell to the rough-and-tumble of the world. Poor Suso was little fitted by nature for that rough-and-tumble: and a large part of his autobiography is concerned with the description of all that he endured therein. The Dark Night for him was emphatically an "active night"; and the more active he was forced to be, the darker and more painful it became. Chapter after chapter is filled with the troubles of the unhappy Servitor; who, once he began to meddle with practical life, soon disclosed his native simplicity and lost the reputation for wisdom and piety which he had obtained during his years of seclusion.

There was not in Suso that high-hearted gaiety, that child-like courage, which made the early Franciscans delight to call themselves God's fools. The bewildered lover of the

---

[1] Leben, cap. xxiii. [2] *Ibid.*, cap. xxv.

Eternal Wisdom suffered acutely from his loss of dignity; from the unfriendliness and contempt of his fellow-men. He gives a long and dismal catalogue of the enemies that he made, the slanders which he endured, in the slow acquirement of that disinterested and knightly valour which had been revealed to him as the essential virtue of the squire who would "ride with the Eternal Wisdom in the lists." [1]

Suso was a born romantic. This dream of a spiritual chivalry haunts him : over and over again he uses the language of the tournament in his description of the mystic life. Yet perhaps few ideals seem less appropriate to this timid, highly-strung, impracticable Dominican friar : this ecstatic "minne-singer of the Holy Ghost," half-poet, half-metaphysician, racked by ill-health, exalted by mystical ardours, instinctively fearing the harsh contact of his fellow-men.

There is no grim endurance about Suso : he feels every hard knock, and all the instincts of his nature are in favour of telling his griefs. A more human transcendentalist has never lived. Thanks to the candour and completeness with which he takes his readers into his confidence, we know him far more intimately than is the case with any of the other great contemplatives. There is one chapter in his life in which he describes with the utmost ingenuousness how he met a magnificent knight whilst crossing the Lake of Constance ; and was deeply impressed by his enthusiastic descriptions of the glories and dangers of the lists. The conversation between the tough man at arms and the hypersensitive mystic is full of revealing touches. Suso is exalted and amazed by the stories of hard combats, the courage of the knights, and the ring for which they contend : but most astounded by the fortitude which pays no attention to its wounds.

"And may not one weep, and show that one is hurt, when one is hit very hard ? " he says.

The knight replies, "No, even though one's heart fails, as happens to many, one must never show that one is dis-tressed. One must appear gay and happy ; otherwise one is dishonoured, and loses at the same time one's reputation and the Ring."

"These words made the Servitor thoughtful ; and he was

[1] "Buchlein von der ewigen Weisheit," cap. ii.

greatly moved, and inwardly sighing he said, ' Oh Lord, if the knights of this world must suffer so much to obtain so small a prize, how just it is that we should suffer far more if we are to obtain an eternal recompense ! Oh, my sweet Lord, if only I were worthy of being Thy spiritual knight ! ' "

Arrived at his destination, however, Suso was visited by fresh trials : and soon forgetting his valiant declarations, he began as usual to complain of his griefs. The result was a visionary ecstasy, in which he heard that voice of his deeper self, to which he always attributed a divine validity, inquiring with ill-concealed irony, " Well, what has become of that noble chivalry ? Who is this knight of straw, this rag-made man ? It is not by making rash promises and drawing back when suffering arrives, that the Ring of Eternity which you desire is won."

" Alas ! Lord," says Suso plaintively, " the tournaments in which one must suffer for Thee last such a very long time ! "

The voice replied to him, " But the reward, the honour, and the Ring which I give to My knights endures eternally." [1]

As his mystic consciousness grows, this instinct pressing him towards action and endurance grows with it. The inner voice and its visionary expression urges him on remorselessly. It mocks his weakness, encourages him to more active suffering, more complete self-renunciation : more contact with the unfriendly world. *Viriliter agite !* He is to be a complete personality ; a whole man. Instead of the quiet cell, the secret mortifications, his selfhood is to be stripped from him, and the reality of his renunciation tested, under the unsympathetic and often inimical gaze of other men. The case of Suso is one that may well give pause to those who regard the mystic life as a progress in passivity, a denial of the world : and the " Dark Night " as one of its most morbid manifestations.

---

[1] Leben, cap. xlvii. So Ruysbroeck, " The gold Ring of our Covenant is greater than Heaven or Earth " (" De Contemplatione "). Compare Vaughan the Silurist (" The World").

> "I saw Eternity the other night,
> Like a great Ring of pure and endless light,
>   All calm as it was bright ;
>
> .   .   .   .
>
>   One whispered thus :
> ' This Ring the Bridegroom did for none provide
>   But for His Bride.' "

It is interesting to observe how completely human and apparently "unmystical" was the culminating trial by which Suso was "perfected in the school of true resignation." "None can come to the sublime heights of the divinity," said the Eternal Wisdom to him in one of his visions, "or taste its ineffable sweetness, if first they have not experienced the bitterness and lowliness of My humanity. The higher they climb without passing by My humanity, the lower afterward shall be their fall. My humanity is the road which all must tread who would come to that which thou seekest : My sufferings are the door by which all must come in." [1] It was by the path of humanity ; by some of the darkest and most bitter trials of human experience, the hardest tests of its patience and love, that Suso "came in " to that sustained peace of heart and union with the divine will which marked his last state. The whole tendency of these trials in the " path of humanity " seems, as we look at them, to be directed towards the awakening of those elements of character left dormant by the rather specialized disciplines and purifications of his cloistered life. We seem to see the " new man " invading all the resistant or inactive corners of personality : the Servitor of Wisdom being pressed against his will to a deeply and widely human life in the interests of Eternal Love. The absence of God whom he loved, the enmity of man whom he feared, were the chief forces brought to play upon him : and we watch his slow growth, under their tonic influence, in courage, humility, and love of his fellow-men.

Few chapters in the history of the mystics are more touching than that passage in Suso's Life [2] " Where we speak of an extraordinary Trial which the Servitor had to bear." It tells how a malicious woman accused him of being the father of her child, and succeeded for the time in entirely destroying his reputation. "And the scandal was all the greater," says the Servitor with his customary simplicity, " because the rumour of that brother's sanctity had spread so far." Poor Suso was utterly crushed by this calumny, "wounded to the depths of his heart." " Lord, Lord ! " he cried, " every day of my life I have worshipped Thy holy Name in many places, and have helped to cause it to be loved and honoured by many men : and now Thou wouldst drag my name through the mud ! " When the

[1] " Buchlein von der ewigen Weisheit," cap. ii.   [2] Cap. xl.

scandal was at its height, a woman of the neighbourhood came to him in secret ; and offered to destroy the child which was the cause of this gossip, in order that the tale might be more quickly forgotten, and his reputation restored. She said further, that unless the baby were somehow disposed of, he would certainly be forced by public opinion to accept it, and provide for its upbringing. Suso, writhing as he was under the contempt of the whole neighbourhood, the apparent ruin of his career—knowing, too, that this calumny of one of their leaders must gravely injure the reputation of the Friends of God—was able to meet the temptation with a noble expression of trust. "I have confidence in the God of Heaven, Who is rich, and Who has given me until now all that which was needful unto me. He will help me to keep, if need be, another beside myself." And then he said to his temptress, "Go, fetch the little child that I may see it."

"And when he had the baby, he put it on his knees and looked at it : and the baby began to smile at him. And sighing deeply, he said, 'Could I kill a pretty baby that smiled at me ? No, no, I had rather suffer every trial that could come upon me !' And turning his face to the unfortunate little creature, he said to it, 'Oh my poor, poor little one ! Thou art but an unhappy orphan, for thy unnatural father hath denied thee, thy wicked mother would cast thee off, as one casts off a little dog that has ceased to please ! The providence of God hath given thee to me, in order that I may be thy father. I will accept thee, then, from Him and from none else. Ah, dear child of my heart, thou liest on my knees ; thou dost gaze at me, thou canst not yet speak ! As for me, I contemplate thee with a broken heart ; with weeping eyes, and lips that kiss, I bedew thy little face with my burning tears ! . . . Thou shalt be my son, and the child of the good God ; and as long as heaven gives me a mouthful, I shall share it with thee, for the greater glory of God ; and will patiently support all the trials that may come to me, my darling son !'" How different is this from the early Suso ; interested in little but his own safe spirituality, and with more than a touch of the religious æsthete !

The story goes on : "And when the hard-hearted woman who had wished to kill the little one saw these tears, when she heard these tender words, she was greatly moved : and her heart was filled with pity, and she too began to weep and cry aloud. The Servitor was obliged to calm her, for fear that, attracted by the noise, some one should come and see what was going on. And when she had finished weeping the Brother gave her back the baby, and blessed it, and said to it, ' Now may God in His goodness bless thee, and may the saints protect thee against all evil that may be ! ' And he enjoined the woman to care for it well at his expense."

Small wonder that after this heroic act of charity Suso's reputation went from bad to worse ; that even his dearest friends forsook him, and he narrowly escaped expulsion from the religious life. His torments and miseries, his fears for the future, continued to grow until they at last came to their term in a sort of mental crisis. "His feeble nature broken by the pains which he had to endure, he went forth raving like one who has lost his senses ; and hid himself in a place far from men, where none could see or hear him . . . and whilst he suffered thus, several times something which came from God said within his soul, ' Where then is your resignation ? Where is that equal humour in joy and in tribulation which you have so lightly taught other men to love ? In what manner is it, then, that one should rest in God and have confidence only in Him ? ' He replied weeping, ' You ask where is my resignation ? But tell me first, where is the infinite pity of God for His friends ? . . . Oh Fathomless Abyss ! come to my help, for without Thee I am lost. Thou knowest that Thou art my only consolation, that all my trust is only in Thee. Oh hear me, for the love of God, all you whose hearts are wounded ! Behold ! let none be scandalized by my insane behaviour. So long as it was only a question of preaching resignation, that was easy : but now that my heart is pierced, now that I am wounded to the marrow . . . how can I be resigned ? ' And after thus suffering half a day, his brain was exhausted, and at last he became calmer, and sitting down he came to himself : and turning to God, and abandoning himself to His Will, he said, ' If it cannot be otherwise, *fiat voluntas tua.*' "[1] The act of submission was at once followed by an ecstasy and vision, in which the approaching end of his troubles was announced to him. " And in the event, God came to the help of the Servitor, and little by little that terrible tempest died away."

[1] *Op. cit., loc. cit.*

Thus with Suso, as with St. Catherine of Siena and other mystics whom we have considered, the travail of the Dark Night is all directed towards the essential mystic act of utter self-surrender ; that *fiat voluntas tua* which marks the death of selfhood in the interests of a new and deeper life. He has learned the lesson of "the school of true resignation": has moved to a new stage of reality. His last state, allowing for temperamental differences, is in essence the same as Madame Guyon's "holy indifference": a complete self-naughting, an utter acquiescence in the large and hidden purposes of the Divine Will.

> "Anzi è formale ad esto beato *esse*
> tenersi dentro alla divina voglia
> per ch' una fansi nostre voglie stesse,"[1]

says Piccarda, announcing the primary law of Paradise. Suso has passed through the fire to the state in which he too can say, "*La sua voluntate è nostra pace.*" The old grouping of his consciousness round "spiritual self" has come to its head and at last broken down. In the midst of a psychic storm parallel to the upheavals of conversion, "mercenary love" is for ever disestablished, the new state of Pure Love is abruptly established in its place. Human pain is the price: the infinite joy peculiar to "free souls" is the reward. We may study the pain, but the nature of the joy is beyond us : as, in the Absolute Type of all mystic achievement, we see the Cross clearly but can hardly guess at the true nature of the resurrection life.

Hence Suso's description of his establishment in the Unitive Way seems meagre, an anti-climax, after all that went before. " And later," he says simply, "when God judged that it was time, He rewarded the poor martyr for all his suffering. And he enjoyed peace of heart, and received in tranquillity and quietness many precious graces. And he praised the Lord from the very depths of his soul, and thanked Him for those same sufferings : which, for all the world, he would not now have been spared. And God caused him to understand that by this complete abasement he had gained more, and was made the more worthy to be raised up to God, than by all the pains which he had suffered from his youth up to that time."[2]

[1] Par. iii. 79. "Nay, it is essential to this blessed being, to hold ourselves within the Will Divine wherewith our own wills are themselves made one."

[2] *Loc. cit.*

CHAPTER X

THE UNITIVE LIFE

WHAT is the Unitive Life? We have referred to it often enough in the course of this inquiry. At last we are face to face with the necessity of defining its nature if we can. Since the normal man knows little about his own true personality, and nothing at all about that of Deity, the orthodox description of it as " the life in which man's will is united with God," does but echo the question in an ampler form ; and conveys no real meaning to the student's mind.

That we should know, by instinct, its character from within—as we know, if we cannot express, the character of our own normally human lives—is of course impossible. We deal here with the final triumph of the spirit, the flower of mysticism, humanity's top note : the consummation towards which the contemplative life, with its long slow growth and psychic storms, has moved from the first. We look at a small but

ever-growing group of heroic figures, living at transcendent
levels of reality which we, immersed in the poor life of illusion,
cannot attain : breathing an atmosphere whose true quality we
cannot even conceive. Here, then, as at so many other points
in our study of the spiritual consciousness, we must rely for the
greater part of our knowledge upon the direct testimony of the
mystics ; who alone can tell the character of that " more abundant life" which they enjoy.

Yet we are not wholly dependent on this source of information. It is the peculiarity of the Unitive Life that it is often
lived, in its highest and most perfect forms, in the world ; and
exhibits its works before the eyes of men. As the law of our
bodies is " earth to earth " so, strangely enough, is the law of
our souls. Man, having at last come to full consciousness of
reality, completes the circle of Being ; and returns to fertilize
those levels of existence from which he sprang. Hence, the
enemies of mysticism, who have easily drawn a congenial moral
from the " morbid and solitary" lives of contemplatives in the
earlier and educative stages of the Mystic Way, are here confronted very often by the disagreeable spectacle of the mystic
as a pioneer of humanity, a sharply intuitive and painfully
practical person : an artist, a discoverer, a religious or social
reformer, a national hero, a " great active " amongst the saints.
By the superhuman nature of that which these persons accomplish, we can gauge something of the supernormal vitality of
which they partake. The things done, the victories gained
over circumstance by the Blessed Joan of Arc or by St. Bernard,
by St. Catherine of Siena, St. Ignatius Loyola, St. Teresa,
George Fox, are hardly to be explained unless these great
spirits had indeed a closer, more intimate, more bracing contact
than their fellows with that Life "which is the light of men."

We have, then, these two lines of investigation open to us :
first, the comparison and elucidation of that which the mystics
tell us concerning their transcendent experience, secondly, the
testimony which is borne by their lives to the existence within
them of supernal springs of action, contact set up with deep
levels of vital power. In the third place, we have also such
critical machinery as psychology has placed at our disposal ;
but this, in dealing with these giants of the spirit, must be used
with caution and humility.

The Unitive Life, though so often lived in the world, is never of it. It belongs to another plane of being, moves securely upon levels unrelated to our speech ; and hence eludes the measuring powers of humanity. We, from the valley, can only catch a glimpse of the true life of these elect spirits, transfigured upon the mountain. They are far away, breathing another air : we cannot reach them. Yet it is impossible to over-estimate their importance for the race. They are our ambassadors to the Absolute. They vindicate humanity's claim to the possible and permanent attainment of Reality ; bear witness to the practical qualities of the transcendental life. In Eucken's words, they testify to "the advent of a triumphing Spiritual Power, as distinguished from a spirituality which merely lays the foundations of life or struggles to maintain them" : [1] to the actually life-enhancing power of the Love of God, once the human soul is freely opened to receive it.

Coming first to the evidence of the mystics themselves, we find that in their attempts towards describing the Unitive Life they have recourse to two main forms of symbolic expression : both very dangerous, very liable to be misunderstood : both offering ample opportunity for harsh criticism to hostile investigators of the mystic type. We find also, as we might expect from our previous encounters with the symbols used by contemplatives and ecstatics, that these two forms of expression belong respectively to mystics of the transcendent-metaphysical and of the intimate-personal type : and that their formulæ, if taken alone, appear to contradict one another.

(1) The metaphysical mystic, for whom the Absolute is impersonal and transcendent, describes his final attainment of that Absolute as *deification*, or the utter transmutation of the self in God. (2) The mystic for whom intimate and personal communion has been the mode under which he best apprehended Reality, speaks of the consummation of this communion, its perfect and permanent form, as the *Spiritual Marriage* of his soul with God. Obviously, both these terms are but the self's guesses concerning the intrinsic character of a state which it has felt in its wholeness rather than analyzed : and bear the same relation to the ineffable realities of that state, as our clever theories concerning the nature

---

[1] "Der Sinn und Wert des Lebens," p. 140.

and meaning of life bear to the vital processes of men. It is worth while to examine them ; but we shall not understand them till we have also examined the life which they profess to explain.

The language of "deification" and of "spiritual marriage," then, is temperamental language : and is related to subjective experience rather than to objective fact. It describes on the one hand the mystic's sudden, astonished awareness of a profound change effected in his own personality [1]—the transmutation of his salt, sulphur, and mercury into Spiritual Gold—on the other, the rapturous consummation of his love. Hence by a comparison of these symbolic reconstructions, by the discovery and isolation of the common factor latent in each, we may perhaps learn something of the fundamental fact which each is trying to portray.

Again, the mystics describe certain symptoms either as the necessary preliminaries or as the marks and fruits of the Unitive State : and these too may help us to fix its character.

The chief, in fact the one essential, preliminary is that pure surrender of selfhood, or " self-naughting," which the trials of the Dark Night tended to produce. Only the thoroughly detached, "naughted soul" is "free," says the " Mirror of Simple Souls," and the Unitive State is essentially a state of free and filial participation in Eternal Life. The chief marks of the state itself are (1) a complete absorption in the interests of the Infinite, under whatever mode It happens to be apprehended by the self, (2) a consciousness of sharing Its strength, acting by Its authority, which results in a complete sense of freedom, an invulnerable serenity, and usually urges the self to some form of heroic effort or creative activity : (3) the establishment of the self as a " power for life," a centre of energy, an actual parent of spiritual vitality in other

---

[1] Compare Dante's sense of a transmuted personality when he first breathed the air of Paradise :—

> " S' io era sol di me quel che creasti
> novellamente, Amor che il ciel governi
> tu il sai, che col tuo lume mi levasti " (Par. i. 73).

" If I were only that of me which thou didst new create, oh Love who rulest heaven, thou knowest who with thy light didst lift me up."

men. By collecting together these symptoms and examining them, and the lives of those who exhibit them, in the light of psychology, we can surely get some news—however fragmentary—concerning the transcendent condition of being which involves these characteristic states and acts. Beyond this even Dante himself could not go :—

> " Trasumanar significar *per verba*
> non si poria." [1]

We will then consider the Unitive Life (1) As it appears from the standpoint of the psychologist. (2) As it is described to us by those mystics who use (*a*) the language of Deification, (*b*) that of Spiritual Marriage.   (3) Finally, we will turn to the lives of its initiates ; and try, if we can, to perceive it as an organic whole.

(1) From the point of view of the pure psychologist, what do the varied phenomena of the Unitive Life, taken together, seem to represent ? He would probably say that they indicate the final and successful establishment of that higher form of consciousness which has been struggling for supremacy during the whole of the Mystic Way. The deepest, richest levels of human personality have now attained to light and freedom. The self is remade, transformed, has at last unified itself ; and with the cessation of stress, power has been liberated for new purposes.

" The beginning of the mystic life," says Delacroix, " introduced into the personal life of the subject a group of states which are distinguished by certain characteristics, and which form, so to speak, a special psychological system. At its term, it has, as it were, suppressed the ordinary self, and by the development of this system has established a new personality, with a new method of feeling and of action. Its growth results in the transformation of personality : it abolishes the primitive consciousness of selfhood, and substitutes for it a wider consciousness : the total disappearance of selfhood in the divine, the substitution of a Divine Self for the primitive self." [2] If he be a psychological philosopher of Eucken's school, the psychologist will say further

---

[1] Par. i. 70.   [2] Delacroix, " Études sur le Mysticisme," p. 197.

that man, in this Unitive State, by this substitution of the divine for the "primitive" self, has at last risen to true freedom, "entered on the fruition of reality."[1] Hence he has opened up new paths for the inflow of that Triumphing Power which is the very substance of the Real; has wholly remade his consciousness, and in virtue of this total regeneration is "transplanted into that Universal Life, which is yet not alien but our own."[2] From contact set up with this Universal Life, this "Energetic Word of God, which nothing can contain"—from those deep levels of Being to which his shifting, growing personality is fully adapted at last—he draws that amazing strength, that immovable peace, that power of dealing with circumstance, which is one of the most marked characteristics of the Unitive Life. "That secret and permanent personality of a superior type"[3] which gave to the surface-self constant and ever more insistent intimations of its existence at every stage of the mystic's growth—his real, eternal self—has now consciously realized its destiny: and begins at last fully to *be*. In the travail of the Dark Night it has conquered and invaded the last recalcitrant elements of character. It is no more limited to acts of profound perception, overpowering intuitions of the Absolute: no more dependent for its emergence on the psychic states of contemplation and ecstasy. The mystic has at last resolved the Stevensonian paradox; and is not truly two, but truly *one*.

(2) The mystic, I think, would acquiesce in these descriptions, so far as they go: but he would probably translate them into his own words and gloss them with an explanation which is beyond the power and province of psychology. He would say that his long-sought correspondence with Transcendental Reality, his union with God, has now been finally established: that his self, though intact, is wholly penetrated—as a sponge by the sea—by the Ocean of Life and Love to which he has attained. "I live, yet not I but God in me." He is conscious that he is now at length cleansed of the last stains of separation, and has become, in a mysterious manner, "that which he beholds."

---

[1] "Der Sinn und Wert des Lebens," p. 12.

[2] *Ibid.*, p. 96.

[3] Delacroix, *op. cit.*, p. 114 (*vide supra*, p. 327.

In the words of the Sūfi poet, the mystic journey is now prosecuted not only *to* God but *in* God. He has entered the Eternal Order; attained here and now the state to which the Magnet of the Universe draws every living thing. Moving through periods of alternate joy and anguish, as his spiritual self woke, stretched, and was tested in the complementary fires of love and pain, he was inwardly conscious that he moved towards a definite objective. In so far as he was a great mystic, he was also conscious that this objective was no mere act of knowing, however intense, exultant, and sublime, but a condition of being, fulfilment of that love which impelled him, steadily and inexorably, to his own place. In the image of the alchemists, the Fire of Love has done its work : the mystic Mercury of the Wise—that little hidden treasure, that scrap of Reality within him—has utterly transmuted the salt and sulphur of his mind and his sense. Even the white stone of illumination, once so dearly cherished, he has resigned to the crucible. Now, the great work is accomplished, the last imperfection is gone, and he finds within himself the " Noble Tincture "—the gold of spiritual humanity.

(A) We have said that the mystic of the impersonal type—the seeker of a Transcendent Absolute—tends to describe the consummation of his quest in the language of *deification.*

The Unitive Life necessarily means for him, as for all who attain it, something which infinitely transcends the sum total of its symptoms : something which normal men cannot hope to understand. In it he declares that he "partakes directly of the Divine Nature," enjoys the fruition of reality. Since we "only behold that which we are," the doctrine of deification results naturally and logically from this claim.

"Some may ask," says the author of the " Theologia Germanica," "what is it to be a partaker of the Divine Nature, or a Godlike [*vergottet*, literally deified] man ? Answer : he who is imbued with or illuminated by the Eternal or Divine Light and inflamed or consumed with Eternal or Divine Love, he is a deified man and a partaker of the Divine Nature." [1]

Such a word as " deification " is not, of course, a scientific term. It is a metaphor, an artistic expression which tries to hint at a transcendent fact utterly beyond the powers of human

[1] " Theologia Germanica," cap. xli.

understanding, and therefore without equivalent in human speech : that fact of which Dante perceived the "shadowy preface" when he saw the saints as petals of the Sempiternal Rose.[1] Since we know not the being of God, the mere statement that a soul is transformed in Him may convey to us an ecstatic suggestion, but will never give exact information : except of course to those rare selves who have experienced these supernal states. Such selves, however—or a large proportion of them—accept this statement as approximately true. Whilst the more clear-sighted amongst them are careful to qualify it in a sense which excludes pantheistic interpretations, and rebuts the accusation that extreme mystics preach the annihilation of the self and regard themselves as co-equal with the Deity, they leave us in no doubt that it answers to a definite and normal experience of many souls who attain high levels of spiritual vitality. Its terms are chiefly used by those mystics by whom Reality is apprehended as a state or place rather than a Person :[2] and who have adopted, in describing the earlier stages of their journey to God, such symbols as those of rebirth or transmutation.

The blunt and positive language of these contemplatives concerning deification has aroused more enmity amongst the unmystical than any other of their doctrines or practices. It is of course easy, by confining oneself to its surface sense, to call such language blasphemous : and the temptation to do so has seldom been resisted. Yet, rightly understood, this doctrine lies at the heart, not only of all mysticism, but also of much philosophy and most religion. It pushes their first principles to a logical end. "The wonder of wonders," says Eucken, whom no one can accuse of a conscious leaning towards mystic doctrine, "is the human made divine."[3] Christian mysticism, says Delacroix with justice, springs from "that spontaneous and half-savage longing for deification which all religion contains."[4] Eastern Christianity has always accepted it and expressed it in her rites. "The Body of God deifies me and feeds me," says

[1] Par. xxx. 115–130 and xxxi. 1–12.
[2] Compare p. 153.
[3] "Der Wahrheitsgehalt der Religion," p. 433.
[4] *Op. cit.*, ix. But it is difficult to see why we need stigmatize as "half-savage" man's primordial instinct for his destiny.

Simeon Metaphrastes, "it deifies my spirit and it feeds my soul in an incomprehensible manner."[1]

The Christian mystics justify this dogma of the deifying of man, by exhibiting it as the necessary corollary of the Incarnation—the humanizing of God. They can quote the authority of the Fathers in support of this argument. "He became man that we might be made God," says St. Athanasius.[2] "I heard," says St. Augustine, speaking of his pre-converted period, "Thy voice from on high crying unto me, 'I am the Food of the full-grown : grow, and then thou shalt feed on Me. Nor shalt thou change Me into thy substance as thou changest the food of thy flesh, but thou shalt be changed into Mine.'"[3] Eckhart therefore did no more than expand the patristic view when he wrote, "Our Lord says to every living soul, 'I became man for you. If you do not become God for me, you do me wrong.'"[4]

If we are to allow that the mystics have ever attained the object of their quest, I think we must also allow that such attainment involves the transmutation of the self to that state which they call, for want of exact language, "deified." The necessity of such transmutation is an implicit of their first position : the law that "we behold that which we are, and are that which we behold." Eckhart, in whom the language of deification assumes its most extreme form, justifies it upon this necessity. "If," he says, "I am to know God directly, I must become completely He and He I : so that this He and this I become and are one I."[5]

God, said St. Augustine, is the country of the soul: its Home, says Ruysbroeck. The mystic in the unitive state is living in and of his native land ; no exploring alien, but a returned exile, now wholly identified with it, part of it, yet retaining his personality intact. As none know the spirit of England but the English ; and they know it by intuitive participation, by mergence, not by thought; so none but the "deified" know the secret life of God. This, too, is a knowledge conferred only by participation : by living a life, breathing an atmosphere : by "union with that same Light by which they see, and which they see."[6] It is one of those

[1] Divine Liturgy of the Orthodox Eastern Church. Prayers before Communion.
[2] Athanasius, De Incarn. Verbi, i. 108.   [3] Aug. Conf., bk. vii. cap. x.
[4] Pred. lvii.   [5] Pred. xcix. ("Mystische Schriften," p. 122).
[6] Ruysbroeck, "L'Ornement des Noces Spirituelles," l. iii. cap. v.

rights of citizenship which cannot be artificially conferred. Thus it becomes important to ask the mystics what they have to tell us of their life lived upon the bosom of Reality: and to receive their reports without prejudice, however hard be the sayings they contain.

The first thing which emerges from these reports, and from the choice of symbols which we find in them, is that the great mystics are anxious above all things to establish and force on us the truth that by *deification* they intend no arrogant claim to identification with God, but as it were a transfusion of their selves by His Self: an entrance upon a new order of life, so high and so harmonious with Reality that it can only be called divine. Over and over again they assure us that personality is not lost, but made more real. "When," says St. Augustine, "I shall cleave to Thee with all my being, then shall I in nothing have pain and labour; and *my life shall be a real life*, being wholly full of Thee." [1] "My life shall be a real life" because it is "full of Thee." The achievement of reality, and deification, are then one and the same thing: necessarily so, since we know that only the divine is the real. [2]

Mechthild of Magdeburg, and after her Dante, saw Deity as a flame or river of fire that filled the Universe; and the "deified" souls of the saints as ardent sparks therein, ablaze with that fire, one thing with it, yet distinct. [3] Ruysbroeck, too, saw "Every soul like a live coal, burned up by God on the hearth of His Infinite Love." [4] Such fire imagery has seemed to many of the mystics a peculiarly exact and suggestive symbol of the transcendent state which they are struggling to describe. No longer confused by the dim Cloud of Unknowing, they have pierced to its heart, and there found their goal: that uncreated and energizing Fire which guided the children of Israel through the night.

By a deliberate appeal to the parallel of such great impersonal forces—to Fire and Heat, Light, Water, Air—mystic writers seem able to bring out a perceived aspect of the Godhead, and of the transfigured soul's participation therein, which no

---

[1] Aug. Conf., bk. x. cap. xxviii.
[2] Cf. Coventry Patmore, "The Rod, the Root, and the Flower," "Magna Moralia," xxii. [3] Par. xxx. 64.
[4] "De Septem Gradibus Amoris," cap. xiv.

merely personal language, taken alone, can touch.   Thus
Boehme, trying to describe the union between the Word and
the soul, says, "I give you an earthly similitude of this.   Behold
a bright flaming piece of iron, which of itself is dark and
black, and the fire so penetrateth and shineth through the iron,
that it giveth light.   Now, the iron doth not *cease to be ;* it is
iron still : and the source (or property) of the fire retaineth its
own propriety : it doth not take the iron into it, but it penetrateth (and shineth) through the iron ; and it is iron then as well
as before, *free* in itself : and so also is the source or property of
the *fire*.   In such a manner is the soul set in the Deity ; the
Deity penetrateth through the soul, and dwelleth in the soul,
yet the soul doth not comprehend the Deity, but the Deity com-
prehendeth the soul, but doth not alter it (from being a soul)
but only giveth it the divine source (or property) of the
Majesty." [1]

Almost exactly the same image of deification was used,
five hundred years before Boehme's day, by Richard of St.
Victor ; a mystic whom he is hardly likely to have read.
"When the soul is plunged in the fire of divine love," he says,
"like iron, it first loses its blackness, and then, growing to white
heat, it becomes like unto the fire itself.   And lastly, it grows
liquid, and losing its nature is transmuted into an utterly
different quality of being."   "As the difference between iron that
is cold and iron that is hot," he says again, "so is the difference
between soul and soul : between the tepid soul and the soul
made incandescent by divine love." [2]   Other contemplatives
say that the deified soul is transfigured by the inundations
of the Uncreated Light : that it is like a brand blazing in the
furnace, transformed to the likeness of the fire.   "These souls,"
says the Divine voice to St. Catherine of Siena, "thrown into
the furnace of My charity, no part of their will remaining
outside but the whole of them being inflamed in Me, are like
a brand, wholly consumed in the furnace, so that no one can
take hold of it to extinguish it, because it has become fire.
In the same way no one can seize these souls, or draw them
outside of Me, because they are made *one thing* with Me
through grace, and I never withdraw Myself from them by

---

[1] "The Threefold Life of Man," cap. vi. 88.
[2] "De Quatuor Gradibus Violentae Charitatis" (Migne, Patrologia Latina cxcvi.).

sentiment, as in the case of those whom I am leading on to perfection."[1]

For the most subtle and delicate descriptions of the Unitive or Deified State, understood as self-loss in the " Ocean Pacific " of God, we must go to the great genius of Ruysbroeck. He alone, whilst avoiding all its pitfalls, has conveyed the suggestion of its ineffable joys in a measure which seems, as we read, to be beyond all that we had supposed possible to human utterance. Awe and rapture, theological profundity, keen psychological insight, are here tempered by a touching simplicity. We listen to the report of one who has indeed heard "the invitation of love" which "draws interior souls towards the One" and says "Come home." A humble receptivity, a meek self-naughting is with Ruysbroeck, as with all great mystics, the gate of the City of God. "Because they have given themselves to God in every action, omission or submission," he says of the deified souls, " they possess a peace and a joy, a consolation and a savour, that none can comprehend ; neither the world, nor the creature adorned for himself, nor whosoever prefers himself before God. These interior souls, these men of lucid vision, have before their eyes whensoever they will the invitation of love, which draws them towards the One, and which says, Come home. . .

Thus the spirit is caught by a simple rapture to the Trinity and by a threefold rapture to the Unity, and yet *never does the creature become God :* never is she confounded with Him. The union is brought about by Love ; but the creature sees and feels between God and herself an eternal and invincible distinction. However close the union may be, yet heaven and earth, which have come forth from the hands of God, still hide impenetrable secrets from the spirit of the contemplative. When God gives Himself to a soul, the chasm between herself and Him appears immense : but the powers of the soul, reduced to simplicity, suffer a divine transformation. . . . The spirit feels the truth and splendour of the divine union, yet still feels in itself an essential propensity towards its ancient state ; and this propensity safeguards in it the sense of the gap which is between God and itself. There is nothing more sublime then the sense of this distance : for the Unity is a force which draws

[1] Dialogo, cap. lxxviii.

towards Itself all that which it has put into the world, both natural and supernatural. Further, illuminated men are caught up, above the reason, into the domain of naked vision. There the Divine Unity dwells and calls. Hence their bare vision, cleansed and free, penetrates the activity of all created things, and pursues it to search it out even to its heights. And this bare vision is penetrated and impregnated by the Eternal Light, as the air is penetrated and impregnated by the sun. The naked will is transformed by the Eternal Love, as fire by fire. The naked spirit stands erect, it feels itself to be wrapped round, affirmed and fixed by the formless immensity of God. Thus, far above reason, the created image is united by a threefold bond with its eternal type, the Source and Principle of its life." [1]

"When love has carried us above all things," he says in another place, "above the light, into the Divine Dark, there we are transformed by the Eternal Word Who is the image of the Father; and as the air is penetrated by the sun, thus we receive in peace the Incomprehensible Light, enfolding us and penetrating us. What is this light, if it be not a contemplation of the Infinite and an intuition of Eternity? We behold that which we are, and we are that which we behold, because our being, without losing anything of its own personality, is united with the Divine Truth which respects all diversity." [2]

Here the personal aspect of the Absolute seems to be reduced to a minimum: yet all that we value in personality—love, action, will—remains unimpaired. We seem caught up to a plane of vision beyond the categories of the human mind: to the contemplation of a Something Other—our home, our hope, and our passion, the completion of our personality, and the Substance of all that Is. Such an endless contemplation, such a dwelling within the substance of Goodness, Truth, and Beauty, is the essence of that Beatific Vision, that "participation of Eternity," "of all things most delightful and desired, of all things most loved by them who have it," [3] which theology presents to us as the objective of the soul.

Those mystics of the metaphysical type who tend to use

[1] Ruysbroeck, "Samuel" (Hello, pp. 199–201).
[2] *Ibid.*, "De Contemplatione" (Hello, p. 145).
[3] St. Thomas Aquinas, "Summa Contra Gentiles," bk. iii. cap. lxii.

these impersonal symbols of Place and Thing often see in the Unitive Life a foretaste of the Beatific Vision : an entrance here and now into that absolute life within the Divine Being, which shall be lived by all perfect spirits when they have cast off the limitations of the flesh and re-entered the eternal order for which they were made. For them, in fact, the " deified man," in virtue of his genius for transcendental reality, has run ahead of human history : and attained a form of consciousness which other men will only know when earthly life is past.

In the " Book of Truth " Suso has a beautiful and poetic comparison between the life of the blessed spirits dwelling within the Ocean of Divine Love, and that approximate life which is lived on earth by the mystic who has renounced all selfhood and merged his will in that of the Eternal Truth. Here we find one of the best of many answers to the ancient but apparently immortal accusation that the mystics teach the total annihilation of personality as the end and object of their quest. " Lord, tell me," says the Servitor, " what remains to a blessed soul which has wholly renounced itself." Truth says, " When the good and faithful servant enters into the joy of his Lord, he is inebriated by the riches of the house of God ; for he feels, in an ineffable degree, that which is felt by an inebriated man. He forgets himself, he is no longer conscious of his selfhood ; he disappears and loses himself in God, and becomes one spirit with Him, as a drop of water which is drowned in a great quantity of wine. For even as such a drop disappears, taking the colour and the taste of wine, so it is with those who are in full possession of blessedness. All human desires are taken from them in an indescribable manner, they are rapt from themselves, and are immersed in the Divine Will. If it were otherwise, if there remained in the man some human thing that was not absorbed, those words of Scripture which say that God must be all in all would be false. *His being remains, but in another form, in another glory, and in another power*. And all this is the result of entire and complete renunciation. . . . Herein thou shalt find an answer to thy question ; for the true renunciation and veritable abandonment of a man to the Divine Will in the temporal world is an imitation and reduction of that self-abandonment of the blessed, of which Scripture speaks : and this imitation approaches its model more or less according as men are more or less united with God and become more or less one with God. Remark well that which is said of the blessed : they are stripped of their personal initiative, and changed into another form, another glory, another power. What then is this other form, if it be not the Divine Nature and the Divine Being whereinto they pour themselves, and which pours Itself into them, and becomes one thing with them ? And what is that other glory, if it be not to be illuminated and made shining in the Inaccessible Light? What is that other power, if it be not that by means of his union with the Divine Personality, there is given to man a divine strength and a divine power that he may accomplish all which pertains to his blessedness and omit all which is contrary thereto? And thus it is that, as has been said, a man comes forth from his selfhood."[1]

All the mystics agree that the stripping off of personal initiative, the I, the Me, the Mine, utter renunciation, or "self-naughting"—self-abandonment to the direction of a larger Will —is an imperative condition of the attainment of the unitive life. The temporary denudation of the mind, whereby the contemplative made space for the vision of God, must now be applied to the whole life. Here, they say, there is a final swallowing up of that wilful I-hood which we ordinarily recognize as ourselves. It goes for ever, and something new is established in its room. The self is made part of the mystical Body of God ; and, humbly taking its place in the corporate life of Reality, would " fain be to the Eternal Goodness what his own hand is to a man."[2] That strange " hunger and thirst of God for the soul," " at once avid and generous," of which they speak in their most profound passages, here makes its final demand and receives its satisfaction. " All that He has, all that He is, He gives: all that we have, all that we are, He takes."[3]

The self, they declare, is devoured, immersed in the Abyss ; "sinks into God Who is the deep of deeps." In their efforts

---

[1] Suso, " Buchlein von der Wahrheit," cap. iv.
[2] " Theologia Germanica," cap. x.
[3] Ruysbroeck, " De Contemplatione " (Hello, p. 151).

towards describing to us this, the supreme mystic act, and the new life to which it gives birth, they are often driven to the use of images which must seem to us grotesque, were it not for the flame which burns behind: as when Ruysbroeck cries, " To eat and be eaten! this is Union! . . . Since His desire is immensity itself, to be wholly devoured of Him does not greatly amaze me." [1]

(B) At this point we begin to see that the language of deification, taken alone, will not suffice to describe the soul's final experience of Reality. The personal and emotional aspect of man's relation with his Source is also needed if that which he means by " union with God " is to be even partially expressed. Hence, even the most " transcendental " mystic is constantly compelled to fall back on the language of love in the endeavour to express the content of his metaphysical raptures : and forced in the end to acknowledge that the perfect union of Lover and Beloved cannot be suggested in the arid though doubtless accurate terms of religious philosophy. Such arid language eludes the most dangerous aspects of "divine union," the pantheistic on one hand, the "amoristic" on the other ; but it also fails to express the most splendid side of that amazing vision of truth. It needs some other more personal and intimate vision to complete it : and we shall find in the reports of those mystics of the "intimate" type to whom the Unitive Life has meant not self-loss in an Essence, but self-fulfilment in the union of heart and will, just that completing touch.

The extreme form of this kind of apprehension of course finds expression in the well-known and heartily abused symbolism of the Spiritual Marriage between God and the Soul : a symbolism which goes back to the Orphic Mysteries, and thence descended *via* the Neoplatonists unto the stream of Christian tradition. But there are other and less concrete forms of it, wholly free from the dangers which are supposed to lurk in " erotic " imagery of this kind. Thus Jelalu 'd Din, by the use of metaphors which are hardly human yet charged with passionate feeling, tells, no less successfully than the writer of the Song of Solomon, the secret of this union in which " heart speaks to heart."

[1] Hello, p. 223.

"With Thy Sweet Soul, this soul of mine
        Hath mixed as Water doth with Wine.
Who can the Wine and Water part,
        Or me and Thee when we combine?
Thou art become my greater self;
        Small bounds no more can me confine.
Thou hast my being taken on,
        And shall not I now take on Thine?
Me Thou for ever hast affirmed,
        That I may ever know Thee mine.
Thy Love has pierced me through and through,
        Its thrill with Bone and Nerve entwine.
I rest a Flute laid on Thy lips;
        A lute, I on Thy breast recline.
Breathe deep in me that I may sigh;
        Yet strike my strings, and tears shall shine." [1]

What the mystic here desires to tell us is, that his new life is not only a free and conscious participation in the life of Eternity—a fully-established existence on real and transcendental levels—but also the conscious sharing of an inflowing *personal life* greater than his own; a tightening of the bonds of that companionship which has been growing in intimacy and splendour during the course of the Mystic Way. This companionship, at once the most actual and most elusive fact of human experience, is utterly beyond the resources of speech. So too are those mysteries of the communion of love, whereby the soul's humble, active, and ever-renewed self-donation becomes the medium of her glory: and "by her love she is made the equal of Love"—the beggar maid sharing Cophetua's throne.

Thus the anonymous author of the "Mirror" writes, in one of his most daring passages, "'I am God,' says Love, 'For Love is God, and God is Love. And this soul is God by her condition of love: but I am God by my Nature Divine. And this [state] is hers by the justice of love. So that this precious one loved of Me, is taught, and is led of Me out of herself. . . . This [soul] is the eagle that flies high, so right high and yet more high than does any other bird; for she is feathered with fine love.'" [2]

The simplest expression of the Unitive Life, the simplest

<hr />

[1] Jalulu 'd Din, "The Festival of Spring" (Hastie's translation, p. 10).
[2] "The Mirror of Simple Souls," f. 157, b.

interpretation which we can put on its declarations, is that it is the complete and conscious fulfilment here and now of this Perfect Love. In it certain elect spirits, still in the flesh, " fly high and yet more high," till " taught and led out of themselves " they become, in the exaggerated language of the " Mirror," "God by condition of love." Home-grown English mysticism tried as a rule to express the inexpressible in homelier, more temperate terms than this. " I would that thou knew," says the unknown author of the " Epistle of Prayer," " what manner of working it is that knitteth man's soul to God, and that maketh it one with Him in love and accordance of will after the word of St. Paul, saying thus : ' *Qui adhaeret Deo, unus spiritus est cum illo* ' ; that is to say : ' Whoso draweth near to God as it is by such a reverent affection touched before, he is one spirit with God.' That is, though all that God and he be two and sere in kind, nevertheless yet in grace they are so knit together that they are but one in spirit ; and all this is one for onehead of love and accordance of will ; and in this onehead is the marriage made between God and the soul the which shall never be broken, though all that the heat and the fervour of this work cease for a time, but by a deadly sin. In the ghostly feeling of this onehead may a loving soul both say and sing (if it list) this holy word that is written in the Book of Songs in the Bible, '*Dilectus meus mihi et ego illi*,' that is, My loved unto me, and I unto Him ; understanding that God shall be knitted with the ghostly glue of grace on His party, and the lovely consent in gladness of spirit on thy party." [1]

I think no one can deny that the comparison of the bond between the soul and the Absolute to " ghostly glue," though crude, is wholly innocent. Its appearance in this passage as an alternative to the symbol of wedlock may well check the uncritical enthusiasm of those who hurry to condemn at sight all " sexual " imagery. That it has seemed to the mystics appropriate and exact is proved by its reappearance in the next century in the work of a greater contemplative. " Thou givest me," says Petersen, " Thy whole Self to be mine whole and undivided, if at least I shall be Thine whole and undivided. And when I shall be thus all Thine, even as from everlasting

---

[1] " The Epistle of Prayer." Printed from Pepwell's edition in " The Cell of Self-knowledge," edited by Edmund Gardner, p. 88.

Thou hast loved Thyself, so from everlasting Thou hast loved me: for this means nothing more than that Thou enjoyest Thyself in me, and that I by Thy grace enjoy Thee in myself and myself in Thee. And when in Thee I shall love myself, nothing else but Thee do I love, because *Thou art in me and I in Thee, glued together as one and the selfsame thing*, which henceforth and forever cannot be divided." [1]

From this kind of language to that of the Spiritual Marriage, as understood by the pure minds of the mystics, is but a step. [2] They mean by it no rapturous satisfactions, no dubious spiritualizing of earthly ecstasies, but a life-long bond " that shall never be lost or broken," a close personal union of will and of heart between the free self and that " Fairest in Beauty " Whom it has known in the act of contemplation.

The Mystic Way has been a progress, a growth, in love: a deliberate fostering of the inward tendency of the soul towards its source, an eradication of its disorderly tendencies to "temporal goods." But the only proper end of love is union: "a perfect uniting and coupling together of the lover and the loved into one." [3] It is "a unifying principle," the philosophers say; [4] life's mightiest agent upon every plane. Moreover, just as earthly marriage is understood by the moral sense less as a satisfaction of personal desires, than as a part of the great process of life—the fusion of two powers for new purposes—so such spiritual marriage brings with it duties and obligations. With the attainment of a new order, the new infusion of vitality, comes a new responsibility, the call to effort and endurance on a new and mighty scale. It is not an act but a state. Fresh life is imparted by which our lives are made complete: new creative powers are conferred. The self, lifted to the divine order, is to be an agent of the divine fecundity: an energizing centre, a parent of transcendental life. " The last perfection," says Aquinas, to "supervene upon a thing, is its becoming the cause of other things. While then a creature

[1] Gerlac Petersen, "Ignitum cum Deo Soliloquium," cap. xv.

[2] Compare Pt. I. Cap. VI. It seems needless to repeat here the examples there given.

[3] Hilton, " The Treatise written to a Devout Man," cap. viii.

[4] Cf. Ormond, " Foundations of Knowledge," p. 442. "When we love any being, we desire either the unification of its life with our own, or our own unification with its life. Love in its innermost motive is a unifying principle."

far she is from wishing to be esteemed in the least thing! When she possesses the ceaseless companionship of her Bridegroom, how could she think of herself? Her only thought is to please Him, and to seek out ways in which she may show Him her love. It is to this point, my daughters, that orison tends ; and, in the design of God, this spiritual marriage is destined to no other purpose but the *incessant production of work, work !* And this, as I have already told you, is the best proof that the favours which we receive have come from God." [1] "To give to our Lord a perfect hospitality " she says in the same chapter, " Mary and Martha must combine."

When we look at the lives of the great theopathetic mystics, the true initiates of Eternity—inarticulate as these mystics often are—we find ourselves in the presence of an amazing, a superabundant vitality: of a "triumphing force" over which circumstance has no power. "The incessant production of work, work" seems indeed to be the object of that Spirit, by Whose presence their interior castle is now filled.

We see St. Paul, abruptly enslaved by the First and Only Fair, not hiding himself to enjoy the vision of Reality, but going out single-handed to organize the Catholic Church. We ask how it was possible for an obscure Roman citizen, without money, influence, or good health, to lay these colossal foundations : and he answers, " Not I, but Christ in me."

We see Joan of Arc, a child of the peasant class, leaving the sheepfold to lead the armies of France. We ask how this incredible thing can be : and are told " Her Voices bade her." A message, an overpowering impulse, came from the supra-sensible: vitality flowed in on her, she knew not how or why. She was united with the Infinite Life, and became Its agent, the medium of Its strength, " what his own hand is to a man."

We see St. Francis, " God's troubadour," marked with His wounds, inflamed with His joy—obverse and reverse of the earnest-money of eternity—St. Ignatius Loyola, our Lady's knight—incurably romantic figures both of them—go out to change the spiritual history of Europe. Where did they find— born and bred to the most ordinary of careers, in the least spiritual of atmospheres—that superabundant energy, that genius for success which triumphed best in the most hopeless situations ?

[1] "El Castillo Interior," Moradas Sétimas, cap. iv,

Ignatius found it in the long contemplations and hard discipline of the cave of Manresa, after the act of surrender in which he dedicated his knighthood to the service of the Mother of God. Francis found it before the crucifix in St. Damiano, and renewed it in the ineffable experience of La Verna ; when " by mental possession and rapture he was transfigured of God."

We see St. Teresa, another born romantic, pass to the Unitive State after long and bitter struggles between her lower and higher personality. A chronic invalid over fifty years of age, weakened by long ill-health and by the terrible mortifications of the Purgative Way, she deliberately breaks with her old career, leaves her convent, and starts a new life : coursing through Spain, and reforming a great religious order in the teeth of the ecclesiastical world. Yet more amazing, St. Catherine of Siena, an illiterate daughter of the people, after a three years' retreat, consummates the mystic marriage, and emerges from the cell of self-knowledge to dominate the politics of Italy. How came it that these apparently unsuitable men and women, checked on every side by inimical environment, ill-health, custom, or poverty, achieved these stupendous destinies ? The explanation can only lie in the fact that all these persons were great mystics, living upon high levels the theopathetic life. In each a character of the heroic type, of great vitality, deep enthusiasms, unconquerable will, was raised to the spiritual plane, remade on higher levels of consciousness. Each by surrender of selfhood, by acquiescence in the large destinies of life, had so furthered that self's natural genius for the Infinite that their human limitations were overpassed. Hence they rose to freedom and attained to the one ambition of the "naughted soul," " I would fain be to the Eternal Goodness what his own hand is to a man."

Even Madame Guyon's natural tendency to passive states breaks down with her entrance on the Unitive Way. Though she cannot be classed amongst the greatest of its initiates, she too felt its fertilizing power, was stung from her "holy indifference " to become, as it were, involuntarily true to type.

"The soul," she says of the self entering upon Union—and we cannot doubt that as usual she is describing her own carefully docketed "states"—"feels a secret vigour taking more and more strongly possession of all her being : and little by little she receives a new life, never again to be lost, at least so far as one can be assured of anything in this life. . . . This new life is not like that which she had before. It is a life in God. It is a perfect life. She no longer lives or works of herself: but God lives, acts and works in her, and this grows little by little till she becomes perfect with God's perfection, rich with His riches, and loves with His love. . . . She lives only with the life of God, Who being the Principle of Life, this soul cannot lack anything. How greatly has she gained by her losses! She has lost the created for the Increate, the nothing for the All. All is given her : but not in herself but in God, not to be possessed of herself but to be possessed of God. Her riches are immense; for they are nothing less than God Himself.[1]

" I confess," she says again, " that I do not understand the risen and deified state of certain persons who remain, in spite of it, all their lives long in a state of impotence and deprivation : for here the soul resumes a veritable life. The acts of a risen man are vital acts: and if the soul after her resurrection remains without life, I say that she is dead or buried, but not risen. To be *risen*, the soul should be capable of all the acts which she performed before the time of her losses ; and perform them without difficulty, since she performs them in God." [2]

This new, intense, and veritable life has other and even more vital characteristics than those which lead to "the performance of acts" or "the incessant production of work, work." It is, in an actual sense, as Richard of St. Victor reminded us, fertile, creative, as well as merely active. In the fourth degree of love, the soul brings forth its children. It is the agent of a fresh outbirth of spiritual vitality into the world ; the helpmate of the Transcendent Order, the mother of a spiritual progeny. The great unitive mystics are each of them the founders of spiritual families, centres wherefrom radiates new transcendental life. The "flowing light of the Godhead" is focused in them, as in a lens, only that it may pass through them to spread out on every side. So, too, the great creative seers and artists are the parents, not merely of their own immediate works, but also of whole schools of art ; whole groups of persons who acquire or inherit their

---

[1] "Les Torrents," pt. i. cap. ix.   [2] *Op. cit.*, pt. ii. cap. i.

vision of beauty or truth. Thus within the area of influence of a Paul, a Francis, an Ignatius, a Teresa, an atmosphere of reality is created ; and new and vital spiritual personalities gradually appear, meet for the work which these great founders set in hand. The real witness to St. Paul's ecstatic life in God is the train of Christian churches by which his journeyings are marked. Wherever Francis passed, he left Franciscans, "fragrant with a wondrous aspect," where none had been before.[1] The Friends of God spring up, individual mystics, here and there through the Rhineland and Bavaria. Each becomes the centre of an ever-widening circle of transcendent life, the parent of a spiritual family. They are come, like their Master, that men may have life more abundantly: from them new mystic energy is actually born into the world. Again, Ignatius leaves Manresa a solitary: maimed, ignorant, and poor. He comes to Rome with his company already formed, and ablaze with his spirit ; veritably his children, begotten of him, part and parcel of his life.

Teresa finds the order of Mount Carmel hopelessly corrupt : all its friars and nuns blind to reality, indifferent to the obligations of the cloistered life. She is moved by the Spirit to leave her convent and begin, in abject poverty, the foundation of new houses, where the most austere and exalted life of contemplation shall be led. She enters upon this task to the accompaniment of an almost universal mockery. Mysteriously, as she proceeds, novices of the spiritual life appear and cluster around her. They come into existence, one knows not how, in the least favourable of atmospheres: but one and all are salted with the Teresian salt. They receive the infection of her abundant vitality: embrace eagerly and joyously the heroic life of the Reform. In the end, every city in Spain has within it Teresa's spiritual children : a whole order of contemplatives, as truly born of her as if they were indeed her sons and daughters in the flesh.

Well might the Spiritual Alchemists say that the true "Lapis Philosophorum" is a *tinging stone ;* which imparts its goldness to the base metals brought within its sphere of influence.

This reproductive power is one of the greatest marks of the theopathetic life ; the true " mystic marriage " of the individual

[1] Thomas of Celano, Legenda Secunda, cap. xii.

soul with its Source.   Those rare personalities in whom it is found are the *media* through which that Triumphing Spiritual Life which is the essence of reality forces an entrance into the temporal order and begets children; heirs of the superabundant vitality of the transcendental universe.

But the Unitive Life is more than the sum total of its symptoms: more than the heroic and apostolic life of the "great active": more than the divine motherhood of new "sons of the Absolute." These are only its outward signs, its expression in time and space. I have first laid stress upon that expression, because it is the side which all critics and some friends of the mystics persistently ignore. The contemplative's power of living this intense and creative life within the temporal order, however, is tightly bound up with that other life in which he attains to complete communion with the Absolute Order, and submits to the inflow of its supernal vitality.

In discussing the contributions of the mystical experience to the theories of Absolutism and Vitalism,[1] we saw that the complete mystic consciousness, and therefore, of course, the complete mystic world, had a twofold character. It embraced, we perceived, a Reality which seems from the human standpoint at once static and dynamic, transcendent and immanent, eternal and temporal : accepted both the absolute World of Pure Being and the unresting World of Becoming as integral parts of its vision of Truth, demanding on its side a dual response. All through the Mystic Way we caught glimpses of the growth and exercise of this dual intuition of the Real.   Now, the mature mystic, having come to his full stature, passed through the purifications of sense and of will and entered on his heritage, must and does take up as a part of that heritage not merely (a) a fruition of the Divine Goodness, Truth, and Beauty, his place within the Sempiternal Rose, nor (b) the creative activity of an agent of the Eternal Wisdom still immersed in the River of Life : but both together—the twofold destiny of the spiritual world.   To use the old scholastic language, he is at once patient and agent : patient as regards God, agent as regards man.

In a deep sense it may be said of him that he now participates according to his measure in that divine-human life which

---

[1] *Supra*, Pt. I. Cap. II.

mediates between man and the Eternal, and constitutes the "salvation of the world." Therefore, though his outward heroic life of action, his divine fecundity, may seem to us the best evidence of his state, it is the inner knowledge of his mystical sonship, "the mysterious peace dwelling in activity," says Ruysbroeck,[1] which is for him the guarantee of absolute life. He has many ways of describing this central fact; this peculiar consciousness of his own transcendence, which coexists with, and depends on, a complete humility. Sometimes he says that whereas in the best moments of his natural life he was but the "faithful servant" of the eternal order, and in the illuminated way became its "secret friend," he is now advanced to the final, most mysterious state of "hidden child." "How great," says Ruysbroeck, "is the difference between the secret friend and the hidden child! The first makes lively, impassioned, but measured ascents towards God. But the second presses on to lose his own life upon the summits, in that simplicity which knoweth not itself. . . . It is then that, caught up above all things by the sublime ardours of a stripped and naked spirit, we feel within ourselves the certitude and the perfection of the children of God; and obtain the immediate contact of the Divine because we are immersed in the Nothingness."[2]

Though the outer career of the great mystic, then, be one of superhuman industry, a long fight with evil and adversity, his real and inner life dwells securely upon the heights; in the perfect fruition which he can only suggest to us by the paradoxical symbols of ignorance and emptiness. He dominates existence because he thus transcends it: is a son of God, a member of the eternal order, shares its substantial life. "Tranquillity according to His essence, activity according to His Nature: absolute repose, absolute fecundity": this, says Ruysbroeck again, is the twofold property of Godhead: and the secret child of the Absolute participates in this dual character of Reality—"for this dignity has man been made."[3]

Those two aspects of truth which he has so clumsily classified as static and dynamic, as Being and Becoming, now find their final reconciliation within his own nature: for that nature

---

[1] "De Contemplatione" (Hello, p. 167).
[2] *Op. cit., loc. cit.*
[3] *Ibid.*, p. 175. *Vide supra*, p. 42.

has become conscious in all its parts, has unified itself about its highest elements. That strange, tormenting vision of a perfect peace, a joyous self-loss, annihilation in some mighty Life that overpassed his own, which haunts man throughout the whole course of his history, and finds a more or less distorted expression in all his creeds, a justification in all his ecstasies, is now traced to its source: and found to be the inevitable expression of an instinct by which he recognized, though he could not attain, the noblest part of his inheritance. This recognition of his has of necessity been imperfect and oblique. It has taken in many temperaments an exaggerated form, and has been further disguised by the symbolic language used to describe it. The tendency of Indian mysticism to regard the Unitive Life wholly in its passive aspect, as a total self-annihilation, a disappearance into the substance of the Godhead, results, I believe, from such a one-sided distortion of truth. The Oriental mystic "presses on to lose his life upon the heights"; but he does not come back from the grave and bring to his fellow-men the life-giving news that he has transcended mortality in the interests of the race. The temperamental bias of Western mystics towards activity has saved them as a rule from such one-sided achievement as this; and hence it is in them that the Unitive Life, with its "dual character of activity and rest," has assumed its richest and its noblest forms.

Of all these Western mystics none has expressed more lucidly or more splendidly than Ruysbroeck the double nature of man's reaction to Reality. It is the heart of his vision of truth. In all his books he returns to it again and again: speaking, as none familiar with his writings can doubt, the ardent, joyous, vital language of first-hand experience, not the platitudes of philosophy. He might say with Dante, his forerunner into the Empyrean:—

> "La forma universal di questo nodo
> credo ch' io vidi, perchè più di largo
> dicendo questo, mi sento ch' io godo." [1]

It is then from Ruysbroeck that I shall make my quotations: and if they be found somewhat long and difficult of com-

[1] Par. xxxiii. 91. "I believe that I beheld the universal form of this knot: because in saying this I feel my joy increased."

prehension, their unique importance for the study of man's spiritual abilities must be my excuse.

First, his vision of God :—

"The Divine Persons," he says, "Who form one sole God, are in the fecundity of their nature ever active : and in the simplicity of their essence they form the Godhead and eternal blessedness. Thus God according to the Persons is Eternal Work : but according to the essence and Its perpetual stillness, He is Eternal Rest. Now love and fruition live between this activity and this rest. Love would work without ceasing : for its nature is eternal work with God. Fruition is ever at rest, for it dwells higher than the will and the longing *for* the well-beloved, *in* the well-beloved ; in the divine nescience and that simple love where the Father, together with the Son, enfolds His well-beloved in the abundant unity of His Spirit, above the fecundity of nature. And that same Father says to each soul in His infinite lovingkindness, ' Thou art Mine and I am thine : I am thine and thou art Mine, for I have chosen thee from all eternity. ' "[1]

Next, the vision of the self's destiny : " Our duty is to love God : our fruition is to endure God and be penetrated by His love. There is the same difference between love and fruition as there is between God and His Grace. When we unite ourselves to God by love, then we spiritualize ourselves : but when He Himself draws us in a flight of the spirit, and transforms us in His spirit, then, so to speak, we are fruition. And the spirit of God Himself pushes us out from Himself by His breath, in order that we may love, and may do good works ; and again He draws us to Himself, in order that we may repose in peace and in fruition. And this is Eternal Life ; even as our bodily life subsists in the indrawing and outgoing of our breath." [2]

" Understand," he says again, " God comes to us incessantly, both with and without intermediary ; and He demands of us both action and fruition, in such a way that the action shall not hinder the fruition, nor the fruition the action, but they shall reinforce one another reciprocally. And this is why the interior man [*i.e.*, the contemplative] possesses his life according to these two manners ; that is to say, in rest and in work. And in each of

---

[1] " De Septem Gradibus Amoris," cap. xiv.   [2] *Ibid.*, *loc. cit.*

them he is wholly and undividedly; for he dwells altogether in
God in virtue of his restful fruition and altogether in himself in
virtue of his active love.   And God, in His communications,
incessantly compels him to renew both this rest and this work.
And because the soul is just, it desires to pay at every instant
that which God demands of it; and this is why each time it is
irradiated of Him, the soul is introverted in a manner that is
both active and fruitive, and thus that man is strengthened in
all virtues and ever more profoundly immersed in fruitive love.
. . . He is active in all loving work, for he sees his rest.   He
is a pilgrim, for he sees his country.   For love's sake he strives
for victory, for he sees his crown.   Consolation, peace, joy,
beauty and riches, all that can give delight, all this is shown to
the mind illuminated in God, in spiritual similitudes and without
measure.   And through this vision, in the contact of God, love
continues active.   For such a just man has built up in his own
soul, in rest and in work, a veritable life which shall endure
for ever; but which shall be transformed after this present
life to a state still more sublime.   Thus this man is just, and
he goes *towards* God by inward love, in eternal work, and he
goes *in* God by his fruitive inclination in eternal rest.   And
he dwells in God; and yet he goes out towards created things,
in a spirit of love towards all things, in the virtues and in
works of righteousness.   *And this is the supreme summit of
the inner life."* [1]

Compare this description with the careers of the theopathic
mystics; in whom, indeed, " action has not injured fruition, nor
fruition action," who have, by some secret adjustment—some
strange magic, as it seems to other men—contrived to " possess
their lives in rest and in work " without detriment to inward
joy or outward industry.

Bear in mind as you read these words—Ruysbroeck's last
supreme effort to tell the true relation between man's free spirit
and his God—the great public ministry of St. Catherine of
Siena, which ranged from the tending of the plague-stricken to
the reforming of the Papacy; and was accompanied by the
inward fruitive consciousness of the companionship of Christ.
Remember the humbler but not less beautiful and significant
achievement of her Genoese namesake: the strenuous lives of

[1] Ruysbroeck, " L'Ornement des Noces Spirituelles," l. ii. cap. lxxiii.

St. Francis of Assisi, St. Ignatius, St. Teresa, outwardly cumbered with much serving, observant of an infinitude of tiresome details, composing rules, setting up foundations, neglecting no aspect of their business which could conduce to its practical success, yet "altogether dwelling in God in restful fruition." Are not all these supreme examples of the state in which the self, at last fully conscious, knowing Reality because she is wholly real, pays her debt? Unable to rest entirely either in work or in fruition, she seizes on this twofold expression of the superabundant life by which she is possessed: and, on the double wings of eagerness and effort, takes flight towards her Home.

In dwelling, as we have done, on the ways in which the great mystic makes actual to himself the circumstances of the Unitive State, we must not forget that this state is, in essence, a fulfilment of love; the attainment of a "heart's desire." By this attainment, this lifting of the self to free union with the Real—as by the earthly marriage which dimly prefigures it—a new life is entered upon, new powers, new responsibilities are conferred. But this is not all. The three prime activities of the normal self, feeling, intellect, and will, though they seem to be fused, are really carried up to a higher term. They are unified, it is true, but still present in their integrity; and each demands and receives full satisfaction in the attainment of this final "honour for which man has been made." The intellect is immersed in that mighty vision of truth, known now not as a vision but as a home; where St. Paul saw things which might not be uttered, St. Teresa found the "perpetual companionship of the Blessed Trinity," and Dante, caught to its heart for one brief moment, his mind smitten by the blinding flash of the Uncreated Light, knew that he had resolved Reality's last paradox: the unity of "*cerchio*" and "*imago*"—the infinite and personal aspects of God.[1] The enhanced will, made over to the interests of the Transcendent, receives new worlds to conquer, new strength to match its exalted destiny. But the heart too here enters on a new order, begins to live upon high levels of joy. "This soul, says Love, swims in the sea of joy: that is, in the sea of delight, the stream of divine influences."[2]

[1] Par. xxxiii. 137.
[2] "The Mirror of Simple Souls," f. 161.

"*Amans volat, currit et laetatur : liber est et non tenetur,*"[1]
said A Kempis: classic words, which put before us once and
for ever the inward joyousness and liberty of the saints.
They "fly, run and rejoice"—those great, laborious souls,
often spent with amazing mortifications, vowed to hard and
never-ending tasks. They are "free, and nothing can hold
them," though they seem to the world fenced in by absurd
renunciations and restrictions, deprived of that cheap licence
which it knows as liberty.

That fruition of joy of which Ruysbroeck speaks in majestic
phrases, describes as constituting the interior life of mystic
souls immersed in the Absolute—the translation of the Beatific
Vision into the terms of a supernal feeling-state—is often
realized in the secret experience of those same mystics, as
the perennial possession of a childlike gaiety, an inextinguishable gladness of heart. The transfigured souls move to the
measures of a "love dance" which persists in mirth without
comparison, through every outward hardship and tribulation.
They enjoy the high spirits peculiar to high spirituality: and
shock the world by a delicate playfulness, instead of exhibiting
the morose resignation which it feels to be proper to the
"spiritual life." Thus St. Catherine of Siena, though constantly
suffering, "was always jocund and of a happy spirit." When
prostrate with illness she overflowed with gaiety and gladness,
and "was full of laughter in the Lord, exultant and rejoicing."[2]

Moreover, the most clear-sighted amongst the mystics
declare such joy to be an implicit of Reality. Thus Dante,
initiated into Paradise, sees the whole Universe laugh with
delight as it glorifies God:[3] and the awful countenance of
Perfect Love adorned with smiles.[4] Thus the souls of the
great theologians dance to music and laughter in the Heaven
of the Sun;[5] the loving seraphs, in their ecstatic joy, whirl
about the Being of God.[6] "*O luce eterna che . . . ami ed arridi,*"
exclaims the pilgrim, as the Divine Essence is at last revealed
to him,[7] and he perceives love and joy as the final attributes

---

[1] "De Imitatione Christi," l. iii. cap. v.

[2] Contestatio Fr. Thomae Caffarina, Processus, col. 1258 (E. Gardner, "St.
Catherine of Siena," p. 48).

[3] Par. xxvii. 4.   [4] *Ibid.*, xx. 13.   [5] *Ibid.*, x. 76, 118.
[6] *Ibid.*, xxviii. 100.   [7] *Ibid.*, xxxiii. 124–26.

of the Triune God. Thus Beatrice with "*suoi occhi ridenti*"—so different from the world's idea of a suitable demeanour for the soul's supreme instructress—laughs as she mounts with him the ladder to the stars. So, if the deified soul has indeed run ahead of humanity and "according to his fruition dwells in heaven," he too, like Francis, will run, rejoice and make merry: join the eager dance of the Universe about the One. "If," say Patmore, "we may credit certain hints contained in the lives of the saints, love raises the spirit above the sphere of reverence and worship into one of laughter and dalliance; a sphere in which the soul says:—

> "'Shall I, a gnat which dances in Thy ray,
> *Dare* to be reverent?'"[1]

Richard Rolle has expressed this exultant "spirit of dalliance" with peculiar insight and delicacy. "Among the delights which he tastes in so sweet love burning," he says of the true lover who "in the bond of lovers' wills stably is confirmed," "a heavenly privity inshed he feels, that no man can know but he that has received it, and in himself buries the electuary that anoints and makes happy all joyful lovers in Jesu; so that they cease not to hie in heavenly seats to sit, joy of their Maker endlessly to use. Hereto truly they yearn in heavenly sights abiding; and inwardly set afire, all their inward parts are glad with pleasant shining in light. And themselves they feel gladdened with merriest love, and in joyful song wonderfully melted. . . . But this grace generally and to all is not given, but to the holiest of holy souls is taught; in whom the excellence of love shines, and songs of lovely loving, Christ inspiring, commonly burst up, and as it were a pipe of love new-made, in sight of God more goodly than can be said, joying sounds. The which (soul) the mystery of love knowing, with great cry to its Love ascends, in wit sharpest, and in knowledge and in feeling subtle; not spread in things of this world but into God all gathered and set, that in cleanness of conscience and shining of soul to Him it may serve Whom it has purposed to love, and itself to Him to give.

[1] Coventry Patmore, "The Rod, the Root, and the Flower," "Aurea Dicta," xxxix.

Surely the clearer the love of the lover is, the nearer to him and the more present God is. And thereby more clearly in God he joys, and of the sweet Goodness the more he feels, that to lovers is wont Itself to inshed, and to mirth without comparison the hearts of the meek to turn." [1]

The last state of burning love, said Rolle, than which he could conceive no closer reaction to Reality, was the state of Sweetness and Song : the welling up of glad music in the simple soul, man's natural expression of a joy which overpasses the descriptive powers of our untuneful speech. In the gay rhythms of that primordial art he may say something of the secret which the more decorous periods of religion and philosophy will never let him tell : something, too, which in its very childishness, its freedom from the taint of solemnity and self-importance, expresses the quality of that inward life, that perpetual youth, which the " secret child " of the Transcendent Order enjoys. " As it were a pipe of love " in the sight of God he " joying sounds." The music of the spheres is all about him : he is a part of the great melody of the Divine. " Sweetest forsooth," says Rolle again, " is the rest which the spirit takes whilst sweet goodly sound comes down in which it is delighted : and in most sweet song and playful the mind is ravished, to sing likings of love everlasting." [2]

When we come to look at the lives of the mystics, we find it literally true that such " songs of lovely loving commonly burst up " whenever we can catch them unawares ; see behind the formidable and heroic activities of reformer, teacher, or leader of men, the *vie intime* which is lived at the hearth of Love. " What are the servants of the Lord but His minstrels?" said St. Francis,[3] who saw nothing inconsistent between the Celestial Melodies and the Stigmata of Christ. Moreover the songs of such troubadours, as the hermit of Hampole learned in his wilderness, are not only sweet but playful. Dwelling always in a light of which we hardly dare to think, save in the extreme terms of reverence and awe, they are not afraid with any amazement : they are at home.

The whole life of St. Francis of Assisi, that spirit trans-

---

[1] Richard Rolle, "The Fire of Love," bk. ii. cap. vii.
[2] *Op. cit.*, bk. i. cap. xii.
[3] " Speculum Perfectionis," cap. c. (Steele's translation).

figured in God, who " loved above all other birds a certain little bird which is called the lark,"[1] was one long march to music through the world. To sing seemed to him a primary spiritual function : he taught his friars in their preaching to urge all men to this.[2] It appeared to him appropriate and just to use the love language of the troubadours in praise of the more perfect Love which had marked him as Its own. " Drunken with the love and compassion of Christ, blessed Francis on a time did things such as these. For the most sweet melody of spirit boiling up within him, frequently broke out in French speech, and the veins of murmuring which he heard secretly with his ears broke forth into French-like rejoicing. And sometimes he picked up a branch from the earth, and laying it on his left arm, he drew in his right hand another stick like a bow over it, as if on a viol or other instrument, and, making fitting gestures, sang with it in French unto the Lord Jesus Christ."[3]

Many a time has the romantic quality of the Unitive Life— its gaiety, freedom, assurance, and joy—broken out in " French-like rejoicings"; which have a terribly frivolous sound for worldly ears, and seem the more preposterous as coming from people whose outward circumstances are of the most uncomfortable kind. St. John of the Cross wrote love songs to his Love. St. Rose of Lima sang duets with the birds. St. Teresa, in the austere and poverty-stricken seclusion of her first foundation, did not disdain to make rustic hymns and carols for her daughters' use in the dialect of Old Castile. Like St. Francis, she had a horror of solemnity. It was only fit for hypocrites, thought these rejuvenators of the Church. The hard life of prayer and penance on Mount Carmel was undertaken in a joyous spirit to the sound of many songs. Its great Reformer was quick to snub the too-spiritual sister who " thought it better to contemplate than to sing": and was herself heard, as she swept the convent corridor, to sing a little ditty about the most exalted of her own mystical experiences: that ineffable transverberation, in which the fiery arrow of the seraph pierced her heart.[4]

[1] " Speculum," cap. cxiii. [2] *Ibid.*, cap. c.
[3] *Ibid.*, cap. xciii., also Thomas of Celano, Vita Secunda, cap. xc.
[4] *Cf.* G. Cunninghame Graham, " Santa Teresa," vol. i. pp. 180, 300, 304.

But the most lovely and real, most human and most near
to us, of all these descriptions of the celestial exhilaration
which mystic surrender brings in its train, is the artless, unin-
tentional self-revelation of St. Catherine of Genoa, whose inner
and outer lives in their balanced wholeness provide us with one
of our best standards by which to judge the right proportions of
the Mystic Way.   Here the whole essence of the Unitive Life is
summed up and presented to us by one who lived it upon heroic
levels : and who was, in fruition and activity, in rest and in
work, not only a great active and a great ecstatic, but one of
the deepest gazers into the secrets of Eternal Love which the
history of Christian mysticism contains. Yet perhaps there is
no passage in the works of these same mystics which comes to
so unexpected, so startling a conclusion as this; in which St.
Catherine, with a fearless simplicity, shows to her fellow-men
the nature of the path that she has trodden and the place that
she has reached.

   "When," she says, in one of her reported dialogues—and
though the tone be impersonal it is clearly personal experience
which speaks—"the lovingkindness of God calls a soul from the
world, He finds it full of vices and sins; and first He gives it an
instinct for virtue, and then urges it to perfection, and then by
infused grace leads it to true self-naughting, and at last to true
transformation.   And this noteworthy order serves God to lead
the soul along the Way: but when the soul is naughted and
transformed, then of herself she neither works nor speaks nor
wills, nor feels nor hears nor understands, neither has she of
herself the feeling of outward or inward, where she may move.
And in all things it is God Who rules and guides her without
the mediation of any creature. And the state of this soul
is then a feeling of such utter peace and tranquillity that it
seems to her that her heart, and her bodily being, and all both
within and without is immersed in an ocean of utmost peace ;
from whence she shall never come forth for anything that can
befall her in this life. And she stays immovable, imper-
turbable, impassible. So much so, that it seems to her in
her human and her spiritual nature, both within and without,
she can feel no other thing than sweetest peace. And she
is so full of peace that though she press her flesh, her nerves,
her bones, no other thing comes forth from them than peace.

Then says she all day for joy such rhymes as these, making them according to her manner:—

> " '¸Vuoi tu che tu mostr'io
> Presto che cosa e Dio?
> Pace non trova chi da lui si partiò.' " [1]

"Then says she all day for joy such rhymes as these"—nursery rhymes, one might almost call them: so infantile, so naïve is their rhythm. Who would have suspected this to be the secret manner of communion between the exalted soul of Catherine and her Love? How many of those who actually saw that great and able woman tirelessly labouring in the administration of her hospital—who heard that profound and instinctive Christian Platonist instructing her disciples, and declaring the law of universal and heroic love—how many of these divined that "questa santa benedetta" who seemed to them already something more than earthly, a matter of solemn congratulation and reverential approach, went about her work with a heart engaged in no lofty speculations on Eternity; no outpourings of mystic passion for the Absolute, but "saying all day for joy," in a spirit of childlike happiness, gay and foolish little songs about her Love?

Standing at the highest point of the mystic ladder which can be reached by human spirits in this world of time and space, looking back upon the course of that slow interior alchemy, that "noteworthy order" of organic transformation, by which her selfhood had been purged of imperfection, raised to higher levels, compelled at last to surrender itself to the all-embracing, all-demanding life of the Real; this is St. Catherine's deliberate judgment on the relative and absolute aspects of the mystic life. The "noteworthy order" which we have patiently followed, the psychic growth and rearrangement of character,

---

[1] "Dost thou wish that I should show
All God's Being thou mayst know?
Peace is not found of those who do not with Him go."
(Vita e Dottrina, cap. xviii.)

Here, in spite of the many revisions to which the Vita has been subjected, I cannot but see an authentic report of St. Catherine's inner mind; highly characteristic of the personality which "came joyous and rosy-faced" from its ecstatic encounters with Love. The very unexpectedness of its conclusion, so unlike the expressions supposed to be proper to the saints, is a guarantee of its authenticity. On the text of the Vita see Von Hügel, "The Mystical Element of Religion," vol. i., Appendix.

the visions and ecstasies, the joyous illumination and bitter pain
—these but "served to lead the soul along the way." In the
mighty transvaluation of values which takes place when that way
has at last been trod, these "abnormal events" sink to insig-
nificance. For us, looking out wistfully along the pathway to
reality, they stand out, it is true, as supreme landmarks, by which
we may. trace the homeward course of pilgrim man. The
importance of their study cannot be overrated for those who
would study the way to that world from this. But the mystic,
safe in that silence where lovers lose themselves, "his cheek on
Him Who for his coming came," remembers them no more. In
the midst of his active work, his incessant spiritual creation, joy
and peace enfold him. He needs no stretched and sharpened
intuition now : for he dwells in that "most perfect form of contemplation" which "consists in simple and perceived contact
of the substance of the soul with that of the divine."[1]

The wheel of life has made its circle. Here, at the last point
of its revolution, the extremes of sublimity and simplicity are
seen to meet. It has swept the soul of the mystic through
periods of alternate stress and glory ; tending ever to greater
transcendence, greater freedom, closer contact with "the
Supplier of true life." He emerges from that long and
wondrous journey to find himself, in rest and in work, a little
child upon the bosom of the Father. In that most dear relation
all feeling, will, and thought attain their end. Here all the
teasing complications of our separated selfhood are transcended.
Hence the eager striving, the sharp vision, are not wanted any
more. In that mysterious death of selfhood on the summits
which is the medium of Eternal Life, heights meet the deeps :
supreme achievement and complete humility are one.

In a last brief vision, a glimpse as overpowering to our
common minds as Dante's final intuition of reality to his
exalted and courageous soul, we see the triumphing spirit, sent
out before us, the best that earth can offer, stoop and strip
herself of the insignia of wisdom and power. Achieving the
highest, she takes the lowest place. Initiated into the atmosphere of Eternity, united with the Absolute, possessed at last
of the fullness of Its life, the soul, self-naughted, becomes as a
little child : for of such is the kingdom of heaven.

[1] Coventry Patmore, "The Rod, the Root, and the Flower," "Magna Moralia," xv.

CONCLUSION

WE have traced, as well as our limitations allow us, the Mystic Way from its beginning to its end. We have seen the ever-changing, ever-growing human spirit, emerging from the cave of illusion, enter into consciousness of the transcendental world: the "pilgrim set towards Jerusalem" pass through its gates and attain his home in the bosom of Reality. For him, as we have learned from his words and actions, this journey and this End are all: their overwhelming importance and significance swallow up, of necessity, every other aspect of life. Now, at the end of our inquiry, we are face to face with the question—What do these things mean for us; for ordinary unmystical men? What are their links with that concrete world of appearance in which we are held fast: with that mysterious, ever-changing life which we are forced to lead? What do these great and strange adventures of the spirit tell us as to the goal of that lesser adventure of life on which we are set: as to our significance, our chances of freedom, our relation with the Absolute? Do they merely represent the eccentric performances of a rare psychic type? Are the matchless declarations of the contemplatives only the fruits of unbridled imaginative ·genius, as unrelated to reality as music to the fluctuations of the Stock Exchange? Or are they the supreme manifestation of a power which is inherent in our life: reports of observations made upon an actual plane of being, which transcends and dominates our normal world of sense? The question is vital: for unless the history of the mystics can touch and light up some part of this normal experience, take its place in the general history of man, contribute something towards our understanding of his nature and destiny, its interest for us can never be more than remote, academic, and unreal.

Far from being academic or unreal, that history, I think, is vital for the deeper understanding of the history of humanity. It shows us, upon high levels, the psychological process to which every self which desires to rise to the perception of Reality must submit: the formula under which man's spiritual consciousness, be it strong or weak, must necessarily unfold. In the great mystics we see the highest and widest development of that consciousness to which the human race has yet attained. We see its growth exhibited to us on a grand scale, perceptible of all men: the stages of its slow transcendence of the sense-world marked by episodes of splendour and of terror which are hard for common men to accept or understand as a part of the organic process of life. But the germ of that same transcendent life, the spring of the amazing energy which enables the great mystic to rise to freedom and dominate his world, is latent in all of us; an integral part of our humanity. Where the mystic has a genius for the Absolute, we have each a little buried talent, some greater, some less; and the growth of this talent, this spark of the soul, once we permit its emergence, will conform in little, and according to its measure, to those laws of organic growth, those inexorable conditions of transcendence which we found to govern the Mystic Way.

Every person, then, who awakens to consciousness of a Reality which transcends the normal world of sense—however small, weak, imperfect that consciousness may be—is put of necessity upon a road which follows at low levels the path which the mystic treads at high levels. The success with which he follows this way to freedom and full life will depend on the intensity of his love and will; his capacity for self-discipline, his steadfastness and courage. It will depend on the generosity and completeness of his outgoing passion for absolute beauty, absolute goodness, or absolute truth. But if he move at all, he will move through a series of states which are, in their own small way, strictly analogous to those experienced by the greatest contemplative on his journey towards that union with God which is the term of the spirit's ascent towards its home.

As the embryo of physical man, be he saint or savage, passes through the same stages of initial growth, so too with spiritual man. When the "new birth" takes place in him, the new life-process of his deeper self begins, the normal individual, no less than the mystic, will know that spiral ascent towards higher levels, those violent oscillations of consciousness between light and darkness, those odd mental disturbances, abrupt invasions from the subliminal region, and disconcerting glimpses of truth, which accompany the growth of the transcendental powers; though he may well interpret them in other than the mystic sense. He too will be impelled to drastic self-discipline, to a deliberate purging of his eyes that he may see: and, receiving a new vision of the world, will be spurred by it to a total self-dedication, an active surrender of his whole being, to that aspect of the Infinite which he has perceived. He too will endure in little the psychic upheavals of the spiritual adolescence: will be forced to those sacrifices which every form of genius demands. He will know according to his measure the dreadful moments of lucid self-knowledge, the counterbalancing ecstasy of an intuition of the Real. More and more, as we study and collate all the available evidence, this fact—this law—is borne in on us: that the movement of human consciousness, when it obeys its innate tendency to transcendence, is always the same. There is only one road from Appearance to Reality. "Men pass on, but the States are permanent for ever."

I do not care whether the consciousness be that of artist or musician, striving to catch and fix some aspect of the heavenly light or music, and denying all other aspects of the world in order to devote themselves to this: or of the humble servant of Science, purging his intellect that he may look upon her secrets with innocence of eye: whether the higher reality be perceived in the terms of religion, beauty, suffering; of human love, of goodness, or of truth. However widely these forms of transcendence may seem to differ, the mystic experience is the key to them all. All in their different ways are exhibitions here and now of the Eternal; extensions of man's consciousness which involve calls to heroic endeavour, incentives to the remaking of character about new and higher centres of life. Through each, man may rise to freedom and take his place in the great movement of the universe: may "understand by dancing that which is done." Each brings the self who receives its revelation in good faith, does not check it by self-regarding limitations, to a humble acceptance of the universal law of knowledge: the law that "we behold that which we are "; and hence that "only the Real can know Reality." Awakening, Discipline, Enlightenment, Self-surrender, and Union, are the essential processes of life's response to this fundamental fact : the conditions of our attainment of Being, the necessary formulæ under which alone our consciousness of any of these fringes of Eternity—any of these aspects of the Transcendent—can unfold, develop, attain to freedom and full life.

We are, then, one and all the kindred of the mystics ; and it is by dwelling upon this kinship, by interpreting—so far as we may—their great declarations in the light of our own little experience, that we shall learn to understand them best. Strange and far away though they seem, they are not cut off from us by some impassable abyss. They belong to us. They are our brethren ; the giants, the heroes of our race. As the achievement of genius belongs not to itself only, but also to the society that brought it forth ; as theology declares that the merits of the saints avail for all ; so, because of the solidarity of the human family, the supernal accomplishment of the mystics is ours also. Their attainment is the earnest-money of our eternal life.

To be a mystic is simply to participate here and now in that real and eternal life ; in the fullest, deepest sense which is possible to man. It is to share, as a free and conscious agent— not a servant, but as a son—in the joyous travail of the Universe : its mighty onward sweep through pain and glory towards its home in God. This gift of " sonship," this power of free co-operation in the world-process, is man's greatest honour. The ordered sequence of states, the organic development, whereby his consciousness is detached from illusion and rises to the mystic freedom which conditions, instead of being conditioned by, its normal world, is the way he must tread if that sonship is to be attained. Only by this deliberate fostering of his deeper self, this transmutation of the elements of character, can he reach those levels of consciousness upon which he hears, and responds to, the measure " whereto the worlds keep time " on their great pilgrimage towards the Father's heart. The mystic act of union, that joyous loss of the transfigured self in God, which is the crown of man's conscious ascent towards the Absolute, is the contribution of the individual to this, the destiny of the Cosmos.

The mystic knows that destiny. It is laid bare to his lucid vision, as plain to him as our puzzling world of form and colour is to normal sight. He is the "hidden child" of the eternal order, an initiate of the secret plan. Hence, whilst "all creation groaneth and travaileth," slowly moving under the spur of blind desire towards that consummation in which alone it can have rest, he runs eagerly along the pathway to reality. He is the pioneer of Life on its age-long voyage to the One: and shows us, in his attainment, the meaning and value of that life.

This meaning, this secret plan of Creation, flames out, had we eyes to see, from every department of existence. Its exultant declarations come to us in all great music ; its wild magic is the life of all romance. Its law—the law of love—is the substance of the beautiful, the energizing cause of the heroic. It lights the altar of every creed. It runs like ichor in the arteries of the universe. All man's dreams and diagrams concerning a transcendent Perfection near him yet intangible, a transcendent vitality to which he can attain—whether he call these objects of desire, God, grace, being, spirit, beauty, "pure idea"— are but translations of his deeper self's intuition of its destiny ; clumsy fragmentary hints at the all-inclusive, living Absolute which that deeper self knows to be real. This supernal Thing, the adorable Substance of all that Is—the synthesis of Wisdom, Power, and Love—and man's apprehension of it, his slow remaking in its interests, his union with it at last ; this is the theme of mysticism. That twofold extension of consciousness which allows him communion with its transcendent and immanent aspects is, in all its gradual processes, the Mystic Way. It is also the crown of human evolution ; the fulfilment of life, the liberation of personality from the world of appearance, its entrance into the free, creative life of the Real.

Further, Christians may well remark that the psychology of Christ, as presented to us in the Gospels, is of a piece with that of the mystics. In its pains and splendours, its dual character of action and fruition, it reflects their experience upon the supernal plane of more abundant life. Thanks to this fact, for them the Ladder of Contemplation—that ladder which mediaeval thought counted as an instrument of the Passion, discerning it as essential to the true salvation of man—stretches without a break from earth to the Empyrean. It leans against the Cross; it leads to the Secret Rose. By it the ministers of Goodness, Truth, and Beauty go up and down between the transcendent and the apparent world. Seen, then, from whatever standpoint we may choose to adopt—whether of psychology, philosophy, or religion—the adventure of the great mystics intimately concerns us. It is a master-key to man's puzzle: by its help he may explain much in his mental make-up, in his religious constructions, in his experience of life. In all these departments he perceives himself to be climbing slowly and clumsily upward toward some attainment yet unseen. The mystics, expert mountaineers, go before him : and show him, if he cares to learn, the way to freedom, to reality, to peace. He cannot rise in this, his earthly existence, to the awful and solitary peak, veiled in the Cloud of Unknowing, where they meet that " death of the summit," which is declared by them to be the gate of Perfect Life : but if he choose to profit by their explorations, he may find his level, his place within the Eternal Order. He may rise to freedom, live the " independent spiritual life."

Consider once more the Mystic Way as we have traced it from its beginning. To what does it tend if not to this ?

It began by the awakening within the self of a new and embryonic consciousness : a consciousness of divine reality, as opposed to the illusory sense-world in which she was immersed. Humbled, awed by the august possibilities then revealed to her, that self retreated into the " cell of self-knowledge " and there laboured to adjust herself to the Eternal Order which she had perceived, stripped herself of all that opposed it, disciplined her energies, purified the organs of sense. Remade in accordance with her intuitions of reality, the " eternal hearing and seeing were revealed in her." She opened her eyes upon a world still natural, but no longer illusory ; since it was perceived to be illuminated by the Uncreated Light. She knew then the beauty, the majesty, the divinity of the living World of Becoming which holds in its meshes every living thing. She had transcended the narrow rhythm by which common men perceive but one of its many aspects, escaped the machine-made universe presented by the cinematograph of sense, and participated in the " great life of the All." Reality came forth to her, since her eyes were cleansed to see It, not from some strange far-off and spiritual country, but gently, from the very heart of things. Thus lifted to a new level, she began again her ceaseless work of growth : and because by the cleansing of the senses she had learned to see the reality which is shadowed by the sense-world, she now, by the cleansing of her will, sought to draw nearer to that Eternal Will, that Being which life, the World of Becoming, manifests and serves. Thus, by the complete surrender of her selfhood in its wholeness, by the perfecting of her love, she slid from Becoming to Being, and found her true life hidden in God.

Yet the course of this transcendence, this amazing inward journey, was closely linked, first and last, with the processes of human life. It sprang from that life, as man springs from the sod. We were even able to describe it under those symbolic formulæ which we are accustomed to call the "laws" of the natural world. By an extension of these formulæ, their logical application, we discovered a path which led us without a break from the sensible to the supra-sensible ; from apparent to absolute life. There is nothing unnatural about the Absolute of the mystics : He sets the rhythm of His own universe, and conforms to the harmonies which He has made. We, deliberately seeking for that which we suppose to be spiritual, too often overlook that which alone is Real. The true mysteries of life accomplish themselves so softly, with so easy and assured a grace, so frank an acceptance of our breeding, striving, dying, and unresting world, that the unimaginative natural man—all agog for the marvellous—is hardly startled by their daily and radiant revelation of infinite wisdom and love. Yet this revelation presses incessantly upon us. Only the hard crust of surface-consciousness conceals it from our normal sight. In some least expected moment, the common activities of life in progress, that Reality in Whom the mystics dwell slips through our closed doors, and suddenly we see It at our side.

It was said of the disciples at Emmaus, " Mensam igitur ponunt, panes cibosque offerunt, et Deum, quem in Scripturae sacrae expositione non cognoverant, in panis fractione cognoscunt." So too for us the Transcendent Life for which we crave is revealed, and our living within it, not on some remote and arid plane of being, in the cunning explanations of philosophy ; but in the normal acts of our diurnal experience suddenly made significant for us. Not in the backwaters of existence, not amongst subtle arguments and occult doctrines, but in all those places where the direct and simple life of earth goes on.   It is found in the soul of man so long as that soul is alive and growing : it is not found in any sterile place.

This fact of experience is our link with the mystics, our guarantee of the truthfulness of their statements, the supreme importance of their adventure, their closer contact with Reality. The mystics on their part are our guarantee of the end towards which the Immanent Love, the hidden steersman which dwells in our midst, is moving : our " lovely forerunners " on the path towards the Real.   They come back to us from an encounter with life's most august secret, as Mary came running from the tomb ; filled with amazing tidings which they can hardly tell. We, longing for some assurance, and seeing their radiant faces, urge them to pass on their revelation if they can.   It is the old demand of the dim-sighted and incredulous :—

> " Dic nobis Maria
> Quid vidisti in via ? "

But they cannot say : can only report fragments of the symbolic vision :—

> " Angelicos testes, sudarium, et vestes "—

not the inner content, the final divine certainty.   We must ourselves follow in their footsteps if we would have that.

Like the story of the Cross, so too the story of man's spirit ends in a garden : in a place of birth and fruitfulness, of beautiful and natural things.   Divine Fecundity is its secret : existence, not for its own sake, but for the sake of a more abundant life.   It ends with the coming forth of divine humanity, never again to leave us : living in us and with us, a pilgrim, a worker, a guest at our table, a sharer at all hazards in life.   The mystics witness to this story : waking very early they have run on before us, urged by the greatness of their love.   We, incapable as yet of this sublime encounter, looking in their magic mirror, listening to their stammered tidings, may see far off the consummation of the race.

According to the measure of their strength and of their passion, these, the true lovers of the Absolute, have conformed here and now to the utmost tests of divine sonship, the final demands of life. They have not shrunk from the sufferings of the cross. They have faced the darkness of the tomb. Beauty and agony alike have called them : alike have awakened a heroic response. For them the winter is over : the time of the singing of birds is come. From the deeps of the dewy garden, Life—new, unquenchable, and ever lovely—comes to meet them with the dawn.

> Et hoc intellegere, quis hominum dabit homini?
> Quis angelus angelo?
> Quis angelus homini?
> A te petatur,
> In te quaeratur,
> Ad te pulsetur,
> Sic, sic accipietur, sic invenietur, sic aperietur.

APPENDIX

A HISTORICAL SKETCH OF EUROPEAN MYSTICISM FROM THE BEGINNING OF THE CHRISTIAN ERA TO THE DEATH OF BLAKE

I F we try to represent the course of Mysticism in Europe during the Christian period by the common device of a chronological curve, showing, by its rises and falls as it passes across the centuries, the absence or preponderance in any given epoch of mystics and mystical thought; we shall find that the great periods of mystical activity correspond with a curious exactness with the great periods of artistic, material, and intellectual civilization. Rather, they come immediately after, and seem to complete such periods : those stupendous outbursts of vitality in which man makes fresh conquests over his universe, apparently producing as their last stage a type of heroic character which extends these victories to the spiritual sphere. When science, politics, literature, and the arts—the domination of nature and the ordering of life—have risen to their height and produced their greatest works, the mystic comes to the front ; snatches the torch, and carries it on. It is almost as if he were humanity's finest flower ; the product at which each great creative period of the race had aimed.

Thus the thirteenth century expressed to perfection the mediaeval ideal in religion, art, philosophy, and public life. It built the Gothic cathedrals, put the finishing touch to the system of chivalry, and nourished the scholastic philosophers. It has many saints, but not very many mystics ; though they increase in number as the century draws on. The fourteenth century is filled by great contemplatives ; who lifted this wave of activity to spiritual levels, and brought all the romance and passion of the mediaeval temperament to bear upon the deepest mysteries of the transcendental life. Again, the sixteenth century, blazing with an intellectual vitality which left no corner of existence unexplored, which produced the Renaissance and the Humanists and remade the mediaeval world, had hardly reached its full development before the great procession of the post-Renaissance

mystics, with St. Teresa at their head, began.   If Life, then—the great
and restless life of the race—be described under the trite metaphor of a
billowy sea, each great wave as it rises from the deep bears the mystic
type upon its crest.

Our curve, then, will follow close behind that other curve which
represents the intellectual life of humanity.   Its course will be studded
and defined for us by the names of the great mystics ; the possessors
of spiritual genius, the pathfinders to the country of the soul.   These
starry names are significant not only in themselves, but also as links in
the chain of man's growing spiritual history.   They are not isolated
phenomena, but are related to one another.   Each receives something
from the past : each by his personal adventures enriches it, and hands
it on to the future.   As we go on, we notice more and more this cumulative power of the past.   Each mystic, original though he be, yet owes
much to the inherited acquirement of his spiritual ancestors.   These
ancestors form his tradition, are the classic examples on which his
education is based ; and from them he takes the language which they
have sought out and constructed as a means of telling their adventures
to the world.   It is by their help too, very often, that he elucidates for
himself the meaning of the dim perceptions of his amazed soul.   From
his own experiences he adds to this store ; and hands on an enriched
tradition of the transcendental life to the next spiritual genius evolved
by the race.   Hence the names of the great mystics are connected by a
thread ; and it becomes possible to treat them as subjects of history
rather than of biography.

I have said that this thread forms a curve, following the fluctuations
of the intellectual life of the race.   At its highest points, the names of
the mystics are clustered most thickly, at its descents they become
fewer and fewer, at the lowest points they die away.   Between the first
century A.D. and the nineteenth, this curve exhibits three great waves
of mystical activity ; besides many minor fluctuations.   They correspond with the close of the Classical, the Mediaeval and the Renaissance
periods in history : reaching their highest points in the third, fourteenth,
and seventeenth centuries.   In one respect, however, the mystic curve
diverges from the historical one.   It rises to its highest point in the
fourteenth century, and does not again approach the level it there
attains ; for the mediaeval period was more favourable to the development of mysticism than any subsequent epoch has been.   The fourteenth century is as much the classic moment for the spiritual history
of our race as the thirteenth is for the history of Gothic, or the
fifteenth for that of Italian art.

The names upon our curve, especially during the first ten centuries

APPENDIX

of the Christian era, are often separated by long periods of time. This, of course, does not necessarily mean that these centuries produced few mystics : merely that few documents relating to them have survived. We have now no means of knowing, for instance, the amount of true mysticism which may have existed amongst the initiates of the Greek or Egyptian Mysteries ; how many inarticulate contemplatives of the first rank there were amongst the Alexandrian Neoplatonists, the pre-Christian communities of contemplatives described by **Philo,** the deeply mystical Alexandrian Jew (B.C. 20–A.D. 40), the innumerable Gnostic sects which replaced in the early Christian world the Orphic and Dionysiac mystery-cults of Greece and Italy, or later, amongst the thousands of monks and hermits who peopled the Egyptian Thebaid in the sixth and seventh centuries. Some real mystical inspiration there must have been, for we know that from these centres of life came many of the doctrines best loved by later mystics : that the Neoplatonists gave them the concepts of Pure Being and the One, that the New Birth and the Spiritual Marriage were foreshadowed in the Mysteries, that Philo anticipates the theology of the Fourth Gospel.

As we stand at the beginning of the Christian period we see three great sources whence its mystical tradition might have been derived. These sources are Greek, Oriental, and Christian—*i.e.*, primitive Apostolic—doctrine or thought. As a matter of fact all contributed their share : but Christianity, destined to absorb the virtue of both the others, seems at first to have given least. Of course the Christian religion, by its very nature, must always have had its mystical side. Putting the personality of its Founder outside the limits of the present discussion, **St. Paul** and the author of the Fourth Gospel are obvious instances of mystics of the first rank amongst its earliest missionaries. The inner history of primitive Christianity is still in confusion ; but in what has been already made out we find numerous, if scattered, indications that the mystic life was indigenous in the Church and the natural mystic had little need to look for inspiration outside the limits of his creed. Not only the epistles of St. Paul and the Johannine writings, but also the earliest liturgic fragments which we possess, and such primitive religious poetry as the " Odes of Solomon " and the " Hymn of Jesus," show how congenial was mystical expression to the mind of the Church : how eagerly that Church absorbed and transmuted the mystic element of Essene, Orphic, and Neoplatonic thought.

Towards the end of the second century this tendency received brilliant literary expression at the hands of **St. Clement of Alexandria** (*c.* 160–220), who first adapted the language of the pagan Mysteries to the Christian theory of the spiritual life. Nevertheless, the first person after St. Paul of whom it can now be decisively stated that he was a practical mystic of the first rank, and in whose writings the central mystic doctrine of union with God is found, is a pagan. That person is **Plotinus,** the great Neoplatonic philosopher of Alexandria (A.D. 205-*c*. 270). His mysticism owes nothing to the Christian religion, of which he was a determined opponent. Intellectually it contains elements drawn from Platonic philosophy, from the Mysteries, and probably from the Oriental cults and philosophies which ran riot in Alexandria in the third century. These things, however, merely served Plotinus on his mystical side as a means of expressing as much of his own sublime experience as he chose to tell the world. Ostensibly a metaphysician, he possessed transcendental genius of a high order: and was consumed by a burning passion for the Absolute. He has left it on record that he attained three times in his life to ecstatic union with " the One."

The Neoplatonism of which Plotinus was the greatest exponent became the vehicle in which most of the mysticism—both Christian and pagan—of the first six centuries was expressed. But, since the emergence of mysticism always means the emergence of a certain type of character or genius, not the emergence of a certain type of philo-sophy, Neoplatonism as a whole, and the mysticism which used its language, must not be identified with one another. Thus Porphyry (233-304), the pupil and biographer of Plotinus, inherits his master's philosophy, but not his mysticism. Neoplatonism as a whole was a confused, semi-religious philosophy; containing many inconsistent elements. Appearing at the moment in which the wreck of paganism was complete, but before Christianity had conquered the educated world, it made a strong appeal to the spiritually minded; and also to those who hankered after the mysterious and the occult. It taught the illusory nature of all temporal things, and in the violence of its idealism outdid its master Plato. It also taught the existence of an Absolute God, the "Unconditioned One," who might be known in ecstasy and contemplation; and here it made a direct appeal to the mystical instincts of men. Those natural mystics who lived in the time of its greatest popularity found in it therefore a ready means of expressing their own intuitions of reality. Hence it is that the early mysticism of Europe, both Christian and pagan, has come down to us in a Neo-platonic dress; and speaks the tongue of Alexandria rather than that of Jerusalem, Athens, or Rome.

The influence of Plotinus upon later Christian mysticism was enormous though indirect. During the patristic period all that was best in the spirit of Neoplatonism flowed into the veins of the Church.

St. Augustine (A.D. 354–430) and **Dionysius the Areopagite**
(writing between 475 and 525) are amongst his spiritual children.
So too is **Proclus** (412-c. 490), the last of the pagan philosophers.
Through these there is hardly one in the long tale of the European
contemplatives whom his powerful spirit has failed to reach.

The mysticism of St. Augustine is partly obscured for us by the
wealth of his intellectual and practical life: yet no one can read the
"Confessions" without being struck by the intensity and actuality of
his spiritual experience, and the characteristically mystical formulæ
under which he apprehended Reality. In the period in which he
composed this work it is clear that he was already an advanced
contemplative. The marvellous intellectual activities by which he is
best remembered were fed by the solitary adventures of his soul. No
merely literary genius could have produced the wonderful chapters in
the seventh and eighth books, or the innumerable detached passages in
which his passion for the Absolute breaks out: and later mystics,
recognizing this fact, will be found to appeal again and again to his
authority.

The influence of St. Augustine on the later history of mysticism,
though very great, was nothing in comparison with that exercised by
the writings of the strange and nameless character who chose to ascribe
his works to Dionysius the Areopagite, the friend of St. Paul, and to
address his letters upon mysticism to Paul's fellow-worker, Timothy.
The pseudo-Dionysius was probably a Syrian monk. The fact that he
quotes the works of Origen proves that he cannot have written before
A.D. 475 ; it is most likely that he flourished in the early part of the
sixth century. His chief works are the treatises on the Angelic
Hierarchies and on the Names of God, and a short but priceless tract
on mystical theology. Few persons now look at the works of Dionysius : but from the ninth century to the seventeenth they nourished the
most spiritual intuitions of men, and possessed an authority which it
is now hard to realize. In studying mediaeval mysticism one has always
to reckon with him. Particularly in the fourteenth century, the golden
age of mystical literature, the phrase "Dionysius saith" is of continual
recurrence : and has for those who use it much the same weight as
quotations from the Bible or the great fathers of the Church.

The importance of Dionysius lies in the fact that he was the first,
and for a long time the only Christian writer who attempted to describe
frankly and accurately the workings of the mystical consciousness, and
the nature of its ecstatic attainment of God. So well did he do his
work that later contemplatives, reading him, found their most sublime
and amazing experiences reflected and partly explained. Hence in

describing those experiences, they adopted in their turn his language and metaphors; which afterwards became the classic terms of contemplative science. To him Christian literature owes the paradoxical concept of the Absolute Godhead as the "Divine Dark," the Unconditioned, "the negation of all that *is*"—*i.e.*, of all that the surface consciousness perceives—and of the soul's attainment of the Absolute as a "divine ignorance," a way of negation. This idea is common to Greek and Indian philosophy. With Dionysius it enters the Catholic fold.

Whilst he gave a Christian significance to the most mystical aspects of Neoplatonism, much of his teaching is clearly founded upon personal experience, not upon metaphysical speculations. Its accent of ardour and sincerity is alone enough to prove this. Taken in its entirety it probably represents a mystical tradition current in the Syrian convents and partly derived from Oriental sources: but this tradition has passed through the temperament of a great natural mystic in the course of attaining to literary expression.

About A.D. 850 the works of Dionysius were translated from Greek into Latin by the great Irish philosopher and theologian, **John Scotus Erigena,** one of the scholars assembled at the court of Charlemagne; and from this event we must date the beginning of a definite tradition of mysticism in Western Europe. John the Scot, many of whose own writings exhibit a strong mystical bias, is the only name in this period which the history of mysticism can claim. We are on the descending line of the "Dark Ages": and here the curve of mysticism runs parallel with the curves of intellectual and artistic activity. The lowest point is reached with the "terrible year" A.D. 1000; when all Christendom expected the end of the world, and apathy seemed to invade every department of life.

During the eleventh century the arts revived: and by the beginning of the twelfth the wave of new life had reached the mystic level. France now made the first of her many contributions to the history of mysticism in the person of **St. Bernard** (1091–1153), the great Abbot of Clairvaux: and was the adopted country of another mystic almost as great, though now less famous: the Scotch or Irish **Richard of St. Victor** (*ob. c.* 1173), whom Dante held to be "in contemplation more than man." Richard's master and contemporary, the scholastic philosopher **Hugh** (1097–1141) of the same Abbey of St. Victor at Paris, is also generally reckoned amongst the mystics of this period, but with less reason; since the subject of contemplation occupies a smaller place in his theological writings, and is there treated in a formal and dogmatic manner which it is hard to believe inspired by personal experience. In spite of the deep respect which is shown towards him by Aquinas and other theologians, Hugh's influence on later mystical literature was slight. The spirit of Richard and of St. Bernard, on the contrary, was destined to dominate it for the next two hundred years. With them the literature of mediaeval mysticism, properly so called, begins.

This literature falls into two classes : the autobiographical and the didactic. Sometimes, as happens in a celebrated sermon of St. Bernard, the two are combined; the teacher appealing to his own experience in illustration of his theme.

In the works of the Victorines, the attitude is purely didactic : one might almost say scientific. In them, mysticism—that is to say, the degrees of contemplation, the training and exercise of the spiritual sense—takes its place as a recognized department of theology. It is, in Richard's favourite symbolism, " Benjamin," the beloved child of Rachel, emblem of the Contemplative Life : and in his two chief works, " Benjamin Major " and " Benjamin Minor," it is classified and described in all its branches, with a wealth of allegorical detail which too often obscures the real beauties and ardours beneath. Richard of St. Victor was one of the chief channels through whom the antique mystical tradition, which flowed through Plotinus and the Areopagite, was transmitted to the mediaeval world. In his hands, that tradition was codified. Like his master, Hugh, he had the mediaeval passion for elaborate allegory, neat arrangement, rigid classification and significant numbers in things. As Dante parcelled out Heaven, Purgatory, and Hell with mathematical precision, and proved that Beatrice was herself a Nine ; so these writers divide and subdivide the stages of contemplation, the states of the soul, the degrees of Divine Love : and perform terrible *tours de force* in the course of compelling all the living spontaneous and ever-variable expressions of man's spiritual vitality to fall into orderly and parallel series, conformable to the mystic numbers of Seven, Four, and Three.

The same baneful passion obscures for modern readers the real merits of St. Bernard, though it did but enhance his reputation with those for whom he wrote. His writings, and those of Richard of St. Victor, quickly took their place amongst the living forces which conditioned the development of later mystics. Both have a special interest for us in the fact that they influenced the formation of our national school of mysticism in the fourteenth century. Translations and paraphrases of the " Benjamin Major," " Benjamin Minor," and other works of Richard of St. Victor, and of various tracts and epistles of St. Bernard, are constantly met with in the MS. collections of mystical and theological literature written in England in the thirteenth and fourteenth centuries. An early translation of the " Benjamin Minor," sometimes attributed to the "father of English mysticism," Richard Rolle, was probably made by the anonymous author of the "Cloud of Unknowing," who was also responsible for the first appearance of the Areopagite in English dress.

The curve of mystical life, then, travelling through the centuries, has moved, like all waves of spiritual vitality, from east to west.   By the twelfth century it has reached France : and shown, in the persons of Richard of St. Victor and St. Bernard, at once the intellectual and political strength of the mystic type.   At the same time there appear in Germany the first of the long line of women mystics : the first, at any rate, whose literary works and authentic records have survived.

With **St. Hildegarde** (1098–1179) and **St. Elizabeth of Schoenau** (1138–1165) the history of German mysticism begins. These remarkable women, visionaries, prophetesses, and political reformers, are the early representatives of a type of mysticism of which St. Catherine of Siena is the most familiar and perhaps the greatest example.   Exalted by the strength of their spiritual intuitions, they emerged from an obscure life to impose their wills, and their reading of events, upon the world.   From the point of view of Eternity, in whose light they lived, they attacked the corruption of their generation.   Already in the letters which St. Hildegarde sent like firebrands over Europe, we see the German romanticism and the German practicality struggling together ; the coarse and direct description of abuses, the flowery charm of the vision by which they are condemned.   These qualities are seen again in the South German mystics of the next century : the four Benedictine women of genius, who had their home in the convent of Helfde. These are the **Nun Gertrude** (Abbess 1251–1291) and her sister **St. Mechthild of Hackborn** (*ob*. 1310), with her sublime symbolic visions : then, the poet of the group, the exquisite **Mechthild of Magdeburg** (1212–1299), who, first a *béguine* at Magdeburg, where she wrote the greater part of "The Flowing Light of the Godhead," came to Helfde in 1268 ; lastly the celebrated **St. Gertrude the Great** (1256–1311).   In these contemplatives the political spirit is less marked than in St. Hildegarde : but religious and ethical activity takes its place.   St. Gertrude the Great is a characteristic Catholic visionary of the feminine type : absorbed in her subjective experiences, her often beautiful and significant dreams, her loving conversations with Christ and the Blessed Virgin.   Close to her in temperament is St. Mechthild of Hackborn ; but her attitude as a whole is more impersonal, more truly mystic. The great symbolic visions in which her most spiritual perceptions are expressed are artistic creations rather than psycho-sensorial hallucinations, and dwell little upon the humanity of Christ, with which St. Gertrude is constantly occupied. The terms in which Mechthild of Magdeburg, half poet, half seer, describes her union with God, while intensely individual and apparently owing nothing to earlier writers, are singularly free from sensuous imagery. The works of this Mechthild, early translated into Latin, were read by Dante. Their influence is traceable in the " Paradiso " ; and by some scholars she is believed to be the Matilda of his Earthly Paradise, though others give this position to her sister-mystic, St. Mechthild of Hackborn.

Another precursor of Dante begins for us the history of Italian mysticism : **St. Francis of Assisi,** poet and mystic (1182–1226), one of the greatest figures of the mediaeval world. It might truly be said of St. Francis, as was untruly said of his disciple St. Bonaventura, that all his learning was comprised in the crucifix. His mysticism owed much to nature, nothing to tradition ; was untouched by the formative influence of monastic discipline, the writings of Dionysius and St. Bernard. It was the spontaneous and original expression of his personality, the rare personality of a poet of the Infinite, a " troubadour of God." It showed itself in his few poems, his sayings, above all in his life : the material in which his genius expressed itself best. He walked, literally, in an enchanted world ; where every living thing was a theophany, and all values were transvaluated by love.

None of those who came after him succeeded in recapturing his secret, which was the secret of spiritual genius of the rarest type : but he left his mark upon the history of Europe and the influence of his spirit has never wholly died. Italian mysticism descends from St. Francis, and in its first period seems indeed to be the prerogative of his friars. In the thirteenth century we see it, in all its detachment, freshness, and spontaneity, in four very different temperaments. First in **St. Bonaventura** (1221–1274), biographer of St. Francis, a theologian and doctor of the Church. Perhaps the least mystical of the four, he has had the greatest influence on later mystics. He combined a contemplative nature with considerable intellectual powers. A student of Dionysius, whose influence pervades his writings, it was he who brought the new spirit into line with the tradition of the past. Next, in the beautiful figure of **St. Douceline** (*n.* 1214), the lady of Genoa turned *béguine,* we find a spirit which, like that of its master, could find its way to the Divine through flowers and birds and simple natural things. The third of these Franciscan contemplatives, **Jacopone da Todi** (*ob.* 1306), the converted lawyer turned mystical poet, lifts Franciscan mysticism to the heights of ecstatic rapture and of literary expression. Jacopone's work has been shown by Von Hügel to have had a formative influence on St. Catherine of Genoa; and has probably affected many other Italian mystics.

The **Blessed Angela of Foligno** (1248–1309), last of the four in time though not in importance, was converted from a sinful life to become a tertiary hermit of the Franciscan order; and has left in her " Divine Consolations " the record of a series of profoundly significant visions and intuitions of truth. By the sixteenth century her works, translated into the vernacular, had taken their place amongst the classics of mysticism. In the seventeenth they were largely used by Madame Guyon and other Catholic contemplatives. Seventeen years older than Dante, whose great genius properly closes this line of spiritual descent, she is a link between the thirteenth and fourteenth centuries in Italian mysticism.

We are now approaching the Golden Age of Mysticism: and at the opening of that epoch, dominating it by their genius, stand that astonishing pair of friends, St. Bonaventura, the Franciscan, and **St. Thomas Aquinas,** the Dominican (1226–1274). It is commonly stated that fourteenth-century mysticism on its formal side derives from St. Bonaventura, and represents an opposition to scholastic theology; but as a matter of fact some of its greatest personalities—in particular Dante and the whole of the German Dominican school— are soaked in the spirit of Aquinas, and quote his authority at every turn.

Most of the mystical literature of the late thirteenth and early fourteenth centuries is still in MS., and much probably remains unidentified. An interesting example has lately come to light in " **The Mirror of Simple Souls** "; a long treatise, translated and edited by an unknown English contemplative in the late fourteenth or early fifteenth century from a lost French original, which was probably written under Franciscan influence between the years 1280–1309. The Mirror, which its prologue declares to be full of "high ghostly cunning" dangerous for common men, is certainly a piece of mystical literature of an advanced kind. Strongly influenced by Dionysius, by Richard of St. Victor, and by St. Bonaventura, it probably influenced in its turn the English writers who produced in the next century " The Cloud of Unknowing " and other profound treatises upon the inner life: and these are in fact the works which most nearly resemble it in substance, though its manner is its own.

With " The Mirror of Simple Souls " we bridge not only the gap between the mysticism of England and of France, but also that be-

tween the thirteenth and fourteenth centuries. In Europe the mystic
curve is now approaching its highest point. In the East, as we might
expect, that point has already been passed. Sūfi, or Mahommedan
mysticism, which appears in literature in the twelfth century in the
Confessions of **Al Ghazzali,** has its classic period in the thirteenth in
the works of the mystic poets 'Attar (*c.* 1140–1234), **Sādi** (1184–1263),
and the saintly **Jelalu 'd Din** (1207–1273). Its tradition is continued
in the fourteenth century by the rather erotic mysticism of **Hafiz**
(*c.* 1300–1388) and his successors : and in the fifteenth by the poet
Jámi (1414–1492).

Whilst Hafiz already strikes a note of decadence for the mysticism
of Islam, the year 1300 is for Europe a vital year in the history of the
spiritual life. In Italy, England, Germany, and Flanders mystics of
the first rank are appearing, or about to appear. In Italy **Dante**
(1265–1321) is forcing human language to express one of the most
sublime visions of the Absolute which has ever been crystallized into
speech. He inherits and fuses into one that loving and artistic reading of reality which was the heart of Franciscan mysticism, and that
other ordered vision of the transcendental world which the Dominicans
through Aquinas poured into the stream of European thought. For
the one the spiritual world was all love : for the other all law. For Dante
it was both. In the " Paradiso " his stupendous genius apprehends
and shows to us a Beatific Vision in which the symbolic systems of all
great mystics, and many whom the world does not call mystics—of
Dionysius, Richard, St. Bernard, Mechthild, Aquinas, and countless
others—are included and explained.

In Germany at the moment when the " Commedia " was being
written, another mighty personality, the great Dominican scholar
Meister Eckhart (1260–1329), who resembles Dante in his combination of mystical insight with intense intellectual power, was laying the
foundations at once of German philosophy and German mysticism.
These two giants stand side by side at the opening of the century,
perfect representatives of the Teutonic and Latin instinct for transcendental reality.

Eckhart, though only a few years younger than St. Gertrude the
Great, seems to belong to a different world. His commanding personality, his strange genius for the supra-sensible, moulded and
inspired all whom it came near. The German and Flemish mystics of
the fourteenth and fifteenth centuries, differing enormously in temperament from their master and from each other, have yet something
in common : something which is shared by no other school. This
something is derived from Eckhart ; for one and all have passed under

his hand, being either his immediate disciples, or the friends or pupils of his disciples. Towards the end of his life he fell into disgrace. A number of propositions extracted from his writings, and representing his more extreme views, were condemned by the Church as savouring of pantheism and other heresies: and certainly the violence and daring of his language easily laid him open to misconstruction. In his efforts to speak of the unspeakable he was constantly betrayed into expressions which, though doubtless as near as he could get to his sublime intuitions of the Absolute, were bound to seem paradoxical and exaggerated to other men. Eckhart's influence, however, was little hurt by ecclesiastical condemnation. His pupils, though they remained loyal Catholics, contrived also to be loyal disciples, and to the end of their lives their teaching was coloured—often inspired—by the doctrines of the great, if heretical, scholar.

The contrast in type between Eckhart and his two most famous disciples is an interesting one. All three were Dominican friars, all were devout followers of St. Augustine, the Areopagite, St. Bernard, and Aquinas: all lived and worked in the valley of the Rhine. The mysticism of Eckhart, so far as he allows us to see it in his sermons— the only literary works he has left—is objective; one might almost say dogmatic. He describes with an air of almost terrible certainty and intimacy, not that which he has felt, but the place or plane of being he has known—"the desert of the Godhead where no one is at home." He is a learned mystic. A great scholar, a natural metaphysician, he had taught in the schools at Paris and Cologne: and his sermons, though addressed to the people and delivered in German, give evidence of his culture at every turn.

Of his two pupils, **John Tauler** (*c.* 1300–1361), friar-preacher of Strassburg, was a born missionary: a man who combined with great theological learning and mystical genius of a high order an overwhelming zeal for souls. He laboured incessantly to awaken men to a sense of their transcendental heritage. Without the hard intellectualism occasionally noticeable in Eckhart, or the tendency to introspection and the excessive artistic sensibility of Suso, Tauler is the most virile of the German mystics. The breadth of his humanity is only equalled by the depth of his spirituality. His sermons—and these are his only authentic works—are trumpet-calls to heroic action upon spiritual levels. Tauler, like Eckhart, keeps himself and his own experience in the background of his work. Only by implication, by unconscious self-revealing touches, can we assure ourselves that he speaks from personal knowledge. He has sometimes, and most unfairly, been described as a precursor of the Reformation. Such a claim could only be made by those who look upon 'all pure Christianity as a form of Protestant heresy. He attacked, like St. Catherine of Siena and many other mediaeval mystics, the ecclesiastical corruption of his period : but in the matter of belief his writings, if read in unexpurgated editions, prove him to have been a fervent and orthodox Catholic.

Tauler was one of the leading spirits in the great informal society of the **Friends of God,** which sprang into being in Strassburg, spread through the Rhenish province, and worked in this moment of religious decadence for the spiritual regeneration of the people. In a spirit of fierce enthusiasm and whole-hearted devotion, the Friends of God set themselves to the mystic life, as the only life worthy of the name. A tremendous outburst of transcendental activity took place: many visions and ecstasies were reported: amazing conversions occurred. The movement had many features in common with that of the Quakers, excepting that it took place within, instead of without, the official Church. With it was connected the third of the trio of great German Dominican mystics, the **Blessed Henry Suso** (c. 1300–1365), a natural recluse and ascetic, and a visionary of the most exuberant Catholic type.

To Suso, subjective, romantic, deeply interested in his own soul and his personal relation with God, mysticism was not so much a doctrine to be imparted to other men, as an intimate personal adventure. In his autobiography—a human document far more detailed and ingenuous than St. Teresa's more celebrated Life—he has left us the record of all his griefs and joys, his pains, visions, ecstasies, and miseries. Even his mystical treatises are in dialogue form, as if he could hardly get away from the personal and dramatic aspect of the spiritual life.

Around these three—Eckhart, Tauler, Suso—are gathered other and more shadowy personalities : members of this mystical society of the Friends of God, bound to the heroic attempt to bring life—the terribly corrupt and disordered religious life of the fourteenth century —back into relation with spiritual reality, to initiate their neighbours into the atmosphere of God. From one of these nameless members comes the literary jewel of the movement : the beautiful little treatise called the **"Theologia Germanica,"** one of the most successful of many attempts to make mystic principles available for common men. Others are known to us only as the authors of letters, descriptions of conversions, visions, and spiritual adventures—literature which the Friends of God produced in enormous quantities. No part of the history of mysticism has been more changed by recent research than that of the

Rhenish school: and the work is still but partly done. At present we can only record the principal names which we find connected with the mystical propaganda of the Friends of God. These are first the nuns **Margaret Ebner** (1291–1351) and her sister **Christina**, important personages in the movement, upon whose historicity no doubts have been cast. Margaret appears to have been a psychic as well as a mystic: and to have possessed, like Madame Guyon, telepathic and clairvoyant powers. Next the rather shadowy pair of laymen, **Henry of Nordlingen** and **Nicholas of Basle.** Lastly the puzzling and fascinating figure of **Rulman Merswin** (c. 1310–1382), whose story of his conversion and mystic life, whether it be regarded as fact or "tendency literature," is a psychological document of the first rank.

In immediate dependence on the German school, and like it drawing its intellectual vigour from the genius of Eckhart, is the mysticism of Flanders: best known to us—though not so well as it should be—in the work of its most sublime representative, **John Ruysbroeck** "the Admirable" (1293–1381), one of the very greatest mystics whom the world has yet known. In his early years a parish priest, in old age a recluse in the forest of Groenendael, Ruysbroeck's influence on his own generation was great. In that mystic age great mystics were recognized, and their help was eagerly sought. Through his disciple **Gerard Groot** (1340–1384), founder of the Brotherhood of the Common Life, his spirit touched in the next generation the very different character of **Thomas à Kempis** (1380–1471). In the fifteenth century Denis the Carthusian was a close student of his works, and calls him "another Dionysius," but "clear where the Areopagite is obscure"—the highest praise he knew how to bestow. His works, with those of Suso, appear in English MSS. early in the fifteenth century, taking their place by the side of St. Bernard, St. Bonaventura, and the great English mystic Richard Rolle. The influence of his genius has even been detected in the mystical literature of Spain. In Ruysbroeck's works the metaphysical and personal aspects of mystical truth are fused and attain their highest expression. Intellectually indebted to Eckhart, and probably to Richard of St. Victor, his value lies in the fact that the Eckhartian philosophy is merely the medium by which he expresses the results of profound experience. He was both saint and seer : truly a " God-intoxicated man."

England, so closely akin to Flanders in religious thought and art, first appears in the history of mysticism at the end of the thirteenth century, with the shadowy figure of **Margery Kempe** (probably writing c. 1290), the anchoress of Lynn   We know nothing of this woman's life; and only a fragment of her "Contemplations" has survived. With the next name, however, **Richard Rolle of Hampole** (c. 1300– 1349), the short but brilliant procession of English mystics begins. Rolle, educated at Oxford and widely read in mystical theology, became a hermit in order to live in perfection that mystic life of " Heat, Sweetness, and Song," to which he felt himself to be called. Richard of St. Victor, St. Bernard, and St. Bonaventura are the authors who have influenced him most; but he remains, in spite of this, one of the most individual of all writers on mysticism. Rolle already shows the practical temper destined to be characteristic of the English school. His interest is not philosophy, but spiritual life. There is a touch of Franciscan poetry in his descriptions of his communion with Divine Love, and the "heavenly song" in which it was expressed; of Franciscan ardour in his zeal for souls. His works greatly influenced succeeding mystics.

He was followed in the second half of the fourteenth century by the unknown author—or possibly group of authors—of "**The Cloud of Unknowing**" and its companion treatises, and by the gracious spirit of **Walter Hilton** (ob. 1396). With "The Cloud of Unknowing" the spirit of Dionysius first appears in English literature. It is the work of an advanced contemplative, deeply influenced by the Areopagite and the Victorines, who was also an acute psychologist. From the hand that wrote it came the first English translation of the Theologia Mystica, " Dionise Hid Divinite": a work which, says an old writer, "ran across England like deere," so ready was the national conscious- ness for the reception of mystical truth.

Hilton, though also influenced to some extent by Dionysius, addresses a wider, less advanced audience. He is pre-eminently a lover, not a metaphysician : a devout and gentle spirit anxious to share his certitudes with other men. The moment of his death coincides with the completion of the most beautiful of all English mystical works, the Revelations of Love of **Julian of Norwich** (1343–1443?), "theodidacta, profunda, ecstatica," whose unique personality closes and crowns the history of mediaeval mysticism. In her the best gifts of Rolle and Hilton are transmuted by a "genius for the infinite" of a peculiarly beautiful and individual type. She was a seer, a lover, and a poet. Her mysticism, owing little to her predecessors, results from a direct and personal vision of singular intensity.

Julian's life takes us on into the fifteenth century. Before her death —if we accept its traditional date—that century produced two mystical works of the first rank: the exquisite "Imitation of Christ" (written 1400–1425) and the more amazing, less celebrated " Fiery Soliloquy

with God " of À Kempis's contemporary **Gerlac Peterson** (*c.* 1411)—
last gleams from the setting sun of the mediaeval world.   Her later life
saw the birth and death of **Blessed Joan of Arc** (1412–1431), and of
a Flemish mystic of a type less congenial to the modern mind, the
suffering visionary **St. Lydwine of Schiedam** (1380–1432).

Already before the completion of Julian's revelations another woman
of supreme genius, **St. Catherine of Siena** (1347–1380), had lived and
died.   The true successor of Dante as a revealer of Reality, and next
to St. Francis the greatest of Italian mystics, Catherine exhibits the
Unitive Life in its richest, most perfect form.   She was a great active
and a great ecstatic: at once politician, teacher, and contemplative,
holding a steady balance between the inner and the outer life.   With
little education she yet contrived, in a short career dogged by persistent
ill-health, to change the course of history, rejuvenate religion, and compose, in her Divine Dialogue, one of the jewels of Italian religious
literature.

With the first half of the fifteenth century it is plain that the mystic
curve droops downwards.   The great period is over: the new life of the
Renaissance, already striving in other spheres of activity, has hardly
touched the spiritual plane.   France gives us two names only : Joan
of Arc, the last gift of the Middle Ages, and **Denis the Carthusian**
(1402–1471), a theologian and contemplative deeply read in mystical
science.   He was a close student and passionate admirer of the
Areopagite and of Ruysbroeck; and his works, now forgotten but
very popular during the three succeeding centuries, helped to carry
over into the modern world the best traditions of Christian mysticism.

With the second half of the century the scene shifts to Italy, where
a spiritual genius of the first rank appeared in **St. Catherine of
Genoa** (1447–1510).   She, like her namesake of Siena, was at once an
eager lover and an indomitable doer.   More, she was a constructive
mystic, a profound thinker, as well as an ecstatic: an original teacher,
a busy and practical philanthropist.   Her influence lived on, and is
seen in the next generation in the fine, well-balanced nature of another
contemplative: the **Venerable Battista Vernazza** (1497–1587), her
goddaughter and the child of one of her most loyal friends.

Catherine of Genoa stands alone in her day as an example of the
sane and vigorous mystic life.   Her contemporaries were for the most
part visionaries of the more ordinary female type; such as **Osanna
Andreasi of Mantua** (1449–1505), **Columba Rieti** (*c.* 1430–1501),
and her disciple, **Lucia of Narni.**   They seem to represent the slow
extinction of the spirit which burned so bright in Catherine of Siena.

That spirit reappears in the sixteenth century in Spain; a country

which seems to have been almost untouched by the outburst of
mystical life which elsewhere closed the mediaeval period. Spanish
mysticism, discernible as an influence in the writings of Luis of Leon
and Luis of Granada, first attained definite expression in the life and
personality of **St. Ignatius Loyola** (1491–1556), the great founder of
the Society of Jesus. The concrete nature of St. Ignatius's work, and
especially the direction in which it afterwards developed, has blinded
historians to the fact that he was a true mystic; own brother to such
great actives as St. Teresa and our own George Fox, actuated by the
same vision of reality, passing through the same stages of psychological
growth. His spiritual sons exercised an enormous influence on
the inner life of the great Carmelite, **St. Teresa** (1515–1582): an
influence shared by another and very different mystic, the gentle but
ardent Franciscan saint, **Peter of Alcantara** (1499–1562).

Like St. Catherine of Siena, these three mystics—and to them we
must add St. Teresa's greatest disciple, the poet and contemplative
St. John of the Cross (1542–1591)—seem to have arisen in direct
response to the need created by the corrupt or disordered religious life
of their time. They are the "saints of the counter-Reformation";
and, in a period of ecclesiastical chaos, flung the weight of their genius
and their sanctity into the orthodox Catholic scale. Whilst St.
Ignatius organized a body of spiritual soldiery, who should attack
heresy and defend the Church, St. Teresa, working against heavy odds,
infused new vitality into a great religious order and restored it to its
duty of direct communion with the transcendental world. In this she
was helped by St. John of the Cross; who, a scholar as well as a great
mystic, performed the necessary function of bringing the personal
experience of the Spanish school back again into touch with the main
stream of mystic tradition. All three, practical organizers and profound contemplatives, exhibit in its splendour the dual character of the
mystic life. They left behind them in their literary works an abiding
influence, which has guided the footsteps and explained the discoveries
of succeeding generations of adventurers in the transcendental world.
The true spiritual children of these mystics are to be found, not in
their own country, where the religious life which they had lifted to
transcendent levels degenerated as soon as their overmastering
influence was withdrawn: but amongst the innumerable contemplative
souls of succeeding generations who have fallen under the spell of the
"Spiritual Exercises," the "Interior Castle," or the "Dark Night of
the Soul."

The Divine fire which blazed up and exhausted itself so quickly in
Spain, is next seen in the New World: in the beautiful figure, too little

known to English readers, of **St. Rose of Lima** (1586–1617), the Peruvian nun. It appears at the same moment, under a very different aspect, in Protestant Germany; in the person of one of the giants of mysticism, the " inspired shoemaker " **Jacob Boehme** (1575–1624).

Boehme, one of the most astonishing cases in history of a natural genius for the transcendent, has left his mark upon German philosophy as well as upon the history of mysticism. William Law, Blake, and Saint-Martin are amongst those who have sat at his feet. The great sweep of Boehme's vision includes both Man and the Universe: the nature of God and of the Soul. In him we find again that old doctrine of Rebirth which the earlier German mystics had loved. Were it not for the difficult symbolism in which his vision is expressed, his influence would be far greater than it is. He remains one of those cloud-wrapped immortals who must be rediscovered and reinterpreted by the adventurers of every age.

The seventeenth century rivals the fourteenth in the richness and variety of its mystical life. Two main currents are to be detected in it: dividing between them the two main aspects of man's communion with the Absolute. One, symbolic, constructive, activistic, bound up with the ideas of regeneration, and often using the language of the alchemists, sets out from the Teutonic genius of Boehme. It achieves its successes outside the Catholic Church: and chiefly in England, where by 1650 his works were widely known. In its decadent forms it runs to the occult: to alchemy, Rosicrucianism, apocalyptic prophecy, and other aberrations of the spiritual sense.

The other current arises within the Catholic Church, and in close touch with the great tradition of Christian mysticism. It represents the personal and intimate side of contemplation: tends to encourage passive receptivity: and produces in its exaggerated forms the aberrations of the Quietists. It has its chief field in the Latin countries: France, Italy, and Spain.

In the seventeenth century England was peculiarly rich, if not in great mystics, at any rate in mystically-minded men. Mysticism, it. seems, was in the air; broke out under many disguises and affected many forms of life. It produced in **George Fox** (1624–1690) the founder of the Quakers, a "great active" of the first rank, entirely unaffected by tradition; and in the Quaker movement itself an outbreak of genuine mysticism which is only comparable to the fourteenth-century movement of the Friends of God. At the opposite end of the theological scale, and in a very different form, it shows itself in **Gertrude More** (1606–1633) the Benedictine nun, a Catholic contemplative of singular charm.

Gertrude More carries on that tradition of the communion of love which flows from St. Augustine through St. Bernard and Thomas à Kempis, and is the very heart of Catholic mysticism. In the writings of her director, and the preserver of her works, the **Venerable Augustine Baker** (1575–1641)—one of the most lucid and orderly of guides to the contemplative life—we see what were still the formative influences in the environment where her mystical powers were trained. Richard of St. Victor, Hilton and the "Cloud of Unknowing"; Angela of Foligno ; Tauler, Suso, Ruysbroeck ; St. Teresa and St. John of the Cross ; these are the authorities to whom Augustine Baker most constantly appeals, and through these, as we know, the line of descent goes back to the Neoplatonists and the first founders of the Church.

Outside that Church, the twins **Thomas Vaughan** the spiritual alchemist and **Henry Vaughan**, Silurist, the mystical poet (1622–1695) show the reaction of two very different temperaments upon the transcendental life. Again, the group of "Cambridge Platonists," **Henry More** (1614–1687), **John Smith** (1618–1652), **Benjamin Whichcote** (1609–1683), and **John Norris** (1657–1711) developed and preached a rational philosophy which is nevertheless deeply tinged with mysticism. In the saintly **Bishop Hall** (1574–1656) the same spirit takes a devotional form. Finally, in the crowd of Rosicrucians, symbolists, and other spiritually minded occultists—above all in the extraordinary sect of Philadelphians, ruled by **Dr. Pordage** (1608–1698) and the prophetess **Jane Lead** (1623–1704)—we find mysticism in its least balanced aspect, mingled with mediumistic phenomena, wild symbolic visions, and apocalyptic prophecies. The influence of these Philadelphians, who were themselves strongly affected by Boehme's works, lingered on for a century, appearing again in Saint-Martin the "Unknown Philosopher."

The Quietistic trend of seventeenth-century mysticism is best seen in France. There, at the beginning of the century, the charming personality of **St. Francis de Sales** (1567–1622) sets the key of the spiritual life of the time, with a delicate but slightly sentimental application of the principles of mystic love to popular piety. Under the brilliant worldly life of seventeenth-century France, there was something amounting to a cult of the inner life. Such episodes as the careers of St. Jeanne Françoise de Chantal and St. Vincent de Paul, the history of Port Royal, the apostolate of Madame Guyon, the controversies of Bossuet and Fénelon, and the interest which these events aroused, indicate a period of considerable vitality. The spiritual life threatened to become fashionable. Hence, its most satisfactory initiates are those least in touch with the life of the time ; such as the simple

Carmelite, **Brother Lawrence** (1611–1691). Lawrence shows the passive tendency of French mysticism in its most sane, well-balanced form. He was a humble empiricist, laying claim to no special gifts : a striking contrast to his contemporary, the brilliant and unhappy genius **Pascal** (1623–1662), who fought his way through many psychic storms to the final vision of the Absolute.

The earliest in date and most exaggerated in type of the true Quietists is the Franco-Flemish **Antoinette Bourignan** (1616–1680) : a strong-willed and wrong-headed woman who, having renounced the world with Franciscan thoroughness, founded a sect, endured considerable persecutions, and made a great stir in the religious life of her time. An even greater uproar resulted from the doctrinal excesses of the devout Spanish priest **Miguel de Molinos** (1640–1697); whose extreme teachings were condemned by the Church, and for a time brought the whole principle of passive contemplation into disrepute. Quietism, at bottom, was the expression of a need not unlike that which produced the contemporary Quaker movement in England : a need for personal contact with spiritual realities, evoked by the formal and unsatisfying quality of the official religion of the time. Unfortunately the great Quietists were not great mystics. Hence their unbalanced propaganda, in which the principle of passivity—divorced from, and opposed to, all spiritual action—was pressed to its logical conclusion, came dangerously near to nihilism : and resulted in a doctrine fatal not only to all organized religion, but to the healthy development of the inner life.

Madame Guyon (1648–1717), the contemporary of Molinos and one of the most interesting personalities of the time, though usually quoted as a typical Quietist, taught and practised a far more balanced mysticism. Madame Guyon is an instance of considerable mystical genius linked with a feeble surface intelligence. Had she possessed the robust common sense so often found in the great contemplatives, her temperamental inclination to passivity would have been checked, and she would hardly have made use of the unfortunate expressions which brought about the official condemnation of her works. In spite of the brilliant championship of Fénelon, and the fact that she really continues the tradition of feminine mysticism as developed by Angela of Foligno, St. Catherine of Genoa, and St. Teresa—though lacking the wide, impersonal outlook of these mystics—she was involved in the general condemnation of " passive orison" which the aberrations of the extreme Quietists had called forth.

The end of the seventeenth century saw a great outburst of popular Quietism   some within and some without the official Church

Amongst the more respectable of these quasi-mystics—all of whom appealed to the general tradition of mysticism in support of their one-sided doctrine—were **Malaval**, whose " Théologie Mystique " contains some beautiful French translations from St. Teresa, and **Peter Poiret** (1646–1719), once a Protestant pastor, then the devoted disciple of Antoinette Bourignan.   Later generations owe a considerable debt to the enthusiasm and industry of Poiret, whose belief in spiritual quiescence was combined with great literary activity.   He rescued and edited all Madame Guyon's writings ; and has left us, in his " Biblioteca Mysticorum," the memorial of many lost works on mysticism.   From this unique bibliography we can see how " orthodox " was the food which nourished even the most extreme of the Quietists : how thoroughly they believed themselves to represent not a new doctrine, but the true tradition of Christian Mysticism.

With the close of the seventeenth century, the Quietist movement faded away.   The beginning of the eighteenth sees the triumph of its " completing opposite "; that other stream of spiritual vitality which arose outside the Catholic Church and flowed from the great personality of Jacob Boehme.   If the idea of surrender be the main-spring of Quietism, the complementary idea of rebirth is the main-spring of this school.   In Germany, Boehme's works had been collected and published by an obscure mystic, **John Gichtel** (1638–1710) ; whose life and letters constantly betray his influence.   In England, where that influence had been a living force from the middle of the seventeenth century, when his writings first became known, the Anglo-German **Dionysius Andreas Freher** was writing between 1699 and 1720.

In the early years of the eighteenth century, Freher was followed by **William Law** (1686–1761), the Nonjuror : a brilliant stylist and one of the most profound of English religious writers.   Law, who was converted by the reading of Boehme's works from the narrow Christianity to which he gave classic expression in the " Serious Call " to a wide and philosophic mysticism, gave, in a series of writings which burn with mystic passion, a new interpretation and an abiding place in English literature to the " inspired shoemaker's " astounding vision of Man and the Universe.

The latter part of a century which clearly represents the steep downward trend of the mystic curve, gives us three great personalities ; all of whom have passed through Boehme's school, and have placed themselves in opposition to the official Church of their day.   In Germany, **Eckartshausen** (1752–1803), in " The Cloud upon the Sanctuary " and other works, continued upon individual lines that tradition of esoteric and mystical Christianity, and of rebirth as the price of man's entrance into Reality, which found its best and sanest interpreter in William Law. In France, the troubled spirit of the transcendentalist **Saint-Martin** (1743–1803), "the unknown philosopher," was deeply affected in his passage from a merely occult to a mystical philosophy, by the reading of Boehme and Eckartshausen; and also by the works of the English "Philadelphians," Dr. Pordage and Jane Lead, who had long sunk to oblivion in their native land. In England, one of the greatest mystics of all time, **William Blake** (1757–1827), shines like a solitary star in the uncongenial atmosphere of the Georgian age.

The career of Blake, poet, painter, visionary, and prophet, provides us with a rare instance of mystical genius forcing not only rhythm and words, but also colour and form, to express its vision of truth. So individual in his case was this vision, so strange the elements from which his symbolic reconstructions were built up, that he failed in the attempt to convey it to other men. Neither in his prophetic books "dark with excessive light," nor in his beautiful mystical paintings, does he contrive to transmit more than great and stimulating suggestions of "things seen" in some higher and more valid state of consciousness.

An impassioned Christian of a deeply mystical type, Blake, like Eckartshausen and Saint-Martin, was at the same time a determined and outspoken foe of conventional Christianity. He seems at first sight the Ishmael of the mystics, wayward and individual, hardly touched by tradition; but as a matter of fact his spirit gathered up and expressed the scattered threads of that tradition, parted since the Reformation amongst divergent groups of explorers of the unseen. It is for this reason that his name may fitly close and complete this short survey of European mysticism.

Whilst his visionary symbolism derives to a large extent from Swedenborg, whose works were the great influence of his youth, Blake has learned much from Boehme, and probably from his English interpreters. But, almost alone amongst English Protestant mystics, he has also received and assimilated the Catholic tradition of the personal and inward communion of love. In his stupendous vision of "Jerusalem," St. Teresa and Madame Guyon are amongst the "gentle souls" whom he sees guarding that Four-fold Gate which opens towards Beulah— the gate of the contemplative life—and guiding the great "Wine-press of Love" whence mankind, at the hands of its mystics, has received, in every age, the Wine of Life.

INDEX

Printed in Great Britain by
Whitstable Litho Ltd., Whitstable, Kent